French Cinema

The Student's Book

French Cinema

The Student's Book

Alan Singerman
Davidson College

Focus Publishing / R. Pullins Co.
Newburyport, MA

Copyright 2006 Alan Singerman

ISBN 1-58510-205-9

10 9 8 7 6 5 4 3 2 1

For Gary, Carolee, Dave & Mark
with my love

Table of Contents

Introduction.. xi

Film Terms xiii

History of Cinema I: The Beginnings 1

History of Cinema II: The Nineteen-Twenties......................................7

"Reading" a Film 19

Poetic Realism 37

Jean Vigo, *Zero For Conduct* (1933)...39

Jean Renoir, *A Day in the Country* (1936, 1946) 55

Jean Renoir, *Grand Illusion* (1937) 75

Jean Renoir, *The Rules of the Game* (1939) 97

Marcel Carné, *Daybreak* (1939)... 121

Marcel Carné, *Children of Paradise* (1945) 139

Jean Cocteau, *Beauty and the Beast* (1946) 161

René Clément, *Forbidden Games* (1952) 177

Jacques Tati, *Mr. Hulot's Holiday* (1953) 189

Robert Bresson, *A Man Escaped* (1956) 205

The New Wave 229

François Truffaut, *The 400 Blows* (1959)... 233

Alain Resnais, *Hiroshima mon amour* (1959) 253

Jean-Luc Godard, *Breathless* (1960) 271

François Truffaut, *Jules et Jim* (1962) 289

Eric Rohmer, *My Night at Maud's* (1969) 309

Alain Resnais, *My American Uncle* (1980).. 333

Agnès Varda, *Vagabond* (1985) 353

Historical Context of the Films 375

To Broaden Your Knowledge of French Cinema 377

For Further Research on French Films 383

Name Index 385

Credits 391

Illustrations

1. Louis and August Lumière, inventors of the Cinematograph.
2. The Cinematograph, the first camera-projector (1895).
3. Georges Méliès, *A Trip to the Moon* (1902).
4. Luis Buñuel and Salvador Dalí, *An Andalusian Dog*: the cutting of the eye.
5. Jean Vigo, *Zéro For Conduct*: the pillow fight.
6. Jean Renoir, *A Day in the Country*: Henri (Georges Darnoux) and Henriette (Sylvia Bataille) on the island.
7. Jean Renoir, *Grand Illusion*: Lieutenant Maréchal (Jean Gabin) and Captain de Boëldieu (Pierre Fresnay) arrive at the first officers' camp.
8. Jean Renoir, *The Rules of the Game*: Christine (Nora Grégor) welcomes André Jurieu (Roland Toutain) and Octave (Jean Renoir) to her castle.
9. Marcel Carné, *Daybreak*: François (Jean Gabin) and Valentin (Jules Berry) argue over Clara (Arletty).
10. Marcel Carné, *Children of Paradise*: Baptiste (Jean-Louis Barrault) and Nathalie (Maria Casarès), his future wife.
11. Jean Cocteau, *Beauty and the Beast*: Belle (Josette Day) at the Beast's (Jean Marais) castle.
12. René Clément, *Forbidden Games*: Michel (Georges Poujouly) and Paulette (Brigitte Fossey) play together.
13. Jacques Tati, *Mr. Hulot's Holiday*: Hulot (Jacques Tati) gives the photographer-"voyeur" a kick in the pants.
14. Robert Bresson, *A Man Escaped*: Fontaine (François Leterrier) in his cell at the Fort de Montluc prison.
15. François Truffaut, *The 400 Blows*: Antoine (Jean-Pierre Léaud) scolded by his parents after starting a fire in the apartment.
16. Alain Resnais, *Hiroshima mon amour*: "She" (Emmanuelle Riva) and "He" (Eiji Okada) on location during the shooting of the film against the atomic bomb.
17. Jean-Luc Godard, *Breathless*: Patricia (Jean Seberg) kisses Michel (Jean-Paul Belmondo) in the street.
18. François Truffaut, *Jules et Jim*: Catherine (Jeanne Moreau) makes "faces" for Jules (Oscar Werner) and Jim (Henri Serre).
19. Eric Rohmer, *My Night at Maud's*: Jean-Louis (Jean-Louis Trintignant) joins Maud (Françoise Fabian) on her bed.
20. Alain Resnais, *My American Uncle*: René Ragueneau and Veestrate fight at the office (metaphorically).
21. Agnès Varda, *Vagabond*: Mona, the vagabond (Sandrine Bonnaire), on the move.

Acknowledgements

I would like to express my deepest gratitude to all those who supported and encouraged me during the four years it took to develop, write, and prepare this textbook for publication. I would like to thank above all Brigitte Humbert of Middlebury College, who was my most valuable and faithful source of support from the beginning. Her careful readings and criticisms of each chapter of the French edition of this book forced me countless times to reformulate my ideas to produce a more readable text. I am likewise grateful to Michèle Bissière of the University of North Carolina at Charlotte for her meticulous reading of the major part of my French manuscript and for her stylistic advice. As regards the present edition, I am deeply indebted to Professor of English Emeritus J. Gill Holland of Davidson College, who read and criticized the language of each chapter with uncompromising frankness, persistently leading me toward clarity of expression and eradicating many Gallic turns of phrase.

I benefited as well from the advice and moral support of a large number of colleagues who are film teachers, including Rebecca Pauly of West Chester University, Marc Buffat of the University of Paris VII, Jean Mottet of the University of Paris I, Laurent Déchery of Gustavus Adolphus College, Alan Williams of Rutgers University, Rémi Fournier Lanzoni of Elon University, Roch Smith of the University of North Carolina at Greensboro, and Jonathan Walsh of Wheaton College. I would also like to acknowledge here a major debt to Franck Curot of the University of Montpellier, the director of my Master's thesis on cinema, who taught me the basics of film history, esthetics, and analysis.

I would like to express my gratitude as well to the personnel of the Bibliothèque du Film (BIFI) in Paris for their cordial, competent, and always helpful support of my research in their establishment. I owe a special thanks to Bernard Roemer of the Centre National de la Cinématographie (CNC) in Paris, to Joe Gutekanst of Interlibrary Loan at Davidson College, and to Raymond Cauchetier, André Heinrich, and Agnès Varda (who reviewed with me the whole chapter devoted to her film!). I am grateful to all of the studios, film journals, and publishers — too numerous to name here — who gave me permission, many of them at no charge, to reproduce in my book either frames from films or excerpts of articles and books bearing on the films presented in this work.

I realize that this book would not exist without the contributions of my French cinema students at Davidson College, who tolerated more or less patiently my pedagogical experiments during the elaboration of the numerous versions of my cinema course over the years. I am grateful to Davidson College also for granting me several subsidies which enabled me to conduct essential research at the BIFI in Paris and to obtain the permissions necessary for the publication of this book. In the course of the preparation of the manuscript, I was most appreciative of the moral and practical support offered by Ron Pullins, Linda Robertson, and Cindy Zawalich of Focus Publishing.

I've left for the end those to whom I owe the most: the members of my family, who endured with only moderate complaining the years of endless viewings in our living room of the French films that I was teaching in my courses. I offer my deepest thanks to my wife Véronique, always the first reader and critic of my French manuscripts for over a quarter century. Her unconditional support has helped me to overcome many misgivings and to bring this project to fruition.

Introduction

This book grew out of the desire to provide students with a textbook which would introduce them to some of the most important French film directors and help them to reflect in depth upon their best works. For those colleagues who are teaching this course in French, or who have in their cinema class students proficient in French, a French language version of this book, *Apprentissage du cinéma français. Livre de l'étudiant* (2004), is also available through Focus Publishing. Although this textbook begins with two chapters on the early stages of French and world cinema, *French Cinema. The Student's Book* is not a history of cinema, just as it is not the study of a specific period, genre, or theme of cinema. This book offers an in-depth study of a number of widely recognized masterpieces, any of which might be included in the syllabus of a course on French film.

Each chapter of *French Cinema* includes a synthesis of the best critical thought surrounding the film featured in that chapter, followed by a study guide designed to facilitate the students' reflection on that film. The chapters are completed by a critical dossier composed of a selection of excerpts from the best articles and books I was able to find during research conducted primarily at the Film Library (Bibliothèque du Film, or BIFI) in Paris. I have provided these excerpts to promote yet more sophisticated reflection by the students on the various films by encouraging them to take into account a variety of critical viewpoints, some of which are quite divergent.

Any instructor who uses this textbook in conjunction with his or her course on French film will, of course, ask the students to read the chapters which are the most relevent to the particular films included in the course. The sheer number of masterpieces of French cinema presented in this book — eighteen, if we count the short subject *An Andalusian Dog* — is too large to include all of these films in a one-semester course. I thought it best to provide the instructor with a choice of great films rather than attempt to dictate the precise content of the course. Moreover, some colleagues who may be less interested than others in early cinema may prefer to skip one or both of the short chapters on the origin and beginnings of moviemaking from the nineteenth century to the end of the nineteen-twenties. I consider it very important, however, no matter which films are on the course syllabus, to include the chapter on "'Reading' A Film," in which the students learn the technical vocabulary and concepts essential for film analysis.

It goes without saying that this book does not pretend to present all of the masterpieces of French cinema; this would simply be impossible. It was necessary to select works from the corpus of great films which have by and large been consecrated by tradition. My criteria of selection were related primarily to the richness of content and the formal originality of each film, that is, the film's thematic and esthetic interest in the history of French and world cinema. It should be emphasized that the choice of films in this book is not intended to be restrictive as regards course content. It would be perfectly normal for an instructor to include in his or her course other films — more recent French films for example — which seem particularly important or interesting to that instructor, while leaving out some of the films presented in this volume. In this area, I would recommend strict adherence to the latitudinarian motto of Rabelais's Abbey of Thélème: "Do as you please!"

As for classroom use of the three parts of each chapter (introduction, study guide, and critical dossier), here is the approach I have developed with my own students, teaching the class on a Tuesday-Thursday schedule. I first ask them to read the introduction before seeing the film, to focus their attention immediately on the most important and interesting elements when they come to the projection. This preliminary reading would be less important if the students had the time to see each film several times, but they rarely have that luxury. In the class following the projection of the film, normally Thursday, we discuss the various themes and characters. Since the following class is on Tuesday, they have a substantial period in which to prepare the next assignment, which is more demanding. For this class I ask the students to read the study guide (with the director's remarks, important quotations from the dialogue, and reflection topics) and a selection of readings from the critical dossier. I also ask them to study and answer questions on a series of film excerpts which I make available to them electronically. When the students come back to class, we discuss selected elements in the above material, varying the focus from film to film. We always include substantial discussion of the most important formal aspects of the film, as well as the relationship between the form and the themes, by analyzing together some of the excerpts they have studied out of class.

I've attempted to present in this textbook an abundance of pedagogical and critical materials so that each instructor has a wide range of pedagogical options. It is difficult to discuss everything in the study guide and critical dossier, and the instructor is free to decide which exercises are most appropriate to assign to his or her students to prepare the class discussions. This is a choice which is dictated quite naturally, I believe, by each instructor's personal sense of what is most important in each film.

Alan J. Singerman
Davidson College

Film Terms

Auteur: A director ("author") who imposes a recognizable personal style on his or her films.

Camera Angle: The position of the camera in relationship to the subject being filmed (for example, an upward or a downward angle — see **Shot** below).

Cinéaste: A filmmaker.

Cinemascope: A wide-screen process.

Cinéma Vérité: Refers generally to documentary-style filmmaking; originally associated with the New Wave style of hand-held cameras, small crews, and interviews.

Continuity: Smoothness of transition between shots (the responsibility of the **script girl** — see below).

Credits: The beginning and end of a film which show the title of the film, and the names of the actors, the director, and everyone who participated in the making of the film.

Cross-Cutting: An editing technique in which shots of two actions are alternated regularly for a certain time to suggest the simultaneity of the two actions involved; often used to create suspense.

Cut: A simple transition between two shots accomplished by simply joining two pieces of film together (see also **Editing**).

Deep Focus: A type of photography in which the focal length and the light permit objects or characters in both the foreground and the background to be in focus at the same time. Also referred to as **depth of field**, this shooting technique facilitates dramatic effects which depend on the interplay between actions in the foreground and background of the **field** (see below).

Découpage: Last stage in the preparation of the shooting script. The screenplay is cut into sequences and numbered shots, usually with detailed notes regarding the specific camera angles and movements. It refers to the general arrangement of the shots in a film.

Dissolve: Link between two shots in which the first image disappears progressively while the second appears superimposed on the first and remains alone when the first image has disappeared completely (see also **Transition** and **Superimposition**).

Dubbing: Technique which involves replacing the original sound track with another which contains the dialogues in a different language. The new sound track is coordinated with the images so that the words correspond as closely as possible to the lip movements of the actors.

Editing: Process in which the finished shots of a film are assembled according to the narrative thread. Special attention is paid in this stage of post-production to the **links** between shots and the rhythm of the film (the respective lengths of the shots). There are various editing styles, for instance, fast, slow, cut, parallel, cross-cutting, etc. (see separate entries for "**Parallel Editing**" and "**Cross-Cutting**").

Fade-Out: An editing technique in which the image disappears progressively until the screen is completely black. It is usually a form of punctuation used to end a sequence. The opposite technique, a **Fade-In**, is primarily used to begin a new sequence: the image appears progressively beginning with a black screen.

Fast Motion: An effect obtained by projecting at normal speed (24 frames per second) images which have been shot at a slower speed. If the cameraman shoots at 8 frames per second, for example, the action will be three times faster than normal when projected.

Field: The portion of space that is framed by the cameraman during a take. Characters may enter or leave the field (i.e., the image on the screen) during a shot.

Flash: A very short shot used for special effect (e.g., brusqueness, brutality, rapidity).

Flashback: A shot or sequence of shots which represent a return to an earlier time in the chronological narrative.

Flash-Forward: A shot or sequence of shots which represent a jump forward in time with respect to the chronological narrative.

Frame: Refers to a single photograph of the 24 photographs (frames) which are shot in one second. The same term also refers to the space of the entire image (the field) that the spectator sees on the screen. The cameraman **frames** a portion of space. The **framing** of a shot involves the camera angle and the arrangement of everything (characters and objects) that is in the field.

Freeze Frame: A single frame is reproduced a certain number of times and then spliced into the film, creating an effect of a photograph or of frozen action.

Insert: Usually a close-up of an object or character which is added during the editing process to clarify the action or make a special point.

Iris: A special type of shot used at the end of a sequence in which the image disappears by means of a black circle which progressively fills the screen until there is only a point of light left at the center, which then also disappears. This shot is referred to as an **iris out**. The opposite shot, in which the image appears as a widening circle, is called an **iris in**. This type of shot was common in the silent film era but is rarely used today, except as a reference to early cinema.

Jump Cut: Abrupt "jump" from one shot to the next by removing a small segment of the film, which breaks the normal continuity of the action. It is actually a cut within a scene rather than between scenes. It is normally used to create a special effect, as in J.-L. Godard's *Breathless* (see also **Editing**).

Maquette: Scenery built in miniature which is intended to be taken for an authentic setting.

Mask: A shield which is put in front of the camera lens while shooting. Part of the surface of the shield is opaque, while part is transparent, permitting the recording of an image on a specific part of the film only. A mask is often used to present multiple images, side by side, in the same **field** (see above).

Match Cut: A shot which is similar in size and composition to the preceding shot.

Mixing: Post-production process which involves "mixing" together the several sound tracks of a film (dialogue, music, sound effects) and varying the volume of each according to its importance at a given moment. The result of the mixing is the final sound track, synchronized with the images.

Off-Camera: Refers to the invisible space which is adjacent to the field which appears on the screen in a given shot. This space is an extension of the field and exists in the spectator's imagination.

Panning: A movement in which the camera pivots horizontally around its vertical axis while the tripod remains stationary. The **pan** is used most commonly to "describe" a setting by sweeping over it or to follow the movement of a character or object. A **swish pan** is a type of link between shots which consists of an extremely rapid pan which produces a blurred horizontal movement on the screen.

Parallel Editing: An editing technique in which shots are juxtaposed to suggest a metaphorical or symbolic connection between them.

Post-Synchronization: A post-production technique which consists of adding the dialogue and sound effects after the film has been shot.

Rear Screen Projection: Projection of a moving image on a screen behind the actors in a studio, giving the impression that the scene was shot on location (inside a moving car, for example).

Reframing: Using camera movements (**pans** and **tracking shots**) instead of beginning a new shot to change the framing or the camera angle (typically used during **sequence shots**).

Screenplay: The written script, also called the **scenario**, which is cut up into scenes and includes the dialogues.

Script Girl: The person who is responsible, during the shooting of a film, for all the links between the shots, that is, for the film's "**continuity**" (see above). She also usually times all the shots to keep track of the length of the film.

Sequence: A series of shots which constitutes a narrative unit. It is the loose equivalent of a scene in a play or a chapter in a novel.

Shot: The basic unit of a film. A shot includes any continuous series of images recorded between the moment when the camera is started ("Camera!") and when it is stopped ("Cut!") each time.

Sizes of Shots:

Close-Up: Shot which features a character's face or singles out an object. An extreme close-up is a shot which frames a small detail, either an object or a part of the face.

Establishing Shot: Very long shot in which the general locale of the film is established (e.g., a prairie or a city).

Long Shot: Shot encompassing a large space (e.g., a street) in which characters can be identified; they must be framed full-length.

Medium Shot: Shot in which characters are framed from the knees up; called an "*American shot*" by the French, because of its wide use in American films of the 1930s.

Near Shot: Shot in which the characters are framed from the waist or from the chest up.

Types of Shots:

Angle-Reverse Angle Shot: A technique generally used to film dialogues. In a sequence in which two characters A and B exchange remarks, the camera frames A and B alternately, the angle changing each time to show one or the other character. These shots are also called **match cuts** (see above), since they are similar in size and composition.

Down Shot: Shot in which the camera is placed above the subject being filmed and angled downward (also called a **high angle shot**). An **up shot** is the opposite of a "down shot": the camera is placed below the subject being filmed and angled upward (also called a **low angle shot**).

Iris Shot: See entry above.

Point-of-View Shot: Shot in which the perspective is intended to represent the viewpoint of a character in the film (also called **subjective camera**).

Sequence Shot: Also referred to as a **lengthy take**, this is an unusually lengthy shot which constitutes an entire sequence by itself. It commonly includes a number of camera movements and the use of **deep focus** photography (see separate entry).

Static Shot: Shot in which the camera doesn't move in any way.

Tilt: Shot in which the camera is tilted up or down around its horizontal axis.

Tracking Shot: See entry below.

Two Shot: A shot which frames two people; a ***three shot*** includes three people.

Slow Motion: An effect obtained by projecting at normal speed (24 frames per second) images which have been shot at a faster speed. If the cameraman shoots at 96 frames per second, for example, the action will be four times as slow as normal when projected.

Soft Focus: Shot in which the image is slightly blurred

Special Effects: Any unusual effect achieved through cinematographic or theatrical means or devices. A good example is **stop-action photography**, in which the camera is stopped after filming a shot, then a new subject is placed before the camera or the first subject is simply removed. When the film is projected, the spectator is given the impression, in the first case, that the subject has been suddenly transformed; in the second case one has the impression that the subject has suddenly disappeared as if by magic.

Superimposition: A technical procedure which involves recording a second image over a first one, so that the two images are visible at the same time (for example, titles appearing over a moving background, supernatural events, phantoms). The superimposition is an integral part of a **dissolve** (see above).

Synopsis: A short summary of the action of a film.

Title Card: Written text placed between shots. In silent films the dialogue was presented on title cards, but the title card may also contain information to clarify the action.

Tracking Shot: Camera movement which usually involves placing the camera on a dolly (which is then rolled on tracks) or on a crane, or holding the camera in the hands while moving forward or backward. Cameras may track forward, backward, vertically, or laterally. Also referred to as a **traveling, trucking**, or **dolly shot**.

Transition: Any means of going from one shot to the next. This is normally accomplished in such a way that the transition, or link, seems natural to the spectators. Links must take into consideration such things as scenery, costumes, the actors' movements, the general rhythm of the film, etc. When any of the above elements are not respected, a transition is considered to be bad. The most common types of transitions include **cuts**, **fades**, and **dissolves** (see separate entries and **Editing**).

Voice-Over: The voice of a character who is off-screen or who is visible on-screeen but is not speaking. Voice-over is thus often used to express the thoughts of a character or as a narrative voice.

Wipe: A technique in which one image is pushed off the screen by another (with a vertical line moving horizontally across the screen). A wipe normally indicates a change in subject, place, or time.

Zoom: A simulated **tracking shot** (see above) achieved by use of a lens with variable focal length while the camera remains stationary.

Louis and August Lumière, inventors
of the Cinematograph. Courtesy of
Museum of Modern Art Film Stills
Archive

The Cinematograph, the first camera-projector (1895). Courtesy
of Museum of Modern Art Film Stills Archive

History of Cinema I: The Beginnings

SOME TECHNOLOGICAL LANDMARKS

The invention of cinema can be traced to technological discoveries which took advantage of a psychological and optical phenomenon recognized in the 1820s: the retention of images in our memory. Because of short-term visual memory, the perception of an image lasts a fraction of a second after the disappearance of the image, resulting in an impression of continuity between two separate images if they follow each other in rapid succession. Thus, as an English doctor demonstrated in 1823, if you spin a disk with the picture of a bird on one side and a cage on the other, you see the bird in the cage. In the case of a movement broken down into a series of consecutive images, you only have to project the series of images at a speed of 16 per second to produce the illusion of continuous movement, in spite of the actual discontinuity of the images. The illusion becomes perfect at 24 images per second, which has become the standard in modern cinema. **Joseph Plateau**, a Belgium physicist, was the first to synthesize movement successfully by inventing in 1832 a toy that he named the *phenakistiscope* (a combination of the Greek words for "deceive" and "observe"). His invention works in the following manner: "A disk with slots cut in it spins around its axis. On the other side there are drawings which are reflected in a mirror. By looking through the slots, you can see the drawings move because of the phenomenon of the retention of the image combined with the narrowness of the slots" (Prédal, p. 16). In the course of the 19th century Plateau's device was gradually perfected. A man named **Hoerner** notably invented the *zootrope*, which was used by the French physiologist **Etienne-Jules Marey** and the American photographer **Eadweard Muybridge** to study the movements of a cantering horse and of birds in flight. The use of photographic images in place of drawings represents a critical step in the invention of cinema.

A few years later (1882), Marey went even further by inventing the *photographic rifle*, which permitted him to obtain 12 consecutive images per second on a round photographic plate. In 1888, taking advantage of the invention of celluloid film by the American **George Eastman** a few years earlier, he replaced the plate with a length of film in a new device, the *chronophotographe*, which is the immediate ancestor of the camera. What was still lacking was the perforation of the film on its sides, which permits the film to be pulled forward smoothly as the camera records. It is the famous American inventor **Thomas Edison** who achieved this feat, producing in 1889 rolls of perforated film 35 millimeters wide which he put into use as early as 1891 in his *kinetograph* (Greek for "to write movement"), the first modern camera. This invention was soon followed (1893) by the *kinetoscope* ("to watch movement"), a large box in which a film plays, producing moving pictures. The major drawback to this device, in addition to the small size of the images, is that only one spectator at a time can watch, through a small viewer.

While Edison is the inventor of the first camera with a viable (pronged) mechanism to advance the film, he never found the solution to the problem of projecting the images onto a screen, which is the essential element in the creation of the cinema as a form of mass entertainment. This obstacle was cleared, successively, by two French scientists. The principle of marginal perforation was discovered in 1889 (the same year as Edison's discovery) by French physicist **Emile Reynaud,** who was especially interested in the animation and projection of comic strips made of paper. By adapting the mechanism of the bicycle (a wheel with teeth pulled the perforated comic strip forward), he was able to project a series of animated comic strips in front of a large crowd of spectators. His perfection of the *praxinoscope* thus made him the inventor of the cartoon as well, which proved to be immensely successful. Between 1892 and 1900, 12,800 showings at the Grévin Museum in Paris were seen by a half-million spectators (*Emile Reynaud*, p. 8). However, the credit for the invention of the device which marks the true birth of modern cinema goes to another Frenchman, **Louis Lumière**, assisted by his older brother **Auguste**, the sons of a big manufacturer of photographic plates in Lyons. Inspired by the work of Marey, Edison, and Reynaud, the Lumière Brothers' *Cinematograph*, which was invented in 1895, is a small camera which can be converted into a projector. It uses perforated celluloid film both to record the images and then to project them. Its name, like that of Edison's kinetograph, comes from the Greek word *kinêma* (movement) and *graphein* (to write).

The great discovery of Louis Lumière guarantees for the first time the perfection of the impression of movement and the stability of the images when they are projected. Here is how he describes his discovery: "One night when I couldn't sleep, the solution just came to me by itself. It consisted of adapting to the needs of the camera the device known as the foot in the mechanism for moving the fabric forward in a sewing machine" (Sadoul, "La Dernière Interview de Louis Lumière"). The mechanism of the sewing machine (replacing that of the bicycle) permits the intermittent but regular forward movement of the film. In very simple terms, here is how it works both in the camera and in the projector: prongs which fit into the sprocket holes on the side of the film pull the film forward, then release the film and move upwards in a circular movement toward the following perforations. In the time it takes for the prongs to move up and grab the next set of perforations (1/32 of a second), while the film is stationary, the shutter of the lens (a semi-circular plate which spins) allows the light to enter and record the image. The shutter then shuts while the prongs pull the film forward again (always at 1/32 of a second) to prepare the recording of the next image. The result is 16 photographs per second.

The mechanism works the same way to project the film. The device is placed in front of a light source, but the intermittent movement of the film only lets the light through when a photograph is motionless before the lens. For the first time a series of photographic images was successfully projected, perfectly stable, onto a screen. It is for this reason that many film historians consider Louis Lumière to be the true inventor of the cinema. A first public projection took place on March 22, 1895, before the members of the National Society for the Encouragement of Industry. It was followed on December 28, an historic date, in the basement of the Grand Café in Paris, by the first film program of the Cinematograph Lumière for a paying public. Thirty-five people paid one franc to see ten films, each lasting less than one minute.

The modern movie business was born that day.

Georges Méliès, *A Trip to the Moon* (1902). Courtesy of Museum of Modern Art Film Stills Archive

EARLY FRENCH CINEMA: LUMIÈRE AND MÉLIÈS

Louis Lumière made his first films himself, documentaries on daily life shot outside in natural light. The most famous of these little films, made between 1895 and 1896, are *Workers Leaving the Lumière Factory in Lyon*, *Arrival of a Train at the Station in La Ciotat*, and *Feeding the Baby*. Although these films are slightly staged, they are generally considered to be the first documentaries. Lumière quickly added a second film genre to his repertory: newsreels. He sent cameramen all over the world to record important people and public events, such as *The King and the Queen of Italy Getting into Their Carriage* or *The Crowning of Czar Nicholas II*. In addition, among his very first films Lumière made the first "fiction film," a short comic skit known variously as *The Sprayer Sprayed* (*L'Arroseur arrosé*) or *Watering the Gardener*. One of his cameramen, Alexandre Promio, made the first tracking shot ever by placing his camera in a gondola to film *The Grand Canal in Venice* in 1897. In the same period he also produced the first reverse projection shot, *The Diane Baths in Milan*, showing divers coming out of the water feet first and back up onto the diving board (Mitry, I, p. 113). Between 1895 and 1900 he produced more than 2,000 films, many of them constituting a documentary on the life of the upper-middle class of that time.

While Lumière restricted his filmmaking to documentaries and current events, one of his countrymen developed the concept of staging in filmmaking, effectively creating the genre of the fiction film. **Georges Méliès**, a professional magician and director of a theater in Paris, attended the first public showings of the Lumière

Cinematograph at the Grand Café. He immediately understood the potential of the invention in the world of entertainment and began in 1897 to adapt his most spectacular magic tricks to the cinematic medium. He is widely recognized as the inventor of most of the special effects used in cinema: *stop-action photography* (in which the camera is stopped during a shot and a new subject placed before the lens), *superimpositions* (where two or more images are superimposed), *masks* (which permit multiple shots, side by side, in the same frame), *fades to black* and *dissolves* (in which an image disappears or is progressively replaced by another image), *blurred shots, fast-motion* and *slow-motion shots*. In addition to ingenious magic tricks like *The Man with the Rubber Head* (1901), the most famous Méliès films are imaginary voyages such as *The Trip to the Moon* (1902) and *The Conquest of the Pole* (1912), the staged retelling of current events (the best-known of these being *The Dreyfus Affair* in 1899), devil tales like *The Four Hundred Tricks of the Devil* (1906) and fairytales, including *Cinderella* (1899), *Blue Beard* (1901) and *The Fairy Kingdom* (1903).

Compared to Lumière's films, some of Méliès's productions are already "long films," *The Dreyfus Affair* lasting twelve minutes and *The Trip to the Moon* sixteen. More importantly however, as Sadoul observes, the great success of Méliès's fiction films, and especially that of *The Trip to the Moon*, "imposed throughout the world the practice of staging" (*Georges Méliès*, p. 43), which will be the major trend in modern cinema. As regards Méliès's cinematography, the classical film historians (Sadoul and Mitry notably) generally emphasize the similarities between Méliès's films and his theatrical productions, going so far as to speak of "canned theater" and of "tableaux." They note that Méliès uses mostly static medium shots, his camera's viewpoint usually being that of a spectator sitting in the middle of the orchestra. The actors tend to enter the frame as if they were coming from the wings of a stage.

More recent scholars like Pierre Jenn consider this assessment of Méliès's cinema too categorical and feel that the notions of "theatrical framing" and "single viewpoint" are in fact "myths." Jenn points out, for example, the important role of movements toward and away from the camera, the characters sometimes approaching the camera until they are in close-up or moving away from it, producing effects which are impossible in theater. He cites examples of the varying of shot sizes in specific films such as *The Trip to the Moon* and *Cinderella or the Mysterious Slipper* (pp. 20-24, 47-54).

There is little doubt that Méliès's films are not so dominated by theatrical aesthetics as previously thought. Méliès's techniques nonetheless reflected the cinematographic conventions of his time. Although he even used tracking shots and pans from time to time, he hadn't yet understood how to utilize cinema's narrative potential. Narrative language, in the modern sense of the term, will include for expressive purposes the use of the whole range of shot sizes (including close-ups), as well as narrative editing and temporal ellipses, among other techniques. Most of these techniques were already being used in fact by the first British filmmakers, those belonging to the Brighton School (1896-1905), but they would not be generalized until the triumph of American cinema — that is, the films of **D.W. Griffith**, **Thomas Ince**, and **Mack Sennett** — in the World War I period.

THE RISE AND FALL OF FRENCH CINEMA

a) The Big Studios

The film production of Lumière and Méliès remained at the level of a cottage industry. The industrial phase which guaranteed the domination of French cinema in the age of the pioneers was launched by another Frenchman, **Charles Pathé**. Founded in 1896, Pathé Brothers' Productions soon monopolized French cinema and become a major player throughout the world: "Not only did he manufacture the cameras and projectors but the film stock as well. He built factories to process the film, installed studios everywhere, distributed his own films, and owned numerous movie houses" (Betton, p. 7). Despite the general mediocrity of their products, beginning in 1900 the Pathé studios at Vincennes produced an enormous quantity of films in every genre, selling several hundred thousand copies throughout the world. By 1908 "Pathé was selling twice as much film footage in the United States as the entire American output" (Prédal, p. 22).

Pathé's success gave birth to competitors, like the production companies of **Léon Gaumont** and the Éclair film company, among others. The commercial superiority of French cinema lasted until 1913, when "of 2,754 films produced worldwide, 882 are French, 643 Italian, 576 American, 308 German, and 268 English" (Prédal, p. 32).

b) French Films

In this early period French cinema was particularly renowned for three genres: filmed theater, comedies, and serial films (*ciné-romans*). The vogue of filmed theater, called "Film d'art," grew from the ambition to increase the prestige of cinema which, after having been a vulgar form of amusement found in fairs, had become dominated by melodramas and slapstick comedies. In the "Film d'art," films were made of plays featuring big stars from the Comédie Française like Sarah Bernhardt and Réjane. The most famous of these films is *The Assassination of the Duc de Guise* (1908; 15 min. and in color), with original music by a famous composer — a first for the movies — Camille Saint-Saëns. With the same goal of enhancing the reputation of the movies, other studios specialized in adaptations of well-known novels like Zola's *L'Assommoir*, a 45-minute film considered to be the first French feature film (Prédal, p. 33), and Hugo's *Les Misérables* (1912), which lasted…three hours!

Alongside the "literary" films there was a sharp growth in the number of comedies, a genre which soon dominated French production. The French school of comedy produced the first international superstar of the movies, **Max Linder**, who reached the summit of his career after 1910 with such films as *Max, professeur de tango* and *Max toreador*, both in 1913. Linder's most celebrated fan was Charlie Chaplin himself, who readily acknowledged the influence of the French comic on his own style. At the same time the fashion of serials, or episodic films, was on the rise. The most successful serials were Victorin Jasset's *Nick Carter*, the first police series in cinema (beginning in 1908), and the serials by **Louis Feuillade**, *Fantômas* (1913-14), *Les Vampires* (1915-16), and *Judex* (1916). Long undervalued, Feuillade's films are now recognized as masterpieces of early cinema.

c) Cinema Outside France: The Americans

This first period (1895-1914), in which French film is dominant throughout the world, may be considered as its "golden age." At the same time, however, cinema was developing rapidly in other countries, notably in the United States but also in Italy, Russia, Germany, Great Britain, and Denmark, to mention only the major players. **D.W. Griffith** established himself as the top filmmaker in America between 1908 and 1913, directing hundreds of films in every genre for the Biograph production company. Griffith is generally credited with perfecting the narrative language of silent films by generalizing the use of the whole scale of shots (from the establishing shot to the close-up) in narrative editing. He also popularized the utilization of the iris to open and close shots, as well as the use of lens filters, cross-cutting (to depict simultaneous actions), ellipses, and even mental images, including the flashback. In 1914, having become an independent filmmaker, Griffith made his most famous film, *The Birth of a Nation*, the greatest commercial success of American cinema until *Gone With The Wind* in 1939. Two years later he made his magnum opus, *Intolerance*. His body of work will exercise a strong influence on the most important filmmakers in every country. At the same time two other important American directors were honing their talents, one in the western (**Thomas Ince**), the other in comedy (**Mack Sennett**).

If the rise of French cinema was exhilarating, the fall was all the more brutal. From the beginning of World War I, which would prove to be disastrous for France, the production of French films (like Italian films) plummeted. Although the war years (1914-18) permitted a talented young director named **Abel Gance** to learn the fundamentals of his craft (seventeen films), the world was inundated by American cinema, led by Griffith, Ince, Sennett, and **Charlie Chaplin**. Pathé was forced to sell its factory to Eastman Kodak, and the French film industry was reduced for the most part to importing foreign films, mostly from the United States.

WORKS CONSULTED

Betton, Gérard. *Histoire du cinéma*. Paris: Presses universitaires de France, 1984.

Emile Reynaud. Peintre de films. Paris: Cinémathèque française, 1945.

Franju, Georges. *Le Grand Méliès*. Armor Films. New York: Interama Video Classics, 1994.

Jenn, Pierre. *Georges Méliès, cinéaste*. Paris : Albatros, 1984.

La Bretèque, François de. "Les Films Lumière : des témoins de la fin de siècle?" *Cahiers de la Cinémathèque* 62 (mars 1995), 7-15.

Mitry, Jean. *Histoire du cinéma*, I. Paris: Editions universitaires, 1967.

Prédal, René. *Histoire du cinéma*. Condé-sur-Noireau: CinémAction-Corlet, 1994.

Sadoul, Georges. *Georges Méliès*. Paris: Seghers, 1961.

.........*Le Cinéma français*. Paris: Flammarion, 1962.

........."La Dernière Interview de Louis Lumière," *L'Ecran français* 155 (15 juin 1948).

History of Cinema II:
The Nineteen-Twenties

CINEMA OUTSIDE FRANCE

The post-war years and the nineteen-twenties brought a period of intense creativity and innovation to the cinema world. It is the period when silent movies blossomed, reached their maturity, and became an authentic art capable of mobilizing all of its resources. The first important European currents are born: **Expressionism** and the ***Kammerspiel*** in Germany and the **montage** school in the Soviet Union.

The films of Robert Wiene (*The Cabinet of Dr. Caligari*, 1920), of F.W. Murnau (*Nosferatu the Vampire*, 1921), and of Fritz Lang (*Dr. Mabuse*, 1922, *The Niebelungen*, 1923-24, *Metropolis*, 1926) dazzled the public, which came to consider German cinema as the best in the world until the beginning of that country's great economic crisis in 1924. German expressionism eschewed realism in favor of morbid supernatural topics like phantoms and vampires and the representation of subjectivity. It reinvented staging, turning studio scenery — deformed and stylized — into a metaphorical or symbolic expression of abnormal states of mind. The masterpiece of the *Kammerspiel* — a genre characterized by its return to realism — Murnau's *The Last Laugh* (1925), was hailed in the United States as "the best film in the world" (Betton, p. 20).

In the Soviet Union **Lev Koulechov** explored in his Moscow school the potential of film editing in the creation of meaning in cinema, using D.W. Griffith's films as his principal source of inspiration. **Dziga Vertov** put into practice the discoveries of such research by producing sophisticated documentaries, the most famous of which, *The Man With A Camera* (1929), constitutes a reflection on the representation of reality in film. **Sergei Eisenstein**, Koulechov's most celebrated student, transformed film language, bringing the art of film editing to perfection with the production of his great masterpieces *Battleship Potemkin* (1925) and *October* (1927). At the same time his countrymen **Vsevolod Pudovkin** (*Mother*, 1926) and **Aleksandr Dovzhenko** (*Earth*, 1930) were directing exceptional works, charged with emotion and bathed in lyricism.

American cinema continued its domination throughout the world, most notably in the area of comedy. Charlie Chaplin directed his first feature films, all enormous box-office successes: *The Kid* (1921), *The Gold Rush* (1925), and *City Lights* (1930). Other great comic actors broke through, like Harry Langdon, Harold Lloyd, and above all Buster Keaton, who made *The General* in 1926. Elsewhere the documentaries of Robert Flaherty, including *Nanook of the North* (1921), were appreciated by a wide public, as were the early westerns of John Ford — especially *The Iron Horse* (1924) and *Three Bad Men* (1926). Cecil B. DeMille, specializing in epic spectaculars, enjoyed a resounding success with *The Ten Commandments* in 1923 (a film he will remake, just as successfully, in 1956). A number of great European directors, attracted by Hollywood, also contributed important films to American cinema. Among them we note the famous "naturalist" film *Greed* (1924) by the Austrian director Erich Von Stroheim, *Sunrise* (1927) by Murnau, *The Wind* (1928) by the Swede Viktor Sjöstrom, and the comedies by the German filmmaker Ernst Lubitsch.

CINEMA IN FRANCE

Abel Gance

If Jacques Feyder's *L'Atlantide* (1921) was the first big French film to appear after the war (Mitry, II, p. 435), the most important French director between the end of the Great War and the beginning of the talkies (1927) was most certainly **Abel Gance**. Gance's most significant films are *J'accuse* (1918), *The Wheel* (*La Roue*, 1921-23), and, above all, *Napoleon* (1925-27), an enormous fresco of nearly four hours which features some of the central episodes of the emperor's life and career. Heavily influenced by both Griffith and Murnau, Gance nevertheless exhibited a very personal boldness, developing narrative technique far beyond what was customary in French cinema. In *The Wheel*, for instance, he exploited the technique of rhythmic editing, that is, cutting a series of shots progressively shorter to produce an impression of acceleration and increase tension. He was at his most innovative, however, in *Napoleon*. Characterized as a "filmmaker of crisis and excess" by Prédal (p. 54), he created a supercharged atmosphere through the use of multiple superimpositions, blurred shots, camera movements, and fast editing. Like Eisenstein he created striking metaphors by using parallel editing, as he does in the scene of the "storm" which batters both the Convention (during the French Revolution) and the little boat in which Napoleon crosses the sea after fleeing Corsica. Gance's boldest technical innovations were nonetheless his point-of-view shots combined with tracking shots, as well as the use of the triple screen during the last segment of the film, the Italian campaign.

Owing to the French invention of ultra-light portable cameras, no longer constrained by the hand-turned crank, Gance was able to integrate into his film the viewpoint of characters in a variety of positions and movements. Let's read the description provided by Sadoul: "For the chase scene in Corsica a camera was placed on a galloping horse to obtain the viewpoint of Bonaparte as he fled. Then they took another automatic camera, enclosed in an airtight box, and threw it from the top of a cliff into the Mediterranean below to record Bonaparte's viewpoint as he fell. When they came to the Toulon siege, a miniature portable camera was tucked into a soccer ball, which was then tossed violently into the air to yield the viewpoint of a soldier thrown into the air by a cannon ball" (*Le Cinéma français*, pp. 32-33). As for the triple screen, which was called "polyvision," the use of three screens at once permitted Gance to juxtapose three different subjects. In one sequence, for example, he shows simultaneously the army on the march (the conquest of Italy), images of Josephine (Napoléon's thoughts, his sentimental life), and an image of a globe (the emperor's ambitions). At certain times Gance went further yet, multiplying the images on each of the three screens by utilizing masks or superimpositions to create a "visual symphony" (Sadoul, p. 32). Speaking of film in general, Prédal does not hesitate to describe Gance's special effects as "visual fireworks which mark one of the high points of the art of silent cinema" (p. 55).

While Gance's films stand out because of their narrative innovations, the nineteen-twenties in France are remembered mostly as a period of revolt, provocation, and formal experimentation, which all fall outside the development of narrative art as such. It is the period of Impressionism, Dadaïsm, and Surrealism.

Impressionism

For the moviemakers of the Impressionist school — the most "poetic" current of the avant-garde — it was more important to create an atmosphere or to depict a fantasy or a dream fragment than to tell a story. They launched into formal experiments (visual and rhythmic) of all kinds. The most typical characteristics of the movement were the systematic utilization of fast editing and blurred images (both of which were relatively new to the movies), of slow motion, superimpositions, light play, point-of-view shots, and various deformations of the image. Under the aegis of Louis Delluc, the first authentic French critic-theoretician of cinema, the impressionists attempted to foreground in their films the very specificity of film art, its autonomy with respect to both narrative literature and theater, by emphasizing its poetic potential and its relationship to painting as a mode of artistic expression. The most prominent impressionist directors and films include Germaine Dulac (*La Fête espagnole*, 1919, *The Smiling Madame Beudet*, 1922), Delluc himself (*Fever*, 1921, *The Woman From Nowhere*, 1922), Marcel L'Herbier (*Eldorado*, 1921), and Jean Epstein (*Faithful Heart*, 1923) — and of course Jacques Feyder's admirable *Crainquebille* (1922), a harbinger of the poetic realism which will sweep over the decade of the thirties. The first film of Jean Renoir, *The Whirlpool of Fate* (*La Fille de l'eau*, 1924) was no less a product of the impressionist current, which persevered until the end of the decade.

At the same time, influenced by German filmmakers another type of experimental cinema was developing in France, a very abstract form of expression whose rather unrealistic ambition was to approximate musical composition by using moving shapes to achieve a visual representation of pure rhythm. In 1925 Germaine Dulac, the theoretician of "pure cinema," characterized this ambition quite aptly: "The ultimate film which we all dream of composing is a visual symphony made of rhythmic images that only an artist's sensitivity is capable of coordinating and projecting onto the screen" (quoted in Mitry, II, p. 444). Among the most noted directors of abstract films are **Fernand Léger** and **Dudley Murphy** (*Ballet mécanique*, 1924), **Jean Grémillon** (*Photogénie mécanique*, 1925), **Marcel Duchamp** (*Anémic cinéma*, 1925), **Henri Chomette** (*Cinq minutes de cinéma pur*, 1926), and **Germaine Dulac** (*Disque 957*, 1927).

Dadaïsm — René Clair, *Entr'acte* (1924)

The "Dadaïst" movement, which affected poetry, theater, painting, and cinema, only lasted a brief moment in France at the beginning of the twenties. It is the most virulent expression of the spirit of revolt which swept over the literary and artistic circles of this period: revolt against conventions, against the decorum and comfortable attitudes of the bourgeois world, and against intellectual ossification in general. The dadaïsts sought above all to surprise, shock, and provoke in order to take the public out of its comfort zone. The undisputed masterpiece of "dadaïst" cinema (and the only film produced by this current still watched today) is *Entr'acte* (1924) by **René Clair**.

Actor and film critic, then filmmaker, René Clair was the most famous and the most popular director in France at the beginning of the nineteen-thirties, that is, at the beginning of the talkies. After making a hugely popular adaptation of a madcap comedy by Eugène Labiche, *The Italian Straw Hat* (1927), he consolidated his celebrity with three major sound films, *Under The Roofs of Paris* (*Sous les toits de Paris*, 1930), *Le Million* (1931), and *Liberty Is Ours* (*A nous la liberté*, 1931). After 1935 he left France to make films first in England and then in the United States during the German Occupation of France. When he returned to France after the war, he never again achieved the success he had enjoyed at the beginning of his career. If Clair's major films have aged somewhat, his very first film, *Entr'acte,* continues to amuse and intrigue the public.

Entr'acte is a short subject lasting around 15 minutes. It was made to be shown during the intermission of *Relâche*, a ballet written by the poet-painter Francis Picabia, with music by Erik Satie, for a performance by Rolf de Maré's Swedish Ballet in Paris in 1924. The provocative character of Clair's film is obvious to everyone, as Jean Mitry points out: "*Entr'acte* was made, it's quite clear, to 'shock' the spectator and slap him in the face, to surprise and flabbergast him, to mystify and demystify him at the same time. It was a sort of manifesto, a kind of revolt against bourgeois academism, against official art, against art period, an uprising against everything which was 'for,' and for everything which was 'against'" (II, p. 447). This is not to say that the film is humorless. Picabia added that "the only thing it respects is the desire to burst out laughing" (René Clair, "Picabia, Satie et la première d'*Entr'acte*," p. 7). The cast consists of the authors Picabia and Satie, the producer Rolf de Maré, the painter-filmmaker Marcel Duchamp, and the playwright-screenwriter Marcel Achard.

Described as "liberated images" ("images en liberté") by Clair, *Entr'acte* is in fact a carefully calculated montage of shots intended to amuse the bourgeois public while simultaneously ridiculing what it revered. The film begins by making fun of the ballet itself, filming in slow motion (and eventually from below) the legs of a ballet dancer who turns out to be…a man with a heavy black beard and a pince-nez. In the main scene of the film Clair ridicules a religious ceremony, a funeral, by showing the audience a hearse pulled by a camel and followed by a gaggle of gentlemen in top hats and black suits running in slow motion. Later in the film the hearse breaks loose from the camel and goes out of control, followed by the whole crowd sprinting madly behind it in faster and faster motion. Suddenly we find ourselves on the Luna Park rollercoaster, the funeral procession becoming in Mitry's hyperbolic terms "a toboggan which plunges down a steep slope, rushes forward, leaps up to the top of the hills, speeds around corners, plunges again and swallows up the oblique lines of the surrounding landscape in dramatic swerves. The back and forth and the front and back blend together and rush forward in a breathtaking jumble. Snatching up, crushing, kneading the depths of the void, the vertiginous dash bursts into a shower of sparks" (II, p. 447). And to top it off, one of the characters shoots another dead with a rifle — which doesn't prevent the dead man from reappearing triumphantly at the end of the film to make all the other characters disappear with strokes of his magic wand (in a series of stop-action shots), before making himself disappear in the same manner.

In the process of creating this hallucinatory gag-filled work, Clair implements the whole gamut of specifically cinematographic techniques, such as slow and fast motion shots, forward and backward tracking shots, swish pans, superimpositions, divided screens (masks), dissolves, reverse projections, stop-action shots, high and low angle shots, blurring, point-of-view shots, and fast editing. Unlike most of the other avant-garde films of the period, *Entr'acte* was highly successful, garnering praise from the film critics and an enthusiastic reception from the public. Benjamin Péret remarks on the poetic character of the film and the originality of the images, while Paul Souday notes the "considerable technical qualities" of the film, adding that "it is stunningly comical and crazy." The great poet Robert Desnos is no less enthusiastic, stating that "*Entr'acte* is the finest film of the year" (critics quoted in René Clair and Francis Picabia, *L'Avant-Scène Cinéma*, p. 7). As Prédal remarks, the success of Clair's film helped to "popularize the less appealing experimental works by dadaïst and surrealist filmmakers" (p. 50). Let us look then at "surrealist" cinema.

Surrealism — Buñuel and Dalí

An Andalusian Dog (*Un chien andalou*, 1929)

Surrealism was a politically left-leaning artistic movement founded by the poet-essayist **André Breton**. He defined the concept in 1924 in his first *Manifeste du surréalisme*: "A pure psychic automatism by which we propose to examine either verbally, by writing, or by any other manner how thought really functions. Dictates of thought in the absence of any rational control and with no esthetic or moral considerations" (p. 37). Breton recruited a circle of poets (including Louis Aragon, Phillipe Soupault, Robert Desnos, and Paul Eluard) who had, like him, broken with the Dadaïst movement. Inspired by the writings of Freud and the poet Lautréamont, he conceived poetry as a form of "automatic writing" whose goal was to reproduce the content and the functioning of unconscious thought by liberating its expressive power from the control of logic and morality. Like Freud's concept of dreams, poetry must become the expression of the deep-rooted psychological reality of man. As Breton says in his *Manifeste*: "I believe in the future reconciliation of these two ostensibly contradictory states, dream and reality, in a sort of absolute reality, a *surreality* so to speak" (pp. 23-24). While dreams are the locus of the language of the subconscious, the mission of poetry is to reproduce this language.

It is hardly surprising that cinema was attracted to surrealism, considering the central role of the image both in dreams and on the screen. However, few truly "surrealist" films have been made. One might mention two short films by Man Ray, the most important being *Starfish* (*Etoile de mer*, 1928), a "cinépoème" based on the poem by the same name by Robert Desnos. The principal examples of surrealist cinema remain however two films by the Spaniard Luis Buñuel, *An Andalusian Dog* (1928), based on his own screenplay co-authored with the painter Salvador Dalí, and *The Golden Age* (*L'Age d'or*, 1930). André Breton himself, after seeing the first showing of *An Andalusian Dog*, declared that it was a "surrealist" film, and some people went so far as to consider it "the cinematographic equivalent of the surrealists' automatic writing" (Kyrou, "Un itinéraire exemplaire," p. 9). Few films have provoked so much controversy as regards their interpretation as *An Andalusian Dog*, a short subject less than 17 minutes long shot in two weeks in Le Havre. It takes its name — which

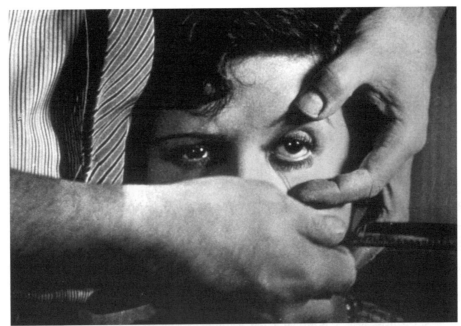

Luis Buñuel and Salvador Dalí, *An Andalusian Dog*: the cutting of the eye. © Les Grands Films
Classiques F-Paris

is totally unrelated to its content — from a volume of poems by Buñuel, *Le Chien
andalou* (1927). If everyone agrees on the provocative character of the film, which
"disturbs the moral comfort of bourgeois society" (Prédal, p. 51) with its troubling,
indeed, shocking images, there are striking differences in the interpretations given its
content. Let's look then at the content.

An Andalusian Dog begins with a title card, "Once upon a time…" Then, in a
short "prologue," we see a man (played by Luis Buñuel) slice through a woman's eye
with a straight razor, right after he watches an elongated cloud cut across the moon.
After a second card, "8 years later," a young man in a suit (Pierre Batcheff), decked out
in frilly white ruffles, rides down a street on a bicycle in the rain. A box with diagonal
stripes hangs from his neck. In a room the young woman we saw in the prologue
(Simone Mareuil) is reading a book on painting that she tosses aside to go look out
the window. She sees the cyclist fall on his side in the street beneath her. She hurries
down and covers him with kisses.

Back in the room she opens the little box and takes out a striped necktie, whose
pattern resembles that on the box. We then see her standing before the bed staring at
the things the young man was wearing, placed on the bed in the same configuration
as if he were wearing them still. Suddenly the tie ties itself. The woman turns around
and sees the man staring intently at his hand. A close-up shows a troop of ants pouring
from a black hole in the center of his hand.

We next see the man and the woman together looking out the window at an
androgynous individual — a woman with a male haircut and attire — who is using
a long stick to poke at a human hand lying in the street. A policeman puts the hand
into the striped box we saw before and gives it to the woman. In the next scene the
woman in the street is run over by a car, which seems to titillate the man in the room.

He grabs the young woman and rubs her breasts through her dress. In his imagination (apparently) he then caresses her naked breasts, which, in a dissolve, become her buttocks; his features become distorted, and he begins to slobber. When the woman tears herself free and takes defensive action, the man harnesses himself to a series of objects including some corks and melons, followed by two Christain churchmen lying on the floor and two grand pianos upon which are lying the carcasses of putrefying donkeys. He tries with all his might to drag them toward the woman, who escapes into another room in the apartment. The man pursues her and tries to follow her into the room, but his hand is caught in the door when she tries to close it behind her. We again see the ants climbing out of the hole in his hand. Suddenly the woman turns around and sees the man lying on the bed, again wearing the white frills, with the striped box on his chest.

A title card, "Around 3 o'clock in the morning," introduces the arrival of an older man, perhaps the hero's father, who proceeds to scold him severely. He tears off the feminine accoutrements and the box, throwing them out of the window one after the other before making the young man go stand in the corner. A new title card intervenes, "16 years before," after which the older man (who now appears identical to the hero) picks up two books from a pupil's desk, orders the young man to hold out his arms in the position of the cross, and places a book in each hand. The young man revolts as the two books change into revolvers with which he fires at and kills his … double. The latter man collapses in a park beside a half-naked woman. A group of men strolling in the park arrive and carry off his corpse.

Back in the room we witness a confrontation between the man and the woman during which the man's mouth disappears and is replaced by a tuft of hair from the woman's armpit. With an expression of disgust and scorn, the young woman sticks out her tongue at him and leaves the room. Outside the room, the woman finds herself looking at a beach where she runs to meet another man (Albert Duverger). They walk along the beach together until they come upon debris which we recognize as the former striped box, as well as pieces of white cloth and of the bicycle. A final card, "In the spring," precedes the last image in the film: the main character (or is it the new lover?) and the young woman blinded, wearing tattered clothing and buried in the sand to the chest.

What is this film supposed to mean? *An Andalusian Dog* has been the object of innumerable studies since it first came out, studies which propose interpretations of all stripes, often conflicting — not unlike the commentaries of the filmmaker himself. Buñuel takes pleasure in confounding the would-be exegetes, declaring, "Nothing in the film symbolizes anything," but adding immediately afterwards, "The only valid way of interpreting the symbols would perhaps be through psychoanalysis" (Buñuel, "Notes," p. 30). We also know that Buñuel and Dalí agreed in the spirit of surrealism on a simple rule before beginning to write the screenplay for the film: "not to accept any idea, any image which would lend itself to a rational explanation, psychological or cultural. Open all the doors to the irrational. Only accept images which we find striking, without making any attempt to understand why" (Blanco, p. 64). In essence the two writers are resorting to the method preferred by all surrealist artists, "automatic writing," that is, the free association of ideas and images. Indeed, here is what Buñuel says about the beginning of his association with the surrealist group in

Paris in 1929: "Since I was the only filmmaker in the group, I decided to bring the esthetics of surrealism to the screen" (Aranda, p. 17). However, we also know that he declared in 1929, in an issue of *La Révolution surréaliste*, that his film wasn't an aesthetic experiment but rather "a desperate, passionate call for murder" (Kyrou, "Un itinéraire exemplaire," p. 9).

The contradictory messages are enough to discourage any potential commentator, and certain of them, Sadoul for example, conclude simply that there is no logical plot to be found in the film: "The film's universe, which is poetic, transposes sentiments and moods through the use of metaphors whose only goal is to surprise and shock" (*Le Cinéma français*, p. 38). Buñuel nonetheless indicates, as if by accident, several paths to pursue: "*Un chien andalou* is not an attempt to narrate a dream, but it develops a mechanism which is analogous to that of a dream" (Liebman, p. 155); "the protagonists' acts are determined by subconscious drives" (Aranda, p. 17) — statements which rather clearly authorize psychoanalytic hypotheses on the meaning of the film. Aranda considers in fact that "we find an amalgam of surrealist esthetics and Freud's ideas" in Buñuel's film (p. 17). We know moreover that before writing the scenario for *Un chien andalou*, Buñuel and Dalí had decided to tell each other their dreams, and that this is the origin of their film project (Blanco, p. 64). One may conclude with Kyrou that dream representation in Buñuel's film is only an "expression of human anguish" (p. 19). However, if we recall that dream language, according to Freud, is the language of the unconscious mind (and that the working title of the film was *It is dangerous to look inwards*), it does not seem unreasonable to use Freud's theories as a possible interpretive grid in analyzing Buñuel's film.

Certain images, like the famous mutilation of the eye in the prologue, the feminine attire of the hero, the molestation scene, the punishment of the hero and the murder of his "double," may be interpreted in the context of Freud's theories on the Oedipus complex. The obvious allusions include the subconscious desire for union with the mother, fetishism, castration fear (in the male infant who fears punishment by his father for desiring his mother), and the wish for the father's death — as well as the Eros/Thanatos thematics (sexual desire and death). As regards the shot of the eye being sliced, for example, we recall Freud's comment that "the study of dreams, of fantasms, and of myths has taught us that fear for the eyes, the fear of becoming blind, is a frequent substitute for the fear of castration" (in Dubois, p. 42). We cannot forget of course the final gesture of Oedipus, who blinds himself when he realizes that he has had an incestuous relationship with his mother. Moreover, the theme of castration is again suggested by the severed hand lying in the street. The feminine flounces that the main character wears recall the fetishism that Freud interprets as a sign of the male child's refusal to accept the difference between himself and his mother. The man who chides the hero, forcing him to take off the pieces of white flounces and the box, suggests the fear of punishment by the father (related to the superego) which is an integral part of the Oedipus complex. The theme of the relationship between eroticism and death is carried by the music of the film, which includes an Argentine tango (dance in dreams, according to Freud, connotes sexual relations) and passages from the Liebestod ("dying from love") in Wagner's opera *Tristan and Isolde*. The "dream mechanism" is suggested moreover by the treatment of time in the film, the apparently groundless movement between present, past, and future — a temporal incoherence characteristic of dreams.

In addition, the film is rife with objects whose sexual symbolism, as deciphered by Freud, can hardly be due to chance. In the classification of objects which appear regularly in dreams, for example, Freud distinguishes between objects which represent the masculine sexual organ and those which symbolize the feminine organ. Among the latter are included everything which is concave, like a box or a mouth, but also objects such as books and landscapes. The former includes everything which has an elongated shape, like sticks, ties, revolvers, and certain parts of the body. Thus, in the scene where the box hanging from the hero's neck turns out to contain a tie, or in the one in which the severed hand is put into the box and given to the androgyn, the mixing of signs of gender seems intentional. The whole set of Freudian motifs leads certain critics like Linda Williams (to whom the foregoing psychoanalytical analysis owes a great deal) to perceive in *An Andalusian Dog* a latent text whose reference is quite clear: the "successive stages of the psycho-sexual development of the main character" ("La Rhétorique de l'inconscient," p. 56). Williams's interpretation is not unlike Renaud's conclusion that *An Andalusian Dog* is "the adventure of a man struggling with his homosexual instincts and his ordinary desires" (p. 150).

In addition to the psychoanalytical hypotheses that Buñuel seems to encourage, the various individual elements of *An Andalusian Dog* have been subjected to a multitude of interpretations — and none more so than the sliced eye, "one of the most famous images in the history of cinema" (Leutrat, p. 94). Buñuel obtained this image by slicing the eye of a dead calf, after applying eye liner. The filmmaker claims that it is only a reference to a dream that he had in which he saw both a cloud move across the moon and an eye being cut; the two images are simply juxtaposed in the film. When he shot the eye being cut, he adds later, it was solely to "produce a traumatic shock in the spectators from the outset, to prepare them for what was to follow" (Blanco, p. 65). For the filmmaker Jean Vigo, nonetheless, the image has a concrete meaning. It is meant to convey to the spectators that "in this film, they will be expected to see in a different way" (p. 10). Vigo's hypothesis seems supported by the fact that it is the filmmaker himself who plays the role of the man who slices the eye. For another critic, "the cutting of the eye may represent an entrance into the realm of sexuality: deflowering, with its unbearable side" (Renaud, p. 151). Leutrat reminds us, moreover, that "the association of the eye and the female sexual organ is a wide-spread concept among those who were connected to surrealism at the end of the twenties and at the beginning of the thirties" (p. 94). On the subject of the striped box, Leutrat completely eschews Freud's sexual symbolism of objects appearing in dreams, declaring that this motif "seems to have no other meaning than the mystery created by its surprising reappearances and the objects which it contains" (p. 96).

Many interpretations, some contradictory, have also been proposed for the scene of the donkey carcasses lying across the grand pianos. It has been perceived negatively as an expression of "the dead weight of the hero's past, of his childhood and his education" (Drummond, p. 120), or of the moral and cultural disapproval of sexual desire. But it has also been interpreted positively: "The man sacrifices his convention-ridden past to the woman he wishes to conquer, in order for their love to blossom without restrictions" (Renaud, p. 152). Other interpretations are clearly at the extreme limit of credibility, like the hypothesis that the scene contains an international pun on the words "asses" (donkeys) and the French word for grand pianos, "pianos à queue" ("queue" being a slang term for the male sexual organ), with the resulting suggestion of sodomy... (*loc. cit.*).

Critics agree more and more today on the principle that it is impossible to establish clearly the meaning of *An Andalusian Dog*. Some are beginning to focus on formal questions, such as the organization of space and the variations on certain motifs in the film, like the "chain of destroyed eyes" (Drummond, p. 124). Leutrat reflects also on images which express the theme of *renversement*, or reversal (the tango, for example). Images of reversal, he claims, "become the principle of the whole film, in its smallest as in its largest units, beginning with the young woman with the male haircut who is *renversée* (run over) by a car" (p. 96).

It is certain in any case that *An Andalusian Dog* astonished everyone in its own time and that it continues to fascinate the public today. While Buñuel may utilize techniques developed and made fashionable by the cinematographic avant-garde in general — superimpositions, dissolves, stop-action photography, slow-motion, iris shots — his film contrasts starkly with the purely formal experiments conducted by his impressionist and dadaïst predecessors. As Renaud remarks, " If *An Andalusian Dog* occupies an important place in the history of cinema, it is less due to the technique Buñuel employs (which is rather rudimentary) than to the expression — very original for the period — of an idea, of a situation, and of a plot with images which apparently have nothing in common with the theme being treated" (p. 156). By demonstrating that French cinema was capable of treating the most serious and complex subjects, of competing with the most subtle poetry, Buñuel helped put the "seventh art" on an equal footing with the classical literary and artistic genres.

Despite its importance, Buñuel's film did not create a school in French cinema. Moreover, his surrealistic feature film made the following year, *The Golden Age* (*L'Age d'or*), which was dedicated to passionate love (*l'amour fou*) and to the spirit of revolt, was a resounding failure — despite the fact that it was crammed full of scandalous images and themes. If we are to believe Buñuel, it very nearly led to the excommunication of the film's financier, the viscount of Noailles. We are at the beginning of a new era. The end of the twenties coincides with the virtual end of silent cinema, its death knell tolling with the opening of the first sound film, *The Jazz Singer* by the American Alan Crosland. The masterpiece by the Dane **Carl Dreyer,** *La Passion de Jeanne d'Arc* (1928), ranked among the "twelve best films of all time" in 1958, would remain the definitive monument to the art of silent film.

The reign of the talkies begins with the decade of the thirties, as does the progressive triumph of the principal current of the "classical age" of French cinema, **poetic realism**. This "movement," which includes films of various stripes, is characterized above all by a profoundly human, thematic, and metaphorical richness. The first of the following chapters bearing on individual films will thus be devoted to several French filmmakers whose work is representative, each in its own way, of poetic realism: **Jean Vigo, Jean Renoir,** and **Marcel Carné**.

But let's look first at how a film is analyzed.

WORKS CONSULTED

Aranda, Juan Francisco. "La Réalisation d'*Un chien andalou*," *Revue belge du cinéma* 33-35 (1993), 17-21.

Betton, Gérard. *Histoire du cinéma*. Paris: Presses universitaires de France, 1984.

Blanco, Manuel Rodriguez. *Luis Buñuel*. Paris: BiFi-Durante, 2000.

Breton, André. *Manifestes du surréalisme*. Paris: Gallimard, 1977.

Buñuel, Luis. "Notes on the making of *Un chien andalou*" in Stauffacher, Frank, ed. *Art in Cinema*. San Francisco: San Francisco Museum of Art, 1947 (pp. 29-30).

Buñuel, Luis, and Salvador Dalí. "Un Chien andalou" (screenplay). *L'Avant-Scène Cinéma* 27-28 (juin 1963), 3-22.

Clair, René. "Picabia, Satie et la première d'*Entr'acte*," *L'Avant-Scène Cinéma* 86 (novembre 1968), 5-7.

Clair, René, and Francis Picabia. *Entr'acte* (screenplay). *L'Avant-Scène Cinéma* 86 (novembre 1968), 3-18.

Drummond, Phillip. "L'Espace textuel : la séquence des ânes et des pianos," *Revue belge du cinéma* 33-35 (1993), 119-126.

Dubois, Philippe. "Plans de coup(e) d'œil," *Revue belge du cinéma* 33-35 (1993), 40-42.

Kyrou, Ado. *Luis Buñuel*. Paris: Seghers, 1962.

.........."Un itinéraire exemplaire," *L'Avant-Scène Cinéma* 27-28 (juin 1963), 9-10.

Leutrat, Jean-Louis. "Liberté grande," *Revue belge du cinéma* 33-35 (1993), 93-98.

Liebman, Stuart. "Le Traitement de la langue," *Revue belge du cinéma* 33-35 (1993), 155-161.

Mitry, Jean. *Histoire du cinéma*, II. Paris: Editions universitaires, 1969.

Prédal, René. *Histoire du cinéma*. Condé-sur-Noireau: CinémAction-Corlet, 1994.

Renaud, Pierre. "Symbolisme au second degré : *Un chien andalou*," dans *Etudes cinématographiques* 20-23 (1963), 147-157.

Sadoul, Georges. *Le Cinéma français*. Paris: Flammarion, 1962.

Vigo, Jean. *"Un chien andalou,"* *Avant-Scène Cinéma* 27-28 (juin 1963), 10.

Williams, Linda. "La Rhétorique de l'inconscient," *Revue belge du cinéma* 33-35 (1993), 47-60.

.........*Figures of Desire*. Urbana, IL: University of Illinois Press, 1981.

"Reading" A Film

In their *Introduction To Film Analysis*, Vanoye and Goliot-Lété remind us that film is "a cultural product inscribed in a socio-historical context" (p. 43). As regards the precise character of the relationship between a film and its context, they add:

> In a film, whatever its goal (to describe, entertain, criticize, denounce, or militate), society is less *shown* than staged. In other words a film makes choices, organizes elements, borrows from both reality and the imagination, and constructs a virtual world which entertains complex relations with the real world [...]. Whether a reflection or a rejection, a film constitutes a *viewpoint* on this or that aspect of the contemporary world. It represents society in the form of a spectacle or drama (in the broadest sense of the word), and it is this representation which is the analyst's object of study (pp. 44-45).

This very apt conception of the object of film analysis implies of course the description by the analyst of the type of representation which is presented in the film. This may be the depiction of society or of a character's inner life or of any fictional universe posited by the director. If it is generally agreed that "the analysis of films is above all descriptive" (Aumont and Marie, p. 11), this undertaking is not a simple affair. As many theoreticians, including Aumont and Marie, recognize, description is also an interpretative activity. To describe a film — that is, to analyze it — it is necessary first to break it up into its component parts. This critical first step is then followed by an attempt to understand the relationship between those parts in order to gain an appreciation of the manner in which the film produces its various meanings. This second activity, which is reconstructive in nature, itself produces meaning, to such an extent that the film reader's perspective (informed by his/her personal culture, opinions, and biases) tends to be superimposed on the viewpoint which is inscribed in the film. I mention from the outset this particular complication in order to emphasize both the role of description in film analysis and the importance of keeping constantly in mind the perspectives which are developed in the film itself so as not to substitute our personal preoccupations. Aumont and Marie propose the following general rule: "Never perform an analysis which loses sight of the film being analyzed; to the contrary, always return to the film whenever possible" (p. 56). Vanoye and Goliot-Lété concur completely, formulating the same principle slightly differently: "The film is thus the point of departure and the destination of the analysis" (p. 10). This being said, what do we mean precisely by the "description" of a film?

FILM "LANGUAGE"

Let's discuss immediately the notion of "film language." For some theoreticians, like André Bazin or Marcel Martin, the cinematographic medium is an authentic language to the extent that it disposes of "innumerable means of expression which it uses with the flexibility and effectiveness of a verbal language" (Martin, p. 15). Martin goes on to state (quoting Alexandre Arnoux) that "cinema is a language of images with its own vocabulary, syntax, inflections, ellipses, conventions, and grammar" (p. 15). He recognizes nonetheless that film language most closely resembles poetic language, a realm where the image reigns supreme also. For linguists, however, the basis elements of cinematographic representation are not equivalent to the elementary units of meaning in natural languages — phonemes, morphemes, or even words — because of the analogical character of images and the "continuity" of the visual signifier. Since a natural language, like English or French, is neither analogical (in general words do not physically "resemble" what they signify) nor continuous (it is a concatenation of discrete phonemes), we can only refer to film as a "language" in a metaphorical sense. Understood literally or metaphorically, the notion of "film language," referring to the whole gamut of techniques used in cinema, is extremely useful in discussing how one reads a film. Like verbal narrative language, which can be divided into units of meaning from a single word to sentences, paragraphs, chapters, and even a whole novel, a film lends itself to a similar segmentation — called ***découpage*** — into signifiying units. This is where the description of a film must begin.

THE FILMIC IMAGE

Martin is right to insist on the following point: "*You must learn to read a film*, to decipher the meaning of images just as you decipher the meaning of words and ideas, to understand the subtleties of cinematographic language" (p. 29). Film is like any other area of knowledge (mathematics, biology, psychoanalysis, linguistics, etc.): to understand it you must learn its language, because you learn its fundamental concepts along with its language. The basic element of film is the ***image***. In narrative terms, the image is the (metaphorical) equivalent of the word, and the film will be built on images combined with sound. We note immediately that the filmic image has its own specific character. It is always "in the present" — in movies the past is constructed mentally by the spectator, aided by the temporal context or by technical indications, as we shall see below. It is "realistic" — that is, it creates through movement, as the semiotician Christian Metz notes, an "impression of reality" (pp. 16-19). It is polysemous (i.e., it contains multiple meanings) and lends itself therefore to diverse interpretations, although its significance is anchored, at least partially, by its context, by the soundtrack, and by its combination with other images (film "montage," which we will discuss below). Given the polysemous nature of the image, it is generally agreed that the analysis of a film is never "over," its meaning never exhausted by a given interpretation.

To finish this introduction to the image, we note that the filmic image is always circumscribed by a ***frame***, just like a photograph. When the director of photography (or the cameraman) "frames" a space, this space (corresponding to the image we see on the screen) is called the ***shot***. When we discuss an image, we speak of what is in the shot and, conversely, what is ***off-screen***. The off-screen space is an imaginative continuation of the visible space of the shot; it is the invisible space where are located "all of the elements (characters, settings, etc.) which, not being included in the shot, are nonetheless attached to it by [the spectator's] imagination" (Aumont et al., *Esthétique du film*, p. 15). In a film the ***voice-over*** (a voice that we hear without seeing the person speaking on-screen), for example, often belongs to a character located off-screen.

SHOT, SEQUENCE, SCENE

If we pursue the comparison with the linguistic model, just as words combine to make a sentence, individual images combine to create a larger unit that is also called a *shot*. A shot is the portion of film which is recorded between a single starting and stopping of the camera. A series of shots which form a distinct dramatic unit (like a "scene" in a play) is called a *sequence*, which may also be compared to a paragraph or a chapter in a written narrative text. A single shot, on the other hand, may constitute by itself a dramatic unit of a film: this is called a *sequence shot* (or a lengthy take), a technique perfected by Jean Renoir, as we shall see in the chapters devoted to his films.

Christian Metz's reflections on film language permit us to make a useful technical distinction between a sequence and a *scene*. The latter refers, in Metz's taxonomy, to a type of sequence which takes place in real time, whereas the term "sequence" is reserved for sequences which contain temporal ellipses (pp. 130-131). All of the sequences and scenes taken together constitute the entire film, as the set of chapters constitutes the novel. To understand the dramatic structure of a film, one needs to know how to analyze its *découpage*; that is, how to identify in a film the various sequences which compose it and the manner in which they are connected. To be able to appreciate the nuances of a filmmaker's style, you also have to be able to identify the shots in a given sequence and know how to describe them, as well as how they are linked together. In the following paragraphs we will speak of the fundamental characteristics of the various types of shots, including the relative size and the length of the shots, the camera angles and movements, the types of transitions between plans, and finally the use of deep focus.

SHOT LENGTHS AND SIZES

Though the average length of a shot is 8 to 10 seconds, a shot can vary from a fraction of a second to a whole reel (the latter being of course extremely rare!). The various lengths of the shots determine the rhythm of the film. A series of very short shots creates, for instance, a tense, nervous, or even violent atmosphere, whereas a very lengthy shot which emphasizes the passage of time may give an impression of calm, reflection, or monotony — or it may create suspense. A professional film analyst, working on an editing table, may go so far as to time each shot to be able to draw conclusions as to the rhythmic style of a film.

Among the important characteristics of a shot, the spectator needs to be sensitive to its relative size, which is generally determined by the distance between the camera and its subject, although size can also be determined optically by varying the focal length of the lens. Shot sizes range from the extreme close-up to the vast establishing shot. The conventional "rhetoric" of film formulated very early in the history of cinema dictated the use of an extremely long shot, or *establishing shot*, at the beginning of the film to reveal the geographic context of the action. In a western, for example, this could be a wide plain dotted with buttes. This initial shot was then followed by a *long shot* which normally depicted people in a setting; e.g., a western town with people in the streets. This would be followed by a *medium shot* framing characters in a precise décor, such as the interior of a saloon. It was not unlike the description of the physical and social environment at the beginning of a Balzac novel in the 19ᵗʰ century, although considerably more cursory. This convention is no longer widely respected in cinema. We see numerous films which do not begin with a long shot, like Jean Renoir's *Grand Illusion*, for instance, which begins with a close-up of a record spinning on a turntable.

The scale of shots closer than the long shot is best illustrated in relation to the characters in the film. In descending order we move from the long shot, in which we see characters from head to toe, to the medium shot, in which they are framed from the knees up. The French refer to the medium shot as an ***American shot*** because it is the typical shot in American comedies from the thirties. According to André Bazin it is also the shot which "best corresponds to the spontaneous gaze of the spectator" (p. 72). A ***near shot*** frames the upper body of the actor, whereas a ***close-up*** focuses on the actor's face and the ***extreme close-up*** (or ***insert***) on a small detail of the actor's body, such as the tearful eye of Henriette in a famous shot near the end of Renoir's *A Day in the Country*. It should be understood that the range of shots just described (with the exception of the "American shot") applies to settings and objects as well as to characters.

Among the various shot sizes it is important to note the particular character and role of the long shot and the close-up, the two most specifically cinematographic shots insofar as there is no real equivalent in the theater. The long shot serves above all to situate the character in the world, to objectify it and reduce it to its proper proportions. At the same time, it creates a wide range of atmospheres: pathetic or threatening, dramatic or comical, lyrical or epic, to name a few. The long shot often sets the tone for the film. The close-up on the other hand is one of the most powerful and expressive devices of cinema. As Martin remarks, "It is in the close-up of the human face that the psychological and dramatic significance of a film are depicted most powerfully" (p. 42). When the camera moves forward until it frames a character's face in close-up, we have the impression that we are coming into contact with the character's inner being. As a corollary, the close-up of a face often suggests "a high degree of mental stress in the character" (p. 44), if not out and out anguish. We see this clearly in the case of François in Marcel Carné's *Daybreak*, just before the besieged factory worker begins to search his memory to understand the murder he has just committed. Likewise, very close shots and close-ups produce tension in the spectator. Alfred Hitchcock's films have amply demonstrated that the suspense rises as the camera approaches a character (especially if it is in the middle of the night in a forest or in a dark basement…)! In the case of an object, the close-up dramatizes its presence and endows it with meaning — even if we do not understand immediately what meaning — as in the case of the twitch in the Japanese lover's hand in Alain Resnais's *Hiroshima mon amour*.

CAMERA ANGLES

In addition to the shot size, the director must choose the camera angle which best suits the subject, that is, the particular perspective from which he or she is going to show the subject. If the camera is positioned above the subject (above the normal level of the eyes), so that we are looking downwards, the director is producing a ***high angle shot*** or a "***down shot***." Conversely, if the camera is placed below the subject, we are seeing a ***low angle shot*** or an "***up shot***." Although it is not a general rule, camera angles which are not at normal eye level may have a specific psychological function. An up shot which frames a character gives that person a dominant position in relationship to whomever he or she is looking at. The object of the character's gaze (as well as the spectator, who is in a similar position) feels diminished. On the other hand, in the case of the down shot, it is the character being filmed who feels dominated and diminished by the gaze; the spectator is on the side of the character who is in the superior position. In extreme cases, to produce a striking effect, we may see vertical up or down shots. In the famous dormitory sequence in *Zero For Conduct*, for example, Jean Vigo places his camera near the ceiling to shoot from above, nearly vertically, the children running wildly across the beds. In *Entr'acte*, René Clair films a dancer from below, in a vertical up shot through a glass floor, to provoke the bourgeois public.

In the area of camera angles, finally, we should mention two sparingly used angles, ***sideways tilts*** and what Martin calls "***disorderly shots***." In the first the camera is tilted on its side to the left or the right. If we are dealing with a point of view ("subjective") shot, a tilt may suggest a psychologically or morally aberrant state of mind, as in the case of a drunken or deranged individual. In the case of "disorderly shots," the camera is turned every which way, such as the scene in *Napoleon* when Abel Gance puts his portable camera inside a soccer ball and then throws it into the air to simulate the viewpoint of a soldier who is tossed end over end by an exploding artillery shell.

CAMERA MOVEMENTS

At the beginning of cinema, the camera rarely moved. It simply recorded action taking place in front of it. According to the theoretician Alexandre Astruc, "The history of cinematographic technique, reduced to its simplest terms, is the history of the liberation of the camera." Liberation means movement: the camera has become mobile and can henceforth represent the spectator's gaze as well as the viewpoint of a character in the film. There are two principal types of camera movements: the ***panning shot*** (or **pan**) and the ***tracking*** (or ***traveling***) ***shot***. A ***pan*** is a rotation of the camera around its vertical or horizontal axis without moving the tripod on which it is mounted. In other words, when the camera pans, it simply pivots towards the right, towards the left, upwards, or downwards (the latter two movements are referred to as ***tilts***). While pans often just accompany the movement of a character, vehicle, or object, they can also have an important descriptive function. This function may be purely objective, as when the camera's eye sweeps across Von Rauffenstein's room at Wintersborn in Renoir's *Grand Illusion*, or subjective, as when it represents Antoine's gaze as the adolescent examines the police station through the bars of his cell in François Truffaut's *The 400 Blows* (see our analysis of this sequence at the end of this chapter).

The tracking shot (also called a "dolly shot," a "crane shot," or a "tracking shot," depending on the method used) involves moving the camera, which leaves its horizontal or vertical axis to move closer to or further away from its subject, or to accompany its movement. If the camera approaches the subject, we say that it "tracks forward"; if it moves away from it, it is "tracking backward." If the camera moves parallel to a motionless subject, we speak of a "lateral tracking"; if the tracking shot follows a moving person or object, it is, quite logically, a "follow shot." In the case of tracking both forward and backward, the camera movement can be simulated, as we mentioned above, by optical means, allowing the cameraman to approach or move away from the subject without the camera moving physically. This is called a ***zoom***. Like the pan, a tracking shot can be objective or subjective. When the camera represents a character's point of view, which occurs frequently in films, we may speak of a ***subjective*** (or ***point-of-view) tracking shot***. Tracking shots of all sorts — including vertical dolly shots — have invaded the cinema, for both descriptive and dramatic reasons. As we saw in the case of François in *Daybreak,* tracking forward to a close-up of a character's face materializes his state of mind and suggests unusual psychological stress. Tracking backward produces various effects depending on the context, including an impression of solitude or alienation. A striking example of this may be found in the famous police van sequence in *The 400 Blows* in which Antoine stares out the back window as the vehicle drives through and away from the Pigalle neighborhood where he lived, on the way to prison.

Finally, we note that panning and tracking shots may be combined in a relatively complicated movement that Martin calls a "trajectory." The trajectory shot is often used at the beginning of a film, during the credits for example, to introduce us to the diegetical (fictional) world in which the action is going to take place. At the beginning of *The 400 Blows* the camera tracks rapidly through the streets of Paris while panning over the fronts of the buildings, before sweeping around the Eiffel Tower and panning upward to look at the Tower in a low-angle shot. In Renoir's films pans are often choreographed with tracking shots in complicated sequences like the celebrated "Danse macabre" scene at the marquis's castle in *The Rules of the Game.*

FILM EDITING

As Gérard Betton states, "editing is the element most specific to cinematographic language" (p. 72), to the extent that it presides over the organization of the film's component units. In its most elementary sense editing is the assembling of the shots of a film in the order decided by the director. In conventional ***narrative editing***, the most common type of editing, it involves ordering the shots in such a way that the logical progression of the action is assured. If the shots and sequences are presented in chronological order, we are dealing with ***linear editing***. Linear editing may include ***cross-cutting***, in which shots of two different actions are alternated to suggest simultaneity. We see this often in westerns where, in order to create suspense, shots of the fort under attack by Indians are alternated with shots of the cavalry galloping to the rescue. In other cases the chronological order of the action may be interrupted by a series of flashbacks, which mix the past with the present.

In addition to narrative coherence, the editing creates the rhythm of the film through the choice of the size and length of the shots. As we suggested above, the shorter the shots, the greater their intensity and dynamism. Accordingly, series of short shots tend to dominate action films, while lengthy shots are more characteristic of psychological films, insofar as they emphasize the characters' state of mind (sadness, boredom, introspection, etc.). The level of intensity varies similarly according to the size of the shots: the closer the shot the higher the psychological tension.

It is generally agreed that the American filmmaker D.W. Griffith is the principal pioneer in narrative editing. More than anyone else, Griffith exploited the potential of editing, giving the art its modern form by varying the length and size of shots for expressive and narrative purposes. As regards expressivity, however, it is above all the Soviet school which led the way by showing the entire world of cinema that editing is not simply the logical organization of shots to tell a story. Referred to as *montage* (the French term for editing), it is also the art of juxtaposing shots to produce emotions and ideas. As the most famous Soviet theoretician and filmmaker Sergei Eisenstein says, "Montage is the art of expressing or signifying through the juxtaposition of two shots such that their combination gives rise to an idea or expresses something which is not contained in either of the two shots alone. The whole is superior to the sum of the parts" (quoted in Betton, *Esthétique*, p. 75). More simply put, "montage produces an idea which is born of the shock created by bringing together two distinct elements" (Eisenstein, p. 49).

The discovery that the confrontation of two shots can produce a meaning that is not in either of the shots separately belongs however to one of Eisenstein's teachers, Lev Koulechov, who conducted a now famous experiment. In one of the several versions of the story, Koulechov edited a series of shots together alternating close-ups of the actor Ivan Mosjoukine with a blank look on his face and shots depicting a bowl of steaming hot soup, a revolver, a child's casket, and an erotic scene. The spectators invited to view this short sequence were amazed at how subtly Mosjoukine's facial expressions (his face was blank, we remember) conveyed the feelings of hunger, fear, sadness, and desire. Specific meanings were thus produced solely by the juxtaposition of the shots: this is the now famous "Koulechov Effect."

Eisenstein elaborated a complete theory of montage in which he described the different methods of editing at the filmmaker's disposal. Explaining the precise effect that each is intended to have on the spectator, he distinguished between *metric montage*, based on the length of the shots, *rhythmic montage*, based on both the length of the shots and movement within the frame (the content of the shot), *tonal montage*, based on the "emotional resonance," the "general tone" of the shot, and, finally, *intellectual montage*. This last form of editing, which Eisenstein described somewhat abstrusely as "the conflicting combination of concomitant intellectual affects" (p. 71), is the basis for the *ideological montage* for which the Soviet director is most famous. This method of editing shots together produces either an emotion or a precise idea through the shock of their juxtapostion. *Parallel editing* is a particular case of ideological montage in which the combination of two or more shots produces a symbolic or metaphorical effect. One of the best-known examples of this is found in the first film by Eisenstein, *Strike* (1924). A shot of workers being mown down by Cossacks is followed by a shot of animals being killed in a slaughterhouse. The spectator draws the obvious conclusions. In this case the parallel editing of the two shots creates a metaphor, which explains why it is sometimes referred to as *metaphorical montage*. As J. Aumont et al. note, this classification of editing techniques and the theory surrounding it is "generally outmoded" today (p. 49). It nonetheless remains important as regards the discovery of the specifically cinematographic techniques which are available to narrate a story, provoke emotional responses, produce meaning, and create atmosphere.

TRANSITIONS (CONTINUITY EDITING)

To be able to speak about the editing of a given film, an analyst needs to understand how the transition is effected from one shot to the next and between sequences. Such transitions constitute the ***continuity editing*** of a film, and the techniques used for this purpose are tantamount to the "punctuation" of the film. As regards the transition between shots, the simplest and most common type is a ***cut***, where two shots are simply set side by side, the second replacing the first. In principle the cut is neutral; it does not in and of itself add any meaning to the passage from one shot to the next. But cut editing, because of its abrupt nature, may produce a shock. It is not by chance that Eisenstein's films, in which the shock of images produces meaning, are dominated by simple cuts between both the shots and the sequences.

In the case of editing between sequences, several types of transitions are commonly used in classic cinema. When the linkage between two sequences is effected by a particular technique, the technique is always chosen (at least in good films) with the goal of producing a particular effect and a certain meaning. For example, to indicate the end of a sequence filmmakers often use a ***fade out***, that is, the progressive disappearance of the image until the screen becomes black. This is a very strong punctuation mark which tells the spectator that it is the end of a segment of the narrative. Conversely, a ***fade in***, the progressive appearance of an image beginning with a black screen, indicates the beginning of a new action following the one which has just ended. In old films, especially in silent cinema, the ***iris in*** and the ***iris out*** were frequently used. This is a particular type of fade in which the image appears or disappears by means of a circle of light which expands or shrinks, from or to the black screen. The iris shot was frequently used to focus attention on a particular detail of the image. Rarely seen in cinema today, this technique is sometimes used in modern films when the director wants to allude to the origins of cinema, or to emphasize cinema as a theme, as Jean-Luc Godard does in a scene in *Breathless* (1960).

One of the most frequently used and most expressive transition techniques in classic cinema is the ***dissolve***, in which an image fades out as the following image fades in, the second image superimposed for a moment on the first. The dissolve most frequently indicates the passage of time between two sequences. It is normally a simple moving forward in time (with an ellipsis), but when the dissolve is drawn out, it may signal a flashback, as in the case of François in *Daybreak*. The dissolve may also be used inside a sequence, as in the train episode in *Grand Illusion* where the long series of dissolves signifies both the passing of time and the transfer of the French officers from prison to prison. We see a similar use of the dissolve in Antoine's interview with the psychologist at the juvenile delinquent facility in *The 400 Blows*, where a series of dissolves on the boy's face implies temporal discontinuity (jumping ahead in time) in spite of the apparent continuity of the dialogue.

We note, finally, the use of ***sound dissolves***, in which the linkage of two sequences is effected by music or sound effects which gradually replace the sound accompanying the preceding image. An exceptionally successful example of this transition technique may be seen at the end of the sequence in *Daybreak* where François, lost in the memory of his first confrontation with Valentin at the cabaret, returns slowly to the present.

DEEP FOCUS

When we speak of "depth of field" in photography, we are referring to the range of distances, from close to far, at which the subject framed by the camera remains in focus. If there is very little depth of field, the characters or objects which are in the foreground or background of the shot will be blurry. To shoot in deep focus (with depth of field) means therefore that everything that is in the shot will be in focus. In use since the very beginning of cinema, depth of field will take on a new significance with the move from the esthetics of silent film to the techniques of the talkies in the thirties and forties. If we are to believe André Bazin, "the talkies are the death knell of a certain kind of esthetics of film language" (p. 78). Silent film had perfected the art of montage, and the nature of montage is fragmentation of space. Bazin insists that fragmentation is inimical to the principal goal of cinema, which is the realistic representation of the world. To the extent that it preserves unity of space, deep focus, often combined with camera and actor movements, " places the spectator in a relationship with the image that is similar to the one he has with reality" (p. 75).

Bazin considers moreover that deep focus has a liberating effect on the spectator, whereas liberty is lost in the process of classical découpage, which constantly directs the spectator's attention and imposes certain meanings. In this perspective montage takes away an essential aspect of reality, its fundamental ambiguity. Roland Barthes conjectures, in fact, that Eisenstein's cinema, which is based on montage, tends to destroy the ambiguity of reality (quoted in Aumont et al., p. 59). Depth of field and its corollary, the sequence shot, would thus grant the spectator greater liberty, while at the same time soliciting his active participation in the construction of the meaning of the film.

There is no unanimity, however, on the concept of the liberating function of deep focus. Marcel Martin, for instance, expresses strong reservations about the real liberty offered by depth of field (pp. 197-198). Many techniques — words, movements, objects, sound effects, music, organization of space — serve in fact to focus the spectator's attention and anchor certain meanings. A good example may be seen in the servants' meal sequence in *The Rules of the Game*, which is analyzed at the end of this chapter. Martin nonetheless points out other advantages of deep focus, such as the possibility of representing several actions at the same time (in both the foreground and the background, for instance) and of highlighting the psychological drama by framing characters in a given decor in lengthy fixed shots (p. 194). But the importance of depth of field in the evolution of cinema is clear to everyone, for "it implies a whole concept of staging and even of cinema itself" (Martin, p. 189). In the hands of a great filmmaker, such as Jean Renoir or Orson Welles, the conscious use of deep focus tends to create "a cinematographic narrative which is capable of expressing everything without cutting up the world; it is capable of revealing the hidden meaning of beings and things without destroying their natural unity" (Bazin, 78).

Whatever position one takes, the opposition between Bazin's esthetic bias (based on the representation of reality) and Eisenstein's (based on the construction of meaning) represents one of the most important ideological debates in the history of world cinema. It is about the very conception of cinema, for Bazin's theory promotes the notion of the "transparency" of the filmic narrative — the spectator's attention is focused wholly on the illusion of reality — whereas Eisensteinian montage foregrounds cinema itself, drawing the spectator's attention to the techniques which are specific to the seventh art (Aumont et al., p. 52).

SOUND

The great masters of silent film attacked the talkies violently at the end of the twenties when they first appeared on the scene, accusing them of having a negative impact on the most specifically cinematographic techniques. Chaplin accused them for instance of ruining the art of pantomime, which was a fundamental part of silent film, while Eisenstein and his Soviet colleagues claimed that it destroyed the art of montage. Today everyone agrees that sound is an essential and fundamental component of cinema which has transformed its very esthetics.

There is little doubt that the sound track contributes greatly to the impression of reality which characterizes cinema in general, just as it reinforces the impression of the continuity of the visual representation (which, we remember, is a series of discrete photographs). The use of sound effects and talking permitted filmmakers to do away with the title cards containing dialogue or explanations which were part and parcel of silent cinema. It also obviated the need to use certain metaphors or symbols to communicate ideas — like the hands vigorously shaking the mixer to represent the sound of the doorbell in *An Andalusian Dog*. In addition, the technique of voice-over "opens up to cinema the rich domain of in-depth psychology by making it possible to exteriorize the most intimate thoughts" (Martin, p. 130). Voice-over enriches cinematographic representation in general by greatly increasing the relevance of off-screen space in comparison to silent cinema.

Music, finally, plays a critical role in sound cinema — provided that it is not a simple paraphrasing of the image, as is too often the case. In the best of scenarios the music either has a dramatic function, since it creates an atmosphere which supports the action, or it constitutes an additional source of meanings which complements those which are located in the images. Examples of music which are absolutely essential to the success of a given scene are numerous in French cinema. One need only consider the famous music by Maurice Jaubert in the dormitory scene in Jean Vigo's *Zero For Conduct*, the music by the same composer in Marcel Carné's *Daybreak*, the music by Joseph Kosma in Jean Renoir's *A Day in the Country*, the use of Saint-Saëns' *Danse macabre* in the party sequence in Renoir's *Rules of the Game*, or, more recently, Giovanni Fusco's score for Alain Resnais's *Hiroshima mon amour* — to mention only a few of the most famous examples of remarkable film music.

COMMENTARIES OF SELECTED SEQUENCES

We offer here three examples of analyses of film sequences (or sub-sequences) in which we put into practice some of the concepts presented in the foregoing discussion of how to read a film. Excerpts from three major films are featured: Renoir's *The Rules of the Game* (1939), Godard's *Breathless* (1960) , and Truffaut's *The 400 Blows* (1959). The excerpt from *The Rules of the Game*, the servants' meal sequence, is a striking example of a sequence shot (lengthy take), a technique for which Renoir is famous and in which deep focus and camera movements play a principal role. On the other hand, in *Breathless* we have chosen an excerpt in which the esthetics of film editing reaches a kind of apogee: the sub-sequence toward the beginning of the film in which the protagonist, Michel, shoots and kills one of the policemen who had been chasing him for a traffic violation. The sequence in *The 400 Blows*, finally, taken from the episode of Antoine's incarceration, has a more "classical" character, integrating several shots of medium length into a fairly conventional ensemble but dominated by camera movements. Unless otherwise indicated, the transitions between shots are simple cuts.

Sequence 1. The servants' meal in *The Rules of the Game*

The beginning of the servants' meal shows that their world is homologous to that of their masters, insofar as it is structured by a similar hierarchy. The majordomo Corneille reigns over this world, while Lisette, as chambermaid to Madame (the wife of the marquis de la Chesnaye), is second in line. Lisette even answers in English (with consummate snobbism!) when one of the servants asks for mustard. Her "If you please" recalls the conversation in English between the two aristocrats Boëldieu and Rauffenstein in *Grand Illusion* (1937), by the same director. The servants' conversation at the table, before the beginning of the excerpt we will discuss here, reflects moreover the same concern for social proprieties — and the same prejudices — that characterize their employer's society. Their conversation revolves around the impropriety of the presence of André Jurieu, whom everyone assumes to be Madame's former lover, and expressions of prejudice toward the marquis, who is of German Jewish extraction. This is the context for the remarkable sequence shot lasting nearly two minutes which begins with the arrival of the marquis's game warden Schumacher, Lisette's husband. During the following sequence Schumacher's departure marks the arrival of Marceau, a poacher whom the warden detests but whom the marquis has just hired to work as a domestic in the castle. The attraction between Marceau and Lisette quickly becomes apparent.

The large table at which the servants are dining is located in the foreground of a spacious hall adjacent to the kitchens, which we can see far off in the background. During most of the scene in question, which takes place in real time, Renoir plays on the great depth of field to integrate the action more effectively into the world of the servants, which is precisely the world of kitchens and work.

Shot 1 (1 min. 50 sec.): Medium up shot on Schumacher as he stops on a short stairway to answer a question someone has asked him. Schumacher: "*I don't know what you're talking about; I just got here.*" Pan downwards and to the right following Schumacher's descent into the hall. Slight tracking forward to meet the head chef who stops in a near shot just behind the two servants sitting at the table. Behind the chef, as he speaks, we can see from time to time a cook moving in the kitchens in the far background, which emphasizes the great depth of field. The chef: "*Speaking of Jews, before coming here I was in the service of the baron d'Epinay. I can assure you that there are no Jews there. But I can also assure you that they ate like pigs. And that's why I left them.*" While the chef moves toward the rear, short pan towards the right to frame Schumacher in a near shot just behind Lisette. Shcumacher: "*Will you be long, Lisette?*" Lisette: "*I don't know. Madame needs me a while longer.*" Pan in the opposite direction to frame again the chef, who returns and stops again in a near shot in front of the table and begins to speak again: "*La Chesnaye, even though he's a foreigner, summoned me the other day to bawl me out for a potato salad. You know, or rather you don't know, that for this salad to be edible you have to pour the white wine on the potatoes when they are boiling hot — which Célestin hadn't done because he doesn't like to burn his fingers. Well, the boss caught that immediately! You can say what you will, but that's a real connoisseur.*"

While the chef is speaking, Schumacher moves away from the table to go back up the stairs. When the chef leaves again, the camera pans towards the left to accompany Schumacher's departure just as the warden passes Marceau coming down the stairs. The two men (and the camera) stop briefly; they exchange glances before the pan resumes accompanying Marceau's descent. Marceau then moves back toward the camera and stops in a medium shot behind the servants seated at the table. During Marceau's arrival we hear a servant say in voice-over: "*Who's that guy?*" Marceau: "*I'd like to speak to M. Corneille.*" Corneille" "*How may I help you, my good fellow?*" Marceau: "*I'm the new servant. The marquis must have told you about me.*" Corneille: "*What do you know how to do, my good fellow?*" Marceau: "*What I know how to do? Oh, I don't know…a little bit of everything.*" Corneille: "*Do you know how to polish boots?*" Marceau: "*Yes, indeed, M. Corneille. For anything concerning clothes and all, I'm a real specialist.*" Corneille: "*Good. Tomorrow morning you'll go get the boots outside the rooms and do them.*" Marceau: "*O.K., M. Corneille.*" During this exchange the domestic who is serving the other servants at the table comes up from the back of the hall. We can see the chef and the other cook moving back and forth in the kitchens in the background. As we mentioned above, Renoir is clearly emphasizing the unity of space in order not to cut the action off from its socio-cultural context.

Leaning toward Corneille, Marceau asks, "*Is this where we eat?*" Corneille: "*Yes, my good fellow.*" Pan towards the right stopping on the male servant seated beside Lisette. He gets up, saying, "*I've got to get back to work.*" Slight pan towards the left to greet Marceau as he stops beside Lisette, who asks the servant to set a place for Marceau before asking him, "*What's your name?*" Marceau: "*Marceau. And you, Mademoiselle?*" Lisette: "*Madame. My name is Lisette. I'm Mme Schumacher.*" Marceau is taken aback and begins to walk away. Lisette calls him back, laughing: "*Oh, don't let that stop you from sitting down!*" At this moment the space is divided into three parts, which draws attention to its depth, by the arrival of the female servant from the right side, midway between the foreground where Lisette and Marceau are placed and the background occupied by the chef and the kitchens. Marceau comes back to the table and sits down. Voice-over of two male servants speaking of the coming hunt provides the transition to the following shot.

Shot 2 (7 sec.): Near shot of the two male servants seated at the table, who continue to speak, but on screen now. Slight tracking forward, then short pan to the left to frame Lisette who is smiling at Marceau, whose head is cut by the left edge of the frame, in the foreground.

Shot 3 (10 sec.): Reverse angle near shot of Marceau, with Lisette's head cut by the right edge of the frame in the foreground this time. Marceau leers at her as he eats.

Shot 4 (3 sec.): A close-up of the face of a radio followed by a dissolve to a clock on the mantelpiece upstairs returns us to the world of the marquis and his guests.

This two-minute ten-second sequence, which is dominated by the long sequence shot lasting a minute fifty seconds at the beginning, only includes four shots. To appreciate Renoir's feat here, and the esthetics of the sequence shot, one must understand that in a conventionally edited film (that is, most films at that time), shots only last five to ten seconds. A sequence such as this, shot by a conventional director, would have been composed of around twenty shots, continually fragmenting the space. Insofar as possible Renoir refuses this fragmentation, for the reasons we have indicated in the section on deep focus above (**pp. 15-17**). His technique is nonetheless quite risky, for it implies a precise choreography of movements and dialogues, entries and departures of characters, and camera movements which highlight this "ballet." If there is the slightest misstep, you have to start all over again — and that is expensive. For Renoir it is worth the risk, because his principal goal is to represent reality as a unified whole: the fewer the shot changes (reminding the spectator that it is a film), the more realistic the impression. This doesn't stop him of course from using classical editing when necessary. We see a good example of this in the conventional angle-reverse angle shot at the end of the sequence shot, where he highlights the mutual attraction between Marceau and Lisette which is going to provoke the circumstances leading to Jurieu's death.

Séquence 2. The death of the motorcycle policeman in *Breathless*

The death of the policeman comes at the end of the second sequence of the film, in which Michel, having stolen a car in Marseilles, is driving towards Paris on Highway 7. In the first part of the sequence Michel's character is established: he's an arrogant, pretentious little punk, but sentimental and likeable. At the beginning of the film he says to the girl who has helped him steal the car, "*I gotta run, Hon.*" He is, in fact, a character who never stops "running"; he seems obsessed by speed. But speed leaves him no time to think about what he is doing. It seems that the whole murder episode, whose editing style emphasizes speed, occurs with no reflection on Michel's part, as if a malevolent destiny were dictating his actions.

The excerpt of nineteen shots which interests us here is preceded by a momentary slowing of the action. Michel has to slow down because of roadwork. But he is chafing at the bit, and at the first opportunity he passes.

Shot 1 (1 sec.): In the very brief shot which begins this sub-sequence, we see in a near shot the front of the car crossing the solid line on the highway. This detail is important because it is this act which materializes Michel's status as an "outlaw." He "crosses the line" and moves both outside the law and into the public domain. He will remain in this situation until his death at the end of the film.

Shot 2 (2 sec.): Point-of-view (POV) shot through the windshield: Michel sees two motorcycle policemen on the side of the road. Michel: "*Oh shit, the cops!*"

Shot 3 (4 sec.): Michel's car passes a truck framed in a near shot and accompanied by a rapid lateral pan.

Shot 4 (1 sec.): Long shot of the truck through the back window of Michel's car.

Shot 5 (3 sec.): Long shot of the two policemen who begin the chase. The transition from the previous shot is a jump cut, an abrupt cut which startles because it violates the classical principle that the continuity editing should not be perceived by the spectator. At the end of the shot the camera pans laterally from the back window to Michel's back.

Shot 6 (1 sec.): Medium shot of Michel's car, accompanied by a pan from left to right as it passes another car.

Shot 7 (2 sec.): Long shot, with a pan, of the two policemen speeding from right to left — in the *opposite direction* of the preceding shot, which again violates conventional editing principles.

Shot 8 (5 sec.): Close shot of Michel's car as it turns off the highway into a small side road (with an accompanying pan) and stops. Michel: "*Oh! The wire's come off*" (he had hotwired the car to steal it).

Shot 9 (1 sec.): Long shot of the highway, seen from the side road. A policeman speeds by.

Shot 10 (4 sec.): Medium shot of Michel, who opens the hood of the car. Michel: "*Piece o' crap!*"

Shot 11 (1 sec.): Repeat of shot 9 (long shot of the highway): the second policeman speeds by.

Shot 12 (4 sec.): Medium shot of Michel trying to repair the wire he used to steal the car.

Shot 13 (3 sec.): Same long shot of the highway, but this time the policeman has turned around and come back to the side road where Michel's car is parked.

Shot 14 (3 sec.): Near shot of Michel followed by a lateral pan accompanying him to the car door. Framed from behind, he leans through the open window into the car. The voice-over of the policeman provides a sound transition to the following shot in which the sentence is ended: "*Don't move or you're a dead man!*"

Shot 15 (1 sec.): In a close-up of Michel's profile, the camera pans from his hat to his arm.

Shot 16 (1 sec.): Jump cut followed by an extreme close-up of Michel's arm and a lateral pan to his hand, which is holding a revolver.

Shot 17 (1 sec.): Extreme close-up of the cylinder of the revolver. Loud click followed by a pan to the barrel of the gun. Loud detonation of the revolver which provides the transition to the following shot.

Shot 18 (2 sec.): Medium shot of the policeman falling beside a tree. We note that this shot is introduced by a clearly faulty transition (probably intended by Godard), since the pistol shot is accompanied by a pan to the right, whereas the policeman falls to the left (Marie, p. 82).

Shot 19 (14 sec.): Long shot, angled slightly downward, with a pan accompanying Michel as he runs across a field. The camera comes to a stop and maintains a fixed shot as Michel runs off into the twilight. Fade out. On the soundtrack we hear loud jazz music underlining the dramatic nature of the event.

It would be difficult to take the esthetics of fast editing any further than this. We note that these nineteen shots, eleven of which are no longer than two seconds, last only 54 seconds in all. The combination of fast editing, camera movements, jump cuts, and reverse movements has a dizzying effect on the spectators which draws them into Michel's sphere of experience. We identify with Michel, seeing the action largely through his eyes from the beginning of the sequence. The rapidity and intensity of the action create the impression of a hellish moment in which, as we indicated above, reflection is impossible. Michel is not thinking about what he is doing. He just reacts to the situation he provoked by yielding to his desire to go faster, to live "breathlessly." The death of the motorcycle policeman is the sign of Michel's destiny; the rest of the film is the chronicle of an unavoidable fate which will track him down until it finishes him off.

Sequence 3: Antoine in the lock-up in *The 400 Blows*

The sub-sequence that we are going to discuss here is part of the long sequence in which Antoine enters the prison world toward the end of the film. It begins with the discussion between Antoine's stepfather and the police chief, followed by Antoine's statement in which he admits stealing a typewriter from his stepfather's office. He is then taken to the holding cells in the basement where suspects are kept until they are transferred to prison. Antoine is put in a large cage with an adult. The camera tracks backward with a dissolve into the next shot. Our sequence of thirteen shots begins at this point and includes the arrival of three prostitutes, Antoine's move to a new cell, and his transfer to the prison where he will await his assignment to a center for juvenile delinquents.

Shot 1 (35 sec.): The dissolve ends in a close-up of the hands of two policemen playing a kids' board game. The camera tracks backward, then pans to the right where we see a third policeman reading the paper, then a dumbwaiter which comes up and stops, empty. The camera stops in front of the cage in which we see the adult prisoner sleeping in a sitting position (near shot through the wire mesh). The camera tracks slightly forward, then pans to the left and downward to frame Antoine asleep on another bench, in a near shot angled downward — still through the wire mesh. We hear off-screen the noise of a vehicle arriving, a motor running. A policeman (off-screen): "*Hey, here come the honeys.*"

Shot 2 (22 sec.): Medium shot framing from behind three prostitutes followed by a policeman who puts them in the cage where Antoine and the adult man have been sleeping. First prostitute, sitting down: "*I saw a police station in a film once; it was a heck of a lot cleaner.*" Music begins, soft and melodious. Second prositute: "*I've seen dirtier ones.*" Third prostitute: "*Well, I've seen more cheerful ones.*" The camera tracks slowly forward to a near shot of the people in the cage, then pans to the left to follow Antoine as he is taken from the large cage and put into a smaller one. The policeman (shoving Antoine): "*Move it.*"

Shot 3 (20 sec.): The music continues, with no other noise. POV shot seen through Antoine's eyes: the camera pans to the right revealing first, in a near shot, the adult prisoner sitting in the big cage (seen through both the wire mesh of Antoine's cage and the mesh of the large cage). The pan (Antoine's field of vision) moves down to frame the prostitutes, maintaining the near shot, then moves slightly upward to frame a poster on the wall with sanitation regulations. In the same shot the pan then moves back down diagonally in a near shot of the back of a policeman and stops in a near shot on the board game which is cut by the frame on the right. The music stops just before the end of the shot.

Shot 4 (16 sec.): Near shot of Antoine, with a slight tracking backward. Through the wire mesh we see Antoine sitting in his cell. Off-screen sounds of steps, then a motor. Antoine is cold; he pulls his turtleneck up over his mouth and crosses his arms.

Shot 5 (26 sec.): The camera pans to the right following in a near shot a policeman who slings his machine gun over his shoulder and goes over to Antoine's cage. A second policeman gets to his feet just as the first one stops walking and joins the pan, which continues on to the right. The camera stops in a near shot in front of the big cage and frames the prostitutes as they pass just in front of the camera. The camera then pans to the left to accompany the exit of the man who had been sharing the cage with the prostitutes. It stops to let the man pass just in front of it, as did the prostitutes. A policeman tells Antoine as he begins to follow the others, "*Put on your jacket.*" Antoine obeys as he passes in front of the camera like the others, but accompanied by a pan.

Shot 6 (20 sec.): Long static shot outside in the street in front of the police station. The group begins to get into the police van parked next to the sidewalk. The camera tracks slightly forward to a near shot of Antoine who zips up his jacket, climbs into the wagon, and takes a seat beside the male prisoner and one of the policemen. Near shot on the back door of the van, which slams shut. We can see Antoine and the two men beside him through the bars on the back door. The slamming of the door seems to set off background music which accompanies the departure of the police van as it moves away from the motionless camera. This music, emphatically sentimental, will last until the end of the sequence.

Shot 7 (5 sec.): POV shot (Antoine), with a backward tracking shot of the wet pavement, since the camera is located in Antoine's place in the wagon. Slight down shot before the camera pans up and to the left (still Antoine's viewpoint) to frame and sweep over the buildings which the van is leaving in the distance.

Shot 8 (18 sec.): The camera tracks forward to a near shot of Antoine behind the bars (the camera is now following the van). The camera, clearly hand-held and bobbing up and down constantly, falls a little further behind the wagon. Antoine makes a small gesture with his hand as if to ask the cameraman to come closer. The camera tracks forward to a tight near shot through the bars. (At this point we note a flagrant error in the continuity: the two men seated beside Antoine at the beginning of the journey have been replaced by two prostitutes.)

Shot 9 (14 sec.): The camera tracks backward again, placed this time in the police van beside Antoine, whose face is cut by the frame on the left, as if we were seated beside him. He continues to stare out at the street. A car following the van closely begins to pass.

Shot 10 (3 sec.): Very rapid shot, with continuity provided by a pan following the movement of the car which was passing the van in the preceding shot. The van passes just in front of the camera, creating the effect of a rapid swish pan, accentuated by a pan accompanying the van as it moves rapidly away.

Shot 11 (20 sec.): Near follow shot of Antoine through the bars (same as shot 8) with the prostitutes smoking behind him now. As the camera tracks forward, it approaches the van then falls back a little, seeming to sway in time with the sentimental music.

Shot 12 (7 sec.): Repeat of shot 9: backward tracking shot with Antoine's face still cut by the frame on the left, staring at the streets and buildings. We see with him the large neon signs of the nightspots of Pigalle: "The Most Gorgeous Nude Women in the World" and "Narcissus."

Shot 13 (20 sec.): Near follow shot of Antoine through the bars (repeat of shot 11). The camera, still swaying, moves to a close-up of Antoine's face. The swaying suddenly stops, and we see tears streaming down Antoine's cheeks. Dissolve with a pan to the right on a blackened wall in a prison hallway. The music comes to a stop at the beginning of the shot following the dissolve.

In a rather remarkable analysis, Anne Gillain demonstrates Truffaut's great originality in this sequence. By playing on the continual camera movements, on musical effects, and on other clever techniques, Truffaut successfully masks the sordid side of Antoine's incarceration (pp. 106-111). From the first shot, replacing the guards' traditional card game by a children's board game, Truffaut places the whole episode in the frame of childhood. Whether we watch Antoine or share his gaze, we live the experience with him, from his viewpoint. The camera movements and the complete absence of fixed shots render the scene livelier and prevent it from becoming morose. Truffaut's camera, like Renoir's, creates the impression that there is an invisible guest beside the characters in the film, a curious, compassionate guest who is constantly moving, following everyone else's movements and particularly Antoine's. Ultimately the guest identifies completely with Antoine by joining him behind the bars and seeing through his eyes. This guest is the spectator — us. It is perhaps our solicitous attitude, combined with that of the policeman who tells Antoine to put on his jacket, that produces "the strangely comforting character of this sequence" noted by Gillain (p. 109).

To make this episode less grim, Truffraut also alludes to the cinema, whether it be the remark by the prostitute, the presence of the well-known film director Jacques Demy in the role of one of the guards, or, more subtly, the "quotation" of a famous film by Renoir, *The Bitch* (*La Chienne*, 1931), which begins with a shot of a dumbwaiter in a restaurant. Whatever the precise reason, we receive the impression that Antoine is experiencing his incarceration serenely, as if he hasn't yet understood the seriousness of his situation, the fact that he is being excluded from society. By its tritely romantic melody, the music which accompanies the arrival of the prostitutes, as well as Antoine's gaze in his cage and the whole trip in the police van, contributes powerfully to the softening of reality in this sequence. The episode in the police station is thus bathed in a detached atmosphere, suggesting Antoine's alienation from reality at this point.

Reality will set in near the end of the subsequence in the police van, in which Antoine witnesses through the bars his exclusion from the Pigalle neighborhood where he had grown up. Here again we are either beside him in the van or sympathetic witnesses of his plight, following closely behind the van. The melancholy music emphasizes the nostalgia felt by Antoine as he leaves the world he loves; the tears gleaming on his cheeks betray the emotion which finally overcomes him. The reassuring *intermezzo* (reprieve?) created by Truffaut is over. The music stops with Antoine's official entrance into the prison world, just the other side of the dissolve. Reduced to silence during this whole sequence (which contains scant dialogue in any case), Antoine had already lost the right to speak. With his imprisonment he loses the rest of his rights.

WORKS CONSULTED

Aumont, Jacques, and Michel Marie. *L'Analyse des films*. Paris: Nathan, 1989.

Aumont, Jacques, Alain Bergala, Michel Marie, and Marc Vernet. *Esthétique du film*. Paris: Nathan, 1983.

Bazin, André. *Qu'est-ce que le cinéma?* (pp. 63-80). Paris: Editions du Cerf, 1981.

Betton, Gérard. *Esthétique du cinéma*. Paris: Presses universitaires de France, 1983.

Eisenstein, S.M. *Le Film: sa forme, son sens*. Paris: Christian Bourgeois, 1976.

Gillain, Anne. *Les 400 Coups*. Coll. "Synopsis." Paris: Nathan, 1991.

Marie, Michel. *A bout de souffle*. Coll. "Synopsis." Paris: Nathan, 1999.

Martin, Marcel. *Le Langage cinématographique*. Paris: Les Editeurs Français Réunis, 1977.

Metz, Christian. *Essais sur la signification au cinéma*, I. Paris: Klincksieck, 1978.

Vanoye, Francis, and Anne Golio-Lété. *Précis d'analyse filmique*. Paris: Nathan, 1992.

Poetic Realism

It has become customary to refer to the first great period of modern French cinema, which stretched from the beginning of the talkies (1930) to the Liberation (1945), as the "French School." Owing to one of its most pronounced tendencies, it is also known as the era of "poetic realism." Like the denomination "New Wave" thirty years later, poetic realism is in fact only a general term, in this case borrowed from literature, tying together loosely a very heterogeneous group of filmmakers including René Clair, Jean Vigo, Jean Grémillon, Julien Duvivier, Jean Renoir, Marcel Carné, Jacques Becker, Jacques Feyder, Marcel Pagnol, and Sacha Guitry. From the whimsical and slapstick comedy of the films of René Clair, such as *Le Million* (1931), to the dark pessimism of the Marcel Carné-Jacques Prévert duo in *Port of Shadows* (*Quai des Brumes*, 1938) or *Daybreak* (*Le Jour se lève*, 1939), without forgetting the humanism of Jean Renoir in *Toni* (1934) or *Grand Illusion* (1937), poetic realism encompasses the most disparate currents, the most personal preoccupations, and the most diverse influences. In Jean Vigo's films, for instance, we note the traces of the surrealism of the twenties, the strangeness and fantasy so striking in *Zero For Conduct* (*Zéro de conduite*, 1933) and in *L'Atalante* (1934). Renoir's films, on the other hand, may bear the imprint of Impressionist painting, as in *A Day in the Country* (*Partie de campagne*, 1936) or the mark of the literary populism and naturalism of Emile Zola in *The Human Beast* (*La Bête humaine*, 1938). For their part Carné and Prévert tended to propagate the tradition of expressionism, with the creation of evocative scenery and lugubrious atmosphere which dominate all of their films.

If we were to attempt to describe the major characteristics of this "school," we would have to observe first and foremost the thematic richness of its masterpieces. In poetic realism, reality is constantly used as a springboard for themes which are often expressed in metaphors and symbols. We might refer to this as the "poeticizing" of reality. We may think, for example — among a wealth of examples — of the theme of liberty in *Zero For Conduct*, the metaphor of fishing in *A Day in the Country*, or the theater motif in *Grand Illusion*; the symbolic value of the toy bear and the brooch in *Daybreak* or of the mechanical dolls in *The Rules of the Game* (1939). However, the trademark of poetic realism may be located in the thematic nexus dominating the works of a particular group of filmmakers, beginning with Jacques Feyder, whose films introduce a sordid and pessimistic social realism. Born of the traumatic economic, social, and political turmoil of the thirties, this pessimism was developed mostly by Julien Duvivier in films such as *They Were Five* (*La Belle Equipe*, 1936), *Pépé le Moko*, (1937) and in the films of Marcel Carné and his regular screenwriter Jacques Prévert. Despite the momentary measure of hope brought by the triumph of the Popular Front and its government (1936-37), the Nazi threat which hung over Europe had a sobering and depressing effect on the population. We see the effects of this gloomy outlook in many films of the period, including Jean Renoir's greatest masterpiece, *The Rules of the Game*.

Although Carné preferred the term "social fantastic" to "poetic realism," two of the films he made with Prévert are considered to be the most typical of this current: *Port of Shadows* and *Daybreak*. In Carné's works pessimism becomes out-and-out despair, which is conceived as an inevitable product of man's destiny. His heroes, working-class people, are condemned to misfortune by a tenacious and malevolent fate: the search for happiness — through love — is always doomed to failure. René Prédal characterized Carné-Prévert's poetic realism well when he observed that their films develop "a set of themes (the weight of destiny, unhappy love, failure), an atmosphere (oppressive, scummy surroundings, empty rain-splashed cities, gray nights), and a style (polished dialogues, lavish camera movements) which all seem made for cinema" (p. 76). It is nonetheless above all the idea of the abjection of a world in which the scum triumph over good people, in which escape through happiness is impossible, which emanates from this collaboration.

To conclude, during the Occupation the current that was still called poetic realism took on quite a different character. The filmmakers who continued to make films in France during this period — Carné, Jean Delannoy, and Jean Cocteau, for instance — responded to the need of the French to find relief from their difficult daily existence under the Nazis. They cultivated an escapist cinema sometimes featuring the fantastic situated in far-off periods, at other times taking refuge in estheticism. With Jean Cocteau as his screenwriter, Delannoy made *The Eternal Return* (*L'Eternel Retour*, 1943), a modernized version of the medieval Tristan and Isolde myth. Carné had major successes with *The Devil's Envoys* (*Les Visiteurs du soir*, 1942), whose action is set in a legendary Middle Ages, and with *Children of Paradise* (*Les Enfants du paradis*, 1945), considered by many to be his major work. The latter film is a story of unhappy love at the height of the romantic period (1820-1840), combined with a reflection on the intimate relationship between theater and life. These are the most successful films, along with Jean Cocteau's *Beauty and the Beast* (*La Belle et la Bête*, 1946), in this final metamorphosis of poetic realism.

WORKS CONSULTED

Betton, Gérard. *Histoire du cinéma*. Paris: Presses Universitaires de France, 1984.

Mitry, Jean. *Histoire du cinéma*, IV. Paris : Delarge, 1980 ("Le réalisme poétique en France," pp. 325-352).

Prédal, René. *Histoire du cinéma*. Courbevoie: CinémAction-Corlet, 1994.

Sadoul, Georges. *Le Cinéma français*. Paris: Flammarion, 1962.

.........*Histoire du cinéma mondial des origines à nos jours*, 9ᵉ éd. Paris : Flammarion, 1949 ("Le réalisme poétique français," pp. 267-293).

Jean Vigo

Zero For Conduct
Zéro de conduite

(1933)

Jean Vigo, *Zero For Conduct*: the pillow fight.
© Gaumont

Subtitle .... "Young Devils in School"
Director .... Jean Vigo
Original Screenplay and Dialogues.................................. Jean Vigo
Director of Photography .... Boris Kaufman
Music... Maurice Jaubert
Songs ....Charles Goldblatt
Film Editor .... Jean Vigo
Sound .... Royné et Bocquet
Producer ....Argui-Films
Length ....43 minutes

Cast

Louis Lefèbvre (*Caussat*), Coco Goldstein (*Bruel*), Gilbert Pruchon (*Colin*), Gérard de Bedarieux (*Tabard*), Jean Dasté (*the new supervisor Huguet*), Delphin (*the Principal*), Robert Le Flon (*the supervisor Parrain, called "Nasty"*), Blanchar (*the head supervisor, called "Lamppost"*), Léon Larive (*the chemistry teacher*), Mme Emile (*Mme Colin, called "Ma Bean"*), Louis de Gonzague-Frick (*the Prefect*).

STORY

Summer vacation is over. Caussat and Bruel, two junior high students, find themselves together in the train which will take them to their private school in the provinces. They show off their new toys, play kids' games, and smoke cigars. A man shares their compartment, fast asleep. When they arrive at their destination, they are met by a supervisor, Monsieur Parrain. The man who was sleeping in the train introduces himself to M. Parrain. He is the new supervisor, M. Huget. René Tabard, a student with effeminate clothes and haircut, arrives with his mother.

In the dormitory, at bedtime, three students, Caussat, Bruel, and Colin, are punished unjustly. The next morning, having refused to obey the order to get out of bed, all three are given a "zero for conduct" and detention the following Sunday. Angry at being grounded each Sunday, the three boys plot against the school authorities during recess. They are preparing their revenge and escape from the school. The new supervisor, Huguet, becomes the boys' accomplice, standing in front of them to hide their activity from the other supervisors. Then he plays with the children in the schoolyard and imitates Charlie Chaplin's gait. Meanwhile the head supervisor "Lamppost" goes into the study hall and noses about the students' personal items, stealing chocolate and other objects.

After recess Caussat discovers that his chocolate has been stolen. Furious, he empties several bottles of glue into his hiding place. Huguet supervises study hall, then amuses the students by walking on his hands. Still standing on his hands — on top of his desk — he then draws a caricature of the head supervisor which becomes an animated cartoon, changing into a woman, then into Napoleon.

Huguet takes the children on a walk through town while the Principal, a dwarf, speaks in his office with the head supervisor. He is concerned about the friendship, too intimate for his taste, between Tabard and Bruel. Huguet strolls through town day-dreaming while the students run off in various directions — only to come back and line up behind him on their own as he follows a pretty woman down the street. When the boys return from their walk, the Principal calls Tabard into his office to warn him against temptation. He manages to make him feel deeply guilty, although the boy has no idea what he is supposed to have done wrong.

Caussat spends Sunday afternoon at the home of his host family, where he submits patiently to the games of a little girl. At the same time, Bruel convinces Colin to include Tabard among the plotters. That evening in the cafeteria the meal degenerates into a riot. The students revolt against the bad food and pelt each other with beans until Caussat and Bruel put a stop to the racket, suddenly remembering that the cook "Ma Bean" is their friend Colin's mother. The next morning during chemistry class the teacher notices that Tabard isn't taking notes. He pats him on the head and then covers the boy's hand with his. Traumatized by the Principal's remonstrations, Tabard reacts angrily, screaming, "Go to Hell!" at the teacher. Enjoined by the Principal to apologize to the teacher in public, in front of the whole school, Tabard balks and repeats his insult.

In the dormitory that night the children announce that the revolt has begun. They go berserk, running wildly around the dormitory and messing up the beds while Parrain makes futile attempts to stop them. On the roof of the school, Tabard attaches to the chimney the flag of revolt, which bears a skull and crossbones. The children begin a pillow fight, the feathers from the torn pillows soon filling the room. The scene comes to an end with a phantasmagorical parade of children in nightshirts moving in slow-motion through a cloud of feathers, accompanied by strange, surrealistic music. The next morning, in a mock crucifixion, the four ringleaders tie the sleeping supervisor Parrain to his bed and stand it upright, placing in front of it a double Chinese lantern.

It is the day of the annual school celebration. When the guests of honor arrive, the four boys, lying in ambush on the roof of the school, bombard the crowd with all the objects they had laid in store for the occasion. Their schoolmates, joined by the supervisor Huguet, cheer them on from below. When the school officials rush up to the attic to catch the rebels, the four boys "escape" by climbing up the roof toward the sky as they sing in unison.

CRITICAL RECEPTION

Zero For Conduct was presented on April 7, 1933, in a private showing for distributors, cinema directors, and representatives of the press, as well as the members of the crew, including the children in the film and their friends. The film was not well received, to say the least. Two years later a spectator commented, "The spectators, as befits their bourgeois mentality, were quite shocked by the behavior of the children as depicted by Vigo. During the projection the film had to be stopped several times and the lights turned on; the showing almost turned into a fistfight" (Salès Gomès, p. 154). These remarks are apparently an exaggeration, according to Salès Gomès, who adds, "If the truth were known, nearly all the distributors and cinema managers were indeed shocked, but more by the lack of commercial potential of the film rather than for moral reasons" (p. 154). Nonetheless, the few newspaper articles devoted to the film in the following days were hardly enthusiastic, and some were downright hostile, as we see in the following piece:

> "An exceptional work, which will be derided and discussed. It is hard to understand why a major commercial distributor [Gaumont] has taken on this film. Hateful, violent, destructive, spiteful, it seems to be shot through with all the bitterness the author obviously still harbors from his miserable experience in school. Infected with vulgarity, harsh and noxious, his film stigmatizes vicious, obtuse teachers and sings a desperate hymn to liberty. Badly muddled photography, which adds to the anguished character of the story. Bold, fiery work" (quoted in Salès Gomès, p. 156).

Not a single critic in Vigo's time recognized the poetic character of *Zero For Conduct* or its stylistic interest. On the other hand, the Catholic press had an immediate and violent reaction. It focused on the "subversive ideas" in the film and considered its denigration of teachers to be an attack on morality. Under pressure from the government, and apparently fearful that the film might provoke public disorder, the censuring body simply cancelled the public showing scheduled several days later. Although the film was banned for being "anti-French," it is thought that the commission's action was due at least in part to Vigo's identity as the son of a famous anarchist who had died in prison under rather suspicious circumstances (see below).

Since *Zero for Conduct*'s commercial career was stifled by the banning, the film was reduced to showings in cinema clubs until November, 1945, when it had its first real opening in France. In Belgium on the other hand, where there was intense interest in Vigo's work, the critics were more "lucid." *Zero For Conduct* was projected for a month in the fall of 1933 in a Brussels theater before being relegated to the Belgium film clubs. Vigo's film was not really rehabilitated until the 1950s, when the "damned" filmmaker came to be known as the "Rimbaud" of the cinema. The young critics of the *Cahiers du cinéma* (see the Introduction to the New Wave), beginning with François Truffaut and Jean-Luc Godard, recognized in Vigo a precursor of poetic realism. They also saw in his work an expression of surrealism (the spirit of revolt, for example) and the model for an autobiographical cinema which would serve as an inspiration for certain filmmakers of the New Wave. French television eventually showed Vigo's films over and over again, introducing them to an ever-larger public.

BEFORE AND AFTER *ZERO FOR CONDUCT*

Jean Vigo's complete cinematographic work consists of only two hours and forty minutes of film. The young filmmaker died at the age of 29 after a long illness. Vigo was strongly influenced by the political ideas of his father Miguel Vigo, called Almereyda, a militant anarchist and a notorious opponent of the military. He was no less influenced by the film-editing theories of the great Soviet filmmaker, Sergei Eisenstein (see "How To Read A Film," **pp. 45-47**). At age 25 he made his first film, *A propos de Nice* (1930), which was political in nature. It is a "social" document, or what Vigo prefers to call a "documented viewpoint," on the city of Nice which highlights the contrast between the life led by the wealthy bourgeois in the upscale neighborhoods and the life of the inhabitants of the slums. The film received critical praise but had little commercial success.

After making another short subject, a commissioned film on a champion swimmer, *Taris or Swimming* (*Taris ou la natation*, 1931), Vigo made *Zero For Conduct* and the year after his only feature film, *L'Atalante* (1934). This film, his last, is a lyrical depiction of the life of a bargeman and his wife, newlyweds, on a barge on the Seine river. This story about "mad love" — another surrealist theme — is highly poetic in spite of the fact that it was badly mutilated by the distributor. Film critics heaped praise on the film, but its reception by the public was lukewarm. Gravely ill, Vigo insisted nonetheless on attending the opening of the film. He died the following month from blood poisoning.

THE ORIGIN

When Jean Vigo was twelve, towards the end of the "Great War" (the First World War, 1914-18), his father was accused — falsely, by all appearances — of contact with the enemy. Arrested and incarcerated in the Fresnes prison, he was found dead by hanging a few days later. It has never been determined if it was suicide or murder. For his own protection during the dangerous vindictive period following the war, the child was enrolled under a pseudonym, Jean Salles, at a private school in Millau where he would live for four years. In *Zero For Conduct* (originally titled *The Dunces*), Vigo depicts his existence as a schoolboy. He describes the life of the students in private schools in the French provinces around 1920 as "petty, unhealthy, and sometimes cruel" (Sand, p. 14). He remembers all too well the "zero for conduct" and the inevitable punishment of "Sunday detention" which prevented him and his friends from leaving the school that day. At the school in Millau Vigo met Caussat and Bruel, while Colin, the third conspirator in the film, was in fact a friend from his high school in Chartres transplanted to the middle school in Millau. Vigo's personal traits are recognizable in all three children, but especially in Tabard. The filmmaker confirms the autobiographical nature of his work in an interview during the shooting of the film: "This film is so full of my life as a kid that I can't wait to finish it and get on to something else" (quoted in André Négis, p. 68). As for the adults in the film, we know that the nicknames "Lamppost" and "Nasty" recall the supervisors in the school in Millau, but the characters are such a product of Vigo's imagination that the originals are no longer recognizable: "Vigo's adult characters are rooted in reality, but a reality seen through the eyes of a rebellious, bruised child who is now an adult seeking revenge through satire" (Salès Gomès, p. 121). The model for the Principal is easily recognizable in the director of the high school in Chartres — a small, rather kind bearded man, very unlike the pompous, ridiculous character in Vigo's film. The model for the likeable Huguet character is a Millau supervisor who only stayed at the school a few weeks.

THE SHOOTING, THE ACTORS, THE EDITING

The Gaumont studios, co-producers of the film, only granted Vigo eight days of studio time to shoot all the indoor shots, during the last week of December, 1932, and the first week of January, 1933. Vigo was thus forced to work rapidly and to cut a number of planned sequences, resulting in the somewhat disjointed, muddled character of the final version of the film. Moreover, since the dialogues he had written for the original screenplay turned out to be inadequate, he had to write new ones each morning as the shooting progressed, usually in the train he took to the studio. Vigo's director of photography was Boris Kaufman (the brother of the renowned Soviet filmmaker and theoretician Dziga Vertov) who worked with Vigo on *A propos de Nice* and later stayed with him to shoot *L'Atalante*.

In the main roles Vigo cast children of friends and from his neighborhood in Paris. The role of Caussat was given to Louis Lefèvre, "the terror of the neighborhood and a fascinating kid, weird and crude" (Salès Gomès, p. 124). The twenty-some children hired as extras all came from various working-class neighborhoods in Paris, especially the 19th district, with its numerous spirited and rebellious youths. The role of the head supervisor, Lamppost, is played by M. Blanchar, the manager of the building where Vigo lived, that of Ma Bean the cook by Mme Emile, the owner of the bistro where the film crew ate, and other adult roles by friends of the director. There are only three professional film actors in the cast: those who play the roles of the supervisor Parrain (Nasty), the revolting chemistry teacher, and the Principal. The new supervisor Huguet is played by Jean Dasté, a talented theater actor who began a long career in film in *Zero For Conduct*. He also plays the main role in *L'Atalante*. We will soon meet him again in Renoir's *Grand Illusion* (*La Grande Illusion*, 1937) and even in Alain Resnais's *My American Uncle* (*Mon oncle d'Amérique*, 1980), nearly a half-century later.

Given the severely restricted studio time, the rhythm of the shooting is intense. Since Vigo is working with a rudimentary shooting script, he is forced to improvise constantly. Many of the extras recruited in the street are veritable hellions, undisciplined and very difficult to direct. Their poor diction, combined with the inferior quality of the sound recording, produced a marginal soundtrack. Vigo's fragile health suffered severely from the exhausting shooting sessions; by the end of December he was down with the flu and had lost his voice. For the dormitory scenes he was reduced to whispering his instructions into one of his assistant's ear, who then shouted them to the boys. Worn out and feverish, on the edge of pneumonia, Vigo was finally confined to his bed for five days and didn't finish shooting in the studio until January 7. To finish on time, most of the scenes could now only be shot once, while others were simply cut out of the screenplay.

The shooting on location was completed in ten days, between January 10 and 22, in a railroad station in the Paris suburbs (the beginning scenes), in the town of Saint-Cloud where Vigo had lived as a child, and in the Saint-Cloud middle school. With rain and snow occasionally halting the shooting, Vigo was again forced to cut out scenes and, as in the studio, to shoot each scene only once.

When Vigo began editing at the end of January, he was forced to cut out still more scenes; his film still exceeded the limits which had been imposed on him. As a result, he had to add several title cards to make the story comprehensible. The editing was completed at the beginning of March, Maurice Jaubert's music and the sound track at the end of the month. The film was ready at the beginning of April.

STRUCTURE

Zero For Conduct is organized loosely into four parts. Introduced by a title card stating "Vacation is over. Back to school," the first part begins in a train compartment where two students, Caussat and Bruel, entertain themselves by playing children's games. It ends the following day in the dormitory when the two boys and Colin, the school's three troublemakers, are penalized with a "zero for conduct" and are "grounded Sunday." A new title card, "Children's Plots," announces the beginning of the second part at recess where the three students, fed up with being grounded, prepare a revolt against an authority they perceive as abusive. This part of the film establishes as well the complicity of the new supervisor Huguet and the odious character of the head supervisor "Lamppost."

The third part of the film, which is not introduced with a title card, could have been named "Adult Suspicions," a parallel to "Children's Plots." The scene of the children's walk through the town with Huguet is imbued with an atmosphere of liberty and innocence. It is cross-cut with a scene in the office of the Principal, who expresses strong suspicions about the friendly relations between Tabard and Bruel. This "chapter" ends with Tabard's refusal to sit next to Bruel, which immediately follows the scene in which the principal makes Tabard feel guilty.

The third section of the film consists of a kind of interlude in which Caussat spends Sunday with his host family playing angelically with their little girl, followed by a scene in Ma Bean's kitchen which serves as a prelude to the final part of the film. The final movement is dominated by the spirit of revolt. The riot of the children in the dining room, who are disgusted with the bad food, foreshadows the open revolt initiated by Tabard's angry "Go to Hell!" to the chemistry teacher, an outburst he will repeat in front of the whole school. The general revolt breaks out that evening in the dormitory and culminates the following morning with the boys' attack on the dignitaries assembled for the annual school celebration.

THEMES

The principal theme of *Zero For Conduct* is abundantly clear: children's desire for liberty in a world peopled by despotic adults. And it is in the name of liberty, presented as an essential ingredient of happiness, that the children prepare their revolt — another major theme developed from the beginning of the film. Lherminier calls it "a film about absolute revolt, a lyrical explosion of liberation which is its own justification and its own end" (p. 72). As such, *Zero For Conduct* is manifestly related to the Surrealist movement. Although Vigo never officially belonged to André Breton's group, the definition of Surrealism offered by Gaëton Picon leaves little doubt of the allegiance of the film to the movement: "A refusal of human and social existence in its present form, Surrealism is born in a spirit of revolt. It denounces a society composed of curbs, prohibitions, and injustice."

As for the autobiographical question, if Vigo begins from his own experience in school, his film goes far beyond its personal side. It becomes an expression of the world of children in general and especially of their psychological life, their imagination, their fantasy, their need to blossom. Vigo throws the child's world, with its purity and quasianarchical craving for liberty, against an adult world dominated by interdiction, injustice, and oppression. Even worse, adults cast over the innocent world of children a shadow of guilt, treating simple boyhood friendships as sexually suspicious. The childrens' revolt grows out of a feeling of injustice which becomes a clear theme in the scene where the boys place the double Chinese lantern which recalls the scales of justice before the supervisor Parrain, "crucified" in his bed. In addition to these major themes, we note also the motif of "playing," whose importance in the child's world is established in the first sequence, as well as the themes of plotting, friendship, and homosexuality — this last theme shown as a product of perverted adult minds.

STYLE

In spite of its undeniably autobiographical character, one should not mistake *Zero For Conduct* for a realistic documentary about provincial private schools or about adults. We cannot forget that Vigo is transforming his schoolboy experience, filtering it through the children's perspective in such a way that we are left with a caricature of adults and of life in a boarding school. As Pierre Lherminier observes, "Starting from a personal experience which he wants both to protest and surmount (his 'life as a kid'), he goes on to describe in fact a dreamlike and mythical world which is far removed from his own life" (p. 62). Jean Mitry sees in Vigo's film "a lavish poem, both caricatural and dreamlike, a sort of waking nightmare in which memories and their psychical deformations collide. The real and the imaginary melt together into a global vision" (p. 333). This mixture of the real and the imaginary best characterizes the style of *Zero For Conduct*, whose combination of realism and poetry has often been praised. While related to the Surrealist movement through its cry of revolt, Vigo's film is no less considered, and justly so, as a precursor of the "poetic realism" which dominated the French cinema of the thirties, especially the films of Jean Renoir and Marcel Carné.

The style of *Zero For Conduct*, both poetic and farcical — the gags are nonstop — makes itself felt through the cultivation of the bizarre and the fantastic. This is apparent in the highly whimsical games of the children in the train at the beginning of the film, as in the startling camera angles in the dormitory and in special effects such as the balloon which disappears and reappears in Caussat's hand. Huguet's behavior is even more fantastic. He walks on his hands in the study hall and then, in the same position, draws a caricature of Lamppost which, we remember, becomes an animated cartoon transforming the head supervisor first into a woman, then into Napoleon. And just as strange is the carnival booth scene with its grotesque oversized dolls, which are bombarded as they sit in the gallery just behind the school officials — not to speak of the ferocious and irony-laden caricaturing of the adults in the film, ultimately identified with the puppets they sit beside on the benches. Mockery has rarely been taken so far in a film.

But no scene in the film better illustrates the poetic dimension of the style of *Zero For Conduct* than the famous revolt episode in the dormitory. Numerous commentators have noted the strange editing of the scene when the students go on a rampage in their dormitory, which is followed by a dreamlike parade of children in nightgowns, advancing in slow motion through a cloud of feathers accompanied by the hallucinatory music of Maurice Jaubert. Lherminier refers to the scene aptly as a "lyrical paroxysm" (p. 68). It is the height of the bizarre in the film and the emblem of its style.

MUSIC

The music is an integral part of the style of *Zero For Conduct*. If, as Gilles Jacob says, "Vigo was one of the first to understand the importance of music to film" (p. 90), we cannot emphasize too greatly the contribution of the composer Maurice Jaubert to the success of the work. To create the extremely bizarre music for the dormitory sequence near the end, for instance, Jaubert had the ingenious idea of recording his score backwards, the musicians beginning at the end and reversing the order of the notes. When the sound track was added to the film, Jaubert then reversed the recording back to the original order of the score, producing the weird, "surrealistic" impression of a dream world. The union of music and image to create a particular atmosphere has rarely achieved such a degree of perfection in film. Jaubert's genius shines through in other sequences as well, like Huguet's walk in town with the children or the beginning scene in the train: "In a period when everyone was crazy about realistic sound effects [...], daring to replace the classical train sounds in *Zero For Conduct* with a leitmotif composed by Jaubert was boldly innovative" (Jacob, p. 90). As Salès Gomès adds, "The score of *Zero For Conduct* was a total success, and it was clear from that moment on that Jaubert was the leading film composer in France" (p. 135).

STUDY GUIDE

Director's Comments

"Fantasy is the only interesting thing in life. My ambition is to push it to the level of the absurd."

"Now I can feel the anguish. You are going to see *Zero For Conduct*, and I'm going to see it again with you. I watched it grow up. How puny it seems to me now! Not even convalescing, like my own child; it's no longer my own childhood. It's useless to stare wide-eyed. I just don't recognize my own memories. Is it so far off already? [...] Of course I recognize my two friends in the train compartment, their vacation over, returning to school. Of course I can see there the dormitory I lived in for eight years as a boarder, with its thirty identical beds, and I see Huguet also, whom we liked so much and his colleague, the supervisor Nasty, and the ever-mute head supervisor, with his phantom-like crepe-soled shoes. In the glow from the nightlight, will the little sleepwalker haunt my dreams again tonight? And perhaps I'll see him again standing at the foot of my bed as he did the day before the Spanish flu took him away in 1919 [...].

"Yes, I know, my pals Caussat, Bruel, Colin the cook's son, and Tabard, whom we called the girl and whom the school administrators spied on and tortured, while what he really needed was a big brother, since his mother didn't love him [...].

"Everything is there, the cafeteria with its beans, the class, and the study hall where one day one of us said out loud, twice, what we were all thinking.

"So I'll watch again the preparation of the plot which we worked so hard at, the night in the attic, the rioting in the dormitory, the crucifixion of Nasty, the school celebration we disrupted on the aptly named Saint-Barbe Day.

"Will I again leave the attic, our only private space, by the roof, towards more promising skies?" (Excerpted from the "Presentation of *Zero For Conduct* " in Brussels, October 17, 1933).

Excerpts for Discussion

Excerpt 1 (1'00-4'00): The sequence at the beginning in the train compartment (the two boys try to impress each other with their toys).

Excerpt 2 (12'30-13'10): The schoolyard at recess (the children's plot, the complicity of the new supervisor Huguet).

Excerpt 3 (14'10-14'25): The supervisor Huguet and Charlie Chaplin.

Excerpt 4 (16'40-18'30): Huguet's acrobatics in study hall.

Excerpt 5 (20'00-24'35): The Principal's office and the walk in town.

Excerpt 6 (34'20-37'40): The dormitory sequence (the revolt of the children, the parade in slow motion).

Excerpt 7 (40'10-43'00): The school celebration (the bombardment of the officials, the denouement).

Quotations for Comment

Caussat: "My friends, here's the plan: the plot is ready. We're grounded every Sunday; we have to escape."

Bruel: "By the attic?"

* * *

The Principal: "…what you are saying worries me. In conclusion, Mr. Sant, according to you, Mr. Head Supervisor, Tabard and Bruel are behaving like little children, like kids. This will not do, not at all… [shots of Huguet and the children walking in town]… and have you considered our responsibility from the moral standpoint? [Return of the children in the rain, Tabard and Bruel sharing a cape.] You see! Together again. This friendship is becoming excessive. You are right, Mr. Head Supervisor; we will have to keep an eye on them."

* * *

The Chemistry Teacher: "Well, little fellow, you aren't taking notes this morning?"

[Nervously Tabard takes out his notebook and begins to write. The teacher places his fat, greasy hand on Tabard's left hand.]

Teacher: "That's better!"

[Furious, Tabard abruptly pulls his hand away.]

Tabard: "Leave me alone!"

Teacher: "I'd watch what I say, Sonny!"

Tabard: "Yeh, well you can go to hell!"

* * *

Title Card: "The next morning fatigue helps the four boys."

Caussat, Tabard, Bruel, and Colin arrive fully dressed. Without awakening Parrain, they tie him to his bed with a scarf, stand the bed on end, and place in front of the sleeping supervisor a double Chinese lantern to stand for scales: scales of blind justice?!

© *L'Avant-Scène Cinéma*

Questions/Topics for Reflection

1. Depiction of the children's world in the train sequence.
2. The relationship between "zero for conduct" ("Sunday detention") and the revolt of the children; the attitude of the children toward the power of the adults.
3. Introduction of the theme of revolt (when?).
4. Depiction of the adults (and of the school).
5. The character of the new supervisor Huguet; his role.
6. The character of Tabard and his friendship with Bruel.
7. The incident which sets off the revolt.
8. The dormitory sequence: camera angles, objects, special effects, music.
9. The denouement of the film: optimistic? pessimistic? "lyrical"?
10. "Poetic realism": realism and poetry in *Zero For Conduct*.

CRITICAL DOSSIER

James Agee — A Cinema Poem

Zero For Conduct is one of the rare great cinema poems. It's a film which creates its own world freely and precisely, from the beginning to the end and from the interior towards the exterior ("*Zéro de conduite* et *L'Atalante*," p. 75).

André Négis — The Torments of Shooting

We're at the Gaumont studios, and Jean Vigo is shooting the indoor scenes of his film *Zero For Conduct*, which we will soon see on the screen […].

It's no small feat, let me tell you, to direct, to discipline, to get something out of these twenty kids recruited here and there, grabbed in a back room, a school, a garret, or off the street. Vigo selected only Paris's "best." He would follow them in the street sometimes, at the risk of being taken for a degenerate. But whatever this fellow wants he goes after it.

So, at this very minute, with his sunken eyes and hollow cheeks, his flu-induced cough, his 102-degree fever, he should have stayed in bed. But they're shooting, the meter's running, and he's there voiceless, aggravated, shouting, cursing. But since he can't make a sound, Riera lends him his magnificent voice, a real electro-dynamic loud-speaker. Vigo whispers the words into Riera's ears, and Riera bellows:

— Lie down, kids, g... d... it! Lie down and close your eyes!! Are you ready? O.K, let's rehearse one last time!

Lights. Camera. You think you got it in the can and you don't. You have to shoot the scene again, give just the right shape to this tough, unpliable dough: kids who have never acted and who think they're just there to screw around […] ("On tourne *Zéro de conduite*," p. 66).

Pierre Lherminier — Pure Childhood

Starting from a personal experience which he wants both to protest and surmount (his 'life as a kid'), [Vigo] goes on to describe in fact a dreamlike and mythical world which is far removed from his own life. One might be content to see in this film just a vitriolic documentary about certain educational methods formerly in use in boarding schools — and that's exactly what was seen in 1933 by the censors who condemned it to oblivion for twelve years. Its "realism" seemed to be a blatant attack on the honor and the morale of teachers. But, like them, we would be misconstruing the true character of the film and its fundamental meaning. *Zero For Conduct* is of course a satirical text, an indictment of a whole system of education and of its over-zealous personnel. In the final analysis, however, that is only the pretext for the film, an anecdotal framework which Vigo quickly transcends in order to develop quite different perspectives. The best proof is that this film has lost none of its virulence, and that it affects us perhaps even more today than it did ten, twenty, or thirty years ago, even though its apparent subject, if we restricted ourselves to that, might seem of another age. It is in fact a film which is still young, whose age is only betrayed by the poor condition of the celluloid, whereas a film which was really *realistic* would have become outmoded long ago.

Judged by the criteria of realism alone, *Zero For Conduct* would only be an exaggerated and false film. If it is neither and instead seems to exude truth, it is because we cannot reduce it to the exterior reality that it supposedly depicts. We are confronted here with another reality that it does not depict but of which it is a sort of implicit proof: the secret inner reality of the author. Nothing is truly *real* here, and especially not the grotesque, crudely drawn characters, whose psychological makeup is clearly revealed in their physical presence, their manner of walking and gesturing, like the characters in melodramas, in fairytales, in the ballet, and in animated cartoons [...]. No, nothing is real here, but everything is *true*, if only because we are there, and because we are part of it [...].

In all truth, haven't we in fact inhabited that world? We rediscover in this film the forgotten or misunderstood universe which continues nevertheless to live deep within us, the world of childhood. It is not a manufactured world in which we might catch sight of something which resembles the vague memories of our childhood and which might only awaken in us a diffuse and bitter tasting emotion. It is *the* very world of childhood, the ideal and eternal childhood whose essential impulses and revolt are captured by Vigo, who may be revealing them to us for the first time in the event that, as it sometimes happens, we did not experience them when we were young. Far from being realistic, *Zero For Conduct* is, in this respect, the most beautiful of abstract films [...]. In deciding to make this film, Jean Vigo did not choose the safest path but the riskiest; he ran the risk of becoming a prisoner of the past which was his inspiration. The sign of success is that he avoided the trap. Born from memory, the film becomes a work of pure invention; the narrative becomes creation, the story poetry; reality disintegrates into truth. Beyond Jean Vigo's childhood, *Zero For Conduct* speaks to us of pure childhood (*Jean Vigo*, pp. 62-63).

Jean-Paul Marquet — Vigo's Optimism

When the son of the cook (Ma Bean) hides his heads in his hands and cries, while the rioting children in the cafeteria throw their plates at each other and shout "Ma Bean!", Vigo's whole childhood is in this sentiment of distress — just as his whole adult life is in the bitter spirit of revolt which gushes from the cruel buffoonery and flows over the whole film. He depicts the principal as a midget, shows a supervisor stealing children's snacks, and ends his film with a carnival shooting gallery: a shooting gallery to the second power, however, since the film mows down, in a carnivalesque mode, the childhood demons of the author.

We are moved far less by this buffoonery, however, than by Vigo's deep love for the children and a sort of optimism which transfigures everything. If grownups sully what is pure, the children will escape and triumph over the adult world. It is the only possible attitude faced with the meanness of the world we are forced to live in. It alone purifies. If at the beginning the children seem base, ugly, and wicked, at the end they become pure and angelic by the very fact of their revolt, their victory over the adult world, our world ("Optimisme et pessimisme chez Vigo," p. 93).

Phillipe d'Hugues — Caricature in Vigo

Just as there is a thin line between depicting people and caricaturing them, all Vigo has to do is exaggerate a gesture a little beyond its normal limit, raise his voice a smidgen, or heighten a banal attitude until it has become something else, to discover one of the keys to his art — an art which creates beauty by changing lines. While still a novice, Vigo goes further along this path than any other filmmaker before him. He begins by giving free rein to the tense verve which first strikes us in his work, and we are speaking of *Zero For Conduct* or the memory of youth in revolt. But we musn't be fooled by the caricature: it is not only the means by which Vigo reveals the true nature of things but also his way of rendering them bearable by making us laugh at them, even if we don't want to. At the same time we are dealing with a superior form of irony. Is the school principal dreadful because he's a midget with a long beard? Hardly. He is a midget with a beard because he is already dreadful. If we imagine him without his peculiarities, we're no longer amused. But by making him ridiculous by his physical appearance, Vigo intends to show us his true nature and, at the same time, make a judgment upon it. Ambiguous by nature, caricature thus becomes the instrument of satire and suggests a kind of morality: ugliness is the punishment for wickedness, but wickedness is also the punishment for ugliness. At the very moment they are presented to us, these characters have already been tried and judged ("La Fièvre de Jean Vigo," p. 96).

Paulo Emilio Salès Gomès — The Dormitory Scene

…The principal, impatient, repeats: *"Come on, say what you want to say!"* And once again Tabard explodes: *"Professor, I say…Go to Hell!"*

The next image shows us the dormitory simmering with excitement. Tabard reads a proclamation which we can only hear in part, because his diction is bad and the sound- track even worse: *"Down with the supervisors! Down with the sanctions! Long live the revolt!…Our flag on the roof of the school! We'll bombard them with old books!"*

Panicked, running around in his nightshirt, Nasty tries to intervene but is stopped by the students. When Tabard finishes reading the revolutionary proclamation, an incredible riot begins. The beds are messed up and chambers pots dragged around; the kids throw everything they can lay their hands on. They fight with the pillows and quilts until they burst. Exhausted and in a cloud of feathers, Nasty tries to sit down; the kids pull the chair out from under him, and he tumbles to the floor. Jaubert's music emphasizes the disorder.

At this moment two extraordinary events occur: the music and the images change. The movement in the images goes into slow-motion as an acrobatic boy does a cartwheel, his night shirt rising to expose briefly his naked body before he lands in the chair pulled out from under Nasty a moment before. At the same time the music takes on a bizarre quality. To find the perfect musical equivalent of the action in slow motion, Jaubert had recorded his melody played backwards, then reversed the sound track when the film was edited.

This phantasmal music continues to accompany the torch-lit parade which develops in slow motion behind the acrobat as he is carried off on his chair. All of the little people are in their nightshirts, in an apparent state of ecstasy, surrounded by the gentle movement of the feathers in the air. At the end of the parade we see a little phantom, a child struggling along wrapped in the curtains from the supervisor's quarters (*Jean Vigo*, pp. 146-147).

Pierre Lherminier — Lyricism and the Children's Revolt

Although *Zero For Conduct* clearly illustrates Vigo's spirit of revenge against everyone and everything that had attempted to repress him after having finished off his father, it is especially, above and beyond the preceding, a film about the ontological revolt of childhood. By the same token it is about everything in men which is reminiscent of childhood, that is, their very *openness* to experience. I spoke of *revolt without cause*: the "plot" of *Zero For Conduct* does not contain a precise, logical motive for Bruel, Caussat, Colin, Tabard and their troops to mount an assault against the school and everything which represents authority. The literal pretext for their revolt is trivial and in fact doesn't really count. What counts is that this revolt takes place because it cannot *not* take place. Because it is *the* revolt, whose function is to represent all revolts. The function of Vigo's schoolboys is not to overcome minor difficulties at school but to fulfill their role as rebels. They revolt because they are. They embody childhood's refusal to conform, its radical and fundamental bringing into question of the whole world, its desire to destroy everything and begin anew, its profound, logical, *normal* need to remake the world in its image. And that means rejecting everything that existed before, everything that claims the right to organize this world without its consent and to force it to adopt forms that it, itself, had no hand in creating.

Vigo pushes the limits in this respect. He has to consolidate the absurd revolt of his schoolboys, whom he has charged with the supreme mission. He has to make it eternal, *permanent*, prevent it from ever giving in, exclude once and for all the possibility of its being questioned and threatened by compromise. It is in lyricism that he finds the way. A lyricism which isn't the lyricism of *song* (as it will be later in *L'Atalante*) but the lyricism of the *cry*. A lyricism which is literally a *lyricism of fixation* [...].

It is of course in the extraordinary sequence of the riot in the dormitory that Vigo reaches the apogee in this respect. The slow motion and Jaubert's perfect music give this sequence all its meaning and all its weight. Once the revolt has reached its climax, Vigo maintains it on this extreme orbit and makes it appear eternal [...]. The final images of the film confirm this, but in a different way: after having defied all constituted authority by the irremediable act of bombarding everyone, the students, finally liberated, flee toward the summit of the roof, toward the blue sky, i.e., both nowhere and everywhere. They declare by this very act that what counts for them is not just any liberty but liberty itself, naked and pure, without shores and without form, like everything that is just being born: not liberty at any price, but the most complete liberty at the highest price; not the liberty to change their current life in order to try out the one they can see beyond the gates, but the liberty to change *life* and to begin again from *zero* (*Jean Vigo*, pp. 77, 79).

Bruno Voglino — The Children's Revolt and the Shock of Cultures

Zero For Conduct is about allegorical figures rather than real people constructed with a normal psychological makeup governed by the dialectics of facts and experiences. Indeed, some of them, deformed by the lens of caricature, are among the living dead; they defend a ridiculous, odious culture and morality. The others are the symbol of a new culture and morality. Their abstract, anarchical "angelization" is most clearly expressed in the famous slow-motion procession scene — light, pure, impalpable — in the dormitory ravaged by the rebellion [...].

Fortunately Vigo is not suggesting an "escape from the human condition," or more modestly from the family living room, but the very destruction of the prison of a historically determined society, a revolt against certain educational principles, a rejection of certain rules of behavior in favor of others. In short, he is proposing to construct life in a different manner [...].

The opposition between the adult universe — forbidden, petty, egotistical — and the children's — free, healthy, creative — is not the simple "eternal," non-historical contrast between the adult world and the kids' world. It is not the ideal antinomy between the arid, uncomprehending adult universe and the romantic spontaneity of children [...]. In reality the film is the representation of the shock between two cultures. The revolt of the four boys is a whole group's renunciation of the society in which it is forced to live, and into which it is being integrated according to the norms of the class in power. Vigo rejects the grownup world (and his viewpoint and judgment often coincide with the viewpoint and judgment of his young protagonists), because he recognizes in it the stratification and crystallization of a criminal social order which smothers the man in the child in order to smother in the man the becoming of history.

So rather than being the itinerary of a "difficult" adolescence, *Zero For Conduct* is the struggle between two opposing conceptions of life which collide, one attempting to survive, the other fighting to begin to be ("Un réalisme poétique," pp. 101-102).

JEAN VIGO'S FILMOGRAPHY

1930	*A propos de Nice*
1931	*Taris or Swimming (Taris ou la natation)*
1933	*Zero For Conduct (Zéro de conduite)*
1934	*L'Atalante*

WORKS CONSULTED

Agee, James. "*Zéro de conduite* et *L'Atalante*." *Premier Plan*, 19 (Nov. 1961): 74-76.

Bost, Pierre. "*Zéro de conduite*." *Premier Plan*, 19 (Nov. 1961): 72-73.

D'Hugues, Philippe. "La Fièvre de Jean Vigo." *Premier Plan*, 19 (Nov. 1961): 96-97.

Jacob, Gilles. "Saint Jean Vigo, Patron des Ciné-Clubs." *Premier Plan*, 19 (Nov. 1961): 89-93.

Leutrat, Paul. "Comme une sentinelle...," dans Buache, Freddy, Vinicio Beretta et Franco Vercelotti, ed., *Hommage à Jean Vigo*. Lausanne: La Cinémathèque suisse, 1962.

Lherminier, Pierre. *Jean Vigo*. Paris: Pierre Lherminier, 1984.

Marquet, Jean-Paul. "Optimisme et pessimisme chez Vigo." *Premier Plan*, 19 (Nov. 1961): 93.

Négis, André. "On tourne *Zéro de conduite*." *Premier Plan*, 19 (Nov. 1961): 66-68.

Salès Gomès, Paulo Emilio. *Jean Vigo*. Paris: Seuil, 1957.

Storck, Henri. "Naissance de *Zéro de conduite*." *Premier Plan*, 19 (Nov. 1961): 78-80.

Vigo, Jean. "Mon Journal. Ma petite vie au collège de Millau et pendant les vacances." *Positif*, 7 (May 1953): 88-93.

.........."Présentation de *Zéro de conduite*" (Oct. 17, 1933, in Brussels). *Positif*, 7 (May 1953): 41-45.

........."*Zéro de conduite*" (screenplay), *L'Avant-Scène Cinéma*, 21 (Dec. 15. 1962: 1-28.

Voglino, Bruno. "Un réalisme poétique." *Premier Plan*, 19 (Nov. 1961): 100-104.

Jean Renoir

A Day in the Country
Partie de campagne

(1936, 1946)

Jean Renoir, *A Day in the Country*: Henri (Georges Darnoux) and Henriette (Sylvia Bataille) on the island. © Films du jeudi

Director .... Jean Renoir
Screenplay and Dialogues.. Jean Renoir
Assistant Directors .... Jacques Becker, Henri Cartier-Bresson
Director of Photography ....Claude Renoir
Music...Joseph Kosma
Film Editors ....Marguerite Houllé-Renoir, Marinette Cadicqx
Sound ....Joseph de Bretagne
Art Director ....Robert Gys
Props and costumes...Luchino Visconti
Script Girl (continuity) ....Marguerite Houllé-Renoir
Producer ....Pierre Braunberger
Length ....36 minutes

Cast

Sylvia Bataille (*Henriette*), Georges Darnoux (*Henri*), Jacques B. Brunius (*Rodolphe*), Jane Marken (*Juliette Dufour*), André Gabriello (*Cyprien Dufour*), Paul Temps (*Anatole*), Jean Renoir (*Old Poulain*), Marguerite Houllé-Renoir (*the waitress*), Gabrielle Fontan (*the grandmother*), Alain Renoir (*the little boy fishing*).

STORY

It's a summer Sunday in 1860. M. Dufour, a Parisian hardware store owner, takes his wife and daughter out to the country, along with his mother-in-law and his clerk, Anatole. They decide to have lunch at Poulain's inn. The men are attracted by a nearby river, where they hope they will be able to go fishing, while the women are pleased to see that there are swings.

Inside the restaurant two boaters, Rodolphe and Henri, are about to have lunch. They gripe about being disturbed by the arrival of a swarm of Parisians. However, when Rodolphe sees the beautiful girl Henriette standing and gliding back and forth on a swing, he is smitten and decides to try to seduce her. He enlists his friend to take care of the mother, a rather corpulent but jolly woman who was clearly once attractive.

Once the meal has been ordered, M. Dufour and Anatole walk over to the edge of the river and discuss fishing, while Mme Dufour and her daughter look for a piece of lawn where they can eat lunch. Excited by this unusual contact with nature, Henriette shares her feelings with her mother, who is no stranger to the desires her daughter is experiencing for the first time. This lyrical interlude is interrupted by Anatole, who calls the two women over to admire two beautiful skiffs he has discovered. Seeking a way to meet the two women, Rodolphe and Henri take their spot on the grass and grab Henriette's hat, which she has forgotten there. The hat will be the pretext for speaking to the women.

Despite the gathering storm, Henriette insists on picnicking on the grass. To make a good impression on the ladies, Rodolphe and Henri let them have their place back and return Henriette's hat to her. The young girl is clearly attracted to Henri. The Dufour family and their clerk settle in to eat. After the meal we find M. Dufour and Anatole sleeping off their wine. Aroused sexually but frustrated by the somnolent state of her husband, the mother proves to be receptive to the advances of the two boaters, who offer to take her and her daughter for a ride on the river. While they are enthusiastic, the mother and her daughter cannot accept without M. Dufour's permission. To facilitate things, Rodolphe wins over ("seduces," the French would say) the shopkeeper and his assistant with some fishing poles. While M. Dufour and Anatole happily go off to fish, Henri grabs Henriette by the hand and runs with her toward his boat. Being a good sport, Rodolphe takes the giggling mother. The two couples get into the boats and head down the river.

Recalcitrant at first, then encouraged by her mother's enthusiasm, Henriette agrees to visit an island, where Henri leads her into his "personal hideaway," a little thicket where they are hidden from view. Rodolphe likewise debarks on the island with the mother and amuses himself by chasing her around, acting like Pan the satyr. Henri tries to put his arm around Henriette and kiss her. Although she is deeply moved, the young girl first resists, then gives up and embraces Henri passionately. The storm which has been building finally bursts, and rain beats down on the river.

A few years later, Henri rows alone to the island to visit his "hideaway." To his astonishment, he finds Henriette there, with her husband…Anatole. He confides in the young woman that this place has remained very special to him; emotionally, she responds that she "*thinks of it every night.*"

CRITICAL RECEPTION

Shot in 1936, but not edited until 1946 (see below, "The Origin…"), *A Day in the Country* finally opened in Paris in December, 1946. The reaction of the film critics was fairly mixed. The critics complained about the poor quality of the sound and the uneven quality of the acting, although everyone praised highly the touching interpretation Sylvia Bataille gave to her character. Many appreciated the poetic nature of *A Day in the Country*, and some boldly spoke of an "uncompleted masterpiece." Like all medium-length films, it couldn't be a commercial success, but it was made available to the public in film clubs during the fifties and sixties. Paradoxically, as André Bazin points out, the absence of the few scenes which weren't shot is not detrimental to the film: "The scenes which were not shot, and which would have taken place primarily in Mr. Dufour's hardware store (rue des Martyrs) are insignificant in Maupassant's short story, so it really could be claimed that *A Day in the Country* is a perfectly finished film" (p. 47). Among cinema critics a consensus slowly formed that *A Day in the Country* is an absolute jewel, one of Renoir's most appealing films, and a model for the adaptation of literary works to the screen.

THE ORIGIN AND THE CAST

The story of the filming of *A Day in the Country* is a real saga. The plan to adapt "A Day in the Country," a short story by Guy de Maupassant published in 1881, grew out of Renoir's desire to give a starring role to the young actress Sylvia Bataille, who had played a minor role in *Le Crime de Monsieur Lange* and earned the filmmaker's admiration. (For a summary of Renoir's body of works before *A Day in the Country*, see the introduction to *Grand Illusion*, "Before *Grand Illusion*," **p. 78**). He found the role he was seeking in Henriette's character. In addition, Renoir was very struck by Maupassant's story, observing that "there are few love stories that are so touching" and that "there is everything in this story, a mess of problems, a whole slice of the world." Finally he wanted to make a period film in a pastoral setting far from the studios and a mode of production he found cumbersome. He chose therefore a site out in the country near Fontainebleau (the same area which had inspired some of the paintings of his father, Auguste Renoir) on the banks of the Loing where he had a house.

Assisted by his crew, Renoir spent around two months (May-June, 1936) polishing the screenplay and preparing the shooting of the film. Opposite Sylvia Bataille he cast two veteran film actresses, Jane Marken and Gabrielle Fontan, in the roles of Henriette's mother and grandmother. The foregoing were joined by a cabaret actor, André Gabriello, in the role of the father, the production administrator, Jacques B. Brunius, an inspired dilettante, as Rodolphe, and Georges Darnoux, Renoir's assistant director for several earlier films, as Henri. The cast is completed by novice actors: Paul Temps (Anatole), Marguerite Houllé-Renoir, the script girl for the film and Renoir's domestic partner (the waitress), and Alain Renoir, Renoir's son, in the role of the boy who is fishing at the beginning of the film. Renoir himself plays the role of the inn-keeper, Old Poulain, while several of his friends fill in as the priest and the seminary students who walk by during Henriette's swing scene.

SHOOTING AND EDITING

Despite the family-like "day in the country" atmosphere of the enterprise, things went wrong from the very beginning of the filming (June 27). Renoir insisted on shooting most of the scenes outside with synchronized sound recording, a rather unusual approach for the period. Unfortunately, the work was constantly interrupted by rain, and the shoot, which was only supposed to last a week and a half, was still in progress a month and a half later, in mid-August. Forced to spend their days waiting for a ray of sunlight, the crew members became irritable, and relationships become strained, as Sylvia Bataille herself testifies: "Ah! Let me tell you, the last days got pretty ugly. People were sick of each other, and the atmosphere became downright hateful… Why? Just try to imagine what it's like for a crew to have to wait days on end, ready to work, for the sun and for the money to continue shooting!" (Philippe, p. 75). And it didn't help things that Georges Darnoux (Henri) was a little too attached to the bottle and, again according to Sylvia Bataille, "already drunk in the morning."

Renoir, for his part, couldn't wait to finish the project, so that he could turn to his next feature film, *The Lower Depths* (*Les Bas-Fonds*), an adaptation of the Gorki novel which he was preparing to shoot in Paris. The last shots of *A Day in the Country*, during the second week of August — including, notably, the embarking of the ladies in the skiffs, nearly all the shots on the water, and Rodolphe's satyr act on the island — were in fact done by Renoir's assistants, following his precise instructions (Curchod, p. 21). The film being considerably over-budget by this time, the producer, Pierre Braunberger, concerned moreover about the deteriorating relations between the members of the crew, finally closed down operations on August 15. They had shot neither the scene which was supposed to begin the film (the Dufour family's departure from Paris), nor the scene which was supposed to be placed just before the final sequence on the island when Henri stops at the Dufour hardware store, where he learns that Henriette has been married to the clerk Anatole. Despite Braunberger's desperate efforts to "save" the project by transforming it into a feature film based on a scenario written by Jacques Prévert, the work remained unfinished.

The reels of *A Day in the Country* would sleep in their boxes for ten years, until the Liberation. Then, without consulting Renoir (who was still in the United States, where he had fled the Nazi occupation of France in 1940), Braunberger realized that, to finish the film adequately, it would be enough to add two intertitles to replace the two scenes which weren't shot, the one at the beginning of the film and the one which comes just before the dénouement on the island. From November, 1945, to January, 1946, he had the film edited by Marguerite Houllé-Renoir, who, we remember, served as script girl when the film was made. For the music, he called on Joseph Kosma, one of Renoir's closest collaborators who had composed the music for many of his films, including some of his greatest masterpieces, *Grand Illusion* (1937), *The Human Beast* (*La Bête humaine,* 1938), and *The Rules of the Game* (*La Règle du jeu,* 1939). We should note that in the credits, in the final version of the film, there is a slight modification of the title. Originally titled *Une partie de campagne*, like Maupassant's story, the film was now called simply *Partie de campagne*. This change explains the existence of the two titles in the literature devoted to Renoir's film. First projected at the Cannes Film Festival in September, 1946, *Partie de campagne* finally had a public showing in December in a movie theater on the Champs-Elysées.

STRUCTURE

Renoir intended to make, as he puts it, "a short film which would be complete and would have the style of a feature film." Hence, *A Day in the Country* was to unfold, classically, in five movements, including a prologue (the Dufour's depature from Paris), the main part of the story in three sections, and the epilogue on the island (Henri and Henriette's sad reunion). The prologue, which was not shot, is replaced, as we've seen, by an intertitle which provides the context for the action — although we might consider the arrival of the cart on the bridge to be a short prologue. The first part of the main body of the film includes the introduction of the Dufour group arriving at the inn, followed by the presentation of the two boaters preparing to lunch inside the inn and the seduction plan concocted by Rodolphe after he sees Henriette on the swing. In the second part M. Dufour and Anatole marvel at the mysteries of nature while discussing fishing, while Mme Dufour and Henriette, sitting on the grass where they want to have lunch, are aroused by the contact with nature. In this part the two boaters also manage to meet the Dufour women by using Henriette's hat as a "lure." The third part of the film, beginning after lunch, is devoted to the seduction of the two women: the frustration of Mme Dufour's desires, the offer of the boat ride on the river, the permission of Henriette's father, and the two amorous adventures on the island. We might consider, somewhat schematically, that the first long sequence creates an opposition between the boaters without women and the men in the Dufour group accompanied by the mother and daughter; in the second, Henri and Rodolphe meet the Dufour women and men; in the course of the third sequence, the boaters replace the Dufour men beside their women.

THEMES, METAPHORS, AND SYMBOLS

As regards both characters and themes, the main body of *A Day in the Country* is structured by a series of binary oppositions. From the outset the Parisians, whose attire evokes the city, are set in opposition to the boaters and the countryside which is their natural habitat. The boaters themselves constitute a new opposition, Rodolphe's carefree and spirited nature contrasting with Henri's seriousness and disillusionment. In the second part of the film Renoir develops a major opposition between the themes of knowledge and ignorance of nature which foregrounds both the parallels and the contrasts between the two couples within the Dufour group. On the one hand, the men: M. Dufour shows off his knowledge of nature (fishing) to Anatole, whose ignorance is an indication of his foolishness. On the other hand, the women:

Mme Dufour embodies carnal "knowledge," knowledge of pleasures of the flesh, in opposition to her daughter, whose ignorance is a sign of her innocence, her purity. At the same time the two couples are starkly opposed by the absurd character of the two men, their slapstick side, which reminds us of Laurel and Hardy, and the tenderness and sensitivity which characterize the ties between the two women and nature. Indeed, as soon as the film came out in 1946, the critics were struck by the unusual mixture of styles, the comic episodes alternating with highly emotional scenes.

In the third part the oppositions proliferate, beginning with the fishing motif which underlies the whole film. The two boaters go "fishing" (a metaphor developed at length in the film), with the two Dufour women as their prey. At the same time M. Dufour and Anatole dream of going fishing literally, a dream which is realized when the boaters set them up to fish — in exchange for the boat ride with the two women. The other oppositions are thus complemented, on the rhetorical level, by the contrast of the literal and metaphorical planes. As soon as they are on the island, a new opposition is established between the Rodolphe-Mme Dufour couple, whose grossly lecherous and ludic attraction returns us to the burlesque vein of the film, and the Henri-Henriette couple, who share a brief, intense adventure filled with sentiment and passion. The two adventures are no less parallel: they are both stagings of desire, sensuality, and seduction developed in different modes.

Renoir's film ends with a final, very painful opposition. Henriette's marriage to Anatole, which we learn of in the epilogue at the same moment Henri does, establishes an opposition between the law of Nature — the natural attraction between Henri and Henriette — and the law of Society — the marriage of Henriette to her father's successor in the hardware store. The presence of the fishing poles in this final scene emphasizes ironically that it is the grotesque clerk Anatole who has caught the big fish: social law prevails.

Beside the fishing metaphor, the bad weather which plagues the filming gives birth to a second important metaphor related to water (itself an obvious figure for the flowing of time): the metaphor of the storm. Renoir, famous for his talent at improvisation, manages in fact to integrate the unexpected rainy weather into the thematic texture of the film. The gathering storm seems to be a foreshadowing of the passion which will engulf the two couples in the island. The forces of nature are going to burst loose. The series of short shots on the trees and the reeds bent by the wind and on the ominous clouds, followed by the long tracking backwards on the river pelted by the rain, have thus been interpreted as a metaphor for love-making (Sesonske, p. 252). On the other hand, as André Bazin remarks, the rain beating down on the water, which concludes the brief liaison between Henri and Henriette, seems to express "all the disenchantment, or rather the pathetic sadness after love-making" (p. 47). From this viewpoint the gloomy weather and the sadness that it evokes foreshadow the lugubrious dénouement of the film.

Finally, certain themes are imbedded in symbols in the film. Renoir keeps, for example, the nightingale, a traditional symbol of love present in Maupassant's tale. He adds the transformation of the women's costumes — from Henriette's white dress to the black attire of the grandmother, with the mother's grey clothes in between — into symbols of the wearing down effect of life and of the sad destiny of the petty bourgeois woman (Arnault, p. 152). The somber dress that Henriette wears in the epilogue seems to confirm the symbolic character of the ladies' attire.

STYLE AND MUSIC

It is difficult to speak of the style of *A Day in the Country* without noting its links to the Impressionist movement in painting. The pictorial composition of the shots is obvious to everyone. Curchod points out the "thousand clear references — from Manet to Pissarro, from Caillebotte to Sisley, from Renoir to Monet" (p. 74) — while emphasizing that Renoir is in no way attempting to imitate those artists' works. To some the strong ties to the works of his father are, however, self-evident: "Renoir has managed to identify with his father's pallette; Auguste Renoir's Impressionism is discernable behind his son's images; the same poetry, the same sensuality vibrate with the same touch, the same brief, fluid sentiments" (Allombert, p. 7). One cannot help but think of *Boaters* (*Canotiers*, 1868) and of *La Grenouillère* (1869), but especially of *The Swing* (*La Balançoire*, 1876), which is clearly evoked — with the movement added — in the scene where Henriette swings standing up, as if the son, while paying homage to his father's art, wanted to assert his own originality (or superiority?). In any case, we undeniably find in Renoir's film the most characteristic traits of the Impressionist movement: the cult of nature, with its country scenes, its rivers, and its bridges, the lunch on the grass and the ride in the boat, as well as the emphasis on movement (the swing, the boats, the river water) and the play of light.

The impression of movement is reinforced by a filming style which is typical of Renoir, a style in which the camera movements play a major role. Pans and tracking shots, contrasting with the many static shots, accompany the characters' movements, while the many camera movements limit the fragmentation of the space. Here is what Curchod has to say regarding the most striking panning shots:

> Throughout the film, the camera movements describe a harmonious ballet of rhymes, the most famous being the meeting of Henriette and Rodolphe (converging tracking shots), the entrance into Henri's personal hideaway (a lateral tracking towards the left accompanying the couple), and the final meeting (identical tracking shots which first go to find the young woman, then follow her back in the opposite direction to Henri). During the seduction scene, a single short pan, following the girl when she throws herself back onto the grass to escape her companion's caresses, indicates, by the static shots which precede and follow it, the futility of this attempt to escape (p. 82).

In *A Day in the Country* the camera movements compensate to some extent for the lack of the sequence shots which will soon become one of the principal signatures of Renoir's style (see the sections on style in the chapters on *Grand Illusion* and *The Rules of the Game*). We note, however, the importance Renoir already grants to a depth of field which preserves the unity of space, its "realistic" character. The most striking example of this technique is the scene in which Rodolphe, sitting inside the inn, pushes open the shutters to reveal Henriette swinging in the background.

As for the importance of Joseph Kosma's music, which is an integral part of the style of the film, let's listen once again to Sylvia Bataille: "After the war, when Braunberger showed us the edited film without any music, no one thought that you could show that to the public [...]. But when Kosma spread his marvelous score over it, the film gelled instantly, seamlessly…a real surprise" (*Premier Plan*, p. 226). Added in 1946, without Renoir's involvement, Kosma's score serves, on the one hand, to compensate for the poor quality of the sound track, which the director didn't have time to complete, having abandoned the film before post-production when they would have recorded the "natural" sounds which were missing. On the other hand, from the very beginning of the film the music "introduces a dramatic intensity tempered by melancholy" (Le Loch, p. 27). It sets the tone, the atmosphere, and the emotional texture by alternating cheerful and sad melodies, the themes of joy and bitterness, as the action develops. An additional stroke of genius, Germaine Montero's humming, which accompanies the first tracking shot on the river (from the viewpoint of Henri and Henriette in the boat), intensifies the romantic atmosphere which prepares the couple's tryst on the island. Nonetheless, the music creates a melancholic effect tinged with irony when the same hummed melody accompanies the final separation of the two lovers at the end of the film.

ADAPTING MAUPASSANT'S TALE

The numerous commentators of *A Day in the Country* have studied every detail of Renoir's remarkable adaptation of Maupassant's work. Although the tale, as Curchod observes, "furnished all the dramatic material" (p. 45), the brevity of the piece and the lack of character development allow the filmmaker to "embroider," as he says, on the writer's tapestry. Renoir remains essentially faithful to both the letter and the spirit of the literary work, keeping Maupassant's basic plot and his caricature of the petty bourgeois Parisians and expressing the same warmth and emotion, while sharing the author's pessimism — or should we say cynicism? On the other hand, Renoir develops his characters in far greater depth. He endows the two boaters, who are scarcely developed at all in Maupassant's story, with individualized and starkly contrasting personalities and better defines Anatole's character, which the writer doesn't even dignify with a name. For this purpose he invents dialogues and entire scenes: the boaters lunch in the inn, the episode in which Rodolphe opens the shutters to reveal Henriette on the swing, the comic scene at the river's edge where M. Dufour shows off his "knowledge" about fish, the conversation between Mme Dufour and her daughter about the sensuality of nature and the "vague desire" it produces, and the after-lunch siesta scene, among others. While Renoir simply reproduces the seduction of the two women as it occurs in Maupassant's work, he enriches it with the "fishing" metaphor and adds the storm metaphor — the raging of the natural forces of passion — which replaces the nightingale's song, the overt sexual metaphor employed in the tale. He likewise introduces the satyr act performed by Rodolphe, whose carefree and fun-loving personality, like the clownish characters of M. and Mme Dufour and Anatole, is entirely created by Renoir. The filmmaker thus develops a comic dimension which is scarcely suggested in Maupassant's tale. The result is a rather "Shakespearean" mixing of comic and dramatic styles: the opposition, for instance, between Rodolphe's ridiculous courting of the mother and Henri's earnest seduction of Henriette. Especially notable is the striking contrast between the light, amusing beginning of the film and the serious, indeed pathetic, tone of the ending. As far as "embroidery" goes, the richness and aptness of Renoir's creative enhancements are undeniable; his film appears to be the result of a natural blossoming of Maupassant's tale.

STUDY GUIDE

Director's Comments

"I had wanted for a long while to make a short film which would be as polished as a feature film. Shorts are commonly made in a few days, sloppily, sometimes with poor actors and inadequate technical support. It seemed to me that if you made a short film carefully, it could perhaps be combined with other shorts to make a full-length film [...]. So it was, basically, a first step towards the idea of the collective film.

I made a Maupassant film for a very simple reason: I like Maupassant, and it seems to me that in a little story like "A Day in the Country" you have everything, a whole slice of the world, with a mess of problems. Moreover, there are few love stories which are as touching as "A Day in the Country" [...].

Another thing: this extremely short story left me free, unlike a play which dictates the dialogue. "A Day in the Country" dictated nothing — other than an ideal framework to embroider upon [...].

The most important incident in the shooting of *A Day in the Country* is related to the fact that I had written the scenario for the sun. I had written the scenario for people to be sitting in the dust and sweating. Well, it rained constantly. Although I was able to steal a few rays of sun between the cloudbursts, I finally decided to transform the screenplay into a rain scenario.. And those long rain scenes that you see were thus simply due to the meterological conditions we couldn't escape" (*Entretiens et propos*, pp. 142-144).

"This film arose from my desire to do something with Sylvia Bataille; it seemed to me that a costumed film would be best for her [...]. It occurred to me to use Maupassant's tale because I saw things which suited her voice well [...]. To return to *A Day in the Country*, if certain country scenes and costumes seem to evoke my father's paintings, it's for two reasons: first, because the action takes place in a period and in places where my father did a lot of his work when he was young; and then, because I am my father's son, and people are necessarily influenced by their parents [...]. As the son of a painter, I was necessarily influenced by the painters who surrounded me when I was little" (*Entretiens et propos*, p. 156).

Excerpts for Discussion

Extrait 1 (3'25-5'55): Rodolphe and Henri complain about the arrival of the Parisians; Rodolphe opens the shutters and sees Henriette on the swing; Henriette as the object of multiple (desiring) gazes.

Extrait 2 (8'40-11'25): M. Dufour and Anatole discuss fishing; Henriette discovers sensuality through contact with nature and discusses the "vague desire" she feels with her mother.

Extrait 3 (16'15-18'10): After the meal Mme Dufour has cravings; upset by her sleepy husband's unresponsiveness, she uses Anatole's hiccups as a pretext to throw a fit.

<u>Extrait 4</u> (**27'30-31'45**): Henri and Henriette ride down the river in their skiff; Henriette wants to go back but agrees to visit the island with Henri when his mother shouts that she is going to "go all the way" with Rodolphe; the two couples on the island; the storm bursts.

<u>Extrait 5</u> (**33'00-34'40**): Part of the epilogue on the island, several years later.

Quotations for Comment

Henri: What can I say, my friend! I think like a family man. I find whores boring... society women even more than the others...I find it too dangerous.

Rodolphe: Yeh, you're afraid of catching something.

Henri: No, I'm afraid of the responsibility. Suppose that nice little girl swinging over there falls for you! What would you do with her?

Rodolphe: I'd invite her for a ride in my boat. We'd get off at the island and go to the factory dam. Then, pure pleasure!

Henri: And if you got her pregnant?

Rodolphe: Oh! If you got a girl pregnant every time you had a little fun...we'd have a world population problem.

[...]

Henri: [...] Of course, you would drop her, and there's another life spoiled, ruined... It's not worth it, my friend.

* * *

Henriette: Tell me, mother, when you were young...I mean...when you were my age, did you go out to the country often?

Mme Dufour: No, not very often. Like you!

Henriette: Did you feel real funny...like I do today?

Mme Dufour: Funny?

Henriette: Well, yes...Did you feel a sort of tenderness for everything, for the grass, for the water, for the trees? A kind of vague desire? It starts here, it moves up, it almost makes you feel like crying. Did you feel that, mother, when you were young?

Mme Dufour: Oh, you sweet thing, I still feel it! But...I'm more sensible now.

* * *

Rodolphe: OK, so you're going to participate in this...uh...fishing expedition! How about choosing our gear?

Henri: We'll do fly-fishing. It's the latest rage.

Rodolphe: Fly-fishing! With dead or live bait? Or with artificial lures?

Henri: For women, with a lure of course!

Rodolphe: But are we going to fish from the river bank or from a boat?

Henri: From a boat, my friend, it's more elegant.

* * *

Henriette: Papa, can mother and I go for a boat ride with these gentlemen?

M. Dufour: On the water?

Henriette: Yes, a boat ride!

M. Dufour: In a boat!

Rodolphe, *holding out the fishing poles.* Here, sir. If you like to fish, here's all you need.

[…]

Henriette: Come on, papa, yes or no?

M. Dufour: What?

Henriette: Can we go?

M. Dufour: Where?

Henriette: For a boat ride!

M. Dufour: Ah! With these gentlemen? Yes, of course, I trust these gentlemen completely.

* * *

Stage directions:

Medium shot of Henri trying to kiss Henriette, who resists. She throws herself on her back. He lies on her. Near shot of their faces, Henri trying to find Henriette's lips; she finally stops fighting and embraces him. Close-up of the kiss. Extreme close-up of Henriette's face, held up by Henri's hand.

Dissolve to a medium shot of Henriette, lying beside Henri.

Series of shots of the countryside, indicating rain soon. Reeds bending, dark clouds in the sky. The light dims. Tall poplars are bent by the wind. Again the wildly waving reeds. Large, black clouds. And to finish, a long backward tracking shot on the river.

Drops of rain strike the water.

Fade to black.

* * *

Henri: I often come here. You know, it's where I have my best memories.

Henriette: I think of it every night.

© *L'Avant-Scène Cinéma*

Questions/Topics for Reflection

1. The characters in the film (describe).
2. The forming of couples (comment).
3. Thematic oppositions in *A Day in the Country.*
4. Allusions to Impressionist painting.
5. The importance of sensuality (reference to sensual pleasures) in this film.
6. The mixing of genres (comic and serious).

7. The two principal metaphors of the film: fishing and the storm.
8. Water plays an important role in many of Renoir's films. It's role in this film?
9. Renoir's cinematographic style and the impression of movement which dominates this film.
10. Renoir's original contributions in relationship to Maupassant's tale.

CRITICAL DOSSIER

Hubert Arnault — The Cinematography

With the exception of a few shots inside M. Poulain's inn, *A Day in the Country* is a film composed entirely of outside shots.

The deep focus of nearly all the shots adds to this third dimension which strikes the Dufour family "confronted with the distant horizons."

The luminous quality of the photography lends special importance to the trees with their brilliant leaves, the grass, the river, the sun, and the reeds, as well as to the individuals.

This brightness lights up the screen and gives the film a unity of tone which contrasts with the epilogue, where the lighting is more somber.

The siesta sequence is bathed in a vaporous light: it gives off "a truly unnatural heat."

For these reasons, the photography in *A Day in the Country* is remarkable.

The camera movements are discreet and justified. They never create an action; they simply underline the characters' movements. They are accompanying movements.

We must give particular note to Henriette's swing scene. The camera, fastened to the swing, accompanies Henriette in a slight up-shot. The result is a gentle emotional effect which intoxicates the sensitive spectator. Henriette, smiling, happy, is thus intimately associated with the brilliantly lit natural surroundings.

The camera often glides along the dolly track, simultaneously panning to avoid any break in the shot as the action develops.

This technique is particularly clear in the epilogue, when Henri walks under the foliage on the island. The camera follows him, leaves him, discovers Henriette sitting next to Anatole, accompanies Henriette by tracking backwards, and then, to finish, frames the two lovers in a static medium shot.

The complexity of the camera movement highlights the unforgettable bond between them.

To portray this meeting in a series of fragmented shots would have been a grave error.

A few rare movements do, however, have their own dramatic role. The moves toward the bank during the long tracking shot on the river betray Henri's desire to bring Henriette onto the island with him ("*Partie de campagne* (1936-1946) de Jean Renoir," pp. 151-152).

Jacques Doniol-Valcroze — Sylvia Bataille

But Sylvia Bataille alone, as much or more than the river, the warm grass, or the languid clouds, is the very heart of this day in the country, which is both the object and the cause of her agitated emotional state.

She communicates this agitation, this vague sensuality, this naïve pantheism, this carnal desire, and this exquisite confusion to the whole work with a deeply moving youthfulness. Nothing artificial, no studied behavior, just a slightly astonished gaze, a slightly subdued voice, scarcely audible, something tense yet inviting in her movements. Guileless and perverse, her wordless love scene next to the water, under the foliage rustling with the storm which is gathering in the distance, is doubtlessly one of the most beautiful in our cinematographic anthology ("Une esquisse," pp. 70-71).

Guy Allombert — Love and Tragedy

Renoir made this "tragedy" — for it is indeed a tragedy — with such a light touch, such delicacy in the depiction of the awakening of love between a girl and a young man, that it is impossible to escape the emotional impact. Henriette, an extraordinarily fresh, pure character, incarnates all the grace of youth, whereas Henri, who acts the cynic, soon turns out to be a sensitive, romantic individual. Renoir places them in a setting that guarantees that they are really going to awaken to their natural desires, fall in tune with the quivering life which surrounds them, become sensitive to the elements, in a sort of cosmic opera in which human sentiment is integrated into the sensual joy of luxuriant nature. The joyous character of their meeting is only a brief image; the same nature which smiles at them through the sun is going to separate them by the rain. And that is where *A Day in the Country* becomes tragic. The river may sparkle with a thousand points of light, and the wind may play exquisitely on the surface of the water and in the rushes; they are indifferent to human existence and flow by impassively without end. Renoir is using his father's palette. Auguste Renoir's Impressionism is present behind the son's images: the same poetry, the same sensuality vibrate with the same strokes, the same fugitive and fluid sentiments.

A remarkably beautiful visual poem, Renoir's film unites the joy of living to the melancholy of loves lost almost before they begin. In few films is such bitterness mingled with such a lust for life. Rarely have the brief sentiments which guide beings been so absorbed into the infinite space of nature; and no one who has seen *A Day in the Country* will ever forget Sylvia Bataille discovering love in an embrace after having followed the progression of her sentiments towards an anguish she cannot resist. The photography of Claude Renoir and the music of Joseph Kosma contribute to this perfect tribute to Maupassant in which all of Renoir's themes were developed to perfection: the feeling for nature, the theme of water, the light eroticism and deep sensuality, the love of life, people, the world… ("Variations cinématographiques sur des thèmes de Maupassant," p. 7).

André Bazin — The Love Scene on the Island

The love scene on the island is simultaneously one of the most atrocious and one of the most beautiful ever shown on the screen. It owes its dazzling effectiveness to a few gestures and a look by Sylvia Bataille which contain a heartrending emotional realism. What is expressed there is all the disenchantment, or rather the pathetic sadness, after making love. And then it had to be transposed visually to the screen; that's the admirable storm sequence (*Jean Renoir*, p. 47).

Hubert Arnault — Henri

Although he doesn't realize it, Rodolphe is dominated by Henri. While he seems to take a back seat to Rodolphe, Henri is by far the cleverer and slyer. Henri exploits Rodolphe's reactions, which he provokes at will. Despite his tendency to tease, however, Henri never takes it far enough to endanger the comradeship they share [...]. While Rodolphe is quick to thrust himself forward, Henri only acts later, analyzing the situation and taking effortlessly the course which suits him...at his friend's expense. Essentially a weak individual, Rodolphe accepts the situation gracefully.

Henri loves intensely. He is an introverted sentimental individual, sincere and sensitive. Henriette's first appearance sets his blood flowing. Before such youth, beauty, and innocence, his whole being is filled with desire. Henri has only to give free rein to his desire and seduce Henriette. He does so with great tact, gentleness, and resolution. His "family man" mentality will not allow him to ruin a life; this discovery of a love destined to last is the result of a long wait during which Henri seeks in vain, with prostitutes and society women, an authentic happiness. In the person of Henriette he finds the Woman of his dreams. "I can see her this morning attaching those little flowers before leaving. She has a lot of poise, that girl. I was surprised at how naturally she spoke to you. She is really very nice..."

However, this happiness will be destroyed by the stupidity of others. Social conventions will prevent this union. Henri and Henriette will continue nonetheless to love each other in silence ("*Partie de campagne* (1936-1946) de Jean Renoir," p. 151).

Claude Gauteur et al. — The Role of Nature

The two works thus emphasize the active role of nature in the awakening of sensuality. In the tale, as soon as they arrive at Bezons, M. Dufour, aroused by the surrounding countryside, pinches his wife's calf sharply. Renoir, for his part, establishes a very precise parallel between the agitation of the invisible insects in the grass around Henriette and her mother and the sensual response which makes the two women feel "so strange." In the film, the river plays a major role in this respect: while the amorous couple slides along in their skiff, enjoying the silence, a languorous music can be heard, as if the water were singing. Renoir found this highly poetic way of expressing what, in the tale, is communicated by a veritable personification of Nature. Henriette's emotion, in Maupassant's work, is indissociable from the natural elements. They are the cause and the echo of her turmoil and are omnipresent in the text: "She was deeply agitated by this tête-à-tête *on the water*, in the middle of this countryside emptied of people by the burning *sun*, with this young man [...] whose desire was as penetrating as *the sun*."

[Nature] has nonetheless, in both works, an ultimately destructive effect. Nature only appears gentle, friendly, and exciting in order to achieve its ends. It is only, to quote the philosopher Schopenhauer, a "desire to live" which crushes beings in the spiral of an eternal but aimless desire.

We note, accordingly, in both the tale and the film, that the same nature which favors love changes character as soon as it has accomplished its principal work in bringing the sexes together. In Maupassant's tale, everything changes at that moment; not objectively, of course, but subjectively, the landscape being completely interiorized. "The blue sky," he writes, "seemed darkened to them; the burning sun no longer visible; they only noticed the solitude and the silence." Nature has no further effect to offer; it only subsists in the souls of the characters, and it is ominous.

Renoir is going to take literally this subjective interiorization of the landscape, remaining very faithful to the text here. In the film, indeed, the storm arises immediately after the love scene. And we see a series of eleven short shots showing the storm beginning and the river changing. Heavy clouds pass in the sky; the river's banks grow dark; the grass rustles in the wind. The last shot of this sequence, in which both the disillusionment of love and the treachery of nature are expressed, shows the river, in a rapid backward tracking movement, no longer smooth as before but marred by the spots made by the heavy raindrops pelting the water. This rain, whose negative effect will be amplified by a fade to black, is absent from Maupassant's text (*Une partie de campagne Maupassant, Partie de campagne Renoir*, pp. 66-68).

Claude Gauteur et al. — Forms of comedy

Because he likes actors and uses a lot of dialogue, Renoir introduces a certain comic theatricality into his film. This is due first to the strong emphasis put on the farcical nature of the situation: the film, far more than the tale, is the story of a husband cuckolded by a wife who looks like a shopkeeper and acts like a tart. In addition, Renoir exhibits his dramatic originality in balancing very carefully the romantic couple with the parodical couple formed by Mme Dufour and Rodolphe, the bawdy boater. This exploiting of a simple potential offered by the text (Rodolphe has no name in the tale and scarcely any individual presence) adds to the film a clear reference to classical comedy which, from Molière to Marivaux, indulges frequently in these contrapuntal and mirroring effects.

In addition, Renoir borrows from Boulevard theater M. Dufour's reply built on a play on words ("No, not a horse [*cheval*]! You're unbearable, Anatole! A chub [*chevesne*]!"), or recycles a hackneyed popular joke when M. Dufour says, "We'll write you a letter," to his mother-in-law who is deaf as a doornail.

All of that, the effectiveness of which is clear when the film is shown in public, is also responsible for the exaggerated character of the acting at times. When Rodolphe discovers the girl, or when he entices Mme Dufour into the woods, he becomes a sort of mime: he flutters his eyelashes, strokes his mustache, does a little dance in which his large, supple body parodies the lechery of the faun.

But M. Dufour and Anatole are, of course, Renoir's major comic creations. Here the reference is not only theatrical. The filmmaker chose to turn these two clowns into a ludicrous couple recalling in many respects Laurel and Hardy. This identity is manifested in many ways: the opposition of the fat and thin men, the business suit of Dufour-Hardy, the oversized and clownish outfit of Anatole-Laurel; and especially the pairing of a strong and a weak person. In addition, like the famous duo, the fat, dominant man is ultimately eclipsed by the skinny simpleton: M. Dufour loses in every respect, while Anatole, as is often the case with Laurel, wins slyly at the end of the film. And finally, Renoir deliberately promoted in his staging the impression of a "comic act" in certain sequences with M. Dufour and Anatole. Thus, in the scene where the duo discusses the mysteries of the river, the filmmaker chooses to film his actors from the front (as if they were seen from an orchestra seat) and to have them make their entries and departures from the side of the frame, like actors on a stage (*Une partie de campagne Maupassant, Partie de campagne Renoir*, pp. 61-62).

Olivier Curchod — An "Impressionistic Cinema"

The inspiration of nature, the seizing of ephemeral moments, the impression of movement — it didn't take critics long to see in *A Day in the Country* the model of an "impressionistic cinema," as if, despite the paradox, a pictorial reference authenticated the "naturalism" of the film. Of course, by its landscapes (bridge, open-air café, river bank, and other country subjects) or by the situations that it presents (picnic lunch on the grass, boat rides, romantic outings), the film recalls the subjects of Auguste Renoir and his friends. Of course, the photography by Claude Renoir (the painter's grandson) tries to render the shimmering light speckling the ladies' gowns or the surface of the water. Of course, imitating certain painters, the cameraman cuts across an object or a face, placing the fragment at the border of the frame. But these are all frequently used techniques in cinematographic art. In place of the obvious references which the cultivated commentators will happily list, Renoir indulges in parodical winks which serve as antidotes to the cliché representing the filmmaker as his father's son. Poaching on his father's territory, as soon as a painting comes to mind Renoir consistently falsifies its tint, changes its framing, interchanges the characters, in short, constantly blurs the reference with subtle distortion effects. Wolfram Nitsch has clearly demonstrated that the swing scene, rejecting any formal tribute, literally shatters the motif painted by Auguste Renoir into a series of contradictory shots and frames, to such an extent that the swing in the film, compared to the one in the painting, becomes for him "a futurist or cubist mobile." Organizing an impression of Impressionism in the manner of a trompe-l'oeil, the filmmaker attempts to detach himself from the paternal figure and to assert the prerogatives of his own art. Just as the Impressionist esthetic, born in the sphere of influence of photography, distanced itself from that art to claim the right to recompose reality, we may see the same underlying formal relationship between the painter and the filmmaker. *A Day in the Country* is an illusion (*Partie de campagne.. Jean Renoir*, pp. 79-80).

Jacques Gerstenkorn — "Fishing Trips"

In the very first shot of *A Day in the Country*, unexpectedly sticking up from the bottom of the frame, a fishing pole erupts into the landscape, troubling the serene view. The reference to the painting of papa ("The River Seen From Old Poulain's Bridge") disappears, giving way to Jean Renoir's cinema: a clever kid, his head shaved like a billiard ball, has just caught a fish.

"Are they biting?" Madame Dufour chirps from the cart.

The Parisians on their Sunday outing have noted the catch; they sense this a good place to eat and stop at the nearby inn for some fried fish.

From the outset, Monsieur Dufour, his puny clerk at his side, can only think of one thing: bringing some fish back to Paris. From this viewpoint, the narrative program is set, and one could just as well call the film "Laurel and Hardy go fishing." We recall "Professor Dufour" at the water's edge, impressing Anatole by his knowledge of the secrets of nature, then the awkward expressions of the pair yearning for fishing poles, and finally their disappointment when they see — a real comic book gag — that the big catch of the day is just a rotten old boot.

At the same time, *A Day in the Country* contains another narrative, a second fishing trip, completely metaphorical this time, which quickly surpasses the first one (or the real one). During the lunch, Rodolphe and Henri are far more interested in Henriette's gliding back and forth on the swing — they don't miss a crumb of this show — than in old man Poulain's tarragon omelette. At the end of the meal, Rodolphe describes their program metaphorically: "So, are you going to participate in this…fishing trip? How about choosing our gear," he asks Henri.

After quickly spinning their metaphor, the accomplices agree that "the first order of business is to put out the bait." Henriette's hat, forgotten under the cherry tree, is a choice piece of bait. Rodolphe continues to set his rhetorical nets, using technical terms which eventually annoy his friend, who is clearly more romantic […]. A little later, Rodolphe invites Henri to "strike," then, noticing Henri's increasing interest in the girl, accuses him of "poaching in his waters"… The development of the metaphor is not simply linguistic coquetry; it accompanies, punctuates, and structures a course of action, modeling behavior, relating the erotic conquest to a form of expertise, and limiting the vicissitudes of seduction through the mastery of consecrated techniques.

The composition of *A Day in the Country* does not grow solely out of this insistent and precise motif; it depends even more on a weaving together of the two fishing parties that I've just described. Since we are dealing with a film, this weaving tends to take the form of cross-cutting, although we may not be able to identify it as such, given that the metaphorical net covers the whole narrative and not a particular sequence, and also given that this net is part of a *game*, in that it is flexible and playful, as if Renoir were wary of a systematic composition, overly rigid and rhetorical. The weaving together of the two fishing trips finds its point of intersection — which is also an ironic counterpoint — when the seducers bring the shopkeepers their fishing poles, enabling them to get the ladies into their boats. To each his fishing trip, Renoir says of his characters. Precisely because of this, the film takes different paths from the literary tale, in which the fishing motif does not appear: to each his day in the country, says Renoir, this time addressing himself to Maupassant (*La Métaphore au cinéma*, pp. 96-98).

JEAN RENOIR'S FILMOGRAPHY
(PRINCIPAL FILMS)

1926   *Nana* (silent)

1928   *The Little Match Girl*
        (La Petite Marchande d'allumettes, silent),
        Sad Sack (Tire au flanc, silent).

1931   *Baby Gets a Laxative (On purge bébé)*

1931   *The Bitch (La Chienne)*

1932   *Boudu Saved from Drowning*
        (Boudu sauvé des eaux)

1933   *Madame Bovary*

1934   *Toni*

1935   *Le Crime de Monsieur Lange*

1936   *A Day in the Country*
        (Partie de campagne, edited and shown in 1946)

1936   *The Lower Depths (Les Bas-fonds),*
        People of France (La Vie est à nous)

1937   *La Grande Illusion*

1938   *The Human Beast (La Bête humaine),*
        La Marseillaise

1939   *The Rules of the Game (La Règle du jeu)*

1941   *Swamp Water (L'Etang tragique*, USA)

1945   *The Southerner (L'Homme du Sud*, USA)

1946   *Diary of a Chambermaid*
        (Le Journal d'une femme de chambre, USA)

1950   *The River (Le Fleuve*, India)

1952   *The Golden Coach (Le Carrosse d'or*, Italy)

1954   *French Cancan*

1956   *Elena and Her Men (Elena et les hommes)*

1959   *Picnic on the Grass (Le Déjeuner sur l'herbe)*

1962   *Elusive Corporal (Le Caporal épinglé)*

1969   *The Little Theater of Jean Renoir*
        (Le Petit Théâtre de Jean Renoir)

SOURCES CONSULTED

Allombert, Guy. "Variations cinématographiques sur des thèmes de Maupassant." *Image et son* 110 (March 1958): 4-7.

Amengual, Barthélemy. "*Une partie de campagne :* Un film de Guy de Maupassant et Jean Renoir." *CinémAction TV*, 5 (April 1993): 36-42.

Arnault, Hubert. "*Partie de campagne* (1936-1946) de Jean Renoir." *Image et son*, 150-151 (April-May 1962): 121-153.

Bazin, André. *Jean Renoir*. Paris: Champ libre, 1971.

Berthomé, Jean-Pierre. "Voir un peu d'herbe avant de mourir… Prévert et sa *Partie de campagne*." *Positif*, 408 (Feb. 1995): 84-89.

Bourget, Jean-Loup. "Le fragment, le tableau, le triptyque," *Cahiers de la Cinémathèque*, 62 (March 1995): 31-35.

Comolli, Jean-Louis. "En revoyant *Une partie de campagne…*," *Cahiers du cinéma* 299 (April 1979): 39-40.

Curchod, Olivier. *Partie de campagne. Jean Renoir*. Paris: Nathan, 1995.

Doniol-Valcroze, Jacques. "Une esquisse." *La Revue du cinéma*, 4 (Jan. 1947): 70-71.

Gauteur, Claude, Annie Mottet, Claude Murcia, Francis Ramirez, Christian Rolot. *Une partie de campagne Maupassant, Partie de campagne Renoir*. Coll. "Profil d'une oeuvre" 185-186. Paris: Hatier, 1995.

Gerstenkorn, Jacques. *La Métaphore au cinéma*. Paris: Méridiens Klincksieck, 1995.

Le Loch, Raymond. *Une partie de campagne. De Maupassant à Jean Renoir*. Paris: Bertrand-Lacoste, 1995.

Maupassant, Guy de. *Une partie de* campagne followed by *Une partie de campagne*, screenplay and film dossier by Jean Renoir. Henry Gidel, ed. Paris: Librairie Générale Française, 1995.

Pagliano, Jean-Pierre. "Entretien avec Sylvia Bataille." *Positif*, 408 (Feb. 1995): 90-93.

Philippe, Pierre. "Sylvia Bataille ou l'absence." *Cinéma 61*, 58 (July 1961): 69-78.

Renoir, Jean. *Entretiens et propos*. Paris: Editions de l'Etoile, Cahiers du cinéma, 1979.

………*Une partie de campagne* (screenplay). *L'Avant-Scène Cinéma* 21 (Dec. 15, 1962): 29-42.

Sesonske, Alexander. *Jean Renoir. The French Films, 1924-1939*. Cambridge, MA: Harvard University Press, 1980 (pp. 234-256)

"Une Partie de campagne." *Premier Plan* 22-23-24 (May 1962): 212-226.

Webster, Robert M. "Renoir's *Une Partie de campagne*: Film as the Art of Fishing." *The French Review*, 64.3 (Feb. 1991): 487-496.

Jean Renoir

Grand Illusion
La Grande Illusion

(1937)

Jean Renoir, *Grand Illusion*: Lieutenant Maréchal (Jean Gabin) and Captain de Boëldieu (Pierre Fresnay) arrive at the first officers' camp. © Studio Canal Image

Director .... Jean Renoir
Screenplay and Dialogues.......................Charles Spaak, Jean Renoir
Assistant Director..Jacques Becker
Technical Advisor .... Carl Koch
Director of Photography .... Christian Matras
Cameraman ....Claude Renoir
Music...Joseph Kosma
Film Editor ....Marguerite Houllé-Renoir
Sound .... Joseph de Bretagne
Art Director .... Eugène Lourié
Costumes .... René Decrais
Script Girl (Continuity) ....Françoise Giroud (Gourdji)
Producers .... Frank Rollmer, Albert Pinkévitch
Length .... 1 h 53

Cast

Jean Gabin (*Lieutenant Maréchal*), Pierre Fresnay (*Captain de Boëldieu*), Marcel Dalio (*Lieutenant Rosenthal*), Erich von Stroheim (*Captain then Major von Rauffenstein*), Julien Carette (*Cartier, the actor*), Gaston Modot (*the engineer*), Jean Dasté (*the school teacher*), Dita Parlo (*Elsa*), Carl Heil (*Krantz, nicknamed "Arthur"*), Sylvain Itkine (*Lieutenant Demolder)*, little Peters (*Lotte*).

STORY

In 1916 Captain de Boëldieu's plane, piloted by Lieutenant Maréchal, is shot down during a reconnaissance flight by Captain von Rauffenstein of the German army. Von Rauffenstein greets the two French officers in the German officers' mess and invites them to dine at his table. The meal is interrupted by a German soldier who takes charge of the two prisoners, who are sent to an officers' prison at Hallbach.

At Hallbach, Maréchal and Boëldieu find themselves in a barrack-room with other French officers from a variety of social strata, including a vaudeville actor (Cartier), a provincial school teacher, an engineer, and a wealthy Jewish couturier from Paris (Rosenthal). The French officers are digging a tunnel to escape, while at the same time preparing, with the British prisoners, a variety show for Christmas. The evening of the performance, to which the German officers have been invited, the show is suddenly interrupted by Maréchal, who announces that the Douaumont fortress has been taken back from the Germans. The English and French prisoners mock their guards by singing together "La Marseillaise." Maréchal is punished for his role by several weeks in solitary, rejoining his comrades the day before their planned escape—only to learn with them that they are all to be transferred to other camps the next day.

Several months later, Maréchal and Boëldieu are incarcerated in the medieval fortress at Wintersborn, from which "no one ever escapes." Each of them has made several attempts to escape from other prison camps. The commander of the fortress is none other than the former pilot Rauffenstein, who has been reduced to this function by serious wounds he has received in aerial combat. The two French officers are also reunited with Rosenthal, who is busily preparing another escape attempt.

Rauffenstein tries to strike up a friendship with Boëldieu based on their class affinities, but Boëldieu remains faithful to his comrades and organizes a diversion to help Maréchal and Rosenthal escape. Rauffenstein is forced to shoot Boëldieu and wounds him fatally; devastated, he attends the final moments of his aristocratic counterpart.

Several days later, Maréchal and Rosenthal, exhausted and famished, have a sharp dispute. They make up and finally find refuge at a German farm where Rosenthal can rest until his badly sprained ankle has recovered. They are taken in by a young widowed peasant, Elsa, who lives alone on her farm with her little daughter Lotte. On Christmas eve Maréchal becomes her lover, but has to leave soon after with Rosenthal, He promises to come back for her after the war. At the end of the film the two men cross the border into Switzerland, narrowly escaping shots from a passing German patrol.

CRITICAL RECEPTION

Opening in Paris on June 9, 1937, during the brief triumph of the Popular Front (a left-wing government, from May 1936 to April 1938) and in the excitement of the Universal Exposition in Paris, *Grand Illusion* was an immediate success, in both the eyes of the critics and the general public. As Olivier Curchod remarks, the film "projected continuously from 10 a.m. to 2 a.m., fills the cinema at each showing and beats all the previous attendance records: 1.55 million francs in four weeks, 200,000 spectators in two months in a single theater, the top moneymaker of 1937, and the best film of the year according to a poll of *Le Cinématographie française*" (p. 16). Abroad, *Grand Illusion* was awarded the cup for the best artistic production at the Venice film festival in September, 1937 ("prize invented for the sole purpose of avoiding the necessity of giving us the Mussolini Cup," Renoir explains) and the prize for the best foreign film in New York (December, 1938), where it ran for thirty-six weeks in the same cinema. Subsequently it was be nominated for Best Film at the Oscars, which was a remarkable tribute if one remembers, as Priot points out, that "it is the first time that a foreign film is included in this group, reserved for American films up until then" (p. 17). It is well known, moreover, that President Roosevelt requested a private showing of *Grand Illusion* at the White House for his wife's birthday. He declared afterwards that "all the democrats in the world should see this film." Renoir had become an international celebrity.

On the other hand, most of the fascist regimes in Europe, as well as Japan, quickly censured or banned Renoir's film, owing to its internationalism and pacifism. Goebbels, the Nazi propaganda chief, described *Grand Illusion* as the "cinematographic public enemy number one." Immediately after the declaration of war on Germany, in the autumn of 1939, the French authorities also banned *Grand Illusion*, criticizing the sympathetic portrayal of German soldiers—which didn't prevent the Germans from banning the film, in their turn, for its patriotism. The ban was maintained by the Vichy government, and even after the Liberation, until 1946, on the pretext that the film was anti-Semitic and pro-German.

When the film was brought out again, in August 1946, and despite the fact that several scenes had been cut, it "beats all the attendance records since the Liberation"(Viry-Babel, p. 49). It nonetheless provoked the indignation of the former Resistance press, which deplored the naïveté of the image of the Germans in the light of the horrors perpetrated by the Nazi regime. The film was criticized as "pacifist"(accurately), but also as "collaborationist" and "racist."

In spite of this, beginning in 1952, *Grand Illusion* was finally consecrated as a masterpiece, being selected by fifty-four filmmakers as the fourth best film of all time (tied with *City Lights* by Charlie Chaplin). This honor was confirmed shortly before the third opening of the film, in its original version, in October, 1958: on the occasion of the International Exposition in Brussels, 117 filmmakers and critics from around the world designated Renoir's film as the fifth best film in the world. While it is true that the international critical community would later recognize *The Rules Of The Game* as Renoir's best film, ranked ahead of *Grand Illusion* among the ten best films ever made, the latter film, as Curchod remarks, "remains, in the eyes of the general public, Jean Renoir's masterpiece" (p. 19).

BEFORE *GRAND ILLUSION*

Born in Paris on September 15, 1984, Jean Renoir is the second son of the famous impressionist painter, Auguste Renoir. After working in ceramics for a while, his inheritance from his father, deceased in 1919, allowed him to make his first films, during the silent film era. These included adaptations of Emile Zola's novel *Nana* (1926) and Hans Christian Anderson's fairy tale *The Little Match Girl* (1928), the latter still striking for its poetic qualities. After several other silent films, commercial failures, Renoir finally met financial success in 1931 with his first talking film, *Baby Gets A Laxative* (*On purge bébé*), a hastily produced adaptation of a Georges Feydeau farce. He hit his stride, however, the same year with his first important sound film *The Bitch* (*La Chienne*). *The Bitch* shocked spectators by its flagrant amorality but won over the public by its brilliant conception, its technical mastery, and the rich development of the characters, including "Legrand," played magnificently by one of Renoir's favorite actors, Michel Simon.

The above works are followed by a long series of films which all bear the mark of Renoir's genius as he continued to refine his art. These include *Boudu Saved From Drowning* (*Boudu sauvé des eaux*, 1932), starring Michel Simon again, *Madame Bovary* (1933), *Toni* (1934), *Le Crime de Monsieur Lange* (1935), and *A Day in the Country* (*Partie de campagne*, 1936, edited 1946). Between *A Day in the Country* and *Grand Illusion*, Renoir directed *The Lower Depths* (*Les Bas-Fonds*, 1936), an adaptation of the novel by Maxim Gorki, with two great actors, Jean Gabin and Louis Jouvet. When Renoir began the shooting of *Grand Illusion*, in February, 1937, he had already made seventeen films.

ORIGIN OF *GRAND ILLUSION*

Grand Illusion was inspired originally by the multiple escapes of the French pilot Chief Warrant Officer Pinsard, whom Renoir had met in 1916 when he was himself a pilot. Pinsard had been shot down and imprisoned seven times and, miraculously, had managed to escape each time. When Renoir met him again, while shooting *Toni* in 1934, he asked the former pilot, now a general, to tell him again about his wartime experiences: "I said to Pinsard: 'Come on, old fellow, tell me again about your escapes. Perhaps I can make a film about them.' So he told me his stories and I wrote them all down; they have little to do with the final film, but they were an essential departure point" (quoted in Viry Babel, p. 40).

Renoir took notes and sketched out a story titled "Pinsard's Escape," which had already become "Captain Maréchal's Escapes" when he showed it to the master screenwriter Charles Spaak. The two men then coauthored a detailed synopsis, the first version of the screenplay, which was flatly rejected by the producers and distributors they approached: "No distributor wanted to risk money on a production which had no love story in it" (Priot, p. 6). Renoir complained that he spent three years looking fruitlessly for a producer. During this time he made four other films and even tried to trade the *Grand Illusion* project for the screenplay of *They Were Five* (*La Belle Equipe*), which Spaak was writing for Julien Duvivier. When Spaak proposed the deal to Duvivier, the filmmaker rejected the idea out of hand: "Are you out of your mind? A story about prisoners of war will be of no interest to anyone! You can go shove it, and I don't have to tell you where" (quoted in Priot, p. 6).

In 1936, having finally managed to get a producer interested, the two men wrote together a first screenplay with dialog, now called *Grand Illusion*, in which just a few traces of Pinsard's adventures remained (Maréchal's solitary confinement, the escape from the fortress, his companion's sprained ankle). On the other hand, one is struck by clear borrowings from the recent novel *Kavalier Scharnhorst* (1931), whose author brought suit for plagiarism—unsuccessfully—against Renoir, Spaak, and the producers of the film as soon as it opened. In this version several scenes have disappeared from the previous scenario, notably an episode in which the two escapees (Maréchal and Dolette, a young intellectual) share the sexual favors of the German peasant woman (an episode replaced by the love affair between Maréchal and Elsa), while we see the introduction of several new characters, clear social types like the actor, the teacher, the engineer, and the Jewish couturier Rosenthal. Other modifications and additions—the German officers' mess, the geranium, the edible manger scene, the singing of *La Marseillaise*, for example—can be attributed either to Renoir or to the various members of the crew, including the cast. Curchod evokes very aptly "Renoir's remarkable capacity to integrate everyone's suggestions before shooting" (p. 42).

In the quasi-final version of the screenplay (the continuity script written a few months later by Renoir and Spaak), Dolette's character disappeared from the film, assimilated into Rosenthal's character, which was more fully developed. Several other scenes were likewise dropped, including a dogfight in which Maréchal and Boëldieu's plane is shot down, considered too expensive to shoot. The ending was completely transformed with the decision to cut out a final very pessimistic scene at Maxim's in which the two escapees arrange to meet on Christmas Eve in 1918, and neither of them shows up (first version) or Maréchal shows up and Rosenthal doesn't (second version). Renoir was ready to shoot.

THE CAST

The cast of *Grand Illusion* includes some of the most famous names in the French cinema of the thirties. The main role, that of Lieutenant Maréchal, is played by Jean Gabin, one of the biggest French stars of the period, who has been featured in a series of recent hits by Duvivier, such as *The Brigade* (*La Bandera*, 1934), *Pépé le Moko* (1935), and *There Were Five* (*La Belle Equipe*, 1936). Gabin also played the main role in Renoir's *The Lower Depths* (1936), the film which is awarded the very first Louis Delluc Prize. Gabin's legend continued to grow in the years before the war, during which he triumphs repeatedly in the great films produced by the "poetic realism" current of Marcel Carné and Jacques Prévert: *Port of Shadows* (*Quai des brumes*, 1938), and *Daybreak* (*Le Jour se lève*, 1939). He also triumphs in the films of Jean Grémillon, *Lady Killer* (*Gueule d'amour*, 1937) and *Stormy Waters* (*Remorques*, 1939-41), in addition to Renoir's *The Human Beast* (*La Bête humaine*, 1938). The Boëldieu role is played by Pierre Fresnay, a renowned stage actor and member of the Comédie française but only known in movies for his role in Marcel Pagnol's *Marius* (1929). The two French stars are surrounded by actors who are nearly all well known to the French movie-going public: Marcel Dalio (Rosenthal), Julien Carette (Cartier, the actor),

Gaston Modot (the engineer) and Jean Dasté (the school teacher)—who played the role of the supervisor Huguet in *Zero For Conduct* (*Zéro de conduite*, 1933) and of the bargeman in *L'Atalante* (1934), both directed by Jean Vigo. Dalio and Carette both come from the stage, while Dasté is known on both stage and screen. Gaston Modot had been acting in movies since the silent film period, first appearing in the films of the French avant-garde in the twenties. We will find Carette the following year beside Gabin in *The Human Beast*, while the Dalio-Modot-Carette trio will be reunited the year after, with the filmmaker himself in a starring role this time, in Renoir's greatest film *Rules Of The Game* (*La Règle du jeu*, 1939).

Across from the French superstars Gabin and Fresnay, it was deemed essential to find German actors of sufficient renown to create "a parity between the French and German viewpoints," which Carl Koch, Renoir's German technical advisor, considered necessary to the general balance of the film (Priot, p. 8). Dita Parlo, a German superstar, had already been cast in the role of Elsa, leading the screenwriters to flesh out her character much more fully, develop further her love affair with Maréchal, and give her a daughter, Lotte. A few days before the shooting was to begin, seizing a rare opportunity (without consulting either Renoir or Spaak), the director of production brought on board the legendary Austrian director and actor Erich von Stroheim. He was to play the very minor role of the German officer who shoots down the French plane at the beginning of the film and invites the officers to dine at his table, before disappearing from the film. Overcoming their initial dismay at this unexpected turn of events, Renoir and Spaak had the ingenious idea of combining in a single character, played by Stroheim, the German aviator and the commander of the fortress at Wintersborn: Captain von Rauffenstein is born. Fascinated by Stroheim's personality, Renoir gives him *carte blanche* in the creation of his character, allowing him to choose his costumes, scenery, and diverse props such as the famous neck brace, as well as including him in the writing of his own dialogue. Renoir makes important modifications in the scenario to take advantage of this new addition to the cast, adding the well-known conversation between Rauffenstein and Boëldieu about the dilemma of the aristocracy, the fatal wounding of Boëldieu by the German commandant, and the scene in which the French officer dies. With the addition of Stroheim to the cast, the screenplay achieved its final form and Renoir was ready to shoot.

FILMING

The shooting of *Grand Illusion* begins in January 1937, in Alsace (Colmar), since German-style architecture is needed for the exteriors. After the barracks scenes (the first officers' camp in the film), the crew moves to the Haut-Königsberg castle for the exteriors of the fortress at Wintersborn. The conditions are difficult, as the script girl Françoise Giroud recalls: "God it was cold, and we really froze during the nights when we shot the episodes where Pierre Fresnay plays the flute to help his comrades escape. One of us, in fact—I think it was Claude Renoir, who was at the camera—became pretty sick" (p. 23).

At the beginning of March the shooting resumes at the studio in Paris, to finish the interiors: the two officers' messes at the beginning of the film, the barrack-room scenes and the variety show at the first camp, and the interiors of the fortress, including the famous chapel which serves as Rauffenstein's room. The last sequence of the film, the "epilogue," was shot in two separate sessions: the close-ups of Maréchal and Rosenthal in the studio were done first (the art director, Eugène Lourié, constructing a hole with Epson salts around it to simulate snow), and the crossing of the Swiss border was then directed in Alsace by Jacques Becker, the assistant director, with Gabin and Dalio replaced by stand-ins filmed from behind. *Grand Illusion* was edited during April by Renoir's longtime companion, Marguerite Houllé (called Marguerite Renoir, since she had eventually taken the filmmaker's name).

STRUCTURE

Grand Illusion divides neatly into three parts, corresponding to the three places where the principal action of the film takes place: the first officers' camp at Hallbach, the fortress at Wintersborn, Elsa's farm. These three "acts" are preceded by a short "prologue" (the French and German messes) and followed by an even shorter "epilogue" (the crossing of the Swiss border). The three places are linked by transitional scenes, either transfers by train or the escape of Maréchal and Rosenthal—which might be considered, given its development, as a separate episode.

Inside each part the various sequences are divided clearly into tableaus, "separate little films" (Curchod, p. 45), a structural characteristic we will also find in the films of one of Renoir's greatest admirers, François Truffaut (see the chapter on *Jules et Jim*, p. 295). This is quite clear if we look at the sequences which compose the Hallbach episode: the meal given by Rosenthal, the elaborate staging of the work on the tunnel, the preparation of the variety show, the show itself, and the solitary confinement of Maréchal.

The film is likewise organized—and here the question of structure is clearly related to the thematic side of the work—according to a series of national, social, or racial parallels and oppositions whose paradigm is established masterfully from the outset of the film. In the German officers' mess the opposition between the French officer de Boëldieu and the German officer von Rauffenstein is obscured by the similarity of their aristocratic origins—origins which are set in opposition to the social class of Maréchal and his German worker counterpart whose affinities are in turn parallel to those of the Boëldieu-Rauffenstein couple. We find the same motif at Hallbach, in the series of socio-professional oppositions foregrounded in Rosenthal's meal, as well as in the opposition with the Germans and in the opposition/parallel with the British officers. The theme is formalized in the dialogues of the Wintersborn episode, and especially in the social class solidarity sought by Rauffenstein with Boëldieu, but also in the opposition between Maréchal and the French aristocrat. It reappears again in the racially colored argument between Maréchal and Rosenthal during their flight toward Switzerland and, in the last segment of the film, in the class affinity which brings Maréchal and Elsa together despite the enmity of their respective nations. We will evoke this thematic aspect of the film again below, but it is enough to note here the perfect harmony of structure and theme in *Grand Illusion*, one of the unmistakable marks of an artistic masterpiece.

Joyeux Noël

imagine the speech

THEMES

"I made *Grand Illusion* because I'm a pacifist," Renoir declared in his presentation of his film to the American public in 1937. It is impossible to consider Renoir's film separate from its historical context; it faithfully reflects a number of major contemporary concerns, beginning with the growing threat of war with Nazi Germany. Like many intellectuals of the thirties, Renoir was a fellow traveler of the communists, sharing their pacifism and their ideal of international fraternity. In 1936, during the legislative campaign which would lead to the victory of the leftist Popular Front government, he even made a film promoting the French Communist Party, *Life Is Ours* (*La Vie est à nous*). In 1938 he made *La Marseillaise*, a film on the French Revolution of 1789 financed through subscriptions solicited by the C.G.T., the communist workers' union. Above and beyond politics, however, Renoir simply advocated humanism, being keenly interested in human beings above all. When he was interviewed in 1928 about his principles as a director, Renoir stated, "I consider the human element as the most important thing" ("Propos," p. 20). He liked to quote a sentence from Pascal, "What interests man the most is man" (Truffaut, p. 8).

Renoir will remain faithful to this principle, and nowhere more clearly than in *Grand Illusion*, where he refuses to favor one group over another: the portrait of the German guards is scarcely less sympathetic than that of their French prisoners. Renoir's film, which seems to gloss over the horrors of war, has often been called naïve. It is true that what is referred to as the "Great War" was a veritable hecatomb, producing almost nine million deaths (and twenty-two million wounded) between 1914 and 1918. But Renoir's focus is elsewhere, as he explains before the very first opening of the film in 1937: "This is not a war film. I've tried to show the comradeship which unites the two French officers despite their different social classes, and the mutual esteem between the enemy pilots during the war" ("Propos," p. 29). Renoir wanted to give a lesson about equality and human fraternity to the public; the war remains off camera.

In fact, the film emphasizes especially the differences which separate the social classes and socio-professional categories of the French officers who are housed together at Hallbach and Wintersborn. Maréchal, the factory worker, has absolutely nothing in common with Boëldieu the aristocrat, nor with the wealthy Parisian couturier Rosenthal. The divisions between these characters are perfectly clear, in spite of the bonds of friendship which develop or the spirit of national solidarity which they all share. These divisions are no less evident as regards the other social types which are represented: the vaudeville comic, the engineer, the country school teacher, "Pindar" the scholar. As Bazin reminds us, Renoir has often evoked his theory that "men are less separated by the vertical barriers of nationalism than by the horizontal divisions of cultures, races, classes, professions, etc." (pp. 59-60)—which explains the multiple parallels and oppositions, mentioned above, developed from the beginning of the film. The creation of the Jewish character of Rosenthal, moreover (a character which was absent from the first version of the screenplay), enriches the thematic texture of the film by adding to the difference between social classes the antagonism between races.

The title of the film announces unambiguously the theme which runs throughout the entire work, the "grand illusion." When Renoir was asked, while he was making the film, what the "grand illusion" was, he answered unhesitatingly: "War! With its perpetually unfilled hopes, it's perpetually broken promises" ("Propos," p. 29). This answer, echoing the theme of Jean Giraudoux's recent play *Tiger At The Gates* (*La Guerre de Troie n'aura pas lieu*, 1935), does not begin to account for the multiple "illusions," several of them "grand," which are suggested in *Grand Illusion* (see the excerpt from André Bazin's commentary in the *Critical Dossier*, "The 'Realism' of *Grand Illusion*"). The most explicit reference is doubtlessly Rosenthal's reply at the end of the film, when Maréchal remarks that "we have to finish this goddam war—and it better be the last one." "Man, you're just kidding yourself!" It doesn't matter if we close the Gates of War, as Hector does in Giraudoux's play; they will just open again.

In addition to the "grand illusion," there are illusions of all magnitudes in this film, like Maréchal's self-delusion that the war will be over in a few weeks: "You're kidding yourself," answers the engineer. The theater motif, which is evoked several times in the film (and whose very nature is "illusion"), likewise foregrounds this theme, whether it be the frustrated escape plans (the tunnel at Hallbach), the variety show (the British prisoners dressed as women), or Boëldieu's flute act which facilitates Maréchal's and Rosenthal's escape. At the end of the film Maréchal's plans to come back for Elsa after the war may also be just an illusion.

In the socio-political arena Boëldieu's sacrifice is tied to a vaguely revolutionary theme, insofar as the aristocracy he embodies yields to the interests of the bourgeoisie and the working classes clearly represented by Rosenthal and Maréchal. The romance between Maréchal the French worker and Elsa the German peasant may suggest, in the same manner, an ideal of proletarian solidarity beyond the national divisions and linguistic obstacles. The easy communication between Maréchal and Elsa, despite the language barrier, puts a final positive spin on the theme of the problem of communication so clearly developed in *Grand Illusion*—whether it be due to foreign languages (French, German, English, Russian) or to obstacles of a purely socio-cultural nature.

Finally it should be noted that the thematic interest of *Grand Illusion* evolves and changes as the film opens in different historical periods. In 1937 the aspects of the film that made the strongest impression on the public were its pacifism and patriotism; in 1946, on the heels of the horrors perpetrated by the Nazis, certain spectators were repelled by its germanophilia and accused the film, unjustly, of anti-Semitism; in 1958, in the excitement caused by the creation of the Common Market, Renoir didn't hesitate to evoke the "European" spirit of the film…

STYLE

One of the most consistent stylistic principles of *Grand Illusion* is most certainly "the constant concern to never separate, by the choice of shots, the center of dramatic interest from the general context in which it takes place (physical and human)" (Bazin, p. 58). This concern is expressed in Renoir's insistence on unity in the treatment of time and space; that is, by his resistance to the systematic breaking up of time and space natural to film editing. Renoir substitutes instead, on the one hand, the utilization of depth of field (deep-focus photography), which allows him to better situate the subject in its context, whether it be in relationship to the physical space or to the other characters in its sphere of activity. On the other hand, and for largely the same reasons, he utilizes frequent camera movements and lengthy (sequence) shots to minimize the inevitable fragmentation created by breaking up a scene into several shots. Thus, in the first shot of the film, in the French officers' bar, there are a series of pans, in several directions, to avoid cutting Maréchal off from his environment in any way. Likewise, in the sequence shot of the preparations for the variety show, the depth of field and the camera movements allow Renoir to combine in a unified continuous space the rehearsal of the British officers' musical number and the unpacking of the costumes by the Frenchmen. And at Wintersborn again, the long pan in close-up on the chapel which serves as Rauffenstein's room serves to create the character through the various props which clearly reflect his personal traits. "We thus find in the very technique of the filming," Bazin remarks, "Renoir's search for the truth of the relations between Men and the world in which they are plunged" (pp. 58-59).

Sometimes the camera movements, combined with the scenery, serve to unite particularly disparate spaces, emphasizing both their difference and their place in the same reality. The sequence shot in which the engineer washes Maréchal's feet begins by focusing on the actor outside, in the camp yard, followed by a tracking shot backward through the window and into the room to frame Maréchal and the engineer, who continue their discussion about Rosenthal before moving on to Boëldieu, the subject of the actor's remarks at the beginning of the shot. Here as elsewhere in Renoir's films the window serves as an explicit link between interior and exterior, diversifying the space and suggesting its expanse (Masson, pp. 70-72). The world doesn't stop at the barracks' walls, and the tracking shot inscribes the two men in a broader, richer context.

Renoir's predilection for the sequence shot is explained also by the importance he attributes to the actors, an attitude he has exhibited since the beginning of his career: "To summarize my remarks, the essential element of a film is the acting. Choosing the right actors and directing them properly, that's the principal role of the director" ("Propos," p. 19). To allow the actors a maximum of freedom in developing their character, without using overly static medium shots, Renoir adopts a technique which consists of "beginning with a close-up of the actors, then following them as they move about" (Renoir, p. 143). "*Grand Illusion* is perhaps the film in which I applied this approach most successfully," he adds, referring specifically to Rosenthal's meal scene and the sequence in which the prisoners sing "La Marseillaise" (see *Propos de Jean Renoir* below).

STUDY GUIDE

Director's Comments

"I made *Grand Illusion* because I'm a pacifist. For me, a true pacifist is an authentic Frenchman, American, or German. The day will come when men of good will will find a way to live together in peace. The cynics will say that, in these times, my confidence is a sign of naiveté, but why not? However troublesome Hitler may be, he does not change my opinion about the Germans.

"For as long as I can remember I've liked and respected this people. If, for example, I have a longtime friend who is really dear to me and he gets syphilis, is that a good reason to stop being his friend? With all my heart and with all possible means, I would try to help him get well.

"In *Grand Illusion* I attempted to show that we don't hate Germans in France. The film was very successful. No, it's no better than many other films, but it simply expresses what the average Frenchman, my brother, thinks of war in general.

"People have long had this image of the pacifist as a man with long hair and wrinkled pants who, standing on a soap box, relentlessly foretells calamities and goes berserk at the sight of a uniform. The characters of *Grand Illusion* don't belong to this category of people. They are the very image of what we were, the "class of 14." I was an officer during the war, and I still have a keen memory of my comrades. We felt no hate toward our adversaries. They were good Germans like we were good Frenchmen…" ("*La Grande Illusion*," *Premier Plan*, p. 239).

"The story of *Grand Illusion* is absolutely true and was told to me by one of my war buddies… I'm speaking of course of the war of 1914, and it was Pinsard especially. Pinsard was a fighter pilot, while I was part of a reconnaissance squadron. From time to time I had to go take photos of the German lines. He saved my life several times by intervening when the German fighters became too pesky. He was shot down seven times; he was put in prison seven times and escaped seven times. His escapes are the main source for the story of *Grand Illusion* […].

"Pardon me if I stress once again the authenticity of the facts presented in *Grand Illusion*, but certain scenes, especially those in which the relationship between the French and the Germans are described, may be surprising for some. But one has to remember that in 1914 Hitler didn't exist yet. There was no trace of the Nazis who almost managed to make us forget that Germans are human beings too. In 1914 men's minds hadn't yet been twisted by totalitarian religions and by racism. In certain respects, this world war was still a gentlemen's war, a war between men of good breeding—which doesn't excuse it. Politeness, even chivalry, do not excuse slaughter.

"A story of escapes, no matter how exciting, is not enough to make a film. You have to have a screenplay. For that, I had the collaboration of Charles Spaak. Our collaboration was easy and problem-free. In addition to our friendship, there was our shared faith, our profound belief in the equality and fraternity of men.

"*Grand Illusion* is the story of people like you and me, lost in this distressing adventure we call war [….]" (excerpt of the preview made by Renoir for the opening of the film in 1958, *Premier Plan*, pp. 241-242).

"This theme of grouping men together by professions or by common interests has pursued me throughout my life and follows me still. It's the theme of *Grand Illusion*. It plays a role in virtually all of my works" (*Ma Vie et mes films*, p. 260).

"Another of my preoccupations was and still is to avoid the fragmentation of space, by choosing longer and longer shots and by giving the actor the freedom to develop his interpretation of the dialogue as he sees fit. As far as I'm concerned, it's the only way to insure that the acting is sincere. There are two ways to obtain longer shots. Not counting close-ups, you can use as many medium shots, even long shots, as possible— but then the public is too far from the actors and can't see their expressions because of the distance from the camera. The other approach, which I consider better, consists in beginning with a close-up of the actors, then following them as they move about. That requires great skill on the part of the cameraman, but the results are sometimes exciting. Personally, this pursuit of the subject by the camera has given me some of my greatest emotions, in films by others as well as my own.

"*Grand Illusion* is perhaps the film in which I applied this approach most successfully. Of course, to be perfect, this technique must be invisible, like all techniques, in any case. The spectator musn't be aware that the camera is engaged in a veritable ballet, moving subtly from one actor to another, from one prop to another. A shot of this type, when it's done well, must be like a complete unit unto itself, including the backgrounds—which are all the more difficult to include since the floor is covered with lighting equipment.

"I would illustrate this with two takes from *Grand Illusion* made according to the above principles: the shot of the meal in the prisoners' room in the first camp, in which the camera caresses the elements in the scene and continues its unifying action up to the end of the shot. The other shot is the singing of "La Marseillaise" in the prisoners' theater. The shot begins on Maréchal, standing in the middle of the stage in the little theater, and finishes on the spectators after taking in all the important elements in a 180° pan. The cameraman to whom I owe these shots is my nephew, Claude Renoir. He was as quick as an eel and undaunted by any of the acrobatics required (*Ma Vie et mes films*, pp. 142, 143).

"I spent my life trying out different styles. These changes may be reduced to this: they reflect my various attempts to express interior truth, the only one which counts for me" (*Ma Vie et mes films*, p. 258).

"In *Grand Illusion* I was still preoccupied with realism. I went so far as to ask Gabin to wear my own pilot's jacket that I had kept after my discharge. At the same time, I didn't hesitate to embroider on certain things in somewhat whimsical ways to heighten the effect, as with Stroheim's uniform. His role, trivial at the beginning, was increased ten-fold, because I was afraid that, confronted with the massive presence of Gabin and Fresnay, his character would appear lightweight. In art like in life, everything depends on balance. The problem is to keep the two sides of the scales level. That's why I took liberties with Stroheim's uniform that really weren't compatible with my realistic theories at that time. His uniform is authentic, but much too fancy for a camp commander during the great war. I needed this theatrical flamboyance to balance the grandeur of the Frenchmen's simplicity. In spite of its rigorously realistic appearance, *Grand Illusion* contains examples of stylization which tend toward whimsy. I owe this introduction of illusion into the film to Stroheim, and I am deeply grateful to him. I'm incapable of creating a good show if I don't make room for fantasy" (*Ma vie et mes films*, pp. 145-146).

Excerpts for Discussion

Excerpt 1 (1'25-2'35): In the French officers' mess.

Excerpt 2 (3'30-6'10): In the German officers' mess.

Excerpt 3 (7'15-7'25): Boëldieu and Maréchal (manners).

Excerpt 4 (12'50-14'30): Rosenthal's meal; a social microcosm.

Excerpt 5 (14'30-15'15): The engineer washes Maréchal's feet; tracking shot and unity of space (outside/inside).

Excerpt 6 (25'45-28'35): Preparation of the variety show; sequence shot; dreaming of women.

Excerpt 7 (37'25-38'45): The show — *La Marseillaise* (panning and tracking).

Excerpt 8 (46'10-47'50): Series of dissolves representing temporal ellipses between the imprisonment in different camps before arriving at Wintersborn.

Excerpt 9 (47'50-49'00): Rauffenstein's room in the chapel; descriptive pans and tracking shots.

Excerpt 10 (1h16'40-18'40): The escape — Boëldieu and the flute.

Excerpt 11 (1h29'10-32'10): Maréchal and Rosenthal on the run ; the quarrel.

Excerpt 12 (1h45'40-46'40): Announcing the departure to Elsa (depth of field, the window).

Quotations for Comment

Boëldieu: "May I ask you a question? Why have you made an exception for me, inviting me into your office?"

Rauffenstein: "Why? Because your name is de Boëldieu and you are a career officer in the French Army, and mine is von Rauffenstein and I'm a career officer in the Imperial German Army."

Boëldieu: "But…my comrades are officers too."

Rauffenstein: "A Maréchal and a Rosenthal—officers?"

Boëldieu: "They are very good soldiers."

Rauffenstein: "Yeh…a nice gift from the French Revolution."

Boëldieu: "I'm afraid we can't do anything to stop the march of time."

Rauffenstein: "I don't know who is going to win this war, but there's one thing I do know: the end of the war, however it comes out, will mark the end of the Rauffensteins and the Boëldieus."

Boëldieu: "Perhaps we are no longer of any use."

Rauffenstein: "And you don't think that's regrettable?"

Boëldieu: "Perhaps!"

* * *

Maréchal: "Listen, whatever happens I'd like to tell you…"

Boëldieu: "You know…I'm not doing anything for you personally. And we don't want to become sentimental here."

Maréchal: "Even so, there are certain times in life…"

Boëldieu: "How about we avoid them?"

[…]

Maréchal: "Well, I have to admit that putting on white gloves for this type of event is something which would never occur to me."

Boëldieu: "To each his own."

Maréchal: "[…] We haven't been out of each others' sight for eighteen months, and we still speak to each other formally." [*We use the formal "vous".]

Boëldieu: "I use "vous" with my mother and my wife."

Maréchal: "No!"… […]

Boëldieu: "Want a cigarette?"

Maréchal: "English tobacco makes my throat sore. Good grief, your tobacco, your gloves—we have nothing in common."

* * *

Maréchal: "You slipped! We know you slipped! And if we get caught crawling along at this rate, you're gonna explain to them that you slipped? Clumsy fool! And we don't have anything left to eat; we might as well turn ourselves in right now."

Rosenthal: "You bet, because I'm sick and tired of this too. Sick and tired! If you only knew how much I despise you!"

Maréchal: "How do you think I feel about you! You want to know what you are to me? A deadweight! Yeh, a deadweight, a ball and chain tied to my foot. And you know what else? I've never been able to stand Jews."

Rosenthal: "A little late to remember that. Why don't you just beat it! What are you waiting for? You just can't wait to be rid of me, right?"

Maréchal: "Don't ask me twice!"

Rosenthal: "Get out of here! Get out of here! Right now! I can't stand looking at your dirty mug!"

Maréchal: "Okay, I'm out of here! Screw you! Goodby."

* * *

Rosenthal: "Don't worry: the border is there, drawn by men…nature doesn't give a damn."

Maréchal: "I don't give a damn either… And when the war is over, I'll come back for Elsa."

Rosenthal: "Are you in love with her?"

Maréchal: "I think so!"

Rosenthal: "Don't forget…if we get back to our lines, you'll go back to your squadron and I'll go back to my artillery."

Maréchal: "We have to finish this goddam war…and it better be the last one."

Rosenthal: "Man, you're just kidding yourself!"

Questions/Topics for Reflection

1. Why is this film considered to be an example of "poetic realism"?
2. The fundamental oppositions and parallels which structure *Grand Illusion*.
3. The social significance of the secondary French characters: the actor, the engineer, the country schoolteacher, the scholar.
4. The theme of theater in the film: examples, thematic importance.

5. The use of the sequence shot in *Grand Illusion*: give a good example and discuss it.
6. The symbolism or metaphorical value of the following props: Boëldieu's monocle and his white gloves, Rauffenstein's neck brace, the geranium, the squirrel in the cage.
7. The theme of language.
8. The significance of Boëldieu's sacrifice near the end of the film.
9. The Maréchal-Elsa couple: significance.
10. The character of Rosenthal and the representation of Jews in *Grand Illusion*. Is the accusation of "anti-semitism" justified?
11. How are the ideals of the Popular Front of 1936-38 (solidarity between the social classes, internationalism, pacifism) reflected in Renoir's film?
12. The meaning of the film's title: possible interpretations.

CRITICAL DOSSIER

André Bazin — The "Realism" of *Grand Illusion*

I'm not sure that *Grand Illusion* is the most realistic of Renoir's films, but it is clear that if it has remained an effective work, it's due above all to its realistic elements. The signs of reality are numerous, beginning with the most obvious: the diversity of languages spoken [...]. Well before neo-realism, Renoir bases his film on the authenticity of human relations through language [...]. Here the stroke of genius which gives all its human flavor to this motif is the use of the third language, English, by von Rauffenstein and de Boëldieu, not as a national language but as a class language which separates the two aristocrats from the commoners.

This invention of a third term seems, indeed, to be one of the most successful elements in the structure of *Grand Illusion*, both for the screenplay and the staging. We have noted the doubling of the theme of the aristocracy with Fresnay and Stroheim, but one needs to know also that Rosenthal didn't exist at the beginning. Well, his character, which adds the idea of race to that of class, enriches significantly the meaning of the film, while helping to avoid the potentially schematic nature of the Fresnay-Gabin opposition.

There is realism also—or shall we say truth, or better, veracity—in the human relations [...] that Renoir created between the protagonists in the foreground and the minor characters in the background: the German guards, simple soldiers, non-commissioned officers, and officers are depicted—let's not say with truth, which is relative to personal experience—but with astounding veracity. This realism is not a matter of imitation, but rather a reinvention of a convention-free preciseness which produces details which are both documentary and meaningful. The invention of a character like Mr. Arthur and the subtle complicity he cultivates with his prisoners is a form of creation bordering the sublime. His reaction, during the show, when Carette calls out to him where he is sitting behind his superiors, "You get it, Arthur?" is a moment of pure cinema. And how about those rather brief shots where we see the British officers: a whole civilization is evoked in a few seconds without any of the significant details appearing "typical" or what you'd expect.

It is precisely a question of invention here, and not simply documentary reproduction. The accuracy of the details, in Renoir's films, is as much a function of imagination as of observation of reality; Renoir always manages to single out the essential details while avoiding stereotypes. The most exemplary sequence, in this respect, is certainly the famous scene during the show when the retaking of the fort at Douaumont is announced. Based on this brilliant idea, any talented director would be capable of producing a striking scene. But Renoir adds ten strokes of inspiration which turn it into something other than an anthology piece, beginning with the idea of having the singing of *La Marseillaise* begun not by a Frenchman but by a British officer disguised as a woman.

It is the multitude of these realistic inventions that weaves the solid fabric of *Grand Illusion* and that, still today, preserves its brilliance.

There is realism also in the shooting, or more precisely in the "découpage" of the film. But it is certain that the truthfulness of *Grand Illusion* would not be the same if Renoir hadn't begun by shooting all the exteriors (and even some of the interiors) on location. Since he couldn't do it in Germany, he chose Alsace, as close as possible to the border. And finally—although Renoir developed this technique more in other films—we note his constant concern to never separate, by the choice of shots, the center of dramatic interest from the general context in which it takes place (physical and human). This principle is expressed in a number of techniques: deep focus photography, of course, but especially the use of camera movements instead of changing shots, which entails treating scenes not like fragments, but truly as part of a whole. One example: for certain scenes in the barrack-room which could have been shot in the studio, Renoir had mobile pieces of scenery built and placed in the prison courtyard, which allowed him to film his actors "inside" while at the same time revealing through the window the activity in the camp (the scene of the new recruits marching). We thus find, in the very technique of the filming, Renoir's search for the truth of the relations between Men and the world in which they are immersed.

Without granting too much importance to a title, perhaps we can examine this one: *Grand Illusion*! Historically it can be explained by the denouement of the first version of the script. The two escapees agree to meet at Maxim's to celebrate the first Christmas Eve after the end of the war, but when Christmas of 1918 roles around, their long-reserved table stays empty. For this pessimistic lesson about the grand illusion of friendship, we see that Renoir has substituted a far more optimistic message. It is, of course, possible to detect a sort of proliferation of the theme of illusion in the various episodes of the film (the sexual illusion with the cross-dressers, the illusion of love with the doubtful future of Maréchal's affair with Elsa, the illusion of a quick end to the war and the illusion of liberty with the failed escape attempts)—illusions which are in any case more beneficial than harmful, to the extent that they help the men to transcend their painful situation and give them the courage to persevere.

But we should probably approach the question from a more elevated viewpoint and give the word "illusion" a resolutely positive, even militant, sense. The grand illusions are, on the one hand, the dreams which help us to live, even if it's a simple obsession, like pyrography or the translation of Pindar, but we see here especially the grand illusion of the hate which arbitrarily separates men who are in reality separated by nothing at all, the borders and the war which results, the races, the social classes.

The film's message is thus a demonstration *a contrario* of the fraternity and equality of men. The war, a product of hate and separation, reveals paradoxically the falseness of all moral borders within our consciousness.

If the borders are abolished, they exist no less. And here we see another theme that Renoir holds dear and which he has often expressed in his interviews: men are less separated by the vertical barriers of nationalism than by the horizontal divisions of cultures, races, classes, professions, etc.

Among these horizontal divisions, there is one which receives special treatment in *Grand Illusion*—the opposition between the people and the aristocracy. In all of his films, before or after the war, Renoir consistently expresses his respect for the aristocracy, but the true aristocracy, with or without a title, the aristocracy of the heart, of sensitivity, and especially of art or simply of profession, which puts Boëldieu and Maréchal on an equal footing. Contrary to Rauffenstein, Boëldieu knows and accepts it; he also understands that the manifest signs of his aristocracy are henceforth anachronistic and condemned to disappear. That is why his supreme manner of asserting his nobility is to sacrifice himself for Maréchal (*Jean Renoir*, pp. 56-60).

Another Viewpoint — Obscuring Reality

In Paris in 1937, the film was considered pacifist, without shocking the patriots, and everyone found something to like in it, both the left and the right.

Let's try to make some sense of this mosaic of meanings:

1) *Grand Illusion* is, first of all, a prettified version of war. The story is transformed by the effect of memory. The ocean of mud, boredom, sweat, and death that characterized the war years becomes a sort of chivalry. We shouldn't forget that in '37 the veterans were in their fifties. They were in denial as regards the hideous side of war. Renoir is fantasizing, like the rest of his generation.

2) The prison camps are presented like centers of patriotism. Someone announces that Douaumont has been taken back and the guys all stand at attention, "smartly," in the French manner, while singing the national anthem. Well, in '16 and '17, the morale of the troops was extremely low. Entire regiments refused to fight. Mutinies were put down in pools of blood and soldiers were executed as an example, paying the price of a war which didn't concern them.

3) The patriotic demagogy is combined with an amiable populism. People chatter. Carette clowns around, someone else eats, another reads Pindar. It's Jean Renoir's personal little world; there are a few complainers, of course, but like the old song goes, "all that makes for excellent Frenchmen…"

4) The Haut Koenigsbourg sequences are suddenly more rigorous. Renoir has become more careful. He was now working under the gaze of a film giant, Stroheim, who clearly played the role of a Father substitute for him. The character of the film changes, as if each actor were trying to be worthy of the great man. There is less self-indulgence in the dialogue, less negligence in the staging. Pierre Fresnay himself, who until then had been playing the role of a little Gallic rooster, achieves a

certain truth, and his character, the aristocrat condemned by the flow of History, takes shape in relation to Stroheim.

5) The ending is good. Gabin and Dalio, who were shallow characters, take on human substance. They help and hate each other, are both free and prisoners of themselves [...]; they experience the dialectics of racism. And the romance between Gabin and Dita Parlo occurs outside of the war, against war. Even if Renoir, twenty years later, passes it off, idiotically, as a preamble to the European Economic Community, it delights us (*"La Grande Illusion," Premier Plan*, pp. 235-236).

Olivier Curchod — Renoir's Style (the découpage)

For Renoir style serves dramatic art and carries its meaning, while cultivating the spectator's belief. It is first and foremost at the level of the stage, self-enclosed, that the formal organization of *Grand Illusion* is defined.

The choices in the shooting script (length of shots, size of the frame, angle-reverse angle shots, camera movements, depth of field, etc.) are a function of the dramatization of a scene. During the searching of the prisoners' room at Wintersborn, Renoir uses long shots twice, first to capture the feverish activity of Maréchal and Rosenthal, who fear that their rope will be found, then to record the stiff, methodical search of the German soldiers. In contrast, short shots and angle-reverse angle shots emphasize the role of Boëldieu (who hides the rope) and Rauffenstein (who asks Boëldieu for his word of honor): the distinctions between class and temperament are inscribed in the formal conception of the scene. In the same manner, during the lunch at the German mess, each couple (Rauffenstein and Boëldieu, Maréchal and the soldier who used to work at Gnôme) is isolated from the other through framing and editing; it is only when the funeral wreath enters, off-camera, that they are united in the same shot. Renoir uses a similar technique to film the discussion at the French officers' meal at Hallbach (the angle-reverse angle shots set in opposition Boëldieu and Rosenthal talking about Fouquet's and Maréchal responding to the teacher). But when the fall of Douaumont is announced, the national antagonism is expressed by a sequence shot which opposes, by a 180° pan, the chauvinism of the Germans singing *Die Wacht am Rhein* and the spiteful disappointment of the six Frenchmen standing at their window. Here as elsewhere, the technique has no set meaning. At the end of Christmas Eve, in a scene which concludes by the kiss between Elsa and Maréchal, a clever device gives the impression that it is a sequence shot. At the beginning of the shot, after Rosenthal leaves, the camera shows Elsa and Maréchal alone in front of the table, then, in a circular movement, accompanies Maréchal as he leaves the room and goes to his bedroom, passing through Rosenthal's room, and then returns to Elsa's side, at the same place we had left her, sad and alone. But a discreet cut on Maréchal at the moment he shuts the door between his room and Rosenthal's carefully excludes the latter from the following love scene.

When he films groups, Renoir approaches them progressively, first giving free play to what he likes to call the actors' "ballet," as he does at the beginning of the tunnel-digging scene, at night, when the Frenchmen stand on their beds and cover the window with a blanket while the teacher gets out the equipment. In the scene of the unpacking of the costumes, in the theater, a tracking shot takes in the group of Englishmen rehearsing *Tipperary* and ends up on our friends leaning over the large container. The following conversation about women, becoming more intimate, is filmed in closer and closer shots until the camera is forced to pan to include a newcomer in the group, Private Maisonneuve, who then dresses up, precisely, like a woman. We see how the découpage depends on a certain choreography of the actors, without becoming a simple ornament. Thus, the priest who comes to give the final rites to Boëldieu performs a veritable pas de deux, turning now to the right to meet Rauffenstein's genuflection or to greet him, then to the left to receive his coat or to leave the room; in the process, he prevents the commander from turning back toward the bed, off camera, where his friend is dying.

The frequent close-ups (there are several dozen in the film, principally on objects), in addition to their obvious descriptive function (the French and German officers' messes, Rauffenstein's room, the room in Elsa's house) or symbolic value (the crucifixes, the braided rope, the squirrel in the cage), identify a character by the object with which he is associated, in the style of Balzac [...] (*La Grande Illusion*, pp. 76-79).

Olivier Curchod (cont.) — Renoir's Style (off-camera space)

By frequently using off-camera space to direct the spectator's attention, Renoir reveals a key to his directing technique, expressed unwittingly by Maréchal's remark in reference to Private Maisonneuve: "Let us dream a little. If we see you, we can't use our imagination any more." Thus the funeral wreath at the German mess, imposing its presence off camera by a quick pan to include the whole table, breaks up Maréchal's sentence ("Hey, I'm a mechanic too") and recalls the national enmity, just as, much later in the film, when Maréchal comes back for Rosenthal whom he has insulted and abandoned, all we see of him is a piece of his coat at the extreme right edge of the frame, as if his remorse were keeping the rest of him, momentarily, off camera. Frequently, in an approach which might be considered theatrical, the characters reveal their presence while staying "in the wings," whether it be the engineer to whom Cartier asks a question ("Is he there, 'the monocle'?") or Rauffenstein calling off camera to his orderly, who is showing him a pair of gloves — and although we haven't seen Rauffenstein since the prologue, his voice, immediately identifiable, invites the spectator to solve the riddle of this surprising reappearance. The sound track thus contributes, in a discreet but singular way, to the dramatic structure of *Grand Illusion*: whether it's about evoking Maréchal's beating in the cell, the training of the young recruits in the barracks courtyard, the death of Boëldieu, or the frightening approach of a German column, Renoir chooses off-camera sound; he prefers having the faces of the characters on screen reflect the dramatic events which are occurring off camera. But when Private Maisonneuve shows his "feminine" figure to the dumbfounded prisoners, and when the guards surround Boëldieu at the top of the fortress, a brief stretch of dead silence emphasizes the extreme dramatic tension of the scene (*La Grande Illusion*, pp. 79-80).

JEAN RENOIR'S FILMOGRAPHY
(PRINCIPAL FILMS)

1926	*Nana* (silent)
1928	*The Little Match Girl*
	(La Petite Marchande d'allumettes, silent),
	Sad Sack (Tire au flanc, silent).
1931	*Baby Gets a Laxative (On purge bébé)*
1931	*The Bitch (La Chienne)*
1932	*Boudu Saved from Drowning*
	(Boudu sauvé des eaux)
1933	*Madame Bovary*
1934	*Toni*
1935	*Le Crime de Monsieur Lange*
1936	*A Day in the Country*
	(Partie de campagne, edited and shown in 1946)
1936	*The Lower Depths (Les Bas-fonds),*
	People of France (La Vie est à nous)
1937	*La Grande Illusion*
1938	*The Human Beast (La Bête humaine),*
	La Marseillaise
1939	*The Rules of the Game (La Règle du jeu)*
1941	*Swamp Water (L'Etang tragique,* USA)
1945	*The Southerner (L'Homme du Sud,* USA)
1946	*Diary of a Chambermaid*
	(Le Journal d'une femme de chambre, USA)
1950	*The River (Le Fleuve,* India)
1952	*The Golden Coach (Le Carrosse d'or,* Italy)
1954	*French Cancan*
1956	*Elena and Her Men (Elena et les hommes)*
1959	*Picnic on the Grass (Le Déjeuner sur l'herbe)*
1962	*Elusive Corporal (Le Caporal épinglé)*
1969	*The Little Theater of Jean Renoir*
	(Le Petit Théâtre de Jean Renoir)

SOURCES CONSULTED

Bazin, André. *Jean Renoir*. Paris: Champ libre, 1971 (esp. pp. 50-60).

Braudy, Leo. *Jean Renoir: The World of His Films*. New York: Doubleday, 1972.

Curchod, Olivier. *La Grande Illusion*. Paris: Nathan, 1994.

Durgnat, Raymond. *Jean Renoir*. Los Angeles: UCal Press, 1974.

Faulkner, Christopher. *The Social Cinema of Jean Renoir*. Princeton, N.J.: Princeton University Press, 1986.

Giroud, Françoise. "Ce jour-là." *L'Express* 382 (Oct. 9, 1958): 22-24.

Leprohon, Pierre. *Jean Renoir*. Paris: Seghers, 1967.

"*La Grande Illusion*" in "Jean Renoir." *Premier Plan* 22-24, special issue (May 1962): 235-250.

Masson, Alain. "*La Grande Illusion*. Fenêtres." *Positif* 395 (Jan. 1994): 70-72.

Priot, Franck. "*La Grande Illusion* : histoire du film en dix chapitres." *Archives* 70 (Feb. 1997): 3-13, 15-21.

Renoir, Jean. *La Grande Illusion* (screenplay). *L'Avant-Scène Cinéma*, 44 (Jan. 1965).

.........*Ma Vie et mes films*. Paris: Flammarion, 1974.

........."Propos (1925-1937)." *La Revue du cinéma* 296 (May 1975): 18-29.

Serceau, Daniel. *Jean Renoir, l'insurgé*. Paris: CinémAction, 1981.

Sesonske, Alexander. *Jean Renoir: The French Films (1924-1939)*. Cambridge, MA: Harvard UP, 1980.

Truffaut, François. Préface à *La Grande Illusion*. Paris : Balland, 1975 (pp. 7-13).

Viry-Babel, Roger. "*La Grande Illusion* de Jean Renoir." *Cahiers de la cinémathèque* 18-19 (Spring 1976): 37-63.

Jean Renoir

The Rules of the Game
La Règle du jeu

(1939)

Jean Renoir, *The Rules of the Game*: Christine (Nora Grégor) welcomes André Jurieu (Roland Toutain) and Octave (Jean Renoir) to her castle. © Les Grands Films Classiques F-Paris et Janus Films N.Y.

Director .... Jean Renoir
Screenplay and Dialogues... Jean Renoir
Assistant Directors .... André Zwobada, Henri Cartier-Bresson
Director of Photography ....Jean Bachelet
Music.. Roger Desormières
Film Editor ....Marguerite Houllé-Renoir
Sound .... Joseph de Bretagne
Art Director ....Eugène Lourié
Gowns...Coco Chanel
Script Girl (Continuity) .... Dido Freire
Producers ............N.E.F. (1939), Les Grands films classiques (1959)
Length .... 1 h 52

Cast

Marcel Dalio (*the marquis Robert de La Chesnaye*), Nora Grégor (*Christine, his wife*), Mila Parély (*Geneviève, his mistress*), Roland Toutain (*André Jurieu*), Jean Renoir (*Octave*), Paulette Dubost (*Lisette, Christine's servant*), Gaston Modot (*Schumacher, the marquis's game warden, Lisette's husband*), Julien Carette (*Marceau, the poacher*), Odette Talazac (*Charlotte*), Pierre Magnier (*the general*), Pierre Nay (*Saint-Aubin*), Richard Francoeur (*La Bruyère*), Claire Gérard (*Mme de La Bruyère*), Eddy Debray (*Corneille, the majordomo*), Anne Mayen (*Jackie, Christine's niece*), Léon Larive (*the chef*).

STORY

It is the end of the nineteen-thirties. An airplane lands at the Le Bourget airport amid wild applause from the crowd. The aviator André Jurieu has just beaten the record for a transatlantic flight. Interviewed immediately on the radio, he bitterly reproaches Christine, the woman he loves, for not bothering to come to the airport to greet his arrival. It was for her, he explains, that he had accomplished this feat. Christine is listening to the broadcast in her Parisian residence, as is her husband the marquis Robert de La Chesnaye. Christine gives her husband to understand that Jurieu has misunderstood their relationship, which according to her is only a friendship. Swept away by a surge of love for his wife, Robert decides to break it off with his long-time mistress Geneviève the very next day.

In a state of despair after his scandalous indiscretion on the radio, Jurieu attempts to commit suicide in his car in the company of Octave, his best friend. None too appreciative, Octave criticizes him severely for his lack of respect for the rules of the elevated society to which Christine belongs. Yielding nonetheless to Jurieu's beseeching, Octave agrees to help him see Christine again. Octave has known Christine since her childhood, having been close to her father, who was a famous orchestra leader in Vienna. He manages to convince Christine and Robert to invite Jurieu to join them for a hunting party at their country residence La Colinière in Sologne, where he will be entertaining other guests, aristocrats and wealthy bourgeois acquaintances.

As soon as he arrives at the castle Robert has to resolve a conflict between his Alsatian game warden Schumacher and a local character, Marceau, who is poaching on his land. Amused by Marceau, the marquis solves the problem by offering to employ him as a servant in the castle. When Octave and Jurieu arrive, the aviator is given a hero's welcome by the other guests. Christine takes advantage of the occasion to publicly declare the innocence of her relations with André — which earns her plaudits from the guests but convinces no one. Her husband is nevertheless relieved and proposes, following the hunt, a big party in Jurieu's honor in which all the guests will wear costumes and put on skits. One story below, Marceau joins the other servants at the dinner table and begins to flirt with Lisette (Christine's servant and Schumacher's wife).

The film picks up the next day with the hunt. Beaters flush out pheasants and rabbits, which are then shot by hunters hiding behind blinds. After the hunt, when Robert informs Geneviève of his decision to terminate their romance, his mistress entreats him to embrace her one last time. Their parting kiss is spotted by Christine, who chances to see them through a spyglass and misinterprets their embrace. She is shocked to discover this affair, which had been an open secret for years among their friends.

The evening of the party Christine decides to take revenge by flirting with one of her admirers, Saint-Aubin, who is only too happy to oblige her. During a skit in a darkened room, based on Saint-Saëns's *La Danse macabre*, Jurieu jealously keeps an eye on Christine and Saint-Aubin while Schumacher tries to put a leash on his wife Lisette, who is flirting with Marceau. Eventually Jurieu confronts and fights with Saint-Aubin, before he is himself confronted by the marquis. While Jurieu and the marquis fight, Schumacher pursues Marceau — whom he has caught in the kitchen with Lisette — taking wild shots at him with his revolver. When Schumacher is finally brought under control, he is fired by the marquis along with Marceau. The marquis has made up with Jurieu. Having regained his aristocratic composure, he accepts the idea that his wife is going to leave with the aviator.

Meanwhile Christine has stepped outside with Octave, who confesses that he too is in love with her. She asks him to run away with her immediately. Schumacher and Marceau watch the scene in the darkness, mistaking the marquise for the warden's wife, since Christine is wearing her servant's cloak. The two men decide to take revenge by killing Octave, who has returned to the castle to get his coat. When Lisette persuades Octave that he isn't the man for Christine, he gives his coat to André and sends him to Christine in his place. Schumacher mistakes André for Octave and shoots him dead with his rifle. Marceau relates the tragic event to the people in the castle, then departs along with Octave. Robert makes a speech to the assembled guests describing the incident as "a deplorable accident," his warden having simply mistaken Jurieu for a poacher. The case is closed, and everyone retires to the castle.

CRITICAL RECEPTION

When one sees *The Rules of the Game* today, it is difficult to imagine the storm it provoked when it came out in two Parisian cinemas on July 7, 1939. In a remarkable study of the film's reception André G. Brunelin recounts the experience of the producer Camille François that evening:

> When Camille F… came into the theater, the big party in *The Rules of the Game* was in full swing. On the main floor there was a deafening racket. The catcalls and whistling made it virtually impossible to hear the dialogue. Some outraged spectators were breaking seats, while others were setting on fire copies of *L'Action française* and using them as torches as employees rushed to put them out […]. Camille F… bolted out of the "Colisée." He had seen and heard enough. He ran to his car and, in a panic, drove like a madman to the "Aubert-Palace" on the boulevard des Italiens. When he got there, the film was almost over. The crowd reaction was pretty much the same. The public was less bourgeois and less violent, but the whistling, the mocking laughter, and the gibes were just as loud as at the "Colisée" (pp. 40-41).

The rejection of the film by the public was so general that, at the time, it looked like a cabal organized by extreme right-wing groups to guarantee that Renoir's film would fail. Renoir's left-wing sympathies were well known. Nonetheless, the remarks overheard by Renoir himself (in a café across from the "Colisée" where he had taken refuge after the film) are quite revealing:

> — It's scandalous! someone said. This film is pure filth. It drags French society through the mud. And what's this rubbish about a marquis whose mother is Jewish?...
> — I don't give a damn about the Jewish business, said another. For me, this film is just a piece of crap; it's bad, so bad it's unbelievable! The ending, for instance, is totally incomprehensible (p. 41).

These few sentences give a good idea of the public reaction to Renoir's film: offended patriotism, incomprehension, anti-Semitism in some cases. It's hardly surprising that the French public of 1939, accustomed to chauvinistic themes in the popular films of the time and anguished by the Nazi threat, was not willing to countenance a satirical portrait of their social elite which was basically negative. And it is no less surprising that this same public was perplexed by the tangled plots, the thematic subtlety, and the ambiguous morality developed in the film — not to mention the mixture of comic and tragic registers foreign to the French public's viewing habits. As the publicity for the film trumpeted, *The Rules of the Game* was "a film resembling no other," and the public was not in a mood in those troubled times to tolerate such a slap in the face. The reaction of the critical community is ambivalent: a few voices are raised in defense of the film, but the large circulation papers and magazines, basically right-wing, were uniformly hostile to the film, as Claude Gauteur clearly demonstrates (see "Works Consulted").

Renoir desperately tried to save his film by cutting the shots and sequences which seem to anger the spectators. Cut by cut the film was thus reduced from 1h40 to 1h30 — certain copies to 1h25 — but it was no use. Anticipated as the cinematographic event of the year, *The Rules of the Game* ended its Parisian run after only three weeks. The film's rejection was no less clear in theaters outside Paris, and the foreign distributors, alarmed, broke their contracts. It was a financial disaster for Gaumont, and Renoir's new production company, the N.E.F., went under. Two months after its opening *The Rules of the Game* was banned by the government, along with other French films considered to be "demoralizing" for the public. Continued by the Germans when they occupied France in 1940, the ban lasted until the Liberation in 1945.

The history of *The Rules of the Game* and its reception continued after the Liberation and began to resemble a veritable saga. Three versions of the film circulated in France, primarily in the ciné-clubs, varying in length from 1h30 to 1h20. Finally, in 1956, after several months of painstaking work, a team of film specialists managed to reconstruct the 1h40 version of the film as it came out in 1939, before restoring, under Renoir's direction, the original version of 1h53. The film was projected at the Venice Film Festival in 1959, but the public reaction was not particularly enthusiastic when the film opened again after the festival. However, André Bazin and his young collaborators at the *Cahiers du Cinéma* had been showering praise on *The Rules of the Game* throughout the decade of the fifties. In 1952 *The Rules of the Game* was ranked as the tenth best film of all time; in 1962 it moved up to third place. In time the public came around to the opinion of the new generation of film critics, and in April 1965 the film's new opening enjoyed a solid success at the Studio Médicis in Paris. In 1972 *The Rules of the Game* was ranked second best film of all time, a place it still occupies today.

THE ORIGIN AND THE CAST

Just before Renoir launched into the adventure of the *The Rules of the Game*, his previous film, an adaptation of Emile Zola's famous novel *The Human Beast* (*La Bête humaine*, 1938), was a huge hit with both the critics and the general public. It is the high point of Renoir's "naturalist" phase, a rather pessimistic current which includes, notably, *The Bitch* (*La Chienne*, 1931), *Madame Bovary* (1933), *Toni* (1934), and *The Lower Depths* (*Les Bas-Fonds*, 1936). (For a more complete summary of Renoir's body of works before *The Rules of the Game*, see the chapter on *Grand Illusion*, pp. 78, 82.) Renoir felt the urge to turn the page, to move on to something new, as he remarks in speaking of *The Human Beast*:

> Nonetheless, working on this screenplay made me feel like changing directions and perhaps moving completely away from naturalism toward a more classical, or a more poetic genre. The result of these reflections was *The Rules of the Game* [...]. To help me get into *The Rules of the Game*, I carefully reread Marivaux and Musset [...]. I think that these readings helped me to establish a style, including both realism—not the external kind, but realism all the same—and a certain poetry; in any case, that's what I was trying to do.

On the other hand Renoir also cites baroque music as an important influence on the conception of the film: "You spend an evening listening to records, and it ends up with a film. I can't tell you that French baroque music directly inspired *The Rules of the Game*, but it contributed to my desire to film characters acting in the spirit of this music" (*Ma Vie et mes films*, p. 154). Whatever the case may be, to free himself from his habitual filmmaking, Renoir wanted to make "a merry drama" in a classical style. At the beginning the plan was to do a simple adaptation of Musset's *Les Caprices de Marianne* (1833) and place the action in contemporary times. Renoir in fact wrote a first screenplay in this vein. Virtually nothing remains of this initial version other than the theme of the tragic error, which is the focal point of the denouement of Musset's play (a jealous husband arranges the assassination of the man whom he suspects of being his wife's lover but gets the wrong man). In the following version, not far removed from the definitive scenario, Renoir took his inspiration from eighteenth-century theater classics such as Marivaux's *The Game of Love and Chance* (*Le Jeu de l'amour et du hasard*, 1730), in which the parallels — the mirroring motif — between masters and servants play an important role, and Beaumarchais's *Le Mariage de Figaro* (1784), with its mistaken identities, its focus on the master-servant opposition, and its critical depiction of nobility.

The choice of actors will profoundly affect the development of the scenario of *The Rules of the Game*. At the beginning Renoir had intended to give the role of the marquis's wife to Simone Simon, casting Fernand Ledoux in the role of the game warden; the cast would have thus included the principal stars of *The Human Beast*. Having just returned from Hollywood, Simon has become "too expensive," and

Renoir decided to give Christine's role to a neophyte actress whose aristocratic style had struck his fancy, Nora Gregor (an Austrian princess who elected exile in France as soon as the Nazis arrived in her country). But Nora Gregor was a thirty-something lady who had nothing in common with the capricious young woman in Musset's play — and who spoke French with a heavy German accent to boot. For the role of the marquis Renoir chose Marcel Dalio, the Rosenthal of *Grand Illusion*, who evoked for the French public the stereotype of the Jew — or at the very least the Middle-Eastern foreigner. Renoir was thus forced to modify the biography of his characters: the couple at the top of the French social elite would be a half-Jewish marquis with an Austrian wife. This not only changed the character of the film but was perceived as a form of provocation, indeed an insult, by the French public of 1939. As Pierre Guislain remarks, regarding the character of the marquis: "At a moment when anti-Semitism was on the rise in Europe, only Renoir would dare feature in a film, as Dalio himself will later put it, 'a frizzy-haired foreign-looking marquis,' a character not only unlikely, but downright scandalous for the vast majority of the spectators at that time" (p. 92).

The strange casting by Renoir for *The Rules of the Game* has certainly not gone unnoticed. All of the actors, among the masters at least, seem to be incongruous choices for the characters they play (Guislain, pp. 93-95). In addition to Dalio we note Renoir's controversial decision to cast himself in the role of Octave instead of giving it to his brother Pierre, a seasoned actor who had been brilliant in the role of Louis XVI in the recent Renoir film *La Marseillaise* (1938). Renoir's amateurishness greatly distressed the producers (and was apparently one of the reasons why Simone Simon refused the role of Christine). Moreover, Renoir realized too late that the actress who was playing the marquis's mistress, Mila Parély, would have been much better than Nora Gregor in the role of the wife. Consequently he was led to flesh out much more fully the role of the mistress Geneviève, as well as that of Lisette, played by Paulette Dubost — whose admirable acting only served to highlight the meager talents of the princess. Miraculously, and perhaps because of its very incongruity, Renoir's cast produced an impression of oddness, an ambiguity, a sort of malaise or a premonitory atmosphere which permeates the whole film and can be felt beneath the social and sentimental thematics.

THE SHOOTING

On February 15, 1939, Renoir's crew left Paris for the castle of La Ferté-Saint-Aubin in Sologne, where they would shoot the outdoors scenes of *The Rules of the Game*. A persistent rain forced them to wait two weeks to begin shooting. Renoir used the time to finish writing part of his screenplay, but they fell behind schedule because of the rain and because Renoir was constantly improvising to compensate for the incompleteness of the scenario. It is well known of course that improvisation is inherent to Renoir's filming technique, since he considered the actors to be full partners in the creation of a film and liked to take advantage of their suggestions when he was shooting. As he admitted, speaking of *The Rules of the Game*, "Yes, I improvised quite a bit: the actors are also the film's authors, and when they work, they sometimes produce unanticipated reactions. These reactions are often very good, and I would be crazy not to take advantage of them" (Rivette and Truffaut, p. 4).

Nonetheless, as the shooting stretched out, the film went quickly over budget. Renoir's partners found additional financing, but he was forced to begin shooting quickly at the Joinville studio in Paris, leaving behind his assistants Zwoboda and Cartier-Bresson to shoot the famous hunt sequence, following his precise instructions. This sequence turned out to be extremely difficult to film and required ingenious solutions. To obtain the desired effects without endangering the cameraman, they finally constructed a sort of mobile blockhouse in which they enclosed the cameraman with his equipment:

> The shooters would thus able to kill their rabbits without making mincemeat of them. This approach worked, and the little rabbits ran up and died photogenically before the camera, just as Renoir wanted, while the bullets which missed the target just bounced off the blockhouse (Brunelin, p. 53).

It took them two months to get the sequence, and at the cost of several hundred rabbits. (While the contemporary spectators admired the "documentary" character of the hunt scene, they were nonetheless shocked by the massacre of the rabbits.)

It shouldn't be forgotten that while Renoir was making his film, the growing Nazi threat was creating a climate of apprehension and instability throughout the country. The French government announced a partial military call up, and the studios soon lacked technical personnel. Nevertheless Renoir finished the shooting of the interiors in the studio, while still unsure of how to end his film. Unable to decide, he shot two endings, the first depicting Octave and Marceau's departure in the night, the second the one he would keep. Exhausted, he turned the editing of the film over to Marguerite Houllé, sending her specific instructions. The original version of the film lasts 1h53. Under pressure from the producers, who feared a commercial failure, Renoir agreed to cut seven scenes, over half with his own character Octave, to obtain the 1h40 version which was shown a few days later at the "Colisée" movie theater— with the ugly reception we've described above.

Nine weeks later at the beginning of September France declared war on Germany, which had just invaded Poland.

STRUCTURE

With the knowledge that Renoir was inspired by classical French theater, we are not surprised to note that *The Rules of the Game* seems to divide naturally into five distinct acts, as Francis Vanoye observes (pp. 29-30):

Act I. Presentation of the main characters and of their relations with each other.

Act II. Gathering at La Colinière of all the characters.

Act III. The hunt and the following morning.

Act IV. The party.

Act V. The denouement.

In addition to its "classicism," this conception of the film's structure reinforces the fundamental opposition of the film between social order and the disorder introduced by human passion which threatens this order. Vanoye thus distinguishes five "moments" in the film, corresponding to the five acts, in which order (social, conjugal) is alternatively upset and reestablished among the masters or the servants (pp. 31-32). It is likewise possible to conceive the structure of the film as a four-phase dialectic between modernity and the old social order in which the initial opposition of the two yields to coexistence, then to the ascendancy of modernity before the old established order triumphs in the end (Marty, pp. 22-23).

Other structural hypotheses are moreover just as conceivable in the attempt to account for this complex film: a division in three acts (instead of four or five), for example, in which the first act is still the Parisian episode, whereas the second would contain all of the action from the arrival at the castle to the preparation for the party after the hunt, with the third act including the party itself and the tragic ending (Vanoye, p. 31). The division into three acts has the advantage of foregrounding the progressive tightening of the action and its acceleration in the third act. The absence of ellipses in the final act, contrary to the first two, gives the impression that the action is taking place in real time before the spectator's eyes. For Renoir himself, however, the structure of *The Rules of the Game* is simpler yet: it consists of two major sections separated by the hunt episode and Christine's discovery of her husband's infidelity, a "pivot" which precipitates the chain of events leading to the final tragedy. Whatever structure one prefers, it is also possible to view the work holistically and compare it to a symphony or even a painting, as André Bazin does:

> Renoir has managed to make his film without recourse to dramatic structures. It is essentially an interlacing of references, allusions, and relationships, a carrousel of themes in which reality and moral concepts play off one another with no loss of meaning, rhythm, tonality, or melody. But it is a marvelously constructed film in which there isn't a single useless or misplaced image. It's a work that you have to see over and over, as when you listen to a symphony or contemplate a painting, because each time you gain a better understanding of the interior harmony (p. 76).

The notion of "symphony" is no less a reference to the thematic texture of the film, to which we shall now turn.

THEMES AND METAPHORS

The whole set of themes in *The Rules of the Game* is organized in relationship to a specific social milieu, "high society," composed of aristocrats and the wealthy bourgeoisie. The micro-society presented by Renoir is peopled primarily by very rich, idle individuals whose principal activity is seeking entertainment to fill their rather empty lives. The main character in this universe is the marquis Robert de La Chesnaye, who manages to entertain himself by collecting antique musical dolls, clear symbols of an age long past, a way of life which has virtually disappeared with the Old Regime. The fundamental thematic opposition of the film is established immediately with the arrival of the man of action André Jurieu in his airplane, a symbol of modernism. The symbolism of the airplane, which is linked to that of the radio, another emblem of modernity, creates an instant contrast with the outdated, anachronistic character of the world inhabited by Robert and his spouse. At the same time the automated dolls serve as metaphors for the characters in Robert's milieu, insofar as they only *imitate* life in the absence of any real human sentiment or "sincerity."

The theme of the confrontation of anachronism and modernity which underlies the entire film is joined from the beginning by equally fundamental thematic oppositions between truth and falsehood, appearance and reality, and public and private spheres. Jurieu publicly reveals the reality (the truth) of his feelings for Christine immediately upon landing; the marquise preserves appearances, privately first in relationship to her husband, then publicly in front of their social peers gathered at La Colinière, by apparently lying (including to herself?) about the true nature of her relationship with Jurieu. The problem of the confusion between appearance and reality is introduced later, after the hunt, in the spyglass scene in which Christine errs completely in her interpretation of the rather ambiguous "image" that she captures, the goodbye kiss her husband gives to Geneviève (see Pierre Guislain's metaphorical interpretation of the spyglass as camera in the *Critical Dossier*). The theme of appearances and falsehood is at the very basis of the concept of the "The Rules of the Game": the rule of the game for this milieu is absolute discretion, protecting appearances — by lying if necessary. Scandal must be avoided at all cost. The "scandalous" declarations by Jurieu, which violate the rules which separate the private and public spheres, suggest from the outset his incompatibility with Christine's world, an incompatibility which will be confirmed by the fisticuffs which break out during the episode of the party. At the same time Jurieu's remarks at the airport, followed by Christine's in her boudoir, place at the very center of the film the theme of love or, more generally, the question of the relationship between men and women.

From the beginning Jurieu's *faux pas*, the scandal he provokes, also introduces the theme of disorder, in opposition to the order established by Robert and Christine's society. The same theme will be embodied later by Schumacher, the only other truly passionate character in the film. During the party at La Colinière these two "foreign" elements (by virtue of their sincerity) bring an explosion of disorder into this very orderly world. The famous mechanical organ, the jewel of Robert's collection of automated toys (all of them symbols of order, of well-regulated behavior), is transformed into a metaphor of disorder by going awry at the very moment that the chaos reaches its height during the party.

Within this basic thematic framework there is a swarm of additional themes supported by a series of metaphors. Among the latter set of themes, the idea of "spectacle" is dominant, in its double meaning of "theater" and "human comedy." In a world where only appearances count, how does one distinguish between play-acting and reality, or between truth and falsehood? This problem is emphasized in the party episode, where play-acting in moving from the stage to the hall, invades social space when Christine decides to flirt with Saint-Aubin, while Marceau and Lisette the servants are doing precisely the same thing. The metaphorical character of the show put on by the guests is made quite clear by Christine's declaration ("*I'm sick of this theater, Octave!*"), as by the exchange between Robert and his majordomo in the thick of the chaos ("*Corneille, put an end to this comedy!*" "*Which one, Sir?*"). Octave's dilemma — he has a terrible time getting out of his bear costume — also takes on metaphorical overtones if we consider that his problem suggests how difficult it is to try to stop "acting," to become oneself (i.e., sincere) when pretending and lying (including to oneself) have become a way of life.

"Renoir plays on all conceivable oppositions," Jean Roy notes (p. 45), far too many to mention them all here. A final important thematic contrast we should mention, however, is the opposition between masters and servants in the film. We should speak in fact of a parallel rather than an opposition, for masters and servants obey the same rules in *The Rules of the Game*. As Esnault observes, "The back-and-forth from the drawing rooms to the kitchens reveals a strong similarity between people whose lot in society is quite different" (p. 10). Indeed, Renoir's intentions in *The Rules of the Game* are in no way political, and the servants model themselves unambiguously after their masters. Despite the vacuousness of the masters' lives, Renoir's portrayal of them (as of the servants) is basically sympathetic, and we remember the famous statement by Octave-Renoir which summarizes the filmmaker's humanism: "*Everyone has his reasons.*" Renoir himself says of his film, "The characters are simple human beings, neither good nor bad, and each of them is a function of his social position, his milieu, and his past" (quoted in Esnault, p. 10).

Let us finish this discussion with the theme of death. Introduced at the very beginning of the film — the danger of the pilot's feat, the car accident — the theme of death becomes more and more prominent after the arrival at La Colinière. In the distance we hear gunfire, which will be followed shortly by the fusillade of the hunt scene which, according to Renoir, foreshadows the death of Jurieu. Thematically death is no less foreshadowed by the party which precedes it, and especially the staging of Saint-Saëns's "Danse macabre," a scene begun by a player piano whose mechanical character evokes the "mechanics of death" soon to be set in motion (Guislain, p. 117). The ghosts, incarnations of death, fan out among the guests to "frighten" them before the spectators themselves, masters and servants, begin their own death dance, soon punctuated by Schumacher's gunshots as he pursues Marceau.

Retrospectively, it is tempting to interpret the hunt, the massacre of the innocent rabbits, in its historical context. This carnage may appear metaphorically as "the most striking image of the danger felt by everyone in 1939" before the Nazi threat (Vanoye, p. 55). Renoir admits in fact that "being absolutely convinced that war was inevitable, this feeling pervaded my work in spite of myself" (Rivette and Truffaut, p. 6). In another interview he adds, "My ambition when I began this film was to illustrate this historical comment: 'We are dancing on a volcano'" (quoted in Guislain, p. 61). The whole atmosphere of the film is colored by the pessimistic, premonitory climate which reigned in France between the Munich Accords of September 1938 and the declaration of war a year later — the precise period during which Renoir was writing the screenplay and shooting *The Rules of the Game*. Death was roaming throughout Europe.

In any case the metaphorical function of the massacre of the rabbits as foreshadowing for the murder of Jurieu becomes explicit when Marceau describes the manner in which the aviator dies: "*He rolled over just like a rabbit.*" Ultimately Jurieu is a victim of appearances which, ironically, take precedence over reality, just as in the spyglass scene where Christine misunderstands what is taking place between her husband and Geneviève. In this instance it is the cloak lent to Christine by Lisette which represents the theme of appearances and their danger. But why does Jurieu have to die? The death of Jurieu can of course be viewed as the logical outcome of the murderous folly which grips the social microcosm at the castle. However, Jurieu like Marceau and Octave is also a disturbing element which must be eliminated to reestablish order. He serves in a certain sense as a scapegoat; his murder is interpreted by some as a kind of outlet, a form of release for the underlying violent urges of this social group (Guislain, p. 119; see also "Director's Comments", below). With Jurieu the intruder dead and Octave and Marceau (the two other "outsiders") expelled, this social milieu recovers its cohesiveness, order is imposed, and the rules of the game prevail.

STYLE

We note in *The Rules of the Game*, just as in *Grand Illusion*, Renoir's resistance to fragmentation of space (the editing of a scene into a series of shots) in favor of sequence shots which respect, as Bazin says, "the natural unity" of beings and things: "Jean Renoir [is] the only filmmaker whose experiments with filming, up to *The Rules of the Game*, constitute an attempt [...] to discover the secret of a filmic narrative which is capable of expressing everything without fragmenting the world — which is capable of revealing the hidden significance of beings and things without rupturing the world's natural unity" (*Qu'est-ce que le cinéma?*, p. 78). By shooting in deep focus and employing camera movements (pans and tracking shots), Renoir liberates the actors to develop their characters freely. The same techniques allow him moreover to focus both on the movements of the characters in their physical and social environment and on the relations between the actions which are taking place simultaneously in the foreground and the background. At the same time, by avoiding the directive effect of editing, which constantly orients the spectator's gaze, the use of deep focus liberates the spectator (at least partially) and encourages him or her to participate more fully in the construction of the meaning of the sequences. The use of pans in particular, combined with deep focus, gives Renoir's films their characteristic impression of constant movement and complexity: "The pan is the principal camera movement in *The Rules of the Game*. It accentuates the breadth of field in opposition to the depth of field which emphasizes all the actions whether close to or far from the camera. Panning and depth of field together thus allow Renoir to shoot with a maximum of freedom, speed, and life in a maximum of complexity. Deep focus, panning, speed" (Guislain, p. 148). The hunt scene alone provides a notable exception to this esthetic bias in *The Rules of the Game*. Here Renoir prefers short shots and very fast editing whose shock value emphasizes the violence of the butchery.

When we seek examples of striking sequence shots in *The Rules of the Game*, there are so many it is hard to choose. We may cite, nevertheless, in the servants' meal scene, the nearly two-minute-long sequence shot which plays both on depth of field (the servant's table in the foreground, the kitchen in the background) and the camera movements which accompany Schumacher's arrival, followed by Marceau's as he joins the group of servants at the table (see our commentary of this sequence in the chapter "'Reading' a Film," pp. 29-31). During the "Danse macabre" scene the sequence shot reaches unimagined artistic heights. A series of tracking-panning shots frames first Schumacher as he enters the spectators' space (looking for Lisette), then shows us Christine flirting with Saint-Aubin before reversing direction and stopping on Marceau and Lisette sneaking kisses, followed by a stop on Jurieu, who is keeping an eye on Christine and Saint-Aubin. The camera then reverses direction once again to catch up with Schumacher, who grabs Lisette just as she tries to slip away with Marceau, and then continues its trajectory to catch Christine as she hurries off with Saint-Aubin. The mobility of Renoir's camera here as in virtually all the castle sequences takes on human characteristics: "During the whole last part of *The Rules of the Game* the camera behaves like an invisible guest, strolling through the drawing room and the hallways, watching curiously but with no other privilege than its invisibility" (Bazin, "Renoir français," p. 25).

Since Renoir works primarily in deep focus, here and in his other films, there are relatively few close-up shots in *The Rules of the Game*. However, Renoir often reverses the classical rhetoric of cinema by beginning with a close-up on a small detail of the decor before moving (in the same shot) to an establishing shot which situates the object in its context. *Grand Illusion*, for instance, begins with a close-up of a spinning record, followed in the same shot by camera movements which reveal the French officers' mess. Similarly, the "Danse macabre" sequence begins with a close-up of the keyboard of the player piano before the camera tracks backward and pans up to frame the little stage. In each case the camera movements immediately integrate the object isolated by the close-up into its environment, while at the same time emphasizing the continuity of the space, its "realistic" character—instead of breaking it up by editing shots together. We note the same technique at the beginning of *The Rule of the Game*, where the camera frames the mass of electrical wires in close-up before moving to reveal the radio reporter on the landing strip. The following sequence in Christine's boudoir creates a parallel with the first by virtue of the close-up of the radio tubes at the back of the radio, followed by a pan upwards to frame Christine and Lisette in deep focus. Renoir rarely utilizes close-ups simply to produce an emotional charge in his films, as is frequently done by other filmmakers.

STUDY GUIDE

Director's Comments

"My initial intention was to do a modernization of the *Caprices de Marianne*. It's the story of a tragic mistake: the man who is in love with Marianne is mistaken for another man and assassinated in an ambush. I won't go into the plot any further: I surrounded it with so many other elements that the story itself is reduced to a framework. One important element is the sentimental honesty of Christine, the heroine of the drama. The authors of films or books are generally men, so they tell men's stories. For my part, I like to describe women. Another important element is the purity of the victim Jurieu, who, in trying to become part of a world to which he does not belong, fails to respect the the rules of the game. During the shooting I was torn between my desire to create comedy on the one hand and to tell a tragic story on the other. The result of my ambivalence was the film such as it is" (*Ma Vie et mes films*, p. 155).

Questions put to Renoir:

"What exactly will *The Rules of the Game* be?"

"A precise description of the bourgeois people of our times. I want to demonstrate that for every game there are rules. If you don't follow the rules, you lose [...]."

"And what role will *you* play?"

"The role of a failure! I would have liked to become a musician, but I'm too lazy. So I settle for being a music critic. And I give advice to everyone, resulting in the worst problems and the most impossible complications" ("Jean Renoir, *La Règle du jeu*," pp. 276-277).

"In *The Rules of the Game* the milieu portrayed is extremely wealthy, extremely worldly; not a parvenu milieu but the good, authentic, old bourgeoisie.

The rules of the game are therefore particularly rigorous. Some people try to break loose occasionally. Perhaps our aviator [...] thought he could break the bonds by undertaking his big trek around the world? In reality, he didn't break anything at all. The flight turned him into a hero, but this hero is nonetheless still a member of the grand bourgeoisie.

Christine doesn't believe in the rules. She imagines that she can simply obey the dictates of her heart, remain a faithful spouse or take a lover, how and when she pleases. Big mistake. Romantic questions, or let's say more simply the relations between men and women, play a big role — you might even say a social role, — in our milieu, but they are likewise, and without fail, subject to the the rules of the game.

Christine's husband is, of course, a merciless adherent to these rules, and in his entourage all behavior [...] is subjected to an etiquette which is less apparent but just as rigorous as at the court of Louis XIV" (quoted by Gauteur, *Positif*, p. 37).

"In reality Christine doesn't say so, it isn't shown, and I didn't include any shots explaining this feeling, but I believe that this woman is being abruptly confronted with certain realities of life, realities she doesn't find particularly attractive. She's a woman who, although no longer young, is probably rather innocent, and that's why I found it interesting to have a Viennese woman in this romantic role. And suddenly this romanticism, pure love, eternal love, strolls hand in hand in the moonlight, all of that, suddenly, is replaced by a far more brutal reality, by the purely physical need to be pushed onto a couch and to make love, the love she sees in the eyes of this fellow, in the others, the people who are flirting with her [...]. The party at the castle — which I tried to make somewhat unreal — is a way into reality for Christine, and that immediately provokes a complete change in her conduct. Since life is like that, let's get to it. I'll make love with the first man who comes along. I don't love him, but I'll do it; since those are the rules, well, I'll just apply the rules, and even better than the others" (*Entretiens et propos*, p. 123).

"That's really too clear to be by chance [*the parallel between the death of the rabbit and Jurieu's death*]. It's obvious. I planned Jurieu's death all along — Jurieu was condemned to death before I began the film — but the idea of having him die exactly as he does came to me from the rabbit's death, which was filmed first. My original idea was that the whole hunt was a prelude to the death of Jurieu; Jurieu was innocent, and innocence couldn't survive in this milieu. It's a romantic but rotten world. We happen to be faced with two extremely innocent beings, Christine and Jurieu. One of them has to be sacrificed. If this milieu is to be preserved, we have to kill one of them; the world depends on sacrifices, so we have to kill people to appease the gods. This society is going to survive a few months more, until the war and even longer, and it's going to survive because Jurieu has been killed. Jurieu is the being we sacrificed on the alter of the gods to permit this life style to continue to exist" (*Entretiens et propos*, p. 125).

"You only really know what a film is after finishing the editing. From the very first projections of *The Rules of the Game*, I was assailed by doubts. It's a war film, and yet it doesn't contain a single reference to war. Beneath its benign appearance this film was attacking the very structure of our society. Nevertheless, at the beginning I didn't want to present the public with an avant-garde work, just a good, normal film. People came to the movies thinking they were going to be able to leave their worries behind. Instead I plunged them into their own problems. The imminence of war made everyone more thin-skinned. I gave them very nice, sympathetic characters but showed them a society falling apart. They were looking at people who were already beaten [...], and the spectators recognized them. If the truth were to be known, they recognized themselves. People who are committing suicide don't like to have witnesses" (*Ma Vie et mes films*, pp. 156-157).

"In *The Rules of the Game* I didn't intentionally make a film which would be difficult for the public to accept. On the contrary, I was persuaded that people would really like this story [...].

I was apparently wrong, since the spectators reacted to the film as if they were being lashed with a whip. If *The Rules of the Game* had been made into a romantic film, if I had given them people dissolving into tears, opening their hearts to the public [...], if I had resorted to the whole romantic arsenal, I am sure that the same story would have worked. But the classical style, which is a style in which you try to keep things inside rather then exteriorizing them, is apparently extremely difficult to understand for a public which, for a hundred years, has been submerged in romantic tears. Classicism is a difficult path, and I can assure you that I constantly take my lumps for it [...].

To achieve this classicism, I think we have to establish a distinction between internal and external realism. I can't avoid thinking of Molière: Molière never dealt with external realism. He called his characters Philinte, Orgon, and Cléante, instead of Dupont, Duran, and Dubois; he even put them in costumes which weren't realistic [...]. Nonetheless, Molière's plays are probably among the most realistic. A man like Chaplin never subordinated his work to external realism: Chaplin plays the role of a prospector, but he wears a little bowler hat, big shoes, and a cane, and he looks for gold in the snow. If he were realistic, he would have a fur coat and everything else he would need to fight the cold. Nonetheless, Mr. Chaplin, with his little bowler hat, seems more authentic to me than any ham actor wearing real prospector's garb. What do they look like? They look like crabs with their magnificent disguises; Chaplin on the other hand, with his big shoes and little hat, looks like a real prospector.

Personally I made a lot of films of the 'external realism' type. I tried humbly — perhaps not always successfully — to add internal realism to the mix. I must tell you that, basically, external realism has always been for me primarily a way to reach internal realism. It seems to me that if I were to tell the story of a laundress by placing this laundress in a real laundry, with a real iron, in a real laundress's outfit [...], perhaps, because of these external attributes, with these external tools, I might be able to understand this person more completely, from the inside.

But I believe that the giants — Chaplin, Shakespeare, Molière — don't need external realism; they don't need a real iron to reach the inner truth of the laundress.

Personally I'd really like to get away from external realism" (*Ecrits 1926-1971*, pp. 227-228).

Excerpts for Discussion

Excerpt 1 (1'40-4'50): The beginning of the film, at the airport and in Christine's boudoir (role of the radio, the public/private opposition).

Excerpt 2 (7'05-8'45): In Robert's room — the radio and the mechanical dolls (opposition of the modern and the old worlds).

Excerpt 3 (32'40-34'30): André Jurieu's arrival at the castle; the camera as an invisible guest (tracking around the column).

Excerpt 4 (37'35-39'40): The servants' meal (sequence shot — deep focus and camera movements). *See our commentary of this sequence in "'Reading' a Film," pp. 29-31**.

Excerpt 5 (47'45-49'10): The hunt; "fast" editing, killing.

Excerpt 6 (51'55-55'00): The spyglass scene — modernity, the theme of appearances, metaphorical allusion to the camera.

Excerpt 7 (1h00'20-01'30): The party — the hall and the stage, the real life-theater parallel (play-acting and love).

Excerpt 8 (1h02'35-04'50): The "Danse macabre" sequence; the theme of death.

Excerpt 9 (1h12'50-13'55): The mechanical organ scene.

Excerpt 10 (1h20'00-22'00): Schumacher tries to shoot Marceau; the mechanical organ goes awry (disorder).

Excerpt 11 (1h37'50-40'05): The greenhouse scene; the murder of Jurieu (appearances, mistaken identity, and tragedy).

Quotations for Comment

Jurieu: "I say to her publicly that she is unfaithful!"

* * *

Octave (to Jurieu): "When you're not in a plane, all you do is fall on your face [...]. She's a socialite, and her world has rules — very strict rules."

* * *

Octave (to Robert): "You understand, in this world there is an appalling fact: everyone has his reasons."

* * *

Robert: "Well, I think we should have a party, a big party in honor of Jurieu [...]. We'll all wear costumes and put on skits."

* * *

Robert: "Corneille! Put an end to this comedy!"
Corneille: "Which one, Sir?"

* * *

Christine: "For three years my life was based on a lie. I haven't been able to get this thought out of my mind ever since I saw them together, at the hunt, and suddenly understood."

Octave: "Listen, Christine, that's another thing about our times. We're living in a time when everyone lies: the pharmacists' advertisements, the governments, the radio, the cinema, the newspapers... So how can you expect us, simple individuals, not to lie too?"

* * *

Marceau (concerning Jurieu's death): "He rolled over like a rabbit."

* * *

Robert: "Gentlemen, it's a terrible accident and nothing else! My warden Schumacher thought he saw a poacher, and he shot at him, which is normal. By a whim of fate this error cost André Jurieu his life..."

Topics for Reflection

1. Describe the main characters of the film: Robert de La Chesnaye, Christine, André Jurieu, Octave, Schumacher, Lisette, Marceau.
2. Describe the relationships between the main characters.
3. Discuss the role of the radio at the beginning of the film.
4. Which parallels and oppositions structure *The Rules of the Game*?
5. Describe a sequence shot in this film that you consider particularly interesting.
6. Give an example of the use of deep focus photography.
7. Discuss the themes of "game" or "playing" (*jeu*) and of mistaken identity in *The Rules of the Game*. What are the "the rules of the game"?
8. Discuss the major metaphors in the film: the radio, games (and theater), the mechanical dolls and organ, the hunt, the spyglass, poaching, the storm (etc.?).
9. Discuss the mixing of theatrical genres in *The Rules of the Game*.
10. Discuss the death of André Jurieu. (What is it due to? Fate?)

CRITICAL DOSSIER

Jean Fayard — "What strange sickness…"

How can a talented man go so completely astray? […] You can only shake your head. You wonder, anxiously, what strange sickness could have suddenly befallen an intelligent and gifted man […]. I don't want to be overly cruel, but in all truth and with all the indulgence I can muster I can't find anything to say in defense of the accused. Or perhaps one might plead irresponsibility (*Candide*, July 12, 1939)!

Fauteuil 22 — "Neither intelligence nor talent"

As bungling goes, this is as bad as it gets. It would be difficult to find anywhere else such an accumulation of nonsense and bad taste […]. I can't find the slightest explanation or excuse for this base attempt to stir up prejudice. Mr. Jean Renoir behaves here as if he had neither intelligence nor talent (*La Croix*, July 16-17, 1939).

Marcel Pierre — Mixing genres

In my opinion, what is new in Renoir's film is the proof that heretofore separated styles may in fact coexist. Renoir has shown that the "human comedy" does not enclose its various episodes in well-defined genres. In life the burlesque combines with the tragic, the farcical with the heroic. To its great credit, *The Rules of the Game* succeeds in effecting this synthesis of theatrical styles that we assumed was irreconcilable (*Bordeaux-Ciné*, July 28, 1939).

Nino Frank — "Perhaps a date in the history of cinema…"

The Rules of the Game is the very type of film which is difficult to describe in fifty lines, but about which one could easily write several long articles. It's a film of such richness, and so disconcerting, that you can't understand its character and dimensions with one viewing; you even risk completely missing its importance.

What impression does it make on the spectator who is seeing it for the first time? That it is a rich work, even too rich, too complex and deeply intelligent from beginning to end — but that this very wealth, this pure humanity, this abundance of intentions have taken the author too far, and he hasn't succeeded in mastering entirely the magnificent material he's invented. You may compare *The Rules of the Game* to one of these capricious rivers, with numerous turns and slack expanses, which seem to offer the very image of nature's disorder.

Well! Let's hold on to this comparison: in the end we have to recognize that the disorder of nature is really a little more intelligent that our paltry critical sense, and that in the final analysis this disorder is an order which comes from a superior mind… That's how we are led to revise our hasty evaluation of a work like this and to consider a certain number of things: that *The Rules of the Game* just might be a date in the history of cinema […]; that it is unquestionably the most important film that Renoir has made, and that people will still be talking about it in ten years; that here for the first time is a film which isn't just "cinema," but life in its purest form, with its mixture of muddles and mayhem, of the ridiculous and the profoundly serious;

that we finally discover in a film not the artificial rhythms of pulp literature but the sweeping, powerful, and apparently disorderly rhythm of great novels... But then again perhaps this is all just conjecture, and *The Rules of the Game* is a bad film. We won't know for a few weeks or perhaps a few years (*Pour Vous*, July 12, 1939).

Pierre Leprohon — "What game?"

We are faced with an "amusement," in the 18th-century sense, made clear by the very structure of the work, the parallelism of its double plot and even the music of Mozart which comes in at various moments behind this now tragic, now farcical ballet [...].

What is this form of amusement? "Just what game are we talking about?" writes Jean Prat in the filmographical entry devoted to this film [at the I.D.H.E.C. film school]. It's about life but about the life of a society which has begun to fall apart and which can only prolong its bored and useless existence by dint of an iron discipline and an absolute rule: falsehood. Lying in speech, lying in sentiment, lying in action, the suffocating of all spontaneity beneath a layer of frivolity and politeness. A fragile layer, however, ever at the mercy of an explosion of sincerity such as the one which becomes the subject of the film (*Jean Renoir*, p. 83).

Pierre Guislain — Masters and Servants

The excessive generosity which characterizes the head of the clan played by Dalio is emphasized in the following scenes, in which Renoir introduces a new main character (another one), the poacher Marceau, whose role is played by Carette [...]; he decides to hire the poacher and employ him as a servant in the castle. Lively, impertinent, enjoying the confidence of a master to whom he doesn't hesitate to speak his mind, Marceau fits perfectly the archetype of the valet, an essential character in classical comedy. With the entry of this Figaro the film's structure is now clearly modeled on the plays by Beaumarchais and Marivaux. Like these authors Renoir will proceed to describe two parallel micro-societies, the masters' society on the one hand, the valets' society on the other, which are the two sides of the same world. Like these authors, in describing the valets' society he reveals the foundations of the masters' society — either indirectly by analogy or directly by putting in the valet's mouth, as is done in comedies, truths that the master is constitutionally incapable of stating.

With the exception of Robert and Christine, all the aristocrats with high-sounding names invited to the castle behave exactly like these *nouveaux riches* or upstart bourgeois whose quirks, queer habits, and conversation they've adopted. In this small world where the principal activity is avoiding boredom, the women speak of diets (restricted to sea salt, for example), the men of the performance of their cars. In emphasizing the fading identity of this aristocracy which is being absorbed into the bourgeoisie, Renoir highlights, on the other hand, the authentic nobility (and by that very fact anachronistic) of the "foreigners" (a Jew, an Austrian) that the La Chesnaye couple represent. Resurfacing in the kitchens, around the table where the servants have taken their places, according to their rank, the debate about Robert's origin will permit Renoir to tackle head on the particularly virulent anti-Semitism of the period (*La Règle du jeu. Jean Renoir*, pp. 105-106).

André Bazin — Depth of Field

If only as a reminder, it is necessary to show why and how this dedication to realism, which goes beyond the contents of the image to include the very structures of the staging, led Renoir ten years before Orson Welles to the use of depth of field [...]: "The more I learn about my profession, the more I'm led to use deep focus in my approach to filming. The more I work, the more I move away from confrontations of two actors planted in front of the camera as in a photographer's studio. I find it more advantageous to situate my characters more freely, at different distances from the camera, and to have them move around. For that I need a great deal of depth of field..." This modestly technical explanation is only of course the immediate and practical consequence of the stylistic experimentation we have attempted to define. Depth of field in itself is nothing but the other dimension of this "lateral" liberty which Renoir needs. It's just that our commentary begins with what's on the screen, whereas Renoir's, at the other end of the creative process, is thinking first of his actors.

But clarity in deep focus evokes an additional aspect of research that is not necessarily implied by the lateral mobility related to the movements of the actors; it confirms the unity of the décor and the actor, the total interdependence of all reality, from the human to the mineral. In the representation of space it is a necessary modality of this realism which postulates a constant sensitivity to the world, but which opens onto a universe of analogies, metaphors, and, to use Baudelaire's word, in another no less poetic sense, correspondences ("Renoir français," pp. 28-29).

Pierre Leprohon — A Pure Work of the Cinema

The Rules of the Game is above all a pure work of the cinema, in the sense that it is conceived cinematographically, that it does not transpose a preexisting narrative. This is the source of the stylistic liberty, the lively rhythm, the tightly united audio-visual elements. Never has Renoir achieved such mastery in the organization of an action which juggles motifs, proceeds by jumps and bounds, by shocks, and by symbols, without a single false note throughout. The dialogue resists any dramatic or explicative intention. It is both realistic — by the authenticity of the futility of the ideas expressed — and symbolic — by what it reveals about the characters who express them. The virtually constant refusal to use close-ups or angle-reverse angle shots in favor of deep focus photography, the intelligence of the direct sound recordings and the music assuring with a studied ambiguity the double character of the film (realism and fantasy, humor and drama), the technical novelty, the formal subtlety supporting the thematic originality — all of these things explain the utter confusion of the public in 1939, as well as part of the critical community, and they still require today that we not judge such a complex work on a single viewing. It was of course ahead of its time; if it represents a turning point in Renoir's body of works, it is no less a turning point in the history of cinema. Modern cinema perhaps owes this film its most important discoveries (*Jean Renoir*, p. 85).

Pierre Guislain — The Spyglass

It's at the end of the long hunt sequence that we come to this pivotal scene called the spyglass scene, which will again cause the film to change directions dramatically. While observing with a spyglass some squirrels climbing around in the trees, Christine happens upon the touching goodbye of Robert and his mistress Geneviève. At this moment the character who appears the most sincere, naïve, authentically romantic, and therefore the most completely blind ("Romantic people are blind," says Renoir) begins abruptly to understand what is going on. But in this universe where everything has been long out of step, this new and decisive moment of truth comes, as one would expect, at the wrong time. The only one who is unaware of a love affair which has been going on for years, Christine discovers that her husband is unfaithful at the very moment that, out of love for her, he is in the process of leaving his mistress. Supreme paradox: in discovering the truth she only manages to plunge further into her misconceptions.

It is in putting her eye innocently to the spyglass handed to her by Octave/Renoir that Christine will finally meet reality, a reality she finds much more unattractive of course than the one she has always imagined. As we stated at the beginning of our text, this "marvelous instrument" which enables us to see beings from afar without frightening them, "spying on their personal life" (not only little wild animals but also, as we see, human beings), is remarkably similar to a camera. Much more than an allegory, this scene is a formidable cinema lesson [...]. The camera/spyglass appears here as an instrument which both reveals and obscures reality. Thanks to this instrument Christine indeed sees "something" (the goodbye kiss which Robert gives to Geneviève), but she is completely mistaken about its significance. And this is where the cinema lesson begins. Christine thinks she is (finally) seeing "an image which is just," as Godard would say, whereas what she actually saw was "just an image" and moreover a silent image. Unlike ourselves, the spectators, who have been following this breaking up scene since the beginning, who have known for a long time that it is going to happen, who have heard every word of the exchange which precedes this kiss, the young woman will inevitably misinterpret this admittedly ambiguous act (for the onlooker, nothing distinguishes a goodbye kiss from any other kiss!). What Renoir says is clear: no image, even the most realistic, the most documentary, can in itself tell the truth. You can even make an image, whatever it may be, say one thing and its opposite, its meaning being a function of the preceding and the succeeding images. That is of course the secret of film editing (*La Règle du jeu. Jean Renoir*, pp. 111-112).

Marcel Dalio — The Anti-Semitism of the Critics

Naturally my role gets special attention. In *Les Annales* "Interim" (what a courageous signature!) writes: "The choice of the actors aggravates even more the strangeness of this undertaking. Mr. Dalio plays the role of the marquis: to portray a little country nobleman, they go get the little Jewish officer in *Grand Illusion*!"

Here we go! But Bardèche and Brassillach, in *L'Action française*, express even better what some people are saying under their breath: "An astonishing Dalio, more Jewish than ever, both attractive and sordid, like a hunchback ibis in the middle of the swamp; he's a man from another planet, not just strange but foreign to these the rules of the game which, in all truth, are not his.

"Another odor rises from the depths of time, another race which doesn't hunt, which has no castles, for whom Sologne is nothing and which looks on. The queerness of the Jew has perhaps never been so forcefully, so brutally shown" (*Mes années folles*, pp. 132-133).

Alain Marty — An Ideological Viewpoint

In the France of the period just preceding the war, the major event was the Popular Front and its social and political consequences.

Through its struggles the workers' movement clearly made some important gains (the 40-hour week, with no reduction in salary, paid vacation, and salary increases, especially the lowest salaries...). But above all the new agreements put an end to the isolation of the workers by enabling them to improve their position vis-à-vis the owners.

The bourgeoisie later launched a counter-attack against the workers' movement to take away what it had won: the Vichy regime was the ultimate expression of this.

The intellectuals rallied massively to the Popular Front by proposing their services to the workers' organizations. Thus Renoir, and part of the crew that later made *The Rules of the Game*, produced *People of France* (*La Vie est à nous*, 1936), financed by the French Communist Party, and *La Marseillaise* (1938), which was financed by public contributions supported by democratic and workers' organizations [...].

Since the Popular Front only represented for these intellectuals the forces for change, its "failure" will signify for them the triumph of the old order. This ideological viewpoint alone permits us to understand the problematics, and it determines the choice of signs as well. The film presents us with a society divided into masters and servants: the servants in total subjection to their masters and the masters, the ruling class — half-aristocratic, half-bourgeois — confined to a sealed-off world whose sole activity is to entertain itself and to tend to its leisure activities. Only the middle classes (Jurieu, Octave, Marceau) are bearers of change, but this proves to be impossible. This pessimistic, static vision of reality that the film presents comes from a non-scientific understanding: class struggle does not exist (masters and servants live in harmony) [...].

As a cultural product this film will pass itself off as critical of [the ruling class]. But this criticism — and there is indeed criticism — is located inside the ruling ideology: far from representing a danger to the class in power, it reinforces its domination, since it maintains that nothing can be changed. The film lowers the political consciousness of the spectator in relation to class struggle and renders its criticism ineffectual by suggesting the futility of the struggle ("L'Analyse du film," pp. 26-28).

JEAN RENOIR'S FILMOGRAPHY
(PRINCIPAL FILMS)

1926	*Nana* (silent)
1928	*The Little Match Girl*
	(La Petite Marchande d'allumettes, silent),
	Sad Sack (Tire au flanc, silent).
1931	*Baby Gets a Laxative (On purge bébé)*
1931	*The Bitch (La Chienne)*
1932	*Boudu Saved from Drowning*
	(Boudu sauvé des eaux)
1933	*Madame Bovary*
1934	*Toni*
1935	*Le Crime de Monsieur Lange*
1936	*A Day in the Country*
	(Partie de campagne, edited and shown in 1946)
1936	*The Lower Depths (Les Bas-fonds),*
	People of France (La Vie est à nous)
1937	*La Grande Illusion*
1938	*The Human Beast (La Bête humaine),*
	La Marseillaise
1939	*Rules of the Game (La Règle du jeu)*
1941	*Swamp Water (L'Etang tragique,* USA)
1945	*The Southerner (L'Homme du Sud,* USA)
1946	*Diary of a Chambermaid*
	(Le Journal d'une femme de chambre, USA)
1950	*The River (Le Fleuve,* India)
1952	*The Golden Coach (Le Carrosse d'or,* Italy)
1954	*French Cancan*
1956	*Elena and Her Men (Elena et les hommes)*
1959	*Picnic on the Grass (Le Déjeuner sur l'herbe)*
1962	*Elusive Corporal (Le Caporal épinglé)*
1969	*The Little Theater of Jean Renoir*
	(Le Petit Théâtre de Jean Renoir)

WORKS CONSULTED

Bazin, André. "Renoir français." *Cahiers du cinéma* 8 (Jan. 1952): 9-29.

.........*Jean Renoir*. Paris: Gérard Lebovici, 1989.

.........*Qu'est-ce que le cinéma?* Paris: Cerf, 1985.

Braudy, Leo. *Jean Renoir: The World of His Films*. New York: Doubleday, 1972.

Brunelin, André G. "Histoire d'une malediction." *Cinéma 60* 43 (Feb. 1960): 36 -64.

Dalio, Marcel. *Mes années folles*. Paris: J.-C. Lattès, 1976.

Durgnat, Raymond. *Jean Renoir*. Los Angeles: U of California P, 1974.

Esnault, Philippe. "Le Jeu de la vérité." *L'Avant-Scène Cinéma* 52 (Oct. 1965): 7-15.

Faulkner, Christopher. *The Social Cinema of Jean Renoir*. Princeton, N.J., Princeton UP, 1986.

Gauteur, Claude. "*La Règle du jeu* et la critique en 1939." *La Revue du cinéma* 282 (March 1974): 49-73.

........."Jean Renoir. *La Règle du jeu*." *Positif* 257-258 (July-Aug. 1982): 35-50.

Guislain, Pierre. *La Règle du jeu. Jean Renoir*. Paris: Hatier, 1990.

"Jean Renoir, *La Règle du jeu*." *Premier Plan* 22-24, Special Issue (May1962): 274-293.

Leprohon, Pierre. *Jean Renoir*. Paris: Seghers, 1967.

Marty, Alain. "L'Analyse du film." *La Revue du cinéma. Image et Son* 266 (Dec. 1972): 3-28.

Renoir, Jean. *Ecrits 1926-1971*. Paris: Pierre Belfond, 1974.

.........*Entretiens et propos*. Paris: Editions de l'Etoile, Cahiers du cinéma, 1979.

.........*La Règle du jeu* (screenplay). *L'Avant-Scène Cinéma* 52 (1965).

.........*Ma Vie et mes films*. Paris: Flammarion, 1974.

Rivette, Jacques et François Truffaut, "Entretien avec Jean Renoir." *Cahiers du cinéma* 34 (April 1954): 3-22.

Roy, Jean. "La Règle du jeu à la television." *Cinéma 78* (April 1978): 33-46.

Sesonske, Alexander. *Jean Renoir: The French Films (1924-1939)*. Cambridge, MA: Harvard UP, 1980.

Vanoye, Francis. *La Règle du jeu*. Paris: Nathan, 1989.

Marcel Carné

Daybreak
Le Jour se lève

(1939)

Marcel Carné, *Daybreak*: François (Jean Gabin) and Valentin (Jules Berry)
argue over Clara (Arletty). Courtesy of Collection André Heinrich

Director .... Marcel Carné
Screenplay .... Jacques Viot
Adaptation and Dialogues .... Jacques Prévert
Director of Photography .... Curt Courant,
assisted by Philippe Agostini
Music .... Maurice Jaubert
Film Editor .... René Le Henaff
Sound .... Armand Petitjean
Art Director .... Alexandre Trauner
Costumes .... Boris Bilinsky
Script Girl (Continuity) .... Jeanne Witta
Producers .... SIGMA
Length .... 1 h 29

Cast

Jean Gabin (*François*), Jacqueline Laurent (*Françoise*), Arletty (*Clara*), Jules Berry (*Valentin*), Mady Berry (*concierge*), René Genin (*concierge*), Bernard Blier (*Gaston*), Marcel Péres (*Paulo*), Jacques Baumer (*the Chief of Police*), René Bergeron (*the café owner*), Gabrielle Fontan (*the woman in the stairway*), Arthur Devère (*Monsieur Gerbois*), Georges Douking (*the blind man*).

STORY

Daybreak begins at the end of the story. During a violent quarrel in a hotel room François shoots Monsieur Valentin, who staggers out of the room and dies as he tumbles down the stairs. When the police arrive, François fires at them through the closed door. We don't enter the room and join the troublemaker until the police have retreated and taken cover. The police rapidly surround the building, question the inhabitants, and then begin to fire shots through the window of the room. Trapped in this room, on the top floor of this six-story hotel, without the slightest hope of escaping, François takes refuge in his memories. During the ensuing night, after preventing the police from getting into his room by blocking the door with a heavy wardrobe closet, he chain-smokes as he recalls the principal events which have lead to this tragic set of circumstances.

François is a worker in a metallurgy factory in the Amiens suburbs. He falls in love with Françoise, a pretty little florist who had grown up, like him, in a public orphanage. He wants to marry her, but she demurs. The same evening that he makes his proposal, he follows her to a cabaret where she has gone to meet Valentin, a much older man who performs an act with trained dogs. At the bar François meets Clara, Valentin's assistant and former mistress. Disgusted with his treatment of her, she has abruptly resigned and left him after a three-year love affair. When her former lover takes her to task after his performance, François comes to her defense, thus making an enemy of Valentin. Terribly disappointed to discover the affair between Françoise and Valentin, François becomes Clara's lover while continuing to see Françoise.

After several months, during which François refuses to move in with his mistress Clara, Valentin shows up to quarrel with François about the worker's continuing relationship with Françoise. During their conversation in a café Valentin informs François that he is Françoise's father, a status which gives him certain "rights." Françoise later flatly denies that Valentin is her father, explaining that he is just someone who enjoys lying. François gets back together with Françoise, who gives him a brooch she had been wearing, as a token of her love. When François informs Clara of his intention to break off their affair, she spitefully shows him that she has the same brooch as Françoise. Valentin has the habit of offering one to each woman he sleeps with...

Back in his room in the present François cries out in rage and despair and rejects the appeals from a crowd of friends gathered beneath his window in the fear that he might jump. He doesn't even see Françoise, who calls out his name and collapses in the street. Clara has her brought to her hotel room, where she watches over her.

As dawn begins to break François retreats once again into his memories, recalling Valentin's arrival in his room ostensibly to continue their argument over

François's romance with Françoise. In fact he has come to taunt François, provoking him with offensive comments about his worker's status and making crude allusions to his seduction of Françoise. Outraged, François grabs a revolver which Valentin has placed on the table and shoots him in the stomach. This incident brings us back to the murder at the beginning of the film and thus to the present, where the action will continue to the end.

In Clara's room Françoise becomes delirious, speaking incoherently of the love she shares with François. Policemen on the roof of the worker's hotel crawl toward his window with teargas canisters. François commits suicide by shooting himself in the heart just before one of the policemen tosses a canister through the window. The hero's alarm clock rings while the teargas fills the room. Dawn breaks…

CRITICAL RECEPTION

Daybreak came out at the Madeleine Cinema in Paris on June 17, 1939. While the film was "recognized immediately as a masterpiece by the most knowledgeable of its spectators" (Pérez, p. 65), it nonetheless provoked very diverse and rather ambivalent reactions from many. René Lehmann, for example, praised "the mastery of the découpage," "the beauty of the images," and "the quality of the dialogue" of this "extremely appealing and impressive film," but cautioned that the spectator "may not appreciate its content" (*L'Intransigeant*, 1939). Georges Altman, who admires this "consummate, intransigent work of art," nonetheless emphasized its unattractive side: "The grind, the soulless life, the wilted love, the leaden skies, the suffocating atmosphere of the cities, and the modern distress all give this film a character which makes it understandably difficult to digest" (*La Lumière*, 1939).

From a strictly commercial viewpoint, Carné certainly chose the wrong time to bring out such a dark film. Despite the prestige he still enjoyed from the resounding success of the no less pessimistic *Port of Shadows* (*Quai des brumes*) the year before, the Nazi threat which weighed heavily on France at the time was hardly favorable to his new film. He is the first to recognize it: "*Daybreak* […] didn't come at a very good time, since most filmgoers were looking for cheerfulness and an escape from the danger looming on the horizon. So the lines were not very long at the *Madeleine Cinéma*, which was featuring a film full of melancholy and death" (*La Vie à belles dents*, p. 108).

Moreover, Carné felt that the style of his film "troubled and disturbed" the contemporary spectators both by its unusual temporal structure and by "the rather novel manner of acting" developed in the film (p. 108). Convinced that the film's lack of success was due to the confusing flashbacks, the producers insisted on adding, unbeknownst to Carné, an introductory title: *This film is the story of a man who is locked in his room and reflects on his past…* . To facilitate the spectators' understanding yet further, they added a whispered voice-over from Gabin when he first drifts into his memories, *"Yet, only yesterday, remember…"*.

In any case the film was withdrawn after a short run, at the beginning of the "phony war" in September. Banned by the military authorities as "demoralizing," along with Renoir's *Rules of the Game* (*La Règle du jeu*, 1939), *Daybreak* enjoyed considerable success abroad—in the United States, in Great Britain, and in Sweden, among other countries. Only after the Liberation, however, did Carné's film gain wide recognition as a masterpiece of the cinema. This turnabout was largely the work of André Bazin, the future founder and editor-in-chief of the *Cahiers du cinéma*, who made the film his favorite subject for presentations in film clubs all over France at the end of the forties (see the *Critical Dossier*). The great film historian Jean Mitry supported Bazin's assessment of Carné's film, declaring: "*Daybreak* is a masterpiece. The French—indeed, European—masterpiece of poetic realism […]. From a strictly formal point of view, *Daybreak* is at the top of the French cinema of the thirties" (p. 342). The contemporary filmmaker Claude Sautet gives a good idea of the fascination this film exercised when it came out again after the war: "From *Citizen Kane* to Renoir's masterpieces, many films astounded me with their power, their mastery, and their modernity, but at that time there was only one that I saw seventeen times in one month: *Daybreak*" (p. 126).

BEFORE *DAYBREAK*

Born in 1909, Marcel Carné made his first film, *Nogent, Eldorado du dimanche*, when he was 20. Composed of a series of vignettes showing Parisians frolicking one Sunday on the shores of the Marne, this short documentary was well received by the critics. Already a prize-winning film critic, Carné was hired by the weekly *Cinémagazine*, eventually becoming its editor-in-chief while writing regular columns for several other film magazines. At the same time he became an assistant to the famous filmmaker René Clair, as well as to Jacques Feyder, one of the originators of French "poetic realism." Carné served as Feyder's assistant on several films, including *Pension Mimosa* (1935). The realistic scenery and the "naturalistic" subject of this film—common people, hoodlums, tragic destiny — had a lasting impact on Carné's style of filmmaking.

In 1936 Carné began a long and fruitful collaboration with the poet-screenwriter Jacques Prévert. Together they made Carné's first feature film, *Jenny*, a melodrama which takes place, as would often be the case in the Carné-Prévert collaboration, in a shady lower-class locale—in this case a seedy nightclub, half gambling den, half bordello. The following year Carné and his screenwriter shot a dramatic comedy, both wacky and serious, titled *Bizarre, Bizarre* (*Drôle de drame*), before striking it rich with *Port of Shadows* in 1938. *Port of Shadows,* the tandem's first masterpiece and first big success, was awarded the Prix Louis Delluc, the Grand Prix National du Cinéma Français, the Prix Méliès and, in the United States, the award for the Best Foreign Film. The sordid, tragic climate, the populism, the victims, the abject characters, and the profound pessimism of the film created the Carné-Prévert image and the major example of "poetic realism" (or of "film noir") in France. (Some public figures deplored the demoralizing character of the film and went so far as to declare, after the defeat of 1940, "It's the fault of *Port of Shadows* that we lost the war!")

Carné applied the same formula a second time that year in *Hôtel du Nord*, without Prévert and with notably less success, but the collaboration with Prévert reached its point of perfection the following year in *Daybreak*. Carné and Prévert continued to work together during the Occupation, making the wildly successful *The Devil's Envoys* (*Les Visiteurs du soir*, 1942), a medieval fable with Arletty in the starring role. They also produced in this period their most famous work, *Children of Paradise*

(*Les Enfants du paradis*), appearing during the final battles of the Libération in 1945. The following year they made their last film together, *Gates of the Night* (*Les Portes de la nuit*), which met little success.

ORIGIN, CAST, AND SHOOTING OF *DAYBREAK*

As Carné recounts in his memoirs, the idea of *Daybreak* came from Jacques Viot, his neighbor in Paris, whom he only knew from his reputation as an "adventurer" and as an art connoisseur. One day Viot brought him to read a short synopsis which hit him like a "bolt of lightning." Carné was fascinated by a story which began at the end and then proceeded through a series of flashbacks, a rather unusual idea for the period. After persuading Jacques Prévert and the producer that the project was worthwhile, he managed to interest Jean Gabin in the main role. Gabin's participation was essential to the project. He had starred in *Port of Shadows* and was the most succesful male actor in French cinema in the thirties (as Jean-Paul Belmondo would be in the sixties). Carné's favorite actress, Arletty, one of the most popular actresses of the period, was cast in the role of Clara, while Jules Berry, famous for his portrayal of scoundrels, played the vile Valentin. The principal cast was completed by Jacqueline Laurent, a young inexperienced actress who was given the role of Françoise at the request of Prévert (who apparently had a crush on her). If we are to believe Carné, Prévert wrote the role with her in mind. Viot and Prévert shared the writing of the film, Viot concentrating on the screenplay, Prévert on the dialogue.

The film was shot in February and March, 1939, at the Billancourt studios in Paris, in scenery designed and built entirely in the studio by Alexandre Trauner. After Prévert, Trauner was Carné's most important collaborator. Henri Agel has remarked in fact that "Trauner and Carné are inextricably linked" (p. 174). With the concern for realistic detail which characterizes all of Carné's films, both the square where François's hotel sits and the little street where Françoise's house is located were created from photographs of real buildings. While opinions differ regarding Carné's fanatic devotion to artificial scenery in certain films, this is not the case here, especially as regards François's hotel. As J. B. Brunius observes, "All you have to do is take a glance at the model or at a photo of Trauner's admirable set to see that Carné was right: no real building would have been so expressive or so true as this quintessential industrial suburb" (p. 6).

The room in which François barricades himself posed a particular problem. As Carné explained, he wanted "a completely closed set, to give the impression of a man walled up in the room where he was spending his last night, much like a condemned man in his cell" (p. 107). To achieve this effect the room had to have four walls, not the usual three partitions which allow the members of the crew to get in and out. The solution to this problem was, finally, for everyone to enter and leave the room by the ceiling, that is, by a ladder which was set against the electricians' catwalks hung above the set (see Carné's "Comments" in the "Study Guide").

The staging of *Daybreak* is characterized by the extreme rigor for which Carné has become famous. Nothing is left to chance in the composition of the shots, whose beauty and formal perfection are recognized by everyone. It is well known, for instance, that Carné spent five hours, a whole afternoon, perfecting the scene in which Gabin, trailed by the camera, leaves the window, picks up the teddy bear on the floor, and returns to the window. As for the scene of Valentin's murder, he spent an entire afternoon just rehearsing it before spending two days shooting it. "This whole scene," observes Jean Quéval, "from the arrival of the cabaret performer to the pistol shot, is one of the best ever written for the cinema, and it wasn't written until the last moment [...]. On the screen it creates an unbearable tension and cruelty, and it 'works' magnificently in spite of its verbal mass, owing to the consummate acting [and] to the discrete transcendence of the staging" (pp. 39-40).

THEMES AND SYMBOLISM

Daybreak is an ill-fated love story, of course, but especially a "tragedy of purity and solitude," as André Bazin remarks in the most famous study of Carné's film, which was written shortly after the Liberation (1948) during a round of talks at film clubs and factories. Bazin's brilliant analysis is required reading, and all contemporary studies of *Daybreak*, including the present commentary, are heavily indebted to it (see the excerpts in the *Critical Dossier*). The tragic theme dominates *Daybreak* from the very first shots in which we see a blind man walk up the stairs. This briefly glimpsed character clearly embodies destiny in the film, a theme which recalls the fatality of Greek tragedy and in particular *Oedipus Rex*, where the blindness of the hero, and his anger, produce the act which seals his fate. François's angry act, the pistol shot at the beginning of the film, functions in much the same manner in Carné's film. The rest of the film only serves to show the set of circumstances which lead the hero inexorably to the murder.

If Bazin considers this story a tragedy of "purity," it is because purity is what François thought he had found in Françoise before learning that she had been seduced, sullied, by Valentin. François had seen in Françoise an unexpected chance to achieve happiness and transcend a dreary grinding existence, and he cannot bear the thought of her fall from grace. We see here a constant theme in Carné's films: the impossibility of achieving happiness in a sordid world.

When François murders Valentin, his act is a lightly veiled suicide; with Françoise corrupted, all hope lost, the worker has lost his will to live. He screams his despair to the crowd gathered in the square in front of the hotel, a crowd which may suggest the choir of Greek tragedy: "In the scène where François stands in his window and shouts at the crowd, Prévert injected a familiar lyricism into the tragic character of *Daybreak*. We see here a clever adaptation of the dialogues between the hero and the choir in ancient tragedy" (Damas and Tournier, p. 43). As for Clara, she is too jaded, too "compromised" by life to satisfy the hero's thirst for purity. As we often see in the films that Carné makes with Prévert, the tragic theme is accompanied by a clear opposition between good and evil. The screenwriter's vision of the world is deeply Manichean. Landry states bluntly, "Prévert's films are melodramas which confront faultless heroes with virtueless villains" (p. 104). Opposed to the innocent François, Jules Berry's character is clearly "diabolical," an incarnation of Evil — and Carné connoisseurs know that the same actor will play the Devil himself in Carné's next film, *The Devil's Envoys*.

The theme of destiny is related as well to the social thematics of the film. Having been raised in a public orphanage, both François and Françoise are marked by a sort of curse. Abandoned by their parents, unloved, they are destined for misfortune. To this "original curse" is added, for François at least, his social class. As a sandblaster in a factory, François is sentenced to death by a job which is gradually ruining his lungs. Social injustice is one of Prévert's favorite themes, and the hero of *Daybreak* is clearly a victim of the injustice that society reserves for members of his class. As for Françoise, starved for affection since her infancy, living on clichéd images of happiness and dreams of escape, she easily falls prey to Valentin's smooth line, his worldly and unscrupulous charm.

The set for Carné's film, created by the superbly talented Trauner, plays a fundamental role on the thematic level — realizing one of Bazin's ideals according to which "cinema should treat the decor like an actor in the story" (p. 61, note 1). The general framework of the action, the workers' suburb, produces from the outset a disquieting atmosphere which "weighs heavily, with its troubling obscurity, on the backs of the inhabitants" (Landry, p. 69). The building itself towers over the other houses on the square. It stands out against the sky and strikes the spectator's imagination with the suggestion that it will be the theater of dramatic events. The decor of the rooms, for its part, helps to establish the character and tastes of the protagonists, like the soccer ball and bicycle parts in François's room or the postcards in Françoise's.

The decor, moreover, reflects some of the main themes of the film. Most of the objects surrounding François, which are sometimes called "signifying objects" in the language of cinema, clearly symbolize aspects of his love for Françoise and thus serve both to explain his behavior in the room and to motivate the flashbacks. We are especially struck in this realm by the perfect unity of the literal and figurative levels of the film, which prompts Bazin to note the "unique synthesis between symbolism and realism. "Nothing," he adds, "not a single object or character which doesn't signify more than it is, but not a single one which is anything but itself" (p. 74). Certain objects like the little teddy bear and the brooch suggest clearly, for both François and the spectator, essential moments in the hero's past. The first recalls his love for Françoise, the second her sullying by Valentin. Others have a more subtle signifying function, like the cigarettes which, in addition to their realistic side, come to represent metaphorically the very consumption of the life of the hero. Lacking matches, he lights each cigarette from the preceding one; as long as his cigarette doesn't go out, he will continue to live. As soon as his cigarette goes out, we understand that it is the end; François's life will soon "go out" as well.

Like the act of smoking, when François pushes the heavy armoire against the door, his action has both a realistic explanation and a symbolic meaning. While he is fortifying the door against the attack by the police, he is also "entombing" himself. The mirror, a common object in any room, first suggests a confrontation between François and himself (his memories), before becoming a foreshadowing of his suicide when he shatters it. The alarm clock, finally, a no less common object in a bedroom, figures the irony which surrounds the death of the hero. Not only does it ring immediately *after* the death of François, who will awaken no longer, but it also emphasizes the fact that the hero himself brings about his tragic end: "Isn't it *Gabin himself* who was rewinding his alarm clock when Berry came into the room, he himself who was thus innocently setting the hour of his death" (Bazin, quoted in Chazal, p. 148)!

STRUCTURE, STYLE, MUSIC

Commentators have often noted the "classicism" of Carné's film, which seems to respect the famous "rule of the three unities" best illustrated by Racine's tragedies: the unities of time, place, and action (Landry, pp. 61-75). If we ignore the time and places of François's flashbacks, all of the action in *Daybreak* takes place in less than 24 hours (from nightfall to dawn), in a single place (the hero's room, the building, and the square where it is located), and has one main plot (François's tragedy). Whatever the validity of this analogy, the perfect unity of the film — characters, décor, dialogue, music — is undeniable. The dramatic intensification, the "desire to concentrate the action to the utmost " (Landry, p. 63), which is moreover the principal goal of classical theater esthetics, is no less evident in this film. In both the present and the past, the action leads inexorably to François's tragic end, which is inscribed in the opening shots.

The structure is based on the rigorous alternation of four major sequences in the present and three flashbacks, each introduced by the highly charged objects mentioned above: the teddy bear and the brooch, but also the postcards and the photos of Françoise. While it is true that Carné did not invent the flashback, no filmmaker before him had used the technique to such an extent. As Brunius says, "Never before *Daybreak* had this narrative technique been so intimately and dramatically integrated into a narrative in the present, to such a point that it is almost impossible to imagine the film organized in any other way, chronologically for example. Never before had the cinema so completely fulfilled its manifest destiny, which was to become the most faithful mirror possible of our mental activity" (p. 6).

To distinguish between the shot changes in the present and the transitions from the present to the past, Carné established a simple binary code. When he wishes to convey a change of place within a sequence in the present (as when the action moves from François's room to the square outside), he uses rapid "wipes," that is, vertical lines which sweep across the screen, the new shot "wiping off" the previous one. To make the transition from present to past, when the hero drifts off into his memories (or when he returns from them), he invariably employs unusually long dissolves accompanied by music effects, "as if the surrounding reality just faded into reverie" (Mitry, p. 343). Carné's camera moves are rigorously calculated, whether it be the slow tracking shots toward the hero's face to bring us into contact with his inner drama or the minutely measured and timed pans and trackings which dog him as he moves about the room.

We cannot conclude this introduction without speaking of the music, the last film music composed by Maurice Jaubert, "perhaps the greatest film music composer up to our time" (Bazin, p. 56). The music of *Daybreak* is not reduced to a form of redundancy, to simple paraphrase, as is often the case in film music. It contributes significantly to the meaning of the film, only coming into play "when it adds something to the psychology or the action" (p. 57). It includes two principal themes, a sentimental theme carried by the flute and the oboe and a heavy, oppressive theme rendered by the bass parts and the percussion instruments. These two themes, which we virtually only hear in the present, bring us into contact with the inner life of the hero, with the poignant emotions that he experiences trapped in his room and brooding over his past. When the music stops in the present, it is nearly always the result of a violent incident, like a hail of bullets which jolt the hero out of his reflections. There is occasional "diegetical" music in François's memories (music which is part of the action itself, like the cabaret music), but the general absence of music in the past helps to emphasize the distinction between scenes in the past and in the present. At the end of the film — perhaps as a concession to the public — music bursts forth triumphantly, "as if, the soul of the hero finally being liberated, this musical double emanating from him was unfurling into the serenity of death" (Bazin, p. 57)

STUDY GUIDE

Director's Comments

"The atmosphere and the characters are more important to me than the plot. An interesting story isn't worth much if the characters are conventional" (interview with Chazal, p. 98).

"The only thing that I respect scrupulously is the dialogue. That's why I won't let the actors change it during the shooting" (Chazal, p. 100).

"There isn't only the artistic climate, there's the social climate too. *Daybreak* was only conceivable, for instance, in a period when people had just became aware of a kind of workers' solidarity [...].

So I've never made "committed" films, but often films influenced by the social context. This is frequently the case for many filmmakers and is clearly one of the missions of cinema — provided that one never forgets that the transposition is such that a film can only ever give an impression and not an exact representation" (Chazal, pp. 99-100).

"I'm not a pessimist. I'm not a fanatic of 'film noir,' but the films one makes are always to some extent a reflection of the times. The period just before the war wasn't a particularly optimistic period. A world was going to collapse, and people were vaguely conscious of it" (Chazal, p. 28).

"A few days before the film opened I had organized a showing for Jacques [Prévert], Trauner, Gabin, and Viot. At the end the first two left after a few vague comments. As for Gabin, he said to me rather haughtily, "It's not as good as *Port of Shadows*." I answered in the same manner, "You're wrong. It's better than *Port*. In any case it's a film which won't get old so fast." The next day I received a very long letter from Viot. His thoughts on the film can be summarized in a few words underlined at the end: 'What a miserable failure!' [...]" (Carné, *La Vie à belles dents*, p. 108).

"As for me, there's something I've always regretted about this film. In the last scene between Gabin and Berry, when Berry throws the revolver on the table, his intention isn't clear enough. He does it on purpose because he has nothing left to live for and wants to be killed by his rival. He knows that Gabin will be caught, will go to prison, and will lose Françoise. I can see that there is a shot missing which would have made the scene clearer" (Carné, p. 190).

"...As a rule the décor of a room is composed of three partitions representing its three walls. If it turns out, as is sometimes the case, that a fourth partition is indispensable for a reverse-angle shot, it is mobile. This creates access to the room for the actors, technicians, and other necessary workers, as well as the electrical equipment and the camera. Well, I wanted a completely closed set, to give the impression of a man walled up in the room where he was spending his last night, much like a condemned man in his cell" (p. 107). I had to show him walking back and forth from the door to the window and from the bed to the dresser in front of it in a completely closed decor, so that the camera would reveal the four walls in the same movement.

At the beginning this didn't cause many problems. All the crew members had to do was move with the camera, staying constantly behind it or lying on the floor when it panned on the mirror on the mantelpiece. When the scene was over they got out of the room through the window or the door. It was another story when we began to shoot at the door with real bullets. The window was the first to go; it was impossible to get out that way with the windowpanes half broken, holding together miraculously. Then the door went, after the police sprayed it with bullets to shoot out the lock. The panel and the frame were completely broken up, the lock half torn off, so it was now impossible for the crew to get out that way either.

When I think of the scene of the fusillade, I'm amazed at my recklessness... In order to take a close-up of the lock as it was being hit by the bullets, the camera was placed less than a meter from it, inside the room, with the police shooting from the other side. We were only protected from the bullets by a few sacks of sand piled up about three feet high. Behind the door the noise of the fusillade was so loud that one of the assistants was half deaf for a week afterwards! From this moment on, not being able to use either the door or the window, we found ourselves in a certain sense prisoners in the scenery. That's when we got the idea of exiting by the ceiling. From the catwalks above the studio, which the electricians used to do their work, we went down a ladder onto the set. We all got a kick out of doing this, except for Gabin who complained on principle..." (Carné, pp. 106-107).

Excerpts for Discussion

Excerpt 1 (6'30-7'45): François goes back into his room; the objects (the teddy bear, the mirror, the brooch, the new tie, etc.); the first wipe (new sequence in the present).

Excerpt 2 (10'00-13'40): François's first cigarette, gun shots, music; the first lengthy dissolve.

Excerpt 3 (35'10-36'50): François and Clara at the cabaret bar, visual and sound dissolve, the return of the music in the room.

Excerpt 4 (39'35-41'25): The cigarette butt, gunshots by the police, the heavy wardrobe, the photos of Françoise.

Excerpt 5 (1h07'00-10'15): Clara shows the brooches to François, extremely long dissolve on Clara's face; François throws the brooch and breaks the mirror with the chair.

Excerpt 6 (1h19'55-23'00): Valentin provokes François, the murder, the cigarette goes out.

Excerpt 7 (1h26'00-29'10): The dénouement (suicide of François); role of the music.

Quotations for Comment

Françoise: "… I have no parents."

François: "You're an orphan?"

Françoise: "No, I was in a public children's home."

François: "I'll be darned!… I was in a public home too! That's funny. We're from the same family, since we don't…have any family. And in addition, today is our Saint's Day, both of us."

* * *

Françoise: "You shouldn't smoke; it makes you cough."

François: "It's not the smoke… it's the sand."

* * *

Françoise: "Why are you laughing?… The Riviera is beautiful, you know…"

François: "Have you been there?"

Françoise: "No… but I heard about it, so I know a little about it… There are big red rocks and the sea… the sea with casinos all around […]. The sun is always shining there… and there are flowers, even in winter… mimosas."

François: "[…] The Riviera…mimosas, that's just a bunch of dreams…music."

Françoise: "Perhaps, but there are days when it's so sad here…"

* * *

François: "So what does he want, this guy? What's he looking for?… And you, what are you doing with him? Why do you keep on seeing him?…

Françoise: "[…] He's always been nice to me. He's the only person, before you, who has ever been nice to me. Each time he comes back, he brings me something. He writes to me…"

François: "Oh, yeh, the postcards…"

* * *

Clara: "And what a smooth talker he is, that guy… He has a way of moving his hands when he talks… His sweet talk, you'd think it comes out of his sleeves… He can tell any story and you'd think it's true… The Riveria, for example, all he has to do is talk about it and you think you're there, up to your neck. That's how he got me, with mimosas".

François: "Mimosas?"

* * *

François: "[…] You'll see how happy we're going to be. I haven't been very happy, you know. But I was all alone […] And everything else. Unemployment, or problems with the job. Boy, have I had jobs, never the same ones, always the same […]. I just floated along… It was pretty bad […]. But now that you are with me, all that's going to change."

* * *

François: "I'd like you to have good thoughts of me, because, you know, I won't forget you."

Clara: "If I could forget *you*, I'd forget you right away, let me tell you. Good thoughts, good memories... Do I look like someone who likes to make love with memories? [...] O.K., I'm going to give you a souvenir, a gift, to remind you of me... (She shows him a brooch.) Valentin gave it to me... You're shocked? He has a whole stock of them [...] Look at it, it's really pretty... He gives one to every woman who sleeps with him. She has one too, your little honey, right?"

* * *

François (to the crowd): "Go on, beat it...get out of here...go! Leave me alone...since I'm all alone. I didn't ask anybody for anything. Leave me the hell alone. I'm tired, just plain tired! Washed up. It's over. I don't trust anyone anymore [...] François? Who's that, François? Don't know him... Don't know him! It's over, François doesn't exist anymore. No one does, no one, anywhere. Go away... Go away! Leave me alone... Leave me alone!"

* * *

Valentin: "Curious! I thought that manual laborers weren't the nervous type."

François: "Are you going to shut up?"

Valentin: "You're nervous because you're worried [...] because there are things you don't understand. Women are complicated, huh? Girls are mysterious..."

Valentin (pointing at the brooch): "Pretty trinket. Pretty gift to give a child!"

François: "What are you getting at?"

[...]

Valentin: "It's surprising the strange ideas simple people get about women... love... romance [...]. Sure she loves you. Ah! it's great to be loved. Women don't love me, but they're attracted to me... That's all that counts : attracting them! Well, since she found me attractive, you understand, the girl and I... what was stopping me? I like young women. Interested? You want to hear more?"

François: "You're going to shut your trap"! (He shoots Valentin.) "That's what you get!"

Valentin: "And what about you?"

© *L'Avant-Scène Cinéma*

Questions/Topics for Reflection

1. The metaphorical role of the blind man who discovers Valentin's body at the beginning of the film. His relationship to François's act (Valentin's murder).
2. François social class, life style, and character. In what sense is he a "tragic hero"?
3. What do François and Françoise have in common?
4. The representation of women in *Daybreak*: the opposition between Françoise and Clara.

a drama / film characterized by
exaggerated emotions, stereotyped characters, interpersonal
conflict

5. The Valentin character. Do you think that the following quotation applies to *Daybreak*? "Prévert's films are melodramas which confront faultless heroes with virtueless villains" (B.-J. Landry).

6. The role of the following "signifying objects": Françoise's flowers (at her first meeting with François), the teddy bear, the brooch, the mirror, the cigarettes, the wardrobe, the alarm clock.

7. The importance of the greenhouse scene.

8. The temporal structure of the film.

9. What technical means does Carné use to distinguish between scenes in the present and those in the past?

10. The role of music in this film and the particular role of the principal instruments. In general, when does background music (non-diegetical) accompany the action, in relation to the temporal organization of the film?

CRITICAL DOSSIER

Claude Sautet — "An apogee ... and thus an end"

A year ago I saw *Daybreak* again, with the usual fear of being disappointed. Had the mirage disappeared? Wasn't it just a case of juvenile fascination? No. The twilight effect was still there. Intact. At its zenith, in all the senses of the term: historical, political, and esthetic. An apogee ... and thus a culmination. And that's probably why this "perfect object" couldn't have imitators. The filmmakers who tried to emulate it all failed, while others simply rejected it as an outmoded artifact. Dead. A kind of over-conventional foil. Eternal polemics, understandable but irrelevant today.

I've always suffered from the public and the media infatuation with *Port of Shadows* and *Children of Paradise*, whereas *Daybreak*, always overshadowed, remains for me, by far, the finest accomplishment of the famous Carné-Prévert tandem […].

Fashions come and go, and *Daybreak* remains a masterpiece bathed in its obscure glory. So it goes ("*Le Jour se lève*," p. 126).

André Bazin — François and Purity

The purity of François and his need to believe in the purity of Françoise are going to turn against him. By her strange naïve duplicity Françoise will embody the negation of the unconditional hope that François has placed in her. Because the purity of Françoise — her native, virgin-like purity — is suddenly revealed to be ambiguous and complicit with the supreme impurity of Berry. The problem is not that Françoise has (perhaps) deceived François with Berry — if this were the case, François could reject her — it is that perhaps she has done so while remaining pure. How? This is the mystery which will cause Gabin's death […]. The simple soul of Gabin could only be saved by the simplicity of her purity, and instead he discovers in Françoise an equivocal purity, an inconceivable purity which seems complicit with what Gabin considers to be the very symbol of impurity. François's error consists in not realizing the metaphysical trap that Françoise's purity has set for him. François could be saved if he stopped clinging to the mirage of purity, if he accepted the way out offered by Clara. Clara is of the same race as Gabin, but she knows how to live with impurity.

After François she will take up with some seal trainer or other, not because she didn't really love François, but simply because she has decided to live. Clara's purity is a form of wisdom. She wasn't unworthy of François, but François couldn't see her type of purity, he was so fascinated by the unattainable mirage of Françoise's purity (*Le Cinéma français de la Libération à la Nouvelle Vague*, p. 66).

Pierre Leprohon — Jean Gabin and Tragic Destiny

Well, this dramaturgical conception of the film is exactly like that of *Oedipus Rex*, in which all the events are completed when the curtain rises. That's why we can say that these films are like tragedies in which the character created by Gabin becomes the illustration of a kind of damnation.

This character is that of a criminal without guilt. But circumstances, people, society are all against him. He may be pursued [...] by the police and by the system of justice, but he is pursued first and foremost by destiny.

This is particularly true of *Daybreak*, which will remain one of Carné and Prévert's best films by its technique and the significance of its dramatic construction. No more so than the legionnaire of *Port of Shadows*, the sandblaster of *Daybreak* is not a bad man. Destiny has gripped him in its clutches and led him to a crime which is neither in his nature nor his mentality but which he cannot help committing. The murderer thus becomes the victim of destiny, a victim whom not even human justice, were it to pardon him, could save. For even if a rancorous little punk didn't shoot down the deserter [in *Port of Shadows*], even if the worker trapped in his room didn't commit suicide, their happiness would nonetheless be impossible; their life is finished. In *Daybreak* the tragedy of the hero is explicitly formulated in the scene where Gabin, standing in his window, cries out his misfortune and his anger to the crowd assembled below. And because of certain shots he is not only speaking to the crowd but to the spectators of the film also, to each of us, the witnesses of his dilemma (*Le Monde du cinéma*, pp. 105-106).

André Bazin — Realism and Symbolism of the Props

You may have noticed the role of Gabin's cigarette in this film. The consumption of the package of cigarettes indicates in a certain sense the passage of time. The fact that Gabin has to light one cigarette from the other, because he has no more matches, condemns him to be vigilant. When he is distracted and lets his cigarette go out, we are strangely affected, as if this oversight marked a decisive moment in the development of the tragedy. We have the impression that Gabin would be condemned to despair when the package was empty. This last, absurd pleasure would allow him to continue to live. But he didn't even have the satisfaction of finishing the pack of cigarettes, and the distraction which allowed the cigarette to go out was perhaps really a manner of giving up: the telltale lapsus [...].

While the meaning of the dramatic symbolism of an element like the cigarette is rather clearly understood by the spectator, the use of the wardrobe is more subtle. The famous Norman wardrobe that Gabin pushes against the door, and which is the occasion of an amusing dialogue between the police chief and the concierge, appears to be a simple detail of the plot which strikes us by its realism. We can easily imagine this episode in a newspaper report. In reality the implicit symbolism of this wardrobe is as necessary and rigorous as a Freudian symbol. Gabin couldn't put the dresser, the table, or the bed against the door. It had to be this heavy Norman wardrobe, and he pushes it like you would an enormous stone slab onto a tomb. The manner in which he pushes the wardrobe, the very form of the piece of furniture, conspire to create the impression that Gabin is not barricading himself in his room: he is entombing himself. Even if the final result is the same and if we are not conscious of any difference, the dramatic tone is completely different [...].

We see how Carné's realism remains rigorously faithful to the literal nature of his decor while at the same time transposing it poetically. He does not achieve this by modifying his scenery formally and pictorially, as the German Expressionists did, but by drawing out its immanent poetry, by forcing it to reveal secret affinities with the drama taking place. It is in this sense that one may speak of the "poetic realism" of Marcel Carné [...]. What makes the perfection of *Daybreak* is the fact that the symbolism never precedes the realism; it completes it like a supplement (*Le Cinéma français de la Libération à la Nouvelle Vague*, pp. 61-63).

André Bazin — The Props, "an astonishing social documentary"

The dramatic role of the props, we were saying, but in relationship with what we would have to call the psychology of the props. The props serve to constitute the characters just as much as the acting itself. For example, when we see Berry dead on the concierge's bed, he is lying on newspapers. We can imagine why. The concierge didn't want them to put this guy she didn't know on her bedspread. Since the blood could have stained it, moreover, she went and got some old newspapers from on top of her wardrobe and spread them out on the bed. This little detail of the decor says more about the psychology of the concierge than a long dialogue. It's with details like this, as much as with the action itself, that a character is created. But the props interest us especially in relation to Gabin. This virtually bare room allows us to reconstitute not only the life but the tastes and character of François. His only pastime is sports: cycling and football [...]. The objects related to sports are about the only sign of disorder that he permits himself in his room, because he doesn't consider them to be messy [...]. He maintains a scrupulous cleanliness, as is indicated by the fact that, after Berry's murder, he mechanically drops the ash from his cigarette into the ashtray (finishing the act even after the gunshots) and carefully puts his tie away after removing the price tag. (These acts have a dramatic value, performed at this moment, but at the same time they define François's psychology.) François is an old bachelor. Used to living alone since childhood, he has learned to get along alone (*Le Cinéma français de la Libération à la Nouvelle Vague*, pp. 63-64).

André Bazin — The Music of *Daybreak*

You can discern two principal themes, a sentimental one, carried by the flute, and a dramatic, oppressive one rendered by the bass and percussion instruments. These two themes are mixed together or separate, but always subtly. The oboe theme is constructed in both logical and musical counterpoint with the theme of the kettledrums. It is a high, very melodious theme, whereas the kettledrums are heavy and exclusively rhythmic. Well, each time that we move from a scene in the past to one in the present or vice-versa, there is a change in the music or simply the appearance of a musical element. This corresponds psychologically to a kind of reversal of values. There are even passages in which the music seems to have been played backwards. The music thus creates an atmosphere which gives the physical sentiment of a reversal of the nature of things.

If Marcel Carné had had only the technique of the dissolve at his disposal, the time changes in the action would have been less acceptable. It's largely due to the particular nature of Maurice Jaubert's music that the spectator is psychologically prepared for the kind of dramatic shift that characterizes the return of the memories each time [...].

The music is in no way an accompaniment; it is incorporated into the action. In fact, it constitutes an action in and of itself. It was necessary for the spectator to feel clearly the weight of the past and that the present, when we return to it, remain in the grasp of the past. When the action we see on the screen is in the past, there is no music (except in the love scene in the greenhouse, and we will see why), but when we return to Gabin in his room in the present, the music reinserts itself and remains as long as we are in the present. Very quickly, owing to the repetition of the technique, but especially to the quality of the music, we identify the music with Gabin's imagination. It pervades us just as his memories pervade the hero. There is a scene very characteristic in this respect. Towards the end of the film Gabin, obsessed, stops before the mirror, then picks up a chair and throws it at the mirror. At the sound of the broken glass the music stops, as if this act of anger had liberated the hero from his obsessive state, as if the mirror were the very memory of Gabin instead of only the symbol. After a few moments of silence the throbbing muted theme of the kettledrums reoccupies little by little the dramatic space, before the oboe's theme penetrates irresistibly into the scene and imposes the memory of Françoise [...]. When we said that there is no music in the past, that was with the exception of real music, like in the cabaret. A single exception: the love scene in the greenhouse in which we meet in its purest state the oboe's theme. But that is because this scene is very special, because it is situated in a certain sense outside of time. Carné had to indicate its fundamental difference from the realism of the others (*Le Cinéma français de la Libération à la Nouvelle Vague*, pp. 56-58).

MARCEL CARNÉ'S FILMOGRAPHY
(FEATURE FILMS)

1936	*Jenny*
1937	*Bizarre, Bizarre (Drôle de drame)*
1938	*Port of Shadows (Quai des brumes)*, *Hôtel du Nord*
1939	*Daybreak (Le Jour se lève)*
1942	*The Devil's Envoys (Les Visiteurs du soir)*
1945	*Children of Paradise (Les Enfants du paradis)*
1946	*Gates of the Night (Les Portes de la nuit)*
1949	*La Marie du port*
1951	*Juliette, or Key of Dreams (Juliette ou la clé des songes)*
1953	*The Adultress (Thérèse Raquin)*
1954	*L'Air de Paris*

1956	*The Country I Come From (Le Pays d'où je viens)*
1958	*The Cheaters (Les Tricheurs)*
1960	*Wasteland (Terrain vague)*
1962	*Chicken Feed For Little Birds*
	(Du Mouron pour les petits oiseaux)
1965	*Three Rooms in Manhattan*
	(Trois Chambres à Manhattan)
1968	*Young Wolves (Les Jeunes Loups)*
1971	*Law Breakers (Les Assassins de l'ordre)*
1974	*The Marvelous Visit (La Merveilleuse Visite)*

WORKS CONSULTED

Agel, Henri. *Le Cinéma*. Paris: Casterman, 1954.

Bazin, André. *Le Cinéma français de la Libération à la Nouvelle Vague (1945-1958)*. Paris: Editions de l'Etoile, 1983.

Brunius, Jacques B. "Un des jalons majeurs de l'histoire du cinema." *L'Avant-Scène Cinéma* 53 (1965): 6.

Carné, Marcel. *Le Jour se lève* (screenplay). *L'Avant-Scène Cinéma* 53 (Nov. 1965): 1-40.

.........*La Vie à belles dents. Souvenirs*. Paris: Pierre Belfond, 1989.

Chazel, Robert. *Marcel Carné*. Cinéma d'aujourd'hui. Paris: Seghers, 1965.

Damas, Georges et Jacques Tournier. *Fiche I.D.H.E.C.* No. 19 (in *Le Jour se lève*, *L'Avant-Scène Cinéma* 53 (1965): 43.

Landry, Bernard-G. *Marcel Carné*. Paris: Jacques Vautrain, 1952.

Leprohon, Pierre. *Le Monde du cinéma*. Paris: Pierre Waleffe, 1967.

Mitry, Jean. *Histoire du cinéma*, IV. Paris: Editions universitaires, 1980.

Pérez, Michel. *Les Films de Carné*. Paris: Ramsey, 1994.

Quéval, Jean. *Marcel Carné*. Paris: Editions du Cerf, 1952.

Sautet, Claude. "*Le Jour se lève*." *Positif*, 400 (June 1994): 126-127.

Schimel, Monique. "L'Homme et son destin ou évolution de l'oeuvre de Marcel Carné." *Image et son*, 55 (July 1952): 7-9.

Marcel Carné

Children of Paradise
Les Enfants du paradis

(1945)

Marcel Carné, *Children of Paradise*: Baptiste (Jean-Louis Barrault) and Nathalie (Maria Casarès), his future wife. Courtesy of Collection André Heinrich

Director .... Marcel Carné
Screenplay and dialogues.. Jacques Prévert
Directors of Photography .... Roger Hubert, Philippe Agostini
Music... Maurice Thiriet (Joseph Kosma*)
Music for the mime acts.............Georges Mouqué (Joseph Kosma*)
Film Editor .... Henry Rust
Sound .... Robert Teisseire
Art Directors .... Léon Barsacq, Raymond Gabutti
(Alexandre Trauner*)
Costumes.. Antoine Mayo
Producers ....Société Nouvelle Pathé-Cinéma (André Paulvé*)
Length .... 3 h 00

*Joseph Kosma, Alexandre Trauner, and André Paulvé were all banned from professional activity during the Occupation owing to their Jewish ancestry. Thiriet and Mouqué (music) and Barsacq (art direction) lent their names to the production and carried out instructions from Kosma and Trauner. Barsacq's personal contribution to the film is nonetheless important. Paulvé directed the complete preparation of the film before being removed from his functions by the Occupying authorities in autumn 1943.

Cast

Arletty (*Garance*), Jean-Louis Barrault (*Baptiste Deburau*), Pierre Brasseur (*Frédérick Lemaître*), Marcel Herrand (*Lacenaire*), Louis Salou (*Count Edouard de Montray*), Pierre Renoir (*Jericho, the second-hand clothes peddler*), Maria Casarès (*Nathalie*), Fabien Loris (*Avril*), Etienne Decroux (*Anselme Deburau, Baptiste's father*), Gaston Modot (*Silk Thread, the blind man*), Jane Marken (*Madame Hermine*), Marcel Pérès (*Director of the Funambules Theater*), Paul Frankeur (*the police inspector*), Auguste Boverio (*1st playwright*), Paul Demange (*2nd playwright*), Jean Diener (*3rd playwright*), Rognoni (*Director of the Grand Theater*), Louis Florencie (*the gendarme*).

STORY

Children of Paradise is divided into two "epochs," "Crime Boulevard" and "The Man in White." The first begins around 1827, the second seven years later. The action takes place mainly in the neighborhood of the Boulevard du Temple in Paris, nicknamed "Crime Boulevard" because of all the melodramas and bloody scenarios offered to the largely plebian public each evening. There are two principal theaters. The Théâtre des Funambules ("tightrope walkers") specializes in pantomime, since the authorities do not allow it to use spoken dialogue, which is reserved for the Grand Theater, the "official" theater.

At the beginning of the film we meet Frédérick Lemaître, a young aspiring actor and inveterate womanizer who dreams of becoming a star. He meets and sweet-talks Garance, a beautiful woman who earns her living by exhibiting her physical charms (modestly) in a carnival show. Garance staves off Frédérick's advances and goes to visit one of her acquaintances, Lacenaire, an anarchist in revolt against society. Lacenaire is a proud, dangerous individual who works as a public writer to cover various and sundry shady activities. Shortly thereafter, Garance is accused of stealing a man's wallet while she is listening to a barker (Baptiste's father) in front of the Funambules Theater. Lacenaire is in fact the guilty party. Baptiste, dressed up as Pierrot, saves her from the police by silently acting out the theft, which he has just witnessed. He reveals a great talent, a veritable vocation for pantomime, but also falls immediately and irremediably in love with Garance.

Baptiste's father is one of the stars at the Funambules. The daughter of the theater director, Nathalie, who is a mime also, is deeply in love with Baptiste. Before the performance that evening a used clothes peddler named Jericho reads in her palm that she will marry the man she loves. The old peddler, a suspicious, repugnant character, appears at critical moments throughout the film, moments which are usually related to the future of the other characters. When a fight breaks out that evening between two rival clans of actors, Baptiste and Frédérick manage to calm the crowd down by improvising a mime act, thus saving the day's receipts. The most enthusiastic of the spectators are those seated in "paradise," that is, on the top floor of the balcony where the cheapest seats are located.

Later that night Baptiste catches sight of Garance with Lacenaire and his accomplices in a seedy restaurant, "The Robin." When he invites Garance to dance, he is thrown out of the restaurant by Avril, Lacenaire's partner. He turns the situation around and leaves with Garance, for whom he finds a room at the same boarding house (The Great Post House) where he and Frédérick live. After declaring his love, Baptiste flees Garance's room, despite her clear invitation to stay. Frédérick doesn't have the same scruples. When he hears Garance singing in her room, which is next to his, he quickly joins her.

Baptiste has become the star of the Funambules, performing pantomime numbers with Garance and Frédéric, who have become lovers. Baptiste is tormented by their affair, while Nathalie, who is convinced that she and Baptiste are "made for each other," suffers from his lack of love for her. Garance is visited in her dressing room by the Count Edouard de Montray, a wealthy and cynical dandy who offers her his fortune if she will agree to become his mistress. Garance is repelled by him and mockingly rejects his proposition. The count nonetheless offers her his protection if the need were to arise. She is later unjustly suspected of complicity in an abortive theft and murder attempt by Lacenaire and Avril. To avoid arrest she is forced to appeal to the count for protection. The first part of the film comes to an end with this development.

"The Man in White," the second epoch of the film, begins several years later. Frédérick has become famous as the star of the Grand Theater. A man about town and a spendthrift, he is covered with debts — which doesn't prevent him from devastating the mediocre play in which he currently has the main role by exposing it to ridicule on opening night. Outraged, the play's authors challenge him to a duel. When he returns to his dressing room, Frédérick is confronted by Lacenaire, who intends to rob and kill him. However, the anarchist is an amateur playwright and strikes up a friendship with the actor instead. He serves as Frédérick's second the next morning, when the actor goes to his duel dead drunk.

Baptiste is still enjoying great success as a mime at the Funambules. When Frédérick goes to a performance the day after the duel, he finds himself in the same box as Garance. His former mistress has returned to Paris after having traveled throughout the world with the Count de Montray, who now keeps her. She has been attending the Funambules every night incognito to watch Baptiste perform. She is still in love with him. Frédérick suddenly finds himself jealous for the first time in his life. While the feeling is highly unpleasant, he realizes that his jealousy will help him as an actor. He will finally be able to play the role of Othello, having now experienced the emotions which motivate the character. Garance asks Frédérick to tell Baptiste of her presence, but Nathalie, now Baptiste's wife, is first informed by Jericho. She sends their small son to Garance's box to speak to her of their family's happiness. When Baptiste arrives, the box is empty. When Garance returns to the count's luxurious house, she finds Lacenaire waiting for her. The count is irritated to see such an individual in his home and tries to condescend to him. Lacenaire reacts with threats, showing a knife at his belt. After the anarchist's departure, Garance declares to the count that she will never love him since she is already in love with another man.

Frédérick finally plays the role of Othello. The Count de Montray, who attends the performance with Garance, is convinced that the actor is the man she loves. At the end of the play, the count mocks Frédérick, trying to provoke him into a duel. When Lacenaire takes Frédérick's side, the count insults him. Lacenaire takes revenge by calling him a cuckold and, pulling aside a curtain, reveals Garance in Baptiste's embrace on the balcony. The two lovers spend the night together in Garance's former room at The Great Post House.

The next morning, at a Turkish bath, Lacenaire assassinates the count for humiliating him the night before by having him thrown out of the theater. He then sends for the police himself to meet his "destiny," which is to die on the scaffold. Nathalie has gone to the hotel, where she surprises Baptiste with Garance. Having decided to leave Paris, Garance gets into a carriage which moves off into the frantic Carnaval crowd, a sea of bobbing masks and white pierrots. Baptiste is swept away by the crowd and separated from Garance forever.

CRITICAL RECEPTION

The reaction of the press when the film came out on March 15, 1945, was simply euphoric, as the set of critical excerpts in *L'Avant-Scène Cinéma* (pp. 101-104) clearly demonstrates. "The masterpiece of Marcel Carné, the masterpiece of Jacques Prévert [...]. This film is one of the most important made in the last ten years in the whole world," proclaimed Georges Sadoul (*Lettres françaises*, March 17, 1945). Most of the other film critics agreed that the film was a masterpiece, praising the exactitude of the historical reconstruction (Denis Marion, *Combat*, March 20, 1945), the staging, the photography, and the brilliant dialogues. "Photos, dialogues, rhythm, acting, the extras, everything works together, everything is polished, everything is remarkable," exuded Jean-Jacques Gautier (*Le Figaro*, March 10, 1945). Jacques Natanson declared blatantly, "Here is the monument of French cinema" (*L'Ordre*, March 16, 1945), while Jean-Paul Sassy in a rave review called it a "jewel of pure art, incomparable, perhaps the greatest France has ever produced" (*Volontés*, March 20, 1945). If we take into consideration the historical context — it's the France of the Liberation — we are not surprised at the patriotic fervor which gleamed through the praise for the film. In the piece quoted above, Sadoul stated outright that the quality of Carné's film ... serves the grandeur and the power of our country."

On the other hand, as Carné himself has remarked, the press "was far from unanimous in its praise" (*La Vie à belles dents*, p. 172). Some mild reservations were voiced by critics like Georges Charensol, who felt that the acting, although dazzling, "sins — like the authors — through excessive intelligence" and that the staging tended to be too artificial (*Les Nouvelles Littéraires*, April 12, 1945). Others criticized the "theatrical character" of the film or "its formal perfection at the expense of the dynamism of the action" (quoted in Chardère, p. 48). François Chalais complained that the film was not contemporary, that it did not reflect the hard realities of the postwar period (*Carrefour*, March 17, 1945), while Jean Gély sniffed that it provoked "more admiration than emotion" (*La Marseillaise*, March 22, 1945).

In any case *Children of Paradise* was an unmitigated success both in France and abroad. The film had a 54-week run in Paris, in spite of the high admission charge (twice the normal ticket price), and was a "raging success" in Marseilles as in the other large cities in the provinces (*L'Avant-Scène Cinéma*, p. 108). Destined to become a cult film, it has survived the test of time: "Still today, nearly twenty years after its opening," remarked Robert Chazel, "it is shown constantly and remains a great success in the *present* [...] we see even better today [...] its astounding richness" (p. 46). In the same period, although Carné no longer enjoyed the favor of the critics, one still heard praise of *Children of Paradise* for "the indisputable grandeur of the staging, the beauty of the scenery and the costumes, the deftness of the directing of the actors, and one of the best dialogues of Prévert" (in Sellier, p. 122). A half-century after its premiere we hear Carné's film described as "the most beautiful French film of all time" (p. 121) and recognized as "the most universally famous film in the history of our cinema" (Pérez, p. 6).

CINEMA AND THE OCCUPATION

Paradoxically, despite the immigration of many of the best French actors and directors to the United States and other countries, French cinema was particularly prolific during the Occupation by Nazi Germany (1940-1944). As was the case in many countries during the Great Depression of the thirties, the movies became the principal form of entertainment for the French public during this period. Since there were substantial profits to be made, producers were eager to invest in film projects. While the GNP fell to half its former level during the four years of the Occupation, the level of production of the movie industry thus remained high, especially in Nice, as Gili points out: "With the exception of René Clair, Jean Renoir, and Jacques Feyder, the biggest names in French cinema worked in Nice at one time or another between 1939 and 1945. Julien Duvivier, Jean Delannoy, Jean Cocteau, Abel Gance, Marcel L'Herbier, Marc and Yves Allégret, Jean Grémillon [...], René Clément, Jacques Prévert, Marcel Carné, to name only the most important ones, were active in Nice and the surrounding area" (p. 196). Morevoer, the absence of some of the greatest filmmakers allowed talented beginners like Jacques Becker, Robert Bresson, Claude Autant-Lara, and Henri-Georges Clouzot to make their first films.

The film industry was nonetheless strictly supervised, both by the Occupying authorities and by their collaborators in Vichy, and subjected to very severe censorship. Any film project which touched on contemporary social or political reality was rejected, except for Nazi propaganda films of course. The result is the production of numerous "escapist" films, mediocre comedies and dramas intended for pure entertainment. The most gifted filmmakers took refuge either in the past, making films about famous French artistic or literary figures, or in mythology. The best films of the period thus include *The Devil's Envoys* (1942) by Carné and Prévert and *The Eternal Return* (1943) by Jean Delannoy and Jean Cocteau. The latter film is a modernized version of the medieval Tristan and Isolde myth, whereas Carné's film, which is set in the 15th century, is a dramatic story of love and sorcery bathed in mystery. The first Carné-Prévert film since *Daybreak* (1939), *The Devil's Envoys* was a huge critical and popular success. Winning the Grand Prix of French Cinema prompted the producer André Paulvé to support the following Carné-Prévert project unhesitatingly despite its exorbitant price tag. This project involved creating a broad fresco of the Romantic Period (1820-1840) set in the neighborhood of the popular theaters. The working title of this film was *The Tightrope Walkers* (*Les Funambules*) — before becoming *Children of Paradise*.

ORIGIN

The idea of *Children of Paradise* came from an anecdote told by Jean-Louis Barrault during a chance encounter with Carné and Prévert one day in Nice. It was an episode in the life of a famous 19th-century mime, Baptiste Deburau, who was tried for the apparently accidental murder of a drunkard who had grievously insulted his wife in public. Carné was fascinated at the idea of resuscitating the Romantic Period and the theatrical milieu in which Deburau lived, especially "Crime Boulevard" so full of life and local color. While researching the subject he discovered that "the humble folk of the period called the upper balcony of a theater 'paradise' " (p. 160). In addition, as Carné explained in an interview, in the neighborhood of the Madeleine in Paris he had seen a toy store named "The Children's Paradise" ("Le Paradis des Enfants"), which also contributed to the choice of the definitive title of the film (Stonehill, p. 59). For Carné, in any case, "children of paradise" may refer either to the spectators up in the gallery or the actors who are playing for them.

Prévert and Carné decided to invent a story which would include not only Deburau but also two other historical figures from the romantic period: a great actor of the popular theaters, Frédérick Lemaître, and a famous anarchist-assassin-poet, Pierre-François Lacenaire, whose colorful character fascinated Prévert. In Carné's film certain aspects of the careers of each of the three men are presented, albeit somewhat stylized. The production of *The South-Side Inn* (*L'Auberge des Adrets*) at the Grand Theater in which Lemaître, in the role of Robert Macaire, devastated the play with parody really happened, but in 1823 rather than in the middle of the 1840s where Carné places it. Likewise, the mime show *Clothes Peddler* (*'Chand d'habits*) in the second "epoch" of the film was produced in reality in 1842, probably starring Paul Legrand, a young mime at the Funambules theater, rather than Deburau himself (Turk, p. 255).

It took Prévert six months to write the screenplay for the film, with the aid of Carné and other members of the crew. It was clearly Prévert's screenplay, however, and his influence on the whole conception of the film was so great that Mitry declared — somewhat abusively according to Quéval (pp. 51-52) — that "it is much less a Marcel Carné film written by Prévert than a Jacques Prévert film staged by Carné" (p. 251). Whatever the case may be, Prévert added two fictional characters to the mix: Garance, a "classy, worldly vamp with a mysterious melancholic side" (Siclier, p. 167), and the Count de Montray, a haughty and cynical aristocratic dandy. He also invented the love story at the heart of the film. The complexity of the subject as developed by Prévert raised fears of an excessively long film. Accordingly, the producer Paulvé suggested that they make two films, an idea which is responsible for the division of *Children of Paradise* into two distinct "epochs."

FILM CREW AND CAST

The final step was to get together the crew and the actors. In addition to Prévert, who was making his sixth film with Carné, the director called upon his habitual art director, Alexandre Trauner, and the composer Joseph Kosma. Both men had just participated, secretly, in the making of *The Devil's Envoys*. As we mentioned above, they were banned, like all Jews during the Occupation, from working in the cinema. Hidden in the countryside near Nice, the city where the shooting began, Trauner and Kosma collaborated on the film without their names appearing in the credits. As noted at the beginning of this chapter, their ideas will be put into practice by Léon Barsacq (for the scenery) and Maurice Thiriet (for the music). Thiriet had already lent his name and talent to the music of *The Devil's Envoys*. In both cases, but especially as regards Barsacq, the personal contribution of the stand-ins was considerable. To receive their instructions for the film, Carné commuted constantly between Nice and the little mountain inn where Trauner and Kosma were hiding.

As for the actors, Jean-Louis Barrault was the obvious choice for the role of the mime Deburau. Having accepted the role despite a commitment to the Comédie française (the principal French theater), he was forced to shuttle back and forth between Paris and Nice! Despite her age (46) Arletty was chosen for the role of Garance, having already starred in three Carné films, *Hôtel du nord*, *Daybreak*, and *The Devil's Envoys*. For the role of Frédérick Lemaître they chose one of Prévert's favorite actors, Pierre Brasseur, who had gained a reputation for playing "spineless or wayward characters, eccentric or cynical, always excessive" (Chardère, p. 28). Although Brasseur had roles in numerous films, this would be his most famous. Much the same could be said of the actors who played Lacenaire (Marcel Herrand) and the Count de Montray (Louis Salou). Herrand was an experienced stage actor who had also played in *The Devil's Envoys*, while Salou was a prolific actor throughout the forties. A young stage actress, Maria Casarès, is cast in her first film role as Nathalie — before going on to a brilliant career on stage and screen. The principal cast is completed by a veteran actor, Pierre Renoir (the older brother of Jean), in the role of Jericho. It is generally agreed that rarely has such a perfect cast been brought together for a film.

SHOOTING

It is impossible to discuss the shooting of *Children of Paradise* without taking into account the Occupation. To make his film, Carné had to deal with an extraordinary number of obstacles, both political and material. Under the conditions, it was miraculous that he managed to make his film at all. In August 1943 the Germans had occupied France for over three years. Until the landing of the Americans in North Africa in November 1942 the country had been divided into two zones: the Northern half ("zone occupée") under German administration and the southern half ("zone libre"). The so-called "free zone" was governed from Vichy by Maréchal Pétain and his prime minister Pierre Laval, who were willingly collaborating with the Occupying forces. After the American invasion of North Africa in November 1942, the Germans occupied the whole country, with Vichy maintaining administrative authority over the former free zone. The policies adopted by the occupiers with regard to the cinema had both advantages and disadvantages. On the one hand, the German authorities banned all American and British films in France, a measure which at the same time eliminated most of the competition the French producers had formerly faced. On the other hand, all the films, from production to distribution, were subjected to political censorship and economic controls which put severe limits on the directors.

Since the presence of the Germans was less oppressive in the south, Nice became a favorite location for movie studios. Carné and Prévert had shot *The Devil's Envoys* at the Victorine Studios in Nice the preceding year. They chose the same studio to create one of the most monumental and most expensive movie sets (around five million francs) in the history of French cinema: the set for *Children of Paradise*. This included not only Crime Boulevard but also the interiors of the two theaters, the Robin Restaurant, the count's sumptuous lodgings, and the Turkish baths, to mention only the most important sets.

The history of the shooting is rife with incidents. Begun on August 17, 1943, in Nice, the filming was stopped a month later (September 12), the moment Italy proposed an armistice following the landing of the Allies in Sicily. Carné had hardly begun shooting (three days) the initial scenes on Crime Boulevard, which involved up to 1,800 extras, when he received an order to return to Paris with his whole crew. The shooting began again in Paris in November 1943, but without the participation of the producer André Paulvé, who was banned from working on the film because of his Jewish ancestry. The scenes in the two theaters were shot at the Pathé Studios, which had agreed to step in after Paulvé's dismissal by the authorities.

When Carné and his crew returned to Nice in February 1944 to shoot on location, the Allies were still far away. The work began in the presence of the Germans, who had replaced the Italians in Nice. The crew discovered that the huge set for Crime Boulevard had been severely damaged by a storm. Two months of repairs added another eight hundred thousand francs to the costs. To complicate matters further, the actor who had been playing the role of Jericho, Robert Le Vigan, did not return to Nice with the others. An anti-Semitic collaborator, he had been forced to flee France, like other notorious collaborators, as the defeat of the Germans became more and more imminent. Pierre Renoir replaced Le Vigan in the role of the clothes peddler, forcing Carné to shoot some scenes again. The filming in Nice was finished at the end of March before concluding in Paris in the middle of April 1944. In both cities Carné had to face extremely difficult material conditions, including a severe lack of building materials and a curfew which prevented shooting at night. There were only a few studio shots left, but when the Allies landed in Normandy on June 6, 1944, Carné was determined to delay the opening of the film until France was liberated: "Indeed, as soon as I learned about the landing it became imperative for me to drag out as long as possible the final work on the film, so that it would be the first film to mark the return of peace to our country" (p. 169).

OPENING

Children of Paradise, the most ambitious French production of the Occupation, finally opened in March 1945. Carné simply couldn't put it off any longer. Although Paris, like most of France, has been liberated, fierce battles were still raging and would continue until the surrender of the Germans on May 8. Carné himself was doing battle with Gaumont. Owing to the length of the film (over three hours), the studio wanted to show the two parts of the film simultaneously in two different Parisian cinemas. Carné was vehemently opposed to this plan and eventually got his way: the whole film opened in two Parisian cinemas at the same time. To compensate for the reduction of the number of daily showings from five to three, the distributors doubled the ticket cost. This did not discourage the Parisian public, which filled the cinemas regularly, as we noted above, for 54 weeks in a row. The film then opened throughout France and abroad, enjoying the same enthusiastic reception everywhere.

On the anecdotal side, it should be noted that Carné was subjected to criticism at the Liberation, like most of the directors and actors who exercised their profession in France during the Occupation. A "purging committee" faulted him officially for signing a contract with Continental Studios, the most powerful German studio in France — despite the fact that he never made a film for the Germans. He defended himself by emphasizing his role in the defense of French cinema in the absence of his fellow filmmakers who had taken refuge abroad: "For four years, I stayed here. I did my best for the cause of our cinema" (Sellier, p. 14). Arletty, for her part, was indicted for indulging openly in a love affair with a German officer. She was found guilty and had her head shaven, as was the customary punishment in these cases, before being condemned to eighteen months of house arrest. She missed the opening of *Children of Paradise.* In spite of her star status, Arletty's movie career was essentially over. Although she appeared in around twenty films after the Liberation, she was generally restricted to minor roles.

STRUCTURE

Each epoch of the film, "Crime Boulevard" and "The Man in White," begins with a curtain rising and ends with the curtain falling, creating immediately a parallel with theater. This parallel is rendered explicit by the traditional three raps on the wall that we hear before the beginning of the action in the film. Nonetheless, as numerous critics have observed, the opening scene on Crime Boulevard with its panoramic character recalls the beginning of a Balzac or Stendhal novel in the 1830s, when Romanticism was at its height. Like Balzac's novels, *Children of Paradise* presents a broad socio-historical fresco in the manner of the "human comedy." The film is organized into a series of scenes resembling "chapters," as Perez remarks, rather than acts in a play (p. 82), despite the explicit reference to the theater at the beginning.

The amorous relationship between Baptiste and Garance is at the center of the two sections of the film. As Chion observes, "the action of these two 'epochs' teeming with characters and events is crystallized around a night of love which *doesn't take place* between Deburau and Garance and finishes with this night of love which takes place a few years later in the same room, between the same people" (p. 14). More generally the action is clearly organized in the first part of the film around Garance, who is the object of desire of the four male protagonists. After her appearance at the beginning of the film in the allegorical role of "Truth," she plays scenes successively with Frédérick, Lacenaire, and Baptiste, scenes which reveal the "truth" about each of the protagonists' characters (Chion, p. 14). The rest of the first movement of "Crime Boulevard" centers on the episode of the fight over Garance at the "Robin" restaurant and the lodging of Garance at the same boarding house as Baptiste and Frédérick.

The second movement begins by the metaphorical mime show depicting the relationship which has developed between Garance and the two actors. In the *Palace of Mirages or the Moon Lover* Pierrot idolizes Phoebe the Goddess of the Moon (i.e., Baptiste, who idealizes love, puts Garance on a pedestal), whereas Harlequin takes the goddess off her pedestal and leaves with her (i.e., the more realistic Frédérick treats Garance simply as an available woman). In the second part of the mime show, we see the "goddess" leave on a boat with Harlequin, an event which sends Pierrot into despair. However, when he contemplates hanging himself, a little girl takes the rope from his hands and transforms it into a jump rope. A young laundress (Nathalie) then changes the rope into a clothesline, giving Baptiste an end of the line to hold while she hangs the laundry. We are watching a metaphorical representation of Baptiste's state of mind, followed by a scene foreshadowing his future. Garance having become Frédérick's mistress, the mime sinks into suicidal despair. But the boat scene seems to refer also to Garance's departure to travel the world with the Count de Montray, which will cause Baptiste to fall in yet deeper despair. While Baptiste will eventually marry Nathalie, found a family and share an everyday relationship with her (alluded to in the mime show by the child and the household chores), he remains nevertheless profoundly sad. Garance's departure is clearly suggested at the end of "Crime Boulevard" when the heroine is forced to appeal to the count for protection from the police. It will become a reality, just like Baptiste's marriage and fatherhood, during the intermission, that is, in the seven-year period between the two epochs of the film. The first epoch is thus composed broadly of two forms of discourse, one of them narrative (the action of the film), the other metaphorical (the mime scenes), which relate successively the same tragic love story.

The second epoch of the film, "The Man in White," is organized around the return of Garance. It is structured by three theatrical performances which highlight the genius of Frédérick and Baptiste. Carné places the meeting between Frédérick and Garance in the box at the Funambules Theater between Frédérick's extravagant parody of *The South-Side Inn* and Baptiste's mime show *Clothes Peddler*. This meeting, or rather the jealousy it provokes when Frédérick learns of Garance's love for Baptiste, will enable the actor to create the role of Othello, which he has always wanted to play. Baptiste's show is once again a stylized representation of the mime's personal dilemma and his state of mind. When the old clothes peddler refuses to let him have the new suit he needs to be admitted into the house and rejoin the woman he loves, he kills him. We understand that Baptiste is revolting here against a cruel fate embodied by the old peddler (see "Themes" below). His fate, we know, has separated him from Garance, who now lives with the count in a luxurious dwelling.

Like the first part of the film, the second comprises a series of meetings between Garance and the group of male protagonists. We note this difference, however: all three men from the beginning of the film have now realized their destiny. Frédérick and Baptiste are at the height of their professional glory, and Lacenaire has become a notorious outlaw and assassin. After her discussion with Frédérick at the Funambules, Garance plays successive scenes with Lacenaire and the count before being united with Baptiste after watching *Othello*. The most dramatic scene of the film, the confrontation provoked by the count after the play, brings together for the first time Garance and the four men who are in love with her. The scene takes place in a highly tense atmosphere of jealousy and animosity and a spirit of vengeance which prepares the melodramatic and tragic denouement: the murder of the count and the departure of Garance.

THEMES

Georges Sadoul, who considers *Children of Paradise* to be "the richest and most perfect film of Carné and Prévert," finds their favorite themes in the work: "the impossibility of preserving happiness and love in a poorly conceived world" (p. 95). These are, indeed, the essential motifs of poetic realism — at least the profoundly pessimistic version offered in the Carné-Prévert films. But beside this broad major theme, which underlies the whole work, the film weaves together a profusion of themes whose variety creates a remarkably rich texture. We defer here again to Mitry, who remarks, "There is thus simultaneously an extremely lively description of the theater world, a study of mores, and behind it all — or provoking it — a tragic story highlighting the solitude, isolation, and inability to communicate of people in spite of the love which unites or separates them" (p. 250).

While the theater is both the subject and the context of the film's action, it is also one of its principal themes. When the curtain raises on the Boulevard du Temple at the beginning of *Children of Paradise*, the theater is established as a metaphor for life: life is a grand spectacle, a "comedy." According to Pérez the film shows us the "intense passion [of Man] for playing roles for his fellow men" (p. 75). It highlights the tight bond between theater and life by linking them constantly, beginning with the Don Juan act that Frédérick puts on for the pretty women he meets on Crime Boulevard. Frédérick's character embodies "the Actor," whether it be in the theater or in life — just as Baptiste embodies "the Mime," a person whose existence is based on virtual action ("make believe") rather than on real commitment in life, whether it be in his mime shows or in his amorous relationship with Garance.

The most theatrical character is, of course, Lacenaire, the poet-assassin (despite his resemblance to the master criminel of Balzac's novels, Vautrin). Lacenaire writes plays whose plots curiously resemble those of the film which frames them. He is likewise the person who stages the *coup de théâtre* towards the end of the film by "opening the curtain" to reveal Garance in Baptiste's arms on the balcony of the Grand Theater. And it is he, finally, who stages his life as if it were a bloody melodrama in which he plays the hero. This side of Lacenaire's character becomes explicit when he says to his side-kick Avril, after murdering the count, *"Poor Avril! The play is over, you can go now."* Lacenaire thus seems to embody simultaneously the playwright, the director, and the actor. If we consider the well-known fascination this character exercised on Prévert, it may not be far-fetched to see in Lacenaire a *mise en abyme* of the screenwriter himself, who shares his anarchism, his revolt against society. Moreover, to the extent that the Lacenaire character evokes the stage director, we may also see in him an allusion to Carné (Sellier, p. 112). Openly homosexual, the film director may have identified with the homosexuality of Lacenaire (which is historically established but only intimated in the film) as with the marginality that this lifestyle entailed in Carné's time.

In the same realm, the opposition between French and Shakespearian theater may not only recall the passionate quarrel between the Classics and the Romantics in the 1820s. It seems to suggest also the 20th-century conflict between conventional theater represented by the Comédie française and the avant-garde theater which Jean-Louis Barrault championed. "The film is a devout tribute," Sellier maintains, "to the most innovative theater, the dramatic art that Barrault learned from his great teacher [Charles] Dullin" (p. 49). The opposition between pantomime and dialogued theater produces, on the other hand, a quite different "esthetic" theme: the contrast between silent film and the talkies. The notion of two "epochs" contributes to this theme, especially since the second, "The Man in White," begins with the dialogued play at the Grand Theater. Carné began his filmmaker's career during the silent film period before hitting his stride with the advent of the talkies in the thirties. However, *Children of Paradise* seems to treat the two forms of film art with the same admiration.

Just as it is the love plot which ties together the various elements in the film, it is love, in its various forms, which constitutes the major theme. As Chardère observes (pp. 41-42), the gallery of suitors surrounding Garance represents in fact four different types of love. Baptiste, who shares the dreamy "lunar" character of Pierrot his stage role, embodies passionate love, absolute love which idealizes its object. Frédérick on the other hand represents sensual and self-centered libertine love. Lacenaire's case is more complicated: he expresses scorn for women several times but admits that he "desires" Garance. His love has an intellectual cast and is perhaps only a form of admiration for the only woman he considers to be his equal, "the only free being that he had ever met" (Pérez, p. 87). It may also be a way to hide (from himself?) his attraction to handsome young men, like Avril, whose latent femininity is suggested by the rose tucked behind his ear and his dumb admiration for Lacenaire. The Count de Montray, finally, represents venal love: he wants to possess Garance as a beautiful object that he can buy and keep to himself. This may explain why Garance, who considers herself to be simply a woman, refers to herself as an "art object" (intentional irony?) when her false arrest forces her to seek the count's protection and become his mistress. The opposition between the Garance-Baptiste and Nathalie-Baptiste couples highlights finally the difference between the exaltation of a couple united by a great love and the sad life which is the lot of a couple where passion is not shared. The film is particularly hard on Nathalie's character, which is often treated as "unattractive" or "unrewarding" by the critics, owing perhaps to her fiercely possessive but thoroughly unrequited love.

As in all the major films by Carné and Prévert, "destiny" is an essential theme of *Children of Paradise*. It is a constant of their variety of poetic realism. And as is often the case, this theme is embodied by a character in the film. Here the role is played principally by Jericho the clothes peddler, a sinister individual, omnipresent and elusive. His arrival is often heralded by a trumpet call, an allusion perhaps to the horn which announces destiny in Victor Hugo's famous play *Hernani*, a veritable "manifesto" of Romanticism which appeared at precisely the same period as the action of the film (1830). The appearances of Jericho, which are never motivated by the dramatic action, are generally related to the future of most of the characters, as we noted earlier. They are clearly tied to Lacenaire's criminal career, Nathalie's future marriage with Baptiste, the departure of Garance with the count, the first kiss between her and Baptiste, the missed meeting in the theater box after Garance's return, and the final separation at the end of the film. This explains the violent antipathy that Baptiste feels for Jericho, as well as his murder of the old man in the show *Clothes Peddler*. Baptiste is in fact revolting against a malevolent fate which unrelentingly prevents him from being united with the woman he loves. The fact that the murdered clothes peddler is played by Baptiste's own father, who had mistreated his son at the beginning of the film, is not without interest. It has led certain critics, like Turk and Sellier, to read this scene as a symbolic settling of accounts by Carné with his own father, with whom his relations had been strained for many years.

Unlike *Daybreak*, several characters seem to share the role of destiny in *Children of Paradise*. In addition to Jericho there is the fake blind man Silk Thread, who takes Baptiste to the Robin restaurant where he meets Garance. And there is Garance herself: "The existences of all the men blossom through contact with Garance [...], but at the same time they all discover their own truth — to such an extent that one cannot help wondering if she too is not one of the forms of Destiny, whose ultimate embodiment remains uncertain" (Pérez, p. 76). It is true that Garance, although she is not coquettish, resembles the Helen of Giraudoux's *Tiger at the Gates* (*La Guerre de Troie n'aura pas lieu*, 1935), this "hostage of destiny" which men only touch at their own risk.

Given the historical context of the film, it is natural to speculate about the possibility of allusions in *Children of Paradise* to the situation of the French during the Occupation. In *The Devil's Envoys* some critics saw a work which "in the guise of a medieval fable relates the defeat of the traditional powers of France faced with the 'diabolic' force of Hitler, but also the emergence of a moral resistance embodied by the petrified lover whose heart continues to beat beneath the stone" (Sellier, p. 65). Carné denied that either he or Prévert had these notions in mind when they made the film, but admitted that they "accepted this interpretation, which corresponded [...] to a genuine need of a certain segment of the public at the end of 1942" (p. 156).

Some critics didn't hesitate to subject *Children of Paradise* to a similar exegesis, interpreting the character of Garance as a metaphor of Occupied France. Although she was a kept woman, she retained her moral freedom, just like the French people: under German domination but "free" in their hearts (Turk, p. 247; Sellier, p. 67). Instead of rebelling, "she plays coy with her benefactor-oppressor [...] and bides her time" (Sellier, p. 67) — like most of the French who waited for the end of the Occupation, their revolt burning in their hearts. By his moral turpitude, Jericho could be seen to represent the informers and the black market profiteers who thrived under the Occupation (Turk, p. 250).

As tempting as these hypotheses may be, they remain highly speculative. As Carné himself says in his memoirs, their principal concern was "to avoid provoking the Vichy censors" (p. 157), and they did so by taking refuge in the past. Carné was only concerned with avoiding any problems with the authorities in order to make his film (in Stonehill, p. 60). He had no intention of playing politics, unlike Jean-Paul Sartre, who in his play *The Flies* (*Les Mouches*, 1943) attacked Vichy's politics of repentance and urged his countrymen to resist violently. Nonetheless, nothing prevents the film's spectators from seeing meanings which go beyond the conscious intentions of the authors.

STYLE

In *Children of Paradise*, as in other Carné-Prévert films, there is a remarkable unity between the subject of the film and its form. On a certain level the film is about escape, not only into the past but also into the world of illusion, that is, into the world of theater. Nothing evokes this universe better than Prévert's dialogue, which is somewhat bombastic, laced with sharp repartee and spicy witticisms. While this is the typical style of Prévert's dialogues, which are often criticized as too "literary," it is particularly appropriate in *Children of Paradise*: "In a film which is intended to be a homage to theater," observes Chardère, "the dialogues should have a 'theatrical' character" (p. 42). That Prévert is perfectly aware of this is clear when Garance remarks to Lacenaire at their first meeting in the film: *"You talk all the time; it's like watching a play."* The style of the film is thus intentionally "theatrical," a characteristic which is emphasized by the general immobility of the camera and the framing of the characters from the knees up, "which permits the spectators to appreciate their costumes and their gestures while they speak their lines" (Sellier, p. 76). The camera movements are reduced to a minimum, especially in the first half of the film, where the most striking example is Baptiste's mime show, *The Palace of Mirages*. Since the camera is placed directly in front of the stage, Carné gives the spectator the ideal position to watch a play. The dramatic structure of the film is dominated by a series of conversations and confrontations between two or three characters, a trait which helps to create the impression of theatricality which emanates from the whole film.

STUDY GUIDE

Director's Comments

"For several months [in September 1940 in Paris], the theaters and cinemas had had their doors open again. If the truth were known, they had been showing pretty mediocre fare. All of my films had been banned by the Vichy regime, without any kind of justification. However, I knew the main reason: some featured actors had fled to the United States near the end of the fighting, like [Jean] Gabin, Michèle Morgan, and [Louis] Jouvet. More importantly, most of my films, if not all, had been made with the collaboration of Jewish technicians like Kosma and Trauner.

"To top it off, with the exception of *Daybreak* all of my films had been financed by Jewish producers who had left Germany to escape the Nazis. Moreover, an incredibly stupid rumor had been circulating for some time. In an effort to justify a defeat for which they alone were responsible, the governmental and military authorities reigning in Vichy could think of nothing better than to launch the rumor that "if we had lost the war, it was the fault of *Daybreak*" (*La Vie à belles dents*, pp. 125, 126)!

"It was an ideal situation to have the author, director, and art director living together. We really worked as a team, each one consulting the other whenever a problem arose, or whenever he felt the need for advice. Unfortunately, writing a screenplay, cutting it into shots, and designing the costumes isn't all there is to do. You also have to prepare for the actual shooting and put together a team of actors and technicians. After a few weeks I had to go back up to Paris to contact everyone I needed. Before leaving I had already chosen the actors, the most prestigious group one could imagine!

It would be impossible to put together a more talented cast: Arletty, Barrault, Brasseur, Salou, Herrand, to name only a few" (*La Vie à belles dents*, pp. 160-161).

How do you work with Jacques Prévert?

"It's simple. We collaborate closely from the first version of the screenplay to the final découpage. On the set I don't change a single word, and I require the actors to respect his text scrupulously. If I'm forced to cut something out, I never do it without his consent" (in Chardère, *Les Enfants du paradis*, p. 47).

"A production manager came to inform me that someone was asking to talk to one of the extras [...]. I was suspicious. I questioned him. Who was asking for him and why? He answered that the extra's wife had had an accident and that she had sent two neighbors to get her husband [...]. I hesitated a moment before answering, 'Tell them that he didn't come this morning'. The fellow returned a few moments later. 'The guys won't leave,' he said. 'His wife was run over by a streetcar and had both her legs cut off. She wants to see her husband before dying'. I didn't know what to do. I looked toward the set of Crime Boulevard. They were rehearsing. People were singing, dancing, laughing [...]. 'Do they have a foreign accent? — No'. I still didn't know what to do. And what if it were true? This guy who was probably laughing and carrying on in the crowd would never forgive me for preventing him from seeing his wife a last time. A feeling of pity suddenly overcame my fear. I put my megaphone to my mouth, asked for silence, and pronounced words for which I have never forgiven myself: "M. X is wanted in the production office'.

"Five minutes later the assistant returned. This time he was as white as a sheet. 'They took him away,' he said tonelessly. 'They were two French cops, probably working for the Gestapo'" (*La Vie à belles dents*, pp. 168-169).

Carné is summoned before a "purging committee" after the Liberation.

"So they interrogated me like a defendant before his judges: "Did you work for Continental Studios?" [Continental was the principal German studio in France during the Occupation.] So that was it! Nevertheless, my interrogator was misinformed. 'No,' I replied. — But you signed a contract! — That is correct, but I didn't make any films for them. — Yeh.'

"They returned my contracts to me. Then there was a silence. I understood that the discussion was over before it really began. I left in the same manner as I had arrived, but this time without any amenities. I learned a few days later that I had received a reprimand for having collaborated with Continental, while some of my colleagues who had in fact made several films for that studio were left alone [...].

"In reality, what certain people really resented was the fact that I had made two films which, in spite of the Occupation, had met considerable success. I'm not sure that they would have been unhappy if French cinema had died instead. In any case, that would have been more consistent with their blanket condemnation of everything that happened during the Occupation, despite the fact that our national cinema experienced an exceptional blossoming and expansion during that period. But that would only be recognized a few years later" (*La Vie à belles dents*, p. 179).

Excerpts for Discussion

Excerpt 1 (2'30-5'40) : The beginning of the film — Crime Boulevard, Garance, Frédérick and the theater.

Excerpt 2 (9'30-11'10): Lacenaire and Garance — the romantic anarchist.

Excerpt 3 (15'50-18'50): Baptiste mimes the theft of the watch.

Excerpt 4 (25'35-27'35) : The fight at the Funambules Theater.

Excerpt 5 (58'30-1h03'20) : Baptiste in Garance's room ; Frédérick and Garance.

Excerpt 6 (1h03'50-8'55) : Baptiste's first mime show at the Funambules — *The Palace of Mirages or the Moon Lover* (the first act).

Excerpt 7 (1h09'00-13'30): *The Palace of Mirages or the Moon Lover* (the second act).

Excerpt 8 (1h48'15-51'40): Frédérick destroys the play *The South-Side Inn* at the Grand Theater.

Excerpt 9 (2h04'45-8'30): The second mime show — *Clothes Peddler*.

Excerpt 10 (2h41'50-45'00): Frédérick, the count, Lacenaire (the confrontation after *Othello*) ; the "coup de théâtre" by Lacenaire.

Excerpt 11 (2h54'25-59'45): The dénouement — Nathalie confronts Baptiste and Garance in the room at the Great Post House ; Garance's departure ; Baptiste engulfed by the crowd of pierrots.

Quotations for Comment

Garance: "Still cruel, Pierre-François?"

Lacenaire: "I'm not cruel. I'm logical. I declared war on society a long time ago."

Garance: "And have you killed many people recently, Pierre-François?"

Lacenaire: "No, my angel! [...] But don't worry, Garance, I'm preparing something extraordinary. You're wrong to smile, Garance, believe me. I'm not like other men [...]. Have you ever been humiliated, Garance?"

Garance: "No, never."

Lacenaire: "Me neither...but "they" have tried, and that's already too much for a man like me [...]. But what a prodigious destiny! Loving no one...alone...unloved by anyone...free..." It's true that I love no one. Not even you, Garance, although you, my angel, are the only woman I've ever known for whom I feel neither hate nor scorn!"

* * *

The Clothes Peddler: "Come, come, my pretty, let me see your hand. (He takes her hand and looks at the lines.) What an astonishing line of luck!

Nathalie: "Oh! My luck...!"

The Clothes Peddler: "Nonsense. Everything will work out, it's written here. Take your good old papa's word for it. You'll marry the one you love."

Nathalie: "You really think so?"

The Clothes Peddler: "I'm sure of it. It's engraved in your hand."

* * *

Baptiste: "I'm trembling because I'm happy. And I'm happy because you are there beside me. I love you…do you love me, Garance?"

Garance: "You talk like a child. It's only in books that people love like that, or in dreams. Not in life!"

Baptiste: "Dreams, life, they're the same thing…or life's not worth living […]."

* * *

Garance: "Please, Baptiste, don't be so serious. You give me the chills. You'll have to excuse me, but I'm not…well, I'm not like you dream me. Please understand me, I'm a simple woman, so simple…I'm like I am. When I like someone, I like him to like me, that's all. And when I feel like saying "yes," I can't say "no"… I prefer the light of the moon…and you?"

Baptiste: "The moon, of course! The moon! That's my country, the moon! […] Oh, Garance! You can't know! I wish, yes I wish so much that you loved me like I love you."

* * *

Garance: "Who says I don't love you, Baptiste?"

Nathalie: "I do."

Garance: "What do you know about it?"

Nathalie: "Baptiste? I know, I see, I understand, I guess everything which concerns him!"

Baptiste: "Nathalie, I forbid you to speak like that!"

Nathalie: "That's the way it is, it's true, and you have nothing to say about it. Be quiet! (*To Garance.*) Of course, I'm not saying you're lying, but I know. Yes, I know that all the love there is in the world for Baptiste, I have it, you hear, I have it… There's no room for anyone else. It's engraved, marked down. I've taken everything, I know it. It's just that way!"

* * *

Chief of Police: "What's your name?" (Literal French: "What do you call yourself?")

Garance: "I never call myself, I'm always there. I don't need to call myself. But others call me Garance, if you're interested."

Chief of Police: "That's not a name!"

Garance: It's the name of a flower. But my real name, my maiden name, is Claire.

Chief of Police: "Claire what!" ["Claire" is the feminine form of "clear" in French.]

Garance: "Clear as daylight, Clear as spring water…"

* * *

Frédérick: "Ah! You're a writer! An unknown genius, of course?"

Lacenaire: "Yes, unknown […]. Still, I've written a little trifle which I can't help liking, a little one-acter full of merriness and melancholy. Two beings who are in love, lose each other, find one another again, and lose each other once again…"

* * *

Frédérick: "Over it! Why would I want to be over it so quickly? And what if I liked it…if it helped me to be jealous…if it was necessary even? Thank you, Garance. Thanks to you, thanks to all of you, I'm finally going to be able to play Othello! I was trying to find the character, but I couldn't feel him — he was a foreign being. But now, now he's a friend, a brother. I know him, I've got him! Othello! My fondest dream…"

* * *

The Count: "I want you to love me."

[…]

Garance: "You are an extraordinary person, Edouard. Not only are you rich, but you want to be loved as if you were poor! And what about the poor? Be reasonable, my friend, you really can't take everything away from the poor!"

[…]

Garance: "If it will make you happy, tomorrow everyone in Paris will know not only that I love you, but that I'm mad about you! […] But I say to you, to you alone, my friend: I loved a man and I love him still. I came back to Paris to see him. He let me know that he had forgotten me…and now all I want to do is leave, to go away!"

Questions/Topics for Reflection

1. What is "paradise?" Who are the "children?"
2. What idea or theme is attached to each of the main characters in the film: Garance, Baptiste, Frédérick, Nathalie, Lacenaire, Count de Montray?
3. The treatment of the themes of love and happiness in the film.
4. The relationship between theater and reality.
5. The first mime show by Baptiste at the Funambules Theater: *The Palace of Mirages or the Moon Lover*. Interpretation?
6. Lacenaire and the theater.
7. The appearances of Jericho at certain moments. Baptiste kills his father in the role of the clothes peddlar during the second mime show, *Clothes Peddler*. Possible interpretations?
8. The relationship between the play *Othello* and the plot of the film.
9. The final act of Lacenaire, his behavior.
10. The significance of the dénouement of the film.

CRITICAL DOSSIER

Jacques Siclier — "The Cinematographic Event of 1945"

In their recourse to the 19th century, Prévert and Carné had rediscovered the essence, the atmosphere of the original "poetic realism." The romanticism of 1830, with its spleen, its taste for absolute love and for death, resembled the spirit of the period just before the war and even more so the atmosphere of the Pétain period. Carné grandly orchestrated the movements of hundreds of extras in a world both realistic and mythical, creating a strange climate, somewhere between the diurnal and the nocturnal. Prévert's characters spoke better lines than ever before. His dialogues were in themselves a literary work [...].

The cinematographic event of 1945, *Children of Paradise* must be counted among the great successes of the French cinema of the Occupation [...]. That this film appeared in a liberated France two months before the surrender of Nazi Germany was also a sign for us. When you have lived through all that, you can't help feeling a profound sentimental attachment to *Children of Paradise* (*La France de Pétain et son cinéma*, pp. 168-169).

Georges Sadoul — "An Esthetic Soliloquy"

This magnificent and sumptuous work is a philosophical apologue and an esthetic soliloquy on the relationship between art and life, as well as a comparison of the different forms of art with each other. One after the other the principal genres of the romantic period appear: circus acts, melodrama, parody, high dramatic pantomime, Shakespearean tragedy. The description of each of these genres corresponds to the dramatic climate of the action in the film. On the esthetic plane the dénouement can be interpreted as a blending of men into a sort of universal spectacle in which the creator and the public are coalesced in the same human comedy. In the background, in addition to these forms of theater arts we can perceive a comparison between film and theater and between silent and sound cinema. These subtle and timely considerations were of less importance to the public than the pretexts employed by Prévert and Carné to develop their metaphors: the splendors of romanticism in a Paris borrowed from Balzac and Eugène Sue (*Le Cinéma français*, p. 96).

Michel Pérez — "A Homage to Show Business"

A homage to show business, *Children of Paradise* aggrandizes performers, who are never themselves except when they are on the stage. When Baptiste tears himself away from the stage to go to meet Garance (leaving the Funambules in the middle of *Clothes Peddler*), he commits a fruitless act. Pantomime needs a Baptiste sick from ungratified love to survive, and his amorous misfortune will lead him back to it for the greater glory of art and the artist. Frédérick, a fickle, superficial lover, needs to feel the pangs of jealousy provoked by Garance's love for Baptiste to gain an intimate understanding of Othello and to decide to play him. He needs to transform Garance into a stage character in order to love her seriously, painfully. In fact, it is Desdemona that he loves; he denies the reality of the woman to magnify his own. Lacenaire, in his project to assassinate Frédérick, provokes the most amusing confusion between theatrical fiction and reality, the stage and the wings, embellishing the picturesque side of the only frankly comic episode of of film […]. This first assassination attempt by Lacenaire — this "first step" in a future body of work — establishes an actor-playwright type of complicity between Frédérick and the assassin. This complicity will lead straight to the sequence of the opening of *Othello*, which sees the undoing of this world which cannot survive the *coups de théâtre* of a professional assassin […]. When Lacenaire draws back the curtain, revealing Baptiste embracing Garance, theater invades the already fragile real world. In the end, theater emerges supreme. It is hardly surprising that the tide of carnival masks submerges the screen at the end of the film (*Les Films de Carné*, pp. 86-87).

Jean Mitry — The Symbolism in *Children of Paradise*

The romanticism which combines the climate of the *Mysteries of Paris* [*Les Mystères de Paris* by Eugène Sue, 1842-1843] with the symbolism of the individuals is interesting and colorful, but the symbolic nature of the action and the characters always takes precedence over life. The leitmotif of the film, its keystone, is the opposition or mutual penetration of theater and reality, each encroaching on the other's terrain. Their causes and effects are so intermingled that one can no longer tell when theater is mixed into life with its lies and playacting or when life is on the stage with its sincerity beneath the mask. But it's all theoretical. The action unfurls around Garance, who is a geometrical locus of passions which are only "ideas of passion." Symbols move around her, like Deburau, a symbol of smouldering passion, of awkward love whose excessive idealism renders it incapable of achieving gratification. Frédérick Lemaître is a symbol of self-centered verve, of ham acting, of theatrical deception, but who asserts himself and fulfills his destiny through his very superficiality. Montray is a symbol of cold, aristocratic superiority, while the fake blind man symbolizes destiny and obliging chance. The tightrope walker is a symbol of the perilous path of men on the thread of their destiny. Lacenaire, finally, stands as a symbol of the gratuitous act, a representation of the absurd which asserts itself by crime and fulfills itself by murder. His character adds an appropriately existential note to this gallery of abstract figures who wear their symbols on their sleeves like the crescent in Garance's hair. And all of this is embellished by a carnival which is itself the symbolic representation of the masks, the appearances, the illusion and the vanity which sweeps the world into its diabolical gyrations (*Histoire du cinéma*, p. 252).

The Construction of Crime Boulevard

Crime Boulevard was built on the back lot of the Victorine Studios. Thirty-five tons of scaffolding brought from Paris (with great difficulty, owing to the troubled times and the many restrictions) furnished the framework for more than fifty theater and house fronts. The coating required no less than 350 tons of plaster […]. To put in 300 windows, we located, with all the difficulty one can imagine, 500 square meters of glass. The depth of the scenery, over 160 meters, was increased by a scale model which completed admirably this impressive ensemble in which more than 1,500 extras were moved around […]. Two specialists, framing carpenters from the capital, put up the scaffolding. That only took forty days. Fifteen other carpenters worked doggedly for ninety days; fifty machinists and an equal number of staff plasterers for sixty days;

twenty master plasterers for forty-five days. We estimate that 67,500 total hours of labor were put in (from a review of the period, *Ciné-Miroir*, in *L'Avant-Scéne Cinéma*, p. 106).

Carné and the Obsession of Realism

Last year I had gone to watch the shooting of *Children of Paradise*, and I was witness to a small tantrum by Carné. The set was the one created for Frédérick Lemaître-Brasseur's ridiculing of the play *The South-Side Inn*. I saw Carné approach the orchestra pit where a dozen good fellows were waiting.

— Are you musicians?

— No, we're extras. We just pretend to play!

Carné became angry.

— Ah! You pretend! Well, I want musicians, real musicians!

The production manager broke in: — But it's not necessary, since we are recording the music separately!

— I don't care. I need real musicians!

And Carné wouldn't agree to shoot until he had in the orchestra pit real musicians who pretended to play real music. The best part of the story is that in the film we only see the orchestra leader. As for the "real musicians," all we see of them is the tip of a violin bow here and there... (*L'Avant-Scène Cinéma*, p. 107).

MARCEL CARNÉ'S FILMOGRAPHY
(FEATURE FILMS)

1936	*Jenny*
1937	*Bizarre, Bizarre (Drôle de drame)*
1938	*Port of Shadows (Quai des brumes),*
	Hôtel du Nord
1939	*Daybreak (Le Jour se lève)*
1942	*The Devil's Envoys (Les Visiteurs du soir)*
1945	*Children of Paradise (Les Enfants du paradis)*
1946	*Gates of the Night (Les Portes de la nuit)*
1949	*La Marie du port*
1951	*Juliette, or Key of Dreams (Juliette ou la clé des songes)*
1953	*The Adultress (Thérèse Raquin)*
1954	*L'Air de Paris*
1956	*The Country I Come From (Le Pays d'où je viens)*
1958	*The Cheaters (Les Tricheurs)*
1960	*Wasteland (Terrain vague)*
1962	*Chicken Feed For Little Birds*
	(Du Mouron pour les petits oiseaux)
1965	*Three Rooms in Manhattan*
	(Trois Chambres à Manhattan)
1968	*Young Wolves (Les Jeunes Loups)*
1971	*Law Breakers (Les Assassins de l'ordre)*
1974	*The Marvelous Visit (La Merveilleuse Visite)*

WORKS CONSULTED

Carné, Marcel. *La Vie à belles dents. Souvenirs.* Paris: Pierre Belfond, 1989.

Carné, Marcel, and Jacques Prévert. "*Les Enfants du paradis*" (screenplay). *L'Avant-Scène Cinéma* 72-73 (July-Sept. 1967): 1-106.

Chardère, Bernard. *Les Enfants du paradis.* Paris: Jean-Pierre de Monza, 1999.

Chazal, Robert. *Marcel Carné.* Paris: Seghers, 1965.

Chion, Michel. "Le Dernier Mot du muet." *Cahiers du cinéma* 330 (Dec. 1981): 5-15.

Gili, Jean A. *Le Cinéma à Nice de 1939 à 1945.* Nice: Faculté des Lettres, 1973.

Mitry, Jean. *Histoire du cinéma*, V. The 1940s. Paris: Jean-Pierre Delarge, 1980.

Pérez, Michel. *Les Films de Carné.* Paris: Ramsey, 1994.

Quéval, Jean. *Marcel Carné.* Paris: Editions du Cerf, 1952.

Sadoul, Georges. *Le Cinéma français.* Paris: Flammarion, 1962.

Sellier, Geniève. *Les Enfants du paradis.* Paris: Nathan, 1992.

Siclier, Jacques. *La France de Pétain et son cinéma.* Paris: Henri Veyrier, 1981.

Stonehill, Brian. "Forbidden Games" (interview avec Marcel Carné). *Film Comment* XXVII, no. 6 (Nov.-Dec. 1991): 58-61.

Turk, Edward Baron. *Child of Paradise. Marcel Carné and the Golden Age of French Cinéma.* Cambridge, MA: Harvard UP, 1989.

Jean Cocteau

Beauty and the Beast
Le Belle et la Bête

(1946)

Jean Cocteau, *Beauty and the Beast*: Belle (Josette Day) at the Beast's (Jean Marais) castle. © Société Nouvelle de Cinématographie

Director	Jean Cocteau
Screenplay, adaptation, dialogues	Jean Cocteau
Director of Photography	Henri Alekan
Music	Georges Auric
Film Editor	Claude Ibéria
Sound	Jacques Lebreton, Jacques Carrère
Lighting	Raymond Méresse
Art Director	Christian Bérard
Costumes	Marcel Escoffier
Technical Advisor	René Clément
Script Girl (Continuity)	Lucile Costa
Producer	André Paulvé
Length.	1 h 32

Cast

Jean Marais (*Avenant, the Beast, the Prince*), Josette Day (*Beauty*), Marcel André (*Beauty's father*), Mila Parély (*Félicie*), Nane Germon (*Adélaïde*), Michel Auclair (*Ludovic*), Raoul Marco, with Jean Cocteau's voice (*the usurer*).

STORY

A financially ruined merchant has three daughters. Adélaïde and Félicie, pretty but mean-spirited young ladies, cannot bear living in poverty and dream of money, fancy clothes, and social hobnobbing. The third, who is so good-hearted and attractive that she has been nicknamed "Beauty," is derided by her sisters and forced to work as their servant. The merchant has a son, Ludovic, who lives with him also. Ludovic's friend Avenant is in love with Beauty and wants to marry her. Beauty refuses his overtures because she does not wish to abandon her father, who is suffering greatly from his financial misfortunes.

Returning one night from the city, after his ruin has been confirmed, the merchant must pass through a great forest. He loses his way and discovers by pure chance the enchanted castle of the Beast, where he dines and spends the night. In the morning as he is leaving, he picks a rose for Beauty, who had asked for one. The Beast appears, furious, and condemns the merchant to die unless one of his daughters agrees to replace him as the Beast's prisoner at the castle. Feeling guilty because of the rose, Beauty offers to go in her father's place. Despite Avenant's angry opposition, she goes to live at the Beast's castle and finds him exquisitely courteous to her. However, each evening her host asks her if she will agree to become his wife. Although Beauty steadfastly refuses, she begins to appreciate the fine qualities — kindness, generosity, nobility of sentiment — which are hidden behind the Beast's hideous exterior.

Beauty learns that her father is dangerously ill. She begs the Beast to let her return home for a week, promising to return to the castle. The Beast finally agrees but makes it clear that he will die of sorrow if she doesn't keep her word. Before her departure he gives her the golden key to Diane the Huntress's Pavilion, where all of his treasures are kept. He also gives her a magic glove which allows her to travel between the enchanted world of the castle and the real world. Richly dressed and adorned, Beauty returns home magically.

Beauty's father recovers instantly when he sees his daughter again. Beauty's sisters are jealous of her wealth and happiness, however, and plot ways to make her violate the terms of her visit in the hope that the Beast will devour her as her punishment. In addition, Félicie steals the golden key to allow Avenant and Ludovic to steal the Beast's treasures after killing him. When Beauty looks in her magic mirror and sees the Beast on the verge of dying as a result of her continuing absence, she quickly returns to the castle. Her love for the Beast appears in her gaze at the very moment that Avenant breaks into Diane's Pavilion. The Beast is instantly transformed into Prince Charming, while Avenant, pierced by an arrow shot by the statue of Diane the Huntress, turns into the Beast and dies. Beauty flies off with the prince to his kingdom, where she will become his wife.

CRITICAL RECEPTION

While *Beauty and the Beast* received an enthusiastic response from the public, it was judged severely by the film critics at the Cannes Film Festival in 1946. As Cocteau recalls in his *Entretiens sur le cinématographe*, "The first public contact at the Cannes Festival was disastrous. The staunchly elitist judges considered that the film would go over the heads of children and would seem childish to adults" (p. 46). In the contemporary reviews (see *L'Avant-Scène Cinéma*, pp. 44-46), we note comments such as "pretentious bungling," "stilted," "childish," "false naiveté," "coldness," "inhuman," "estheticism," "failure," and the like. Even André Bazin and Georges Sadoul, who are among the critics with the most dependable judgment, were rough on Cocteau's film when it came out. Sadoul criticized its "outdated esthetics," while Bazin deplored its "overly obvious formal symbolism."

Other voices, many of them prominent, nonetheless took up the film's defense. Alexandre Astruc upbraided the critics: "Preoccupied with condemning the manner in which the poet wields his arms, they don't notice that the blow has already been struck and that it is right on target [...]. Nothing is more troublesome than a certain nobility of tone, especially in the movies. That is why people speak of estheticism, of arrogance perhaps, and of pretension." Some critics like Jean Vidal approved Cocteau's "estheticism" outright: "In the final analysis *Beauty and the Beast* is a work of art, a plastic poem of rare perfection. Pure beauty is everywhere present, a beauty which is based neither in the heart nor in nature; it is a cold beauty, cruel, intellectual, and if I may be so daring, mathematical." Pierre Lagarde called Cocteau's film a "brilliant success," declaring prophetically that "it is a work which will become a classic." Jean Morienval shared Lagarde's judgment: "*Beauty and the Beast* appears to be one of those films which contribute to the development of film art. In a few years it will be referred to as a masterpiece." René Gilson summarized the critical ambivalence which surrounded the film: "*Beauty and the Beast* was either accepted for its formal splendor alone or refused because of that same beauty, which for certain critics served to make the work cold or petrified. For some, the bride was beautiful and they overlooked her birth and flaws; for others, she was too beautiful, to the extent that her very beauty stifled desire" (p. 45).

In spite of the growling and sniping by the film critics, *Beauty and the Beast* was awarded two prizes at the Cannes Film Festival (for production and music) and captured the prestigious Louis Delluc Prize. Some years later, as Honorary President of the Cannes Festival in 1957, Cocteau reflected ironically, "The film of mine which had one of the longest careers, and which is still playing in India and China, is *Beauty and the Beast*, which was shot down by the critics here" (*L'Avant-Scène Cinéma*, p. 52).

BEFORE *BEAUTY AND THE BEAST*

Born on July 5, 1889, Jean Cocteau was certainly one of the most eclectic French literary figures of the first half of the twentieth century. While he thought of himself primarily as a poet, he was also a novelist, playwright, artist, and librettist, as well as a screenwriter, actor, and filmmaker. In the first decades of the century he was one of the most fashionable figures in the Parisian salons, and the interwar period saw intense artistic creativity on his part. He distinguished himself in the theater with *The Eiffel Tower Wedding Party* (*Les Mariés de la Tour Eiffel*, 1924), *The Human Voice* (*La Voix humaine*, 1930), *La Machine infernale* (1934), *Les Parents terribles* (1938), *Les Monstres sacrés* (1940), *The Typewriter* (*La Machine à écrire*, 1941), *The Eagle Has Two Heads* (*L'Aigle à deux têtes*, 1946), and *Bacchus* (1952).

In 1930 Cocteau made his first film, *The Blood of a Poet* (*Le Sang d'un poète*), which bears the mark of the still popular Surrealist movement and the experimental spirit which that implies. The film is striking also by its autobiographical character. The few films directed by Cocteau himself are all part of a sort of diary in which he expresses his personal obsessions and his reflections on his art, as well as on the role of the poet. He considers cinema to be one of the means by which he can express "the unknown character which lives within him." Cocteau waited fifteen years to make his next film, *Beauty and the Beast*, which is a period adaptation of a fairytale written by Mme Leprince de Beaumont in 1757. Between the two films, in addition to his other artistic activities, Cocteau wrote screenplays or dialogues for films by other directors. These include Jean Delannoy's *The Eternal Return* (*L'Eternel Retour*, 1943), a modernized version of the Tristan and Isolde myth, and Robert Bresson's *Ladies of the Park* (*Les Dames du Bois de Boulogne*, 1945), a modernization of an episode from the novel by Denis Diderot, *Jacques The Fatalist and His Master* (*Jacques le fataliste et son maître*, ca. 1770).

ORIGIN AND ADAPTATION

The project was born during the Christmas holidays in 1943 when Jean Marais, who was living with Cocteau, simply said, "I would so much like you to make a film on *Beauty and the Beast*" (Philippe, p. 63). The germ of the idea was planted, and Cocteau began writing his adaptation of the fairytale in spring 1944 while the Allied bombers crisscrossed the sky over Paris in preparation for the Normandy landing on June 6. Cocteau doesn't hide the deeply personal nature of the project, confiding, "I chose this fable because it corresponded to my personal mythology" (*Entretiens*, p. 46). He compares himself to an "archeologist" who digs down into himself to discover the film: "The film exists (preexists). My task is to discover it in the shadows where it is lying dormant, by digging with a pick and shovel" (*Journal d'un film*, October 7, 1945). He adds shortly afterward in his diary on the making of *Beauty and the Beast*: "Little by little I capture the myths and memories from my youth" (October 9). The world of this personal mythology, like Diane's Pavilion in the film, is "the whole world of childhood guarded and inviolable, which cannot be violated but only constantly enriched by the most secret and mysterious part of our inner worlds, of our deepest feelings, which constitutes for the poet in particular […] one of the inexhaustible sources of poetry" (in Gilson, p. 50). As Cocteau says more simply, a few weeks before finishing his film, "I've attempted to make a film for 'children.' I'm trying to speak to the child who remains in each of us" (*L'Avant-Scène Cinéma*, p. 53).

In this process of introspection Madame Leprince de Beaumont's fairytale undergoes a number of critical modifications. Here are the most important innovations and additions by Cocteau: the handsome but debauched character of Avenant (who replaces Beauty's anonymous suitors in the tale), as well as his death and transformation into the Beast at the end; Diane's Pavilion which contains all of the Beast's riches; the evolution of Beauty's sentiments toward the Beast; the Beast's traumatic inner conflict between animal instinct and human nobility of character. In addition to these major changes, there are a number of minor differences. Beauty has only one brother in Cocteau's film instead of the three in the tale, and he is portrayed as a low-life. In the tale, owing to Beauty's generosity her father is able to give her two sisters the ill-fated marriages they desire, and they are both turned into statues at the end as punishment. The magic ring which permits Beauty to travel between the two worlds in Beaumont's tale is replaced in the film by the Beast's glove. Cocteau invents the white horse Magnificent, which serves as a means of transportation between the real world and the Beast's enchanted castle. Contrary to the tale, fairies and dreams play no role in Cocteau's film. As he says, it is a "fairytale without fairies" (*Entretiens*, p. 45).

On the other hand, Cocteau maintains the general structure of the tale, including the tragic financial ruin of the merchant, the castle and rose episode, Beauty's dramatic sacrifice to save her father's life culminating in her falling in love with her beastly jailor, her return home when her father is ill and her sisters' plotting to keep her there beyond the allotted period, her return to the castle just in time to save the dying Beast, and the transformation of the Beast into a prince. The personal traits of the main characters are virtually unchanged: Beauty kind and virtuous, her sisters prideful, envious, and mean, the Beast noble, courtly, and generous. The relationship between Beauty and her father, finally, remains just as ambiguous in Cocteau's film as in Beaumont's fairytale.

THE ACTORS AND THE SHOOTING

Cocteau has no trouble finding financial backers for his film because of the casting of Jean Marais, already a major star in French theater and cinema, in the roles of Avenant and the Beast. The producers became hesitant, however, if we are to believe Philippe (p. 66), when they learned that the hero's face would be hidden beneath a wild animal's mask. For the role of Beauty Marcel Pagnol suggested Josette Day, who had played in numerous films between 1932 and 1940 before turning to the theater. But she had begun her career as a dancer at the Paris Opera, and it is her grace of movement — very important in the scene where Beauty runs in slow motion through the castle — as much as her talent as an actress which convinced Cocteau to cast her in the role. The rest of the cast is composed of seasoned actors, all of them used to acting both on stage and on screen, with the exception of Michel Auclair, who is playing his first film role. We recognize especially Mila Parély, who played the role of Geneviève, Robert de la Chesnaye's mistress in Renoir's *The Rules of the Game* (1939).

Cocteau's technical crew is composed of specialists with whom he had already worked, including some highly talented figures: Henri Alekan as Director of Photography, Christian Bérard as Art Director, and Georges Auric as composer. Auric would, in fact, compose the music for all of Cocteau's films. Since he had very limited experience with filmmaking, Cocteau took on a technical advisor, René Clément, who had just finished making the very successful *Battle of the Rails* (*La Bataille du rail*, 1946). After a year of preparation Cocteau began to shoot on August 26, 1945. During the making of the film he kept a diary in which he describes the film's progress.

This extremely valuable document was subsequently published in 1946 as *La Belle et la Bête: journal d'un film*. In his diary he allows us to follow day by day (until the final day on June 1, 1946) the staging and shooting of the film. He relates all the vicissitudes of the shooting, revealing at the same time how he achieved the numerous special effects which create the magical atmosphere dominating the episodes at the Beast's enchanted castle.

Certain of these techniques are specific to film art, such as the slow motion shots (Belle's run through the castle, Magnificent's emerging from the stable), the use of reverse projection (the self-lighting candelabras, the pearl necklace which forms in Beauty's hand), dissolves (the appearance of Beauty on her bed at the castle or at her father's home), and superimpositions (the transformation of Avenant into the Beast). Other special effects are purely theatrical or mechanical in nature, like the heads of stone (the male caryatids) which turn beneath the fireplace, the arm which pours the wine, Beauty's floating through the castle on a dolly pulled by assistants, or the ears of the Beast which perk up when René Clément pushes them up from behind with a forked stick.

Part of the film is shot on location at the Château de Raray north of Paris, "the oddest park in France" according to Cocteau. The remainder of the work on location was done at Rochecorbon in Touraine a few kilometers from Tours, where Cocteau had discovered by pure chance a country manor which matched perfectly his image of the ruined merchant's estate. As he tells the story himself, "We found the precise structures and grounds which I had feared we were going to have to build ourselves. This piece of property established a style, and this style served as a guide for the rest. The coincidence is greater still: all of the hardware of this little manor represented the Beast" (*Entretiens*, p. 49). Jean Marais's makeup which changed him into the Beast took three to five hours each time. It was such a trial for Marais that Cocteau compares it to the traumatic transformation of Dr. Jekyll into Mr. Hyde. "He did it alone, gluing hair after hair, adjusting the dental piece, fitting the claws onto his fingernails, changing his state of mind as he changed from man to animal [...]. We had to shoot at night. Around six o'clock in the morning he resembled more and more a suffering animal. We can thank the torture of the glue, the hair, and the fatigue for the extraordinary shot where the Beast gazes at Beauty as he lies dying" (in Philippe, p. 68). Marais had to keep his makeup on for up to fifteen hours at a stretch and could only take liquid nourishment or sip purées, through a straw.

Cocteau began shooting only a few months after the German surrender (May 8, 1945). Since the country was ravaged by five years of Occupation and by the battles for the Liberation, the working conditions were extremely difficult. As Cocteau tells it in his *Journal*, it was hard to obtain good quality film. There were constant power failures, and the quality of the laboratory processing was often very marginal. Moreover, several members of the crew fell ill during the shooting — Marais and Parély, but especially Cocteau himself, tormented for months by a skin infection which covered his face with welts and scabs, by terrible toothaches, and by several other physical ailments. He was finally hospitalized for a whole week, which interrupted the shooting from October 24 to the beginning of November. Cocteau was philosophical, attributing his physical woes to the long torture of the Occupation that the French people had just endured: "We are all paying the price of five unbearable years. "Worrying ourselves sick" is not just a figure of speech. We were really sick from five years of hate, fears, and awakening to a nightmare each day. Five years of shame and degradation. We were soaked in it, smeared with it to our very soul. We had to hold on. Wait. It is this nerve-wracking wait that cost us so dearly. Now we have to catch up, whatever the obstacles. France must be brilliant whatever it takes" (*Journal*, October 7, 1945). *Beauty and the Beast* was Cocteau's contribution to the renaissance of France.

THEMES AND SYMBOLS

The moral of Madame Leprince de Beaumont's fairytale is simple and clear: the only solid happiness is founded on virtue and kindness rather than on beauty or cleverness. In Cocteau's film, which does not contradict the tale's moral thesis, the central interest becomes instead love and/or sexual desire. In the two works we are confronted with several thematic oppositions which all refer to human duality: exterior and interior, beauty and ugliness, appearance and reality. These oppositions are related by Cocteau to the film's principal antithesis between the real world inhabited by the merchant and his family and the enchanted universe of the Beast's castle. The creation of the Avenant character by Cocteau completes the antithetical construction of the film by introducing into the real world a counterpart to the Beast. Avenant is in fact the reverse image of the Beast. The true ugliness of Avenant (his character) is interiorized and his external beauty is reduced to deceptive appearance, just as the hideous appearance of the Beast is deceptive. Beauty's gaze, guided by love, will triumph over appearances and discover the true beauty of the Beast, his inner goodness and noble soul. The radical change in Beauty is the most obvious sense we can give to the metamorphosis of the Beast into Prince Charming: he is transfigured in the eyes of Beauty when she falls in love with him. As the prince says at the end of the film, "*Love can turn a man into a beast. Love can also turn an ugly man into a handsome one.*" The spectator can stop there, if he is so inclined, as regards the interpretation of Cocteau's *Beauty and the Beast.*

Nonetheless, this interpretation does not take into account the role of Beauty's father, which, considering the absence of her mother, complicates the story considerably. Beauty is undeniably and deeply attached to her father, so much so that she prefers to remain unmarried rather than leave him, a position which she verbalizes three times in the film. It is hardly surprising that this situation prompts critics to suggest Freudian themes and to speak of an unresolved Oedipal complex and incestuous desire. This perspective is encouraged moreover by the principal symbol of the film, the rose that the merchant picks in the Beast's garden. The rose is tightly linked to Beauty's imprisonment at the castle and reflects on the character of her relationship with both her father and the Beast. Since the Middle Ages in France, the rose has been a symbol for the beloved woman, or for the possession of the woman. In *The Romance of the Rose* (*Le Roman de la rose*), the allegorical poem by Guillaume de Lorris (ca. 1236), for example, the act of picking the rose is symbolic of amorous conquest, which is the goal of the *persona* of the poem. In the light of this deeply rooted symbolism, Beauty's request that her father bring her a rose, as well as her father's act in picking the rose, are necessarily equivocal and suggestive.

If we agree that the main character of the film is Beauty, we must take into account her relationships with both Avenant and the Beast. We note the striking role of fear in both cases. When we see Beauty alone with Avenant at the beginning of the film, he holds her in his arms from behind, "imprisoning" her with the arrow which has just caused such fright when it flew into the room through the window. The obvious phallic symbolism of the arrow's shaft seems to suggest that Beauty's rejection of Avenant's marriage proposal is related to her fear of sexual relations, which she perceives as a danger. This fear would tend to explain Beauty's desire to "remain a maiden" ("*rester fille*"). Beauty's terror, which causes her to faint later at the sight of the Beast, may be explained in a similar manner, insofar as the ugliness of the Beast may be understood as a metaphorical representation of the base, threatening character of libidinal drives, that is, of male sexual desire (DeNitto and Herman, p. 217). The metaphorical sense of the Beast's "bestiality" is suggested moreover by the Beast's clear shame when he apologizes to Beauty after appearing before her covered with blood. Beauty: "*What are you apologizing for?*" The Beast: "*For being a beast ... Pardon me.*" Beauty: "*You should be ashamed of yourself!*" Ashamed, of course, of not being able to control his animal instincts.

As for the dénouement, Diane's Pavilion, where all of the Beast's treasurers are kept and which is defended by the goddess of chastity, clearly exhibits the same sexual symbolism as the rose. In a Freudian perspective a jewel box signifies either the female sexual organs or virginity itself (the young maiden's "treasure"). For this reason Avenant's attempt to break into the pavilion, which costs him his life, may be interpreted symbolically as an attempted rape. It completes the opposition between the frightening brutality of Avenant's virility and the great courtliness of the Beast, his nobility, which reassures Beauty and wins her over in the end. This nobility is perhaps the implied symbolism of the golden key. The scene in which the Beast is transformed by the amorous gaze of the heroine represents from this viewpoint the awakening of Beauty to a normal sexual life. Achieving emotional maturity she surmounts her fear of male virility, which she now finds attractive, as we see when the prince asks her if she is afraid to fly through the sky with him: "*I like to be afraid ... with you.*" The hideous appearance of the Beast thus becomes a metaphor for the repulsiveness of male virility *as Beauty perceived it*, just as the metamorphosis of the Beast is a metaphorical representation of the transformation of Beauty's attitude towards men and towards her own sexuality (DeNitto, pp. 130, 144, 154). Now she can leave her father and be united with another man.

Given the autobiographical character of Cocteau's works, it is also tempting to see in *Beauty and the Beast* a representation of the psyche of the poet himself, of his own Oedipal drives (Pauly, p. 341). Whatever its mode of application, the Freudian perspective is of course just a viewpoint among others on Cocteau's film. A reading of the film which places the Beast rather than Beauty at the center of the narrative, for instance, may lead us to the personal mythology of Cocteau the Poet without having recourse to psychoanalytical hypotheses. Rather than serving as symbols of Man in general, Avenant and the Beast may be interpreted as contradictory facets of the poet's own particular personality, "this series of 'others' that live within the poet or any man devoted to the fulfillment of his being" (Gilson, p. 42). Here it is no longer a question of metamorphosis but, as Gilson suggests, of "phenixology": "The Beast has

Beast as poet

to die by and for love, but the same being is reborn from this death" (p. 42). If the Beast is the protagonist, it is likewise possible to identify it with the poet as "monster." In this interpretation the Beast may be seen as the incarnation of the rejected poet, hated by an obtuse and hostile public. The transformation of the monster into Prince Charming by Beauty's amorous gaze (the judgment of the enlightened public) signifies here the liberation of the poet from the curse of incomprehension (Popkin, p. 105; see the *Critical Dossier*).

STYLE AND MUSIC

In a film which attempts to create a supernatural "fairytale-like" atmosphere full of mystery and magic, style plays a critical role inseparable from the themes. Paradoxically Cocteau the poet makes every effort in *Beauty and the Beast* to avoid creating with his shots what he calls "poeticizing poetry". The poetry must emanate from reality alone, and he fulminated against the "artistic genre," the esthetic effects sought by his Director of Photography Alekan at the beginning of the shooting. "Nothing equals the sublimation of documentary style," he declared in his *Journal*. "That's the style I want him to achieve" (October 5, 1945). Cocteau, who was no less demanding of his actors, required an unusual discipline in their interpretation of their roles. "I'm having a great deal of difficulty getting my actors to understand that the style of the film demands a supernatural depth and stylization. There is little dialogue and no fuzziness in the delivery. The sentences are all very short and precise" (*Journal*, August 29, 1945). Cocteau carefully avoided any picturesque effects, any decorative temptations. "If you try to be picturesque in a fairytale, you are doomed to failure. The unreal has its own realism. The implausible is even more implausible than in other contexts" (*L'Avant-Scène Cinéma*, p. 53). He noted here the invaluable contributions of the Art Director, Christian Bérard, who managed to avoid what the director calls "the false fantastic": "He was the only one who understood that the fairytale world is inimical to vagueness and that mystery only exists in precise things" (Gilson, p. 48).

Rigorousness in the staging of the film begins with the style of the shots. Cocteau made it a point of honor to reduce camera movements to a strict minimum: "This film is going to be the proof that one can avoid camera movements in favor of stationary shots" (*Journal*, September 9, 1945). He insisted on the austere harmony of long static shots with every detail thought out, but without creating a tableau effect. The highly restrained style of the acting — especially in the characters' movements — is highlighted in this approach. The sober and moderate scenery underlines the style of the film: "No profusion, no excessiveness, no pomp either" (in Gilson, p. 46). The lack of dialogue in certain sequence shots makes Georges Auric's music all the more important. "My film includes some very long scenes with no dialogue and in which nothing happens — a character moves from one point to another — in which, rather, nothing seems to be happening. Here is where I have to count on Georges Auric, who wrote the music for *The Eternal Return* and *The Blood of a Poet*. In these moments the film depends entirely on his score" (Philippe, p. 74).

In order to emphasize the opposition between the real world and the Beast's supernatural world, the scenes at the merchant's manor contrast sharply with those at the Beast's castle. In the former the lighting is natural and the furnishings spare and realistic, creating an impression of bareness. With few exceptions there is no background music, and when there is, it is always in reference to the other world (for example, during Beauty's return home, when she speaks of the Beast). Like the composition of the shots, the costumes create a Dutch atmosphere, taking their inspiration from Vermeer and Rembrandt paintings primarily. Le Nain's influence is also perceptible, particularly in the tavern scenes, which are no less stamped with realism. In the castle scenes, on the other hand, we often hear background music, including a choir at the most dramatic moments which adds a mysterious aura to the film. Since the Beast's kingdom is nocturnal, the raw light of day yields to half-light, clouded sometimes by fog or by play of light and shadow. The furnishings and costumes are much richer. For certain shots, like the dining room table in the castle or the exteriors of Diane's Pavilion, Bérard modeled his designs on Gustave Doré's illustrations for fairytales.

To all of the above Cocteau added his special effects — the talking door and mirror, for example, the human arms which hold the candelabras or pour wine, the bed which makes itself — whose surrealism highlights the strangeness, the unreality, of the Beast's universe. In the remarks by Cocteau below, taken either from his diary or from the technical découpage, the filmmaker makes us privy to some additional reflections on the making of his film, including revelations on the creation of some of his most striking special effects.

STUDY GUIDE

Director's Comments

"First direct special effect: the necklace. We lean the camera to the side. The false necklace falls off-camera, the real one into the frame. They seem to be transformed during the fall" (September 7, 1945).

"First shot of the day. Eleven o'clock: Jeannot [Jean Marais] and Michel [Auclair] leave the barn on Aramis [the horse Magnificent]. Aramis rears up. Yesterday he refused to rear up. We get the shot. The third time the horse comes out of the barn but backs up and goes back inside, bucks, dumps Michel and reappears with Jeannot alone. Last shot. At noon. Avenant and Ludovic have to gallop toward us and leave the frame on the left, brushing close to the camera. That's when the problems begin. Aramis bucks or goes out of control. Michel grabs onto Jeannot, who has neither saddle nor stirrups, almost falls off and makes everyone laugh. He tries again, bravely, but his acrobatics become so dangerous (and Jeannot is riding with an open wound) that I order them to stop. We'll use doubles […]. At three o'clock I shoot the gallop. The riding master is disguised as Avenant. Lucile the script girl is dressed up as Ludovic. Aramis no longer has Michel on his rump, but the two riders still annoy him. He becomes difficult. He finally gallops, and I'm sure that at this speed and with the movement no one will notice the artifice" (September 12, 1945).

"I shoot the close-up of Jeannot smelling the stag. Hidden behind his collar, Clément moves his ears with a forked stick. They perk up. The effect is striking" (September 27, 1945).

"After lunch I attacked the scene in the vestibule where the sisters come back from the stable with the magic mirror. I finished at six o'clock by shooting the monkey that Mila sees in the mirror in her place. The monkey was charming. I shot it through a pane of glass placed in the mirror frame, wearing a bonnet like the sisters, its neck adorned with a ruff and sitting on an open book, in the style of Chardin. Tomorrow morning I'll shoot the old hag that Nane sees" (October 18, 1945).

"The mirror will be slightly turned so as not to reflect Adélaïde's face, which is out of the frame. The old woman will move forward until her face is framed in the mirror at the same time as Adélaïde will appear at the edge of the frame" (technical découpage, in Hammond, p. 333).

"The young extras who are playing the role of the stone heads of the caryatids are incredibly patient. Kneeling uncomfortably behind the scenery, their shoulders in a kind of armor, they have to press their plastered-down hair […] against the columns and take the lights right in the face" (November 30, 1945).

"Last night I shot the scenes where the Beast is dying. I had put collars on the swans' necks, but they had them off in an hour […]. I owe to pure serendipity some amazing shots that would have been impossible to plan. The swans became furious with this strange animal whose mane and paw were hanging in the water. They hissed at it and attacked it. With his usual composure Marais didn't move an inch and put up with their attacks. These swans attacking their sick master, stripped of his power, gave an uncanny quality to the scene" (December 28, 1945).

"Yesterday I finished the shots of Prince Charming beside the spring. Marais was the prince, and he was charming. To finish up, I shot him in slow motion as he fell backwards to be able to project the shot in reverse, showing him coming back up to his feet with an otherworldly grace" (January 4, 1946).

"Next week I'll begin editing. It's the phase which gives a work its rhythm. *My style.* (January 4, 1946) […]. The editing process is absolutely fascinating. By cutting and gluing you correct the life you've created. You add, you take away, you rearrange, you add sentences to faces which are listening to them, you jump from one place to another, and you speed things up or you cut a gesture short" (January 23, 1946).

The last shots:

"Special effect for the mantel which jumps up from the ground. Here's how we'll do this shot. The camera frames the knoll where Beauty and the Prince were lying on the mantel. Above the space framed by the cameraman we will build a sort of diving board. Beneath the diving board we'll cover the knoll with a thick layer of foam rubber. The actor and a lady acrobat (a double dressed like the actress) will wait at the edge of the board, standing on the mantel which is hanging below their feet, weighted down at the lower end (off camera). At my signal, when the shot has already begun, the two actors will jump from the board, holding themselves upright, such that the bottom of the weighted mantel comes into the frame before the actors. They will land on the grassy knoll and let themselves fall, the Prince holding Beauty by the shoulders and Beauty hiding her face against his chest. Once they have fallen, they will not move, letting the shot continue a moment as they hold the position in which they fell. If the actor and actress, before jumping, hold the upper ends of the mantel with their arms stretched out, they will be able to draw the corners of the mantel towards themselves once they are lying still on the ground. We will project this shot in reverse. As a result we will see the Prince and Beauty stretched out in a strange position […]. Suddenly they will rise up from the ground and fly up through the top of the frame. We may have to shoot in slow motion. The next shot will show the heads of Beauty and the Prince (up to the chest) with their bodies stretched out, holding the top of the mantel above them. In reality this shot will be made with the two actors standing in front of a mirror and with a fan turning furiously. On the mirror we will see shots taken from an airplane — coasts, waves, the sea — the shot will finish on the magic mantel, far off flying through the clouds [...]. In the tracking shot taken from an airplane we will see the bottom of the mantel flapping at the top of the frame" (technical découpage, in Hammond, pp. 383, 385, 387, 389).

Excerpts for Discussion

Excerpt 1 (6'35-8'30): Avenant asks Beauty to marry him, holding her "prisoner" with the arrow; Beauty refuses.

Excerpt 2 (14'20-19'00): Beauty's father rides through the forest at night and discovers the Beast's castle (special effects).

Excerpt 3 (21'30-23'45): The father picks the rose ; the reparations demanded by the Beast.

Excerpt 4 (28'20-31'45): Beauty arrives at the castle (supernatural atmosphere).

Excerpt 5 (51'50-55'00): Beauty and the Beast; Beauty's attachment to her father; the Beast arrives before Beauty's door in the middle of the night, covered with blood; the Beast is humiliated.

Excerpt 6 (1h01'05-03'45): Beauty returns home (special effects); her tears become diamonds.

Excerpt 7 (1h05'20-06'00): The pearl necklace and the old piece of rope (special effects).

Excerpt 8 (1h25'30-31'30): The dénouement.

QUOTATIONS FOR COMMENT

Avenant: "I love you. Marry me."

Beauty: "No, Avenant. Please don't ask again, it's useless."

Avenant: "You don't like me."

Beauty: "No, that's not it, Avenant."

Avenant: "So what is it?"

Beauty: "I want to remain unmarried and live with my father."

* * *

The Beast: "My heart is good, but I'm a monster."

Beauty: "There are many men who are more monstrous than you and who hide it."

* * *

Beauty: "What are you doing at my door at such an hour? My God! You're covered with blood."

The Beast: "My apologies…"

Beauty: "What are you apologizing for?"

The Beast: "For being a beast … (he murmurs). Pardon me…"

Beauty: "You have no right to ask such a thing. Aren't you ashamed of yourself?"

* * *

The Beast: "Beauty, a rose which played its role…my mirror, my golden key, my horse, and my glove are the five secrets of my power. They are yours."

* * *

Beauty (speaking of the Beast): "He is suffering, father. Half of him is struggling against the other half. He must be more cruel for himself than for human beings."

* * *

The Prince: "Love can turn a man into a beast. Love can also turn an ugly man into a handsome one."   *end of film*

* * *

The Prince: "Let's go . . . You won't be afraid?"

Beauty: "Well . . . I like to be afraid . . . (silence) . . . with you."

© *L'Avant-Scène Cinéma*

Questions/Topics for Reflection

1. The relationship between Beauty and her father, between Beauty and Avenant, and between Beauty and the Beast; psychoanalytical (or other) hypotheses.
2. The merchant picks a rose, provoking the Beast's anger. Comment.
3. The opposition of the world of the merchant's family and the Beast's world.
4. The role of music in the above contrast (when does it play a role?); the special effects and their role.
5. The opposition between Avenant and the Beast.
6. The anguish of the Beast when it is drawn to Beauty's door after hunting.
7. The metaphorical value of the tears which are turned into diamonds and of the pearl necklace which becomes an old piece of rope.
8. The Beast and the poet: autobiographical interpretation.
9. The symbolic value of objects: the arrow, the rose, the mirror, the glove, the golden key, the horse Magnificent, Diane's Pavilion.
10. The dénouement: Avenant's fate, the transformation of the Beast, Beauty's state of mind.

CRITICAL DOSSIER

René Gilson — The Adaptation

Who could have foreseen that from these twenty pages of Mme de Beaumont would arise characters like Jean Cocteau's Beauty and the Beast. The flat, pastel silhouettes of the fairytale take on the shape, the depth, and the formal and moral values of heroes from a most singular dramatic mythology, perhaps the most exceptional of this century. The characters are immersed in sumptuous images, magnificent and exemplary in their rigor and their organization, remarkably true in both the real and the fantastic (*Jean Cocteau*, p. 43).

Claude-Jean Philippe — "The Impossibility of Love"

All of his activity [...] between 1945 and 1950 becomes coherent. From one film to another (*Les Parents terribles*, *The Eagle Has Two Heads*), and even when they are directed by other filmmakers (*The Human Voice* by Roberto Rossellini, *Les Enfants terribles* by Jean-Pierre Melville), Cocteau consistently and tirelessly glorifies the grandeur, the marvels, the excesses, and the infamies of passionate love considered as a sacred possession. The poet sees the specter of his sixtieth year approaching. It is time for him to celebrate the very impossibility of love that the hideousness of the Beast manifests with such force.

Impossiblity. A possibility.

This phonetic play on words could serve to summarize the film. It is inconceivable that Beauty could love the Beast. At the same time each of their meetings gives birth to more hope that the day will come when they will be united.

Cocteau emphasizes the impossibility by refusing to compromise as regards the hideousness of the Beast. The Beast's royal trappings shouldn't deceive us. He is indeed a wild animal who laps up his water from the stream, whose ears perk up at the sight of a doe, and who trembles with contained ferocity at the idea of devouring it. The magnificence of the scene in which he roars with shame and despair before Beauty's door is of the same order as the terror it produces (*Jean Cocteau*, pp. 66-68).

René Gilson — The Sequence of the Sheets

Driving the poles into the ground with his own hands, spreading the wet sheets to increase their transparency, putting on the clothes pins, Jean Cocteau created a labyrinthian *décor*, a theater of white spaces of provocative beauty, or which would have been if the staging had really played on this beauty. Well, it only plays on it very moderately; it doesn't glorify or transfigure it. It only represents it for what it is, which is much better, and is careful not to forget that it is only sheets which are drying. Beauty, dressed like a princess, sees the sheets and asks, "*Who did my laundry?*" — the possessive is marvelous — "*The sheets are not hung right; they are touching the ground,*" she points out. It is she who establishes the realism of the scene and of the décor, by speaking truthfully, in character. Associated with this simple truth and by the absence of any camera movement, the formal and rhythmic serenity of the sequence of the sheets, after the scenes at the castle, can be fully appreciated (*Jean Cocteau*, pp 46-47).

Jean Decock — The Gaze

The talisman which saves is Beauty's "loving gaze." It is enough to save the Beast, whereas the classical tale demanded nothing less than Beauty's hand in marriage. Verbal semantics is changed by Cocteau into a semiology of the gaze. In fact, images have an incomparable power to express, for example, the fascination of Beauty when she discovers in the silent scene at the fountain the Beast's "sad manner and his eyes" as he laps the water, before she moves away pensively. This scene foreshadows the later episode in which Beauty lets the Beast drink from her hands. In Cocteau's film the gaze reassumes its original sense of burning and rape, of possession. *"Beauty, will you allow me to watch you dine?"* — *"You are the Master."* — *"No, you are the only master here."* The Beast, tortured, repeats: *"Your gaze burns me. I can't stand for you to look at me"* ("Surréalisme et symbolisme," p. 11).

Michael Popkin — "The Poet as Monster"

[…] A comparison between story and film shows that Cocteau, by identifying not with the young girl but with the monster, has used the story to deal not only with Belle's dilemma as an inexperienced girl but also with his own dilemma as a poet.

Why, for example, was la Bête placed under a curse? The explanation in the original story is that "a wicked fairy condemned me to keep this appearance until a beautiful woman agreed to marry me." This punishment is totally arbitrary, and serves to emphasize the importance of the free choice and ability to see beneath appearances, of the beautiful girl who will free the unfortunate prince from his spell. In the film the explanation is more elaborate: "My parents didn't believe in fairies, so the fairies punished them through me. I could only be saved by a look of love." The idea that adults have to accept things with the same simple faith that children have, a notion expressed in the introduction to the film, is more complicated than it might at first appear to be. The fascination that Cocteau's own childhood had for him has been amply discussed and has provided a great deal of fuel for various Freudian fires. But it is much easier to explain Cocteau's fondness for childlike faith by pointing out that such faith implies the absence of criticism. For Cocteau poetry has to be felt, not analyzed […]. So Cocteau had an ideal arm with which to fend off criticism of his own work: one had to accept it with the simple faith of a child, and that was that […].

Only if the Beast is supposed to stand for the poet, as Cocteau conceived the role of the poet, does it make it sense to see him as cursed because of a failure to believe in fairy tales. "Children believe what they are told and doubt it not," Cocteau tells his audience. "I am asking of you a little of this naivete now . . .". That kind of audience response — naive acceptance — is the only thing that can free either the poet or monster from the curse of incomprehension. Cocteau changes the Beast's salvation from the original story's marriage, which is Beauty's salvation as much as the Beast's, to "a look of love" because he is thinking of acceptance as a poet, a salvation in which Beauty is, like Eurydice [in *Orphée*], an instrument but not a participant ("Cocteau's *Beauty & the Beast*," pp. 105-107).

poet → what he expects of spectator

JEAN COCTEAU'S FILMOGRAPHY

1930	*The Blood of a Poet (Le Sang d'un poète)*
1946	*Beauty and the Beast (La Belle et la Bête)*
1947	*The Eagle Has Two Heads (L'Aigle à deux têtes)*
1948	*Les Parents terribles*
1950	*Orphée*
1960	*Le Testament d'Orphée*

WORKS CONSULTED

Barchilon, Jacques. "'Beauty and the Beast': From Myth to Fairy Tale." *Psychoanalysis and Psychoanalytic Review* 46 (1959): 19-29.

Cocteau, Jean. *Entretiens sur le cinématographe*. Paris: Pierre Belfond, 1973.

.........*La Belle et la Bête* (screenplay). *L'Avant-Scène Cinéma* 138-139 (July-Sept. 1973): 7-58.

.........*La Belle et la Bête. Journal d'un film*. Monaco: Editions du Rocher, 1958.

Decock, Jean. "Surréalisme et symbolisme." *L'Avant-Scène Cinéma* 138-139 (July-Sept. 1973): 8-11.

DeNitto, Dennis. "Jean Cocteau's *Beauty and the Beast*." *American Imago* 33 (1976): 123-154.

DeNitto, Dennis, and William Herman. *Film and the Critical Eye*. New York: Macmillan, 1975.

Gilson, René. *Jean Cocteau*. Paris: Seghers, 1964.

Hammond, Robert M., ed. *La Belle et la Bête*. New York: New York UP, 1970 (screenplay and dialogues in English and in French).

La Belle et la Bête. Paris: Balland, 1975.

Pauly, Rebecca M. *The Transparent Illusion. Image and Ideology in French Text and Film*. New York: Peter Lang, 1993.

Philippe, Claude-Jean. *Jean Cocteau*. Paris: Seghers, 1989.

Popkin, Michael. "Cocteau's *Beauty & the Beast. The Poet as Monster*." *Literature/ Film Quarterly* 10.2 (1982): 100-109.

René Clément

Forbidden Games
Jeux interdits

(1952)

René Clément, *Forbidden Games*: Michel (Georges Poujouly) and
Paulette (Brigitte Fossey) play together. © Studio Canal Image

Director .... René Clément
Screenplay .... François Boyer
Adaptation .... Jean Aurenche, Pierre Bost, René Clément
Dialogues .... Jean Aurenche, Pierre Bost, René Clément
Assistant Director .... Claude Clément
Director of Photographer .... Robert Juillard
Music (composition and performance) .... Narciso Yepes
Film Editor .... Roger Duyre
Sound .... Jacques Lebreton
Art Director .... Paul Bertrand
Script Girl (Continuity) .... Yvette Vérité
Producer .... Robert Dorfmann, Silver-Film
Length .... 1 h 25

Cast:

Brigitte Fossey (*Paulette*), Georges Poujouly (*Michel Dollé*), Lucien Hubert (*Michel's father*), Suzanne Courtal (*Michel's mother*), Jacques Marin (*Georges Dollé*), P. Mérovée (*Raymond Dollé*), Laurence Badie (*Berthe Dollé*), André Wasley (*Gouard the neighbor*), Amédée (*Francis Gouard*), Denise Perronne (*Jeanne Gouard*), Louis Saintève (*the priest*).

STORY

June 1940. Civilians flee to the south of France before the conquering German army. German planes bombard and strafe the column of refugees, killing the parents of Paulette, a five-year-old Parisian girl. Her little dog, killed along with her parents, is thrown from a bridge into the river below. After recovering the dog's body from the water, Paulette is separated from the column. She walks down a dirt path through the woods, following a horse which has bolted, its broken cart trailing behind.

The horse arrives in a field where the Dollé family is working. When the older son Georges tries to catch the horse, he is wounded by a kick to the stomach. His eleven-year-old brother Michel, who has run after a stray cow, comes upon Paulette and takes her home with him. He convinces his father to take her in by threatening to give her to the Gouards, a neighboring family with whom the Dollés have been feuding for years.

Paulette spends the evening with the Dollé family. Georges is seriously injured and spends a sleepless night. Paulette wakes up screaming, her sleep troubled by nightmares. Michel goes up to the attic to comfort her.

When Paulette goes to find her dog's body the next morning, she meets the local priest. He teaches her how to pray for her dead parents and tries to get her to make the sign of the cross. With Michel's help she buries her dog in an abandoned mill, where the two children decide to create an animal cemetery.

That evening Michel's father becomes angry with him for making too much noise hammering together makeshift crosses for the cemetery. As punishment Michel is deprived of dinner but later is called downstairs to pray for his brother Georges, who is dying. Georges soon expires, his bed surrounded by his helpless family. The next morning while helping his father repair an old horse-drawn hearse, Michel notices several loose crosses on the roof of the wagon.

Mr. Gouard's son Francis, who has deserted during the chaos of the French army's retreat, returns home. He and Berthe Dollé are in love and want to marry despite the feuding between the two families. Michel shows Paulette the crosses he has stolen from the hearse.

During the funeral mass Dollé discovers the disappearance of the crosses from the hearse and is convinced that the Gouards are responsible. Later, after confession, Michel attempts to steal the cross from the church altar. The parish priest catches him and punishes him. In the attic that evening Michel and Paulette make small signs for the graves of the dead animals they have collected and decide to steal some real crosses from the cemetery by the church. When they go to the barn to get the wheelbarrow to transport the crosses, they surprise Berthe and Francis in the hay.

On Sunday morning the members of the Dollé family, followed by the Gouards, go to the cemetery. The Dollés discover that their family crosses have been removed. Blaming the Gouards, Dollé begins breaking the crosses on their family graves. This provokes an altercation between the two fathers during which they both fall into a newly dug grave and continue to fight. The priest stops them by fingering Michel, who takes to his heels. That evening the Dollés try to persuade Paulette to tell them where the crosses are hidden, but the girl refuses to talk. She is supported by Michel, who has crept back into the house by way of the attic.

The next morning Gouard catches Michel in the barn and beats him to make him talk. The boy refuses until the police come to get Paulette to have her taken to an orphanage. When Michel's father seems to agree to keep Paulette, the boy tells him where the crosses are. His father nonetheless allows the police to take the girl away. Furious at his father's deception, Michel runs to the mill and destroys the cemetery by throwing the crosses into the river.

Paulette has been taken to a Red Cross center where a nun puts a card with her name on it around her neck and asks her not to budge. When she hears someone call "Michel," she gets up and disappears into the crowd looking for her friend.

*The original version of the film begins with an rather maudlin "prologue" in which a small boy relates a story to a little girl. At the end there is an equally vapid "epilogue" in which the boy finishes telling the story while the little girl weeps. Clément explained that the producer insisted he add these two scenes for commercial reasons.

CRITICAL RECEPTION

At its opening on May 9, 1952, *Forbidden Games* met both harsh criticism and warm praise. For some critics it was "the finest film by René Clément" (Kast, p. 64), for others "his least successful film" (Fumet, p. 66). The film critic at the *Tribune de Genève* declared categorically, "This young author must be recognized as one of the best of his generation and his latest work as one of the most moving of the post-war period" (Monnet, p. 22). While everyone agreed that the opening sequence of the film depicting the mass exodus was a masterpiece of realism, a veritable anthology piece, and "a moment of great cinema" (Queval, p. 508), Clément was criticized for offering an unjust, overly caricatured, indeed malicious image of French peasants. The Catholic press reacted violently to *Forbidden Games*, calling it "sacrilegious." The Church considered it to be an anticlerical diatribe and "the most violent satire that the cinema has dared to direct against the Catholic religion, including its most solemn rite" (Schimel, p. 8).

On the other hand, viewers were quick to praise the touching depiction of the children's universe, this "totally closed and elusive world" (Kast, p. 65) that Clément succeeded in recreating in his film. Although there was criticism of Clément's tendency to overemphasize style (the search for esthetic effects that characterizes his filmmaking), critics generally appreciated the "poetic quality" of the film, as well as the elegant photography of Robert Juillard.

Forbidden Games was not chosen to represent France at the Cannes Film Festival in 1952, a decision which provoked a minor scandal in the world of French cinema.

Presented nonetheless at Cannes, Clément's film was awarded the Grand Prize for independent films and enjoyed considerable success in the theaters. The same year the film also won in Paris the women's prize for the best French film and the prize awarded by the Critics' Association. *Forbidden Games* was well received abroad, receiving the International Grand Prize at the Venice Film Festival and the Prize for the Best Foreign Film in New York, both in 1952. The *New York Times* remarked that Clément's film "is a brilliant and dramatic reflection on human fragility." To the above list of prizes the film added in 1953 the Oscar for the Best Foreign Film at the Academy Awards in Hollywood, the Japanese Critics Prize in Tokyo, and the Prize for the Best Film Worldwide in London, before winning the Academy Award Critics' Prize in London the following year.

BEFORE *FORBIDDEN GAMES*

Born in Bordeaux in 1913, Clément first studied architecture before turning to the movies. After serving as a cameraman in the French Army's cinematography branch, he made around thirty short documentaries, of which the best known are *At Islam's Door* (*Au Seuil de l'Islam*, 1934), *The Albegensian* (*L'Albigeois*, 1935), *The Upper Garonne* (*La Haute Garonne*, 1935), *The Marshalling Yard* (*Le Triage*, 1936), *Watch Your Left* (*Soigne ton gauche*, 1936, with Jacques Tati), *La Grande Chartreuse* (1937), *Forbidden Arabia* (*L'Arabie interdite*, 1938), *La Grande Pastorale* (1942), and *Those of the Rails* (*Ceux du rail*, 1943).

Clément's last short subject, a documentary on the life of railroad workers, served as a prelude to his first feature film, *Battle of the Rails* (1945), which chronicles one aspect of the French Resistance. This quasi-documentary fiction film is part of the postwar current of neo-realism most prominent in Italy. It launched Clément's career as a major filmmaker when it received the award for Best Director and the Special Jury Prize at Cannes in 1946. Clément served as Jean Cocteau's technical advisor during the shooting of *Beauty and the Beast* the same year, before making three films of modest success, *The Damned* (*Les Maudits*, 1947), *Beyond the Gates* (*Au-delà des grilles*, 1948, with Jean Gabin), and *The Glass Castle* (*Le Château de verre*, 1950, with Michelle Morgan and Jean Marais). Whether it be in the genres of neo-realism, poetic realism, or psychological realism, critics tend to praise Clément's stylistic subtlety and the quality of his photography, while deploring the lack of inspiration as regards the content of his films. *Forbidden Games*, on the other hand, was generally recognized as "one of the major works of postwar French cinema" (Schimel, p. 8).

ORIGIN, ADAPTATION, CAST, SHOOTING

In 1946, in an effort to convince the administrators of the I.D.H.E.C. (Institute of Advanced Cinematographic Studies in Paris) to create a screenwriting department, the novelist-screenwriter Francois Boyer wrote a scenario titled "Cross of Wood, Cross of Iron." Finding no producer interested in his screenplay, despite the enthusiasm it met (by René Clément especially), Boyer transformed it into a novel which was published by the Editions de Minuit. Four years later Clément adapted the novel to the screen under the title *Forbidden Games*.

To write the new screenplay and dialogues Clément hired Jean Aurenche and Pierre Bost, the most famous team of screenwriters in French cinema at that time. Aurenche and Bost were the authors of some of the best-known films produced in the tradition of "French Quality" since the beginnings of the forties. The film maintains the basic situation and the principal events in the novel but replaces the psychological analysis of the little girl, which is emphasized in Boyer's novel, by a study of peasant society. The dialogue is taken virtually verbatim from the novel.

In the spirit of neo-realism, Clément cast no stars in *Forbidden Games*. Both the adult and children's roles are played by unknown or little-known actors. The stars of the film are unquestionably the two children, played by Brigitte Fossey and Georges Poujouly, whom Clément chose after interviewing several hundred children. The natural and spontaneous character of the children's acting was highly praised by the press in general.

The shooting of the film took place between September 1951 and March 1952, largely on location near a village in the Alpes-Maritimes province, whose topography resembles that of the Limousin region where the action of the film is placed in the novel. Some of the scenes in the church and in the cemetery were shot in the studio, with reconstructed settings. In an effort to achieve realism, the actors wore clothes belonging to peasants living in the area, altered to fit them by local seamstresses. In addition they practiced at some length living like peasants: "More than two weeks before the cameras began to turn, all the actors got the feel for their characters by wearing their costumes, learning to handle a pitchfork, load a cart, and harness a mule or a donkey" (Fiche filmographique de l'IDEHC, p. 13).

STRUCTURE

Forbidden Games is divided into seven distinct parts, beginning with the arrival of Paulette in the peasant's world and ending with her departure. The first two major sequences cover the first day, while the ensuing segmentation of the action corresponds to the following series of days:

1) The 1st day: the exodus on the road, the death of Paulette's parents, Paulette's departure into the countryside; Georges Dollé's injury by the bolting horse, Michel's discovery of Paulette in the woods;

2) The 1st day (cont.): Paulette is taken in by the Dollé family, the evening with the Dollés, the first night;

3) The 2nd day: Paulette meets the priest and buries her dog with Michel's help, the idea of the animal cemetery, making wooden crosses, Michel's punishment, Georges' death;

4) The 3rd day: repairing the hearse, return of Francis Gouard and his reunion with Berthe Dollé, Michel steals the crosses from the hearse;

5) The 4th day: Georges' funeral, Dollé discovers the disappearance of the hearse's crosses, Michel tries to steal the cross from the altar, theft of the crosses from the cemetery;

6) The 5th day: the fight in the cemetery, Michel runs away and later slips back into the house;

7) The 6th day: Dollé catches and beats Michel in the loft, the police come for Paulette, Michel destroys the cemetery, Paulette at the Red Cross center.

The above sequence of events shows that from the second day on the main action of the film revolves around the children's cemetery project and its consequences for the adults. The dramatic structure of *Forbidden Games* is organized around the opposition of the world of the adults and the world of the children.

THEMES

Judging by its first sequence, *Forbidden Games* is going to be a realistic war film whose principal subject will be the massacre of innocent people. This impression fades rapidly however as soon as Paulette enters the peasant world. The war film yields, on the one hand, to a depiction of peasant mores, and on the other to a representation of the children's world, with all of its innocence, curiosity, and incomprehension on the part of the adults. This does not mean that the war disappears. On the contrary, it serves as a backdrop throughout the film and is evoked in various ways: by newspaper articles, by the return of the soldier Francis Gouard, and by the flashes and detonations of artillery shells — as well as by the absence of the town doctor who has been called to treat the refugees wounded by the bombarding of the road. The war is transformed moreover into a rhetorical figure, into an ironic metaphor for the petty feuding, the bellicose enmity between the Dollé and Gouard families in their remote little corner of the world. Although the depiction of the peasants — crude, petty, stupid, and brutal — was severely criticized, the grotesque character of the Dollé and Gouard world is largely a reflection of the even more grotesque character of the outside world where the war is being waged in all its horror.

The clear tie between the outside world and the peasant milieu is established by the theme of death, first the killing of Paulette's parents on the bridge, then Georges Dollé's mortal injury by the horse which "came from the war," as his mother says. It is the discovery of death, of course, which fascinates the two children and becomes an obsession for them. Once it becomes a part of their world, they transform it into a form of play, a game, as children are wont to do with any activity. For this very reason death becomes commonplace for the children, just as it becomes commonplace in war, this deadly adult "game." The Christian burial rites lose their sacred aura and are transformed into simple everyday games, into gestures and words which have lost their religious sense and sentiment. For some spectators this is the "sacrilegious" side of the film.

In addition to the theme of death in *Forbidden Games* we can discern the theme of love, in which we find again the opposition between the children's and the adults' worlds. Deprived of love in his family, Michel "falls in love" with Paulette, sharing with her an affection which serves as a shield against the brutality and insensitivity of the adult world. At the same time Clément develops a parody of the Romeo and Juliet story: Francis Gouard and Berthe Dollé are in love and want to marry despite the fierce enmity which separates their two families.

STYLE AND MUSIC

Clément's style in *Forbidden Games* is striking both for its realistic character and for his concern for the quality of the photography, "the formal perfection of each shot" (Kast, p. 64). Contrary to Renoir, Clément uses very few sequence (lengthy) shots. His film is dominated by relatively short shots in which the camera movements, pans, and tracking shots are reduced to a minimum. Close-ups and close shots are used frequently, especially in the children's scenes. The editing plays a particularly important role in the sequence of the exodus at the beginning of the film. Here the tension of the bombardment is maintained by a long series of very brief shots which stops abruptly after the death of Paulette's parents and is followed by a very lengthy close shot of the little girl's face where we can see the shock of the event and her effort to understand what has happened. In this shot, as elsewhere in the film, Clément places his camera at the level of the girl's gaze to emphasize the child's perspective because "it is through the vision of the children that we see the grown-up world" (Mauriac). As Clément says, he was often shooting "70 centimeters from the ground" while making the film.

Narciso Yepes's music, a simple but catchy tune played on the guitar, is clearly related to the children's world. It engulfs Paulette's character especially, expressing her inner life: her child's sensitivity, her emotional turmoil, and her suffering.

STUDY GUIDE

Excerpts for Discussion

Excerpt 1 (2'00-6'55): The beginning of the film (the exodus, the death of Paulette's parents on the bridge).

Excerpt 2 (31'15-35'30): Paulette learns her prayers; Michel is punished.

Excerpt 3 (59'30-1h00'15): Preparation of the signs for the graves; Michel kills the cockroach, Paulette's reaction.

Excerpt 4 (1h03'35-04'35): On the road at night with the stolen crosses (the war's presence).

Excerpt 5 (1h06'35-08'55): The fight in the cemetery.

Excerpt 6 (1h17'20-18'20): M. Dollé beats Michel in the loft, Paulette's reactions.

Excerpt 7 (1h22'45-24'45): Dénouement — Paulette at the Red Cross center.

Quotations for Comment

Paulette: "I want my daddy and mommy. They're on the bridge."

Michel: "They aren't on the bridge anymore."

Paulette: "Why? Where are they?"

Michel: "In a hole."

Paulette: "In a hole?"

Michel: "Yeh."

Paulette: "They tossed them in…like dogs?"

Michel: "Well…yeh."

* * *

Michel: "We're going to make a great cemetery."

Paulette: "What's a cemetery?"

Michel: "That's where you put dead people so that they'll be together."

Paulette: "Why do they put them together?"

Michel: "So they don't get bored."

Paulette: "Then my dog isn't going to be happy all alone!"

* * *

Paulette (burying her dog while continually crossing herself):

"May God receive him in heaven. In the name of the Father and the son…and the Holy Spirit. Amen. May God receive him in heaven. In the name of the Father, the Son, and the Holy Spirit."

* * *

M. Dollé (picking up the cross Michel has just made): "And what's *that*…a prayer? You're making crosses in a house where there's a sick person? You want to cause his death?"

* * *

The Gendarme: "We don't even have a name for her."

Mme Dollé: "She'll tell me. Your name is Paulette what? Hmm, Paulette what?"

Paulette: "Dollé."

Mme Dollé: "Dollé! She says her name is Dollé now."

Paulette: "I want to have Michel's name."

* * *

The Nun (to Paulette, in the Red Cross center): "Now just don't move. Be a good girl."

A Woman: "Michel! Michel!"

Paulette: "Michel, Michel…" (the woman runs toward a man and embraces him). "Mommy! Mommy! Michel, Michel" (she runs off into the crowd and disappears).

© *L'Avant-Scène Cinéma*

Questions/Topics for Reflection

1. What is the "subject" of this film? Are there several?
2. The treatment of the theme of death. Symbolic relationship between the death of Paulette's parents and the death of her little dog. The death of Michel's brother.
3. What are the "forbidden games"? Why are they "forbidden"?
4. The relationship between Michel and Paulette.
5. The depiction of the country folk (their character, customs, hygiene).
6. Signs of the presence of the war in the film.
7. The theme of "war" as a metaphor (the French and the Germans, the Dollé and Gouard families).
8. The Francis Gouard-Berthe Dollé couple: reference to what famous couple? Explain.
9. Depiction of religion in the peasant milieu.
10. Interpretation of the dénouement.

CRITICAL DOSSIER

Monique Schimel — The Horrors of War

The first sequence of the film is constructed around a bridge, a perilous place, the bane of those who in June 1940 lived through the mass exodus on the jammed roads in the French countryside.

By its pitiless and painful realism, by the choice of sound effects, by the editing — sharp and quick like the death showered down by the Messerschmidts — this episode is, by itself, a masterpiece.

This sequence reminded me of the death of the railroad workers in *Battle of the Rails* when we hear the strangely shrill sound of a locomotive siren, and when the last gaze of a man is full of admiration and sympathy for a spider, frail like life itself, resting on the wall against which his body will collapse in a few seconds. Similarly, in *Forbidden Games*, when the little girl runs after her dog and the mother and father run after their little girl, no one thinking of his or her own safety, just the safety of another, we have another example of one of Clément's principal qualities: love of life, devoid of self-interest and pleasure seeking, just the generous love for the life of others, this highest form of optimism ("Après *Jeux interdits*…," p. 7).

R.M. Arlaud — The Kingdom of Childhood

After this brutal overture [the exodus scene], Clément plunges into a lesser known largely forgotten world: the kingdom of childhood, the mixture of imaginary and real worlds where superstition mingles with religion, a world of incantations and naïve love. The author slips as delicately as possible into this universe where everything is pure for those alone who are pure — while remaining what he is, even in this poetic form: a reporter ("Tribune libre autour de *Jeux interdits*," p. 68).

André Farwagi — A "Liberating Psychodrama"

The first sequence of the film is a reconstructed documentary in the manner of *Battle of the Rails* denouncing the fact of war. It is a description of reality. But suddenly our attention is focused on Paulette. The butchery has a traumatic effect on her which sets off mechanisms of self-defense which, in turn, provoke a transfer. At the conscious level all of these chain reactions occur simultaneously. Paulette hasn't really realized that her parents are dead because at that moment all of her attention is focused on the little dog. From the beginning the little girl is plunged into a dazed state which determines her view of things and people and explains her reactions. The game she will invent with Michel will be a kind of liberating psychodrama. It is important to note immediately that Paulette's system reacts in a healthy manner, because the violence of the shock could have caused a case of severe schizophrenia. At the end of the film when Paulette finds herself at the orphanage and bursts into tears, she has absorbed the initial shock. She has returned to normal and realized what has happened to her; she is weeping for her parents.

The whole story will be seen from Paulette's perspective and secondarily through the eyes of her playmate Michel [...]. The adults are directly responsible for the traumatic experience of these children. This is why the opening sequence is so important: without it the film would have no reason to exist. Presented as the depiction of a moment in the war, these games are above all games of death. We remember the shot in which we see a cockroach scurrying across the floor and where Michel, imitating the noise of an airplane diving, kills it with his pen. He is replaying, at his level, the tragedy which was taking place on the bridge near the farm. The children hasten to bury the dead cockroach! They make it a cross which they stick on its grave [...]. In a world in which airplanes kill civilians with machine-guns, morality can only survive in rituals. Faith gives way to fetishism. By imitating with such complete sincerity the adults' burial ceremony, the children denounce its artifice and falsity. Their behavior also reveals that the child's sense of the sacred is purer than the adult's. The burial of the chick becomes the expression of an isolated and vulnerable sensitivity which vibrates intensely in the world which surrounds it. Paradoxically the burial of Michel's older brother, who dies from a kick in the stomach from the horse, seems just as grotesque as his death (*René Clément*, pp. 46-47).

Max Egly — "Neither Perverted Nor Innocent..."

The story is novel in more than one respect. The refusal to make concessions and the hard realism of René Clément shocked a number of spectators. It is rare to find in the cinema (and particularly in French cinema) the theme of a private children's world developing outside of the adult world. It is no less rare to attempt to depict certain aspects of the mountain peasantry.

René Clément has succeeded in highlighting the fundamental difference between children and adults. In general it is difficult for the filmmaker, as for the spectator, to treat themes related to childhood in an objective fashion. We shouldn't forget, first of all, that in most cases when children appear in movies, they are minor characters [...]. The rare films which do have children as heroes are highly unrealistic; their characters generally come straight from trite children's literature, from the mythology of "good" children, or from comic books. Dear little angel or unbearable rascal, the child only appears in films to move the spectators or to appeal to their protective instincts. Inexhaustible treasure of sweetness or source of violence, the child suffers from the brutal opposition of good and evil which is so popular in the cinema. Well, contrary to these characters, Paulette and Michel don't belong to any stereotypical category. They are simply themselves. Neither perverted nor innocent, they remain pure to the extent that they haven't yet been infected by the baseness of adults. Their actions cannot be judged by the moral standards of grown-ups; they have no knowledge of them. They construct their existence in their own manner, inventing ways to struggle against death by appropriating the symbols (crosses, gestures, prayers) of the adults. In this sense, Michel's theft is not a sacrilegious act at all ("*Jeux interdits*," p. 20).

Pierre Kast — The World As It Is

The very subject of *Forbidden Games* is the discovery of burial rites by two children and the invention of a new ritual for themselves. The amazing shrewdness of the subject is not to have two abstract children, citizens of a children's republic, but two children *in real life*, in a political, social and moral context which is absolutely specific. Moreover, the two children express powerfully, in what we call their *games*, the contradictions and mystifications of this context. Accordingly, we are no longer dealing with childhood alone but, by virtue of the law of exemplarity, with what the world makes of its children. Beyond the world of childhood the film is also interesting for the brutal light it sheds on the world of adults. The same people who find Michel and Paulette's game with death morbid don't seem to be aware of the morbidity of their own game with war, and with death. When Michel dive bombs a beetle, it doesn't demonstrate the cruelty of René Clément but rather the blindness of those who accept the phenomenon of dive bombing, or even justify it. It's been a long time since we've seen a French film attack so courageously the moral comfort of those who accept the world as it is ("Le Jeu de grâce des petits anges," pp. 65-66).

RENÉ CLÉMENT'S FILMOGRAPHY
(FEATURE FILMS)

1945	*Battle of the Rails (La Bataille du rail)*
1947	*The Damned (Les Maudits)*
1948	*Beyond the Gates (Au-delà des grilles)*
1950	*The Glass Castle (Le Château de verre)*
1952	*Forbidden Games (Jeux interdits)*
1953	*Knave of Hearts, Lover Boy (Monsieur Ripois)*
1955	*Gervaise*
1958	*This Angry Age (Barrage contre le Pacifique)*
1959	*Purple Noon (Plein Soleil)*
1960	*What Joy of Living (Quelle joie de vivre)*
1962	*The Day and the Hour (Le Jour et l'heure)*
1964	*The Big Cats (Les Félins)*
1967	*Is Paris Burning? (Paris brûle-t-il?)*
1970	*The Passenger in the Rain (Le Passager de la pluie)*

1971	*The House Beneath The Trees*
	(La Maison sous les arbres)
1973	*And Hope To Die*
	(La Course du lièvre à travers les champs)
1975	*La Baby Sitter*

WORKS CONSULTED

Charensol, G. "*Jeux interdits*. Les Sept Péchés capitaux." *Les Nouvelles littéraires* (May 15, 1952).

Clément, René. *Jeux interdits* (screenplay). *L'Avant-Scène Cinéma* 15 (May 15, 1962).

Egly, Max. "*Jeux interdits*." *Image et son* 114 (July 1958): 20-21.

Farwagi, André. *René Clément*. Paris: Seghers, 1967.

Fumet, Stanilas, and R.M. Arlaud. "Tribune libre autour de *Jeux interdits*." *Revue internationale du cinéma* 14 (1952): 65-69.

Kast, Pierre. "Le Jeu de grâce des petits anges." *Cahiers du cinéma* 13 (June 1952): 64-67.

"*Jeux interdits* (1951)." Analysis of the film ("Fiche filmographique") from the Institut des Hautes Etudes Cinématographiques (Jan. 1, 1961).

Mauriac, Claude. "Terre des Petits d'hommes," *Le Figaro littéraire* (May 29,1952).

Monnet, J. Revue des *Jeux interdits*, *Tribune de Genève* (Sept. 22, 1952).

Queval, Jean, "*Jeux interdits*." *Mercure de France* (July 1, 1952): 505-508.

Schimel, Monique. "Après *Jeux interdits* René Clément parmi les grands réalisateurs français." *Image et son* 56 (Oct. 1952): 7-9.

Jacques Tati

Mr. Hulot's Holiday
Les Vacances de M. Hulot

(1953)

Jacques Tati, *Mr. Hulot's Holiday*: Hulot (Jacques Tati) gives the photographer-"voyeur" a kick in the pants. © Les Films de Mon Oncle

Director .... Jacques Tati
Original Screenplay and Dialogues .... Jacques Tati, Pierre Aubert,
Jacques Lagrange, Henri Marquet
Director of Photography .... Jacques Mercanton, Jean Mousselle
Music .... Alain Romans
Film Editors ...... Jacques Grassi, Ginou Bretoneiche, Suzanne Baron
Sound Editing .... Michel-Ange
Sound .... Jacques Carrère, Roger Cosson
Art Directors .... Henri Schmitt, Roger Briaucourt
Producer .... Fred Orain
Length .... 1 h 27

Cast

Jacques Tati (*Mr. Hulot*), Nathalie Pascaud (*Martine*), Michèle Rolla (*her aunt*), Valentine Camax (*the English Woman*), Marguerite Gérard (*the Walker*), René Lacourt (*her husband*), André Dubois (*the commander*), Lucien Frégis (*the hotel owner*), Raymond Carl (*the waiter*), Georges Adlin (*the Latin Lover*), Nathalie Pascaud's husband (*M. Schmutz, the businessman*).

STORY

It's the month of July, at the beginning of summer vacation. A crowd of city-dwellers is waiting for the train which will take them to the beaches. Reacting to the nasal, quasi-incomprehensible voice coming from the loudspeaker, the crowd runs from platform to platform. They dive each time into the underground passage between the platforms until they manage to come up, apparently by chance, beside the right train. Its cargo of vacationers on board, the train leaves the station and flies through the countryside.

At the same time other vacationers in cars speed toward the beaches on the highways. M. Hulot putts along among them in a weird little sports car (an Amilcar), a vehicle which moves along jerkily, backfiring and smoking and losing automobile parts as it bumps over the paving stones of the village streets.

In another city additional vacationers cram into a bus which will take them to a little seaside resort where they will spend the next two weeks or the whole month. We finally arrive at the resort where the story is situated. The Beach Hotel is located at the center of a tiny village. All of the clients, largely people of modest means and/or large families, will take their meals and spend their evenings here during their beach vacation. In this surge of tourists we note many English nationals and a very pretty blond woman, Martine, who moves into her room in a villa overlooking the beach.

From the moment he arrives, Hulot annoys the other vacationers by leaving the hotel door open. A brisk wind sends papers flying and creates a general disturbance. Despite Hulot's exquisite courtesy and consideration towards others, his clumsiness and absent-mindedness will constantly provoke incidents, both minor and major, which will make virtually everyone angry at him: the hotel owner, the waiter, a boat owner, a retired military officer, a bus driver, and a businessman, among others. The latter individual, M. Schmutz, works throughout the vacation, receiving telephone calls from all over the world.

The children, on the other hand, are delighted with Hulot, marveling over both his odd manner and his even odder car. The only adults who seem to enjoy Hulot are an elderly but athletic Englishwoman and "Henry," the elderly husband of another Englishwoman. Henry and his spouse stroll constantly around the village, the wife always out in front, her husband lagging a few steps behind. Henry, who has a talent for observation, seems to be the only person who keeps an eye on Hulot and is aware of his involvement in a number of mysterious incidents which upset the humdrum routine of the holiday community.

Hulot irritates the waiter by arriving late for meals, then disturbs his table companion. In the evening he destroys the calm of the hotel lounge by playing a jazz record at full blast. The next day at the beach, playing sheriff, he delivers a swift kick to M. Schmutz's backside in the mistaken belief that he is playing Peeping Tom as the attractive Martine puts on her clothes in her cabana on the beach. Later he is riding in a canoe which suddenly folds in two, trapping him inside what now looks like a giant shark's jaws. Panic breaks out on the beach. The following day he plays tennis and exasperates all of his opponents, experienced players whom he beats by using a bizarre service technique. Martine, one of the spectators, begins to enjoy Hulot's antics. That evening while playing ping-pong, he disturbs the card players in the hotel lounge — and sets off a fight among them — by constantly searching for lost ping-pong balls around their tables.

Attracted to Martine, Hulot invites the young woman to go horseback riding with him the next day. He eventually has to give up the idea, since his horse becomes irked with him, forcing him to run away and seek cover. Hulot and Martine meet again that evening, however, at a costume ball which is generally ignored by most of the other vacationers. The only adults in costume, they spend the evening dancing together. The next morning, on the way to a big picnic outing, Hulot is forced to stop to change a flat tire. When he tries to jack up the car, it falls and rolls off down a hill with two ladies aboard in the rumble seat. When Hulot returns to the hotel late that evening, with a dog in hot pursuit, he takes refuge in a shed where fireworks are stored. When he lights a match to see where he is, he sets off a spectacular fireworks display. His frantic efforts to douse the fireworks are useless, and everyone in the hotel is awakened.

The next morning marks the end of the holiday. Nearly all the vacationers are angry at Hulot and give him the cold shoulder as they bid each other goodbye. The old English lady and the husband of the stroller, however, as well as all the children, are very grateful to Mr. Hulot for brightening up an otherwise boring vacation. The film ends with Hulot's departure in his strange car. He leaves behind a deserted seaside scene, with the final shot of the film freezing into a postcard bearing a postage stamp...in color!

Tati reedited his film several times. For this chapter we have used the final version, the one which is generally available in video.

CRITICAL RECEPTION

In an article which appeared in *Esprit* in 1953, André Bazin expressed in glowing terms his admiration for *Mr. Hulot's Holiday*: "It is not only the most important comic work in world cinema since the Marx Brothers and W.C. Fields, but is also an event in the history of talking films" (*Qu'est-ce que le cinéma?*, p. 43). Like Bazin, other critics sang praises to Tati's comic genius. Some of them compared him favorably to Chaplin and Buster Keaton, as well as to the great French comic actor of the first quarter of the century, Max Linder, whom Chaplin himself viewed as his model: "But while recognizing that Tati is the first great French comic since Max Linder, we must also recognize that the director of Mr. Hulot is the greater comic of the two" (*Filmforum*, July 1953; in Agel, p. 111).

Although some critics bemoaned the absence of any plot or "dramatic structure" in *Mr. Hulot's Holiday*, the film won the hearts of the French public. It also had an impressive run abroad, if we are to believe Tati: "A big success in England, Germany,

Sweden, Italy, Spain, everywhere." And in America: "Incredible! A huge success! The people scream with laughter at places where spectators only smile in France […]. Wildly enthusiastic articles in the press!" (Doisneau, pp. 46-47). In 1953 the film won the International Critics Grand Prize at the Cannes Film Festival, as well as the Louis Delluc Prize and the Fémina Prize for the Best Actor (awarded to Tati). It likewise won prizes in Brussels, Berlin, Algeria, Sweden, and Cuba. In the United States it was nominated for an Oscar and won the Golden Laurel Award at the Edinburgh Film Festival. In the course of the nineteen-fifties *Mr. Hulot's Holiday* was translated into a dozen different languages throughout the world.

BEFORE (AND AFTER) *MR. HULOT'S HOLIDAY*

Jacques Tati (Tatischeff originally) was born October 9, 1908, near Saint-Germain-en-Laye on the road to Versailles. He came to the cinema from vaudeville, where he had specialized in the miming of sports (boxing, tennis, rugby, swimming). From 1932 to 1938 he collaborated as screenwriter and actor in a series of short subjects, the best-known of which remain *Oscar, champion de tennis* (1932) and *Watch Your Left* (*Soigne ton gauche*, 1936), a pantomime of boxing directed by René Clément.

Tati began to make his own films in 1936, but his real debut as a film director dates from the shooting in 1947 of a short subject, *The School For Postmen* (*L'Ecole des facteurs*), in which he created a new comic character, François the postman. The film was awarded the Max Linder Prize in 1949. The same year he directed his first feature film, *Holiday* (*Jour de Fête*), in which his postman François enjoyed both a commercial and critical triumph in the United States as well as in Europe, winning the Prize for the Best Screenplay at the Venice Film Festival in 1949 and the Grand Prize of French Cinema in 1950. In this highly slapstick film François plays the buffoon, the village idiot, in the little township where he discharges his postman's functions in a most whimsical fashion. After he sees a documentary film about the speed of the American mail, he does his route at top speed on his bicycle, producing a series of gags and daffy scenes.

Although the success of *Jour de fête* made Tati famous virtually overnight, he refused to make a sequel containing a new series of François the postman's adventures —to the great dismay of the producers, who had begged for more of the same. As Tati explained later, "François was too French. I wanted to find a more international form of expression" (Dondey, p. 88). This "more international" character, that is, a character who resembles a human type (in the best French classical tradition), will be of course the hero of *Mr. Hulot's Holiday*. Tati did with Mr. Hulot what he refused to do with the postman: he gave him a series of sequels. The first sequel was *Mon Oncle* (1958), a satire on the modernization and mechanization of life which won a special prize at Cannes in 1958 and the Oscar for the Best Foreign Film at the Academy Awards in 1959. *Mon Oncle* was followed by two other films with Mr. Hulot, *Playtime* (1967), a vast ironic fresco on modern urbanism (whose enormous production expenses bankrupted Tati's studio), and *Trafic* (1974), a slapstick version of automobile trade shows. In his last film, *Parade* (1974), a medium-length video production for Swedish television, he finally abandoned the Hulot character in favor of "Monsieur Loyal," the master of ceremonies of a little Swedish circus in which he returns to sports parody. In 1977 the Cannes Film Festival awarded Jacques Tati a special Ceasar in recognition of his overall contribution to French cinema.

ORIGIN, ACTORS, SHOOTING

The origin of *Mr. Hulot's Holiday*, like that of every Jacques Tati film, is the observation of the human species: "I watch people live. I get around: I go to matches and expositions. I accept invitations to occasional receptions, and I watch cars go by on the turnpike for hours. I listen to conversations, watching for the mannerism, the detail, the style which reveals the personality of each individual [...]. That is what strikes me, what I'd like to express, as well as everything that is related to the smothering of the personality" (Sadoul, p. 261). Tati met the model for his hero, a barber, during his military service (Kyrou, p. 14). The barber's name was not "Hulot," however; that name was borrowed either from a building manager Tati knew (Cauliez, p. 9) or from an architect whose odd way of walking struck Tati (Chion, p. 32).

Other than his casting of himself in the role of Mr. Hulot, Tati engaged either little known professional actors or out and out novices. Nathalie Pascaud, for example, who plays the role of Martine the pretty blond, had had no previous acting experience. Since she was reluctant to be separated from her husband during the shooting, Tati gave her husband, "a respectable businessman," the role of Mister Schmutz, the businessman who spends his vacation on the phone doing business (Dondey, p. 91). Generally, Tati explained, he chose the actors in his films "according to their nature," pointing out, for example, that the naturalness of the old commander's acting was due to the fact that "he is a real commander" (Henry and Le Péron, p. 12).

Tati revealed that he had experienced serious financial problems when he first tried to make *Hulot*. Since he refused to curry favor with the producers by making a sequel to *Jour de fête*, he had considerable difficulty finding funds for his project. He began to shoot in 1951 after seven months of preparatory work on the Channel and Atlantic coasts, primarily at Saint-Marc-sur-Mer (near Saint-Nazaire). He ran out of money, however, and was forced to stop shooting for a whole year. The shooting resumed in July 1952, on location at Saint-Marc for the outdoor shots and at the Billancourt studios in Paris for the indoor scenes. He finished the filming in October. Although Tati had planned to make a color film, his budget didn't allow it. *Hulot* is shot in black and white.

The shooting of the film was complicated by the fact that the Beach Hotel, for which Tati had been forced to build a fake entrance, remained open to clients. Both the film crew and the vacationers did the best they could: "The vacationers — the real ones — although understanding at first soon became impatient. They were either transformed into extras or asked to go tan somewhere outside of the camera's field of vision. Some newcomers tried to enter the hotel by the fake entrance, of course, and ran into a sheet of plywood" (Dondey, p. 91).

While the spirits of the crew remained generally high, the shooting of some of the gags proved to be exasperating. They demanded hours of minute preparation and occasioned a costly loss of time which Tati simply couldn't afford. Dondey describes, for example, the scene in which Hulot attempts to paint his canoe while the can of paint dances back and forth on the waves (pulled around in fact by a nylon thread): "Tati spent a whole day trying to get the paint can sequence on film and finally left the beach frustrated, without a word, furious that the manipulation of a few props had cost him so much precious time" (p. 92). Unlike Renoir, Tati was allergic to improvisation and didn't like to have to deal with the unexpected when he was shooting: " I work on my subject a long time, but I shoot without a screenplay. I know the film by heart and shoot by heart [...]; I don't improvise" (Bazin and Truffaut, p. 11).

To conclude these remarks on the shooting of the film, it should be mentioned that the episode of the canoe which breaks and folds in two, resembling an enormous shark's jaws, was not part of the film made in 1952. As Jacques Kermabon explains (p. 103), this sequence was added some twenty years later, after Tati had seen Stephen Spielberg's film *Jaws* (1975). The "shark" scene was integrated into the film when it was reedited. Moreover, certain scenes which were in the original film were subsequently cut out, like a scene which makes fun of a priest sleeping in a garden. Tati also eliminated the original dénouement in which we see Martine returning home in the train, smiling as she thumbs through a photo album of her vacation in which Hulot figures prominently.

SOUND IN TATI'S FILMS

It is quite obvious that Tati does not shoot with sound; his films are entirely post-synchronized. For him the sound track is just as important as the shots and requires a second "shooting," scene by scene, as soon as the filming with the camera is over. The editing of the film is no different for Tati. His editing of the sound track is as painstaking a process as the editing of the shots and reveals an unusual genius which has attracted the attention of numerous film critics. André Bazin considers that the particular sound tracks that Tati creates are his "stroke of genius and his most original technique" (p. 46; see the *Critical Dossier*). What is most striking in the sound track of *Mr. Hulot's Holiday* is the subtle mixture of completely realistic sound effects: children's and adults' shouts, shreds of conversation or of radio broadcasts, sundry observations, the hotel's bell, etc. As Tati tells us, "I put in my film everything that you usually hear when you're on vacation at the beach. I tried to reproduce the atmosphere" (Kyrou, p. 15). Kermabon discovers nonetheless in Tati's film what he calls the "invention of slapstick sound" (p. 11). The web of sound is completed by certain natural sounds which are rendered surreal by their amplification, like the sound of the waves, the creaking of a door, or the bouncing of a ping-pong ball. Tati also adds a certain number of artificial or fake sounds, like the machine gun effect during the fireworks display set off by Hulot. Nor should we forget the music, especially this trite melody that Tati calls a "rather sad and somewhat annoying refrain which is a good expression of the boredom and the monotony" which reigns (Kermabon, p. 11). The jazz, on the other hand, seems to express both a zest for life and the disruption that Mr. Hulot personifies.

We are no less struck by the fact that the hero of the film hardly ever speaks. He manages to say his name a couple of time, albeit with some difficulty, and to articulate a short sentence about the Schmutz's boy: "He's so nice!" He really only exists by his physical presence, his decidedly odd attire, his pipe, his gestures, and his bizarre way of walking — and by the disturbing effect he has on others. As for the latter, their speech is often little more than a muddle of sound. When their observations are intelligible, they are so trivial and banal that their words are reduced to a sort of background noise, "on the same level as the noise of the waves breaking onto the beach, the hotel bell, or the trite melody" (Parmion, p. 50). Bazin is led to observe that "the shrewdness of Tati consists in destroying the clarity by clarity itself. The dialogues are insignificant rather than incomprehensible, and their insignificance is revealed by their very preciseness" (p. 46). Tati explains, for his part, that sound has very particular functions in *Hulot*. It is through sound, he tells us, that "Hulot's car becomes a very important *character* in the film" (Henry and Le Péron, p. 8). He notes as well the use of sound "to create a certain depth of field," as in the case of the amplification of the sound of the waves on the beach when they are in the background (p. 9; see the *Critical Dossier*).

STRUCTURE AND THEMES

There is no real plot in *Mr Hulot's Holiday*, other than the romance suggested but scantily developed between Hulot and Martine. Tati considers his film to be simply a "slice of vacation life." It presents us, to quote Bazin, with a "succession of events both coherent in their signification and dramatically independent" (p. 44). We are treated to a series of gags which alternate with descriptive scenes. Most of the gags are related to mishaps or absurd incidents provoked in some way or form by Hulot's absent-mindedness or thoughtlessness. The film has of course a chronological structure: the arrival of the vacationers, their stay at the beach, their departure. One can even consider, albeit somewhat arbitrarily, that the structure of the film is pegged to the activities of the little society at the hotel (Agel, pp. 29-30): 1) *vacation life* (arrival at the hotel, the evening meal, the beach, lunch, the tennis match, the evening in the hotel lounge, etc.); 2) *Mr. Hulot's activities* (the canoe incident, the scene at the cemetery, tennis, ping-pong and the card players, the horse episode, etc.); 3) *group activities* (the costume ball, the picnic, the flat tire, the fireworks, etc.).

The "themes" of the film are reduced to a few simple motifs, the principal among them being, obviously, vacation at the beach. However, the vacation is really only a backdrop to highlight a more important theme, which is the empty existence of adults on vacation (if not the emptiness of their existence itself…). Tati's satirical take shows us individuals who are so scelorotic, so set in their habits that they no longer know how to have fun. They continue to pursue at the beach their everyday preoccupations and concerns. "And the hotel residents represent a colorful sampling of vacationers: the ladies, the commander, the old couple, the photographer, the children. Although they've come to the beach to forget their laborious existence, all these people reconstruct a similar life, with its schedule and its constraints. You almost expect them to punch their time card when they enter and exit…" (Cauliez, pp. 27-28).

In *Hulot* as elsewhere Tati is particularly hard on married couples, represented here by the English strollers, who live together but exist in isolation from one another. "After the initial flirting," observes Desbarats, "a couple's life is a web of misunderstandings" in Tati's films (p. 20). This adult world where order reigns, along with the inevitable boredom, is set topsy-turvy by Hulot's arrival. Hulot belongs to the realm of childhood — "it's the spirit of childhood, miraculously latent in each man" (Cauliez, p. 36) — with all the innocence, irresponsibility, and disorder that that implies. Tati's somewhat cruel representation of adult couples is balanced by his sensitivity toward and fondness for children. For Tati childhood is not only a period of innocence, it is a kind of "state of grace," if we judge by the scene of the little boy carrying the two ice-cream cones. The ice cream doesn't fall (and it really should!) when he turns the door handle…

The contrast between Hulot and his fellow vacationers foregrounds another important theme in the film that Bazin calls "the foolishness of people" (p. 48). Put another way, Tati shows us simply the amusing side of human beings, the humor that we can discern in people's behavior in everyday life. "What I tried to do was show that, basically, everyone is amusing" (Bazin and Truffaut, p. 2). This brings us to our final topic: Jacques Tati's particular brand of comedy.

COMIC STYLE

Geneviève Agel summarizes the general opinion when she observes, "comedy is different in Tati from what we are used to seeing in films of this type" (p. 49. It is above all the originality of Tati's comic style that attracts attention, that fascinates those who go to the trouble of trying to understand how it functions. The most singular aspect of Tati's comedy is, as the filmmaker himself says, that "Hulot is not funny in and of himself" (except, of course, when he does his mime acts, like the tennis and ping-pong matches). As has often been noted, Hulot is above all a catalyst. The comic effects develop around him; he is "someone who passes through the world and reveals the weaknesses of an artificial ritual — the ritual of vacation in this case" (Chevassu, p. 108). The humor is created by the reactions of the other characters, such as the waiter and the hotel owner, who have their own life in the film. Or as Bazin puts it, "the character created by Tati is amusing but in an accessory way, and in any case always relative to the world around him. He can be personally absent from the most comical gags, because Mr. Hulot is only the metaphysical embodiment of a disorder which continues to resonate long after he is gone" (p. 43). For Tati in the ideal comic film Hulot would tend to disappear: "What I would like is for the spectators to see him less and less, and for them to see the other characters more and more" (Bazin and Truffaut, p. 6).

On the other hand, one can hardly deny the slapstick nature of Tati's acting, called "superior burlesque" by Amengual (p. 31), in which we find a highly original blend of farce and comedy of manners. However, the humor here tends to provoke a smile — or even affection and sympathy, as Agel reminds us (p. 49) — rather than a belly laugh. The comic effects do not depend on the "stiffness" of the character and his "falling," in the Molieresque tradition as described by Henri Bergson in his famous essay on laughter. They develop instead by little human touches. Contrary to Chaplin, moreover, Tati does not develop his gags to the limit. He prefers to limit himself to the gag itself, which he leaves in a kind of "unfinished state," to borrow Bazin's term. "What is important as regards Hulot," Tati explains, "is that there is no exploitation. Once the gag is over, it's over. I don't try to milk it for all it's worth" (Bazin and Truffaut, p. 7).

On another score, the laughter that *Mr. Hulot's Holiday* provokes, if there's any at all, is rarely a burst of laughter from the crowd. Since Tati often uses medium static shots, depending on deep focus to present simultaneous actions in the foreground and the background, the spectators do not necessarily discover the comic effect at the same time (Kermabon, p. 14). This explains the "ricochet" effect described by Dondey (p. 97) in which the laughter develops sequentially, rippling through the audience as more and more spectators notice the effect — often produced by very banal events.

To explain more clearly Tati's comic style, it is often compared (as we have done above) to Chaplin's style. Tati himself makes the comparison, maintaining that two completely different schools are involved. "Chaplin bases his gags on intelligence. Isn't Hulot more spontaneous, more direct? [...] Mr. Hulot is always natural" (in Doisneau, p. 46). The great difference between Charlot and Hulot is that in Tati's films "the gag is part of life, not separated from it; it is integrated," if not simply "come upon" (Agel, p. 52). In Chaplin's films, the gag is always *created*. Let's listen again to Tati: "Faced with a difficulty, like a bothersome object, Chaplin comes up with ideas, then modifies or interprets the object...Hulot, on the other hand, does nothing on purpose [...]. Hulot participles in gags without even noticing it, without winking to the audience as Charlie does" (Kyrou, p. 15). The gag in Tati's films is always due to chance, to a misunderstanding, or to clumsiness. Tati likes to cite the famous episode in the cemetery in which the inner tube, which has fallen to the ground and is covered with dead leaves, is mistakenly taken for a wreath which Hulot is thought to have brought to the funeral. In a Chaplin film, it would have happened quite differently: "In the cemetery, for example, if Chaplin had found himself in the same situation as Hulot, he would have picked up the inner tube and stuck on the leaves himself, whereas Hulot is not even conscious of what has happened" (Kyrou, p. 15; see the *Critical Dossier*). Charlie Chaplin is ingenious, while Hulot is just unaware. Chaplin masters situations; Hulot suffers them.

STUDY GUIDE

Director's Comments

"Then I said to myself: 'My actors should be moving, not my camera.' I've often been criticized: 'Tati doesn't do enough with his camera!' Excuse me, but I know how to do a tracking shot, and I too can put a camera on a crane and lift it up five or six meters. All you have to do is sit beside the cameraman and say: 'Up!' And you can pan and follow anything you want to. I'm not saying that these techniques are not useful in the dramatic dynamics of a film which absolutely needs them and in which it is indispensable to crawl along with a character to see things from his perspective. But my story is completely different: it's a story which takes place in two spaces, and I want to see my characters develop their roles within those spaces" (Bazin and Truffaut, p. 10).

"In that case we could dot the i's and cross the t's, like you say, because it's clear that in the case of *Mr. Hulot's Holiday* it's easy with dialogue and without asking any effort from the spectator to say: the businessman continues to conduct his business, the young intellectual constantly propagandizes against society, the retired colonel bores everyone stiff with his war stories, the women behave the same way when they go to a party as when they go to the beach, showing off their prettiest pair of shorts, and in fact there are only three characters who really want to have a good time and get away from what they've been doing all year at the office or wherever. No one knew where Hulot came from, and you can tell that the English woman has only come to have fun and that the retired gentleman is just happy not to have to go back to some office. So what's important? I have no idea, but since you're studying sound, it's clear that this is the type of film which needs its sound track. It's its subject, and it's not easy to do, let me assure you. It's the film's scenario, and that's why you have to choose the sound effects like another director chooses the quality of his actors" (Henry and Le Péron, p. 10).

"Hulot arrives at the cemetery. He needs to get his car started and looks for a crank in the trunk. In the process of looking for the crank, he takes out a tire which falls on the ground. The tire is covered with leaves, turning it into a funeral wreath, and the organizer of the funeral thinks that Mr. Hulot has brought it on purpose. You'll say, "Hulot didn't invent the gag." It's true, he didn't. He did what could happen to any absent-minded person, with no comic ingenuity iinvolved. The comic ingenuity comes from the screenwriter or from the situation, but what happens to Hulot could happen to any number of people [...]. He didn't create anything.

"In the case of Chaplin, if Chaplin had considered the gag good enough to put in his film — which is not at all certain — he would have made the same entrance as Hulot. but seeing that the situation was catastrophic (there is a religious ceremony, and his car is in the way), and finding an inner tube in his trunk, he would have stuck the leaves on the inner tube himself *for the spectator's benefit*, transforming it into a wreath. And the spectators would have found him marvelous, because at the very moment that no one could imagine a way out of this situation, he would have invented a gag on screen for the spectators. And it's this gag which would have provoked the laughter and which would have caused the spectators to say, "He was amazing." You can't say that about Hulot. He wasn't amazing, since that could have happened to you, to anyone: you look for something in a car, something falls out, you pick it up, it's nothing unusual. We see here that there are really two completely different schools of comedy, because Hulot is never ingenious" (Bazin and Truffaut, p. 4).

"So to give a very clear example, let's look at *Mr. Hulot's Holiday* and assume there's no sound. If I shot it like Chaplin or Buster Keaton might have done, Hulot's car would be silent. Great, it would be amusing for a few shots because it looks funny, and it's behavior might make people laugh, but with the sound effects Hulot's car becomes an important *character* in the film. With all the trouble we went to make the little pops from the exhaust, the jerks, the *putt, putt, bang, bang*, so that it wakes up the whole hotel and aggravates everyone, the car becomes a more important character than a drunkard who could have awakened the hotel every night with his singing. So the personality of Hulot's car is noisy [...]. And people will often tell you, what I remember is the sound of the door in the hotel in *Mr. Hulot's Holiday*, because above the orders the owner gives to his waiters you can hear the creaking of the door each time one of them pushes it open. So, you can see the importance of sound. You know, since you must suspect that all comedies are a form of protest [...], that while the door itself isn't protesting, the fact that it is disturbing the vacationers in the dining room makes it part of the protest. You're all eating peacefully and *creak!* And here's something else that might interest you: you can also use sound to create a kind of depth of field. Here's something I did: I made the waves on the beach, which are in the background, louder than some trivial event in the foreground, because at that moment the sea is the most important thing, visually and auditorily. It's the star. You arrive at the beach and right away: Ah, the sea!" (Henry and Le Péron, pp. 8-9).

Excerpts for Discussion

Excerpt 1 (9'00-11'40): Mr. Hulot's arrival.

Excerpt 2 (19'40-20'05): The gag with the watch.

Excerpt 3 (25'00-26'20): Hulot and the suitcase.

Excerpt 4 (28'10-29'45): The jazz episode; the hotel owner and the aquarium.

Excerpt 5 (34'10-35'10): The "Peeping Tom" and the kick in the pants.

Excerpt 6 (35'15-38'15): The paint can gag; the shark-canoe.

Excerpt 7 (38'45-4'15): The wet footsteps gag.

Excerpt 8 (53'30-56'20: The ping-pong and card players episode.

Excerpt 9 (1h01'20-03'35): The horse and the rumble seat; the marshmallow gag.

Excerpt 10 (1h17'45-23'20): The jazz scene sequel; waiting for Hulot; the fireworks.

Questions/Topics for Reflection

1. The scene at the train station and the sound effects.
2. The character of Mr. Hulot: his appearance, his personality.   // car
3. The role of Mr. Hulot's car in the gags.
4. Mr. Hulot's arrival at the hotel; its effect on the other vacationers.
5. The use of dialogue and music in this film
6. The cemetery episode; the funeral wreath gag.
7. The tennis and ping-pong games; the card game gag.
8. The depiction of the vacationers.   what quirks
9. Hulot and the children; the old English lady, the strolling husband.
10. Mr. Hulot's role as a "catalyst" in Jacques Tati's comic style.

CRITICAL DOSSIER

Michel Chion — Mr. Hulot

The customery image we have of Hulot, his "police sketch," shows him tall, a pipe in his mouth, dressed in pants with the legs too short, showing his striped socks — always proper moreover, whether he is dressed up or in casual attire, with a bow-tie or an open shirt, a raincoat which is too short or a light jacket, but often wearing a hat that he lifts politely and armed with an umbrella. His manner of walking is unique. Sometimes he strides forward resolutely, driven by some secret decision; sometimes he pussyfoots around, approaching his object with complicated maneuvers. He is never really at rest, even when he's not moving. He always looks like he's going somewhere

— a veritable human turntable. His expression, veiled by the pipe, the hat, and distance, is indefinable, somewhere between worry, stupidity, and polite neutrality. In his attitude as in his movements he acts like someone who's not up to anything and never is. In fact, Hulot always seems to be up to something, but without our knowing what (*Jacques Tati*, pp. 31-32).

Marc Dondey — "This incessant agitation of details"

On the station platform a nervous crowd awaits the train which is to take it to the seaside. Nets and fishing poles get tangled up in the feet of the travelers: whole families, campers with over-stuffed backpacks. A mother slaps her son. The handle of a suitcase breaks at the worst time. At the sound of a nasal, incomprehensible loudspeaker, the travelers rush down into the underground passage and come up on another platform. A train pulls into the station on the track they had just left. Another announcement, followed immediately by a withdrawal of the crowd, which returns to its starting place. But the train is already on its way. The travelers, out of breath, set their paraphernalia down. The loudspeaker crackles. On the furthest platform, to the despair of the vacationers, another train has come to a stop. This half-human, half-mechanical ballet between the crowd and the locomotives, directed by an invisible station chief, this back-and-forth of the vacationers streaming from one platform to another before quickly withdrawing, are a mischievous imitation of the movement of waves. The comic effect of this scene is based both on the emotion that the spectators feel and on a proliferation of extraordinarily true details.

All of the figures in this crowd are drawn with the preciseness of a miniature. The gratuitous slap, the strap which breaks, the two umbrellas whose handles catch when their owners pass one another and which, fallen to the ground, point to opposite directions, like an absurd traffic sign…all little comic events which grab our attention, minute details which disarm the spectator, no sooner seen than they are gone. What gives the scene its unity, its life, and its flavor is this sparkling meeting of the comic and the true, this incessant agitation of details (*Tati*, pp. 95-96).

François Chevassu — "A Masterpiece of Comic Cinema"

You have to be wary of Tati. The humor isn't always where you think it is at first, but rather in the extension of the gag which goes from a typical comic effect to a much more subtle detail. In the hotel lounge Hulot hears a clock chime. He turns his wrist to check his watch. The waiter, who is watching him, does the same. But since he has a glass in his hand, he spills the contents on a client. Loud complaint… That's fine, it's funny, but we've already seen that sort of thing in Laurel and Hardy. It's even a bit of a let down. A couple of shots later the waiter steps out the front door of the restaurant mumbling to himself, as he always does, and checks the time…on his pocket watch (he has no wrist watch).

As we saw in *Jour de fête*, Tati's effectiveness is also related to the fact that he doesn't systematically draw attention to his own comical behavior. Although Hulot is at the center of the action, the world exists around him, and the other characters have their own weight. And they are vivid enough for us to recognize them twenty-four years later on the summer beaches, even if the apparel has changed. The waiter has his own existence and creates his own comic effects. All he has to do is look at his watch, glance over a client's shoulder, stop and stare at a menu, pass through a creaking door, and when he is baffled by Hulot's enigmatic footprints on the floor of the vestibule, he has an equal role in the dramatic development of the scene. Tati's approach consists in teaching us to discover the humor where it is: everywhere around us, and in us as well. Therefore, Hulot cannot be the exclusive subject of the film but only a catalyst, someone who by his very existence reveals the foibles of an artificial ritual. The ritual of vacation here, other rituals elsewhere ("*Les Vacances de M. Hulot*," p. 108).

Ado Kyrou — "Me *and* The Outside World "

The great comic films usually owe their personality to the main character, who is a victim of the world around him. To accomplish this, reality is exaggerated, distorted, and turned upside down, which doesn't mean that it is betrayed. Objects offer resistance, events rush by governed by unexpected rules. The surprise, the shock, or the gag flow from the attitude adopted by the hero. "Me against the outside world" could be the motto of all the great comic actors. Keaton deals with the struggle imperturbably, while Laurel and Hardy defend themselves furiously, provoking additional chain reactions. Chaplin revolts against the world poetically, and Langdon transforms reality to suit himself. W.C. Fields and the Marx brothers destroy this reality.

Tati's motto could be "Me *and* the Outside World." Here — and when I say "here," I'm thinking especially of *Mr. Hulot's Holiday* — there is no distortion of reality. On the contrary, we are offered an almost naturalistic depiction of the outside world against which the hero has no need to revolt. But if there is no struggle, if there is no exaggeration, what makes people laugh?

Tati wouldn't be funny if he weren't addressing his audience through the medium of cinema. A Tati sequence glimpsed in the street would have no effect on us. We all experience daily Mr. Hulot's adventures. These adventures are so banal that they occur right in front of us, as we stroll or as we travel in the subway, without our even noticing them. Tati shows us what is going on all the time everywhere, things which escape us precisely because they are so commonplace [...].

Whether in relation to life or to the cinema, the laughter in Tati's films is due to the fact that the author shows us what the cinema refuses systematically to show us on the screen, and what is nonetheless the marvelous side of life: unvarnished reality, both obvious and sensitive. The noise from a door, a gob of marshmallow falling, an unsuccessful costume ball, embarrassed handshakes are all things of no importance at first glance, but which, in our life, can become terrifying signs — which in any case are our lives. Rather than a "slice of life," Tati gives us "life" ("Tati et le monde extérieur," pp. 9-11).

André Bazin — The Sound Track

Even more than the images on the screen, the sound track gives the film its temporal density. It is also Tati's stroke of genius and his most original technique. It has sometimes been said, mistakenly, that his sound track was composed of a jumble of sound out of which would arise from time to time a sentence fragment, intelligible words which were all the more ridiculous. That is just the impression of someone who's not listening closely. In fact, indistinct sounds are very rare (like the loudspeaker announcements in the station — but in this case the gag is realistic). On the contrary, the shrewdness of Tati consists in destroying the clarity by clarity itself. The dialogues are not incomprehensible but rather insignificant, and their insignificance is revealed by their very precision. Tati manages to do this largely by deforming the relative intensity of the sound that accompanies various shots, going so far sometimes as to maintain the off-camera sound while we are watching a silent scene.

Generally his sound scenery consists of realistic elements: snatches of dialogue, shouts, various and sundry reflections, none of which is placed clearly in a dramatic context. It's in relation to this background that a misplaced noise becomes completely incongruous. For example, during the evening at the hotel when the residents are reading, discussing, or playing cards, Hulot is playing ping-pong. His celluloid ball makes an extremely disproportionate noise, shattering the relative silence like a billiard ball. At each bounce it seems to grow louder. Underlying this film are authentic sounds, recorded at a real beach, to which Tati adds artificial sound effects, no less precise but constantly offset. Out of the combination of this realism and these deformations is born the irrefutable inanity of the sounds produced by this nonetheless human community.

Never has the physical character of words, their anatomy, been so pitilessly emphasized. Accustomed as we are to lending meaning to words even when they don't have any, we don't adopt the same ironic distance from them as we do sometimes from visual phenomena. Here the words file by stark naked, grotesquely indecent, stripped of the social complicity which dressed them in an illusory dignity [...]. Occasionally Tati slips in a sound which is completely false, but it is so bound up in the tangle of sound that it doesn't occur to us to protest. Such is the case of the sound effects accompanying the fireworks, in which it is difficult to identify, unless you make a real effort, the sounds of a bombardment. It is sound which gives M. Hulot's universe its density, its psychological character. Ask yourself what causes this great feeling of sadness at the end of the film, this exaggerated disenchantment, and you'll discover that it's perhaps the silence. Throughout the film, the shouts from the children as they played accompanied all of the beach scenes, and their absence for the first time signifies the end of the vacation ("M. Hulot et le temps," pp. 46-47. Reproduced by permission of the University of California Press/The Regents of the University of California).

André Bazin — "The Flip Side of a Tragedy"

Like all true and great comic actors, Tati makes us laugh at the flip side of a tragedy. His holiday is filled with imbecility, cruelty, and the smugness of a sample of humanity that can only be excused by the uselessness and "relaxation" of summer vacation. Objectively it would be hard to find a gangster film bitterer than this comedy. However, something saves these people who are even too dumb to be bored. From the presence of Mr. Hulot radiates a clumsy but undeniable love. His idiotic initiatives only disturb the established disorder, but they become more often than not strokes of fate. Like the lightning rod which attracts the lightning and neutralizes it. Knight in white with a newspaper helmet, armed with a fishing rod, always on a quest for some Grail or other, Mr. Hulot is the guarantee of a poetry and an idealism on the scale of this human society in which we are forced in spite of ourselves to recognize ourselves (*Liens*, May 1953, in Agel, *Hulot parmi nous*, p. 114).

JACQUES TATI'S FILMOGRAPHY

Short Subjects (screenwriter and actor)

1932	*Oscar, champion de tennis*
1934	*We Need A Brute (On demande une brute)*
1935	*Gay Sunday (Gai dimanche)*
1936	*Watch Your Left*
	(Soigne ton gauche, directed by René Clément)

Director, screenwriter, actor

1947	*The School For Postmen*
	(L'Ecole des facteurs, short subject)
1949	*Holiday (Jour de fête)*
1953	*Mr. Hulot's Holiday*
	(Les Vacances de Monsieur Hulot)
1958	*Mon Oncle*
1967	*Playtime*
1971	*Trafic*
1974	*Parade* (video)

WORKS CONSULTED

Agel, Geneviève. *Hulot parmi nous.* Paris: Editions du Cerf, 1955.

Amengual, Barthélemy. "L'Etrange comique de Monsieur Tati." *Cahiers du cinéma* 32 (Feb. 1954): 31-36.

Bazin, André. *What is cinema?* Berkeley: University of California Press, 1967-1971.

.........."M. Hulot et le temps" (orig. in *Esprit* 1953), article reprinted in *Qu'est-ce que le cinéma?* Paris: Editions du Cerf, 1981 (pp. 41-48).

Bazin, André, and François Truffaut. "Entretien avec Jacques Tati." *Cahiers du cinéma* 83 (May 1959): 2-18.

Cauliez, A.-J. *Jacques Tati.* Cinéma d'aujourd'hui. Paris: Seghers, 1968.

Chevassu, François. "*Les Vacances de M. Hulot.*" *Image et son* 317 (May 1977): 107-109.

Chion, Michel. *Jacques Tati.* Paris: Cahiers du cinéma, 1987.

Daney, Serge. "Eloge de Tati." *Cahiers du cinéma* 303 (Sept. 1979): 5-7.

Decaux, Emmanuel. "Revoir *les Vacances de Monsieur Hulot.*" *Cinématographe* 27: 32.

Desbarats, Carole. *Les Vacances de Monsieur Hulot.* Paris: Yellow Now, 1997.

Doisneau, Robert. "Jacques Tati." *Cinéma 55* 3 (Jan. 1955): 43-47.

Dondey, Marc. *Tati.* Paris: Ramsay, 1989.

Henry, Jean-Jacques et Serge Le Péron. "Entretiens avec Jacques Tati." *Cahiers du cinéma* 303 (Sept. 1979): 8-13.

Kermabon, Jacques. *Les Vacances de M. Hulot*. Paris: Yellow Now, 1988.

Kyrou, Ado. "Tati et le monde extérieur" suivi d'un "Entretien avec Jacques Tati." *Cinéma 56* 12 (Oct.-Nov. 1956): 9-16.

Parmion, Serge. "Enfin Tati revient." *Cahiers du cinéma* 22 (April 1953): 49-50.

Sadoul, Georges. *Chroniques du cinéma français 1939-1967*. Paris: Union Générale d'éditions, 1979.

Villien, Bruno. "Entretiens. Jacques Tati." *Cinématographe* 27 (May 1977): 30-31.

Robert Bresson

A Man Escaped *or* The Wind Bloweth Where It Listeth
Un condamné à mort s'est échappé ou Le Vent souffle où il veut

---

(1956)

Robert Bresson, *A Man Escaped*: Fontaine (François Leterrier)
in his cell at the Fort de Montluc prison. © Gaumont

Director ....Robert Bresson
Assistant Directors .... Jean-Paul Clément, Louis Malle
Screenplay and dialogues..Robert Bresson
Original Story ....André Devigny
Director of Photography ....Léonce-Henry Burel
Cameraman .... Henri Raichi
Music..Mozart, *Mass in C Minor*
Film Editor .... Raymond Lamy
Sound ....Pierre-André Bertrand
Art Director .... Pierre Charbonnier
Script Girl (Continuity) ....Annie Dubouillon
Producer ....Société Gaumont-Nouvelles Editions de Films
Length .... 1 h 39

Cast

François Leterrier (*Fontaine*), Roland Monod (*the pastor*), Jacques Ertaud (*Orsini*), Jean-Paul Delhumeau (*Hébrard*), Roger Tréherne (*Terry*), Maurice Beerblock (*M. Blanchet*), Charles LeClainche (*Jost*).

STORY

Lyon, 1943. Fontaine, a lieutenant in the French Resistance, is in a Gestapo car along with two other prisoners. He is being taken to the Montluc Fortress, which the Germans have turned into a prison. When the car stops for a moment, Fontaine tries to escape but is quickly recaptured and brought back to the car. One of the Gestapo men strikes him on the head with the butt of his pistol. When the car arrives at the prison, Fontaine is severely beaten and bloodied before being taken to his cell on a stretcher. When the German soldiers awaken him, he pretends to be too weak to get up. In retrospect he thinks that this is the only reason he wasn't taken out and shot immediately.

By pulling himself up to a small barred window, Fontaine can see the prison yard. He manages to make contact with Terry, another prisoner, who helps him communicate with the outside world. Terry tosses him some string with which he lowers letters and pulls up small objects, like a razor and a pin, which his friend obtains for him. After a few days Fontaine is led outside to the toilets where, his hands still shackled, he is able to wash up for the first time.

Fontaine is able to communicate with the prisoner in the adjacent cell by tapping on the wall. With the pin and advice from his neighbor he succeeds in taking off his handcuffs, which he puts back on each time his guards come in. He is questioned and gives his word not to attempt to escape — with all the mental reservations we can imagine. He is soon transferred to a new cell where his handcuffs are removed. He is concerned about the silence of his new neighbor, who does not respond to his taps on the wall.

Fontaine learns the prison routine: the meal served in a mess tin, the daily trip to the prison yard to empty the pails which serve as toilets, the quick washing up at the sinks. It is in the washroom that he meets other prisoners, like Hébrard, the pastor, and Orsini, who was betrayed to the Gestapo by his own wife. The prisoners manage to exchange a few furtive words despite the strict interdiction against speaking among themselves. Fontaine becomes accustomed to the periodic salvos of gunshots marking the executions inside the prison. One day in the yard he finally sees his silent neighbor, an elderly man named Blanchet.

Having noticed that his cell door could be taken apart, Fontaine fashions a chisel from an iron spoon by sharpening the handle on his cell floor. In the constant fear of being caught, he begins a long painstaking task, chiseling down and slowly taking apart his door. He finally makes contact with his neighbor Blanchet by helping him get to his feet one day after a fall in the yard. They begin to speak to each other through their adjacent cell windows. Fearing a collective punishment, Blanchet asks Fontaine to stop working on his door, but a friendship develops between the two men.

After a month of patient work Fontaine is finally able to take his door apart, which permits him to step out into the corridor and erase the sanctions written on one of the prisoner's doors. He shares with the other prisoners his plan to escape, without knowing exactly how he's going to go about it. The pastor gives him a note on which he has copied a short dialogue in which Christ says to Nicodemus, "The wind bloweth where it listeth." Since Orsini wants to participate in the escape attempt, Fontaine gives him a note explaining how to dismantle his door. One night Fontaine leaves his cell and goes onto the roof by pulling himself up through the glass ceiling of the corridor. He begins to make a rope with strips cut from his pillow case, then from shirts, bed sheets, and covers — a rope that he strengths with iron wire taken from the springs of his bedstead. Orsini becomes impatient and tries to escape alone, but he is caught, returned to his cell, and beaten. Before his execution Orsini helps Fontaine benefit from his failure by informing him that he will need large hooks to get over the last wall and explaining how to make them.

The Germans confiscate the prisoners' writing materials, threatening to shoot anyone who doesn't obey. Fontaine refuses to give up his pencil, in a silent show of defiance. At the very moment that the guards come to search his cell, he receives a package. The package distracts the guards, who leave without searching his room. The package contains clothes, which Fontaine cuts up to use in his rope. Blanchet has finally begun to believe in Fontaine's escape plan and gives him one of his blankets to help him finish the rope. Fontaine realizes that he will need an accomplice to succeed, but he cannot find anyone. The other prisoners encourage him to make his escape attempt as soon as possible; the longer he waits, the greater the chance of failure.

Fontaine is taken to the Hotel Terminus, the headquarters of the Gestapo in Lyons, where he learns that he has been condemned to death for his activities in the Resistance. He had tried to blow up a bridge. He is relieved upon returning to the prison to find himself in the same cell, because he had hidden there all of the equipment for his escape. He understands that he must act quickly. He is soon faced with a new dilemma, however, when a new prisoner, François Jost, is put in his cell with him. Jost is a young Frenchman who had served in the German army before deserting. Fontaine gives his last will and testament to the pastor.

Suspecting that he may be dealing with a traitor, Fontaine considers the necessity of killing Jost to prevent him from betraying his plans to escape. He eventually decides to take the young man into his confidence and invites him to leave with him. He gives Jost to understand, in any case, that he really has no choice. The night of the escape Fontaine and Jost exit through the glass ceiling, hauling all of their material onto the roof. The roof is covered with gravel and pieces of glass, which crunch under their feet so loudly that they have to wait for the noise of passing trains to cover their movements. Fontaine is forced to descend into the yard to strangle a sentinel who is on watch at the foot of the first wall. When they come to the second wall Fontaine realizes that he wouldn't have been able to make it over without the help of Jost; the two men have to help each other reach the top. On the other side, in a passage between the two walls, another sentinel is making his rounds on a bicycle. Using the large hooks, Fontaine makes a bridge between the last two walls. After waiting for hours, Fontaine suddenly makes his move. He crawls across the space clinging to the rope, followed soon by Jost. The two men jump down on the other side of the wall and move quickly away into the night.

CRITICAL RECEPTION

As in the case of each new film by Bresson, the opening of *A Man Escaped* was viewed by film critics as a bold statement, indeed a clap of thunder, in the world of cinema. As René Briot's remarks demonstrate, the reception was generally euphoric: "The film was almost unanimously acclaimed by the press. Each critic recognized the exceptional quality of the film" (p. 92). A few days before the premiere, François Truffaut raved in his regular column in *Arts*, "*A Man Escaped* is not only the finest film by Robert Bresson but also the most significant French film of the last decade," adding that it is "the first Bresson film which is perfectly homogeneous; every single shot is perfect" (No. 593, p. 3). *Le Film français* echoes Truffaut's opinion: "A Bresson film is always an event. This one — austere, rigorous, confined to a naked setting — is a complete success of minimalist art, moving by its humanity [...]. The tableaux, the shots, are all irreproachable" (p. 9). J.-L. Tallenay goes even further, declaring that Bresson's new film presents a "Copernican revolution in esthetics" (p. 4).

In the same period, after seeing the film a single time, André Bazin was uncharacteristically at a loss for words, stating that he found it easier to describe what the film wasn't (a conventional film which "exploits the dramatic effects of the scenario," a "plausible" film) than what it was. Like everyone else Bazin was struck by Bresson's profound originality in *A Man Escaped*, "this unusual work which resembles nothing that the cinema offers us habitually" (*Cahiers du cinéma* 72, p. 27). After Truffaut, who observed that the film "is radically opposed to all known cinematographic styles" (*Arts*, 596, p. 3), Rohmer pointed out that Bresson escaped any kind of classification and emphasized the similarities between this film and painting: "Constantly original but with no affectation in the framing or the angles of the shots, Bresson, like the great painters, has his touch, his brush stroke identifiable by its purity without hardness, the gentle but never limp inflections" (pp. 42, 45). While likewise insisting that we are dealing with an "unclassifiable" filmmaker, Marcel Martin asserted that "Bresson's direction is masterly" and that "this admirable film would prove, if necessary, the profound unity of inspiration and expression" of his whole body of works (pp. 110-113).

Nonetheless, not everyone succumbed to the spell of Bresson's cinema. There were dissenting voices, including that of Ado Kyrou, who, while recognizing Bresson's talent, commented that "his films are still dry, stilted, and boring." As for *A Man Escaped*, he added, it is "the account of a captivity and an escape. A particularly attractive subject that Bresson systematically ruins. He eliminates one by one all the dramatic elements of a story which could be enthralling" (p. 41). A few months later the jury at the Cannes Film Festival of 1957 ratified the general critical opinion by awarding *A Man Escaped* the Prize for the Best Director. The film also garnered the Prize for the Best Film of 1957 awarded by the Academy of French Film, the Prize of the International Catholic Office of Cinema (OCIC), the Victory Prize of French cinema (based on a poll of *Le Figaro/Cinémonde*), and the Italian Critics' Prize. It is generally considered to be Bresson's best film — the only film, in any case, which enjoyed broad popular appeal.

BEFORE *A MAN ESCAPED*

Born in Auvergne in 1907, Bresson attended secondary school in Sceaux, near Paris, before enrolling in the School of Fine Arts. He was first drawn to painting, specializing in portraits, but at the age of 26 turned to the cinema. From 1933 to 1939 he wrote dialogues and screenplays, worked as an assistant director, and even directed a short comic film around twenty minutes long, *Les Affaires publiques*, in 1934.

When war broke out in 1939 Bresson enlisted in the Army. Captured in Holland when France was defeated in June 1940, Bresson wasn't repatriated until March 1941. After his return to Paris he directed his first feature film, *Angels of the Streets* (*Les Anges du péché*, 1943), which is about the Sisters of Bethany, a religious order devoted to the spiritual and moral rehabilitation of female convicts just released from prison. The dialogues were written by the famous French playwright Jean Giraudoux.

Encouraged by the success of this first film, Bresson undertook the adaptation of the story of Mme de la Pommeraye, the principal episode of an eighteenth-century French novel, *Jack the Fatalist and His Master* (ca. 1770) by Denis Diderot. With dialogues by Jean Cocteau, Bresson succeeded in making *Ladies of the Park* (*Les Dames du Bois de Boulogne*, 1945) despite the enormous material problems posed by the end of the war and the battle for the Liberation of France. His film is a modernized version of Diderot's story in which a society woman takes revenge on her unfaithful lover by tricking him into marrying a call girl. While critics will later recognize the many fine qualities of this film, *Ladies of the Park* is the greatest "failure" (the only film not to win any prizes) of Bresson's career. The contemporary critics were generally severe, finding the film too dry, slow, and monotonous, the characters too inhuman and too cold to communicate the intense human passions at play.

Ladies was followed by a five-year period during which Bresson, working alone this time, wrote an adaptation of a novel by Georges Bernanos, *Diary of a Country Priest* (*Journal d'un curé de campagne*, 1936). The novel is about the solitary, agonizing path toward grace traveled by a young priest in a tiny rural community. Completed in 1950, the film was instantly acclaimed as an indisputable masterpiece. It won numerous awards and turned Bresson into an international celebrity. After two failed projects at the beginning of the fifties — adaptations of the story of Sir Lancelot by the medieval poet Chrétien de Troyes and of Mme de Lafayette's celebrated novel *La Princesse de Clèves* (1678) — Bresson read in a Parisian newspaper in 1954 the story of a spectacular escape from a Gestapo prison during the Occupation. Although the adaptation of this true story was only the fourth feature film by Bresson in thirteen years, he had already become a kind of legend in the world of French cinema. Bresson has both detractors and hard-core supporters, but the latter see in this short series of films a steady march toward "the perfecting, the deepening of an 'extraordinary' body of works, in the strongest sense of the word" (Arbois, p. 3). Arbois added moreover, "There is no secondary film in Bresson's career," his four films being "essential works of inexhaustible richness which will never be diminished by time" (p. 3).

ORIGIN AND SHOOTING

In 1943 Lieutenant André Devigny, who had been in the Resistance from the very beginning of the Occupation, was arrested by the Gestapo and incarcerated in the Montluc Fortress prison in Lyon. After several months of preparation, and only a few hours before his scheduled execution, he miraculously escaped. The Montluc Fortress was a prison from which virtually no one ever escaped. At its entrance is a plaque which we see in the first shot of Bresson's film carrying the following message: "Here suffered under the German Occupation ten thousand prisoners victims of the Nazis and their accomplices. Seven thousand died." Among these seven thousand was the great martyr of the Resistance, Jean Moulin, who was shot at Montluc after being tortured. When Bresson read Devigny's account of his escape published by the newspaper *Le Figaro littéraire* in November 1954, he decided it would be the subject of his next film.

Bresson reflected for six months before going to work. From that point on, the project moved "rapidly" forward, according to Bresson's standards: around three months to write the dialogues and three more months to construct a crew and choose the actors. For the purpose of authenticity Bresson shot on location at Montluc, in the presence of André Devigny himself, who served as his technical advisor for the material details of the escape. Since the fortress was still being used as a military prison, the authorities had to send fifty prisoners to another penitentiary during the thirteen days of shooting. For the interior shots the art director Pierre Charbonnier reconstructed Devigny's cell up to the tiniest detail at the Studio Saint-Maurice. He used the same material as the cell at Montluc so that the noises made by the prisoner as he prepared his escape would be identical. It took Bresson two and a half months to wrap up the shooting (from May 15 to August 2, 1956) and three months to edit the film. It opened on November 10 in Paris.

ACTORS/"MODELS"

Both the choice of the actors and their acting, quite particular in Bresson's films, require a few comments. Following a practice he established in his preceding film *Diary of a Country Priest*, Bresson avoided hiring professional actors for *A Man Escaped*. For the role of the protagonist Fontaine, for example, he chose François Leterrier, a philosophy student who had had no previous experience in movies. In the role of the pastor he cast the journalist Roland Monod, while Blanchet was played by a Belgian translator named Maurice Beerblock and Jost by a young apprentice discovered in a Jesuit orphanage, and so on. The roles of the prison guards and the members of the Gestapo were played by German students living in the German Residence Hall at the university, all amateurs. Bresson's attitude toward film actors has become a part of his legend. He could not tolerate in his films the style of professional film actors, which was, in his opinion, appropriate to the theater but not to cinema. When film actors are "acting," Bresson maintained, all they are doing is recording theater. Cinema had to find its own language: "I believe that cinema has its own particular language, and I think that as soon as an actor begins trying to express himself by mimicry, gestures, and verbal effects, we're no longer dealing with cinema but with filmed theater" ("Propos de Bresson," p. 4). Actors are generally trained to play in a show (*un spectacle*), a conception of cinema that Bresson rejects absolutely: "Cinema is not a *spectacle*, it's a form of writing" (p. 5). In order to avoid any possible identification with conventional cinema, Bresson preferred the term "cinematograph" to "cinema" to describe his work in film. His rejection of conventional acting is thus only one element — but one of prime importance — in a theoretical position which situates Bresson clearly in the current of cinematographic modernity. This tendancy was defined several years earlier in Alexandre Astruc's famous metaphor of the "camera-pen" (*la caméra-stylo*): "I call this new age of cinema the age of the *Caméra-stylo*. This image has a very precise sense. It means that the cinema will free itself little by little from the tyranny of the visual, of the image for the image, of the story, of the concrete to become a means of writing as versatile and subtle as written language" (p. 39).

It is clear in any case that the "Bresson system" of directing actors, what he calls his "mechanics," is irreconcilable with the normal concept of acting. First, Bresson doesn't ask his actors to "embody" a character but rather to be themselves: "By taking infinite pains, my system involves above all finding in the actor not so much a physical resemblance (choosing him because he has blond or brown hair, is big or small) but a moral resemblance, so that from the outset of the filming he only has to be himself" ("Propos," p. 5). Rather than the *appearance* of the actor, Bresson prefers the more authentic *being* of the individual. In speaking of François Leterrier, for instance, Jean Sémolué remarks, "He doesn't play the role of Fontaine; he *is* Fontaine" (p. 172). Once he has found his actors, Bresson forbids them to "act." He doesn't even call them actors but rather "models," a term which corresponds to his conception of his art: "I'm not a director; I'm a painter" (Leterrier, p. 34). He conceives of himself as a sculptor as well, for he insists in fact on "shaping" his actors, on molding them to obtain the result he desires. When filming, remarks Truffaut, "he only sees and hears his actor, whom he shapes patiently and stubbornly until he resembles Bresson himself" ("Bresson tourne *Un condamné à mort s'est échappé*," p. 5). Jules Roy, who was present at the shooting for several days, describes Bresson's method more precisely: "The problem is, these amateurs have to speak. Bresson doesn't send them to the Conservatory. He sticks them in the prison yard with a toilet bucket in their hand and makes them rehearse their text fifty times. One hundred times, if necessary, until they can reproduce Bresson's tone of voice, which may not be entirely realistic, but it's his. Before the camera rolls, he dictates every expression and gesture they will make" (p. 4). All of his "models," moreover, must pronounce their lines in the same flat, toneless manner (Bresson calls it "leveled"), with no vocal effects, no discernable intention. "Don't think about what you are saying," he said to Monod, "just let the words come mechanically. When people speak they don't think about the words they're using. They don't even think about what they mean. Carried away by what they're saying, they just let the words out, simply and directly" (Monod, p. 18). The goal is to achieve a form of expression which Truffaut calls "a false trueness which soon sounds truer than what is true" (*Arts* 593, p. 3).

Bresson believes that by making his actor repeat until he is exhausted, he can seize his inner truth (and the truth of the character he is "playing"), which surfaces spontaneously, unbeknownst to the actor. Since Bresson himself doesn't know exactly when this truth is going to emerge, he repeats the same take over and over, five times, ten times. For *A Man Escaped* he shot 60,000 meters of film but only kept 2,900. It is in the editing process that his creative talents really come into play. Of the multiple copies of the same shot, Bresson is able to recognize in the course of editing the one take in which the nature of his actor — and thus of his character — is most clearly revealed. To cap it off, since Bresson was not satisfied with the dialogues recorded during the shooting of *A Man Escaped*, he summoned all his actors to re-record them in the studio. "There, sentence by sentence, virtually word by word, we repeated our lines after Bresson, ten times, twenty times, thirty times, trying to imitate perfectly the intonations, the rhythm, the very timbre of the director's voice. All of the roles were now being played by Bresson" (Monod, p. 19). Michel Estève was astonished: "This simple line spoken by Fontaine to Jost, "*Lie down and go to sleep*," was recorded sixty times" (p. 117). However idiosyncratic the method, it produced extraordinary results in *A Man Escaped*, so dense and homogeneous is the acting.

The word "paradox" appears often in critical commentaries of Bresson's work. While it is true that Bresson's behavior with his actors has a despotic side — Maria Casarès, the great actress who plays the heroine of *Ladies of the Park*, calls him a "veritable tyrant" on the set — one shouldn't conclude that Bresson knows exactly what he wants from his cast when he shoots each scene. On the contrary, what Bresson is seeking is precisely a "surprise," the revelation of something unexpected in his actor: "In reality what is beautiful in a film, what I'm seeking, is the foray into the unknown. The public has to feel that I'm going toward the unknown, that I don't know in advance what is going to happen [...]. It's marvelous to discover a man gradually as the film develops, instead of knowing in advance what he is...which in fact would be nothing more than the false personality of an actor. In a film you must have the impression that you are discovering something profound in man" ("Propos de Bresson," p. 6).

Despite the rigorousness of his method Bresson, like Renoir before him, gives an essential role to chance in the making of his films. Although Bresson considers "improvisation" very important (if it is preceded by lengthy reflection), unlike Renoir he does not welcome ideas from his collaborators. Bresson is in total command. As Monod remarks, "Robert Bresson works alone. The crew around him —technicians and actors — must all accept this phenomenal imperative of his character and talent. They are all his instruments. He alone creates" (p. 19). Bresson is without the slightest doubt the "author" of his work.

ADAPTATION AND STRUCTURE

At the beginning of *A Man Escaped*, there is a title card stating, "This is a true story. I give it to you as it is, unadorned." It is true that Bresson's adaptation is extremely faithful, including entire sentences verbatim from Devigny's story. Devigny's account includes however a series of highly colorful episodes which do not appear in Bresson's film. The day after his escape, for example, Devigny is recaptured with his companion eight kilometers from Lyon and reincarcerated — only to escape again, alone this time. He remained hidden a whole day in the Rhône river before being sheltered by strangers in Lyon. One can only imagine how another director would have used these dramatic turns of event to spice up his film, to increase the suspense. Not Bresson. Bresson cuts out everything that is not directly involved with Devigny's original escape from Montluc. As

Jean Sémolué observes, "Between the causes of Devigny's imprisonment and the events following his escape, Bresson isolates the escape itself, which is treated as a complete and sufficient moment which he turns into a work of art" (p. 124). Bresson is only interested in the "inner drama" of his character, and he has a single goal: "to depict the birth and the resulting events of the idea of escape in a prisoner" (Briot, p. 84).

After eliminating everything he considered superfluous in Devigny's account, Bresson proceeded to condense certain characters. Orsini, for example, is a composite of two of Devigny's fellow prisoners. Without changing their nature, he also reorganized the events narrated by Devigny in order to create a better balance, a clearer, simpler structure: "The entire film is based on an oscillation: Fontaine and the others — Fontaine by himself" (Sémolué, p. 130).

In the purest classical tradition Bresson's esthetics are composed of concentration, austerity, and contraction — to such an extent that he has been called the "Jansenist of the cinema." As in classical theater, ellipsis plays an essential role in *A Man Escaped*, blurring space and erasing time (Estève, p. 97). The scenes of violence (Fontaine's beating at the beginning, the murder of the sentinel) are occult, relegated to the wings so to speak. It has even been suggested that the film has the five-part structure of a classical play, beginning with Fontaine's incarceration: 1) the prisoner's adaptation to prison life, 2) the idea of escape, 3) perseverance, 4) doubt or ultimate victory over himself, 5) the escape or the achievement of liberty (Chalonge, pp. 1-2).

From another viewpoint, as many critics have observed, Bresson's film exhibits the contrapuntal structure of a musical composition, playing on the relationship between image and sound and between the images and Fontaine's voice-over commentary. The voice-over monologue guarantees moreover the rhythmic unity of the film. An ordinary film is composed of a series of sequences which are tantamount to "chapters" of the story being told. For Bresson, who wants above all to emphasize the extreme concentration of the action and its musical structure, this is not at all the case of *A Man Escaped*: "The découpage includes six hundred shots, but there are no sequences; the entire film constitutes a single sequence" (in Sémolué, p. 130).

FORM AND CONTENT

If there was ever a filmmaker for whom form and content are inseparable, it is Robert Bresson, and nowhere so clearly as in *A Man Escaped*: "Perhaps never in the history of film art has the content so completely inspired the form and vice-versa. In this case to speak of the content is to treat the form " (Agel, "Présentation," p. 267). One of the explanations for the impression of exceptional unity felt by so many critics is the perfect match between the extremely spare style of Bresson and the subject he is treating: a single action (the escape) reduced to its most essential acts in the barest place imaginable (the prison), where characters about whom we know the strict minimum live under the most austere of regimes. As Gilles Jacob remarks about the scenery, "These dimly-lit halls of *A Man Escaped*, these barren walls [...], this is precisely the decor that Bresson is seeking in his quest for the most absolute austerity" (p. 28). As for the hero Fontaine, he remains a complete stranger to us. His character, stripped bare to the point of abstraction, is completely reduced to his will to escape, to regain his liberty.

On the metaphorical plane there is also unity between Rohmer's direction of the film and its subject. Truffaut called *A Man Escaped* "a stubborn film *about* stubbornness," alluding to Bresson' travail as he struggled stubbornly to make his film, to "overcome," just as Fontaine was struggling to "overcome" his cell door and get out of prison. For some critics of the film the two combats, the filmmaker's and the prisoner's, are reflections of each other: the same "creative" effort, the same patient, minute, and solitary work, the same obsessive character — with, at the end, the "liberation." Similarly, Prédal considers the prison to be both a metaphor for existence and for the film set ("La Dimension plastique," p. 4). Having been subjected to two and a half months of "moulding" by Bresson, Leterrier was particularly sensitive to this analogy. "But the escape is perhaps the filmmakers own escape," he says. "He has to make it out of the studio, finish the work he has undertaken, and the condemned prisoner's patience is the best arm of the director who is prisoner of a production" (p. 34). It is hardly surprising that Bresson identifies particularly closely with this film: "Of all his films," notes Jean Pélégri in 1960, "Bresson only ever speaks of one: *A Man Escaped*. He seems to have forgotten the others" (p. 38).

THEMES

The first part of the title of the film, literally *A Man Condemned To Death Has Escaped*, establishes immediately some of its central themes: "escape" of course, but also "prison" and "death." These latter two themes belong moreover to the inventory of fundamental themes in Bresson's movies. Parallel to the theme of escape Bresson likewise develops the themes of stubborn struggle and defiance of the enemy. If the main title reflects the personal exploit of the protagonist, and accordingly the theme of Human Will, the second title, *The Wind Bloweth Where It Listeth*, suggests the no less fundamental role of Grace, of Divine Will, in the success of his escape. In fact, during the shooting of the film Bresson envisioned another title for his film, *Help yourself* (an abridged form of the saying "God helps those who help themselves"), in which the theme of the combination of Fontaine's efforts and Divine Providence stands out more clearly.

Opinions are divided as regards the Christian interpretation of the film, some commentators preferring to see a simple effect of chance or luck in the set of circumstances which lead to the hero's success: the arrival of the package which distracts the guards from searching his cell, the lessons learned from Orsini's failure, the arrival of Jost, whose help will be indispensable, etc. Devigny himself admits in his story that he cannot determine the role of chance and the role of Providence in his escape. For others, like Henri Agel, the film is simply incomprehensible without the Christian perspective, and the long efforts of Fontaine represent the spiritual progress of Man toward salvation, the liberation of his soul (*Le Cinéma et le sacré*, p. 114). The short phrase "The Wind Bloweth Where It Listeth" is taken moreover from a conversation between Jesus and Nicodemus (in the Gospel of John) that the Pastor copies and slips into the hero's hand. The subject of the conversation is the rebirth to spiritual life that divine grace represents.

In addition, no one is unaware of Bresson's interest in spiritual life and in the works of the Holy Spirit, which is the theme at the center of both *Angels of the Streets* and *Diary of a Country Priest*. André Bazin's well-known reflections on the latter film bring the point home clearly: "For the first time the cinema offers us not only a film whose only real events, whose only perceptible movements, are those of inner life, but even more important a new dramaturgy which is specifically religious, indeed, theological: a phenomenology of salvation and grace" ("Le Journal d'un curé de campagne," p. 15).

It is clearly difficult to deny the legitimacy of the Christian interpretation of *A Man Escaped*. "It is perfectly possible," Briot admits, "to give a Christian interpretation to the film by substituting the word 'grace' for the word 'luck'" (p. 94). Bresson's own attitude seems quite clear in his response to a journalist who had commented on the "mysticism" we feel in the film: "What you have just called mysticism must come from what I feel in a prison, that is, as the second title *The Wind Bloweth Where It Listeth* suggests, these extraordinary currents, the presence of something or of someone [...] which indicates that there is a hand directing everything" ("Propos," p. 7). Nevertheless, Bresson is careful to maintain a certain ambiguity. He recognizes, for example, that "it is perhaps chance that brings Jost to Fontaine's cell, or perhaps this wind which blows where it wishes," without deciding for us. Nothing excludes therefore a purely secular understanding of the film, as Prédal reminds us: "This Christian dimension isn't necessary to grasp the deeper meaning of the film. We can be satisfied with the notion of solidarity, a certain humanism if you will" (p. 66). As for the Christian theme of "rebirth," one might also conclude, like Leo Murray, that it is just as much about the "new life" that Fontaine receives by gaining his liberty when he was on the verge of being executed (p. 78).

The unity of form and content discussed above is no less clear in the fundamental thematic dualism which highlights both Fontaine's will and the grace of God. This dualism is expressed in the very structure of the film by the regular alternation of the scenes in which Fontaine labors alone in his cell and those in which he finds himself in the company of the other prisoners. It is in the latter scenes that the idea of "communion" is developed (Murray, p. 74). It is during the communal washing up, for instance, that the pastor slips the verse from Saint John into Fontaine's hand — the same place where, earlier, he had whispered to him that God would save him. Fontaine had answered, however, "It would be too easy if God took care of everything." Men have to do their part too. The clearest critical consensus regards the importance of the solidarity between the hero and his fellow prisoners. Through his example Fontaine the "chosen one" brings the hope of "salvation" to the other prisoners, who, like the old man Blanchet, have sunk into resignation and despair. The others in turn nourish and sustain Fontaine with their encouragement.

MUSIC

As Bresson's cinematographic body of work develops, the music progressively disappears until it is completely absent from his last film, *Money* (*L'Argent*, 1983). What Bresson cannot tolerate is the mood music which plays such a prominent role in conventional films. As he writes in his *Notes sur le cinématographe* (1975), "No accompanying music, no supporting or reinforcing music," before hardening his position by adding, "*No music at all*" (p. 32) outside of diegetical music (i.e., music which is produced within the fictional universe of the film). The music in *A Man Escaped*, which has nothing to do with mood music, is sparse indeed. We hear the beginning of the *Mass in C Minor* by Mozart seven times in the film and only briefly each time. The music has nonetheless inspired very diverse interpretations which reflect the two opposing viewpoints, religious and secular, on the meaning of the film.

The short musical phrase appears most strikingly each time Fontaine goes out into the yard with the other prisoners, including the episode where Orsini attempts to escape. In this latter case we also hear the choir singing a *Kyrie eleison* ("Lord, have pity"), as we do at the end of the film when Fontaine and Jost have gained their liberty. For the secular exegetes Mozart's music denotes either the liberty or the destiny of the hero, or simply Life itself, "the triumph over death" (Arbois, p. 8). Truffaut is surprised to hear the first chords of Mozart's *Mass* swell up at the very moment at which the prisoners in the yard empty their toilet buckets, which adorns this exceedingly prosaic act with a "liturgical character" ("Depuis Bresson…," p. 3). For Abbot Amédée Ayfre Mozart's music is above all a sign of unity, fraternity, and communion (p. 7), while for many others it is a clear reference to Providence, to grace: "We feel," Agel maintains, "the obscure and patient movement of the music through the images; it is the movement of grace which winds its way and little by little unites the men and turns them into a block as hard as a diamond […]; it is this mass which will sustain Fontaine and enable him to escape in the end" (*Le Cinéma et le sacré*, p. 116).

CLOSE-UPS AND STREAM-OF-CONSCIOUSNESS

The principal subject of the film, for Bresson at least, is less Fontaine's escape than the inner drama he experiences (or the spiritual itinerary he follows). This explains the predominance of static close-ups, whether of the hero's face, his hands, or the objects upon which his destiny hangs. In discussing with Truffaut during the shooting of the film, Bresson made his plans clear: "I want to make a film about objects and a film about the soul; you will therefore see primarily hands and gazes. I'm seeking a constant balance between the close-ups of objects and the close-ups of gazes" ("Bresson tourne *Un condamné...*," p. 5). As other commentators have noted, the first sequence of the film illustrates perfectly Bresson's method, which he will apply consistently in the rest of the film. It consists of around twenty shots, largely close-ups, inside the car which is taking Fontaine to prison. We see in rapid succession, with each shot repeated several times, close-ups of the prisoner's hands, of his face, of the door handle (which he tests), and of the gearshift. Fontaine's fate depends here, as later in his cell, on his desire to escape (that we see in his eyes), on the skillfulness of his hands (his only means of action), and on the objects which will serve to facilitate his escape. Nothing else counts for him.

To keep us close to his hero once he is in his cell, to make us share his incarceration, Bresson only uses close-ups and near shots of Fontaine's gaze (the eyes are of course the "windows of the soul") and of what he can see around him. No long shots allow us to distance ourselves from the prisoner. The film presents a fragmented universe which reflects the subjective reality, the limited knowledge of the person who is living in it. The camera movements, mostly brief pans discreetly following the prisoner's movements, are virtually imperceptible. Unlike the leaders of the New

Wave, who erupted onto the scene a few years later, Bresson refused to foreground the camera movements, to draw attention to anything but his subject, which is the inner journey of his character: "In my opinion systematic movement, as in an action film, is one thing, inner movement is another, and I prefer the latter. It would be unthinkable to put acrobatic takes in a work built on nuance and psychological subtleties" (Briot, p. 34). It is no different in the case of the editing together of sequences, which are often linked by discreet dissolves that we hardly notice, so that we have the impression of a continuous seamless action in which time plays no role.

The close-ups are often accompanied by Fontaine's inner voice. Avoiding for the most part simple redundancy (where the commentary does little more than paraphrase the image), Bresson uses the voice-over commentary by the protagonist to provide essential clarifications of his behavior. In addition, the commentary serves to put us in contact with the hero's inner life and, just as important, to maintain a certain tone and rhythm that the series of image alone could not guarantee. As Agel remarks, "There aren't diverse rhythms in this film, just a single rhythm sustained by the toneless voice which relates the escape" ("Présentation de Robert Bresson," p. 269). Fontaine's flat voice, devoid of emotion, allows the spectator to approach the character, not so much to identify with him as to feel more keenly, to imagine better the nightmare he is living. Bresson's art, profoundly classical, is an art of suggestion and understatement. It is the spectator's role to deduce the emotion and create the suspense.

SOUND

"Bresson belongs to this tiny group of creators [...] who consider the soundtrack as important as the image" (Jacob, p. 30). What counts most for Bresson in making a film is the "composition," which includes the element of sound. All of the commentators have been struck by the "musical" character of *A Man Escaped*, which is characterized by Rohmer as "the most musical work that cinema has produced" (p. 44). As Briot observes, the film is composed like a piece of classical music in which the various noises are arranged in counterpoint: "All these noises, voices, sounds of feet, faint sounds from the town, salvos, whistles, trains [...] are in counterpoint with the image. It is not an intellectual counterpoint, that is, a semantic opposition between image and sound, but rather a purely emotional and musical counterpoint" (p. 90). It is true moreover that Bresson wanted "noises to become music," in place of conventional film music (*Notes sur le cinématographe*, p. 32). One of his assistants remarked in fact that during the creation of the soundtrack he "directed the sound effects like a piece of music, in the manner of an orchestra leader" (Kébadian, p. 19). Bresson's esthetics, which place the primary emphasis on rhythm, recall the concept of "pure cinema" dear to Germaine Dulac. In the twenties Dulac emphasized just as strongly the resemblance of cinema to music: "All the arts are movement since there is development, but the art of images is, I believe, the one which is closest to music because of the element of rhythm they have in common" (Magny, p. 21).

The sound engineer Bertrand was astonished by the depth of Bresson's interest in the film's sound track. In order to obtain exactly the sound effect that the filmmaker wanted, "Bertrand was sometimes obliged, for a single scene, to record sounds on twenty-two different tracks, which were then successively eliminated by mixing the noises by groups of six" (Chalonge, p. 4). It is first and foremost the sound effects in the film which produce the impression of realism that Bresson is seeking. No one is unaware of his obsession with authenticity: it was at precisely four o'clock in the morning, the hour at which Fontaine and Jost were thought to have crossed over the last wall and disappeared into the night, on the very site of the events, that Bertrand had to record the blasts from the trains' whistles that we hear in the film.

For Bresson the cinema is an art of suggestion, not of explanation, and the noises, by their evocative power, play a fundamental role in the creation of the prisoner's world. Like the objects, which only take on importance in relation to the hero, all the significant noises we hear are filtered through Fontaine's sensitivity. The "realism" of the noises, as Arbois emphasizes, " is not objective; it is psychological and subjective" (p. 8), such that certain of them, like the sinister clinking of the head guard's keys against the banister on the stairs, are excessively loud, producing a surrealistic effect. The noises reflect metonymically the presence of the world which exists outside the protagonist's cell, especially the world of his oppressors, his jailers.

Although the title of the film, by announcing the hero's escape, implies a refusal of dramatic suspense, the suspense is in fact reintroduced by means of the soundtrack. It is the sounds, above all, which create the tension and the anguish in *A Man Escaped*. As Agel notes, "In Bresson's films each noise is a presage, good or bad, or a premonition" ("Présentation," p. 268), while Puaux adds, "The suspense is based on sound" in this film (p. 242). Martin, on the other hand, emphasizes the symbolic value of the sounds: "We have the distinct impression that they are only important for Bresson insofar as they are symbolic of danger (the clicking of the keys against the bars of the banister), of death (the salvos from the firing squads), or of hope (the streetcars and trains)" (p. 112). The best example of the role of sounds is doubtlessly found in the escape sequence, where the interplay between the silence and the noises, as Chalonge observes, keeps the spectator in suspense: "The pieces of broken glass underfoot, the crunching of the gravel, the clock striking the hour, the creaking of the sentinel's bicycle and, finally, the putting of a moped suddenly symbolizing liberty, all of these noises lend to each moment of the escape its own time and its particular emotion" (p. 4). *A Man Escaped* is unequivocally the best illustration of the predominance of sound over image, which is one of the cardinal principles of a Robert Bresson film.

STUDY GUIDE

Director's Comments

"We take the love of style to the level of fanaticism. A film is the type of work which most clearly demands a style. There must be an author and a text."

"Structure in and of itself embodies an idea."

"I want to make myself be as realistic as possible, only utilizing raw material taken from real life. I cut out pieces of reality and then put them together in a certain order."

"The film director, like any true artist, must be an *orderer*. I mean that he has to arrange in his personal order the diverse elements that life offers him. The cinema is a prodigiously powerful machine, but rather than to *show*, its role should be to *suggest* by means of rhythms, of relationships, of combinations of relationships…"

"It is the inner life which dominates [...]. Only the knots which are done and undone inside the characters give the film its movement, its true movement. It is this movement that I strive to bring out by something or by some combination of things which is not merely a dialogue."

"The cinema's means of expression is not images but the relations between images, which is not at all the same thing. In the same sense a painter does not express himself by colors but by the relations between colors: a splash of blue is blue all by itself, but if it is beside a splash of green, of red, or of yellow, it's not the same blue. It changes. We have to reach a point where a film is playing the images against each other; there is one image, then another which lends value to the first by their juxtaposition. This means that the first image is neutral and that, suddenly, placed beside another, it begins to vibrate, it is filled with life. And it isn't so much about the life of the story or of the characters, it's the life of the film. From the moment the image is brought to life, cinema is being made."

"Painting taught me that what counts is not making beautiful images but necessary images. From a formal standpoint you have to sculpt an idea into a face by light and shadow. There are exchanges and contacts between the lighting and the shadow. Poetry is born of ellipsis, in what is cut out, in the rhythm of the editing."

"In *A Man Escaped* the drama was born from the relations between the tone of the commentary, the tone of the dialogues, and the images. It was like a painting in three colors. The problem is that there was no real tragedy. The tragedy is an invention of novelists. In prison there is no feeling of tragedy. Things are what they are. The prison was what it was — cold, naturally. The glacial tone of the commentary warmed it up by contrast."

"I am like a sculptor who sees something and tries to come close to it. The film is a mystery."

Notes on the Cinematographer

"Two types of film: those that employ the resources of the theatre (actors, direction, etc.) and use the camera in order to *reproduce*; those that employ the resources of cinematography and use the camera to *create*" (p. 5).

"When a sound can replace an image, cut the image or neutralize it. The ear goes more towards the within, the eye towards the outer" (p. 51).

"To your models: 'Speak as if you were speaking to yourselves.' MONOLOGUE INSTEAD OF DIALOGUE" (p. 74).

"Obvious *travelling* or *panning* shots do not correspond to the movements of the eye. This is to separate the eye from the body. (One should not use the camera as if it were a broom)" (p. 89).

"I have dreamed of my film making itself as it goes along under my gaze, like a painter's eternally fresh canvas" (p. 115).

Excepts for Discussion

Excerpt 1 (2'00-4'00): The beginning of the film — Fontaine in the car on the way to prison; his escape attempt.

Excerpt 2 (16'25-18'00): Fontaine leaves the first floor and moves into cell 107 on the top floor; the noise of the head-guard's key along the banister.

Excerpt 3 (22'50-25'00): Fontaine begins working on his door; Terry comes to tell him he's leaving.

Excerpt 4 (30'40-32'40): Fontaine sharpens the second spoon; he breaks the wooden frame which retains the panels of his door.

Excerpt 5 (46'50-48'55): Fontaine is awakened by a salvo from the firing squad during the night (premonition?); Orsini's escape attempt.

Excerpt 6 (1h22'10-24'00): The escape — crossing the first roof; the noises.

Excerpt 7 (1h28'00-31'10): The scene of the murder of the sentinel.

Excerpt 8 (1h34'35-39'00): Crossing the last walls, liberty.

Quotations for Comment

Fontaine: "Terry's departure and the death of the comrade that I had never seen left me very distraught. I nevertheless continued my work. It prevented me from thinking. All that mattered was to get that door opened…I hadn't made any plans for afterwards."

* * *

Blanchet: "Why go through all that?"

Fontaine: "To fight. To fight against the walls, against myself, against my door. You should do the same thing, M. Blanchet. You have to fight and hope."

Blanchet: "Hope for what?"

Fontaine: "To go back home, to be free […]. Is anyone waiting for you?"

Blanchet: "No one […]. If I really had courage, I would kill myself. I tried. I had made a noose with my shoelace. The nail pulled out."

* * *

The Pastor (slipping a piece of paper into Fontaine's hand): "Read this and pray. God will save you."

Fontaine: "He'll save us if we help ourselves."

The Pastor: "Don't you ever pray?"

Fontaine: "Sometimes."

The Pastor: "When things aren't going well? […] That's convenient."

Fontaine: "Too convenient… It would be too convenient if God took care of everything."

* * *

Fontaine (reading the verse from the Gospel of Saint John): "Nicodemus said to him: How can a man be born when he is old? How can he go back into his mother's womb and be reborn? Jesus answered: Do not be surprised by what I have told you. You must be reborn. The wind bloweth where it listeth, and you hear its noise without knowing from whence it comes nor where it goes…Are you listening to me?"

Blanchet: "I'm listening."

A German Soldier (off screen): "Fire!" (A salvo.)

Fontaine: "It's him" [Orsini].

* * *

Fontaine (upon refusing to give his pencil to the guard, at the risk of being shot): "How stupid! And just not to give in to them."

* * *

Blanchet: "Orsini had to fail in order for you to succeed."

Fontaine: "It's extraordinary."

Blanchet: "I'm not telling you anything new."

Fontaine: "Yes you are. What's extraordinary is that it's you, M. Blanchet, who is telling me this."

* * *

Fontaine: "I was struck by the coincidence of his arrival at the same moment as the notification of my death penalty. I didn't have any time to lose. I was going to have to choose: either I was going to take Jost with me or kill him…In the latter case the heaviest of my hooks would be an effective weapon. But would I have the courage to kill this kid in cold blood?"

* * *

Fontaine: "You will not regret following me. Once we're outside I'll take care of you. I'll make sure you make good use of your liberty; I guarantee it."

Jost: "You've done quite a piece of work here…It's tempting."

Fontaine: "Tempting? Listen, Jost, you don't have any choice here. You need to understand that."

Jost: "I'm free to say yes or no."

Fontaine: "Now that you know everything?"

Questions/Topics for Reflection

1. Why did Bresson choose a prison escape as his subject? (What interests him in this event as a film director?)
2. Why does Bresson announce the success of the escape plan in the very title of the film? Why did he give two titles to his film?
3. The main characters of the film: what do we know about them? Why do we learn almost nothing about Fontaine?
4. The role of the close-ups in relation to the viewpoint of the film. Why aren't there any long shots?
5. The role of the voice-over commentary (the inner voice of the hero) in the film.
6. How does Fontaine manage to take his cell door apart? What is his plan when he begins to work on his door?
7. The role of the objects (and their transformation) in this film, as regards the escape plan of Fontaine.
8. The relationship between Fontaine and the other prisoners. Their means of communication. The influence of Fontaine's escape plan on Blanchet his neighbor (as on the other prisoners). The role of the other prisoners for Fontaine.
9. The importance of the sounds (their function, their meaning) in the film.
10. The role of the film music (the beginning of Mozart's *Mass in C Minor*).
11. The role of chance (or luck) in this film. What religious interpretation can one give to Fontaine's success?
12. What other themes are developed in this film?

CRITICAL DOSSIER

Marcel Martin — "A Passionate Analyst of Human Nature"

This film confirms magnificently the qualities that we already associate with Bresson and with the components of his personal universe: the concern for inner life, the striving for the severest simplicity, the predominance of psychological analysis over description of the world, the scenery only coming into play as a counterpoint to feelings. Bresson is not a realist; he only achieves realism as a by-product and always from inside his characters. For him realism is first and foremost a question of psychological and moral truth and not of material resemblance. Is it even necessary to point out that this concept of realism is the only authentic one?

In fact Bresson is unclassifiable. His name has been associated with Jansenism, and critics have considered his work "Racinian." He is above all a passionate analyst of human nature. His camera is a microscope; it takes us into a world in which beings never before seen experience exceptional adventures at a different rhythm from ours ("*Un condamné à mort s'est échappé*," p. 112).

René Briot — An Esthetics of Simplicity

True to his esthetic principles, Bresson made no attempt to express Fontaine's feelings by images but rather *through* them by the interplay of their relations and correspondences [...]. The other prisoners are present only insofar as they play a role in Fontaine's destiny or help us to become aware of it. The only "scenery" is the objects filmed in extreme close-ups and Fontaine's face. There will never be less scenery, in the normal sense of the term, than in *A Man Escaped*. Three quarters of the film take place in the prisoner's cell, which we never see completely. As for the rest, we scarcely see more than a few corners of the yard with the sinks, a hallway, and the tops of a few walls. Everything is calculated so that the hero always takes precedence over the "prison" entity. One might even suspect that this scenery appealed to Bresson precisely because it permitted him, without abandoning his particular type of realism, to achieve the ultimate simplicity and to create a universe in which everything was reduced to the consciousness of one man (*Robert Bresson*, p. 88).

Henri Agel — The Classicism of Bresson's Art

His art belongs to this classicism that Gide defined as the art of suggestion and understatement. The lyricism is concentrated solely in the dramatic progression, and we can only compare Bresson to Racine to characterize appropriately the formal perfection of this film. Like the author of *Andromaque* Bresson says nothing more than what is strictly necessary to approach the mystery. Each detail becomes a sign by transcending any direct and immediate meaning to assume another signification which can only be accessed through meditation ("Présentation," p. 267).

Henri Agel — A Liberating Labor

What is important is not the outcome, the ultimate result of Fontaine's labor. Perhaps this labor [...] is absolutely futile, but what is essential is that it develops in the hero the virtues of patience, stubbornness, and persistency. The work is in itself a form of asceticism. In a certain sense the film achieves its symbolic value when we see Fontaine use ropes, pins, and the wire mesh under his mattress — the most laughable objects — because, if we understand the film, we no longer see these objects. We no longer see his rudimentary craftsmanship but understand that his liberating labor effects a profound transformation in him [...].

A second point: the communal sentiment, the interaction between the men. These men were isolated in their solitude and remain stuck in the sort of forsaken state which people cannot overcome. Nonetheless, the patience and obstinacy of Lieutenant Fontaine, his courage and his hope nourish his companion's souls, even those who have given up all hope. In their turn, they identify intimately with Fontaine's project, even if they had been convinced that their fate was sealed, that it was impossible to get out of this prison. Now they see a man who is playing the role of witness. Fontaine is testimony to the power of faith, of belief, and of hope; he is living proof for everyone that it is possible to fight to the end, to the last drop of blood. Suddenly this testimony begins to radiate among the others. Suddenly, touched by the light emanating from this character, they too begin to hope again. By continuing to struggle, by liberating himself spiritually, Fontaine has thus liberated from despair and dejection all of those around him (*Le Cinéma et le sacré*, pp. 114-115).

René Briot — Silence

The most important element of the sound track of the film is perhaps the silence. This impression of a "film about silence" is probably due in part to Fontaine's inner voice. Fontaine comments on the action in the first person, in a neutral tone [...]. He speaks to himself, which explains why the words sometimes accompany the action, sometimes precede it or pass beyond it as Bresson chooses. Paradoxically these phrases do not seem to disturb the silence of the cell. To the contrary, these brief articulations reinforce the prisoner's isolation. At no time are they felt to be an artifice, because we know very well that Fontaine is not one of those men that prison turns into a caged animal. Fontaine is alone but alone with himself (*Robert Bresson*, p. 91).

Jean Sémoulué — *The Mass in C Minor* by Mozart

Fontaine is thus selected and elected, whereas Orsini is a just man who didn't have grace. Fontaine "has grace" [...]. This quasi-Jansenist concept of salvation, symbolized by the escape of Lieutenant Fontaine, implies that the facts are signs and not only facts. Bresson said of the mass in C minor by Mozart that the "color" of this work seemed to him "to be the color of the film" [...].

After the chorus of the opening credits we hear the music again seven times during the film. It reminds us that the most simple facts hide and reveal the execution of a secret design. It doubtlessly indicates that above and beyond the visible actions another action is playing out whose meaning may escape us but which is orienting us [...].

The first three times the music of the mass accompanies the goings and comings of the prisoners in the prison yard without any chorus. The fourth time the chorus highlights the decisive scene when Orsini, in the yard, leaves his companions to make his escape attempt. It is at this moment that the wind blows, that destiny turns. The following three times, again without the chorus, the music is related to the departure of Orsini, whom Fontaine watches as he is led away by the guards, to another episode in the yard, and to Fontaine's reflections as he tries to decide if he is going to kill Jost or take him with him.

At the end the chorus bursts out again as Fontaine disappears into the night. The words sung by the chorus are a *Kyrie eleison* ("*Lord, have pity*"). This appeal for pity is not heard in the middle of the film, in Orsini's case. After Fontaine's success it rings out like an expression of gratitude, while preserving its painful resonance. The supplication continues for all of those who remain behind the walls crossed by Fontaine, whether they be prisoners or jailors. Above and beyond the characters the plea for mercy seems to concern the human race as a whole (*Bresson*, pp. 152-155).

Michel Estève — Sounds and Objects

Since *A Man Escaped* sounds and objects play an increasingly important role in Bresson's universe [...]. The sounds and objects refer to the external world of course [...], but also to a sentiment or to an abstract idea. For Bresson the auditory realm is more mysterious that the visual realm because it suggests more, and when the image is too concrete, the sound can draw us toward the abstract. An image imposes a viewpoint, a certain perception of space. A sound permits each of us to formulate our own understanding. When Fontaine climbs out the glass ceiling and hears the train whistle blowing, the sound evokes the concrete world but also the desire to escape, the nostalgia for the liberty which is still to be won. A double counterpoint is thus established in relation to the stylized (non "abstract") image: a concrete counterpoint by means of the sound itself; an abstract counterpoint related to the idea or sentiment suggested by the sound (*Robert Bresson*, p. 94).

François Truffaut — No "Bresson School"

Bresson's theories are certainly fascinating, but they are so personal that they can only apply to his work alone. The idea of the creation of a "Bresson School" would make the most optimistic observers shudder. A conception of cinema which is so theoretical, mathematical, musical, and above all ascetic can hardly produce a "current"... ("Bresson tourne," p. 5).

ROBERT BRESSON'S FILMOGRAPHY

1934	*Public Affairs (Les Affaires publiques,* short subject)
1943	*Angels of the Streets (Les Anges du péché)*
1945	*Ladies of the Park (Les Dames du Bois de Boulogne)*
1950	*Diary of a Country Priest* *(Journal d'un curé de campagne)*
1956	*A Man Escaped* or *The Wind Bloweth Where It Listeth* *(Un condamné à mort s'est échappé* ou *Le Vent souffle où il veut)*
1959	*Pickpocket*
1962	*Trial of Jeanne d'Arc (Procès de Jeanne d'Arc)*
1965	*Balthazar (Au hasard Balthazar)*
1967	*Mouchette*
1969	*A Gentle Woman (Une Femme douce)*
1971	*Four Nights of a Dreamer (Quatre nuits d'un rêveur)*
1974	*Lancelot of the Lake (Lancelot du Lac)*
1977	*The Devil Probably (Le Diable probablement)*
1983	*Money (L'Argent)*

WORKS CONSULTED

Agel, Henri. *Le Cinéma et le sacré*. Paris: Editions du Cerf, 1961.

.........*Les Grands Cinéastes que je propose*. Paris: Editions du Cerf, 1967 ("Robert Bresson," pp. 212-223).

........."Présentation de Robert Bresson," *Etudes* (May 1957): 263-269.

Amiel, Vincent. *Le Corps au cinéma*. Paris: Presses universitaires de France, 1998 ("Bresson ou la palpitation des fragments," pp. 37-62).

Arbois, Janick. "*Un condamné à mort s'est échappé* ou *Le Vent souffle où il veut*." *Téléciné* 64 (March 1957), Fiche 295: 2-10.

Arnauld, Philippe. *Robert Bresson*. Paris: Cahiers du cinéma, 1986.

Astruc, Alexandre. "Naissance d'une nouvelle avant-garde: la Caméra-stylo." *L'Ecran français* 144 (March 30, 1948): 39-40.

Ayfre, Amédée. "L'Univers de Robert Bresson." *Téléciné* 70-71 (Nov.-Dec. 1957), no pagination.

Bazin, André. "Cannes 1957." *Cahiers du cinéma* 72 (June 1957): 27-28.

.........."*Le Journal d'un curé de campagne* et la stylistique de Robert Bresson." *Cahiers du cinéma* 3 (June 1951): 7-21.

.........."*Un condamné à mort s'est échappé*" dans *Robert Bresson. Eloge*. Paris: Cinémathèque française, 1997 (pp. 30-32).

Beerblock, Maurice. "Comment je suis devenu acteur de cinema." *Les Nouvelles littéraires*, July 5, 1956 (Film reviews, BIFI).

Bresson, Robert. *Notes on the Cinematographer*. Trans. Jonathan Griffin. London: Quartet Books, 1986.

.........."Une mise en scène n'est pas un art." *Cahiers du cinéma* 543 (Feb. 2000): 4-9.

Briot, René. *Robert Bresson*. Paris: Editions du Cerf, 1957.

Chalonge, Christian de. *Un condamné à mort s'est échappé* ou *Le Vent souffle ou il veut*. Fiche filmographique IDHEC, no. 146 (Film reviews, BIFI).

Chardère, Bernard. "Robert Bresson 1901-1999. Enfin du nouveau sur Bresson." *Positif* 468 (Feb. 2000): 61-62.

Couteau, Daniel. "Son amour du son." *Cahiers du cinéma* 543 (Feb. 2000): 21-22.

Devigny, André. "Prisonnier de la Gestapo." *Le Figaro littéraire* (Nov. 20, 1954): 7-8.

.........."Un condamné à mort s'est échappé." *Le Figaro littéraire* (Nov. 27, 1954): 7-8.

Durand, Philippe. "Dossier Robert Bresson." *Image et son* 156 (Nov. 1962): 8-13.

Durand, Philippe, and Guy Gauthier. "Dossier filmographique de Robert Bresson." *Image et son* 156 (Nov. 1962): 14-19.

Estève, Michel. *Robert Bresson. La passion du cinématographe*. Paris: Editions Albatros, 1983.

Jacob, Gilles. *Le Cinéma moderne*. Lyon: SERDOC, 1964.

Jousse, Thierry. "Bresson souffle où il veut." *Cahiers du cinéma* 543 (Feb.. 2000): 30-31,

Kyros, Ado. "Le cinéma condamné à mort," *Positif* 2, no. 20 (Jan. 1957): 41-42.

Leterrier, François. "Robert Bresson l'insaisissable," *Cahiers du cinéma* 75 (Oct. 1957): 34-36.

Magny, Joël. "Premiers écrits : Canudo, Delluc, Epstein, Dulac," *CinémAction* 60 (July 1991).

Martin, Marcel. "Le Cinéma de l'après-guerre: de Duvivier à Bresson." *CinémAction* 104 (June 2002): 20-24.

.........*"Un condamné à mort s'est échappé."* *Cinéma* 14 (Jan. 1957): 110-113.

Mauriac, Claude. "Le Nouveau Bresson." *Le Figaro littéraire* 552 (Nov. 17, 1956): 14.

Monod, Roland. "En travaillant avec Robert Bresson." *Cahiers du cinéma* 64 (Nov. 1956): 16-20.

Murray, Leo. *"Un condamné à mort s'est échappé"* in *The Films of Robert Bresson.* New York: Praeger, 1970 (pp. 68-81).

Prédal, René. "La Dimension plastique de l'œuvre de Bresson." *Jeune Cinéma* 201 (May-June 1990): 4-11.

.........*"Un condamné à mort s'est échappé* ou *Le Vent souffle où il veut."* *L'Avant-Scène Cinéma* 408-409 (Jan.-Feb. 1992): 63-66.

Puaux, Françoise. "Robert Bresson et la théorie du 'cinématographe'." *CinémAction* 60 (July 1991): 202-205.

.... "L'Evasion: du *Condamné à mort s'est échappé* de Bresson au *Trou* de Becker." *CinémAction* 105 (Sept. 2002): 237-246.

"Propos de Robert Bresson" (stenographer's notes of a press conference). *Cahiers du cinéma* 75 (Oct. 1957): 3-9.

Ranchal, Marcel. "Une leçon de morale." *Positif* 2, no. 20 (Jan. 1957): 39-41.

Rohmer, Eric. "Le miracle des objets." *Cahiers du cinéma* 65 (Déc. 1956): 42-45.

Roy, Jules. "J'ai vu Robert Bresson tourner au fort Montluc la plus extraordinaire évasion de la résistance." *Le Figaro littéraire*, July 14, 1956 (Film reviews BIFI).

Sémolué, Jean. *Bresson.* Paris: Editions universitaires, 1959.

Sloan, Jane. *Robert Bresson. A Guide to References and Resources.* Boston: G.K. Hall, 1983.

Tallenay, J.-L. "La Force d'âme." *Radio-Cinéma-Télévision* 358 (Nov. 25, 1956): 4-5, 39.

Thomas, Chantal. "Les Prisons" dans *Robert Bresson.* Paris: Ramsay Poche Cinéma, 1989 (pp. 11-14).

Truffaut, François. "Bresson tourne *Un condamné à mort s'est échappé."* *Arts* 574 (June 27-July 3, 1956): 5.

.........*"Depuis Bresson, nous savons qu'il y a quelque chose de neuf dans l'art du film."* *Arts* 596 (Dec. 5-11, 1956): 3.

.........*"Robert Bresson dirige *Un condamné à mort s'est échappé."* *Cahiers du cinéma* 60 (June 1956): 33.

.........*"Un condamné à mort s'est échappé."* *Arts* 593 (Nov. 14, 1956): 3.

"Un condamné à mort s'est échappé." *Le Film français* 649 (Nov. 16, 1956): 9.

The New Wave

French cinema seemed to run out of steam as it approached the end of the fifties. The great directors of the "Golden Age" (1930-45) were at the end of their careers: Jean Renoir, René Clair, Sacha Guitry, Marcel Pagnol, and Jean Cocteau. Max Ophuls had already passed away, and both Jean Grémillon and Jacques Becker would leave us soon. Marcel Carné was still making films, but it was just more of the same. Those filmmakers who rose to prominence after the war — Christian-Jaque, Claude Autant-Lara, Henri-Georges Clouzot, Jean Delannoy, and René Clément notably — had proved to be capable of little more than perpetuating the tradition of solidly conventional cinema, what would come to be referred to as "French Quality." But others were waiting in the wings, growing impatient, demanding that they get their turn. They were the directors of the "New Wave" which was soon going to sweep over France.

So what was the New Wave?

It was first of all a term invented by the journalist Françoise Giroud (in *L'Express*) in October, 1957, to describe the new generation of young Frenchmen and Frenchwomen who were beginning to grow impatient and rebel in the middle fifties. This was the period when France was getting entangled in the Algerian War (1956-62), scarcely having had time to digest the painful defeat in Indochina in 1954. The expression "New Wave" was soon borrowed to designate a group of young filmmakers who stunned the film world, both the critics and the general public, in 1959 and 1960. They succeeded against all odds, thumbing their noses at the rules and at their elders in the film industry. We are speaking principally of François Truffaut's *The 400 Blows* (*Les Quatre Cents Coups*, 1959), Alain Resnais's *Hiroshima mon amour* (1959), and Jean-Luc Godard's *Breathless* (*A bout de souffle*, 1960) — but between 1958 and 1962 no less than ninety-seven young French filmmakers made their first feature film before the "revolution" ran its course.

Far from being a "school" with a program, the New Wave referred to a group of filmmakers who were more different than alike. As Truffaut commented humorously, "Our only point in common was our attraction to the pinball machine." He added, however, "The New Wave is neither a movement, nor a school, nor a group; it is just a term invented by the press to group together fifty new names which erupted over a two-year period into a profession which normally only accepted three or four new names each year" (Douin, p. 14). Where did these new filmmakers come from? First, let's not exaggerate the number of true talents among the new film directors. At best we may distinguish two small groups. One of them was associated with the young critics writing for the newly created film review, the *Cahiers du cinéma* (1952) — Eric Rohmer, Claude Chabrol, François Truffaut, Jean-Luc Godard, Jacques Rivette, and Jacques Doniol-Valcroze, notably. The others were seasoned directors of short subjects, like Alain Resnais, Chris Marker, Georges Franju, Pierre Kast, and Jacques Demy. This latter group, with which Agnès Varda was also associated, was often designated by the term "Left Bank," because it was largely distinguished from the first group by its clearly left-wing political orientation, as well as by the literary character of its films.

What the "young Turks" of the *Cahiers du cinéma* had in common was, above all, the idea that filmmaking is a form of "writing." This elevated conception of cinema was formulated in a kind of manifesto-article written by Alexandre Astruc which clearly expresses their ambitions: "Little by little cinema [...] is becoming a language. A language, that is, a form in which and through which an artist can express his thought, no matter how abstract, or communicate his obsessions exactly as is done today in essays or novels. This is why I call this new age of cinema the age of the *Camera pen* [*Caméra stylo*]." The cinema, he continued, was in the process of becoming "a form of writing which is just as versatile and subtle as written language" (p. 39). The directors of the New Wave thus considered themselves to be "authors" in every sense of the word.

In addition, the filmmakers of the New Wave also had in common a passionate love of cinema; they were all film buffs. They knew in depth all of the cinematographic traditions. While they criticized certain directors, they worshiped a group of filmmakers that they considered to be their masters: Jean Renoir, Abel Gance, Max Ophuls, Jean Cocteau, and Robert Bresson in France; Alfred Hitchcock, Howard Hawkes, John Ford, Orson Welles, and Nicholas Ray in the United States; Roberto Rossellini and Luchino Visconti in Italy. The young rebels of cinema were indignant at the general sclerosis of the works produced by the filmmakers in the "French Quality" tradition, films which were technically perfect but filled with thematic and stylistics clichés and all similar to each other. They wanted to rejuvenate French cinema, to help it find new paths, to make it more personal and sincere; in a word, to breathe new life into it.

The main problem for the young people who wanted to make different kinds of films was that it was extremely difficult at that time to become a film director. The National Center for Cinematography (CNC), the association which regulated the film industry, required an aspiring director to attend three workshops, work three times as second assistant director, and work three times as first assistant before being allowed to direct a film. And then, since all films were made in a studio — with a large technical staff and very expensive stars — the cost was prohibitive for newcomers.

However, there was a foreshadowing of the revolt of the new generation. In 1955 Agnès Varda made her first film *La Pointe Courte* without the authorization of the CNC, just as would Louis Malle a few years later with *Elevator to the Gallows* (*Ascenseur pour l'échafaud*, 1957) and Claude Chabrol with *Handsome Serge* (*Le Beau Serge*, 1958). The financing of films by young filmmakers was facilitated, moreover, by the establishment of a "subsidy for merit," a cash advance that the CNC began granting to new directors in 1955 for film projects which were judged worthwhile.

The success of the New Wave was thus both an economic and an esthetic matter. The new directors rejected the burdensome and costly machinery of the studios. They took advantage of new technologies which provided light cameras which could be hand-held and extra-sensitive film which made artificial lighting unnecessary. They shot in natural light, both outdoors and indoors, and executed their tracking shots without rails. With the exception of Alain Resnais, who was a masterful director of short documentaries and an unparalleled film editor, the new filmmakers used largely makeshift methods. The images were less perfect and the actors less famous, but the films were made for only a quarter of the cost of a conventional studio film — and they exuded sincerity, authenticity, and originality. Some of the directors like Godard wrote their own screenplays and improvised during the shooting. They worked with a few friends out in the streets with the curious passers-by staring into the camera (see also the introduction to Godard's film *Breathless*, pp. 274-276).

Speaking more seriously than above, Truffaut observed that the only thing that really united the young filmmakers was "liberty" (Gillain, p. 40). The young directors of the New Wave liberated the cinema from corporatism (administrative and financial difficulties, the demands of the technicians' unions) and from academism (stylistic conventions), but also from the moral proprieties which had been rejected by the youth culture in France. Roger Vadim set the tone by daring to focus on female sexuality in *And God Created Woman* (*Et Dieu créa la femme*), which revealed Brigitte Bardot to the public in 1956. The other new directors followed suit, ridding the cinema of its moral reticence, whether it be in Louis Malle's *The Lovers* (*Les Amants*, 1958), Claude Chabrol's *The Cousins* (1959), *The Four Hundred Blows*, *Breathless*, or *Hiroshima mon amour*. In the following chapters we will examine closely the last three films, which ultimately defined the New Wave.

The success of the New Wave was short-lived. Its last great triumph would be *The Umbrellas of Cherbourg* by Jacques Demy (*Les Parapluies de Cherbourg*, 1964), an iconoclastic work whose dialogue (in everyday language) was sung to music composed by the jazz pianist Michel Legrand. However, if the New Wave only lasted a few years, its influence did not; cinema throughout the world would bear its mark.

WORKS CONSULTED

Astruc, Alexandre. "Naissance d'une nouvelle avant-garde: la Caméra-stylo," *L'Ecran français* 144 (March 30, 1948): 39-40.

Daney, Serge. "La Nouvelle Vague — essai d'approche généalogique" in Passek, Jean-Loup, ed. *D'un cinéma l'autre* (pp. 72-74).

De Baecque, Antoine. *La Nouvelle Vague. Portrait d'une jeunesse.* Paris: Flammarion, 1998.

Douin, Jean-Luc, ed. *La Nouvelle Vague 25 ans après.* Paris: Editions du Cerf, 1983.

Gillain, Anne. *Le Cinéma selon François Truffaut.* Paris: Flammarion, 1988.

Jeancolas, Jean-Pierre. *Histoire du cinéma français.* Paris: Nathan, 1995.

Passek, Jean-Loup, ed. *D'un cinéma l'autre.* Paris: Centre Georges Pompidou, 1988.

Revault d'Allonnes, Fabrice. "Genèse d'une vague bien precise," in Passek, Jean-Loup, ed. *D'un cinéma l'autre* (pp. 76-92).

François Truffaut

The 400 Blows
Les Quatre Cents Coups

(1959)

François Truffaut, *The 400 Blows*: Antoine (Jean-Pierre Léaud) scolded by his parents after starting a fire in the apartment. © MK2

Director	François Truffaut
Original Screenplay	François Truffaut
Adaptation and dialogues	François Truffaut and Marcel Moussy
Director of Photography	Henri Decae
Cameraman	Jean Rabier
First Assistant Director	Philippe de Broca
Music	Jean Constantin
Film Editor	Marie-Josèphe Yoyotte
Sound	Jean-Claude Machetti
Art Director	Bernard Evein
Script Girl (Continuity)	Jacqueline Decae
Producer	Les Films du Carrosse, SEDIF
Length	1 h 37

Cast

Jean-Pierre Léaud (*Antoine Doinel*), Albert Rémy (*M. Doinel*), Claire Maurier(*Mme Doinel*), Patrick Auffray (*René Bigey*), Georges Flament (*M. Bigey*), Yvonne Claudie (*Mme Bigey*), Guy Decomble (*the French teacher, "Little Leaf"*), Pierre Repp (*the English teacher*), Henri Virlojeux (*the night watchman*), Claude Mansard (*the examining magistrate*), Robert Beauvais (*the Principal*), Jeanne Moreau (*the woman with the dog*), Jean-Claude Brialy (*the man in the street who follows the woman with the dog*), Jean Douchet (*Mme Doinel's lover*). The children: Richard Kanayan (*Abbou*), Daniel Couturier, François Nocher, Renaud Fontanarosa, Michel Girard, Serge Moati, Bernard Abbou, Jean-François Bergouignan, Michel Lesignor.

STORY

Antoine Doinel, thirteen years old, lives in a little Parisian apartment with his mother and stepfather. At the beginning of the film, he is punished because of a pinup of a scantily dressed woman which the boys were passing around in class. Made to stand in the corner, he expresses his sense of injustice in a poem he writes on the wall, for which he is punished by an additional writing assignment for the next day. Having forgotten to write the assignment, he is afraid to go back to school the next day and decides to play hookey with his friend René. They spend the day playing pinball in a café, going to the movies, and going on a ride in a local fair. As they are leaving the fair, Antoine spots his mother in the street kissing a man, clearly her lover. Their gazes cross briefly.

The next morning, when Antoine goes back to school, he explains his absence the day before by telling the teacher that his mother died. Contacted by the school, Antoine's parents soon arrive; his stepfather gives him a hard slap in front of the whole class. Since he is afraid to go home after school, he spends part of the night in a printing shop where René takes him and then wanders around the streets until morning. We see him again back in school, where his mother, shaken by his absence, comes to get him and take him back home. She tries to win him over by confiding in him and offers him some money if he gets a good grade on the next French composition. The day he has to write the composition he becomes excited about the subject assigned by the teacher, feeling inspired in part by a Balzac novel he has just finished reading. In a little alcove at home, he constructs a sort of altar to the novelist and lights a candle in it. A catastrophe is narrowly averted when the candle sets on fire a curtain hanging in front of the alcove. To calm everyone's nerves, the family spends the evening at the movies.

Antoine's situation at school gets worse when the teacher accuses him of plagiarizing Balzac and sends him to the principal's office. Antoine rebels, runs away, and seeks refuge at René's, whose parents, well-to-do but irresponsible, let him do whatever he wants. The boys amuse themselves, go to the movies, then watch a puppet show in the Luxembourg Gardens with a crowd of entranced children. To make some money, they steal a typewriter from Antoine's stepfather's office and try to sell it. Unsuccessful, Antoine tries to return the machine to the office but is caught by the night watchman. His stepfather, alerted, takes him to the local police station, where he is locked up with a petty criminal and some prostitutes until he is taken to prison to await the disposition of his case.

In the last part of the film, Antoine is now in a facility for juvenile delinquents in Normandy, where he is subjected to a brutal disciplinary regime. Questioned by a psychologist, he talks at length about his childhood, his parents, and his experiences with girls. When René shows up to visit, he is turned away, but Antoine's mother comes to tell him that, because of a letter Antoine sent to his stepfather (evidently containing complaints about his mother), the two of them are no longer interested in him or his future. During a soccer game Antoine runs away from the center. He runs all the way to the seashore, where, on the beach, he suddenly turns back toward the camera and, in a startling freeze frame, stares into the spectators' eyes.

*It should be mentioned that in the video versions of this film, four short episodes are unfortunately often cut: a conversation between two women in a grocery store, in Antoine's presence, about difficult childbirths; the destruction of Mauricet's goggles (the tattle-tale schoolmate); the sudden entry of René's father into his son's room, where Antoine is hiding; and a scene in which Antoine and René play with peashooters on the Bigey's balcony, bombarding people in the street with paper wads (which explains what happened to the Michelin Guidebook which Antoine's stepfather cannot find).

CRITICAL RECEPTION

It was April, 1959, in the middle of the Algerian War. To everyone's surprise, *The 400 Blows*, François Truffaut's first feature film, was selected by the Cannes Festival Committee to represent France, along with Marcel Camus's *Orfeu Negro*. Although Camus won the Golden Palm for the best film, the young filmmakers and cinephiles were thrilled at the news that Truffaut's film had won the Grand Prix for Best Director. Overnight the young critic of the film journals *Arts* and *Cahiers du cinéma* was consecrated by the success of his film. For years Truffaut had been vilifying and heaping scorn on the films of his elders in his articles, denouncing the sclerosis of French cinema, bogged down in conventional practices, devoid of inspiration or any form of renewal. The year before he had been virtually banned from the Cannes Festival (he was refused his journalist's accreditation) because of his offensive remarks about the festival in *Arts*. When he turned to filmmaking, there were plenty of people waiting in ambush. If his film wasn't successful, Truffaut would be exposed to the revenge of all those he had attacked. Like Renoir at the opening of *La Grande Illusion*, Truffaut suffered from pangs of anxiety when *The 400 Blows* was projected at Cannes. Here is how De Baecque and Toubiana describe the event: "The evening of the showing at the Festival Palace, Truffaut is pale and tense. Jean-Pierre Léaud winks at him when the lights go out. The filmmaker is soon reassured by the applause which, even before the end of the film, had greeted certain scenes. And when the lights come back on, it's a veritable triumph, everyone turning around trying to get a look at the young filmmaker. In an indescribable crush of people, Jean-Pierre Léaud is carried out to meet the press and the photographers, crowded together at the bottom of the stairs. Accompanied by Cocteau, Truffaut greets his admirers and shakes the anonymous hands which reach out toward him" (pp. 197-198).

As the major French newspapers and magazines spread the news of the film, Truffaut quickly became the symbol of the success of the young cinema which had been fighting for recognition for several years. Truffaut's friends at the *Cahiers du cinéma* and at *Arts* were euphoric: Jacques Audiberti declared that "with his '400 Blows' Truffaut has made a masterpiece"; Doniol-Valcroze spoke of the "Truffaut bomb…" and compares his film to a "rocket which has exploded in the middle of the enemy's camp and destroyed it from inside" (p. 42). Throughout the world, many prizes and honors were added to the director's prize at Cannes: the New York Critics Prize for the Best Foreign Film in 1959, the 1959 Méliès Prize, the Belgium Prix Fémina du Cinéma, as well as prizes in Switzerland, Spain, Mexico, Austria, and other prizes in France and the United States, where the film was most successful. The same year, in Hollywood, the film was nominated for an Oscar in the category of "best original screenplay." Opening on June 3 in two cinemas on the Champs-Elysées, the film was a blockbuster in that period, drawing 450,000 spectators and provoking a public debate about bringing up children and parental responsibility.

BEFORE *THE 400 BLOWS*

Before beginning to direct films, Truffaut was a film critic, one of the most brilliant but also "the most detested critic of his generation," it has been said, for the reasons we mentioned above (see also below). But before being a critic, Truffaut was a passionate cinephile, and before that a rebellious schoolboy, a juvenile delinquent, a deserter, and a prisoner in a French military prison in Germany. Not a very auspicious beginning, making all the more amazing his stunning career in the world of cinema.

Truffaut's cinema, and especially his first film, is inseparable from his personal life. *The 400 Blows* evokes, almost literally, the events of Truffaut's adolescence, at home and at school, when he was around twelve or thirteen. It should be mentioned that Truffaut, born in Paris in 1932, was the child of an unmarried seventeen-year-old girl, and he would always recall the family scandal caused by his illegitimate birth; he never met his father. Until age ten, he lived first with a nurse, then with his maternal grandmother, before going to live with his parents in their little apartment (his stepfather having given him his name). His mother, cold and distant toward him, found it hard to bear his presence, but he had a much better relationship with his stepfather, who enjoyed joking around with him at home. His mother had lovers. His parents paid little attention to him in general, often leaving him alone at home for long periods to indulge their passion for mountain climbing. The young child began to steal small sums of money and to lie.

A very good student at first, François began to behave more and more badly at school, often cutting school with, or without, his best friend, Robert Lachenay. He ran away from home now and then, spending the night in the subway or at the home of his friend, whose parents left him to his own devices (his mother was an alcoholic, his father only interested in playing the ponies). One day, as an excuse for missing school, he said that his father has been arrested by the Germans (it is 1943, during the Occupation). Following the financial failure of a film club he had created with his friend and running away from home again, his stepfather turned him in to the police. He spent two nights in cells with prostitutes and local petty criminals (his parents' apartment was in Pigalle) before being sent to a juvenile delinquent center in the suburbs of Paris. André Bazin, the future founder of the *Cahiers du cinéma*, came to his rescue by taking legal custody of him (his parents gave up their parental rights). Several years later, in 1952, it was Bazin again who saved Truffaut by gaining his release from a military prison where he was serving a sentence for desertion. This time Bazin took him into his own home for two years and became the father Truffaut never had.

For anyone who has seen *The 400 Blows*, the relationship between Truffaut's childhood, as we've just described it, and Antoine Doinel's is amply evident. The fact that Truffaut was saved by Bazin, the greatest film theoretician and critic of his time, has a distinct metaphorical dimension, because it was the cinema, as Truffaut himself says, that helped him to survive his youth: "The cinema saved my life. If I plunged into the cinema, it's probably because my own life wasn't satisfying when I was young, during the Occupation [...]. 1941 is an important date for me: it's the period when I began to go see a lot of films. From age ten to nineteen, I was obsessed with films..." (Insdorf, p. 13). If the adolescent Truffaut spent a lot time in the streets, movies and novels were what he loved the most. He often saw three films a day and read three novels a week; when he skipped school, it was often to spend days on end reading Balzac novels at the public library. He put together large files of press clippings on each filmmaker. It was his enormous knowledge about films which attracted Bazin's attention and led him to put him to work at the *Cahiers du cinéma* with other young rebels like Jean-Luc Godard, Jacques Rivette, and Claude Chabrol, as well as Eric Rohmer, their older colleague. In 1953 Bazin let Truffaut begin writing film criticism at the *Cahiers*. The following year Truffaut published the now famous article "A Certain Tendency of French Cinema," in which he lashed out at the big studios—too conventional, too literary, and dominated since the Liberation by a few prestigious directors and screenwriters who constantly rehashed the same themes in their adaptations of novels into films. His article attracted the attention of the editors of the weekly magazine *Arts*, who invited him to write columns on film for them. From that moment on, justifying his new reputation as the "gravedigger of French cinema," Truffaut launched into an all-out attack on the enemy in violent articles which show no mercy, while singing the praises of the favorite directors of the group of young critics at the *Cahiers* (beginning with Renoir, Rosselini, Ophuls, Gance, Bresson, Hawkes, Hichcock, Fuller, Cocteau, and Ray).

When Truffaut tried his hand at directing, he began, like the other young filmmakers, with short subjects. After several projects which didn't work out, including an eight-minute 16mm film, *A Visit* (1954), which would never be shown publicly, he finally made *The Brats* (*Les Mistons*, 1957, 18 minutes), an adaptation of a short story. Filmed in Nîmes, the film is about a group of five little boys who all have a crush on a beautiful young woman (Bernadette Lafont, in her first film) whom they follow everywhere, spying on her dates with her fiancé in town and in the country, tormenting the couple out of jealousy. Truffaut, who narrated the story himself in voice-over, summarized the film in the following manner: "Not being old enough to love Bernadette, we resolved to hate her and persecute her and her fiancé." The children's writing plays an important role in *The Brats* before becoming a major motif in *The 400 Blows*, and we note already the allusions to other films (filmic "quotations") and the insider jokes which will become common fare in New Wave films. *The Brats* was well received by film critics at the end of the year and won the prize for Best Director at the Brussels World Film Festival in February, 1958. When the film came out in Paris the following November, the newspapers followed suit and heaped praise on this first work by the young film critic.

ORIGIN OF *THE 400 BLOWS*

The 400 Blows will be the incarnation of a new conception of cinema advocated by Truffaut in his articles throughout the fifties: "As I perceive the new films, they will be even more personal than a novel, individual and autobiographical like confessions or like a diary. The young filmmakers will express themselves in the first person and will tell us what has happened to them in their life [...], and the public will like it, virtually necessarily, because it will be true and new" (*Arts*, May 15, 1957). Of course, Truffaut was referring to a refusal to adapt novels, a practice he criticized severely in his 1954 article, and he was describing precisely the approach he was going to employ in his first feature film.

In the beginning, in fact, this film was to be a short subject around twenty minutes long titled *Antoine Runs Away From Home*, part of a collective film on childhood. The plan was to film a real episode of Truffaut's life, with slight modifications. It's the story of a child who cuts class several days in a row to read a multi-volume novel at the library; then, when he finally goes back to school, with no written excuse from his parents, he tries to explain it away by saying that his mother died. His father slaps him in front of the whole class. Afraid to go home, he spends the night outside. Considerably developed, this little sketch is at the origin of *The 400 Blows*. The action of the film, while entirely autobiographical, is nonetheless transformed in various ways to constitute a "story." The Antoine Doinel character is a composite figure composed of Truffaut, his friend Robert Lachenay, and the actor Jean-Pierre Léaud, while the film's principal action, which is placed in a period of several days around Christmas at the end of the fifties, actually took place over a five-year period spanning the Occupation and the Liberation (1942-1947). The personalities of Truffaut and of Robert Lachenay are somewhat reversed in the characters of Antoine and his friend René Bigey. Antoine's stepfather, moreover, will be an automobile enthusiast, rather than a mountain climber.

Confronted with a mass of autobiographical material and understandably afraid of lacking objectivity, Truffaut thoroughly researched adolescent psychology, the problems of teenage children, and juvenile delinquency. In addition, he solicited the help of Marcel Moussy, a novelist and screenwriter who had already worked on childhood problems, to fill out his characters, structure his narrative, and write dialogues for the adult characters. They didn't write out the children's dialogues ahead of time. As Truffaut says, "We gave them the situation, and they found their own sentences" (Gillain, p. 44). Since the casting of the boy who would play Antoine Doinel was critical, Truffaut auditioned about sixty children before choosing Jean-Pierre Léaud, the fourteen-year-old son of a screenwriter and an actress. Truffaut quickly realized that he had a lot in common with Jean-Pierre Léaud, who was a difficult child — misbehaving in school, running away from home, rebelling — but very cultivated for his age. Unlike Truffaut, however, he had a very strong personality, which fascinated the filmmaker and led him, as he admits, to "modify the scenario quite often," with the result that, in the end, "Antoine is a fictional character who borrows a little from both of us" (De Baecque et Toubiana, p. 193). The sequence at the very beginning of the film, for example, where Antoine is caught holding a photo of a pinup, was probably inspired by Jean-Pierre Léaud, who was caught in the dormitory, according to his school principal, looking at pornographic pictures. Antoine's parents are played by Albert Rémy, a well-known film actor since the forties, and Claire Maurier, who had worked primarily on the stage.

FILMING

Unlike certain friends at the *Cahiers*, Truffaut was not able to produce his first film without outside financial help and had to submit therefore to a number of institutional practices. He had a complete technical team, even though it was reduced to the strict "union minimum." The filming of *The 400 Blows* began on November 10, 1958 — the very day of the death of André Bazin, the only "father" Truffaut had known. The grim tone of the film, as De Baecque and Toubiana remark (p. 193), is not unrelated to this unfortunate event. *The 400 Blows* is dedicated "to the memory of André Bazin."

The filming began in a tiny apartment in Montmartre, before moving to Pigalle where Truffaut spent his teenage years, and then to other spots in Paris. Filming with a large number of children is never easy — Truffaut had sworn to never again work with five children after making *The Brats* — and there were many incidents during the shooting. Jean-Pierre Léaud, always impertinent, created problems by insulting policemen in the street, and the other children weren't a lot better: "A few days later, on Christmas Eve, the police, called by the owner of the café *The Workers' Rendez-Vous*, interrupt the shooting again. During the sequence with the gym teacher, which required several takes, Jean-Pierre Léaud distracted the café owner with insults each time, while two of his buddies stole silverware and ashtrays" (p. 195)!

In December, shortly before these incidents, the crew had moved to Normandy, near Honfleur, to film the sequences at the juvenile delinquent center and the ending, Antoine's escape and his long run to the seashore (filmed by Henri Decaë in a tracking car). The classroom scenes, with all the children, were shot just after Christmas, in a school closed for vacation.

The 400 Blows was filmed in black and white and Cinemascope (a technique in which the picture is modified to fit into the wide screen), producing a type of stylization which, according to Truffaut, renders the décor less sad and less shabby. At the same time, with Cinemascope Truffaut was able to make longer and fewer shots, with a minimum of camera movement, particularly important when filming in a little apartment: "Just by turning the camera, I was able to follow all the movements of all the characters" (Billard, p. 26). The film is almost entirely postsynchronized, only the classroom scenes and the sequence with the psychologist being filmed with sound. For the interview with the latter, Truffaut gave no written dialogue to Jean-Pierre Léaud, letting him improvise his responses to the questions, which he didn't know in advance, other than their general thrust. The shooting, which took two months, was wrapped up on January 5, 1959, and followed by an initial editing, with Jean Constantin's music added, at the beginning of February.

STRUCTURE

The structure of *The 400 Blows* is not very complicated: it is a classical linear narrative, a series of successive days and nights. The action covers about a week around Christmas, although it is impossible to know exactly how long Antoine stays in the juvenile delinquent center before escaping. The most interesting aspect of the organization of the action is what Truffaut calls the "spiral" (*l'engrenage*), Antoine's progression, by stages, towards the final "tragedy": "I knew that in each scene, each reel, Antoine was fated to do something worse than in the preceding scene" (quoted in Gillain, 1991, p. 48). After the pinup episode comes the forgotten penalty assignment, which leads to cutting school, then to the lie about his mother's death which results in his running away, followed by the plagiarism of Balzac, running away again, the theft of the typewriter and, finally, the escape from the detention center.

At each misstep by Antoine, the adult world — the teacher, his parents, the judge, the personnel at the Center — punishes him harshly, imposing sanctions out of proportion to his misdeeds and nourishing in him a growing sentiment of injustice and revolt. Antoine is indeed caught in a spiral of events which leads him inexorably toward exclusion: from school, from home, from society. Stylistically, as Anne Gillain observes, Antoine's itinerary is summarized by the opposition between the first and the last images of the film: "an establishing shot filled with people [the class in school] is set in opposition to a near shot of a face alone" (1991, p. 50).

On another level the film is structured by an alternation between the sequences indoors (the school, the apartment) and outdoors (the Paris streets). In the former Antoine suffers from the authority of the adults, experienced as a form of oppression, whereas in the streets he breaks loose, he feels free — a sentiment emphasized by the lively, happy music which often accompanies the outdoor scenes. Only at the movies, where imagination reigns, does Antoine feel happy "indoors"; in the cinema he is not rejected, condemned. The cinema episodes are echoed in the rotor scene at the fair, which evokes the kinetoscope, one of the ancestors of the cinematograph; Antoine goes for a dizzying, exalting ride, accompanied by the filmmaker Truffaut (see Collet, "The Rotor Scene," in the *Critical Dossier*). The cinema is salvation, an escape from the world which excludes Antoine.

THEMES

The 400 Blows is dominated, of course, by the theme of unhappy adolescence. Despite the autobiographical character of the film, Truffaut was careful from the outset to avoid appearing to be feeling sorry for himself. To avoid falling into sentimental pandering, he even forbade Jean-Pierre Léaud to smile on-camera, with very few exceptions. He considered his film to be "a chronical of early adolescence" and tried to record, as De Baecque and Toubiana say, "the universal aspects of childhood" (p. 190). But Antoine is clearly unhappy, and his behavior becomes to some extent a clinical case, the portrait of an adolescent in crisis, a fact which didn't pass unnoticed when the film came out: "To appreciate the realism of this film, one only has to pick up any psychology or psychoanalysis textbook and read the chapter on the typical problems of adaptation experienced by juveniles. All the characteristics of adolescence appear in the character and situation of young Antoine Doinel" (Hoveyda, p. 53). All of the themes in the film, all of the aspects of adolescent crisis are marked by the relationship between Antoine and his mother. Since we are dealing with an eminently autobiographical film, which emphasizes the relations between an adolescent and his parents — and above all between him and his mother — it is difficult to avoid psychoanalytic hypotheses on the case of Antoine (as on the case of Truffaut himself). The mirror scene, his mother's sensuality (she parades around in her slip in front of him), her unfaithfulness and the fact that Antoine announces her death, the clandestine complicity which is established between mother and son, may all contribute to Freudian interpretations. They can easily lead critics (Anne Gillain is a good example) to speak of "Oedipal obsessions" (desire of union with the mother), to discover a fantasmatic element in the story, and to conclude that "all of Antoine's actions are determined by his desire" for his mother (Gillain, 1991, p. 84). Such hypotheses, whether of not one agrees with them completely, serve to enrich the thematic texture of Truffaut's film.

Most of the other themes of *The 400 Blows*, without necessarily entering into the Freudian perspective, are clearly organized around the theme of the adolescent crisis, whether it be the theme of writing, a kind of "original sin" of children (see Collet, "Writing and Revolt," in the *Critical Dossier*), theft, fire and play, lack of communication, incomprehension, marginalization, or exclusion. The film becomes a veritable indictment of the adult world, and particularly of Truffaut's parents; for his mother it was, as he says himself, "a stab in the back." To soften the blow, Truffaut vigorously denies the autobiographical character of the film — a denial which fools no one, and Truffaut subsequently recognizes that it is "in large part autobiographical" (Desjardins, p. 37).

Faithful to the spirit of the New Wave, Truffaut laces *The 400 Blows* with a series of *mises en abyme* of cinema. These include the rotor scene, of course, and the movie episodes, but also the numerous references to particular films: Vigo's *Zero for conduct* (the run through the city with the gym teacher), Renoir's *The Bitch* (*La Chienne* — Georges Flament in the role of René's father), Bergman's *Monika* (the photo stolen in the cinema), Jacques Rivette's *Paris Belongs To Us* (*Paris nous appartient* — the Doinel's evening at the movies) — a whole series of winks to the film world's insiders.

THE ANTOINE DOINEL CYCLE

Antoine Doinel doesn't disappear at the end of *The 400 Blows* — far from it. Truffaut had a stroke of genius. He featured Jean-Pierre Léaud in films at various ages as he grew up, always in the role of Antoine Doinel, and always as an alter ego of himself, the director — over a period of twenty years. Léaud thus played Doinel again, three years later, in a short film, *Antoine and Colette* (1962) that Truffaut made for a collaborative film, with a series of episodes by different filmmakers, *Love At Twenty* (*L'Amour à vingt ans*). Truffaut's little film was based on his crush on a girl who broke his heart when he was eighteen. Six years later he made *Stolen Kisses* (*Baisers volés*, 1968), another love story (which has a happy ending this time), followed by *Domicile conjugal* (1970), which chronicles the failure of Antoine's marriage. The cycle ends with *Love In Flight* (*L'Amour en fuite*, 1979), a film no less pessimistic than the others but innovative and unusual in that it includes excerpts from the preceding

Doinel films. The excerpts serve as flashbacks which show us the characters of the final film at different moments of their former lives, played by the actors at different ages. Both alter ego of the filmmaker and his fictional creation, Antoine Doinel, in Gillain's words, "has become a myth which belongs to the archives of cinema" (p. 22).

STUDY GUIDE

Director's Comments

"The idea which inspired us throughout this project was to paint a picture of adolescence, not full of the usual sentimental nostalgia but, on the contrary, as a disagreeable moment in life that will pass."

"My mother couldn't stand noise; well, to be more precise, she couldn't stand me. In any case, I had to make myself invisible, stay on a chair and read — I didn't have the right to make any noise; I had to make her forgot that I existed."

"After *The 400 Blows* came out, my parents divorced. They felt threatened by the film. I don't even think they ever saw it. Their friends told them not to go. There was a strong physical resemblance between my father and the man who played his role in the film. It was the same for the apartment where we did the shooting. It was the same neighborhood where I grew up. For my parents, the film was a great injustice, especially since it won the big prize in Cannes […]. It's only now that I realize how difficult it must have been for them. There's no doubt that I was very bitter at the time. It would be fair to say that the film's dialogues verbalized everything that hadn't been said between us."

"The challenge was to present sympathetically a kid who, every five minutes, does something reprehensible. Everyone said, "You're crazy! This kid is going to be despicable! The public is going to hate it!" And it's true that during the filming, it was shocking to see this kid steal all over the place. It gave the impression of a documentary on juvenile delinquency. I have to admit that the film was affected by these warnings; now I regret it. In fact, no one realized, including myself, that people are always ready to side with a child, and that it's always the parents who take the blame. I tried to create a balance, not understanding that there was no fairness in this area. I was very naïve, but the film seemed clever in its naïvety."

"It should never be forgotten that a child is a pathetic element which will always have the public's sympathy. That is why it is difficult to avoid sentimentality and indulgence. To succeed, the filmmaker has to be willfully hard and uncompromising in the treatment of the subject — which doesn't mean that the style can't be dynamic. Put a child's smile on the screen and you've won. But what really strikes you when you look at life is the seriousness of children compared to the futility of adults. That's why it seems to me that you can achieve a higher degree of truth by filming not children's games but their crises, which tend to be enormous, much more so than conflicts between adults […]. Adolescence introduces the child to injustice, inaugurates the desire for independence, affective freedom, and sexual curiosity. That explains why it's such a critical age, the age of the first conflicts between the absolute and relative morality of adults, between the pureness of heart and the impurity of life; from the viewpoint of any artist, it's the most interesting age to explore."

Excerpts for Discussion

Excerpt 1 (00'10-2'45): Opening credits — tracking shots in Paris.

Excerpt 2 (2'50-6'50): Beginning of the film. Antoine is made to stand in the corner for the pinup photo, can't go to recess; he writes his "poem" on the wall and is punished again.

Excerpt 3 (11'20-14'20): Antoine at home alone: lights the fire, wipes his hands on the curtains, steals some money, sits down at his mother's vanity. His mother comes home, scolds him because he forgot to buy flour.

Excerpt 4 (20'00-24'10): Antoine and René skip school; the rotor scene at the fair; Antoine surprises his mother kissing her lover in the street.

Excerpt (45'10-46'40): Jogging in the city streets with the gym teacher ("quotation" of *Zero For Conduct* by Vigo).

Excerpt 6 (47'10-50'20): Antoine hangs a photo of Balzac in an alcove; the French composition the following day; he sets a candle in the alcove; the curtain catches fire.

Excerpt 7 (1h12'50-17'20): Antoine in a cell at the police station; transfer to the prison in the police van; Antoine enters the prison world. *See the discussion of this sequence in "'Reading' A Film," pp. 33-35.**

Excerpt 8 (1h25'30-28'55): Antoine is interviewed by the psychologist at the juvenile detention center.

Excerpt 9 (1h32'00-36'45): The escape from the center; Antoine runs to the seashore; the freeze frame at the end of the film.

Quotations for Comment

Antoine's poem, written on the classroom wall:

> "Here suffered poor Antoine Doinel
> Unjustly punished by Little Leaf
> For a pinup fallen from the sky…
> From now on, it's an eye for an eye,
> A tooth for a tooth."

* * *

Antoine sees his mother kissing a man in the street:

> "She won't dare tell my father" (that he had skipped school).

* * *

Antoine's return to school:

Teacher: "I'm curious to see what kind of excuse you dragged out of your parents… Let me see your excuse."

Antoine: "I don't have one, M'sieur…M'sieur, it's, it's my mother…M'sieur."

Teacher: "Your mother, your mother, what about her?"

Antoine: "She died."

* * *

Mme Doinel: "If you are...let's see, among the top five on your next French composition, I'll give you a thousand francs, a thousand francs."

Close-up of Antoine, who lowers his eyes, then looks up at his mother.

Mme Doinel: "But you can't let your father know."

* * *

Psychologist: "Why don't you love your mother?"

Antoine: "Well, because first she stuck me with a nurse, and then, when they had more money, they put me with my grandmother [...]. Then I went to live with my parents [...]. I was eight, and I realized that my mother didn't like me very much; she was always bawling me out for nothing, trivial things. And then, when there were fights at home, I learned that...that...my mother...she had me when she was...when she was...she had me before she was married! And one day she had a fight with my grandmother too, and that's when I learned that she wanted to have an abortion, and if I was born, it was because of my grandmother."

Questions/Topics for Reflection

1. The impression created by the tracking shots during the opening credits.
2. The role of writing in the first sequence, as regards the opposition of the adult and the children's worlds; the role of writing in the rest of the film, in relation to the progressive deterioration of Antoine's situation.
3. Antoine sitting at his mother's vanity: he smells her perfume, tries her eyelash curler, looks in the mirror (multiple reflections).
4. The relationship between Antoine and his parents, and between his parents. His parents' character.
5. The representation of adults in this film.
6. The opposition between the indoor and outdoor scenes, as regards Antoine.
7. The rotor sequence at the fair; the presence of Truffaut, the director, in the rotor with Antoine.
8. The theme of "theft," its role in the film.
9. The role of movies in the film.
10. Antoine's imprisonment (his viewpoint, his treatment by the guards); the sequence of the transfer in the police van.
11. The interview with the psychologist at the center (Antoine speaks out); the originality of the style of this sequence (dissolves into the same shot).
12. Antoine's escape: the effect of the long tracking shot; Antoine's gaze into the camera in the freeze frame at the end of the film.

CRITICAL DOSSIER

Fereydoun Hoveyda — Portrait of a Troubled Adolescence

What is Truffaut's film about? Evoking one of the most difficult periods of our existence, a period that adults, with their short memory, often glorify, albeit hypocritically. *The 400 Blows* is an episode of the difficulty of being, of the distress of an individual thrown into the world without asking him his opinion, and who is offered no means of adaptation. It is a faithful rendering of the incomprehension parents and teachers exhibit so often when confronted with the problems that the child has to assume as he becomes an adult. Second birth, for which no one wants to accept the painful responsibility. The child is simply forced to create for himself, with whatever he has at his disposal, an acceptable world. But how can he be expected to escape the daily tragedy while he remains torn between his parents, idols with clay feet, and an indifferent, if not to say hostile, world?

To appreciate the realism of this film, one only has to pick up any psychology or psychoanalysis textbook and read the chapter on the typical problems of adaptation experienced by juveniles. All the characteristics of adolescence appear in the character and situation of young Antoine Doinel.

But Truffaut, with restraint which does him honor, avoids over-individualizing, pushing his hero's "case" to the limit. If he had wanted to create a real tearjerker, he could have turned Antoine into a lost cause. His film would have been more violent and easier to make. But Truffaut, with a kind of artistic masochism, refuses the easy way.

Marcel Moussy and he systematically eliminated from their story any form of exaggeration. Antoine is neither too spoiled nor too unhappy. A simple teenager like so many others. Not at all abused, he just has to deal with indifference. As an unwanted child, he feels out of place, a burden for a couple grappling with the difficulties of existence. In a perpetual state of anguish, he no sooner extracts himself from one complicated situation that he stumbles into another, with a string of lies as stupid as they are inevitable. Whose fault is it? Everyone's and no one's. The film seems to suggest that a set of socio-economic circumstances (the financial situation of the parents, the tiny apartment), family circumstances (the parents' relationship and their relationship with the child), and individual circumstances (Antoine's masochistic attitude with respect to his parents) are all at the source of the boy's fate.

Truffaut's hero thus acquires an ambiguity which has the ring of truth, to the credit of the authors of the screenplay and the dialogues. Antoine is both victim and accomplice. Compare the bravado of the kid with his friends and his submissive attitude at home. There emanates from *The 400 Blows* an impression of reality and fundamental truth that cannot fail to move the spectator.

The film has been called autobiographical. Truffaut claims it's not true. I'm inclined to believe that, like one of his masters, Hitchcock, he is amusing himself by leading the public down false paths. He gives a bundle of mixed signals. But since he doesn't yet possess the whole bag of tricks of the famous Hollywood Englishman, he can't cover all his tracks. In any case, all films are to some extent autobiographical. However it is made, the film absorbs and reflects the author's personality. *The 400*

Blows could be called an imaginary biography, a genre which is just as legitimate as autobiography, and in any case more artistic, since it allows for a free transposition. One could, like certain literary critics, try to distinguish the autobiographical from the fictional. A waste of time, because, once again, who cares about Truffaut the individual here? Let's be satisfied with saying that the subject of *The 400 Blows* is the childhood of Truffaut and Moussy, reconceived and transposed by Truffaut and Moussy as adults.

What is important to emphasize are the qualities of the screenplay and of the directing: phenomenological description of adolescence, characters and action situated clearly from the beginning, complete liberty of the young hero before our eyes. The idea of "liberty" calls for an important remark: one often has the impression that a hidden camera is following Antoine, and that he is not aware he is being filmed. And it is precisely the illusion of filming live action, the illusion of dealing with "raw material," that gives the film this emotive quality which compensates the somewhat shocking, disorderly character of the beginning of the film. The adoption of a television approach for the psychologist's scene, far from constituting a stylistic inconsistency, simply confirms in its turn the general impression of "live action."

Truffaut thus achieves a verisimilitude seldom seen in cinema, supported by his constant concern with realistic details. There is scarcely a shot in which Truffaut doesn't use an element of the décor to cry out, beyond the screen's surface, the profound truthfulness of his subject. He has an innate sense of the relationship of things to people. Like all great novels, the characters in Truffaut's film find themselves confronted with objects, which resist them in a certain fashion. This gives birth to a sentiment of duration quite unusual in films. Truffaut is passionately interested in everything which, at first, appears secondary: papers to be burned, garbage cans to be emptied, curtains the kid uses to wipe his hands, the buffet he takes the silverware from, the banana skin he cuts up, etc. Things become important and help explain the hero's character.

I'm also struck, in this film, by the movement from the particular to the general: the description of adolescence, as I said above, is consistent with what one reads in textbooks. Antoine is both Truffaut and Moussy, you and I. Sartre said, "*You must know how to say* we *to say* I." To speak to us, Truffaut immediately chose the first person plural. His film therefore sometimes seems too general and not adequately individualized. But who cares, since Truffaut is evolving regularly: in *The Brats*, "we" was a group of kids, here it's a single child. That's progress already. It is easy to criticize a certain negligence in the structure, a feeling of underdevelopment in the story. But is there really a story here? Aren't we dealing, like Truffaut himself says, with a *chronicle* of age thirteen?

The ending is very beautiful, stopping the film as the hero turns back toward us, leaving the door to the future open. But it leaves us wanting more: how will Antoine survive his adolescence? Truffaut will doubtlessly treat this subject at another time. Here his intention is only descriptive [...] ("La première personne du pluriel," pp. 53-55).

Jacques Doniol-Valcroze — The Unforgettable Final Sequence

The "great moments" of *The 400 Blows* are mute like great sorrows: in the unforgettable trip through the night in the police van, the only tear shed in the film, almost invisible on Antoine's cheek, is constantly hidden from our view by the movement to and fro of the ride; similarly, the no less memorable final sequence — Truffaut himself said so — is neither optimistic nor pessimistic. Antoine escapes during a soccer game and begins to run; at the end of his dash, there's the sea… but the sea that he's never seen; he looks at it for a moment and turns back toward the camera, the image freezes, the film is over.

In spite of this soberness, this lack of emotion even, our throat tightens; few film endings are so moving. Why? The secret of these final shots cannot be verbalized. We understand the mechanism without being able to analyze it. First, there's the length of time. Antoine runs interminably, filmed in a single tracking shot; when he gets out of breath, grows tired, slows his stride, it's for real. Then, there's the fact that he is running toward the sea, a symbol of the unknown for Antoine, a symbol of his future; we can read in his face instantly, when it finally turns toward us, that a stage has been crossed, a voyage to the end of night completed, that whatever may be his subsequent life and the anguish of that life, a discovery has been made which bears the seed of generosity and moral beauty.

With infinite tenderness, with a quasi-savage love, François Truffaut gives us as an epilogue this pathetic face of youth, so vulnerable and so rich, and this serious gaze which doesn't even settle on us (quoted by Gillain, 1991, p. 120).

Jean Collet — Writing and Revolt

Then, writing comes into the picture. With beautiful English letters which seem to have been written by a teacher, the calligraphy of the opening credits rolls out. At the end of the credits, the first shot of the film shows us a pupil bending over his notebook. He stops writing and takes from his desk a pinup which begins to circulate among the boys, secretly.

Model writing, a pupil's writing, pictures which move, forbidden images which spread like the plague, here's the motif in its original pureness. At the beginning, the conflict between the child and the adult. And not just any conflict. The first of these four hundred blows sets writing in opposition to the image. It's a combat lost in advance. The image is shameful, it hides under the tables; it's banned. It's tied to desire and guilt. It's by following this photo that we discover Antoine Doinel. Antoine is the one who can't hide the pinup. He's going to be caught at the same time as the pinup. At precisely the instant that he is giving her a fine mustache (a manner of denying women, along with desire, but especially a manner of *writing* on the photo, of refusing the image by marking it with a personal sign) […].

Antoine, condemned to the classroom during recreation, takes revenge by writing an epitaph on the wall:

> Here suffered poor Antoine Doinel
> Unjustly punished by Little Leaf
> For a pinup fallen from the sky…
> From now on, it's an eye for an eye,
> A tooth for a tooth.

Is the film going to reproduce this monstrous text, this delinquent writing? While Little Leaf is busy at the blackboard, the camera approaches a tousle-headed boy, little Abbou (Richard Kanayan). Antoine has just gone off-camera to get a sponge — *"or I'm going to make you lick your imbecilities off the wall…"* Abbou begins to write in a big notebook, but he makes a *blot*. He rips out the page. His fingers are covered with ink, which he gets all over the following pages too. So, little by little, in a daffy scene worthy of the Marx Brothers, the pages of the notebook are torn out down to the very last one, while in voice-over Little Leaf continues bellowing out his shrill monologue […].

[Antoine] has to clean the wall so that the teacher's writing can reign without any competition. Instead of that, we see another child, an accomplice, echo the guilty writing. It's as if the graffiti were spreading, spilling out in a river of vengeful ink […]. Against the teacher's order, against the cleanliness of the school, the only possible revolt is to sully, to destroy the pretty notebook. Our laughter at this spectacle is hardly innocent. It's conniving laughter. Along with Antoine and Abbou, that is, along with the film, our laughter says "crap."

A few moments later, at home, Antoine puts coal in an old stove and wipes his hands on the curtains. The same laughter. *In the same movement*, Antoine steals some money hidden by his parents in a buffet: stain, dirtiness, theft, money are linked together in the same dream of revenge.

The transition between these two scenes is provided by an insulting comment by Little Leaf. He shouts at Antoine: *"Well that's just tough, your parents will pay…Ah, France is going to be in a pretty state in ten years!"* Followed by a pan to the inscription above the door: *"Liberty, Equality, Fraternity."* That's what's written on the walls, engraved in stone. But who does the writing? Who has the right to write these fine slogans? Does one have to *pay* to be able to write? Antoine won't pay. He has accepted the teacher's challenge. And the camera which glides slowly back from the inscription to the children is not neutral. It expresses the mute discourse of revolt (*Le Cinéma de François Truffaut*, pp. 41-44).

Jean Collet — The Rotor Scene

The rotor is a prodigious machine. It combines speed and immobility. Like an airplane. Like a bicycle. The camera — which knows no fear — takes position in the middle of the rotor and calmly records the ecstasy of Antoine. Antoine plastered against the wall, imbedded in this wall of boards, is an unforgettable image; it is, for the first time in the film, the *inscription* of Antoine. Better than the fierce epitaph, better than the graffiti and the fleeting mirrors, the film seizes Antoine exactly as it will at the last moment. He is immobile. He defies time, space, and gravity. He shows no trace of the anxiety we'll read in his face in the last shot. He is radiant.

The rotor resembles the apparatus which preceded the cinematograph: the praxinoscope of Emile Reynaud […]. In the rotor we see François Truffaut beside Jean-Pierre Léaud. The rotor is a metaphor for the cinema. Antoine is no longer the same person. Next to the filmmaker, the character is replaced by the actor. All the ambiguity of the relationship between cinema and reality is foregrounded. Antoine's happiness in the rotor is also the happiness of being plunged into a film — as actor or spectator. The cinema is this curious machine which causes us to take leave of our senses, this black cave we go down into in order to take flight. The cinema is this strange wall in which our acts and our face are recorded forever.

Afterwards, you have to return to reality. Emerging from the rotor, Antoine discovers his mother with her lover. Coincidence? In any case, it relates Antoine's transgression to his mother's: "*She won't dare tell my father.*" They are tied together by a guilty silence (p. 47).

Gilbert Salachas — The Rhythm of *The 400 Blows*

What characterizes the style of directing of *The 400 Blows*, at first view, is the movement, in all its forms. First of all, the structure of the shooting script is just as simple as the dramatic development: it's one episode after the other, most often without any kind of transition or artificial link (visual or verbal). Even the simple technique of fading isn't systematically used […]. The movement itself is captured naturally (for example, and it's often, when the children run) or provoked technically by numerous, broad camera movements. These movements, within the shots, are pans, and most frequently pans back and forth which can be taken to represent the action of the human eye. The camera, liberated from all classical prescriptions, runs after one character, then another, returns to the first, etc. The speed of the mobility is variable. To illustrate these gear changes, let's look at the first sequence. The lens moves slowly from one pupil to another, following the trail of the pinup circulating in the classroom; it hesitates a moment on Antoine (who is drawing mustaches or whatever) and suddenly sweeps over the room to frame the teacher at the very moment that he speaks. We find similar examples in the sequence where we meet René's mother. Here again the camera leaps to greet her. Likewise, when Antoine escapes, the camera twice moves back and forth between the pursuers and the pursued. The goal of this jumpy technique, Truffaut admits, is to reduce the number of shots by avoiding the classical angle-reverse angle shots […]. The image is above all dynamic, its contours perpetually changing. This virtually functional instability of the camera lends an unusually dynamic rhythm to the narrative, to the conscious and intentional detriment of the clarity of the image during the camera's travels (pans).

Because they are obvious, these techniques preserve the original rhythm of the film, its particular vivacity; but the traditional angle-reverse angles are also present. They generally connote confrontation, antagonism, struggle (for example, "Little Leaf" vs. his pupils, Antoine vs. his mother, etc…). In this context, we should note, in particular, the scene — capital scene — where Antoine is questioned by the psychologist. The reverse angle is effected by the sound alone, the voice-over by Annette Wadement. On the screen we only see Antoine's face, in stationary shots of variable length and separated by quick dissolves — tantamount to a series of ellipses (*Télé-Ciné*, p. 6).

Richard Neupert — Music and "Closure" in *The 400 Blows*

The musical accompaniment ends temporarily at the soccer game so that the subdued "wild" sounds of the soccer game can prepare the slow, quiet setting from which Antoine will escape. When he does make a break under the fence, the only sound is the shrill noise of the guards' whistles. Other than these whistles, Antoine's escape is only accompanied by the diegetic sounds of his footsteps, dogs barking, and his heavy breathing. This use of wild sounds corresponds to what Gorbman defines as "diegetic silence." Here, the absence of music helps focalize the spectator's attention onto Antoine's plight, and reinforces his isolation. However, by the time Antoine first sees the ocean, the music returns for its final movement, which reassembles all the film's musical motifs and themes. By now those themes have accumulated a vast collection of textually specific connotations and representational significations.

This reprise creates a musical wrap-up or bracket to close the film by echoing or answering the film's opening overture. The strings slowly crescendo into the tragic theme and are then joined by the xylophone and piano, referring again to Antoine's ride in the police van. Then, as the shot continues, Antoine sees the ocean and runs away from the camera while there is a second crescendo, this time bringing in the full orchestra to take over from the piano music. At this point a bell tolls and the xylophone and flute parts dominate. This shift recalls for the audience the formerly playful jazz score that earlier accompanied Antoine and René on their romps through the city's movie theaters and amusement park.

As Antoine nears the water's edge, however, the diegetic sound of the waves begins to challenge the music for volume and dominance. The slow, serious repetition of the waves takes over the rhythm as the orchestra diminishes, leaving only the waves and the plucking violins. During the second half of the final shot the violins also recede until one lone violin plucks out the theme as the final shot freezes on Antoine's close-up. This lone instrument continues, along with the sound of the waves, through the fade to black leader.

Throughout the final scene of *The 400 Blows*, the point of view structures have narrowed the audience's information, moving closer and closer to Antoine and never revealing the location of the pursuing guards. While earlier in the film we were shown events that Antoine could not have known about or witnessed, his escape gradually pares down our vision of the diegesis by a decreasing focalization. While the visual track and point of view structures limit our field to Antoine's face, the musical score dwindles down to a sound track that also concentrates attention on the narrative strategies (the cyclical camera movement, the freeze-frame, and the highly overt nondiegetic musical theme).

Thus, the musical themes in *The 400 Blows* begin as culturally coded motifs, calling upon pitch, rhythm, and melody to prepare the viewer for certain emotions in the film. Hearing a mournful piano theme or a cheerful jazz piece in the beginning, the audience may anticipate the kind of scene that will follow, or at least they may refer to a handy stock of emotional responses that would accompany such culturally coded motifs. In this way, the film's music calls upon the spectator's knowledge and experience of other, pre-textual codes and contexts.

By the film's conclusion, however, these themes have accumulated additional meanings specific to the film. The jazz score, for instance, has accompanied the gym class where Antoine and René evaded the instructor, as well as the comic scene in which they addressed the priest as "Madame." Similarly, the sad plucking violin theme not only recalls Antoine's arrest, but also his wandering alone and hungry at night when he cannot return home. Therefore, the film's concluding medley carries a double significance : first, it maintains its own pretextual emotional connotations that would exist independent of the film, while second, it recalls the specific story of events that accompanied each theme earlier (pp. 28-29).

FRANÇOIS TRUFFAUT'S FILMOGRAPHY

1958	*The Brats (Les Mistons,* short subject)
1959	*The 400 Blows (Les Quatre Cents Coups)*
1960	*Shoot The Piano Player (Tirez sur le pianiste)*
1962	*Antoine et Colette* [second episode of the Doinel cycle, short subject in the collective film, *Love At Twenty (L'Amour à vingt ans)*]; *Jules et Jim*
1964	*Soft Skin (La Peau douce,* third episode of the Doinel cycle).
1966	*Fahrenheit 451*
1967	*The Bride Wore Black (La Mariée était en noir)*
1968	*Stolen Kisses (Baisers volés,* fourth episode of the Doinel cycle)
1969	*La Sirène du Mississippi*
1970	*Domicile conjugal* (fifth epidsode of the Doinel cycle); *The Wild Child (L'Enfant sauvage)*
1971	*The Two Englishwomen And The Continent (Les Deux Anglaises et le continent)*
1972	*A Beautiful Girl Like Me (Une belle fille comme moi)*
1973	*Day For Night (La Nuit américaine,* Oscar for the best foreign film)
1975	*Histoire d'Adèle H.*
1976	*Small Change (L'Argent de poche)*
1977	*The Man Who Loved Women (L'Homme qui aimait les femmes)*
1978	*The Green Room (La Chambre verte)*
1979	*Love In Flight (L'Amour en fuite,* end of the Antoine Doinel cycle)
1980	*The Last Subway Train (Le Dernier Métro)*
1981	*The Woman Next Door (La Femme d'à côté)*
1982	*Vivement Dimanche*

Truffaut died on October 21, 1984, of a brain tumor. He was 52 years old.

WORKS CONSULTED

Aline Desjardins s'entretient avec François Truffaut. Paris: Edilig, 1988 (conversations dating from December 1971, in Montréal).

Baby, Yvonne. "Les Quatre Cents Coups: Une chronique de l'adolescence nous dit François Truffaut." *Le Monde* (April 21): 12 (conversation with Truffaut).

Billard, Pierre. "Les 400 Coups du père François." *Cinéma 59* 37 (June 1959): 25-29, 136-137 (conversation with Truffaut).

………"Introduction à une méthode de travail." *Cinéma 60* 42 (Jan. 1960): 14-22 (four descriptions written by Truffaut on the main characters of the film, followed by the text of the interview with the psychologist).

Cahoreau, Gilles. *François Truffaut 1932-1984*. Paris: Julliard, 1989.

Collet, Jean. *Le Cinéma de François Truffaut*. Paris: Lherminier, 1977 (pp. 41-55).

Collet, Jean, Michel Delahaye, Jean-André Fieschi, André S. Labarthe and Bertrand Tavernier. "François Truffaut." *Cahiers du cinéma* 138 (Dec. 1962): 41-59 (conversation with Truffaut).

De Baecque, Antoine, and Serge Toubiana. *François Truffaut*. Paris: Gallimard, 1996 (pp. 187-211).

Doniol-Valcroze, Jacques. "Les Quatre Cents Coups." *Cahiers du cinéma* 96 (June 1959): 41-42.

Gillain, Anne. *Le Cinéma selon François Truffaut*. Paris: Flammarion, 1988.

………*Les 400 Coups*. Paris: Nathan, 1991.

Hoveyda, Fereydoun. "La première personne du pluriel." *Cahiers du cinéma* 97 (July 1959): 53-55.

Insdorf, Annette. *François Truffaut. Les Films de sa vie*. Paris: Gallimard, 1996.

Neupert, Richard. "The Musical Score As Closure Device in *The 400 Blows*." *Film Criticism* XIV, 1 (Fall 1989): 26-32.

Rivette, Jacques. "Du côté de chez Antoine." *Cahiers du cinéma* 95 (May 1959): 37-39.

Salachas, Gilbert. "*Les Quatre Cents Coups*." *Télé-Ciné* 83 (June-July 1959): 1-11.

Truffaut, François. *Le Plaisir des yeux*. Paris: Cahiers du cinéma, 1987.

………*Les Aventures d'Antoine Doinel*. Paris: Mercure de France, 1970.

Alain Resnais

Hiroshima mon amour

(1959)

Alain Resnais, *Hiroshima mon amour*: "She" (Emmanuelle Riva) and "He" (Eiji Okada) on location during the shooting of the film against the atomic bomb. © Argos Films

Director ....Alain Resnais
Screenplay and Dialogues.....................................Marguerite Duras
Directors of Photography .... Sacha Vierny (France),
Takahashi Michio (Japan)
Music... Giovanni Fusco, Georges Delerue
Film Editors ....Henri Colpi, Jasmine Chasney, Anne Sarraute
Sound ....P. Calvet, Yamamoto, R. Renault
Lighting ....Ito
Art Directors.................................... Esaka, Mayo, Petri, Miyakuni
Script Girl (Continuity) ....Sylvette Baudrot
Producer ....Argos films, Como Films, Daïeï, Pathé Overseas
Length .... 1 h 26

Cast

Emmanuelle Riva (*She*), Eiji Okada (*He*), Bernard Fresson (*the German lover*), Stella Dassas (*the mother*), Pierre Barbaud (*the father*).

STORY

A French actress in her thirties ("She") comes to Hiroshima in August 1959 to play a role in a film about peace. The day before her departure, she meets a Japanese man ("He") with whom she spends the night making love in her hotel room. While they make love, she relates her visit to the Hiroshima museum whose theme is the catastrophic consequences of the atomic bomb which destroyed the city, her visit to the hospital where the victims continue to receive care, and the documentary films she has seen simulating the event. The following day, the Japanese man manages to find the French woman at the shooting location and takes her to his home, where they again make love. The affair with the Japanese man awakens the deeply repressed memory of a love affair she had had with a German soldier during the Nazi Occupation, when she was a young girl, in Nevers, France. The German soldier was shot dead the day before the city was liberated; the girl, disgraced, her head shaven in public, sinks into madness. She tells the whole story to the Japanese lover, partly in his home, partly in a tearoom, the scenes from her past alternating on the screen with returns to the present. Afterwards she wanders through the streets of Hiroshima, returns to her hotel room for a moment, then goes out again into the night, her thoughts oscillating constantly between Nevers and Hiroshima. She is followed in the street for a while by the Japanese man, who tries to persuade her to stay a few days longer with him in Hiroshima. She sits a moment at the train station, then at a café — where she is approached by another Japanese man — before returning to her hotel room, where her Japanese lover quickly reappears. The film ends in the French woman's room, both characters anguished by the thought of their love affair fading from memory, with a final unresolved question. He: "*Perhaps it is possible you will stay...*". She: "*You know very well, that is even more impossible than separating.*"

CRITICAL RECEPTION

Hiroshima mon amour, Alain Resnais's first feature film, brought him fame virtually overnight, in France first, then throughout the international community. Excluded from the films officially representing France at the Cannes Film Festival (out of fear of offending the Americans), but presented at Cannes anyway in response to public pressure, Resnais's film astounded everyone by winning both the prize awarded by the International Federation of the Cinematographic Press (Fipresci) and the Society of Cinema and Television Writers Prize, before being awarded the prestigious Méliès Prize the following year. Subsequently *Hiroshima* enjoyed remarkable success in the international arena, as described by Frédéric de Towarnicki in October, 1960: "Hailed by filmmakers and writers worldwide, this 'difficult' film was rewarded with a six-month run in theaters in Paris and London and five months in Brussels and won the Belgium Critics Prize for the best foreign film. It was applauded wildly in Tel-Aviv, was more popular than *La Strada* [by Fellini] in Germany, and was acclaimed by audiences throughout Europe and South America. It got top billing in Milan and Turin and was awarded prizes in Athens and in Switzerland. Banned at first in Canada, the film eventually received an award from the cinema fans of Montréal. In New York it will very likely soon break all the attendance records of any non-American or British film in its first run" ("Spécial Resnais," p. 9). It received, in fact, the Critics' Prize and the Distributors' Prize in New York. Where did this film that exploded like a bomb in the cinema world come from?

BEFORE *HIROSHIMA*

Before directing *Hiroshima mon amour*, Alain Resnais (born in 1922, in Vannes, in the Brittany region) had earned a reputation as a highly talented film editor, as witnessed by Jean-Luc Godard's remark, speaking of Resnais's short subjects, that he is "the second-best film editor in the world, after Eisenstein" ("Spécial Resnais," p. 40) — which is no small compliment. Resnais's own first films are in fact a series of short documentaries, including, principally, *Van Gogh* (1948), *Paul Gauguin* and *Guernica* (1950), *Statues Die Too* (*Les Statues meurent aussi*, 1950-53), *Night and Fog* (*Nuit et brouillard*, 1955), *All the Memory in the World* (*Toute la mémoire du monde*, 1956), *The Mystery of Studio Fifteen* (*Le Mystère de l'atelier quinze*, 1957) and *The Song of Styrene* (*Le Chant du Styrène*, 1958). With few exceptions, all of Resnais's short subjects won prizes, beginning with *Van Gogh*, which garnered, in France, the Prize for the best artistic documentary, followed by an Oscar at the Academy Awards in Los Angeles. The film which most clearly foreshadows *Hiroshima* is unequivocally *Night and Fog* (awarded the Jean Vigo Prize), in which Resnais evokes the hell of the Nazi concentration camps by alternating shots of a former camp in the present (in color) with excerpts of documentary films from the period of the Holocaust (in black and white). The sound track of the film features a voice-over commentary, both lyrical and grim, by the novelist Jean Cayrol (himself a former prisoner at Mauthausen). The essential elements of the film — the shock produced by the juxtaposition of the past and the present, which evokes traumatic events, the subtleties of the editing, the role of tracking shots and of voice-over narration — all would appear again in *Hiroshima mon amour*.

THE COLLABORATION WITH MARGUERITE DURAS

It was precisely the producers of *Night and Fog*, encouraged by the film's success, who decided to engage Resnais to make a feature film of the same type, but one which would focus on the effects of the atomic bomb. Resnais accepted the commission but, try as he might, could not imagine a documentary which wouldn't be just a repetition of *Night and Fog* — which he could not bring himself to do. Moreover, he knew quite well that there were already very good documentary films on the bombing of Hiroshima. He remained stymied until he met the novelist Marguerite Duras, who had just published *Moderato cantabile* (1958), which developed the same themes, love and death, which would dominate his new film. Duras marveled at *Night and Fog* and also shared Resnais's left-leaning political views; she agreed immediately to write the screenplay for the film. They agreed from the outset not to make a documentary and to create a distance between the characters and the events. As Resnais recalls: "We thought that we could try to make a film in which the characters do not participate directly in the tragic events but either just remember them or identify with them viscerally" (Delahaye, p. 154). They agreed likewise on the idea of "making a film in which no one would speak of the atom bomb, but in which it would still be present" (quoted in Leutrat, p. 32). In nine weeks Duras wrote at Resnais's request a purely literary work, a text which was so poetic that it at times resembled a form of incantation, a screenplay which developed a subtle dialectic between documentary and fiction, past and present, remembering and forgetting, love and death. Beginning with Duras's screenplay, Resnais created a film in which the "literary" was transformed into pure cinematographic material, integrated into a vast "operatic score" (the metaphor preferred by Resnais) where images, voices, music, sounds, past and present resonate and resound together in a cascade of echoes, counterpoints, and repetitions of all kinds. Duras's screenplay, rightfully considered to be an authentic work of literature on its own, was published the following year as a "film-story" by Gallimard.

To lend depth ("roots") to his characters, Resnais asked Duras (as he would ask all his screenwriters) to write what they liked to call the "subjacent continuity" of the film; that is, the complete personal history of each character. Duras thus composed, in addition to the screenplay and a few filming notes, a "Portrait of the Japanese Man" and a "Portrait of the French Woman" (preceded by a text in which the French woman describes her youth in Nevers). The contents of these portraits do not appear in the film, but they enter into the development of the action by helping the filmmaker, as well as the actors, understand better the personality, the psychology, and the psychic makeup of the characters — to *feel* the characters better. Although Duras was not present during the filming — Resnais always insisted on being totally in charge of this phase, as well as the editing process — she recorded her dialogues, "perhaps influencing, by her intentionally neutral diction, the actors' intonation" (Carlier, p. 47).

ACTORS AND FILMING

The Japanese, who financed the film, had their demands too: the film must be shot partially in Japan, partially in France, with local technical crews and a star from each country. Resnais chose for the role of the French woman an actress who had never played in a film, Emmanuelle Riva. He had seen Riva in a play and was struck by the quality of her diction. The importance of this fact becomes clear in Riva's speeches in voice-over, both dialogues and monologues, where language becomes recitative and incantation, turning Duras's literary text into a sort of film music, as Dionys Mascolo remarks during an interview with Marguerite Duras: "But the text has become here a music intended to be listened to [...] like a musical score" (p. 15; see also the text by Gaston Bounoure in the *Critical Dossier*). The male lead will be Eiji Okada, whom Resnais had seen in Japanese films. Although Okada had the personal qualities Resnais was seeking, he didn't speak a word of French; he had to learn his French text phonetically and improve his linguistic performance during the post-synchronization in France. Resnais completed filming in Hiroshima and Tokyo in seventeen days in August and September, 1958. He worked with a Japanese cinematographer (director of photography), Takahashi Michio, and a Japanese crew which spoke no French.

They all knew, however, Jean Cocteau's film *Orpheus* (*Orphée*, 1950), which served as a point of reference when Resnais needed to explain what type of shot he wanted! The shooting in France, in Nevers and Autun, only took twelve days, in December, 1958, with Sacha Vierny serving as director of photography for the first time in a feature film. Vierny was kept in complete ignorance of the shooting in Japan to prevent any kind of imitation. Resnais even had him use a different make of film from the one used in Japan and asked him to film with a telescopic lens. This latter tactic created a slow-motion effect, as if the characters were laboring in their movements, creating a phantasmagorical atmosphere which contributed to the depiction of the painful memories of the heroine's Nevers period: "…in short, what I wanted," said Resnais, "was to create uncomfortable images…" (Leutrat, p. 88).

STRUCTURE AND MUSIC

The screenplay of *Hiroshima mon amour* is divided into five parts, which makes the film resemble, as many critics have remarked, a play in five acts. **I. Prologue**: credits and intertwined bodies; voice-over dialogue; the night of lovemaking between the French woman and the Japanese man in the hotel room. **II. Night and Following Morning**: dialogue between the lovers, their faces now visible; the hotel room in the morning, separation; **III. The Day**: on location — the parade, then the love affair continues at the Japanese man's home, leading to the recounting of the love affair with the German soldier; **IV. The Evening**: the Café du Fleuve, where the French woman recalls the death of her lover, her disgrace, her madness, her recovery; **V. Epilogue**: return to the hotel, then wandering around the city at night, scenes at the train station, at the café "Casablanca," and in the French woman's hotel room. This reference to classical theater, while interesting, is nonetheless superficial, and the film's structure is more reminiscent (as Resnais intended) of a musical work: "Formally, the film's composition is more musical than theatrical," states Durand (p. XIII). To compose the music for the film, Resnais appealed to the Italian composer Giovanni Fusco, who, to the delight of the filmmaker, immediately grasped the meaning and the structure of the film: "At noon I gave him a working copy of *Hiroshima*, and in the evening, at seven o'clock, he explained the film to me. He had completely understood and assimilated it: the play of contradictions, the role of forgetfulness…everything! In one day we reached agreement on the music" (Pingaud, p. 74). Resnais was quite explicit about the importance of the composer in a film's construction, declaring that "the composer can completely change the emotional value of a film. In any case, he is certainly the person who makes a film comprehensible […]. Without Fusco, *Hiroshima mon amour* would have been just an experimental film" (Leutrat, pp. 61-62). This declaration is particularly important since we know that Resnais lends the greatest importance to the affective content of his films, and that he is convinced that the primary function of cinema is to communicate feelings and to provoke emotions, not to transmit messages or to teach anything.

If it is undeniable that the music of *Hiroshima mon amour* plays an essential role in the expression of emotion and in stylistic, tonal, or rhythmic changes in the film — and in establishing the relationship between the sequences in Hiroshima and those in Nevers — it is no less important from the viewpoint of the structure of the work. The most striking function of the music is surely the evocation of the principal themes of the film, whose intertwining is expressed as much by the interplay of melodic motifs as by the organization of the images. Fusco's music develops, in fact, a broad series of "themes" which are related to the themes expressed either by the voices or by the images on the screen: Forgetfulness, Bodies, Museum, River, Lyricism, Nevers, to mention only the principal motifs. These themes return obsessively, in various combinations, but perfectly integrated into the structure of the visual themes of the film, serving as commentaries, echoes, or developments — or as ironic counterpoints, as in the case of the light-hearted music which accompanies the sobering museum visit. The musical composition takes on such importance in *Hiroshima* that it becomes the model for the whole film, as Resnais explains: "Ultimately, I believe that if we defined the film by a diagram on graph paper, we would discover a form similar to the musical structure of the quartet: themes and variations beginning in the first movement, resulting in numerous repetitions which can be unbearable for people who don't enter into the spirit of the film. The last movement especially is a slow, disconcerting movement, like a decrescendo" (Durand, XVIII).

THEMES

The principal themes of *Hiroshima mon amour* are imbedded in the oxymoron created by the title of the film: love and death, the short tryst between He and She contrasted to the tragedy of Hiroshima, in which the whole population was decimated by the atomic bomb. This opposition serves as a paradigm of sorts for the dialectical structure of the film, consisting virtually entirely of contrasts which echo or play on the basic antithesis. The Hiroshima affair with a Japanese man (the former enemy), for instance, recalls the Nevers love affair with a German soldier during the Occupation, which is terminated by the soldier's death. In the heroine's discourse, the same opposition is reflected in the prologue, but recast in terms of pleasure and pain: "*You're killing me. You're making me feel good. You're killing me. You're making me feel good.*" Other thematic oppositions are developed, such as memory and forgetfulness, past and present, war and peace, collective and individual tragedy, public and private, narrative and gaze, He and She, East and West — related to formal oppositions: sound and image, moving shots and static shots, dissolves and fades to black. And there are other oppositions which strangely resemble parallels: the skin of the lovers in the prologue and the badly burned skin of the Hiroshima victims (pleasure and pain), a bicycle twisted by the explosion and the bicycle ridden by the French girl to her meetings with her German lover (love and death), tracking shots in Hiroshima alternating with tracking shots, at exactly the same speed, in Nevers (past and present). Beside the oppositions arises the obsessive theme of Time (which flows) with its metaphorical correlative, the River (which flows), the Ota in Hiroshima, the Loire and the Nièvre in France. Time and its slow obliteration of memories are opposed to the instantaneous, overwhelming disintegration produced by the nuclear explosion — whose corollary (and not equivalent) on the individual level is the psychical disintegration of a young woman in love, she too a victim of the war.

STYLE

Above all, Resnais creates a universe of movement. Panning shots are frequent, of course, but the stylistic feature which best defines Resnais's cinema is the tracking shot, alone or in a series. In *Hiroshima mon amour*, there are no simple descriptive or accompanying dolly shots, but rather metaphorical travellings which become voyages in the worlds of dream or memory, or even in the unconscious mind. Speaking of the series of forward tracking shots in the streets of Hiroshima during the prologue (before we see the two characters), Resnais explains that "it is a kind of long traveling in the clouds of the subconscious which leads to the two characters" (Leutrat, p. 99). Durand perceives in this scene an erotic analogy as well: "By editing together tracking shots at the same speed, Resnais obtains a long, uniform movement through the streets of Hiroshima which corresponds to the real time of the lovemaking" (p. VIII). Elsewhere, alternating between Hiroshima and Nevers, the tracking shots are assimilated to the return to the past, but a past so intensely experienced that it is completely integrated into the present life of the French woman. Resnais categorically denies, moreover, the presence of flashbacks in *Hiroshima*, having asked Marguerite Duras expressly to write a screenplay "in which the past would not be expressed by real flashbacks, but would be present virtually throughout the story" (Durand, p. IX). Resnais places the two stories, Hiroshima and Nevers, as well as the past and the present, on the same plane and considers them to be completely intertwined; to explain his concept to Duras, he uses "the image of two combs interlocked" (Pingaud and Samson, p. 94). In the world of imagination, where Resnais places himself, past and present mingle freely according to the interplay between memory and desire, or between the conscious and unconscious minds. If Resnais's tracking shots, like the river metaphor, "give concrete expression to the horizontal flow of time" (Bounoure, p. 55), they are no less evocative, now and then, of the atemporal quality of psychological reality — or even of Bergson's concept of "pure time," in which there is a "mutual penetration" of present and past states of mind (pp. 76-77; see Bergson in the *Critical Dossier*).

Contrary to Resnais's normal practice, finally, we see in *Hiroshima mon amour* a proliferation of lap dissolves, beginning with the first sequence of the film. The dissolve, in which an image is replaced, more or less slowly, by another, seems to be a logical technique in a film dominated by the psychological back-and-forth of the female protagonist, the interplay between images from the past and the present that we see through her eyes. Past and present alternate constantly in her mind, occasionally laid over one another like a superimposition (which is at the very basis of the dissolve), as in the sequences where the German and Japanese lovers fuse into a single person in the French woman's mind — first in the tearoom, then when she walks through Hiroshima at night remembering Nevers: "*I meet you. I remember you.*" Moreover, as Leutrat observes, the dissolve is the procedure of "appearance and disappearance, of erasure, the procedure which emphasizes a modification" (p. 90): Nevers erases Hiroshima which, in turn, erases Nevers — like the past erases the present and vice-versa. It is likewise the procedure of transformation, of metamorphosis, as in the first sequence, which is dominated by dissolves in which the bodies of the lovers "are subjected to a process which mineralizes and liquefies them, making them shine…" (p. 90). If Resnais employs so many dissolves, he also transforms their function: no longer a simple mode of transition — from one place or one time to another — the dissolve, like the tracking shot, becomes a metaphor.

It is impossible to discuss Resnais's style without evoking the essential role of editing. As noted above, before becoming famous as a film director, Resnais distinguished himself as one of the best film editors of his time. Like Orson Welles, who exploited his mastery of the medium of radio to revolutionize the use of sound in cinema, Resnais, a professional editor, brought the art of film editing to new heights in *Hiroshima*. The words, the images, and the music are masterfully organized to produce varied rhythms and to create parallels and oppositions, but especially visual and auditory counterpoints, harmony, and dissonance. The image (in the past or in the present) and the sound (always in the present: voice-over, voice-in, music, sound effects) echo each other and collide with each other in a dreamlike choreography which attempts, according to Resnais, to approximate "the complexity of human thought, of its mechanism."

STUDY GUIDE

Director's Comments

"Filmmaking is the art of playing with time."

"We are still faced with the old choice between Lumière and Méliès. We go back and forth between these two possibilities and sometimes find ourselves jammed up."

"Film is also, for me, an attempt, still rather crude and primitive, to approach the complexity of human thought, of its mechanism."

"I tried to find in the cinema the equivalent of reading, leaving the imagination of the spectator as free as if he were reading a book. That's the idea behind the recitation, the long monologue."

"I would like to make films that one looks at like a sculpture and that one listens to like an opera."

"Inscribe a love story in a context which includes the knowledge of the misfortune of others and create two characters for whom memory is always present in their actions."

"The great contradiction is that we have the duty and the will to remember, but that to live we must forget."

"We ask of the spectator, it is true, an enormous and still unaccustomed effort to participate comparable to the effort a writer asks of his reader. The theater is a collective phenomenon, but the conditions of cinema are such that one can attempt to speak to each spectator individually, to show confidence in him by leaving room for his imagination and inviting him to fill in what can only be presented schematically. I don't believe that films are effective when they underline every intention several times."

"We thought that we could try to make a film in which the characters do not participate directly in the tragic events but either just remember them or identify with them viscerally. We wanted to create, in a certain sense, anti-heroes; that's not exactly the right word, but it expresses pretty well our intentions. So, the Japanese man didn't experience the Hiroshima catastrophe, but he knows it intellectually, he is conscience of it, just as all the spectators of the film — and all of us — can feel this tragic event deeply, experience it collectively, without ever having set foot in Hiroshima.

"I was astounded and taken aback to read that some critics were putting the explosion of the bomb and the tragedy of Nevers on the same plane, as if one were intended to be the equivalent of the other. That's not it at all. On the contrary, the film opposes the immense, enormous, fantasmagorical side of Hiroshima to the tiny little story of Nevers, which we see through Hiroshima, like the glow of a candle is enlarged and inverted by a lens."

"We never see the Hiroshima event itself. It is evoked by a number of details, like in a description in a novel, where it is unnecessary to enumerate all the characteristics of a landscape or of an event to suggest its totality" (Interview with Michel Delahaye, pp. 6, 8).

Excerpts for Discussion

<u>Excerpt 1</u> (1'35-14'30): Prologue of the film, until *She* says: "What incredibly beautiful skin you have."

<u>Excerpt 2</u> (17'35-18'15): The following morning in the hotel room; the Japanese man's hand moves while he sleeps; rapid flashback.

<u>Excerpt 3</u> (31'00-34'55): *She* and *He* meet on the filming location ; the parade (demonstration).

<u>Excerpt 4</u> (44'10-48'50): At the Café du Fleuve; *She* tells the story of her love affair with the German soldier (her madness, incarceration in the cellar).

<u>Excerpt 5</u> (48'50-52'45): Continuation of the story (shaving of her head).

<u>Excerpt 6</u> (54'05-58'00): Continuation and end of the story (forgetting, the death of the lover, recovery).

<u>Excerpt 7</u> (1h11'45-14'15): *She* wanders through the streets, alternation of shots of Hiroshima and Nevers (stream of consciousness).

<u>Excerpt 8</u> (1h15'50-18'35): At the train station ; continuation of the preceding sequence ("*Dime novel story…I banish you to oblivion tonight*").

<u>Excerpt 9</u> (1h20'25-23'35): At the café "Casablanca," a man hits on the French woman.

Quotations for Comment

He (*off*): "You saw nothing in Hiroshima. Nothing."

She (*off*): "I saw everything…Everything."

* * *

She (*off*): "Like you, I also tried to fight with all my strength against forgetting. Like you, I forgot […]. Why deny the clear necessity of memory?"

* * *

She (*off*): "I meet you. I remember you. Who are you? You're killing me…You're making me feel good… How could I have doubted that this city was made for love?"

* * *

He: "Was he French, the man you loved during the war?"

She: "No, he wasn't French."

* * *

He: "When you are in the cellar, am I dead?"

She: "You are dead…"

* * *

She: "Ah!…it's horrible! I'm starting to remember you less well…Give me some more to drink. I'm beginning to forget you. I tremble at the thought of having forgotten so much love."

* * *

She (*off*): "Dime novel story…I banish you to oblivion…little girl from Nevers, little tramp from Nevers!…Little piece of trash, killed by love in Nevers! Little girl from Nevers with her head shaven, I banish you to oblivion tonight…"

* * *

She: "Hi-ro-shi-ma… Hi-ro-shi-ma…that's your name."

He: "That's my name. Yes. *Your* name is Nevers. Ne-vers-en-Fran-ce."

Questions/Topics for Reflection

1. The relationship between the documentary and the fictional sides of the film.
2. The "anonymous" status of *She* and *He*. What do we know about these two characters?
3. The importance of the Japanese man's hand which moves while he is asleep; the role of his foreign accent.
4. The "film about Peace" that they are making in Hiroshima, in which the French actress is playing the role of a nurse.
5. The slap that the Japanese man gives the French woman in the Café du Fleuve sequence.
6. The relationship between the German and Japanese lovers; the "therapeutic" role of the Japanese lover.
7. The opposition between the themes of forgetting and remembering. What are the other striking dichotomies in this film?
8. The relationship between Hiroshima and Nevers, the past and the present.
9. The dénouement: does she leave? does she stay? Justify your opinion.
10. This film was considered to be "scandalous" by many spectators when it came out. How would you explain this?

CRITICAL DOSSIER

Philippe Durand — A City, A Woman

This poem about explosion "opposes" History — Hiroshima destroyed by the atom bomb — to the story of a love pulverized by war, the rape of humanity opposed to a crime against the dignity of a human being. It is incumbent upon both the city and the young woman, both victims of the general madness which creates the hell and glorifies it, not to forget. The city has of course been rebuilt, the woman has reconstructed a new life based on stable elements: a husband, children, a profession. But neither the aggressive, cold architecture [of Hiroshima], nor the superficial balance of this woman can hide the devastation, the utter desolation of a soul (collective and individual), the incurable deep suffering, which the bombed city and the broken woman have in common ["Hiroshima mon amour (1959)," pp. XII-XIII].

Nathan Weinstock — Memory

The role of memory in this film symbolizes therefore the **domination of the present** by the past: the present has no meaning except in relationship to the past that foreshadows it [...]. The myth of Nevers is formed by the war-love conjunction, which is found again in Hiroshima. That is why, among her numerous love affairs, it is precisely this one which sets off in the French woman the painful process of identification. In "demystifying" the Japanese man, we observe that his reality is completely dependent on the past. Ultimately the Japanese man is a veritable **reincarnation** of the Nevers affair, which he is led to recreate. In this process of identification and of "mystification," it is memory that appears, on the plane of subjectivity, as the mediator between past and present. Nevers and Hiroshima [...] represent the dialectical movement of consciousness, the process of subjectivity. The construction of the film, far from being gratuitous, expresses Resnais's refusal to interrupt the continuity of subjectivity ("Spécial Resnais," *L'Avant-Scène Cinéma*, p. 43).

Jacques Rivette — *She*

[Emmanuelle Riva's] acting supports the sense of the film. It is an immense effort at *reconstitution*. I think that one finds the scheme that I was trying to describe a moment ago: an attempt to glue the pieces back together; within the conscious mind of the heroine, an attempt by her to regroup the diverse elements of her personality and of her consciousness in order to achieve a form of unity with the fragments, or at least what have become fragments within her by the shock of this encounter in Hiroshima. One is justified in thinking that the film begins twofold after the bomb; on the one hand on both the formal and the psychological level, since the first shot of the film is the abstract image of the couple on which the rain of ash falls, and because the whole beginning is a meditation on Hiroshima after the bomb. But one can also say, on the other hand, that the film begins after the explosion *for Emmanuelle Riva*, since it begins after the shock that devastated her, that disintegrated her social and psychological personality, only permitting us to learn afterwards, by allusions, that she is married, that she has children in France, that she is an actress, in short, that she has a structured life. In Hiroshima she undergoes a shock, she receives a "bomb" which breaks her conscious mind asunder, and she is forced, at that moment, to regain her bearings, to reconstitute herself. Just as Hiroshima had to reconstruct itself after the nuclear destruction, Emmanuelle Riva, in Hiroshima, is going to attempt to recompose *her* reality. She succeeds by achieving a synthesis of the present and the past, a synthesis of what she has discovered in Hiroshima and of what she endured long ago in Nevers ("*Hiroshima mon amour,*" *Cahiers du cinema* 97, p. 8).

Bernard Pingaud — Memory, Past, and Present

At the origin of a work there is always an idea. Here's the idea behind *Hiroshima mon amour*: memory being a form of forgetfulness, forgetting can only be totally achieved when memory has totally finished its work. With respect to her Japanese lover, the young actress who is doing a film about the atom bomb in Hiroshima finds herself, fourteen years later, in a situation comparable to one she experienced during the war with a German soldier. The whole logic of the film consists in leading her to discover this similarity, to understand it, and to free herself of it.

The former experience, rendered unbearable by its atrocity, has been forgotten. It hasn't disappeared or been overcome; it is in fact still present and, as the film will show, a crushing presence in its forgotten state. Forgetfulness is thus, in a certain sense, memory. But a memory without distance, a memory without distinction and which, for that reason, doesn't possess the force to *endure* what is crushing it; so it hides it. That is the first movement, prior to the film. The second movement will be the fascinating apparition. A particular present causes the resurgence of a particular past, whose attraction is made all the stronger since it has so long remained repressed from conscious memory. Relating this past to the Japanese man, the heroine looks at it squarely and very nearly falls apart. The Nevers episode has the same density and the same character as the one in Hiroshima, except that the former event cannot be modified in any way. It is this immutability which makes it fascinating, but as soon as it is understood, memory recovers its rights. The obsessive image finally becomes a memory, the past is finally grasped as the past. The third movement consists in distinguishing the two planes that the repetition confuses and in reestablishing a distance between them. What was is no more; the tragedy of her youth loses its paralyzing prestige, it becomes part of history. At the same time, the current adventure, glorified by the past without the heroine realizing it, is stripped of its magical character. Time begins to flow again. Her memory liberated, the heroine regains her sense of reality; Hiroshima dies with Nevers.

One sees immediately that the film could only be conceived as an enormous flashback. But the term just doesn't fit here. The *flashback* normally serves to explain what we see on the screen. Far from questioning memory, it assumes that it remains active; or rather, treating memory like an inexhaustible reservoir, the narrator draws from it the elements of his past that will explain his present. But the heroine of *Hiroshima* doesn't yet have a past, nor does she have memory. The situation she experienced cannot be used to understand a situation which, purely and simply, replicates it. It can only surge into her conscious mind through this repetition. The film, which begins in Hiroshima, gives us the impression that we then return to Nevers; but it is in fact the reverse which occurs. Under the pressure of Nevers, Hiroshima crumbles, and we witness a sort of *return forward* which, at first, recalls one episode through another, then dissolves this second episode in the first by effecting the disappearance of Hiroshima through the disappearance of Nevers […].

The order of appearance of the events of the past is not the order in which they occurred. The order of the narrative is linear, that of recognition circular. Once the memory has been triggered, its work progresses by spirals. The tension rises as the recounting comes closer and closer to the central event of the death of the German lover — like an artilleryman who, after having zeroed in on the target, finally hits it. The narrative would show us this event before revealing its consequences. Blind memory begins by feeling its way around it. It discovers first the "eternity," this period of stupor in which the girl, cloistered in the cellar, is alienated from herself, condemned to an immobility which resembles death, but which is only a simulacrum. It is only afterwards that she can — that she must — probe herself about the eternity, say when the eternity began and why. It is normal that the scenes of the cellar and the awakening precede, in this investigation, the key scenes of the head shaving and the killing of the German: the heaviest events are the last to rise to the surface ("Alain Resnais," pp. 5-9).

Marie-Claire Ropars-Wuilleumier — Cinema, Literature, and Lyrism

"What I wanted was to achieve the equivalent of a reading, to grant the spectator as much liberty, as much imagination as a the reader of a novel. I wanted him to be able to let his imagination rove freely around, behind, and even inside the images, without losing the fascination of the screen." This commentary of *Hiroshima mon amour* by Resnais gives a good idea of the revolution effected by his film: by his mastery of the expression of time, he achieves of course a traditional goal closely related to the development of cinematic writing; but at the same time, through the new relationship he establishes with the spectator, he moves into the final stage of relating cinema to literature, since it is at the very level of the spectator's perception that Resnais breaks the univocal immediacy of filmic communication, in order to appeal to the liberty, and ultimately the creative activity characteristic of the reader's activity […].

One may well wonder what is the precise role of this appeal to literary writing in Resnais's work. The most obvious is related to the appearance of the lyricism that words add to pictures, as in the prologue of *Hiroshima*, or just before the epilogue when Emmanuelle Riva murmurs the recitative of forgetfulness. This addition of literature to cinema bears clear risks when it is the characters themselves that the spectator sees on the screen declaiming literary texts, which undermines the illusion of reality. On the other hand, when the person speaking does not appear on the screen, or at least not during the declamation, the artifice works because the voice becomes the expression of a stream of consciousness, and the lyrical tonality can even penetrate certain dialogues of *Hiroshima*, recited off screen and projected towards a poetic modulation which, precisely because it abandons the appearance of reality, does not strike the spectator as literature. Liberated by the voice-over, words become song and accompany the image without attempting to explain it; cut off from its psychological roots or its dramatic function, it is transformed into an incantation, which places the narrative at its tragic level while at the same time promoting multiple flights of meditation around the visual representation. In the lyrical recitation the character is separated from himself, just as in theater, and sees himself from without; and the acquisition of a poetic language that was only permissible on the stage up to now liberates the cinema even more from its ties to the bastardized heritage of "psychological" theater [...].

Nonetheless, the intrusion of lyricism cannot be sustained throughout the narrative; it is precisely its intrusive function that makes lyricism effective, and it remains dependent on similarly lyrical editing, which is brought to new heights in *Hiroshima* [...] (*De la littérature au cinéma*, pp. 145-151).

Henri Colpi — "Hiroshima Music"

One might say that *Hiroshima*, even more than a film, even more than a poem, is a piece of music, a music of images because of their photographic, formal, beauty, because of the editing, because of the interpenetration of its visual themes. It is without a doubt the underlying musical character of the film which guarantees the sustained interest, the ineffable "bewitchment" that so many spectators have felt [...].

The five recordings of the music involved piano, flute, piccolo, clarinet, alto, viola, bass, cor anglais — and a guitar in two pieces. Such a group of instruments, very unusual in the cinematographic world, demanded precise execution and a richly composed music.

The distribution of the music in *Hiroshima* shows from the outset that the film is circumscribed by the theme of Forgetfulness, a notion which constitutes a line of force in Alain Resnais's work through *Statues Die Too*, *Night and Fog*, and *All the Memory in the World*. The opening credits, based on this single motif, are neither an opening nor a pretext for orchestral flourishes. They play the role of an introduction to the film by creating a strange and sorrowful atmosphere through its repetition of a group of six identical notes. As for the theme Forgetfulness, it doesn't return for a long while, until sequence 51: the stream of consciousness is brought in by the theme Nevers, replaced by the theme Bodies for the final evocation of the German lover, which has already been forgotten — and then the theme Forgetfulness reappears, its inconsistent and desperate monotony dominating the end of the film and terminating it with a cry.

The theme Bodies presents a contrasting warmth and a depth. It is associated with the lovers in the Prologue, but it disappears as soon as the faces appear and the real dialogue begins. It won't reappear until sequence 34 to unite in the heroine's mind the current and the former loves. This connection is still clearly evident in the passage (sequence 49) where the images of Nevers and Hiroshima are intertwined. In the train station, the theme Bodies only applies to the German love affair. The die being cast and forgetfulness fated to triumph, it will make a final timid and brief appearance before the heroine enters the café Casablanca.

The theme Nevers accompanies the happy memories of the young woman. It is gay, impulsive. We notice that the first strong evocation of Nevers is underlined by the theme Bodies, which logically continues until "*and then, he died,*" but that the second part of the evocation brings in the new motif. The heroine first re-experienced her former life through her Japanese lover, through the moments when she is fulfilled by love; then the Nevers period came back and dominated her. The Nevers theme will not swell up again until the young French woman is alone, with her stream of consciousness (the scene of the washbasin in her hotel room, the train station) [...].

The beautiful melodious phrase devoted to River appears in the Prologue. It is related to the views of "the delta estuary of the Ota River" and dissolves into the theme Bodies. It rises again in the morning, when the young woman strolls on the terrace: the river is in the background, and it is at the Café du Fleuve that the lovers met. The theme River is thus closely related to love, or better: it embraces both an object and a feeling which go together, water and sentimental love. It continues the theme Bodies in a more affective, less carnal mode. Beginning in the Japanese man's home "after love," it thus circumscribes the thirty minutes of the café sequence, where the only two instances of music in the film universe are "realistic and justified" (records) [...].

One more word. There are a number of examples of audio-visual counterpoint in the film, especially in the Prologue. But one cannot claim that the theme Bodies accompanying the bicycle rides of the girl (sequence 35) are contrapuntal. There is rather a continuation of the idea of amorous plenitude in relationship to these images. We have here an example of a technique rarely seen in film music: rather than underlying the internal rhythm of the image, the music prolongs an impression within the spectator.

Truly exemplary music [...]; the score is extraordinarily "attuned" to the filmed sequences, the notes virtually "ooze" from the images. There is not a line to be added or eliminated; the music "is" the film ("Hiroshima musique," pp. 18-23).

Gaston Bounoure — The Text as Score; The Five Movements of the Film

It is revealing that *Hiroshima mon amour* cannot be narrated — faithfully at least — in a dramatic mode. This is probably because love just happens and cannot be recounted. But also because the Hiroshima love is a pure internal song. And that is what I hadn't completely realized in my prior reflections on this film. When the film came out, scarcely anyone perceived its purely musical composition. Of course many people were sensitive to the score written by Giovanni Fusco, whose themes, and their relationship to the images, have been very precisely analyzed by Henri Colpi (who edited the film). But the very same people disparaged the literary tone of the text, without noticing that this text constitutes the true score of the film and that the music is only an accompaniment intended to stay in the background and give "color" to the incantatory themes of which the film is completely composed. It is these themes, which determine the deep structure of a work, that traditional film analysis remains incapable of defining. No division into parts, into sequences that we would expect from a dramatic logic, is perceptible here. The film is only a series of "movements." SHE and HE — SHE especially — are no longer characters, but "instruments" which are performing solos or duos. SHE and HE have no names. They know each other when they make love but cannot recognize each other afterwards. HE is Hiroshima. SHE is Nevers. Only love unites them for a moment (theme of bodies); but the Nevers and Hiroshima episodes play in temporal counterpoint, responding to each other according to the melodic and rhythmic mutations which compose the five movements of the film.

In the first movement [...], SHE performs a long "solo," intense and tragic, on the atomic death within which HE attempts, in a futile leitmotif, to make his voice heard [...]. The variation on this single theme is developed in three parts: the time of the museum (with its photographs and its perfect but factitious reconstructions), the time of forgetfulness [...], and the time of the current love affair [...].

In the second movement a single theme: a duo of love during which SHE and HE try to identify each other and unite. But this too is futile, because Nevers begins to seep into Hiroshima [...].

The last movement develops two themes: the memory of Hiroshima and the memory of Nevers. But the "instruments" recede into the background, barely discernable behind the reality to which they yield. Behind the images of the film (that Resnais would have made if he had accepted the commission) that SHE is making in Hiroshima [...].

In the fourth movement, again a single theme: death in Nevers. SHE plays a solo, in the near absence of any decor — they are sitting in the half-light of a nearly empty café — or of any sound: the background music has disappeared, to leave only a real juke-box playing a Japanese tune or an insistent waltz. HE only intervenes with questions, breaking up the long recitative which culminates in her cry:

SHE: "*I can say that I could no longer perceive the slightest distinction between this dead body and my own. I could only find, between this body and mine, glaring resemblances. (She cries out.) You understand? It was my first love.*"

At this moment the slap of Hiroshima — like the little marble of Nevers — wakes her up. And the two voices again join together a moment to complete the theme [...].

The fifth and final movement, returning to the rhythm of the first, is composed of three variations which correspond to those of the beginning.: SHE regains her composure before a mirror (as if she were coming out of her internal museum, out of her memory) [...]; then, in a persistent march through the city, Nevers dead and forgotten possesses the living Hiroshima (with certain modulations of the first movement which return: "*You're killing me. You're making me feel good.*") and imposes the tragic knot of their story [...].

HE: "*Perhaps it is possible you will stay...*".

SHE: "*You know very well; that is even more impossible than separating.*"

...and then, in a sublime finale, the theme of forgetfulness: forgetting Nevers ("*Charming poplars of the Nièvre, I banish you to oblivion. Dime novel story, I banish you to oblivion*"); the forgetting of love imposed by the bizarre, incongruous sound of a voice in English, which suggests the temptation to begin another affair ("*It is very late to be lonely*"); and forgetting oneself [...] (*Alain Resnais*, pp. 47-51).

Henri Bergson — Time in Space

There are two possible conceptions of duration, one pure of any mixture, the other invaded surreptitiously by the idea of space. Pure time is the form taken by our states of consciousness when our mind lets itself go, when it abstains from establishing a separation between the present state and former states. For that, it has no need to immerse itself in whatever sensation or idea that comes along, for then, on the contrary, it would last no longer. Nor does it have any need to forget the former states: it is enough that in recalling these states it does not juxtapose them to the present state like one point to another, but rather organizes them with it, as we do when we recall, as an ensemble, the notes of a melody. Couldn't we say that although these notes follow one another, we still perceive them as part of each other, and that their ensemble is comparable to a living being whose parts, although distinct, are coalesced by the very effect of their unity? [...] This is indubitably the idea of duration which we would expect from a being both identical and changing which had no idea of space. But once familiar with this idea, indeed, obsessed by it, we unknowingly introduce it into our conception of pure succession; we juxtapose our states of consciousness so as to see them simultaneously, no longer in each other, but beside each other; in short, we project time into space, we express time in space, and succession becomes for us a continuous line or a chain whose parts touch but remain separate [...]. There is a real space, without duration, but in which phenomena appear and disappear at the same time as our states of conscience. There is real time, whose heterogeneous moments permeate each other, but each of whose moments may be related to a state of the exterior world that exists at the same time and may separate itself from the other moments by the effect of this very relationship. From the comparison of these two realities is born a symbolic representation of duration, drawn from space. Time thus takes the illusory form of a homogeneous medium, and the link between these two terms, space and time, is simultaneity, which one could define as the intersection of time and space (excerpt from *An Essay on the Immediate Data of Consciousness* in *Œuvres*, pp. 67-68, 73-74) [my translation].

ALAIN RESNAIS'S FILMOGRAPHY
(FEATURE FILMS)

1959	*Hiroshima mon amour*
1961	*Last Year at Marienbad*
	(L'Année dernière à Marienbad)
1963	*Muriel, or the Time of Return*
	(Muriel, ou le temps d'un retour)
1966	*The War is Over (La Guerre est finie)*
1968-69	*Je t'aime, je t'aime*
1973-74	*Stavisky*
1976	*Providence*
1980	*My American Uncle (Mon oncle d'Amérique)*
1983	*Life is a Bed of Roses (La Vie est un roman)*
1984	*Love Unto Death (L'Amour à mort)*
1986	*Mélo*
1989	*I Want To Go Home*
1993	*Smoking No Smoking*
1997	*Same Old Song (On connaît la chanson)*
2003	*Not on the Mouth (Pas sur la bouche)*

WORKS CONSULTED

Bergson, Henri. *Essai sur les données immédiates de la conscience* dans *Œuvres*, 4ᵉ édition. Paris: Presses universitaires de France, 1984 [edit. orig. 1959].

Bounoure, Gaston. *Alain Resnais*. Paris: Seghers, 1962.

Carlier, Christophe. *Marguerite Duras. Alain Resnais. Hiroshima mon amour*. Paris: Presses universitaires de France, 1994.

Colpi, Henri. "Hiroshima musique." *Premier Plan* 4 (Dec. 1959): 18-24.

Cuvillier, Armand. *Textes choisis des auteurs philosophiques*. Paris: Armand Colin, 1967.

Delahaye, Michel. "Un entretien avec Alain Resnais." *Cinéma 59* 38 (July 1959): 4-14.

Durand, Philippe. "Hiroshima mon amour (1959)." *Image et Son* 128 (Feb. 1960), I-XXII.

Duras, Marguerite. *Hiroshima mon amour, scénario et dialogues*. Paris: Gallimard, 1960.

"Hiroshima mon amour." *Cahiers du cinéma* 97 (July 1959): 1-18 (roundtable discussion avec Rivette, Godard, Doniol-Valcroze, Kast, Rohmer, Domarchi).

Leutrat, Jean-Louis. *Hiroshima mon amour*. Paris: Nathan, 1994.

Mascolo, Dionys. "Les Impressions de Marguerite Duras" (interview). *Cinéma 59* 38 (July 1959), 14-15.

Pingaud, Bernard. "Alain Resnais." *Premier Plan* 18 (Oct. 1961): 3-24.

Pingaud, Bernard et Pierre Samson. "Alain Resnais ou la création au cinema." *L'Arc* 31 (1967): 1-124.

Prédal, René. *L'Itinéraire d'Alain Resnais*. Paris : Lettres modernes, 1996.

Ropars-Wuilleumier, Marie-Claire. *De la littérature au cinéma*. Collection "U". Paris: Armand Colin, 1970.

"Spécial Resnais" (screenplay of *Hiroshima mon amour*). *L'Avant-Scène Cinéma* 61-62 (July-Sept. 1966): 5- 82.

Jean-Luc Godard

Breathless
A bout de souffle

(1960)

Jean-Luc Godard, *Breathless*: Patricia (Jean Seberg) kisses Michel
(Jean-Paul Belmondo) in the street. © Raymond Cauchetier-Paris

Director ....Jean-Luc Godard
Screenplay and Dialogues .... Jean-Luc Godard, based on an idea
by François Truffaut
Director of Photography .... Raoul Coutard
Music.. Martial Solal
Film Editors .... Cécile Decugis, assisted by Lila Herman
Sound .... Jacques Maumont
Script Girl (Continuity) ....Suzanne Faye
Producer ....Les Films de Georges de Beauregard
Length .... 1 h 30

Cast

Jean-Paul Belmondo (*Michel Poiccard*), Jean Seberg (*Patricia Franchini*), Van Doude *(the Franco-American journalist)*, Daniel Boulanger (*Inspector Vital*), Henry-Jacques Huet (*Antonio Berruti*), Jean-Pierre Melville (*the novelist Parvulesco*), Richard Balducci (*Tolmatchoff*), Roger Hanin (*Zumbart*), Claude Mansard (*the garageman fence*), Liliane David (*Michel Poiccard's former girlfriend*), Michel Fabre (*Vital's partner*), Jean-Luc Godard (*the informer*).

*The film itself has no credits.

STORY

A young punk, Michel Poiccard, steals a car in Marseilles to drive to Paris, where he wants to pick up some money owed to him for murky reasons. He also hopes to hook up again with a young American student, Patricia Franchini, with whom he has fallen in love during a brief tryst in Nice. He wants to convince her to go to Italy with him. Chased by some motorcycle policemen because he passed illegally, he shoots and kills a policeman and flees on foot in the countryside. Arriving the next morning in Paris, he steals some money from a former girlfriend and then goes to see Patricia, who is selling the *New York Herald Tribune* on the Champs-Elysées. Later, in a travel agency, he finds the friend who has been holding his money for him (Tolmatchoff), but he can't cash the check because it can only be deposited in a bank account. He has to contact another friend, Antonio Berruti, who will be able to cash the check for him.

While waiting, he finds Patricia again and tries to convince her to spend the night with him. She leaves him to go meet a journalist who has promised to help her learn the trade. The next morning, when Patricia comes back to her hotel room, she finds Michel in her bed, where he slept the previous night. They play out a long scene in the room before finally making love, In the afternoon Michel drives Patricia to the Orly airport, where she joins other reporters in an interview of a novelist, Parvulesco.

Meanwhile, the Parisian police inspector Vital, is hot on the trail of Michel, who has been quickly identified as the cop-killer — which Michel learns in reading the newspaper headlines. The police question Patricia and threaten to create trouble for her with her residency card if she is not cooperative, after which they tail her on the Champs-Elysées through a huge crowd watching a parade. Michel and Patricia manage to lose the police, then go to the movies, steal a car in a parking garage, and finally find Berruti that evening in the Montparnasse quarter of Paris. They spend the night in the studio apartment of a friend's mistress while Michel waits for Berruti to bring the money the following morning. Early in the morning, Patricia calls the police to tell them where Michel is hiding. Michel is shot down in the street by Inspector Vital as he tries to run off.

CRITICAL RECEPTION

As shown by Michel Marie, *Breathless* benefited from a huge advertising campaign before it came out (1999, p. 115): numerous articles in the press (with contradictory opinions), many production photos in the newspapers, posters, a record with the music from the film — and even a film-novel, which came out in February 1960. When the film came out in Paris on March 16, 1960 (no one under 18 allowed), it was immediately successful, thanks in part to the advertising hype, but especially because it spoke to a new generation which recognized its own world in the characters' style — their manner of dress, their slangy speech, their sexual relations — as well as in the places they hang out in, as opposed to the artificial world created by the screenwriters of the big studios producing highly polished films. The spectators' appreciation of the film ratified the reaction of the film critics, who applauded loudly the stylistic boldness of Godard, the iconoclasm of his first feature film. The acclaim of the press was confirmed by the awarding of the prestigious Prix Jean Vigo in February, followed by the Golden Bear (the First Prize for directing) at the Berlin Film Festival. The German Critics Prize for photography was awarded to Raoul Coutard.

Breathless quickly became the "manifesto" of the "New Wave," representing both the revolt of the new filmmakers against the narrow classicism of the cinematographic establishment in France and a declaration of new principles. In American colleges and universities, it is today the most frequently watched film of the French "New Wave." Its continuing popularity in the United States was demonstrated, moreover, by Jim MacBride's remake in 1982, *Breathless*, with Richard Gere and Valérie Kaprisky.

BEFORE *BREATHLESS*

Born in Paris on December 3, 1930, Jean-Luc Godard received his early education in Switzerland, then in Paris and Grenoble, before completing a program in ethnology at the Sorbonne at the beginning of the fifties. Passionately interested in cinema, he belonged to a group of young critics writing for the *Cahiers du cinema*, in which he began publishing articles in 1952. He soon turned to making films, beginning with five short subjects: *Operation Concrete* (*Opération béton*, 1954), a rather classical documentary on the construction of a hydroelectric dam in Switzerland; *A Coquette* (*Une femme coquette*, 1955, 16 mm), his first fiction film, based on a Maupassant tale (*Le Signe*) but never distributed; *Charlotte and Véronique* or *All The Boys Are Named Patrick* (*Charlotte et Véronique* ou *Tous les garcons s'appellent Patrick*, 1957), his first success; *A Water Story* (*Une histoire d'eau*, 1958), and, most interesting of all, *Charlotte and Her Guy* (*Charlotte et son Jules*, 1959). The latter film, in which Jean-Paul Belmondo plays the main role, resembles in certain respects a preliminary sketch of the long scene in Patricia's room in *Breathless*. In addition to the short subjects, Godard edited and wrote dialogue for films by other directors, an exercise which gave him training in filmmaking which paid off in *Breathless*. Nonetheless, Godard was the only member of the group of film critics of the *Cahiers* who, in 1959, still hadn't made his first feature film. He caught up fast.

ORIGIN AND ACTORS

Breathless is based on an incident in November, 1952, which caused quite a stir at the time. Michel Portail, a charming young man of rather shady character, fell in love with a young American newspaperwoman in Paris. He stole a car and killed the motorcycle policeman who had simply tried to stop him because he had a bad headlight. Around 1956 François Truffaut used the newspaper item as the basis for a short, four-page story synopsis that he later gave to Godard. Godard developed it into a full-blown screen-play, completely transformed, keeping only the basic story as it was adapted by Truffaut — the theft of the car, the murder of the policeman, the love affair with the American girl and her betrayal of the "hero." All the rest is made up by Godard: the development of the hero's and the heroine's personality, their complex relationship, the principal themes, and the killing of Michel Poiccard at the end of the film. In a letter to Truffaut, Godard summarized his screen play as follows: "Its subject will be the story of a young man who thinks about death and a young woman who doesn't. The action will concern a car thief [...] who is in love with a girl who sells the New York Herald Tribune and takes French civilization courses." Godard wrote all of the dialogues also.

At the outset, Godard wanted simply to imitate an American gangster film like *Scarface* by Howard Hawks (1932) or *Fallen Angel* by Otto Preminger (1945), or at the very least a "B" film like *Gun Crazy* by J.H. Lewis (1949). However, Godard's personal genius is inimical to any servile imitation. Playing off a deep literary and cinematographic culture, he created an entirely new type of film which would represent, in fact, the inauguration of the "New Wave" style.

The two stars of *Breathless*, Jean-Paul Belmondo and Jean Seberg, played a crucial role in the film's success. Godard had noticed Belmondo, a student at the Dramatic Arts Conservatory, in several films in which he played minor roles and considered him unusually gifted as an actor, "tomorrow's Michel Simon and Jules Berry." (As we've remarked above, Godard gave Belmondo the main role in his short subject *Charlotte et son Jules* made a few months before *Breathless*.) Jean Seberg, a 21-year-old American actress, was already an international star, having played the role of Jeanne d'Arc in the Preminger film *Saint Joan* (1956) and the role of the young American high-school girl, Cécile, beside the Hollywood superstars David Niven and Deborah Kerr, in Preminger's adaptation of Françoise Sagan's hit novel *Bonjour Tristesse* (1957). The presence of Seberg in Godard's film was no small factor in its commercial success.

FILMING, EDITING, STYLE

Godard's comment has become famous: "What I wanted was to begin with a conventional story and then to redo, but differently, all the cinema that had ever been made" (Collet et al., p. 22). Godard might be suspected of immodesty, and he certainly didn't reinvent world cinema from top to bottom, but he did succeed, with a single blow, in upsetting long-established habits in the manner of making fiction films — to such an extent that critics were moved to speak of the creation, in *Breathless*, of a new film esthetics. What's it all about?

As far as filming goes, it's above all about going fast. Godard finished the whole film in about a month, from August 17 to September 19, on location in Paris and in Marseilles primarily, working with a very small crew—as opposed to the big studios with their crowds of technicians of every stripe. To be able to work without tripods and cranes, Raoul Coutard, the director of photography, used a hand-held camera. No laying down of tracks for the travelling shots — Coutard just sat in a wheelchair, propelled forward or backward by Godard. To film in the street among the passersby, much the same method was employed, except that the cameraman was hidden in a post office cart. To obviate the need for heavy, cumbersome lights, and the additional personnel that requires, the crew filmed in natural light, both exteriors and interiors, using an extra-sensitive film normally reserved for photographs. No need for sound technicians either; Godard filmed without sound, finding it quicker to add the sound track later, despite the difficulties this entailed. Godard wrote the dialogue in fact at the last moment, each day during the filming. Working without recording the sound allowed him to give the dialogue to the actors as he filmed; this is not only a striking innovation but reduced to a minimum the time required for rehearsal. And finally, the actors didn't even use makeup, so there was no need for the usual bevy of makeup girls who flutter around the sound stages of the studios. In any case, Godard didn't use studio set-ups, preferring to film in real interiors and exteriors. The result: not only did Godard make his film in record time, but it cost only a third (45 million francs) of a normal feature film.

In another innovative move, Godard integrated into his film television-style reporting. To the technique of the hidden camera mentioned above, he added scenes which evoke television interviews (the novelist Parvulesco at the airport) and news shorts (the filming of the crowd which has gathered to see De Gaulle and Eisenhower ride down the Champs-Elysées). Finally, Godard rejected the classical angle-reverse angle technique in filming the dialogues. He filmed Michel and Patricia together, for instance, in a long sequence shot, while they walked down the Champs-Elysées, or he allowed Patricia to move off-camera, then return, during her dialogue with Michel in her hotel room, instead of alternating shots of the two characters as was usually done. In short, Godard refused to respect the conventions and do as everyone else did.

It is in the editing of the film, however, that Godard's originality, his scorn for traditional practices, is the most striking (see the analysis of the Highway 7 sequence by Michel Marie, in the *Critical Dossier*). As in the filming, the style of editing is characterized by speed. In fact, Godard alternated long sequence shots with very short shots, but he creates the impression of a quick, nervous rhythm which underlies and accentuates the behavior of the hero: "As we move from shot to shot the film jumps forward impatiently, with a syncopated rhythm that suggests and emphasizes the impulsive demeanor of the hero in his descent toward destiny" (quoted in Bordwell, p. 90). The impression of rapidity is due, of course, to the quick cutting, but also to the rather revolutionary use of "jump cuts," which give the impression of "jumping" from one shot to the next, breaking the continuity of the action. Critics have often spoken of errors in the continuity editing of *Breathless*, and Georges Sadoul declared, when the film came out, "a competent film editor can't watch *Breathless* without wincing: the continuity between every other shot is faulty." Sadoul, who was very savvy, added however, "Who cares? These aren't spelling errors but stylistic flourishes." It is true

Jump cut   cut within scene more than betw.
scenes (remove a part of
a scene)

276   *French Cinema - The Student's Book*

that we are not dealing with real mistakes in editing here. The jump cuts are due to a deliberate decision by Godard to shorten his film, which was forty-five minutes too long, by cutting fragments from within the shots, rather than cutting out whole shots (or even entire sequences). Critics have counted up to 75 jump cuts in the film, certain sequences containing multiple jump cuts, such as the segment where Michel drives the stolen car at the beginning of the film, the scene at the café where the newspaperman tells his story to Patricia, or the long scene in Patricia's room. The most striking case is certainly the sequence in the convertible where we see eleven successive jump cuts in shots of Patricia's head and neck during her dialogue with Michel, who remains off-camera. Godard has explained how this came about: "…there was a sequence with Belmondo and Seberg in the car, and we alternated shots between him and her as they conversed. In this case, instead of shortening each of the shots a little, we flipped a coin to decide which character's shots we would keep, while eliminating entirely the shots of the other. Seberg won."

The use of jump cuts is hardly a new phenomenon in movies, as David Bordwell demonstrates ("La sauté et l'ellipse"), but the systematic use by Godard—the series of successive jump cuts—turns it into a basic stylistic characteristic of an original conception of film form. Godard created, in fact, a new film esthetics based on the principle of discontinuity, diametrically opposed to conventional practice which had always aspired, from the beginning of the fiction film, to produce (by hiding the editing) an impression of spatiotemporal continuity, of "transparency," of "reality." The jump cuts in *Breathless* intentionally destroy this impression, drawing attention both to the means of expression, the form, and the intervention of the filmmaker. At the same time, Godard's style constituted an act of provocation, an insolent challenge, indeed a thumbing of the nose to the whole cinematographic establishment. This gesture of revolt expressed the spirit of the New Wave and spoke clearly to the hearts and minds of the generation of the sixties which was inaugurated by Godard's film.

SOUND TRACK AND LANGUAGE

The sound track of *Breathless* makes no small contribution to the rhythm and style of the film, beginning with the music composed by Martial Solal. Although the use of jazz in films was not invented by Godard—Marcel Carné had used jazz music in *Les Tricheurs* (*The Cheaters*) in 1955, for example, as well as Roger Vadim in *Les Liaisons dangereuses 1960* in 1959—the music supports the fast editing and the jump cuts by reinforcing the feeling of speed and energy, the impression of a breathless and exhausting headlong dash suggested by the title of the film. The improvised style of jazz is perfectly suited, moreover, both to the cavalier behavior of the hero, who improvises constantly to survive, and to the very technique of Godard, who gives the impression (although it isn't always true) of improvising his film.

Jazz

The sound effects, post-synchronized like the dialogues, are clearly indicative of Godard's desire to create a realistic, everyday atmosphere: horns blaring, the sound of car engines, snatches of radio shows, and so on. This penchant for realism is detectable in the personal language of the hero, who employs a familiar, spontaneous style of speech full of rather crude street slang which was unheard of in French film before Godard: "*Oh, shit, the cops,*" "*Piece o' crap,*" "*What a pain in the ass,*" "*Beat it, you lousy bitch."* Godard's style was heavily indebted to a recent film by the ethnologist Jean Rouch, *Moi un noir* (*Me, A Black Man*, 1958), whose "cinéma vérité" style, familiar language, use of spontaneous monologue and speech directed at the public in the theater, and the general originality of the sound track all clearly influenced the making of *A bout de soufflé*. On the other hand, literary quotations, cultural references (painting, music), and philosophical reflections are scattered throughout the film, to such an extent that incongruity becomes one of its defining characteristics.

THEMES

François Truffaut relates that Godard "was really in despair when he made this film. He felt the need to film death..." (Collet, p. 172). Death is, of course, a major theme of *Breathless*, which begins with the murder of the motorcycle policeman and finishes with the death of the hero, with the traffic death of the man on the scooter sandwiched between the two. Allusions to death occur throughout the film, sometimes explicitly (Michel: "*Do you think about death sometimes? I think about it all the time,"* or the quotation from Lenin: "*We are all dead people on leave*"), sometimes more subtly, like the role of the motorcycle policemen who remind us of the messengers of death in Jean Cocteau's *Orphée* (Marie, 1999, p. 84). An even more subtle reference to death may be seen in the use of the Clarinet Concerto by Mozart in the studio apartment scene near the end of the film, a piece written shortly before the composer's decease and thus foreshadowing Michel's own demise.

Just as in *Le Jour se lève* (*Daybreak*, 1939), Marcel Carné's masterpiece, the theme of death is closely linked to that of fate. Like François's, Michel's "destiny" is set from the beginning of the film; the die is cast as soon as he kills the policeman. This act certainly explains in part Michel's obsession with death. The fate which holds him in its grasp is rendered tangible throughout the film by the photos and the headlines of the newspaper *France-Soir*, which trace the progress of the investigation into the highway policeman's murder. The newspaper items are relayed by the huge lighted sign on the building in Paris which continues to foretell Michel's doom as the police close in on their target: "*The net is tightening around Michel Poiccard,"* followed by "*Michel Poiccard: Arrest is imminent."*

Other major themes of the film are speed (the role of cars, for instance) and love, suggesting together the "rage to live," a wild pursuit of gratification. The theme of liberty develops as a counterpoint to love in the film; for Michel on the one hand, for whom love is a shackle which prevents him from leaving Paris, from fleeing; for Patricia on the other, for whom the yearning for freedom seems to be the cause of her profound ambivalence toward Michel. A certain pessimism can be perceived as regards the relationship between the sexes, due largely to the lack of communication which prevents the hero and the heroine from understanding each other. Language itself becomes a theme in the film, as an obstacle. In both the literal and figurative senses, Michel and Patricia don't speak the same language; they don't live in the same world. As Godard puts it, "Patricia the American lives on a psychological plane, while Michel lives on a poetic plane. They use words—the same words—which don't have the same meaning.

Cinema itself, finally, is transformed into a theme in *Breathless* by the repeated explicit references in the film. In addition to the particular films which are introduced (and which we will speak of below), we note, for example, the role of cinema as a means of escape: Patricia succeeds in losing the plainclothes cop who has been tailing her by ducking into a cinema; Michel and Patricia take refuge in a cinema to hide from the police. There is, in addition, the issue of the *Cahiers du cinéma* that the girl is selling in the street, the presence of filmmakers in the film (Jean-Pierre Melville in the role of the novelist Parvulesco, Godard himself as the informer), and even the use of old-fashioned punctuation techniques like the iris out and iris in, which evoke early cinema. And we cannot exclude the possibility of an intentional reference to cinema in the parallel established between the character of Michel, who scorns social conventions, and Godard himself, who scorns cinematographic conventions. Godard and Poiccard are undeniably similar in their "improvisational" style, as we mentioned above, but also because both suffer from a lack of money, and both have to go fast if they want to survive. As Truffaut observes, "While he was making *Breathless*, Godard didn't have enough change in his pocket to buy a subway ticket; he was just as destitute—actually more—than the character he was filming" (quoted by Marie, 1989, p. 54). Michel's character, who identifies with movie heroes, seems to evoke the theme of cinema on several registers.

CINEMATIC QUOTATIONS, INTERTEXTUALITY

Godard openly admitted his penchant for "quotations" (references to other films in his own films), a taste he shared, moreover, with the whole gang at the *Cahiers du cinema*. The *mise en abyme* (inscription) of cinema in *Breathless* creates an intertextual network which enriches the film for everyone and delights in particular cinephiles who are capable of recognizing the subtle allusions. The explicit references are already rather numerous, beginning with the cinema posters for recent American films such as *The Harder They Fall* by Mark Robson (1956), with Humphrey Bogart (Michel's model), *Ten Seconds To Hell* by Robert Aldrich (1959), with its caption "Live dangerously to the end," or *Westbound* by Budd Boeticher (1959).

Other quotations are more refined, less direct, as Dudley Andrew demonstrates with multiple examples (pp. 14-18): the scene where Michel knocks a man out in the restroom to rob him comes right out of *The Enforcer* by Raoul Walsh (1951); the shot where Patricia looks at Michel through a rolled-up poster recalls a similar scene in *Forty Guns* by Samuel Fuller (1957) in which we look through the barrel of a rifle; the teddy bear that Michel plays with in Patricia's room, as well as the ever-present cigarette, recalls the character of Jean Gabin in Marcel Carné's *Daybreak*; the episode in the car in which Michel fires three shots at the sun is a clear reference to an act by the hero of *The Tiger of Bengal* by Fritz Lang (1959); the man lying in the street after being run down by a car is an homage to Jean Rouch's *Me, A Black Man*, in which the protagonist exhibits the same nonchalant attitude toward death as Michel. And we cannot overlook the alias of Michel, "Laszlo Kovacs," borrowed from the Resistance leader in Michael Curtiz's famous film *Casablanca* (1942), whose hero is played by none other than Humphrey Bogart. *Breathless* is thus shot through with intertextual references which render the film far denser, far more complex than one might suspect at the first viewing.

Chèque barré : for deposit only, not cash

STUDY GUIDE

Director's Comments

"Our first films were pure cinephile films. You can use what you've already seen in films to make deliberate references. That was my case especially. My thought was informed by purely cinematographic considerations. I used certain shots in imitation of those I had seen in films by Preminger, Cukor, etc. [...]. It is closely related to my penchant for quotations, which I've never lost.

In addition, *Breathless* was the type of film in which there were no limits; that was its nature. Whatever the actors did, it could be integrated into the film. That was actually my point of departure. I thought: there's been Bresson; we've just had *Hiroshima*; a certain type of cinema has just drawn to a close; maybe it's over, so let's finish it off, let's show that there are no limits. What I wanted to do was to start with a conventional story and redo, but differently, all the cinema that had already been done. I also wanted to create the impression that we had just discovered the basic film techniques for the first time. The iris in showed that we had the right to return to the origins of cinema, and the dissolve came all by itself, as if we had just invented it [...].

If we used a hand-held camera, it was so we could go fast, that's all. I didn't have the luxury of using all the normal equipment, which would have added three weeks to the shooting. But that shouldn't be taken as a rule; the type of filming you do is always a function of your subject [...].

What was difficult for me was the ending. Was the hero going to die? At the beginning I thought I would do the opposite of *The Killing*: the gangster wins and leaves for Italy with his money [...]. I finally decided, since I had set out to make a typical gangster film, that I shouldn't try to deviate systematically from the genre: the guy had to die. If the Atrides stop killing each other, they just aren't the Atrides any more" (Collet et al., "J.-L. Godard," p. 22).

"*Breathless* is my film, but not a film I wrote. It's just a variation on a theme of Truffaut's, who wrote the original story.

Based on Truffaut's theme, I wrote the story of an American girl and a young Frenchman. They don't get along because he thinks about death and she doesn't. I thought that if I didn't add this idea to the story the film wouldn't be interesting. The young man has been obsessed with the idea of death for a long time; he has premonitions. That's why I filmed the street scene where the guy gets run over and dies. I quoted these words by Lenin: "We are all dead people on leave," and I chose the Concerto for Clarinet that Mozart wrote shortly before his death [...].

Patricia the American lives on a psychological plane, while Michel lives on a poetic plane. They use words—the same words—which don't have the same meaning. It happens…

When she betrays her lover to the police, Patricia pushes herself to the limit, and that's why I find her touching. In the film we don't see the night before the betrayal. I prefer showing the scene where the girl acts [...].

I didn't improvise anything. I had jotted down a mess of disorganized notes and written some scenes and dialogues. Before beginning the film I put these notes in order and had a general plan. This structure was enough for me to compose, each morning, the eight pages for the sequence I was going to shoot that day. With the exception of certain scenes previously worked out, I stuck to this work schedule and wrote my daily several minutes of film. The director of photography, Raoul Coutard, worked with the camera on his shoulder, with no artificial lighting and on location. The shooting took four weeks. How do I direct actors? I give a lot of small suggestions and try to get the essential gestures from them…" (Interview with Yvonne Baby, *Le Monde*, January 18, 1960).

Excerpts for Discussion

Excerpt 1 (00'10-1'40): The beginning of the film, at the Old Port of Marseilles (Michel's character).

Excerpt 2 (3'55-5'20): Michel driving the stolen car; the murder of the motorcycle policeman (quick cutting, continuity questions). ***See the analysis of this sequence in "'Reading' a Film," pp. 31-33.**

Excerpt 3 (9'40-13'30): Michel and Patricia on the Champs-Elysées; Patricia runs across the street and kisses Michel (long aerial down shot); close-up of the cinema poster ("Live dangerously to the end"); girl selling the *Cahiers du cinéma*; death of the pedestrian in the street; the newspaper.

Excerpt 4 (13'30-16'05): Michel meets Tolmatchoff at the travel agency (long sequence shot).

Excerpt 5 (18'10-19'00): Michel standing in front of the poster of the film starring Bogart; thumb across the lips gesture; iris out, then iris in.

Excerpt 6 (21'45-23'10): Patricia in the convertible with Michel: Michel's voice-over and a series of jump cuts between shots of the back of Patricia's head and neck.

Excerpt 7 (24'15-25'15): Patricia's dark thoughts; the newspaperman tells his story about the girl he was supposed to sleep with (series of jump cuts).

Excerpt 8 (34'20-38'10): Michel and Patricia together in her room (the camera work, posters, dialogue) ; the theme of death.

Excerpt 9 (44'20-47'05): Close-ups, love, Faulkner (sorrow and oblivion).

Excerpt 10 (54'30-55'40): Michel and the informer in front of the Herald-Tribune office, the headlines; the role of Godard in the film.

Excerpt 11 (1h09'00-10'55): The parade on the Champs-Elysées; Patricia tailed by a policeman, who is tailed by Michel; escape through cinema.

Excerpt 12 (1h25'50-29'15): The denouement on the rue Campagne-Première; Michel's death.

Quotations for Comment

Michel: "Do you think of death sometimes? I think of it all the time."

* * *

Patricia (quoting Faulkner): "Between sorrow and oblivion, I choose sorrow."
Michel: "I choose oblivion."

* * *

Patricia: "It's wrong to betray."

Michel: "No, it's normal. Traitors betray, burglars burglarize, killers kill, lovers love…".

* * *

Michel: "When we talked together, I talked about myself and you about yourself, whereas you should have been talking about me and I about you."

* * *

Patricia: "I don't want to be in love with you…that's why I called the police…If I'm mean to you, that proves that I'm not in love with you…now you have no choice but to leave."

distancing in the film?

Questions/Topics for Reflection

1. Michel Poiccard's character. What is he seeking in life?
2. The theme of death (allusions in the film).
3. How does Godard emphasize the theme of "fate" in his film? *Compare to Camus*
4. Patricia Franchini's character, her ambivalence. What is she seeking in life?
5. The role of love (or desire) in the film.
6. The problem of communication between Michel and Patricia; the question of language. *Compare to Renoir*
7. The theme of speed; the role of cars.
8. The denouement of the film.
9. References to cinema in *Breathless*; the "role" of cinema. *Compare to Truffaut*
10. Innovations in film editing by Godard.

Is below. Hiroshima & 400 blows What aspects of modern life does he represent?

CRITICAL DOSSIER

Louis Séguin — "A Film for Fools"

   …*Breathless* is nonetheless the most contrived, the most rigged of films, and its techniques are the most simplistic. You have your characters say one thing, then, a little later, just the opposite, and then you just pass off this stupid contradiction as an example of the ambiguity of life itself. And the same goes for the style. You try to appear "objective" by following your characters' peregrinations with "dazzling" camera movements while not bothering to supply transitions between the various shots. The film becomes chaotic, and you try to pass that off as a flash of genius.

   Claiming, like the director and the "Communist" film critic quoted above [Georges Sadoul], that the hero of this film is a new and improved version of the outlaw of *Port of Shadows* (*Quai des brumes*, 1938) is an aberration. The nineteen-thirties deserter was respectable because he was part of a leftwing, albeit phony, mythology. The little hoodlum of 1960, who says he likes the police, and his girlfriend who, according to Godard, affirms her personality by betraying him to the cops, belong to another mythology, just as artificial and perfectly detestable, since it's reactionary in nature. Gabin the anarchist was made of the same stuff as the fighters in the International

Brigades; Belmondo the anarchist is like the little creeps who write "Death to Jews!" on the walls of the subway, and misspell it ("Quoi de Neuf," p. 49).

Marcel Martin — Godard

Whatever you say, this joker is talented. It doesn't really matter that his film's style is a function of his incompetence, as someone said: cinema isn't defined by the grammatical correctness of its continuity. By thumbing his nose at all the rules, he's managed to create a new style, even if the references are clear. And I'm not talking about his scorn for technical conventions; that's not what's important. What counts is the dynamic boldness of a narrative which shows no concern for logical or chronological continuity, the creation of a spatiotemporal universe which is specifically cinematographic because it is deliberately non-realistic and absolutely subjective: the fluid camera movements, the free-wheeling editing, the disruption of our familiar world of sounds all contribute to the creation of a quasi-surreal universe in which the fantastic is not born of the strangeness of things but of the strangeness of the filmmaker's vision ("*A bout de souffle*," p. 118).

Luc Moullet — "An Attempt at Liberation Through Cinema"

[…] the Godard-Seberg pair yielded magnificent results, probably because we find in Seberg this dialect that Godard likes so much. Although she tries to appear masculine, with her manner of living and her boyish haircut, it just makes her more feminine. Everyone knows that a woman is much sexier in pants and short hair, because it eliminates everything superficial from her femininity.

Patricia becomes more admirable when she places her call to the police. It is an act of courage. She finally decides to make a move to extricate herself from the terrible imbroglio she has gotten herself into. But, like all courageous acts, it's the easy way out. And Michel reproaches her bitterly, because he, on the other hand, accepts wholeheartedly his own nature: he plays the game, doesn't like half-measures, and embraces completely his perpetual dilemma. But he plays the game too well: his death will be the natural penalty demanded by logic, the spectator, and morality. He's gone too far…

It's at this point that we realize that Godard, who identifies literally with his hero, distances himself from him slightly, thanks to his other personality, that of the objective, cruel, entomological filmmaker. Godard is Michel and is not Michel, since he is neither an assassin nor dead, far from it. Why does the author have this slight, disturbing superiority over his character? Because Michel is only a potential double for Godard. He does what Godard only dreams of doing. The scene where Michel goes and pulls up the Parisian girl's dress shows the difference clearly. Some have accused *A bout de souffle* of having an essentially psychoanalytical justification. While there is no doubt the cinema begins where psychoanalysis ends, when the filmmaker is conscious of the peculiarities of his soul and of their vanity, they can become a source of beauty. *A bout de souffle* is an attempt at liberation through cinema: Godard is not — is no longer — Michel because he made *Breathless*, and Michel did not ("Jean-Luc Godard," pp. 32-33).

Jean-Luc Douin — Michel and Patricia

[…] Like Jean Seberg, Patricia is charming. She stumbles over words, walks on top of the metal "nails" of the cross-walks, balancing herself, enrolls in the Sorbonne and compares her profile to that of Renoir's model, talks to herself in the mirror, pulls up the strap of her sexy striped sweater in public. Like Belmondo, Poiccard is a seductive blowhard, amoral and childish, who enjoys singing off-key, gets into bed with his white socks on, is whacky about the countryside and the Place de la Concorde at night, and puts on his hat to use the telephone. Nonetheless, it's a tragedy.

They are in love with each other, but they're afraid to love each other. Patricia would like to know what there is behind Michel's face; she looks at him for ten minutes but she knows absolutely nothing. She wants to be loved, then she doesn't. Michel can't live without Patricia, or perhaps he could but doesn't want to; he wants to go to bed with her, but she doesn't want to; she's carrying his child but he doesn't want it; he's sick and tired of being interested in girls who aren't his type; he wants her to give him a smile or he'll strangle her, and perhaps if she gives him a smile, it's because she's a coward.

Cowardice. *Breathless* is a film about foreboding, betrayal, death stalking and providing relief. There's a guy who gets run over and dies on the Champs-Elysées. There's this poster: "*Live dangerously to the end.*" There's this saying by Lenin: "*We're all dead people on leave.*" There's this concerto for clarinet that Mozart wrote just before his death. There is fatigue and confusion. "*I'm fed up, I'm tired. In prison no one will talk to me*"; the obsession: "*Do you think about death sometimes? — "I think about it all the time.*"

Breathless is a film about opaqueness, the difficulty people living in this society have being what they claim to be, knowing what they are, accepting the ambiguity of people and sentiments. "*I don't know if I'm unhappy because I'm not free, or if I'm not free because I'm unhappy.*" Patricia is free and unhappy […].

Godard, for his part, wants to bet on love. Because it's the only good alternative to Nothingness. The nothingness of Patricia, who, her eyes closed, tries to plunge into oblivion and, her head in her hands, would like to "*think of something, but I don't know what, I just can't think.*" The nothingness of Poiccard who behaves like a rebel, a forerunner of Mai 68, an older brother of tomorrow's young toughs, a censor of a "disgusting" world. Poiccard who, "*between sorrow and nothingness,*" contrary to Faulkner, chooses nothingness because "*sorrow is a compromise.*" Poiccard who, in fact, didn't choose nothingness; he's just in it […] (*Jean-Luc Godard*, pp. 122-123).

David Bordwell — Jump Cuts in *Breathless*

If we move now to 1960, the third moment of the jump cut's insertion into commercial fictional cinema, we can see again some specific formal circumstances governing its perception. Consider how *A bout de souffle* employs cutting as a technique. Whereas the Soviet montage films included many types of temporal discontinuity (ellipsis, overlapping, repetition), Godard's film makes use only of ellipsis. Here a discontinuous cut always signifies that on the visual track some time has been skipped: sometimes a great deal of time, sometimes only a little. In this film visual time always moves forward, albeit in leaps. Moreover, *A bout de souffle* provides a great deal more spatial continuity than its Soviet predecessors: we are usually well-oriented to the overall space of the action. Add to this that the shots are on the average much longer (over eleven seconds) and the jump cuts tend to occur in clusters of two or more, and we can see how on purely internal grounds the jump cut is foregrounded in *A bout de souffle* [...].

With *A bout de souffle*, "Godard" the author became a figure of the cinematic institution, and reviewers responded. *A bout de souffle* "establishes that he has a style of his own and a point of view." "What is especially interesting is the original style that Godard has devised to tell his story." One component of this style was the jump cut and now critics noticed it. "The montage often skips like a needle on a record." "Often there are cuts made within the same shot." Some reviewers even called these disjunctions jump cuts. (The earliest usage of the term in print seems to be *Variety's* 1960 review of *A bout de souffle*.) Most important, the film's jump cuts were interpreted along now-familiar lines. There was, for instance, the appeal to character psychology. "At each cut the film jerks ahead with a syncopated impatience that aptly suggests and stresses the compulsive pace of the hero's doom-ward drive." The cuts shift our attention "as abruptly as the young man himself loses interest in one matter and goes on to the next." The film's style is thus "the style cultivated by Michael as an expression of impermissible masculine virtuosity." The jump cuts were also naturalized as realism: they do not tell a story but render "a sensation or an experience with the kind of chances and hazards that intervene in life." Alternatively, the jump cuts were read as Godard's own asides, his specific "tone of voice," his "personal signature, an index of his modernity," or his sheer virtuosity: "Godard tries more cinematic tricks than most moviemakers risk in an entire career." The art cinema's canons of character subjectivity, verisimilitude, authorial presence and personal style engendered a criticism prepared to see films in these terms; the jump cut in *A bout de souffle* was suitable for all these functions.

Just as Hollywood cinema eventually domesticated Soviet montage, so the norms of classical narrative filmmaking absorbed the jump cut in certain ways [...]. "When he wanted to move Belmondo from his bedroom to the street across town where Jean Seberg is peddling the *Herald Tribune*, he simply cut from the bedroom to the street." Jump cuts in the sense I have been considering here are of course anathema to mainstream filmmaking, but [...] Godard's film supplied a rationale for slightly expanding the range of permissible discontinuities... ("Jump Cuts and Blind Spots," pp. 8-10).

Michel Marie — The Highway 7 Sequence

This second sequence of the film lasts about 3 minutes and 40 seconds and includes 41 shots. And it is particularly difficult to cut up into shots because they are often so short and the continuity editing between the shots can only be perceived in slow-motion, frame by frame.

The sequence is downright brilliant from a rhythmic standpoint. It is a veritable demonstration of the power of editing and a rejection, by its example, of the hackneyed character of the conventional approach to continuity.... [The spectator] is captivated by the rapidity of the shots, the elliptical treatment of the action, and the free-wheeling tone of the character. This relationship is made clear by the famous remark by Poiccard:

"If you don't like the sea, if you don't like the mountains, if you don't like cities… go screw yourself!" From the outset, *Breathless* attacks the spectator in order to destabilize him, to dumbfound and charm him. The Godardian strategy is brutal. Take it or leave it. Forty years later, this radical attitude makes the same innovative impression. It's what establishes the work as a manifest, literally thrown in the spectator's face, questioning him directly as if he were sitting in the back seat of the American car that Poiccard is driving […].

The long dissolve between Sequence 1 and Sequence 2 brings into view the road as the driver sees it. The first shot of Sequence 2 is relatively long also (18 seconds). The camera's eye is that of the driver. Everything is arranged to make the spectator identify with Michel's viewpoint. The spectator drives along with him. He's happy and sings joyously *"La la lala…la la lala…"* on the tune of the song whose refrain he sings: *"Buenas noches, mi amor…"* He hasn't yet pronounced Patricia's name, but the song is the prelude.

Godard recreates here, with an extraordinary authenticity, rare in movies, the typical monologue of a guy driving alone, in a hurry to get where he's going. Simultaneously, and very cleverly, he reveals the intentions of his hero through the monologue: *"So, I'm going to get the money, I'll ask Patricia if she's coming or not, and then…Buenas noches, mi amor…Milano! Genova! Roma!"*

[…] The editing alternates close-ups of the driver and quick shots of the road. The first three jump cuts [while Michel sings *"Pa…pa…papapapa…Patricia!"*] move the action forward in the same direction; they contribute to the dynamic character of the trip in the car, in much the same way as the musical and verbal rhythm. Rapid swish pans emphasize the car's movement forward (accompanied by a loud honking of the horn).

The monologue […] helps us appreciate Michel's behavior: his fascination with speed, his arrogance, his aggressive, ostentatious misogyny, matching his sentimentality (he is in love with Patricia and is obsessed with her name).

Shot 33 [where Michel arrives at the spot where men are working on the road] is the longest of this sequence: 22 seconds, which represent a pause, a break in the rhythm: *"You shouldn't ever put on the brakes… ."* From shot 34 to the end of the sequence, there is an uninterrupted series of moving shots lasting from one to several seconds, joined by jump cuts or continuity errors. It's the logic of the chase scene and the events which are put into motion. By shooting at the sun, Michel, like the architect hero of the *Tiger of Bengal* by Fritz Lang, has challenged destiny. The motorcycle cops, like the messengers of death in Jean Cocteau's *Orphée*, attack him from all sides (the two policemen who are chasing the car suddenly go by from right to left, in the opposite direction they were going before). The absurdity of Michel's act [killing the policeman] is conveyed by the speed of the series of images and the unrealistic decomposition of the act of shooting. When Michel gets ready to shoot the motorcycle cop, there is first an extreme close-up of his profile, before the camera moves from his hat to his forearm and then to his hand. A first shot change goes from his arm to his hand. A second change links to a lateral tracking shot in extreme close-up on the cylinder and the barrel of the gun, accompanied by the sound of the shot. One can discern two jump cuts. The length of these shots is less than a second.

[…] The only real continuity error involves the death of the motorcycle cop, because […] the editing contradicts the directional logic: the gun is pointed to the right when the shot rings out, but the policeman falls to the left (*A bout de souffle*, 1999, pp. 69, 79-84).

JEAN-LUC GODARD'S FILMOGRAPHY (FEATURE FILMS)

1959	*Breathless (A bout de souffle)*
1960	*The Little Soldier (Le Petit Soldat)*
1961	*A Woman is a Woman (Une femme est une femme)*
1962	*My Life To Live (Vivre sa vie)*
1963	*The Soldiers (Les Carabiniers)*, *Contempt (Le Mépris)*
1964	*Band of Outsiders (Bande à part)*,
	A Married Woman (Une femme mariée)
1965	*Alphaville*
1966	*Masculin-Féminin,*
	Made in U.S.A.,
	Two Or Three Things I Know About Her
	(Deux ou trois choses que je sais d'elle)
1967	*La Chinoise, Weekend*
1968	*Joyful Wisdom (Le Gai savoir),*
	One plus One
1972	*Everything's Fine (Tout va bien)*
1979	*Every Man For Himself [Sauve qui peut (la vie)]*
1981	*Passion*
1982	*First Name: Carmen (Prénom Carmen,*
	Golden Lion at the Venice Film Festival 1983)
1983	*Hail Mary (Je vous salue, Marie)*
1984	*Détective*
1986	*Grandeur et décadence d'un petit commerce de cinéma*
1987	*Keep Up Your Right*
	(Soigne ta droite, Prix Louis Delluc 1987),
	King Lear
1990	*New Wave (Nouvelle Vague)*
1993	*Oh, Woe is Me (Hélas pour moi)*
1996	*For Ever Mozart*
2001	*In Praise of Love (Eloge de l'amour)*

WORKS CONSULTED

A bout de souffle. Bibliothèque des Classiques du cinéma. [Paris]: Balland, 1974.

Andrew, Dudley. "Au Début du Souffle : le culte et la culture d'*A bout de soufflé.*" *Revue belge du cinéma*, 16 (Summer 1986): 11-24.

Baby, Yvonne. Interview with J.-L. Godard in *Le Monde*, Jan. 18, 1960.

Bordwell, David. "Jump Cuts and Blind Spots." *Wide Angle* 6, no. 1 (1984): 4-11.

Cerisuelo, Marc. *Jean-Luc Godard*. Paris: Lherminier, 1989.

Collet, Jean, Michel Delahaye, Jean-André Fieschi, André S. Labarthe and Bertrand Tavernier. "J.-L. Godard." *Cahiers du cinéma*, 138 (Dec. 1962): 21-39 (interview with Godard).

Douin, Jean-Luc. *Jean-Luc Godard*. Paris: Rivages, 1994 [Orig. ed. 1989].

Godard, Jean-Luc. *A bout de souffle* (screenplay). *L'Avant-Scène Cinéma* 79 (March 1968).

Lefevre, Raymond. *Jean-Luc Godard*. Paris: Edilig, 1983.

Marie, Michel. "*A bout de souffle*: une tragédie du langage et de la communication impossible." *Le Cinéma selon Godard, CinémAction*, 52 (July 1989): 53-63.

.........*A bout de souffle*. Paris: Nathan, 1999.

Martin, Marcel. "A bout de soufflé." *Cinéma 60*, 46 (May 1960): 117-119.

Moullet, Luc. "Jean-Luc Godard." *Cahiers du cinéma* 106 (April 1960): 25-36.

Ropars-Wuilleumier, Marie-Claire. "L'Instance graphique dans l'écriture du film." *Littérature* 46 (May 1982): 59-81.

Séguin, Louis. "Quoi de Neuf (suite)." *Positif* 33 (April 1960): 49.

Villain, Dominique. "*A bout de souffle*, film 'in-montable'" in *Le Montage au cinéma*. Paris: Cahiers du cinéma, 1991 (pp. 133-142).

François Truffaut

Jules et Jim

(1962)

François Truffaut, *Jules and Jim*: Catherine (Jeanne Moreau) "makes faces" for Jules (Oscar Werner) and Jim (Henri Serre). © Raymond Cauchetier-Paris

Director ....François Truffaut
Screenplay and dialogues................ François Truffaut, Jean Gruault
Director of Photography .... Raoul Coutard
Music..Georges Delerue;
                       "Le Tourbillon" by Cyrus Bassiak
Film Editor .... Claudine Bouché
Art Director and Costumes .... Fred Capel
Script Girl (Continuity) ....Suzanne Schiffman
Producer ....Les Films du Carrosse, SEDIF
Length .... 1 h 44

Cast

Jeanne Moreau (*Catherine*), Oscar Werner (*Jules*), Henri Serre (*Jim*), Cyrus ("Boris") Bassiak (*Albert*), Marie Dubois (*Thérèse*), Vanna Urbino (*Gilberte*), Sabine Haudepin (*Sabine*), Michel Subor (narrator's voice-over).

STORY

The story begins around 1912 in Paris where Jules, a German, and Jim, a Frenchman, meet and become friends for life. Although very different from each other, they discover profound affinities, sharing a taste for literature, theater, sports, and women. Jim has a lot of success with women, whom he often passes off to Jules one after the other, but Jules isn't as fortunate as his friend — until the arrival of Catherine.

Catherine has the mysterious seductive smile of a statue that Jules and Jim had gone to see on an island in the Adriatic Sea. Jules falls in love instantly and gives his friend to understand that this isn't a woman he wants to share: *"Not this one, right, Jim?"* Jules and Catherine invite Jim to go out with them, with Catherine disguised as a man. They have a foot race which Catherine wins by cheating, after which she invites both Jules and Jim to go to the seashore with her. Having asked Jim to stop by her lodgings to help her with her baggage, she proceeds to burn a pile of love letters, setting her dressing gown on fire in the process. Only Jim's rapid action avoids a disaster.

Leaving the following morning, the three friends spend their vacation together at the beach strolling in the woods, biking, and playing dominos. Jules asks Catherine to marry him, but she can't make up her mind. Back in Paris Jim takes his friends to the theater to celebrate a piece of good news: his autobiographical novel has just been accepted by a publisher. When they leave the theater, Jules makes some clumsy comments about women. Catherine puts him in his place by jumping into the Seine. Riding home in a carriage with the two men sitting in stunned silence, Catherine asks Jim to meet her the next evening at a café. She arrives very late and just misses Jim, who had finally left after waiting a long time. The next morning Jules and Catherine telephone Jim to announce that they are going to get married. A few days later (it is 1914), World War I breaks out.

The screen is filled with a series of images of the war: bombardments, trench warfare, and deaths. Forced to fight for their respective countries, Jules and Jim both live in fear of killing each other. After the war Jules invites his friend, a journalist now, to visit him in Germany, where he is living in a rustic chalet with Catherine and their little girl Sabine. Jules informs Jim that despite appearances his marriage with Catherine is on the rocks. She has had lovers and has even gone off with another man for six months. He is afraid that she will leave for good with Albert, a former friend of Jules and Jim who lives in the area. Jules isn't jealous, but he doesn't want to lose Catherine. One evening Catherine entices Jim out into the fields where they spend the night talking. She admits to him that her marriage with Jules is a failure and that they no longer have conjugal relations. The next day Albert arrives to practice a song, *The Whirlpool Of Life* (*Le Tourbillon de la vie*), which Catherine sings while he accompanies her on the guitar.

Jules is quite aware of the desire which has begun to grow between Catherine and Jim and encourages his friend to give free rein to his sentiments. He gives him to understand that he prefers to see them together, even married, as long as he can continue to see Catherine. Jim leaves the inn where he's been staying and moves into the chalet, where he becomes Catherine's lover. The three friends enjoy a month of carefree bliss before Jim has to go back to Paris for his work. He rejoins his mistress Gilberte, but informs her of his intention to marry Catherine. Grievously offended by Jim's infidelity, Catherine takes her revenge by spending a few nights with Albert: "*Albert is my Gilberte.*" Jim and Catherine make up and try to have a child together to crown their union. When they fail, Catherine becomes exasperated and decides to send Jim away for a few months. Jim goes back to Paris and to Gilberte. Shortly afterwards Catherine writes Jim to announce excitedly that she is carrying his baby. Jim is skeptical about the baby's paternity; he soon learns from Jules, in any case, that Catherine has had a miscarriage and doesn't want to see him.

After an indeterminate period Jules and Jim meet by chance in Paris. Catherine drives them to an inn for lunch, then unexpectedly abandons them to spend the night there with Albert. Early the next morning Catherine telephones Jim, begging him to meet her. He goes to her house but rejects her overtures and announces his intention to marry Gilberte and start a family. Catherine is crushed, then becomes furious and takes out a revolver. She threatens to kill Jim, who flees through a window.

Jules, Catherine, and Jim meet a final time by chance in a Parisian cinema — at the beginning of the thirties, when the Nazis are taking power in Germany. Catherine proposes a ride in her car, and the three friends stop at a café beside a river. Catherine invites Jim to follow her, telling Jules to watch. She gets back into the car with Jim, drives onto a wrecked bridge, and plunges the car off the end of the bridge into the water. Jules accompanies the two caskets and attends the cremation of the bodies.

CRITICAL RECEPTION

The critical reaction to *Jules et Jim* was almost uniformly positive. Jean Renoir, deeply moved by the film, wrote to Truffaut: "I wanted to tell you that *Jules et Jim* is, in my opinion, the best expression of contemporary French society that I've ever seen on the screen" (De Baecque and Toubiana, p. 263). The press was overwhelmingly flattering, speaking for example of "a feast of tenderness and intelligence" and of the "first really enchanting film of the New Wave." Opening January 24, 1962, in Paris, *Jules et Jim* played for three months. Because of its "indecent" character the film was forbidden to spectators under eighteen in France; this commercial handicap didn't prevent it from having a solid run: more than 320,000 tickets sold in six months (compared to 450,000 for *The 400 Blows*). It will be counted among the most successful films of the year in France (Le Berre, p. 16). In Italy the film was flatly banned by the government until the intellectuals protested and forced the censors to back down. The film didn't open in Rome until September. In the meanwhile Truffaut travelled throughout Europe, then went to North and South America to help promote *Jules et Jim*. Audiences everywhere were enthusiastic, except in the province of Alberta, Canada (where the film was banned because it was judged "morally reprehensible, degrading, and offensive"). When the film came out in New York in April, the newspapers sang its praises, calling it "one of the most original and most enchanting works of French cinema." "Counting all countries," Gilles Cahoreau remarks, "the film won eight awards and prizes" (p. 207), including the prize for Best Director in Argentina and in Mexico, a Critics' Prize in Spain, the Oscar for the Best European Film of the Year in Denmark, and the prize for best film of the year bestowed by the Italian film press.

ORIGIN AND ADAPTATION

(For a summary of the life and works of Truffaut before *Jules et Jim*, see the chapter on *The 400 Blows*, pp. 236-238.) Between *The 400 Blows* and *Jules et Jim* Truffaut made *Shoot The Piano Player* (a parody of the *film noir*, the American gangster film), a mixture of tragedy and comedy which was a commercial failure despite the critical acclaim it garnered. In addition to this personal failure, the climate surrounding Truffaut's new project was not very promising. The popularity of the New Wave had already begun waning a year after its consecration at Cannes, and the victims of the young rebels at the *Cahiers du cinéma* — such as the screenwriter Michel Audiard — were beginning to gloat and take their revenge: "The New Wave [Nouvelle Vague] is dead. And it's becoming clear that it was more vague than new" (quoted in De Baecque and Toubiana, p. 251). In the political arena Truffaut supported the opponents of the war in Algeria (1956-62) and, along with other prominent personalities, ran the risk of getting into serious trouble with the police by encouraging insubordination among the soldiers. Fearful of getting arrested for subversive behavior, Truffaut went into hiding in the country to devote himself to the writing of the screenplay for *Jules et Jim*.

As we emphasized in the chapter on *The 400 Blows* (pp. 235-237), regarding Truffaut's famous article "A Certain Tendency of French Cinema" (1954), his favorite target was the pedestrian nature of film adaptations of novels in French cinema (see Gillain, in the *Critical Dossier*). When he undertook the adaptation of *Jules et Jim* (1953), the first novel of seventy-year-old Henri-Pierre Roché, Truffaut could not afford any missteps. If his adaptation was no more innovative than the ones he criticized so severely, or if his film failed, he would be exposed to merciless attacks. It is not surprising therefore that the writing of the screenplay was painstaking. He brought in the highly talented screenwriter Jean Gruault, who elaborated the scenario and the dialogue with him. They used both the novel and the *Notebooks* of Roché, a sort of diary in which the writer recorded his numerous affairs with women and the story of his friendship with the German writer Franz Hessel. His diary contains the story of a sixty-year-long love triangle between him, his friend, and a German woman, Helen Grund. The story is only slightly transformed in his novel, where he depicts himself as Jim and Franz as Jules. Roché's story is thus scrupulously autobiographical, with the exception of the denouement; the triangle doesn't end of course with the death of Roché and Helen! The screenplay written by Truffaut and Gruault is faithful to Roché's novel, despite the addition of several new episodes. The plot was nonetheless simplified, concentrated, and accelerated. A few episodes were cut out, and many feminine characters in Roché's novel are not in the film. Catherine's character took on certain traits of some of the women who had been eliminated, while the Thérèse character was simply lifted from Roché's second novel *Two Englishwomen and the Continent* (1956) — which Truffaut would also adapt to the screen. The voice-over narration, which emphasizes the literary origin of the film, is an elaborately worked and reworked text. The screenwriters primarily used sentences from the novel, occasionally rewritten and not always in the same order in which they appear in Roché's work. Certain elements of the voice-over text and of the dialogue were likewise borrowed from *Two Englishwomen*. In any case, the screenplay was constantly modified before and during the shooting itself.

THE CAST

As Le Berre observes, "Truffaut is constantly concerned with the necessity of rendering and keeping his characters sympathetic despite the scabrous nature of the situations…" (p. 29). It was particularly important that the actress who plays Catherine win over the spectator by her charm and her intelligence, despite her morally questionable behavior. Truffaut was quite aware of this: "Since the situation was extremely scabrous, in constant danger of becoming distasteful, we needed a very intelligent actress who could get the audience to tolerate certain things…" (Cukier and Gryn, p. 10). He chose Jeanne Moreau, whose natural charisma turned out to be crucial to the success of the film. Some commentators, such as Gilles Cahoreau, were convinced that Moreau played a critical role in the very conception of the film: "When all is said and done, Truffaut's film was inspired as much by the vitality of Jeanne Moreau, the richness of her personal existence, as by Roché's novel" (p. 201). At the peak of her glory, extremely popular, she clearly fascinated Truffaut, who saw no difference between the actress and the character Catherine: "Through Catherine's character, Jeanne Moreau represents for Truffaut the supreme woman, both fragile and dangerous, intelligent and spontaneous, funny and tragic, free, sovereign, refusing any compromise in the gratification of her desires" (De Baeque and Toubiana, p. 257). Kathe, the young German woman in Roché's novel, thus becomes a young French woman named Catherine in Truffaut's film. The intellectual side of Jeanne Moreau which Truffaut appreciated so much, and which he considered essential to the character, necessitated important modifications of Roché's heroine, as Garrigou-Lagrange remarks: "…what she gains in intelligence or more precisely in cerebrality, she loses in spontaneity and, without exaggeration, in innocence. Kathe drank life to the fullest, by huge gulps; Catherine — more introverted, more refined — chooses her experiences reflectively" (pp. 4-5).

Jim is played by an actor new to the cinema, Henri Serre, chosen partly because of his physical resemblance (tall and thin) to Henri-Pierre Roché when he was young. The role of Jules was given to an Austrian stage actor, Oskar Werner, famous in Germany and Austria but little known in France. Truffaut intentionally chose unknown actors to play beside his star: "I like the idea of having a well-known actor, but I think that the film is more effective if the star is surrounded by unknown actors […] so that the public isn't treated to a *contest*, but a *film*" (quoted in Billard, pp. 7-8). Marie Dubois, the female lead in *Shoot the Piano Player*, was chosen for the role of Thérèse. Albert is played by the young composer Cyrus Bassiak, the author of *The Whirlpool of Life* sung by Jeanne Moreau in the film, accompanied on the guitar by Bassiak. The voice-over narration is read by the film actor Michel Subor.

FILMING

The filming of *Jules et Jim* took place over eleven weeks, from April 10 to June 28, 1961, with a minimal technical crew owing to the difficulty of financing the project, which frightened off most producers. The film required numerous location changes: Truffaut filmed in Normandy, then in the Parisian region, in Paris itself, and then in the south of France. The most critical scenes, which take place in the chalet in Germany, were filmed over a three-week period in the Vosges mountains in Alsace. Truffaut rented a helicopter for the aerial scenes and shot in "day for night" (using a special filter transforming day into night) when he did the long sequence shot of the conversation between Catherine and Jim in the meadow at night. Just as in his first two films, he utilized Cinemascope, in black and white. Cinemascope has an embellishing effect, and the large screen produces both striking close-ups and broad expanses, often with large empty spaces. The filming style of Raoul Coutard, "the best French director of photography" according to Truffaut, is "mobile, fluid, and acrobatic" in *Jules et Jim*. Coutard used both 360° pans and swish pans which emphasize the impression of speed which dominates a good part of the film (Le Berre, p. 19).

EDITING AND STYLE

The editing and postsynchronization of *Jules et Jim* proved to be long and difficult, taking four whole months. When the mixing began, Truffaut realized that the voice-over is sometimes inaudible because of the volume of Delerue's music. Since he didn't want to sacrifice either the voice-over or the music, he was forced to rewrite and record again many sentences in the commentary, changing their place in the soundtrack.

The style of the film is expressed well in the metaphor of the "whirlpool of life," the song Catherine sings in the chalet which describes the infernal but broken rhythm of the spiral in which the three characters are caught: "The style of Truffaut and the life style of his characters are composed of a series of leaps forward and backwards, of dashes interrupted by halts, of plunges into life or into a void, falling or soaring and weaving the plot of a rocky but deeply coherent voyage" (Delahaye, p. 39). As in Resnais's *Hiroshima mon amour*, the director's style becomes clearer in the editing, which is marked by the alternation between ellipses — series of short shots representing the passage of time and accompanied by the voice-over narration — and moments of intensity, with dialogue, composed of lengthier shots in real time. The voice-over, which Truffaut made intentionally "very neutral and very rapid, without intonation," translates the "invisible," "telegraphic" style of Roché. It contributes to the rapid rhythm of the film, along with the fast editing (series of brief shots) and the camera movements accompanying the characters, At the same time it helps to concentrate the action and fill the blanks, an important function in a story which is spread over more than twenty years and thus cannot be represented visually in its entirety. The voice-over serves also as a form of stream-of-consciousness. It reveals Jim's thoughts especially and draws us into his perspective, while providing additional information about the three characters and their adventures (Le Berre, p. 67). The voice-over, an integral part of Truffaut's esthetic of adaptation in *Jules et Jim*, allows the reading of the narration to alternate with the scenes of dialogue, so that the most striking prose passages can be preserved. This has the effect of inscribing the novel in the film instead of replacing it by the adaptation. Truffaut considers *Jules et Jim* to be a "cinematographic book" rather than a "literary film."

STRUCTURE

Beginning "around 1912," the story narrated in *Jules and Jim* comes to an end in the early thirties with the Nazis' rise to power, which is evoked by movie newsreels showing people burning books in the street. With the exception of World War I (1914-1918), the passage of time is indicated by light touches: Jim and Albert shave off their mustaches after the war; Catherine begins to wear glasses; the men wear different hats. More subtly, Picasso's paintings on the walls from different periods of his body of work suggest the passage of time — although the time between the paintings, from 1900 to 1921, does not correspond precisely to the chronology of the novel. The three characters on the other hand — and this is a conscious, anti-realist, choice by Truffaut — do not grow physically old during the twenty years of their story (see Salis in the *Critical Dossier*). The cyclical structure of the film is organized around the separations and reunions of the three characters, notwithstanding the reversal of the roles of Jules and Jim in relation to Catherine.

The war images aside, the film divides neatly into five parts: 1) a "prologue" showing the life of the two men in Paris before Catherine's arrival; 2) their life with Catherine until the declaration of war; 3) Jim's first stay at the chalet in Germany; 4) Jim's return to Paris and his second stay at the chalet, followed by another return to Paris; 5) an "epilogue" which extends from Jules and Jim's chance meeting at the gymnasium in Paris to the end of the film (Le Berre, pp. 60-61). Within each part the film is fragmented, organized into quasi-autonomous segments, each appearing as a little separate episode with its beginning, middle, and end. The result is an intensification: "All of the sequences are virtually independent, owing to their extreme density, their particular character, as if the author only wanted to retain these intense moments [...]. These particularly joyful and sad instants follow and eradicate each other, so that it is impossible to preserve their violent, agitated effect" (Salis, pp. 20-21). Globally the first three parts feature the happiness of friendship and love, but this happiness is threatened in the third part with the failure of Jules and Catherine's marriage and the presence of Albert. The last parts bear the stamp of unhappiness and are marked by painful separations and reunions up to the final tragedy.

THEMES

In an interview granted by Truffaut just before the opening of *Jules et Jim* the filmmaker sums up the principal themes of his film (referring to the love triangle): "Ultimately there are only two themes: the theme of the friendship of the two men which attempts to survive this situation, and the theme of the impossibility of the three of them living together. The basic idea of the film is that the couple is not a satisfactory situation, but that there simply aren't any other solutions, or that all the other solutions are bound to fail" (in Billard, p. 7). Beyond friendship and love, the principal themes, there are of course other important themes to discover in Truffaut's film. The theme of women's liberation is clearly developed (along with the theme of sexual freedom), although Truffaut denies any identification with the feminist movement of the following decade. Catherine rejects the famous "double standard"; she demands the same rights as men and doesn't hesitate to use infidelity to strike back when she feels offended. Her search for equality is first expressed in the scene where she dresses up like a man, an episode which also introduces the theme of inversion, a figure which occurs in several forms in the film (see Delahaye, in the *Critical Dossier*).

Just as in *The 400 Blows*, fire represents a major motif in *Jules et Jim*. It is the principal metaphor for the character of Catherine, this *femme fatale* who burns in men's hearts and has such a burning desire for life that it will consume her. Fire is strongly tied here to its opposite, water. The two elements are united in vitriol ("firewater") and together evoke the danger represented by passionate love, the grave risk of "playing with the sources of life," as Jim says, and of trying to reinvent love by ignoring social conventions. Catherine and Jim meet their fate under the sign of water (the river where they are drowned) and the sign of fire (the crematorium).

Finally, placing Catherine's song "The Whirlpool Of Life" (see below) strategically in the middle of the film foregrounds its thematic matrix, the tortured relations between the three characters, the constant back-and-forth of Catherine between the two (three) men. Moreover, Catherine assumes the role of the masculine character (another example of the heroine's sexual inversion) who is supposedly singing, uniting within herself in the song the three partners and establishing her absolute domination. The theme of "embrace" at the end of the song is echoed by Picasso's painting *The Embrace*, which is on the wall of Jules's room in the chalet after decorating his room in Paris at the beginning of the film. In addition to their temporal function, the other Picasso paintings also seem to echo the film's themes. This is especially true of the last canvas, *Mother and Child*, on the wall of Catherine's room in the converted mill where Jim declares his intention to marry Gilberte and to have children with her, after having failed with Catherine (Coffey, pp. 2-7).

"THE WHIRLPOOL OF LIFE"

She had rings on each finger,
All kinds of bracelets round her wrists,
And she sang with a voice
That bewitched me instantly.
She had eyes, opal eyes,
That fascinated me, fascinated me.
There was the oval of her femme fatale's
Pale face which was fatal to me (repeat).
We met, we recognized each other.
We lost sight of each other and did so again,
We reunited, we warmed each other up,
Then we separated.
We each went our own way
In the whirlpool of life.
I saw her again one evening, hey, hey, hey
It had really been ages (repeat).
I recognized her by the sound of the banjos.
Her curious smile which I liked so much.
Her voice so fatal, her beautiful pale face

Moved me more than ever.
I got drunk just listening to her.
Alcohol helps one forget time.
I awoke with the odor
Of her kisses on my burning forehead (repeat).
We met, we recognized each other.
We lost sight of each other once and then again,
We reunited, we warmed each other up,
Then we separated.
We each went our own way
In the whirlpool of life.
I saw her again one evening, ah, la, la.
She fell into my arms.
When we met,
When we recognized each other,
Why lose sight of each other,
Lose sight of each other again.
Why did we separate?
So we both again were swept into
The whirlpool of life.
We went on turning
In each other's embrace
In each other's embrace.
(Cyrus Bassiak, translated by A. Singerman)

STUDY GUIDE

Director's Comments

"I used throughout the film a voice-over commentary each time that the text seemed impossible to transform into dialogues or too beautiful to be amputated. Rather than a classical adaptation, transforming by any means a book into a play, I prefer an intermediary form which alternates dialogue and voice-over commentary creating a kind of filmed novel."

"Beginning with the most scabrous situation imaginable — two men and a woman living together all their life — we had to make a successful love film, the 'purest' love possible, because of the innocence of the three characters, their moral integrity, their tenderness and, especially, their personal dignity — owing also to the form of friendship between the male characters."

"It is through their life that the characters make their impact on the spectators. Their life has to transcend any ideas that the spectators may have had about it. We have to make the exceptional appear natural. We have to get people not to judge the characters by their own moral standards. We have to prevent the spectators, and ourselves first of all, from dominating the characters. It is essential to leave the characters both a chance at salvation and their contradictions."

"The lover is always the prestigious character, the husband the thankless character. I reversed the situation so completely that the spectator, who confuses the character and the actor, prefers Oscar Werner to Henri Serre."

"However, despite its 'modern' character this film is in no way polemical. Of course the young woman in *Jules et Jim* wants to live like a man, but this is only a peculiarity of her character and not an aggressive feminist position."

Excerpts for Discussion

Excerpt 1 (10'10-11'00): Catherine's arrival at Jules's home; Catherine's face.

Excerpt 2 (11'50-14'00): Jules and Jim arrive at Catherine's apartment; she dresses up as "Thomas"; foot race which Catherine wins by cheating.

Excerpt 3 (14'25-16'35): Jim at Catherine's place; the love letters, the fire, the vitriol.

Excerpt 4 (21'50-23'05): In the country, Jules and Jim play dominos; Catherine slaps Jules then makes a series of "faces" (with freeze frames).

Excerpt 5 (24'35-27'40): After the theater, Jules makes disagreeable remarks about women; Catherine jumps into the Seine river.

Excerpt 6 (37'00-38'40): Jim at Jules and Catherine's chalet after the war (shot reverse-angle shots, then swish pans between their faces, close-ups).

Excerpt 7 (56'30-58'50): Catherine and Albert's song, "The Whirlpool of Life."

Excerpt 8 (1h15'05-16'35): Jim and Catherine in bed, "They glided high in the air..." (aerial travelling); "The promised land took a leap backwards" (aerial zoom backwards).

Excerpt 9 (1h38'10-41'00): Jules, Jim, and Catherine at the café on the river; the car plunges into the river; cremation of Jim's and Catherine's bodies.

Quotations for Comment

Catherine (voice-over):

"You told me: I love you.

I told you: Wait.

I was going to say: Take me.

You said: Go away."

* * *

Jules: "Do you think I'm right in wanting to marry Catherine?" (Pause) Answer me frankly."

Jim: "Is she made to have a husband and children? I'm afraid that she may never be happy in this world. She is an apparition for everyone but perhaps not a woman for just one person."

* * *

Narrator (voice-over): "From his room at the inn Jim could see the chalet. Catherine was over there, the radiant queen of the household, ready to fly away. Jim wasn't surprised: he remembered Jules's mistakes with Thérèse, with Lucie, with all of them. He knew that Catherine was terribly exacting. Jim felt enormously sad for Jules, but he couldn't judge Catherine. She plunged into men like she plunged into the Seine.... A menace hung over the house."

* * *

Jules: "Jim, Catherine doesn't want me any more. I'm terrified at the idea of losing her and of her disappearing completely from my life. The last time I saw you and Catherine together you looked like a couple. (Pause) Jim, love her, marry her, and let me see her. What I mean is, if you love her, stop thinking of me as an obstacle."

* * *

Narrator (voice-over): "Catherine had said: 'One only loves completely for one moment,' but for her, that moment kept returning."

* * *

Jules: "No, no, Jim ... you know very well: Catherine takes everything to the extreme, one thing at a time. She is a natural force which expresses itself in cataclysms. She lives in any circumstances bathed in her clarity and her harmony, guided by the conviction of her innocence."

Jim: "You talk about her as if she were a queen!"

Jules: "But she is a queen, Jim! [...] Catherine isn't particularly pretty nor intelligent nor sincere, but she's a real woman ... she's a woman that we love ... and that all men desire. Why did Catherine, solicited on all sides, bestow her presence nonetheless on us? Because we are completely devoted to her like to a queen."

* * *

Catherine: "Yes, Jim, believe me, it's the only way for us to create something good. Albert equals Gilberte. (A silence) You have nothing to say? We have to begin again from zero."

* * *

Narrator (concerning the relationship between Catherine and Jim when they separate for three months): "So for Jules their love was relative, whereas *his* was absolute."

* * *

Catherine to Jim: "I'm finally pregnant [...]. I'm sure, absolutely sure, that you are the father. I beg you to believe me. Your love is a part of my life. You live in me. Believe me, Jim, believe me. This paper is your skin, this ink is your blood. I'm pressing hard so that it enters. Write back quickly."

* * *

Narrator (after Catherine's miscarriage): "Thus together they hadn't created anything. Jim thought, 'It's fine to try to rediscover human laws, but how practical it must be to follow the existing rules. We played with the sources of life, and we lost."

* * *

Jim to Catherine: "I think like you that the couple isn't the ideal form of love. All we have to do is look around us. You wanted to construct something better by refusing hypocrisy and resignation. You wanted to invent love … but pioneers have to be humble and not self-centered. No, we have to be realistic, Catherine, we've failed, we've made a mess of everything […]. I've given up all hope of marrying you. I have to tell you this, Catherine, I'm going to marry Gilberte. She and I can still have children."

Questions/Topics for Reflection

1. The relationship between Jules and Jim; the women in their lives.
2. The "literary" character of the film (role of the voice-over narration, allusions to writing).
3. Catherine disguises herself as a man ("Thomas") and goes out with Jules and Jim; foot race that Catherine wins by cheating.
4. After the evening at the theater, Jules and Jim discuss women. Catherine, who has been walking on the wall, suddenly jumps into the Seine.
5. The role of fire and water in the film.
6. The love triangle (Catherine's behavior, Jules' and Jim's attitudes).
7. Failure of Jim and Catherine as a couple. The importance of the child they can't have.
8. The revolver scene and the denouement.
9. Relationship between Truffaut's style (editing, camera movements) and the life-style of his characters.
10. Did Truffaut succeed in "equalizing the characters so that they have the same claim on our sympathy, and so that we will have the same affection for them"?

CRITICAL DOSSIER

Anne Gillain — Literary Adaptation

The problem of literary adaptation during Truffaut's years as a literary critic was his favorite target; he couldn't tolerate the prevailing custom of reducing novels — *Le Diable au corps* for example — to the illustration of critical elements of the dialogue in a cinematic mode, that is, with no respect for the style of the writer. Truffaut replaces this approach with what he calls a "filmed reading," modeled on Robert Bresson's adaptation of Bernanos's novel *Diary of A Country Priest*. To accomplish this, it is necessary to alternate "scenes constructed not like scenes in a theater, but scenes with dialogue and acting and then purely narrative elements, the commentary." The novelist's text thus accompanies the film in voice-over. This will be the approach used in the adaptation of *Jules and Jim* (*Les 400 Coups*, p. 27).

Pierre Billard — *Jules et Jim* and Morality

I think that *Jules et Jim* is one of the boldest films, morally speaking, that we've seen for a long time. Just consider the reaction of the censors (R-rating for the film, after the representative of the family associations had demanded a total ban […]). Consider especially the reaction of at least part of the public that I've seen several times laughing nervously from discomfort. What embarrasses these censors and spectators of course is the frankness and purity of the protagonists […]. The heroes of *Jules et Jim* are not your typical fine upright people, those hypocritical little libertines […] who find in their miserable lies the indispensable stimulant of their miserable debauchery. These are pure beings, totally sincere and truthful, morally superior beings for whom the happiness of the other is just as important as one's own, and who can only achieve happiness by experiencing deeply, contradictions included, the powerful, authentic sentiments which move them ("Jules et Jim," pp. 103-104).

Jean Rochereau — *Jules et Jim* and The Moralizers

The New Wave again! Once again the ambiguity and misunderstanding. Those people use the same words as we do: tenderness, love. But they give them meanings that appear absurd to us. This is what they call constructing a new morality. It would be ridiculous if it weren't odious. Especially if their stubborn error were to attract the weak and draw support from particularly unexpected quarters. The third feature film by François Truffaut is receiving passionate accolades from aesthetes on all sides. That's normal and even justified. Technically the film is very well done. But for *Jules et Jim* to be considered by certain moralists to be a moral film, that's just disconcerting, distressing, and downright stupefying (*La Croix du Nord*, February 21, 1962).

Carole Le Berre — The Women in *Jules et Jim*

Elusive, changing, enigmatic, Catherine is all women in one — including androgyny, since she becomes Thomas the second time we see her. She transforms herself into a boy for the first true coming together of the trio, just after Jules, in the stairway, tells Jim she's off limits to him. She is especially a form of energy, a force ("a natural force," says Jules, who expresses himself in cataclysmic terms) which passes through the film and sweeps the two men along with it. Erupting into their orderly life, she creates, like the smiling statue before her, an opening to movement, space, and light: movement from the interior towards the exterior (towards "the test of the street," which Catherine, disguised as Thomas, insists on undergoing immediately), speed of the race on the bridge, invitation to the trip. The bright light of the south of France (the house which is "white outside and inside") repeats the burst of light replacing the darkness of the Parisian apartment where Albert projects his slides, as the light of the Adriatic island where they go to see the statue. Catherine the luminous, dressed completely in white when she appears for the first time at the top of the stairway in Jules's yard, Catherine the unpredictable, who cannot stay in one place and decides just as suddenly to go back to Paris and cannot bear her sedentary existence in the chalet after the war ("*Our life is ordered as if we were in a convent,*" she says to Jim). It is always she who initiates the movement, proposes a race, a trip, a ride, she who rides out in front on her bike exposing the nape of her neck to Jim, she again who owns and drives a car, remaining until the end of the film in charge of the itinerary.

Catherine's appearance is soon associated to the shot of a train crossing the countryside. Catherine is a locomotive-woman like Thérèse, who is to a certain extent her incomplete double. We first see Thérèse imprisoned in Merlin's arms, then free, running, catching up with Jules and Jim and dragging them along in her mad run, just as Catherine will do later. Thérèse is a will-o'-the-wisp who devilishly encircles Jules and embodies gaiety, speed, and perpetual movement. A collector like Catherine and perhaps even more than she […], she lacks her depth and magnetic force […].

On the other hand the stable and patient Gilberte is the exact opposite of Catherine: "*reasonable and patient, she will wait for me forever*," says Jim. Gilberte is always moderate, whereas Catherine is always excessive; she simply calls Jim a scoundrel when he leaves her early in the morning to maintain his independence, or prefers to hide her distress when he informs her that he is going to marry Catherine. The opposition is developed throughout the film, including the spaces assigned to each of the two women: Gilberte is associated with the interior, the city, the enclosed spaces of apartments or cafés (we only see her once outside, walking with Jim on leave during the war, with the horizon blocked by a wooden fence covered with military posters). Catherine is related, from her very first appearance in Jules's yard, to the outside, to nature, to the wide-open spaces of the south of France or of the chalet (and it's a mill beside the Seine which replaces the chalet when she and Jules come to live in France) […].

"*I'm afraid that she may never be happy in this world. She is an apparition for everyone, but perhaps not a woman for just one person*," Jim says prophetically to Jules. An incarnation of vitality, Catherine also carries within herself a simmering violence which can boil over at any moment. Catherine is excessive and sometimes brusque, abusive, and tyrannical, often compared to Napoleon ("*It's what I've always thought: she's Napoleon too*," Jim says to Jules when he confides Catherine's escapades: the voice-over describes her after she jumps into the Seine as "*a modest young general after his Italian campaign*"; in the south, she reveals her dream about meeting Napoleon in an elevator; and we can make out a little portrait of Napoleon on the wall of her room in Paris). She is impatient, willing to cheat (the race on the bridge), occasionally manipulative (the episode of the white pyjama), gifted for dramatics and staging (the love letters she burns before Jim or the plunging of the car into the river: "*Watch us*," she calls to Jules, turning him into the spectator of their death before she drives Jim with her onto the wrecked bridge […].

Oblivious to moderation, unable to tolerate failure, preferring […] the death she shares with her lover to the resignation and degradation of love, Catherine is obsessed with the absolute. She is a woman thirsty for life and love, a free woman especially, lucid and ahead of her time — although Truffaut refused, I repeat, the description of his character as feminist — whose personal morality, both retrograde and modern (establishing a balance, getting even to begin anew), demonstrates a desire for equality which, refusing hypocrisy, attempts to renew or reinvent love. Burning with a profound dissatisfaction ("*When everything is going too well*, says Jules, *she sometimes grows unhappy; she becomes a different person and lashes out at everything, physically and verbally*"), confronted also perhaps — whether it be Jules's gentleness or

Jim's indecisiveness — with men who are too weak to rise to the level of her demands, Catherine is broken. She is a woman who suffers, pathetic and sincere when she asks Jules insistently, "*Do you think Jim loves me?*", devastated, infinitely touching when Jim informs her that he wants to have children with another woman. But she recovers instantly, her traits harden, she takes out her revolver and threatens Jim. The relationship that Truffaut creates between Catherine and the spectator is never simple nor one-dimensional (*Jules et Jim*, pp. 84-87).

Madeleine Garrigou-Lagrange — Jules

His warmth radiates on everything around him. If he has neither Catherine's vitality nor her passion for life, he possesses an autonomy, an integrity which are foreign to the young woman. Nonetheless he is clumsy at life, at expressing himself, at loving. Before meeting Catherine he had had, we know, a considerable number of failed relationships with women. "*It was the generosity, the innocence, the vulnerability of Jules which appealed to me,*" Catherine explains to Jim. Yet he was unable to keep her: Catherine's capricious nature is partially responsible but also a certain incapacity of Jules to understand and satisfy the deep-rooted needs of the woman he loves. Everything considered he is more successful at friendship than at love; his gift of comprehension, his total absence of self-centeredness, exercise a powerful attraction on others: Catherine will continually depend on him as her most attentive confidant.

Jim compares him to a Buddhist monk, and he has indeed acquired the calm serenity of a man who continues to be moved by the passions of others, without his own deep-set equilibrium being affected. I say "has acquired," because between the Jules of Paris and the man in the Swiss chalet, marriage, war, and suffering have taken their toll. At the beginning a carefree young man who holds forth on the banks of the Seine, declaring that in a couple only the faithfulness of the woman counts, the man's being secondary, we see him now accepting, fully conscious of what he is doing, the role of spectator, indeed confidant, of a scandalous love affair between his wife and his best friend. Not that he behaves like the indulgent husband of an unfaithful spouse; he just doesn't feel he has the right or the power to control her […].

The Austrian Oscar Werner, blond, short, and thickset, plays Jules. Thanks to him, to his smiling simplicity which sometimes masks impatience or suffering, his character — peaceful man, faithful friend, and deceived husband — not only never becomes ridiculous but earns the respect of the spectator. Werner pulls off this difficult role with a discretion and a delicacy which preserve the mystery of Jules while revealing all his endearing human traits ("Jules et Jim," pp. 5-6).

Michel Delahaye — Inversion in *Jules et Jim*

To express what a negation, subversion, or inversion of social norms represents, this film, in which there is no homosexuality, has recourse to motifs which in another context would signify actual sexual inversion. At the beginning Catherine changes her sex and becomes Thomas. After her first plunge into the river Jules says to her twice: "*Tu es fou,*" a simple linguistic error perhaps, but a very significant one. On the linguistic plane again, Jules points out to Jim the inversion of masculine and feminine genders which occurs when one goes from French to German. In addition, the song that Catherine sings is written to be sung by a man, and Jim's "Gilberte" and

Catherine's "Albert" are curiously similar in sound ("Les Tourbillons élémentaires," p. 42).

Carole Le Berre — Catherine and Fire

The sequence introduces elements which, weaving together incessant similarities, will return throughout the film. Thus Jim approaches for the first time the back of Catherine's neck, object *par excellence* of his desire, which he will only be able to see from a distance before finally being allowed to touch it. And there is especially fire, with which Catherine plays metaphorically as well as literally, the fire of the love which will ignite between Jim and Catherine. This apparently prosaic fire has nonetheless long been charged with seduction by the cinema. It passes from one smoker to the next, and Jim has already given Catherine fire, after drawing her mustache, by offering her a cigar that he lights for her in front of Jules. He gives it to her once again here, handing her his box of matches for her sentimental auto-da-fé (and Coutard's camera accompanies quickly Jim's gesture in order to isolate the brief moment when the box moves from one hand to the other, joined thus in the center of the screen). There is deadly fire also, which devours papers as the fire seen in the newsreel will later devour books; dangerous fire, whose flames lick Catherine's nightgown, just like those which consume her from the inside — and those which will reduce her body to cinders after the plunge of the car at the end. There is fire which reappears as soon as it is extinguished, bound to water as vitriol, liquid fire which, poured out, changes instantly into smoke. In all its forms fire is indelibly linked to Catherine, a fiery, sparkling woman as bright as a flame, as destructive also, burning herself with what she has set afire. One of the great strengths of the sequence comes from the fact that Truffaut loads it with elements which awaken multiple echoes in our imagination (fire, vitriol, or these "lies" that Catherine wants to burn which are in fact only crumbled papers, and which we assume immediately to be love letters).

[...] The sequence is devoid of voice-over narration, and the thoughts of the characters remain unknown, Jim's most strikingly, so that no interpretation is given to the scene. Impossible to know how much of Catherine's dramatics in front of Jim are part of a calculated plan and how much to innocence or just plain impulsiveness. And it is the *acte manqué* of the nightgown catching on fire — an accident which lends a certain fragility to Catherine and makes her accessible and attractive to Jim, while at the same time revealing her to be a woman with whom one risks getting burned — which brings them together physically for the first time (to put out the fire) and functions as a natural preparation for the second time, when Catherine asks him for help in fastening her dress (*Jules et Jim*, pp. 106-108).

René Salis — "Poetry of the Moment"

In *Jules et Jim* there remain a series of sequences which appear each like a little separate film in which are recorded the most revealing moments of the private existence of the three protagonists. Truffaut captures the privileged moment of a triangle and reproduces it with all of its transient truth, with its brilliant and ephemeral richness. He presents with the same detachment apparently insignificant fragments in which the most intimate relationships are established and the most secret inclinations revealed. Each scene is virtually a complete unit. They are so dense, each so completely unique as if the author had only wanted to retain these intense moments of life — those moments, bitter or sweet, which provoke an overflow of fleeting impressions, those in which the enchantments and disillusionments of friendship and love come delicately together. Thus is life reconstituted with its movement back-and-forth between shadow and light. The moments of keen pleasure and muted sadness succeed and drive off one another, making it impossible to preserve their violent and short-lived perfume. Sometimes the artist freezes abruptly the flow of time in order to savor completely the dense and discrete flavor of a privileged second. This manner of dilating fragments of life and capturing their imponderable and fragile impulses gives them an incisive ephemeral character. The characters and their environment seem integrated into the irreversible flow of time. The movements of the heart and the acts of the heroes pursue irresistibly their course, and the commentary, by its neutral and crisp nature, only emphasizes the permeating nature of time. Linked to the end of a sequence and leading directly to the next, the connecting text rips each scene brutally from the eyes of the spectator and impresses upon him the irrepressible passage of events [...].

The final images (the cremation of the two heroes) hammer in just as intensely the inexorable course of life and bring to an end this story marked by the seal of passing time. The deaths of Jim and Catherine happen suddenly; they add a tragic almost unexpected note to the casual flow of events [...]. In *Jules et Jim*, as in Truffaut's preceding works, this death also expresses the impossibility for his heroes to achieve any durable happiness; the events always manage to plunge them back into their solitude [...].

The time of the action flows by ineluctably, but the characters remain fixed in time. From this opposition, in part, arises the moving beauty of *Jules et Jim*. Each scene seems to exist beyond the present moment as if frozen in eternity. The characters evolve in a quasi-immaterial world from which all possible appearances of external contingencies and daily triviality have been excluded. History never penetrates into the life of the three friends, who are isolated from the rest of the universe. Beginning with the first appearance of Catherine, any human or social background disappears, and the heroes remain alone with nature as the only setting. The passage from one period to another is suggested by the posters from Picasso's exhibitions. Truffaut deliberately chose not to let his characters age physically; thus the material presence of the exterior world tends to disappear. Everything tends, in fact, to render the characters eternal, to remove them from contact with daily life. The perfect sincerity and the great purity of the sentiments which are present throughout the film thus find an arena in which to express themselves [...].

From the exemplary harmony of the different components comes the accuracy of tone and the thematic subtlety which confer on the work its most striking signification. With *Jules et Jim*, François Truffaut's profound, sensitive poetic inspiration is confirmed ("Poésie de l'instant," pp. 19-25)

FRANÇOIS TRUFFAUT'S FILMOGRAPHY

1958   *The Brats (Les Mistons,* short subject)
1959   *The 400 Blows (Les Quatre Cents Coups)*
1960   *Shoot The Piano Player (Tirez sur le pianiste)*
1962   *Antoine et Colette* [second episode of the Doinel cycle,
        short subject in the collective film, *Love At Twenty*
        (L'Amour à vingt ans)];
        Jules et Jim   adaptation
1964   *Soft Skin*
        (La Peau douce, third episode of the Doinel cycle).
1966   *Fahrenheit 451*
1967   *The Bride Wore Black (La Mariée était en noir)*
1968   *Stolen Kisses*
        (Baisers volés, fourth episode of the Doinel cycle)
1969   *La Sirène du Mississippi*
1970   *Domicile conjugal*
        (fifth epidsode of the Doinel cycle);
        The Wild Child (L'Enfant sauvage)
1971   *The Two Englishwomen And The Continent*
        (Les Deux Anglaises et le continent)
1972   *A Beautiful Girl Like Me (Une belle fille comme moi)*
1973   *Day For Night*
        (La Nuit américaine, Oscar for the best foreign film)
1975   *Histoire d'Adèle H.*
1976   *Small Change (L'Argent de poche)*
1977   *The Man Who Loved Women*
        (L'Homme qui aimait les femmes)
1978   *The Green Room (La Chambre verte)*
1979   *Love In Flight*
        (L'Amour en fuite, end of the Antoine Doinel cycle)
1980   *The Last Subway Train (Le Dernier Métro)*
1981   *The Woman Next Door (La Femme d'à côté)*
1982   *Vivement Dimanche*

*Truffaut died on October 21, 1984, of a brain tumor. He was 52 years old.

WORKS CONSULTED

Auzel, Dominique. *Truffaut. Les Mille et Une nuits américaines*. Paris: Henri Veyrier, 1990 (pp. 52-58).

Baby, Yvonne, "Entretien avec François Truffaut sur *Jules et Jim*." *Le Monde*, Jan. 24, 1962.

Billard, Pierre. "En attendant Jules et Jim." *Cinéma 62*, 62 (Jan. 1962): 4- 13.

.........."Jules et Jim." *Cinéma 62*, 64 (March 1962): 103-105.

Cahoreau, Gilles. *François Truffaut 1932-1984*. Paris: Julliard, 1989 (pp. 197-208).

Coffee, Barbara. "Art and Film in François Truffaut's *Jules and Jim* and *Two English Girls*." *Film Heritage*, 9.3 (Spring 1974): 1-11.

Collet, Jean. *Le Cinéma de François Truffaut*. Paris: Lherminier, 1977 (pp. 69-80).

Cukier, Dan A., and Jo Gryn. "Entretien avec François Truffaut." *Script*, 5 (April 1962): 5-17.

De Baecque, Antoine, and Serge Toubiana. *François Truffaut*. Paris: Gallimard, 1996 (pp. 255-267).

Delahaye, Michel. "Les Tourbillons élémentaires." *Les Cahiers du cinéma*, 129 (March 1962): 39-44.

Garrigou-Lagrange, Madeleine. "Jules et Jim." *TéléCiné*, 105 (June-July 1962): 1-11.

Gillain, Anne. *Les 400 Coups*. Paris : Nathan, 1991.

Insdorf, Annette. *François Truffaut. Les Films de sa vie*. Paris: Gallimard, 1996 (pp. 118-127).

Le Berre, Carole. *Jules et Jim*. Paris: Nathan, 1995.

Salis, René. "Poésie de l'instant." *Script*, 5 (April 1962): 19-25.

Rabourdin, Dominique, ed. *Truffaut par Truffaut*. Paris: Editions du Chêne, 1985 (pp. 73-76).

Truffaut, François. *Jules et Jim* (screenplay). *L'Avant-Scène Cinéma* 16 (June 1962).

.........*Le Plaisir des yeux*. Paris: Cahiers du cinéma, 1987.

Eric Rohmer

My Night at Maud's
Ma nuit chez Maud

(1969)

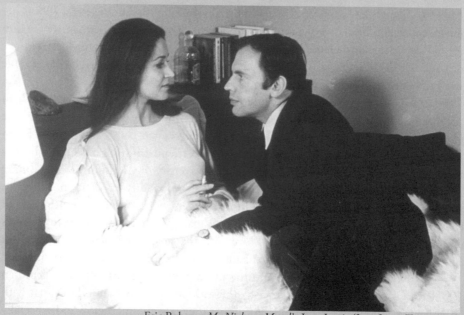

Eric Rohmer, *My Night at Maud's*: Jean-Louis (Jean-Louis Trintignant) joins Maud (Françoise Fabian) on her bed. © Les Films du Losange

Director .... Eric Rohmer
Screenplay and dialogues .... Eric Rohmer
Director of Photography .... Nestor Almendros
Cameraman .... Emmanuel Machuel
Music .... Mozart
Film Editor .... Cécile Decugis
Sound .... Jean-Pierre Ruh
Art Director ....Nicole Rachline
Mixing .... Jacques Maumont
Producer .... Barbet Schroeder, Pierre Cottrell
(Les Films du Losange)
Length .... 1 h 50

Cast

Jean-Louis Trintignant (*the narrator, the protagonist*), Françoise Fabian (*Maud*), Marie-Christine Barrault (*Françoise*), Antoine Vitez (*Vidal*), Father Guy Léger (*the priest*).

STORY

The narrator of the film, who is also the protagonist, is an engineer at the Michelin tire plant in Clermont-Ferrand. Since his name is never heard in the film, it has become customary to refer to the main character by the actor's name, "Jean-Louis."

Having worked for several years in Canada and South America, Jean-Louis has only been back in his native region for two months. Just before Christmas, we see him one Sunday at mass, where he notices a young blonde woman whom he doesn't know. He suddenly decides that this young woman will be his wife. However, he has trouble meeting her to make his feelings known.

Jean-Louis's hobby is mathematics, and he is particularly interested in calculating probabilities. While browsing in a bookstore in Clermont after mass one day, he happens upon a copy of Blaise Pascal's *Thoughts* (ca. 1660) and buys it. Later, upon entering a brasserie, he meets Vidal, an old friend from high school who has become a Marxist philosophy professor at the University of Clermont. While dining together they discuss probabilities (the statistical probability of their meeting, for example), and in this context Pascal's famous "wager," which concerns betting for or against the existence of God. The next evening Vidal takes Jean-Louis to a lady friend's apartment for dinner. He is clearly in love with the lady, whose name is Maud, but they don't get along well enough, he explains, even to consider getting married. Maud is a pediatrician, recently divorced and the mother of a little girl. She belongs to an old Clermont family of freethinkers. An atheist, Maud is visibly amused to spar with a practicing Catholic like Jean-Louis. At dinner they talk about religion and especially about Pascal. Jean-Louis disapproves of Pascal's Jansenist morality, which is so severe that it even condemns good food.

After dinner Maud and Vidal, convinced that Jean-Louis has a girl friend, kid him about his love life. He denies steadfastly that there is any woman in his life. Vidal invents a pretext to go home, leaving Jean-Louis alone with Maud, who urges him to stay the night to avoid driving home in a snowstorm. In the following conversation Maud confides that her husband and she both had had love affairs, her husband with a young Catholic girl that Maud had insisted he stop seeing. Maud's lover died in an accident when his car slipped on an icy road. When Maud goes to bed, Jean-Louis realizes that there is no guest room. He rolls himself up in a cover and stretches out in an armchair, resisting the obvious seduction attempt on the part of the young woman. Towards dawn he nonetheless lies down beside her on the bed to sleep. He soon finds himself in Maud's arms and begins to kiss her before tearing himself from her embrace. Deeply offended, Maud leaves the bed, after which the hero beats a quick retreat.

Once outside, Jean-Louis sees the blonde girl go by on her moped, runs after her and finally speaks to her. The young woman, Françoise, agrees to meet him the next day. During the day Jean-Louis goes for a mountain hike in the snow with Maud and Vidal (and Vidal's date), then meets Françoise by chance in the city that evening. Since it is snowing and the roads are treacherous, he convinces her to let him drive her to the student residence in the suburbs where she lives. When Jean-Louis's car gets stuck in the snow and ice, Françoise invites him to spend the night in an empty room in her dormitory apartment. The next morning, when Jean-Louis becomes romantic, she is reticent. She finally explains to him, some time afterwards, that she had just broken off an affair with a married man with whom she was deeply in love. She doesn't feel worthy of Jean-Louis's love. To calm her scruples, he tells her that the morning they met he had just spent the night with another woman. When Jean-Louis again tries to contact Maud, with whom he had developed a warm relationship, he discovers that she has left Clermont to begin a new pediatric practice in Toulouse.

Five years later Jean-Louis and Françoise are on vacation at the seashore with their little boy. They run into Maud, who has remarried. Jean-Louis is surprised to learn that the two women already know each other and notices that Françoise is quite embarrassed by the meeting. He explains to his wife that it was with Maud that he had spent the night just before meeting her. He is on the point of confessing that nothing had happened between them when he suddenly understands that the young Catholic woman with whom Maud's ex-husband had had an affair was none other than Françoise. He decides therefore not to reveal to his wife that Maud was not his mistress.

CRITICAL RECEPTION

When *My Night at Maud's* was shown at the Cannes Film Festival on May 16, 1969, the critical reaction was lukewarm at best. As Michel Ciment later remarked, "Although they pleased some spectators, the games of love and wit that he developed in his film left the jury cold" (p. 42). What was most striking was the general ambivalence of the critics. Henry Chapier, for example, referred disparagingly to this "ultra-civilized chamber cinema" but couldn't help but admire this "marvelously insightful and subtle chronicle, this admirable recreation of a social milieu which resists the pressure of time" (p. 13). Jacqueline Lajeunesse exhibited the same conflicted attitude, calling the film's "Marivaudage" (sophisticated banter) of limited interest but at the same time recognizing that "Eric Rohmer has created a subtle and brilliant work" (p. 186). Jean de Baroncelli, on the other hand, was much less ambivalent, speaking of "verbal fireworks" and referring to the film as "marvelously old-fashioned," which was a rebuttal of one of the principal criticisms of the film (p. 11). As Jean Collet observed, "Everyone agrees at least on one thing: *My Night at Maud's* is not a fashionable film" (p. 182). Running counter to the type of cinema made fashionable in France by the New Wave, Rohmer's film returns to classical narrative style with its ideal of "transparency." It doesn't foreground its own techniques; it doesn't draw attention to filmic creation as such. It simply tells a story. Moreover, it is characterized by long dialogues in largely static shots. There are no editing effects and —the last anachronistic straw — the film is in black and white. While noting the traditional character of the film, only a few critics like Gilles Jacob perceived the qualities which were going to charm the Parisian public a month later: "*My Night at Maud's* by Eric Rohmer is just the opposite of a revolutionary cry. It touches us by the most classical qualities: psychological analysis, subtlety, sensitivity, rigor [...]. Rohmer proves brilliantly the stature of a filmmaker when intelligence takes over [...]. Here, it is the refinement, the spontaneity, and the accuracy of the tone which triumph" (*Nouvelles littéraires*, p. 14).

The appreciation expressed by Jacob was ratified by the public, which scorned the opinion of the judges at Cannes. The broad success of the film made Rohmer famous both in France and abroad. Many critics began to share the public opinion. In the article quoted above, Ciment described Rohmer's film as "a rare product, keenly intelligent," while noting also, like many critics, the beautiful images produced by Nestor Alemendros, the director of photography. Franz Gévaudan, among others, praised the "great quality of the dialogues" and the "dazzling performance" of the four main actors, as well as the "extraordinary lucidity of the staging" (p. 26). Janick Arbois was struck by a "mischievousness" and a "quality of humor" in Rohmer's film which were quite singular in French cinema (p. 38), while Gaston Haustrate remarked on the "astonishing originality of *Maud*," which he called a "masterpiece of intelligence."

The film continued nonetheless to draw fire from critics like Pascal Bonitzer, who found it "intentionally ideological" and accused it of promoting a conservative agenda which glorified the conjugal and maternal role of women (p. 59). Having been included in the French films selected for the Cannes Film Festival in 1969, *My Night at Maud's* won the Max Ophuls Prize the same year. In both London and New York the critics and public alike gave the film a warm welcome. In 1970 *Maud* was nominated at the Academy Awards for the Best Foreign Film. Its director was nominated for the best original screenplay and the best story. Rohmer finally joined his former colleagues at the *Cahiers du cinéma* (Truffaut and Godard especially) on the stage of world cinema.

BEFORE *MY NIGHT AT MAUD'S*

Born Jean-Marie Maurice Schérer in Tulle (in the Corrèze region in the center of France) in 1920, Eric Rohmer is the most "private" of the famous French film directors. As regards his private life outside of the cinema, we only know that he married in 1957, that he has two sons, and that he was a French professor in a number of Parisian high schools. As Magny points out, Rohmer long refused even to allow his picture to appear in the press. He shouted one day at a photographer, "No, I won't have it! No photos, ever. I'm against the star system. I want to remain in the shadows [...]. The author only exists by his work" (p. 7). It is said that Rohmer's decision to adopt a pseudonym and to avoid publicity was an effort to hide his profession as a filmmaker from his mother, who would have been scandalized at the thought of her son, a respectable professor, "lowering himself to make films" (Magny, p. 9). If Rohmer indeed stayed "in the shadows" during the first part of his career, his role in the world of cinema was no less important, as Molinier's chronology (pp. 29-32), summarized below, bears witness.

Ten years older than the "young Turks" — Truffaut, Godard, Chabrol, and Rivette, notably — whom he joined at the *Cahiers du cinéma*, Rohmer began a career as a film critic at the end of the forties. Between 1948 and 1963 he published around a hundred articles in various Parisian film magazines. In 1950 he created his own review, *La Gazette du cinéma*, which disappeared after five issues for financial reasons.

He was a member of the editorial staff of the *Cahiers du cinéma* from their beginning in 1951 and became editor-in-chief in 1958 after the death of André Bazin. (It was at this time that Rohmer finally abandoned his career as a high school teacher.) As early as 1950 he began making short fiction films, none of which have survived other than two films in the *Charlotte and Véronique* series, *Charlotte and Her Steak* (1951, 1961) and *Véronique and Her Dunce* (1958). He also wrote the screenplay for J.-L. Godard's short in the same series, *All The Boys Are Named Patrick* (1957).

Rohmer didn't make his first feature film, *The Sign of Leo* (*Le Signe du Lion*) until 1959, the same year that Truffaut's *The 400 Blows* and Resnais's *Hiroshima mon amour* appeared. Rohmer met considerable difficulty finding a distributor, which prevented the film from coming out until 1962. Unlike Truffaut's and Resnais's first films, which were both highly acclaimed and commercially successful, *The Sign of Leo* was a financial failure, despite very good critical reviews. Undiscouraged, Rohmer launched into a series of films that he baptized *Six Moral Tales* (*Six Contes moraux*; see below). The first two films, *The Girl at the Monceau Bakery* (*La Boulangère de Monceau*, 1962, 26 mins.) and *Suzanne's Career* (*La Carrière de Suzanne*, 1963, 52 mins.) were made in the most rudimentary conditions. Shot in 16 mm, they were never distributed and remain unknown to the broad public. In 1963 the *Cahiers du cinéma* underwent a dramatic upheaval. The majority of the critics wanted the review to adopt a more politicized (left-leaning) orientation. Since Rohmer was strongly opposed, he was replaced as editor-in-chief by Jacques Rivette.

To make a living, and to be able to continue his career as a filmmaker, Rohmer began making pedagogical films for public television. From 1964 to 1970 he directed around twenty films intended for distribution in the French schools. These works include *Diderot's Salons* (art criticism), *Cervantes's "Don Quixote,"* *La Bruyère's "Characters,"* and — especially notable as regards *My Night at Maud's* — *A Conversation About Pascal* (in 1965). In 1965 he also directed a short subject, *La Place de l'Etoile*, for a collaborative film (with several episodes by different directors) entitled *Paris, seen by...* This film marked the beginning of a long collaboration with a highly talented director of photography, Nestor Almendros, who would be responsible for the shooting of every Rohmer film from that point on.

In 1966 Rohmer had his first taste of success, both critical and commercial, with his third "moral tale," *The Collector* (*La Collectionneuse*), a feature film which won the Silver Bear Award for the Best Film at the Berlin Film Festival. This success, combined with financial help from Truffaut, permitted him in 1969 to make *My Night at Maud's*.

SIX MORAL TALES

My Night at Maud's was the eventual third film in the series of films that Rohmer calls *Six Moral Tales*. (This series would be followed by two other series of films, *Comedies and Proverbs* in the eighties and *Tales of the Four Seasons* in the nineties. See the *Filmography* at the end of the chapter.) The "moral tale" is a literary genre which may be traced back to the eighteenth century, when it first came into prominence with J.-F. Marmontel's *Moral Tales* (1755-59). As Rohmer explains, his tales were first produced in literary form (they were subsequently published as a book in 1974), before he began thinking of making films. Dissatisfied with the literary versions, which were poorly done in his opinion, he later decided to turn them into films.

Before discussing Rohmer's moral tales, it is important to clarify the meaning of the word "moral" here. Rohmer's tales belong to a centuries-long literary current in France referred to as the "moralist tradition." This tradition goes back as far as Montaigne's essays (sixteenth century) but is more generally associated with many of the greatest French authors of the classical period (second half of the seventeenth century) such as Pascal, Molière, Racine, La Rochefoucauld, La Fontaine, and La Bruyère. All of these writers tend to focus either on the psychological analysis of human behavior or on the study of the social mores of their time, if not on both.

Rohmer's *Six Moral Tales* are closely attached to this tradition, especially its focus on psychological analysis and the study of human character. His tales have no *moralizing* intention, which is related to another meaning of the word "moral." As he explained, "What I call a 'moral tale' is not a tale with a moral, but a story which describes less what people do than what is going on in their heads when they do it. Films which depict moods and thoughts as well as actions" (in Nogueira, p. 45). Rohmer added moreover that he uses the word "moral" in opposition to the word "physical" simply "to make it clear that the whole dramatic structure of these films is based on the evolution of the characters and not on external vicissitudes [...]. It is only the heroes' thoughts which give meaning to their acts" (in Simsolo, p. 88).

The series of six moral tales is conceived as a set of variations on the same thematic scheme, in which Rohmer simply tries to show, as he puts it, "a man attracted to a woman at the very moment that he is going to enter into a serious relationship with another woman" ("Lettre à un critique," p. 90). While this description is only applicable in a very general sense to the six films, it is clear that in each case a man is tempted by a woman who is not the one on whom he had originally set his sights or with whom he already has an amorous relationship. And in each case he returns to the first woman. In *Claire's Knee* (*Le Genou de Claire*, 1970), for example, Jérôme is a mature man who is engaged to be married. He is tempted by two adolescents, one after the other, when he is separated for a few days from his fiancée. At the end of the film he leaves to marry her. The narrator of the last film in the series, *Chloe in the Afternoon* (*L'Amour, l'après-midi*, 1972), is a married man who is severely tempted over a period of time by a former acquaintance who wants to seduce him. He escapes at the very last moment one afternoon by going home and making love...to his wife.

ACTORS, ORIGIN, AND SHOOTING

If *My Night at Maud's*, the "third" moral tale according to the order established by Rohmer, was in fact made after *The Collector*, it was due to the fact that Jean-Louis Trintignant was not free. Rohmer preferred to wait two years rather than cast a different actor in the role of the narrator. He was adamant about Trintignant playing this difficult role, and Trintignant's presence in the film was clearly a major factor in its success. Trintignant had been well known in France since his role in Roger Vadim's most famous film, *And God Created Woman* (1957), where he was cast opposite Brigitte Bardot. He was without a doubt one of the most famous actors in France at the end of the sixties, playing in twenty-four films between 1965 and 1969. In 1969 he played the main role not only in Rohmer's film but also in Costa-Gavras's *Z*, which was selected for the Cannes Festival in 1969 along with *Maud*. Trintignant won a Cesar for the Best Actor for his work in *Z*.

The other main actors, who also received critical raves, are all professionals, unlike the casts in Rohmer's preceding films where financial considerations forced him to use amateurs. All three were nonetheless relative unknowns, although Françoise Fabian, who plays the title role, had just appeared in Luis Buñuel's *Belle de jour* (1967). Antoine Vitez is known primarily as a stage director, and Marie-Christine Barrault (the niece of the famous mime, Jean-Louis Barrault), a young stage actress, was playing her first role in a film. She was to have a brilliant career as a movie actress.

My Night at Maud's was the product of a long gestation: "*Maud* was a subject that I had been carrying inside me since 1945. It has since undergone enormous modifications. The initial idea was a character forced to share a room with a woman by external circumstances" (in Bonitzer et al., 1970, p. 49). However, he added, these "circumstances" were "the curfew during the war and not the snow." In the end Rohmer decided, as he usually does, to place the action of his film in the present, a decision which was related to the "realism of his subject." He avoids "showing things which risk becoming too outmoded" (p. 49). However, the choice of snow was no accident: "The snow represents for me the movement from the 'tale' to the film. Snow has a great cinematographic value for me. It creates a stronger situation in the film, more universal that the external, historical circumstance of the Occupation" (p. 49).

The dialogue of *My Night at Maud's* was written two years before the shooting of the film — with the exception, Rohmer explains, of the "Marxist" ideas expressed by Vidal (Nogueira, p. 47). A Marxist in his personal life, Vitez collaborated with Rohmer on the writing of the lines for Vidal, the character he plays, when Vidal uses Pascal's wager (see below) to strengthen his Marxist faith in the meaning of history. As he does for each of his films, Rohmer demanded that his actors respect the text of the screenplay scrupulously, even seasoned actors like Trintignant. With few exceptions he refused improvisation during the filming, probably because he had grown accustomed in his earlier films to doing only one take per scene to keep the costs down. In any case, Rohmer claimed that "it is easier to get a perfect shot with a single take rather than with several" (in Nogueira, p. 46), because repeated takes are detrimental to the spontaneity of the actors. That is the approach he adopted for the shooting of *Maud* in general, except for the long dinner sequence at Maud's, which required several takes. As for his crew, Rohmer worked without a script girl and, again to save money, used neither costumes nor make-up. In addition Rohmer never puts mood music in his films. Other than the voice-over of the narrator, the few times we hear it in the film, there are no non-diegetical sound effects or music — only those that belong to the film's fictional universe. Rohmer attaches considerable importance to the actors' intonations, their vocal modulations. The "musical side" of Rohmer's films, as he says, is "the music of the voices" (in Nogueira, p. 48). We will speak later of the importance of dialogue in Rohmer's films.

Insofar as possible Rohmer shoots his films on location, at the places where the action is situated. Therefore, he shot *Maud* at Clermont-Ferrand, which he doubtlessly chose not only because it is a prototypical provincial city, but also because it is where Pascal lived. Extremely attached to realism, Rohmer highlights the precise topography of the city of Clermont. As he says, "The cinema shows real things. If I show a house, it's a real, complete house, not a cardboard house. When I show traffic in the streets, it's the real traffic in the city in question, at the period in question" (in Bonitzer et al., 1970, p. 49). We recognize in fact the Place de Jaude in the center of Clermont, the café *Le Suffren*, the Notre-Dame du Port church, and, outside the city, the Puy de Pariou which the narrator climbs in the snow with Maud. The only exception is the long dinner scene at Maud's, which was shot in the studio in artificial scenery — a first for Rohmer, who had always shot interiors in real apartments. But it was also the first time that Rohmer shot with sound, "which corresponds better to his taste for realism and for seizing the moment" (J. Magny, p. 132), instead of resorting to post-synchronization of the sound track.

As he did in his first two tales, and despite a positive experience with color in *The Collector*, Rohmer chose to shoot *Maud* in black and white, to widespread consternation since everyone was filming in color by this time. This choice may be explained by his habit of cutting costs but also by the symbolism to which the stark contrast of black and white, as well as the opposition of light and dark, lends itself. But we will discuss that later.

PASCAL AND JANSENISM VS. JESUITISM

Before making films Rohmer taught French literature in high school for many years. He knew very well the great writers of the classical period, as well as those of the French Enlightenment, and we see allusions to Rousseau in *The Collector* and in *Claire's Knee*, as well as to Diderot in *Chloe in the afternoon*. But no classical author plays a more central role in a Rohmer film than does Pascal, the famous mathematician and author of *Thoughts*, in *My Night at Maud's*. As we know, near the beginning of the film the narrator begins rereading Pascal, whom he had read in high school. Pascal was an adherent of Jansenism, which is a Catholic movement based on a very strict moral code. It had many members in France between 1640 and 1715, before being condemned and banished as a heresy. The Jansenists' center was located at Port-Royal outside of Paris, under the direction of the theologians Antoine Arnauld and Pierre Nicole. They subscribed to the morality promoted in the doctrine of Saint Augustine, which condemned as forms of "concupiscence" the three principal "passions" which attach men to the world: sensual pleasures, scientific curiosity, and ambition. If Pascal refused to grant any importance to tasty food and to the good local wine (Chanturges), as Jean-Louis reproaches him, it is because these are "sensual pleasures." If Pascal condemned mathematics and science at the end of his life (a position which "shocks" the hero), after having been one of the most illustrious mathematicians of his time, it is because interest in science, for the Augustinians, is only "futile curiosity," a profane activity which distracts men from God.

The allusions to *Thoughts* in *My Night at Maud's* recall some of the most famous reflections in Pascal's work, such as:

"Man is only a reed, the most feeble being in nature; but he is a thinking reed [...]. All of our human dignity consists in our ability to think."

The two infinities: "For what is Man in nature? Nothing with respect to infinity, everything with respect to nothing, a midpoint between nothing and everything."

The part of the text of *Thoughts* that the narrataor looks at when he leafs through the book in the bookstore (the part about diminishing the passions by adopting the gestures of faith) is found near the end of the famous passage on the "wager." The wager was basically a stratagem to coax some friends who were dedicated gamblers into accepting the Christian faith. He suggests to them the following reasoning: "Let's suppose that either God exists or he doesn't exist. Which way shall we lean? Reason is useless in this case." So we are obliged to make a wager. "Let's compare what we can gain with what we can lose by wagering that God exists. If you bet on God and you win, you win everything; if you bet on him and you lose, you lose nothing. So go ahead and bet that he exists [...]; there is an infinity of infinitely happy life to gain as opposed to a finite number of chances of losing..." (*Thoughts*, pp. 127-128). It is this logic that Vidal applies to his "faith" in the Marxist interpretation of history. But it is precisely this "lottery" side of the wager that offends Jean-Louis as a Christian.

The staunchest enemies of the Jansenists were the Jesuits (members of the Society of Jesus, founded in the sixteenth century by Saint Ignatius of Loyola). To provoke Jean-Louis during the dinner, Vidal accuses him of "Jesuitism." The creation of the Jansenist movement (like that of the Reformed Church in the sixteenth century) was principally a reaction against the lax morality of the Catholic Church, of which the "casuistry" of the Jesuit moralists was the best example. Casuistry is a subtle type of reasoning ("ratiocination") whose purpose was to permit the sinner to shirk his moral duty. Commentators have referred, for example, to the "casuistic discourse of Jean-Louis in *My Night at Maud's*" as regards marriage (Serceau, *Eric Rohmer*, p. 111). To accuse someone of "Jesuitism" is to suggest that his morality is suspect and that he is a hypocrite.

We should mention finally that Pascal's *Thoughts* have a very particular status in the moralist tradition in France. Although unfinished, the *Thoughts* were intended to be a vast vindication of Christianity, a characteristic which ties the work closely to the Christian moral tradition. At the same time Pascal offers an in-depth study of human character and of the human condition, which integrates his work into the secular moralist tradition described above. If Rohmer chose to place the *Thoughts* at the very center of *My Night at Maud's*, it was certainly in order to play on both registers at the same time. This broad two-sided appeal of the work would explain the surprising public reception which the film enjoyed and which far exceeded the expectations of the filmmaker himself. The secular spectators were attracted by the study of social mores and the psychological analysis of the hero (his hypocrisy notably), while the faithful undoubtedly appreciated the reflection on the moral dilemma which temptation poses to the serious Christian in today's world, as well as the "virtuous" choice of the hero in the end. Moreover, the choice of the *Thoughts* as the focal point of the film seems to reflect, in a kind of *mise en abyme*, the importance that Rohmer attaches, as he often remarks, to the study of the "thoughts" of his characters, the "moral" side of his tales.

With this digression on Pascal, Jansenism, and Jesuitism, we have already introduced a certain number of the important ideas in this film. Let's look more closely now at the dense thematic fabric of *My Night at Maud's*.

THEMES

"*My Night at Maud's* may be considered," Marion Vidal remarks, "to be the most representative of the *Moral Tales*. The basic motif is illustrated in an exemplary fashion here: the meeting of the chosen woman, the intervention of the seductress, then the return to the chosen woman" (p. 85). These two feminine figures, "the chosen woman" and the "seductress" (or the "temptress"), who revolve around the narrator of the *Moral Tales*, find their ultimate incarnation in the opposition of "Maud the Dark" and "Françoise the Light" (p. 85). The hero loves the blond Catholic, whom he doesn't even know, is tempted for a moment by the beauty, intelligence, and sensuality of Maud, but resists temptation and succeeds in marrying Françoise as he had resolved to do. Although it is an apparently simple and edifying story, if one looks more closely it is neither so simple nor so edifying. Although ambiguity is characteristic of all of Rohmer's films, it is in *My Night at Maud's* that he develops most deeply the ambiguity of his characters, "this contrast [...] between the behavior of the characters and a backdrop of nebulous intentions and unavowed motives that we suspect" (Vidal, pp. 98-99). This begins with the testimony of the narrator himself, whose viewpoint we share but whom we increasingly suspect of "bad faith" (hypocrisy) — which constitutes one of the principal themes of the film. Let's begin however at the beginning.

The film is dominated from the outset by the themes of chance and probability. The hero's meetings, whether it be with Françoise (three times) or with Vidal, are due strictly to chance. The calculation of probabilities (the hero's favorite pastime) leads to an allusion to Pascal's "wager," first by Vidal, who distorts its Pascalian meaning to justify his Marxist faith in history, as we've noted above. The theme of the wager then reappears at Maud's dinner, where Jean-Louis expresses his repugnance: "*No, what I dislike about the wager is the idea of exchanging something, of buying one's ticket like in a lottery.*" Nonetheless, his plan to marry Françoise, whom he doesn't yet know — he doesn't even know if he'll ever see her again — resembles curiously Pascal's wager: despite the very small probability that he will marry her, if he succeeds in doing so, his gain may be infinite. Therefore, when he gets out of the car to approach the girl in the street at night, without even being sure that it is she, he says to her: "*Even if there had only been one chance out of ten that it was you, I would have stopped.*" The potential gain compensated the slender probability.

As important as the wager may be here, the Pascalian thematics go far beyond to include the condemnation of the "distractions" of life, of all the worldly passions, including scientific curiosity, which distract us from our higher interests, the salvation of our soul. Jean-Louis is a practicing Christian who appreciates good food and wine and enjoys the other sensual pleasures of life as well (he has cohabited with several different women). Moreover, his favorite hobby is the science of mathematics. It is hardly surprising that he revolts against Pascal's Jansenist moral code: "*Insofar as I am Catholic, or at least am trying to be, that goes against the grain of my understanding of Catholicism. It is precisely because I am a Christian that I protest against this rigorism.*" Vidal, who doubts Jean-Louis's sincerity, declares to Maud, "*He hates Pascal because Pascal is his bad conscience, because he knows that Pascal is alluding to him, stigmatizing his false Christianity.*" He adds, turning the knife, "*He is Jesuitism incarnate,*" that is, a perfect hypocrite. This theme will be taken up again later by Maud herself, who, despite being a freethinker, will tell the hero that she is "shocked" by his attitude, the ease with which he reconciles his bachelor's love life, his lack of chastity, and his Christian faith. Noting the contradiction between his moral principles and his behavior, she criticizes him for being "*a guilt-ridden Christian combined with a guilt-ridden Don Juan.*"

The particular relationship between secular love and Christian morality is thus at the very heart of the debate which is developed in this film, and the narrator insists on their complementarity by declaring that "*religion enriches love, but love enriches religion as well.*" On another plane, but still related to Christianity, Rohmer develops the theme of "luck" to which the hero returns several times, congratulating himself on always "having been lucky" in life. The theme of luck is related to those of destiny and Christianity. Clearly believing in Divine Providence, the narrator seems convinced, without daring to say so, that he has a special destiny, that God is watching over him in particular: "He simply believes that he has grace" (Vidal, p. 90). For her part, Maud complains that she has never been lucky with men, having been disappointed in both of her marriages and having lost a man she loved deeply in a car accident.

Among the other "secular" themes of the film, we note especially the motif of libertinism — or simply womanizing — which is a constant in the *Moral Tales*. Represented by Vidal in particular, the tendency to womanize — as in the case of Vidal's one night stands at scholarly conventions — serves here as a foil to the hero's morality, to the Christian conception of love that he is trying to defend. Ironically Vidal speaks of "*going to mass to pick up girls,*" a comment which alludes to the way in which Jean-Louis first noticed Françoise, although Vidal has no way of knowing this. Another secular theme, perhaps the most important in the film, is lying. To be perfectly frank, the narrator lies. He lies about trivial things but also about very important things, as when he tells Françoise that he had "slept" with a woman just before meeting her. Just as he will lie by omission when he understands, at the end of the film, that Françoise was the mistress of Maud's husband.

SYMBOLS AND METAPHORS

As a number of critics have noted, the choice of black and white for *My Night at Maud's* is particularly appropriate for this film. Black and white "corresponds to the austerity of the subject and the characters," as it does to the season (winter and snow) (Magny, p. 132). For Vidal the use of black and white emphasizes the fact that *Maud* is "a work of snow and night" (p. 85). The snow itself has a particular thematic value in the film, serving as an "instrument of destiny" (Vidal, p. 85) in that it is the snow which forces Jean-Louis to spend the night at Maud's, as later in Françoise's student foyer.

Moreover, the cold suggested by the snow serves explicitly as a metaphor in several respects. On the one hand, the cold and snow are related here to lucidity and to a sort of force of character (which Jean-Louis seems to lack). When the narrator leaves Maud's apartment early in the morning, he shares with the reader (in the written version) his confused feelings: "*Outside, the cold and the whiteness of the snow, far from comforting me, brought me to my senses and made me feel ashamed for lacking the courage either to reject clearly Maud's overtures or, having begun to respond to her, to finish what*

I had started" (*Six Contes moraux*, p. 107). In addition, the coldness of the winter is related to the "cold feelings" of the narrator, his lack of passion as regards Maud. When Jean-Louis kisses her during the hike up the Puy de Pariou, remarking that he likes her cold lips, she answers, *"It's just like your feelings."*

The theme of "coldness" is closely tied as well to the theme of marriage, which appears again and again in the film, and especially in relation to love. In *My Night at Maud's*, as in the other moral tales, marriage seems to be opposed to love, indeed, to be inimical to it. Love is scarcely a factor in the narrator's decision to marry Françoise; it is dictated by his tastes (she's blond) and his principles (she's a practicing Catholic). Jean-Louis's lukewarm sentiments, if not to say his coldness, escapes neither Maud nor Françoise, who both recognize that his behavior toward women is based on his "principles." However, Françoise is no less cold, and one might well suspect her of being frigid. In this respect she is completely characteristic of the "chosen woman" (the woman that the hero marries) in the *Moral Tales*: "The chosen woman is a lukewarm individual, often cold, virtually devoid of sensuality, who does not stimulate the hero sexually […]. The wife is above all an idea, an element in the intellectual and moral project of the narrator, his anchoring point and his lifebelt" (Magny, p. 69). Hardly an encouraging image of marriage or of conjugal life to come!

To conclude this discussion, we should mention that another element of winter, the ice on the roads (which was responsible for the death of Maud's lover, whose car slid off the road), also contains metaphorical dimensions. It may evoke, as Molinier suggests, the risk of moral "slippage" that the narrator faces during his night at Maud's (p. 78). She convinces him to stay over — perhaps ironically — precisely because of the danger of his car "slipping." Just as ironic is the fact that it is the slipping of his car on the ice which leads Jean-Louis to spend the night at Françoise's foyer, where he runs no risk of slippage of any kind given the lack of passion between them.

FORM OF THE NARRATIVE AND CINEMATOGRAPHIC STYLE

In the first three tales (in the order in which they were made, despite the eventual numbering), the narrator relates his adventure in voice-over throughout the films. This represents a kind of retrospective stream-of-consciousness, a commentary to which the spectator is made privy as well as to the dialogues of the characters. In *Maud*, quite on the contrary, we only hear the inner voice of the narrator twice: once towards the beginning when he has the abrupt "revelation" that Françoise will be his wife, a second time at the very end when he suddenly understands that Françoise was the mistress of Maud's husband. Rohmer explains this change in narrative technique by the proliferation of the hero's lines in the dialogue: "In *My Night at Maud's* […] the protagonist explains his positions so completely in the presence of his different partners that it would have been difficult to include longer asides from him to the public. Therefore, he will only assert his presence as narrator in the title of the film and by two brief statements intended simply to clarify the situation" ("Lettre à un critique," pp. 90-91). Rohmer added that he had concluded that the inner voice of the narrator could be detrimental to his character: "However, one of the reasons I didn't develop

Trintignant's commentary more is precisely because of that: the character would have become more distant, more antipathetic" (Bonitzer et al., p. 54).

As we indicated at the beginning of this chapter, Rohmer's cinema is worlds apart from the type of filmmaking which was in favor in this period. This is largely owing to the prominence of language, of dialogue, in his films. Contrary to the New Wave style which had become the critical standard, Rohmer does not foreground camerawork in his films, the various techniques related to the shooting (close-ups, tracking shots, striking camera angles), and even less any special editing effects. In *Maud*, for example, there are no tracking shots (other than the sequences shot in Jean-Louis's car) and only four zooms, all of them bringing us closer to Françoise. The dominant camera movement is the pan, which is used subtly in the interplay between the characters without drawing attention to itself.

Rohmer's ideal, which is thoroughly classical, is "transparency," the complete absence of the camera. What Rohmer refuses is the tendency in "modern" French cinema to highlight the work of the filmmaker, to turn cinema into its own subject: "The concrete evidence of the artist's work in the cinema is something *shocking*, much more shocking than in the other arts […]. The greatest danger for cinema is precisely this vanity of the filmmaker who says, I have a style and I want to exhibit it" (in Bonitzer et al., p. 53). As Magny remarks, "Rohmer's directing is based on a spontaneous and unaffected apprehension of reality: the goal of each shot, devoid of any stylistic pretensions, seems to be to show us as clearly and as simply as possible what the filmmaker has chosen to offer to our gaze, to our judgment" (p. 19). Rohmer's principal concern in making a film is "the most precise recreation of reality" (p. 21), which explains why he almost always shoots with sound and on location — whether interiors or exteriors — and why he insists on using natural light, even if that means waiting hours to get the light which corresponds to the exact moment of the day he wants to record.

Rohmer's films are dominated by conversation. He refuses the notion that dialogue is not "cinematographic," insisting that words are an integral part of life, and that it is life that he wishes to film. Verbal communication between people is no less a subject for cinema than the representation of their actions, "and to those people who tell me that this isn't cinema," says Rohmer, "I've often responded that most of the situations I've met in life are situations *in which people speak*. Those in which people don't speak are the exception" (in Séailles, p. 15).

Nonetheless, this does not mean that the technique employed by Rohmer in his films is of no interest — far from it. The long sequence of the evening at Maud's, which takes up almost half of the film, is one of the best examples of the subtlety of Rohmer's technique in filming long conversations. It consists largely of a very calculated type of interplay between image and voice-over in which the typical angle-reverse angle shots of conventional dialogue scenes are often replaced (but not always) by very discreet and fluid camera movements which maintain the unity of space, its "realism," while emphasizing the relations between the characters. As Vidal points out, "The camera is often focused on the person who is listening and not on the one who is speaking" (p. 101), so that the spectator can observe the reactions, the gestures, and the facial expressions of the interlocutor. When Rohmer changes shots to indicate that the conversation has entered a new phase, this change is all the more striking since it is in stark contrast to the fluid style of the preceding dialogue. Rohmer plays subtly on the size of the shots as well. While long shots or knee-length shots are frequent in the first part of the evening at Maud's (when the focus is not on Maud and Jean-Louis), near shots become more and more prevalent as soon as Vidal leaves. This technique serves to "underline the increased intimacy" between the narrator and Maud (Vidal, p. 103).

In Rohmer's films everything contributes in the end to an impression of authenticity. This is a veritable obsession of the filmmaker, "the very foundation of Rohmer's cinema," according to Magny, who adds, "To the realism which dictates the choice of everything which is placed before the camera's lens corresponds the realism of the images: angles, focal lengths, lighting, everything is designed to make the camera disappear so that the screen becomes a window which opens onto the world, so that nothing comes between the spectator and the universe of the film. Rohmer's primary goal is the transparency of the images, and the force of his cinema is based on the radical nature of this approach" (p. 22). In the face of the hegemony of what is referred to as "modern" cinema, Rohmer seems to win his wager. If Maud doesn't succeed in seducing the narrator, the filmmaker does indeed succeed in seducing his public. Whether they be believers, agnostics, or atheists, his spectators follow him, somewhat mystified, in this long reflection on the ambiguous relations between morality and human behavior.

STUDY GUIDE

Director's Comments

"My intention was not to film the events themselves but the events as related by someone. The story, the choice of the facts, their organization, and the manner of understanding them were all a function of the main character and not of my treatment of this character. One of the reasons why the *Tales* are called "moral" is that they are practically devoid of physical action: everything happens in the narrator's head. If the story had been told by someone else, it would have been different or it wouldn't have existed at all. Somewhat like Don Quixote, my heroes see themselves as characters in a novel, but perhaps there is no novel" (*Six Contes moraux*, p. 12).

"Where do I find my subjects? I find them in my imagination [...]. I don't do portraits of real people. Within the narrow limits that I set for myself, I present various plausible human types, female as well as male."

"It's important to understand what *I say*. What my characters say is not necessarily what my film says [...]. Neither the commentary nor the dialogues are my film: they are things that I film, just like the countryside, the faces, the movements, the gestures [...]. Like images, words are part of the life that I'm filming [...]. Basically I'm not *saying*, I'm showing. I'm showing people who act and speak" (Prédal, p. 34).

"The main character of my films is above all self-indulgent. He is constantly a dupe [...] of his own philosophy, which he uses to justify himself. My view of him is fairly critical. His complacency is always denounced by his partners. On the other hand my feminine characters are more sympathetic, or at least more lucid. You should never get the impression that I'm justifying the masculine character, especially when he is justifying himself. Not at all. It's just the opposite. My masculine characters are intentionally antipathetic" (Nogueira, p. 53).

"All the characters are depicted as dogmatic but uncertain. On the one hand the Catholic, on the other the Marxist, but also Maud, who clings to her upbringing as a freethinker, a radical-socialist. Faithfulness is one of the major themes of my *Moral Tales*, with betrayal as the foil" (Bonitzer et al., "Nouvel Entretien avec Eric Rohmer," p. 50).

"What I don't like about many films, especially "poetic" films, is that they are spoiled by the music, which is often very trite and not at all necessary. I really don't see what music is good for, other than patching up a bad film. A good film can do without it. In fact it is not a modern feature of cinema; it is just a holdover from silent film, when there was a piano playing in the movie theater. Associating some sort of music to leaves on the trees, to clouds passing by, or even to someone opening his door is the worst of conventions, a totally outmoded practice. In my *Moral Tales* there is only real music, when the characters listen to records or the radio. There is absolutely no other music, not even during the titles" (Biette et al., p. 56).

Excepts for Discussion

Excerpt 1 (6'00-8'20): After mass Jean-Louis (in his car) follows the blond girl (on her moped) in the streets of the old quarters of Clermont-Ferrand.

Excerpt 2 (37'50-39'40): The evening at Maud's. Vidal asks Jean-Louis what he would do if Maud gave him to understand that she would like to make love with him. Maud and Vidal question Jean-Louis about the woman they suspect he is in love with. (Jean-Louis: "*No !...I was talking about before*" up to Jean-Louis: "*No...no, I find this amusing...much more amusing than you can imagine*").

Excerpt 3 (1h03'50-7'20): The "seduction" scene. Jean-Louis has just turned out the lights. He turns around and sees that Maud is naked under the covers. They sleep "together." At dawn Maud draws Jean-Louis into her embrace. He responds, then breaks loose; Maud leaves the bed abruptly...

Excerpt 4 (1'10'30-12'35): Jean-Louis approaches Françoise in the street.

Excerpt 5 (1h39'30-40'25): Jean-Louis and Françoise meet Vidal in the center of Clermont; Jean-Louis notices that Françoise knows Vidal already. Vidal informs Jean-Louis that Maud is going to leave for Toulouse the next day (Rohmer's technique in filming conversation scenes).

Excerpt 6 (1h45'40-49'50): Epilogue, last sequence. Jean-Louis meets Maud at the seashore. He rejoins Françoise and their child on the beach, speaks to her of Maud. The couple runs towards the sea with their child.

Quotations for Comment

Jean-Louis (voice-over): "That day, on Monday, December 21, the idea came to me, abruptly, precisely, definitively...that Françoise would be my wife."

* * *

Vidal: "He hates Pascal because Pascal is his bad conscience...because he knows that Pascal is alluding to him, stigmatizing his false Christianity."

Maud: "Is that true?"

Vidal: "He is Jesuitism incarnate."

Jean-Louis: "No…I said that I didn't like Pascal, because Pascal has a…very particular conception of Christianity."

* * *

Jean-Louis: "I had affairs with girls that I loved and that I was considering marrying, but I've never gone to bed with a girl just for that… If I didn't, it wasn't for moral reasons, it's because I just don't see the point of it."

Vidal: "Yes…but suppose you found yourself on a trip with a beautiful girl you knew you'd never see again. There are circumstances in which it's difficult to resist temptation."

Jean-Louis: "Fate, and I don't mean God, has always spared me that kind of circumstance."

* * *

Maud: "You know, you really shock me."

Jean-Louis: "*I* shock you! It's him! He's the one who keeps saying terrible things about me."

Vidal: "Well, am I lying?"

Jean-Louis: "No, you aren't lying, but…"

Maud: "I thought that a Christian was supposed to stay chaste until he got married."

Jean-Louis: "Like I said, I don't pretend to be a model."

* * *

Jean-Louis: "Perhaps I'm going to shock you again, but that's too bad. Running after women doesn't separate you from God anymore than — I don't know — doing mathematics."

* * *

Maud: "You know, what annoys me the most about you is that you're slippery. You won't take responsibility for yourself. You're a guilty-ridden Christian combined with a guilt-ridden Don Juan. That takes the cake."

* * *

Jean-Louis: "Each time I was involved with a girl […], it helped me to understand a moral problem that I was unaware of, which I had never had to face before. I was forced to take a position which for me was beneficial, which revived me morally."

Maud: "But you could very well have benefited morally without getting involved physically."

Jean-Louis: "Yes, but the moral side didn't appear…didn't exist…Well yes, of course, I know, anything is possible! But the physical and moral sides are indissociable. You have to be realistic."

* * *

Maud: "Well, even so, you seem terribly devious to me."

Jean-Louis: "Devious?"

Maud: "Yes. I thought that Christians believed that a man is judged by his acts…and you don't seem to attach much importance to that."

Jean-Louis: "To my acts? Sure I do. Tremendous importance. But for me it's not a particular act that counts, it's the sum of one's life."

* * *

Jean-Louis: "What is essential is pureness of heart. When a man really loves a woman, he has no desire to sleep with another one."

* * *

Maud (in her apartment): "You know, what I don't like about you is…your lack of spontaneity."

Jean-Louis: "But I've bared my soul to you. What more do you want?"

[…]

Maud: "I'm talking about the way you calculate everything, the way you predict and classify. 'My wife has to be Catholic,' for instance. Love is secondary."

* * *

The Priest (in the church): "But above and beyond our fears, we must have a faith […] which simply reminds us that God loves us…and that this man, this Saint that we are called to be is only a man who is constantly wrestling, on the one hand, with certain difficulties of living, of being…of living with his existence as a man, with his passions, his weaknesses, his affections but, on the other hand, with the difficulty of living his desire to be a disciple of Jesus Christ."

* * *

Jean-Louis (after Françoise's confession): "I'm going to tell you something in confidence. The very morning we met, I had just left a girl's apartment. I had slept with her."

Françoise: "Why don't we just never speak about all this again, OK? Do you agree?"

* * *

Jean-Louis (voice-over, at the beach, concerning his night at Maud's): "I was going to say, 'Nothing happened between us,' when I suddenly understood that Françoise's embarrassment had nothing to do with what she was learning about me; it was about what she had guessed I had learned about her — and that I had just discovered in fact at that moment and not before. So I said instead, "Yes, that was my last fling."

Questions/Topics for Reflection

1. The personal situation of the main characters: Jean-Louis, Maud, Vidal, Françoise.
2. The circumstances under which the hero meets Françoise; the beginning of his courtship of her.
3. The themes of chance, of probability, and of Pascal's wager.
4. The themes of luck and fate.
5. Jean-Louis's Catholicism and his past (his love affairs); the problem of hypocrisy.
6. The development of relations between Jean-Louis and Maud.
7. The development of relations between Jean-Louis and Françoise.
8. The meaning of the denouement (the epilogue at the seashore).
9. The thematic importance of the season (winter) and of the setting of the action (Clermont-Ferrand).
10. Rohmer's style and the role of language.

CRITICAL DOSSIER

René Prédal — Rohmer's "Classical" Style

Rohmer's staging is based on what is self-evident, and if the ultimate solution he adopts each time is the simplest, it's not because it was the first one he thought of but, on the contrary, because it was the one which was finally retained after all the others were rejected. It is therefore always the richest choice, the one which expresses the most in the simplest way: the static shot chosen after having considered the wildest tracking shots, the front view chosen after having tried all the other angles, the Howard Hawks approach preferred to Orson Welles's.

If Rohmer wishes to communicate, he insists on doing it in the most challenging manner; that is, by the purity of his style and not by the weirdness of his staging. He does it by a subtle interweaving of micro-sequences closely related to the chronology and the topography and not organized with the intention of producing a brilliant or an unusual montage. But purity is not poverty, and his cinematographic language can transmit the most subtle impressions, express the most fleeting sentiments, inject humor into the most serious maxims by appealing to the intelligence of a spectator immediately charmed by his measured discourse [...].

His style is referred to as classical because it highlights values which are not in fashion as this century draws to a close. Indeed, his manner of expression tends toward clarity and rigorous unity of action; the narrator only recounts what is directly related to the psychological situation in question. Rohmer shows little interest in the context. He concentrates his linear narrative on a limited subject, eliminating any secondary themes, characters, or episodes. Since the stories he tells are concentrated in time and take place in a very limited number of places, commentators are likely to discover the principal characteristics which define a classical style" ("Les Ecritures d'Eric Rohmer," pp. 47-48).

Marion Vidal — Filming Conversation Scenes

The meal sequence is a game of hide-and-seek in which Vidal, Maud, and Jean-Louis observe each other and attempt to unmask each other without giving themselves away. The filmmaker frames the character who is speaking, moves to the listener, remains on him while he answers and even when the first person has begun to speak again, then returns to that person to record the end of his comments. It stays on him while we hear the other person, in voice-over, resume the dialogue. This frequent disjunction between the camera and the character who is speaking and this slow gliding toward the interlocutor give the conversation scenes an incomparable flow that would be difficult to produce with a classical découpage in which angle-reverse angle shots are used automatically throughout the dialogue.

Joël Magny — The Rohmerian Hero

Like the libertine, the Rohmerian hero wants above all to reserve for himself the privilege of choosing, even if it means justifying his irrational inclination, after the fact, by suggesting that it was a choice dictated by virtuous principles. Moreover, even those who choose, in what they try to pass off as an act of pure will, the one woman, the chosen one, the wife to whom they will swear faithfulness, never seem to do so in a leap of passionate love. Reason prevails over any demands of sentiment. The narrator of *My Night at Maud's* spends the whole film justifying an intellectual decision intended to protect him from a life of dissipation.

Michel Serceau — Jean-Louis and Love

His words and his behavior during the long evening at Maud's leave the impression of an individual who [...] claims to have had a love life in which pleasures of the flesh were always subordinated to the dictates of the heart and intentions to marry. Without going into the "Jesuitism" of the character (evident when Maud brings out his contradictions regarding the moral problems he attempts to gloss over), let's just note that the function of Maud and Vidal is to force the hero to admit or demonstrate that his pretense of refusing carnal pleasures for themselves, of refusing sensual pleasure without love is simply an element in an ideological positioning, in a project he is developing, that is, the wager he is making on Françoise.

What happens at the end of this night shows the falseness of the position taken the previous evening, according to which "when a man really loves a woman, he has no desire to sleep with another woman." As we see in the excerpt of the *Thoughts* shown in the bookstore, we are dealing with an individual who is trying to believe in a love which subsumes carnal desires, who is trying to convert to a type of love which diminishes the passions which are, to paraphrase the end of Pascal's text, "the great obstacles" ("Mythes et masques de l'amour," p. 72).

Marion Vidal — "Maud The Dark, Françoise The Light"

My Night at Maud's may be considered to be the most representative of the Moral Tales. The scenario is exemplary as regards the paradigm established by Rohmer: the meeting of the chosen woman, the attempts to make her acquaintance, the intervention of the temptress, then the return to the chosen one [...]. No hesitation here, no ambiguity. Françoise is instantly recognized by the narrator as *"the One, the Incomparable, the Sum of All Perfections Ever Imagined or Desired."* Maud is the first active seducer in the whole series of films. Owing to her beauty, intelligence, and distinction, she is the perfect temptress. Maud the dark, Françoise the light — the two women are diametrically opposed in every way. For once the combat is equal: the incontestable superiority of the seducer compensates effectively for the handicap posed by the narrator's bias toward the chosen woman. Finally, the role of fate and chance in the hero's life, as well as the moral implications of his acts, are studied in depth. Placed on a metaphysical and religious plane, the level of reflection is brought to new heights within the *Moral Tales* (*Les Contes moraux d'Eric Rohmer*, p. 85).

Marion Vidal (cont.) — Maud and Seduction

Maud may appear to be an unscrupulous vamp, a black widow implacably spinning the web in which Jean-Louis will become entangled [...]. It is true that she doesn't hesitate to lie about the existence of a guest room and that this lie is troubling, coming from such an honest person. The manner in which she gets rid of Vidal, who is sick with jealousy beneath his cocky manner, may also seem cruel [...].

The manner in which Maud draws in the narrator is clearly a strategic masterpiece. Having intentionally slipped into her bed so that she cannot move, she obliges him to serve her. She asks him first for cigarettes, then a glass of water, little by little taming him and subjugating him. She turns against him the reasons he offers for leaving her. He says that he should leave out of courtesy and tact, but she proves to him that he is only concerned with respectability and that he should keep her company if only out of compassion and Christian charity. But does she really want to seduce him? Isn't she just in need of some company and human warmth in those difficult days following her divorce? [...] So what are we to think of the early morning embrace? Is it the natural reaction of a sensual, uninhibited woman responding half-asleep to the appeal of a male body? Or is it part of a calculated seduction plan? Did Maud want to seduce Jean-Louis? And if she did, why? Because she is in love with him? To punish Vidal? Or was it just to prove that the charms of an atheist could triumph over the scruples of a true believer? To take vengeance on the mysterious blond girl who reminds her, and justifiably so, of her rival for her husband's affections? As usual, the mystery is far from being resolved (*Les Contes moraux d'Eric Rohmer*, pp. 97-98).

Maria Tortajada — Picking up Girls

Does a man marry a girl he picks up? The analyses of this film which emphasize that marriage represents the renunciation of seduction tend to forget that the so-called ideal woman is a girl who has been picked up in the street. In principle she's just as good as any other woman. In *My Night at Maud's* the narrator, who is a practicing Catholic, doesn't hesitate to follow the young woman he had noticed at church, or to approach her in the street. Of course he can use the alibi of marriage, since he had thought of it even before speaking to her. Nonetheless, to all outside appearances he is picking her up. The hero in fact runs after Françoise in the street just after having spent the night in Maud's bed [...]. The difference between the blond Catholic girl and the atheist brunette is not overly apparent. Ultimately, what distinguishes serious love from a simple love affair? [...] Of course, these depictions of men picking up women in Rohmer's films don't have exactly the same tone as the short films produced at the beginning of the New Wave. Picking up girls has become more ambiguous as it is treated with a more serious tone by certain characters. However, the shadow cast by this prosaic type of seduction envelops the later works of the filmmaker and imbues with ambiguity, if not irony, seduction attempts which are passed off as "honorable" (*Le Spectateur séduit*, pp. 71-74).

Pascal Bonitzer — A Narrative Invaded By Lies

I'm going to tell this story in my own way, as I see it — the narrator of *Maud* seems to say — *but be forewarned that there is another way of seeing things which would totally contradict my version.* In this text at least [the literary version of the tale], which is like a diffracted reflection of the film, Rohmer appeals implicitly to the critical sense of the readers, who are also the spectators. We shouldn't base our understanding of this story just on what it seems to be saying but also on what isn't said, on what is concealed. In the overt text of the narrative lurks perhaps another text, another narrative, a latent narrative, a subtext which is quite different from the one which is given to us […]. Rohmer is a storyteller filmmaker, a raconteur, but every story in his films — following a program announced long ago — is invaded by lies, certain types of lies (*Eric Rohmer*, pp. 13-14).

Pascal Bonitzer (cont.) — Conjugal Bliss and Illusion

[Vidal] is radically diminished by the episode to the advantage of Jean-Louis, whose charm, by contrast, works effortlessly. But Maud is lonely also, and if she is more dignified, she appears no less sad at the end of the film in comparison to the obvious happiness of Jean-Louis and his family.

Nonetheless, does the film tell us that we should be happy with (like) Jean-Louis and Françoise and not unhappy like the others? Are we to reduce the work to a vindication of the Catholic, bourgeois marriage, indeed, to a propaganda film in favor of the family? In other words, is the narrator expressing here the viewpoint of the author (*Eric Rohmer*, p. 59)? […]

We are left with another moral of the story. If all of this is nothing but illusion and lies, one illusion at least, one lie at least, bears in itself its reward: peace of mind and heart — in short, happiness. This is the illusion offered by marriage, provided that marriage is chosen and desired for itself. The misfortune of the modern world is, on the contrary, that people don't want to have any illusions, especially about love. They don't believe any longer in fate and even less in happy endings. This is perhaps why Rohmer's characters […] are in a certain sense heroes, and doubly so. Guided blindfolded by the notion of happiness as a couple, they are on the one hand opposed to the barbarous commandments of the modern world with its ephemeral, risky, chaotic, and hopeless relations. On the other hand, by this very aspiration they become the heroes of a classical narrative (*Eric Rohmer*, p. 123).

ERIC ROHMER'S FILMOGRAPHY
(PRINCIPAL FILMS)

1959	*The Sign of Leo (Le Signe du lion)*
1962	*The Girl at the Monceau Bakery (La Boulangère de Monceau. 26 min., Six Moral Tales I)*
1963	*Suzanne's Career (La Carrière de Suzanne, 52 min., Six Moral Tales II)*
1965	*Place de l'Etoile*, in the collective film *Paris seen by... (Paris vu par...)*
1967	*The Collector (La Collectionneuse. Six Moral Tales IV)*
1969	*My Night at Maud's (Ma nuit chez Maud, Six Moral Tales III)*
1970	*Claire's Knee (Le Genou de Claire, Six Moral Tales V)*
1972	*Chloe in the Afternoon (L'Amour, l'après-midi, Six Moral Tales VI)*
1975	*La Marquise d'O.*
1978	*Perceval le Gallois*
1980	*The Aviator's Wife (La Femme de l'aviateur ou On ne saurait penser à rien, Comédies et proverbes).*
1981	*A Good Marriage (Le beau marriage, Comédies et proverbes).*
1982	*Pauline at the Beach (Pauline à la plage, Comédies et proverbes).*
1984	*Full Moon in Paris (Les Nuits de la pleine lune, Comédies et proverbes).*
1985	*Summer (Le Rayon vert, Comédies et proverbes).*
1986	*Four Adventures of Reinette and Mirabelle (Quatre aventures de Reinette et Mirabelle, Comédies et proverbes).*
1987	*My Girlfriend's Boyfriend (L'Ami de mon amie, Comédies et proverbes).*
1989	*A Tale of Springtime (Conte de printemps, Tales of the Four Seasons).*
1991	*A Tale of Winter (Conte d'hiver, Tales of the Four Seasons).*
1992	*The Tree, The Mayor and the Mediatheque (L'Arbre, le maire et la médiathèque).*
1995	*Rendezvous in Paris (Les Rendez-vous de Paris).*
1996	*A Summer's Tale (Conte d'été, Tales of the Four Seasons).*
1998	*Autumn Tale (Conte d'automne, Tales of the Four Seasons)*
2001	*The Lady and the Duke (L'Anglaise et le duc)*
2004	*Triple Agent*

WORKS CONSULTED

Allombert, Guy. "Ma nuit chez Maud." *Image et son: Revue du cinéma* 232 (Nov. 1969): 128-130.

Arbois, Janick. "Ma nuit chez Maud." *Téléciné* 154 (July 1969): 38.

Baroncelli, Jean de. "Ma nuit chez Maud." *Le Monde*, June 7, 1969, p. 11.

Biette, J.-C., Jacques Bontemps, and Jean-Louis Comolli, "L'Ancien et le nouveau." *Cahiers du cinéma* 172 (Nov. 1965) : 33-42, 56-59.

Billard, Pierre. "Sous le signe de Pascal." *L'Express*, June 9-15, 1969, p. 90.

Bonitzer, Pascal. *Eric Rohmer*. Paris: Editions de l'Etoile/Cahiers du cinéma, 1999.

………."Maud et les phagocytes." *Cahiers du cinéma* 214 (July-Aug. 1969): 59.

Bonizer, Pascal, Jean-Louis Comolli, Serge Daney, and Jean Narboni. "Nouvel Entretien avec Eric Rohmer." *Cahiers du cinéma* 219 (April 1970): 46-55.

Bonitzer, Pascal, and Serge Daney. "Entretien avec Eric Rohmer." *Cahiers du cinéma* 323-324 (May 1981): 29-39.

Bory, Jean-Louis. "Cinéma : Un film-torche." *Le Nouvel Observateur*, June 30, 1969, pp. 44-45.

Chapier, Henri. "Du beau 'cinéma de chambre' d'Eric Rohmer." *Combat*, May16, 1969, p. 13.

Ciment, Michel. "*Ma nuit chez Maud*, d'Eric Rohmer." *Positif* 107 (Summer 1969): 42.

Collet, Jean. *Le Cinéma en question*. Paris: Editions du Cerf, 1972.

Estève, Michel, ed. *Eric Rohmer 1. Etudes cinématographiques* 146-148. Paris: Minard, 1985.

Gévaudan, Franz. "*Ma nuit chez Maud* d'Eric Rohmer." *Cinéma 69* 138 (July-Aug. 1969): 26.

Haustrate, Gaston. "Ma nuit chez Maud." *Témoignage chrétien* 138 (July 3, 1969).

Jacob, Gilles. "Cannes." *Nouvelles littéraires* (22 mai 1959): 14.

Lajeunesse, Jacqueline. "Ma nuit chez Maud." *Image et son* 230-231 (Sept.-Oct. 1969): 186.

Magny, Joël. *Eric Rohmer*. Paris: Payot & Rivages, 1995 (orig. ed., Rivages, 1986).

Molinier, Philippe. *Ma nuit chez Maud*. Clefs Concours. Paris: Atlande, 2001.

Nogueira, Rui. "Entretien avec Eric Rohmer." *Cinéma* 153 (Feb. 1971): 43-58.

Pascal, *Pensées*. Paris: Garnier-Flammarion, 1973.

Prédal, René. "Les Ecritures d'Eric Rohmer." *Eric Rohmer 1* (see above Estève), pp.19-50.

Rohmer, Eric. *Le Goût de la beauté*. Paris: Editions de l'Etoile, 1984.

………."Lettre à un critique (*à propos des Contes moraux*)." *Le Goût de la beauté*, pp. 89-91.

.........*Ma nuit chez Maud* (screenplay). *L'Avant-Scène Cinéma* 98 (Dec. 1969): 7-40.

.........*"Pour un cinéma parlant." *Le Goût de la beauté*, pp. 37-40.

.........*Six Contes moraux.* Paris: Editions de l'Herne, 1974.

Serceau, Michel. *Les Jeux de l'amour, du hasard et du discours.* Paris: Editions du Cerf, 2000.

.........*"Mythes et masques de l'amour." *Eric Rohmer 1* (see above Estève), pp. 63-103.

Séailles, André. "Entretien avec Eric Rohmer." *Eric Rohmer 1* (see above Estève), pp. 5-17.

Showalter, English, ed. *My Night at Maud's.* New Brunswick, NJ: Rutgers University Press, 1993.

Simsolo, Noël. "Entretien avec Eric Rohmer." *La Revue du cinéma* 235 (Jan. 1970): 88-92.

Tortajada, Maria. *Le Spectateur séduit. Le Libertinage dans le cinéma d'Eric Rohmer et sa fonction dans une théorie de la représentation filmique.* Paris: Kimé, 1999.

Vidal, Marion. *Les Contes moraux d'Eric Rohmer.* Paris: Pierre Lherminier, 1977.

Alain Resnais

My American Uncle
Mon oncle d'Amérique

(1980)

Alain Resnais, *My American Uncle*: René Ragueneau and
Veestrate fight at the office (metaphorically). © MK2

Director ....Alain Resnais
Screenplay and dialogues...Jean Gruault
Inspired by the works of...Henri Laborit
Assistant Directors ....Florence Malraux, Jean Léon
Director of Photography .... Sacha Vierny
Cameraman ....Philippe Brun
Music..Arié Dzierlatka
Film Editor .... Albert Jurgenson
Sound ....Jean-Pierre Ruh
Art Director .... Jacques Saulnier
Costumes..Catherine Leterrier
Script Girl (Continuity) ....Hélène Sébillotte
Producer ....Philippe Dussart, Andréa Films and T.F. 1
Length .... 2 h 00

Cast

Gérard Depardieu (*René Ragueneau*), Nicole Garcia (*Janine Garnier*), Roger-Pierre (*Jean Le Gall*), Marie Dubois (*Thérèse Ragueneau*), Nelly Borgeaud (*Arlette Le Gall*), Pierre Arditi (*Zambeaux*), Gérard Darrieu (*Veestrate*), Philippe Laudenbach (*Michel Aubert, Jean's friend*), Henri Laborit (*himself*), and with Max Vialle (*Laugier, the stage director*), Jean Dasté (*M. Louis*), Alexandre Rignault (*Jean's grandfather*), Gaston Vacchia (*René's uncle*), Véronique Silver (*Janine's mother*), Laurence Badie (*Mme Veestrate*), Jacques Rispal (*the man René bumps into*), Héléna Manson (*René's landlady*).

STORY

By intertwining three separate narrative voices, *My American Uncle* tells the story of three lives, of three individuals from completely different social milieus whose fates mingle for a moment by chance. **Jean Legall** is born into a wealthy Breton family, is a brilliant student, and dreams of becoming a writer. He marries, has children, and settles for a life as a teacher in a Parisian high school. Through connections he lands some assignments from the Ministry of Education and twenty years later has risen to the position of News Director at the State Radio Bureau. **Janine Garnier** is born in Paris to militant communist workers. She develops a passion for theater and dreams of becoming an actress. Discouraged by her parents, for whom the theater is not a serious occupation, she leaves home and by pure luck lands the main role in an avant-garde play which has a long run on the Left Bank. **René Ragueneau**, finally, is the practicing Catholic son of a small farmer. He has to work hard to get his elementary school diploma, then studies business by correspondence. His dream is to escape from the farm and make a career in the business world. Finding employment in a family-owned textile factory, by dint of hard work and study he succeeds in climbing the ladder to the position of technical director. In what little leisure time he enjoys, he becomes a gourmet cook.

We learn moreover that each of these three characters harbors a fascination for a different French movie star, mythical figures of cinema who appear episodically in brief shots (always in black and white) which are juxtaposed to the corresponding character. For Jean the star is Danielle Darrieux; for Janine it is Jean Marais; and for René it is Jean Gabin.

Parallel to the three narratives which develop the lives of the three main characters, there is a fourth discourse which comes from a real-life character, the scientist Henri Laborit. Moving around his laboratory, Professor Laborit intervenes periodically to discuss his hypotheses on the biology and psychology of human behavior, which elucidate, to a certain extent, the actions and reactions of the three fictional characters.

It is at the very moment (1975) at which each of the three main characters is enjoying the most success in his or her chosen career that the action really begins, that is, when the three destinies begin to converge. When Jean takes his wife to see the play in which Janine is starring, he falls in love with her and soon leaves his wife and children to move into her apartment. René learns that the factory he has been working for is going to be acquired soon by a larger competitor. He is going to have to tolerate the constant presence in his office of Veestrate, his rival for the position of technical director.

Both of the above situations turn out badly. Having displeased his minister, Jean is abruptly fired as News Director. To make matters worse, he begins to suffer acutely from renal colic caused by kidney stones. Anguished by his fear of losing his position, René develops a stomach ulcer. His fears come true: the position is given to Veestrate, who is more abreast of modern production techniques. To compensate him, his new employers offer him a position as director of a new clothing factory in Cholet, 600 kilometers away from his home in Roubaix. Forced to accept, he leaves for his new position without his wife Thérèse, who refuses to leave her teaching job and uproot their children. At the same time Jean's wife Arlette attempts to get her husband back by convincing Janine that she is very ill and is going to die soon. Janine falls into the trap and provokes an argument with Jean to have a pretext to break up with him.

Two years later Jean and Janine meet again by chance on the little Breton island which belongs to Jean's family. Janine, whose career as an actress was short-lived, has become a style consultant in the textile company for which René Ragueneau works. Jean had returned to his teaching position after his downfall, but he has just published a polemical book about his experience at the Radio Bureau. He is preparing to run as a candidate in the next elections for the national legislature. In their conversation Janine learns that Jean's wife Arlette had never been ill and understands that she had duped her to get her husband back. Devastated, she nonetheless goes to a business meeting in Cholet with Zambeaux, the CEO of her company, and René, whose factory is having financial difficulties.

Zambeaux suggests to René that he accept the lower position of technical director of his factory, under the authority of a new director. Indignant at this proposal, René abruptly leaves the restaurant where the meeting is taking place. However, he soon returns and apologizes. Familiar with René's talents as a cook, Janine offers him, with Zambeaux's approval, an executive position in a chain of gourmet food stores. This is the last straw for René. Deeply humiliated, he goes back to his room and hangs himself. Saved just in time by his landlady, he is taken to the hospital where he receives treatment and is soon out of danger.

Meanwhile Janine goes to Jean's home to discuss their situation with him. After a confrontation with his wife Arlette, who clearly scoffs at her, she finally finds Jean at a wild boar hunt. He informs her that Arlette had confessed to everything the night before and gives her to understand that he has decided to side with his wife. Overcome with indignation, Janine strikes Jean repeatedly as he tries to fend her off. Meanwhile, René has regained consciousness at the hospital and finds his wife at his side in tears. Janine and Jean continue to fight in the field where they had met, while their struggle is juxtaposed with shots of a wounded boar running around and around in circles, on the point of collapsing. The film comes to an end with a series of shots of a slum neighborhood in New York City.

CRITICAL RECEPTION

My American Uncle came out on May 21, 1980, in Paris and its outskirts. It enjoyed immediate and broad popular success which even its Special Jury Prize at the Cannes Film Festival did not explain; more than 400,000 tickets were sold in the first ten weeks of its run in selected cinemas. When it opened abroad, it won the New York Film Critics' Prize for the Best Foreign Film in 1980.

Although critical opinion on the formal qualities of the film was unanimously favorable, the film's content provoked widely diverse, even contradictory reactions, as illustrated by the samples of articles in the review *L'Avant-Scène Cinéma* (Resnais, pp. 71-72). For some critics it was an accurate and forceful analysis of both contemporary society and of our social behavior: "No film better analyzes the atmosphere of our time than does *My American Uncle*," asserts Michel Perez the day of the film's opening. This opinon was supported by Philippe Pilard, who commented, "This film translates the type of impasse, the malaise, which characterized French society at the end of the seventies." For his part Marcel Martin appreciated "this intelligent attempt to get away from the well-trodden path of French psychological realism" (p. 24).

This favorable viewpoint was not shared by the critic for the Communist newspaper *L'Humanité*. Françoise Lazard-Levaillant accused Resnais of playing into the hands of the right-wing government by promoting "reactionary theses" according to which "men and social phenomena are biologically determined." Several months later Christian Zimmer charged in *Le Monde* that *My American Uncle* was "a scientific imposture" and "the worst kind of pedagogical film." The commentators could not even agree on the nature of the relationship between Resnais's and Laborit's complementary discourses in the film. Some, like Albert Jacquard, maintained that "each scene presented by the filmmaker illustrates one of the biologist's theses," whereas others like Michel Delain are just as certain, on the contrary, that Resnais "surely does not intend to illustrate the theses of the biologist." The truth is most likely somewhere in between.

BEFORE *MY AMERICAN UNCLE*

As you may read above in the chapter on *Hiroshima mon amour* (p. 255), Resnais began his career as a film editor before making a series of short documentaries whose brilliance purely and simply transformed the genre. In his first feature film, *Hiroshima mon amour* (1959), we already find the themes which will haunt a large segment of his work: love and death, memory and forgetting, and the interweaving of past and present (if not the future). The film won numerous prizes and turned Resnais into an international celebrity virtually overnight. His following film *Last Year at Marienbad* (*L'Année dernière à Marienbad*, 1961), won the Golden Lion at the Venice Film Festival and the prestigious Meliès Prize in France. It both fascinated and confused the public with its mysterious characters and enigmatic plot. A banal story of adultery — a man tries to lure a woman away from her husband — is transformed into a dream-like (or better, nightmarish) ceremony, a succession of phantasmal events whose meaning is elusive.

Next, in *Muriel, or The Time of Return* (*Muriel, ou le temps d'un retour*, 1963),

Resnais returns to his meditations on the problem of time in human relations, as well as on the problem of war, themes that he had treated in *Hiroshima*. In Boulogne a woman who receives a visit by a former lover (their affair dated from the Second World War period) is forced to accept the fact that the effects of time have separated them irremediably. At the same time the woman's stepson, who has just returned from military service in Algeria, tries to face his anguished memory of the acts committed by the French soldiers during the war there. Resnais's following film, *The War is Over* (*La Guerre est finie*, 1966), is a reflection, as Marcel Ohms says, of "the existential problems of political struggle" (p. 104). The hero is an underground militant of the Spanish Communist Party living in exile in France. He experiences an identity crisis during which he questions whether his struggle against Franco's government is still worthwhile. Here again past and present are confronted as the political militant realizes that he may be living in a past whose realities are not pertinent to the present situation.

In *Je t'aime, je t'aime* (1968) Resnais treats familiar subjects in a new manner: as science fiction. Returning once again to the themes of death and the problems of memory — as well as the frequent dream-like climate of his films — he offers us the story of a man who, following a failed suicide attempt, participates in a scientific experiment in which he is sent back into his own past. When the machine goes awry, the order of his memories is upset. The following film *Stavisky* (1974) is probably the most atypical of Resnais's films by its realism and its apparent conventionality — despite a certain unreality produced by the depiction of an extremely opulent world. It is also one of his most "politicized" films. Resnais offers a half-historical, half-fictional version of the "Stavisky Affair," the story of a huge swindle which was all over the news at the beginning of 1934. It had deep repercussions for some of the most prominent political figures in France. Finally, *Providence* (1976), a film which won the Cesar for the Best Director at Cannes in 1978, treats both the problem of aging and death, as well as that of artistic creation. We follow the anguished phantasms of the main character, an aging writer who intertwines in his nightmares the members of his family and the characters of his next novel. His phantasms are profoundly influenced by his bad conscience, his fear of growing old, and his obsession with death.

ORIGIN AND ACTORS

According to Resnais *My American Uncle* began as a failed project for a brief commercial. A pharmaceutical company asked Henri Laborit to make a short film about "a product which helped the memory." The biologist had been very impressed by Resnais's representation of "the mechanisms of the brain which structure human behavior" in *Last Year at Marienbad*, so he only agreed to the film project if it would be directed by Resnais (Chapsal, p. 22). The short subject was never made, but the project brought Resnais and Laborit together. This meeting bore fruit two years later after Resnais had become familiar with the scientist's writings. Collaborating with Laborit and the screenwriter Jean Gruault, he went to work on a feature film closely related to the biologist's work. As he tells us, he wanted to "tell a story on the one hand, and on the other have a scientist — in this case Henri Laborit — talk about his work. It would be interesting to place them side by side, an amusing challenge to find the right dramatic structure" (Decaux et al., p. 15). As regards the story, Gruault was the source of the idea of the three parallel lives, while Resnais was responsible for the idea of using film excerpts in which famous, quasi-mythical actors would provide examples of behavior. Resnais had even briefly considered the possibility of making a film composed entirely of film excerpts with stars from countries around the world: "The cinema is in fact a repository of all types of behaviors. There are enough films to create an illustration of all of Laborit's theories" (Decaux et al., p. 15). Realizing that the project was impossible, Resnais soon abandoned it, but the idea of the inserts of shots of stars was retained for the new film.

As for the actors, Resnais explained that he always chose them in relation to each other, with the idea of "provoking interactions" which might give interesting results. "In this case it was the Garcia/Depardieu/Roger-Pierre combination that I found interesting. If I had had to change one of the actors, I would have perhaps changed all three" (Chapsal, p. 15). The choice of Nicole Garcia and Gérard Depardieu, both well-known movie stars, for the roles of Janine Garnier and René Ragueneau needs no comment. It is a different story for Roger-Pierre, whose casting in the role of Jean Le Gall was somewhat surprising. Roger-Pierre was a Parisian vaudeville performer, well known in the popular theaters but with little experience before the camera. Resnais's decision to give him the role of Jean was governed, he tells us, by "the desire to have him play a dramatic role, but with the possibility of using his gifts as a vaudeville actor" (Benayoun, *Arpenteur*, pp. 250-251).

The filmmaker doesn't hide the fact that he wants the public to find *My American Uncle* "funny." Roger-Pierre's manner, always bordering on ham acting, does help bring out the underlying humor which Resnais is trying to create in his film — a humor which often escapes critics but which plays an important role in attenuating the didactic character of the film. The choice of Laborit to play his own character in the film underlines the intentionally pedagogical side of the work, but that is not all. As Resnais says, Laborit's character "straddles reality and fiction" (p. 6). Casting Laborit as himself is an ingenious manner of playing with the frontier between reality and fiction while suggesting the close relationship between the two.

As regards the development of the subject of *My American Uncle*, it is well known that Resnais always asks his screenwriters for "imaginary biographies" of all of the characters, including the most minor ones. As an example, here is the "description card" for Arlette Le Gall, Jean's wife (Resnais, p. 8):

> Arlette is the daughter of the owner of the biggest butcher shop in town. She is slightly younger than Jean, who, in any case, is marrying beneath his station. This is one of the reasons why he marries her discretely in Paris (1958). But the evolution of social mores will enable him to bring her back to live with him in his home town (1979). His father-in-law, who has become a wealthy property owner and a member of the Left Radical party, may even be able to help him in his political career after he has to leave the Radio Bureau.

Here also is the description of a very minor character, Anne Guesdon, the young actress who refuses to submit to the demands of the stage director and whose departure allows Janine to debut in the theater in the role of Julie de Lespinasse (p. 9):

Born May 14, 1953, in Grenoble to a father who is a judge. Enlightened cultural milieu. Attends the Lycée Fénelon in Paris. Her acting aspirations are encouraged by her parents. Simon School of Acting. Begins acting very young in films and in minor roles in the popular theaters. She wants to try avant-garde theater but gives up quickly because she can't stand amateurism. Lands an important role in a successful play by Marcel Achard, then stars in the latest comedy by Françoise Dorin. Brilliant career in the cinema (unlike her friend Janine Garnier). Favorite reading: Derrida, Barthes, Lacan, Lévi-Strauss. She will write her memoirs one day.

As we noted in the chapter on *Hiroshima mon amour*, while these biographies may not have any direct bearing on the action of the film, they do help the actors to create the characters they are playing and to give them greater depth.

THE INSERTS

The famous movie stars — Jean Marais, Danielle Darrieux, and Jean Gabin — who appear in the inserts (the short excerpts of old films) were chosen because, as Resnais remarked, "it was the most logical choice for each of our three heroes." Moreover, he added, they had to be stars — and there are not many of them — whose careers extended over several generations, which gave them "an air of immortality" (Benayoun, p. 249). Danielle Darrieux was a logical choice for Jean Le Gall, given her personal elegance and her frequent casting as an upper-class character, as in Pierre Billon's *Ruy Blas* (1948), Anatole Litvak's *Mayerling* (1953), or Max Ophuls's *Madame de...* (1953). Her acting career began in 1931 and included around fifty films before the opening of *My American Uncle*.

Jean Marais's career covers approximately the same period as Darrieux's. He became famous in France beginning with his role of a modern Tristan in the Jean Delannoy and Jean Cocteau Occupation-era film *The Eternal Return* (1943). Considered by some to be "the most handsome man in the world," he became Cocteau's favorite actor. He played in Cocteau's most famous films, including *Beauty and the Beast* (1946), *Ruy Blas* (adapted by Cocteau), *Les Parents Terribles* (1948), and *Orpheus* (1950). This did not prevent Marais from starring as a romantic hero in numerous adventure films like *The Count of Monte-Cristo* (1955), *Captain Fracasse* (1961), or *The Iron Mask* (1962). These films reflect perfectly the romantic mentality of Janine Garnier, who "never misses cloak and dagger films on television" (*L'Avant-Scène Cinéma*, p. 12).

Jean Gabin, finally, one of the greatest legends of French cinema, played in more than ninety films over six decades until his death in 1976. In the 1930s he was the ultimate man of the people and romantic hero, before becoming a patriarchal figure and an anti-hero (of the "Godfather" type) in the sixties. He is a perfect match for René Ragueneau both by his identification with the lower social classes and by the strong personal will which often characterizes his roles.

STRUCTURE

Like *Hiroshima mon amour*, which resembles a play in five acts, with a prologue and epilogue, the scenario of *My American Uncle* is divided into four distinct acts preceded by a short prologue and followed by an equally brief epilogue. The prologue consists of a shot of a red plastic heart which we can hear beating, followed by a rapid series of static images representing the natural and cultural environments of man. The whole sequence is accompanied by a scientific commentary in voice-over by Henri Laborit and, for a moment, by the completely intertwined voice-over statements of the three main characters, who speak of their respective beginnings.

In the first "act" we learn about the social origins of the three characters, as well as their upbringing, their schooling, and their ambitions. These succinct biographies begin with the intertwined, barely intelligible, voices of the characters. They are then continued in the images, still woven together and accompanied at the beginning by a female narrator in voice-over, until each character takes over the narration in the first-person, still in voice-over. From the beginning the life stories of the three characters are interwoven with a scientific discourse by Laborit, likewise in voice-over (for the most part) on the behavioral biology of human beings. The whole first act is interspersed with inserts from old black and white films starring the three French actors discussed above. The three characters progressively begin to speak on screen as they become adults, leave home, and begin their personal lives. When the first act draws to a close in 1975, the three protagonists have all achieved professional success, each in his or her own manner.

In the second act the lives of the three characters continue to play out, but we are now in the present. The voice-over narration disappears, incuding Laborit's, to be replaced by the on-screen action. The inserts of the three movie stars continue to appear sporadically. Janine's life has come together with Jean's, who leaves his wife to live with her. Their joint existence continues to be intertwined, on the narrative plane, with that of René. When the situations go badly, they create stressful conditions which produce a stomach ulcer for René and renal colic for Jean, as noted above. Yielding to sentimental blackmail by Jean's wife, Janine forces him to leave her. René, for his part, has to leave his family to take a position in another city. It is now 1977.

The action picks up two years later in the third act. Jean and Janine meet by chance on a little island he owns. Jean's conduct when he discovers Janine's presence on the island is juxtaposed to the behavior of a laboratory rat which Henri Laborit reappears in the film to discuss. The meeting between Jean and Janine, in which Janine understands that his wife duped her to get her husband back, alternates with Laborit's commentary as he establishes a parallel between the rat's behavior in a stressful situation and that exhibited by men in a similar situation. The action on the island and the shots of the rats alternate with brief shots (some of which have already been seen in the first part of the film, from another angle) which highlight either the upbringing that each of the three characters has received, or certain critical moments of their adult lives. In this part of the film, which is devoted especially to the development and illustration of Laborit's theories, the inserts of old movies have disappeared.

The fourth act, which is dominated by confrontations and crises, follows immediately on the heels of the episode on the island. Janine, who serves as a link between Jean and René, whose lives are otherwise completely separate, goes to a meeting between René and their boss Zambeaux. Confronted with his professional failure, René tries to commit suicide. Janine seeks out Jean to explain her earlier behavior, but their meeting proves to be useless, which leaves her in a state of frustration. As in the first two acts, the movie stars intervene at decisive moments in the action, but only those related to René and Janine. At the end of the film Laborit appears on the screen a final time (like his rat) to draw conclusions, in a scene which is interrupted by several shots which recall the lives and theories developed in the film. The film finishes with a short "epilogue," a series of tracking shots in the streets of a slum neighborhood of New York. The tracking shots stop on a large building whose wall is covered with a painting representing a forest. They are succeeded by a series of rapid shots of the wall whose size diminishes progressively until we are left with an extreme close-up of a few bricks.

THEMES

A first theme of *My American Uncle* is revealed in the title of the film. As Resnais explained, "The American Uncle refers to a happy event that we wait for in the expectation that it will solve all of our problems" (p. 7). This "European myth," which nourishes the imagination of each of the main characters, is expressed the most explicitly by Janine when she confides in her boss Zambeaux, "I was like most of the people who spend their lives waiting for happiness like you wait for an inheritance, something which you think you have a right to. The inheritance of an American uncle." The myth of the American Uncle is representative in any case of all of the myths, both conscious and unconscious, which inhabit the lives of everyone — a phenomenon which is illustrated by the shots from old movies in *My American Uncle*, to which we shall now turn.

"Mythical" stars like Gabin, Darrieux, and Marais seem to be behavioral models which serve as a form of commentary on the actions and reactions of people in their social relations. Their influence seems to be linked to what Laborit calls the "associative brain," the brain among the three superimposed brains which is responsible for the faculty of imagination in human beings (see "Henri Laborit's Theories" at the end of this introduction). The cinema, the novel, and the theater provide all imaginable models, for, as Resnais observes, the three genres "illustrate all possible behaviors" (p. 7). Since without realizing it the characters "imitate" the behavior of their favorite movie stars, their imaginary models, Resnais slips into his film the theme of life imitating art, which is the corollary of the traditional theory according to which art imitates life.

Generally the themes of the film, like the theme of the American Uncle, are linked to Laborit's theories on the biological bases of human behavior. Resnais has in effect, as he says, "stuck" a documentary film on a fiction film (and vice-versa). The two discourses, the biologist's and the filmmaker's, intertwine and reflect each other. The behavior of Resnais's fictional characters illustrates for the most part Laborit's theories, despite the fact that the filmmaker insists that what the characters do "doesn't necessarily demonstrate what the biologist says" (Chapsal, p. 8). Although the parallel is in no way systematic, there is a clear association, as Michel Delain remarks, between "the man with the camera" and "the man with the microscope" (Resnais, p. 71).

Moreover, Resnais's and Gruault's plans for their characters are unambiguous in this respect: "We put them in situations in which they will either have to act or become inhibited. That is the subject of the film" (Resnais, p. 6). Accordingly, the fundamental behaviors described by Laborit — gratification, flight, struggle, and inhibition — figure prominently among the principal themes of the film.

In his editing of the shots in the film's "prologue" and in certain subsequent scenes, Resnais strives to express the themes of both nature and culture. According to Laborit these are the two principal forces which shape human character and influence our behavior. By depicting the lives of people who come from different social strata — the bourgeoisie, the working class, and the peasantry — Resnais is suggesting the universality of the main behavior patterns described by Laborit, which are based on constants in nature and on the upbringing given to children. The parallels between characters, despite the class differences, are explicitly established by undeniable behavioral similarities. One of the most striking of these similarities is the "flight behavior" exhibited by the characters at certain moments, when they are prompted to flee a painful situation. The other is related to the "contemporary disorders" from which both Jean and René suffer, illnesses which are produced by the excessive stress created by the workplace in contemporary society. The inability of individuals to escape the situation which is responsible for this stress produces an "inhibition behavior," one of the principal behaviors described by Laborit. Certain remarks by the characters emphasize the parallel that Resnais is trying to establish between them, such as the question formulated by both Jean and René, "What's this mess?" or Jean's "Who do you mean, 'they'?" which echoes an identical question by René's wife.

Theater and cinema are themselves important themes in *My American Uncle*. Through the film excerpts the theme of cinema is clearly inscribed in the film. It is easy to see that Resnais is suggesting a connection between cinema and life, that is, the influence of movies on our behavior. However, since Resnais's film is presented explicitly as a play in four acts in the screenplay, and the heroine is a passionate theater devotee, the theme of theater also is embedded within the film. Resnais suggests in fact a close relationship between theater and life, or more precisely, the theatrical character of life. Indeed, concerning the characters in this film, he observes "They are always performing," to which he adds, "but we all are, in our daily lives, as soon as we are in the presence of others" (p. 7). Arlette's "I'm dying" performance for Janine is the most poignant example of "theater in real life" in the film. Since theater becomes a "struggle behavior" within Arlette's efforts to recover her husband, the theme of theater is effectively integrated into the theories of Laborit illustrated in the film.

Independent of any scientific theory, however, *My American Uncle* contains important social thematics. Critics like Marcel Oms have noted that the film is a "reflection of a society," "a film in which we find, as regards the middle class, all of the socio-economic mutations of the France of 1980" (p. 138). Decaux goes further, describing Resnais's film as a "cruel satire of contemporary capitalist society" (p. 23). Bonnet agrees, finding in the film "a strong satire of competition in French society [...] which rests almost entirely on the fear of being fired" (p. 24). Others take a particularly dark view, ignoring the humorous intentions of the film and only seeing in it "a profoundly desperate film," owing to what they perceive as a lack of hope for progress in man.

STYLE

Contrary to Resnais's reputation, his style in *My American Uncle* is not characterized by multiple series of tracking shots (with the exception of the short "epilogue" in the New York slum). We are struck on the other hand by the rapid editing of static shots at the beginning of the film, following the initial close-up of the blinking plastic heart accompanied by Laborit's voice-over commentary. The following shot features a small round beam of light which is played over a photo montage representing objects, characters, and human habitats — like a camera shooting in extreme close-up or a microscope. This image is joined by the narration of the three characters in voice-over, but at the level of a barely intelligible heap of words. In the next shot Laborit continues his own commentary, which accompanies short shots of objects which belong either to the natural or the cultural realms. His commentary then yields again to the intertwined off-screen voices, more and more distinct now, of the three characters, combined with the same photo montage as before. Laborit's voice then reasserts itself over shots of various animals and of Jean as a child, but soon yields to the voice-over narration of a woman who begins the biography of the three characters.

Resnais explains to us, "I wanted to begin with a kind of 'mishmash,' so that the spectator would have the impression of approaching the main characters little by little" (Decaux, p. 20) — the mishmash suggesting perhaps the original chaos which preceded the organization of the natural world. Whether this was Resnais's intention or not, there is no denying the parallel between the scientist and the filmmaker. As Bonnet points out, "The photo montage which begins and ends the film serves as a metaphor for the system of the film [...]. It is Resnais's way of establishing a parallel between both the filmmaker's and Henri Laborit's laboratory" (p. 24).

In fact, the style of *My American Uncle* is defined by the "experiment" that Resnais and Gruault have set up, which includes both theory and fiction in the same film, "a little like playing with mirrors or weaving completely different types of threads into a rug" (Chapsal, p. 7). The mirror play, the weaving, can only be accomplished by editing, and it is clearly the editing technique which determines the style of the film. As is well known, Resnais was unsurpassed in the art of editing. In the film that we are studying, he uses mainly parallel editing, or what Benayoun called "juxtaposition editing," to tie together the documentary and the fictional threads. He resorts to the same kind of editing to relate the three biographies which constitute the narrative, adding into the mix, at strategic moments, the inserts of "mythical" movie stars. The inserts were only added at the end of the editing process.

The parallel editing of Laborit's scientific discourse and Resnais's fictional discourse lends a pedagogical and rather serious character to the film. As mentioned above, the director attempts to use humor to diminish, if not eliminate entirely, the impression of didacticism and pedantry. Resnais emphasizes in fact the intentionally comic side of his film, which Laborit appreciated in particular: "What I really like," he said, "is the playful side of the film. The comic elements return constantly" (in Chapsal, p. 23). Other than the acting of Roger-Pierre, the comedy is produced primarily by editing effects, beginning with the juxtaposition of the laboratory rats and the characters of the film — when it's not the outright transformation of the characters into rats. The episode of the rat men, which Resnais himself considered a "joke of questionable taste," makes the rivalry between René and Veestrate appear ridiculous.

The comic element is related as well to the black and white film inserts of legendary movie stars. Generally presented in slow motion, these short shots serve as a rather ironic commentary on the role of stereotypes in the imagination of the three characters. Like the comical scenes with the rats, the inserts are part of what Bonnet calls "the art of distancing" in Resnais's films. They are techniques which create reflective distance for the spectator both in relation to the characters and to the behavioral theories which are presented in the film. The music in the film, which Resnais wanted to be "sometimes ironical, sometimes mocking," also contributes to this distancing through humor.

STUDY GUIDE

Henri Laborit's Theories in *My American Uncle*

"A human being's sole reason for existing is to be [...]. It is self-preservation."

"We may thus distinguish between four principal types of behaviors. The first is the consumption behavior, whose purpose is to satisfy basic needs [eating, drinking, copulating]. The second is a gratification behavior. When someone experiences an event which leads to pleasure, he tries to repeat it. The third is a behavior which responds to punishment either by fleeing to avoid it or by fighting to destroy the source. The last is an inhibition behavior. The person doesn't act or react at all. He submits to the tension and is subject to anguish. Anguish is the impossibility to dominate a situation."

"In animals' brains we find very primitive forms. There is a first brain [...], the reptilian brain [...] which sets in motion survival behaviors essential to the animal's survival. Eating and drinking, which permit it to maintain itself physically, and copulating, which permits it to reproduce. As soon as we arrive at the level of mammals, a second brain is added to the first [...], the affective brain. I prefer to call it the brain of memory. Without the memory of what is agreeable or disagreeable, it is not possible to be happy, sad, or anguished. It is not possible to be angry or in love. One could almost say that a living being is a memory in action [...]. Then a third brain is added to the first two, and we call this the cerebral cortex. In human beings this brain is very developed. We call it an associative cortex [...]. That means that it has an associative function. It associates the underlying paths of the nervous system which have recorded past experiences [...], which means that it is going to be able to create an imaginary process [...]. In a human being's brain these three superimposed brains still exist. Our unconscious drives are still the very primitive urges of the reptilian brain."

"These three stages of the brain have to function together, and to do so they have to be tied into bundles. One of them may be called the reward bundle. Another may be called the punishment bundle, which results in fleeing or fighting. Still another inhibits action. For example, the caresses a mother gives to her child [...] or the applause which follows an actor's speech liberates chemical substances in the reward bundle and leads to pleasure for the person concerned.

"What is easy for a rat in a cage is much more difficult for a man living in society [...]; he can rarely satisfy his needs by resorting to fighting when flight is not possible."

"The rat cannot flee. It will therefore be subjected to a punishment which it cannot escape. This punishment will produce an inhibition behavior. It learns that any action is useless, that it can neither flee nor fight. It becomes inhibited, and this inhibition, which is accompanied in men by what we call anguish, is also accompanied by extremely deep-seated biological disturbances [...]. These biological troubles result in what we call 'contemporary disorders' [*maladies de civilisation*], that is, psychosomatic illnesses such as ulcers, high blood pressure, insomnia, and fatigue; in a word, unhappiness."

"When his aggressiveness can no longer be used against others, it can still be used against himself [...]. He can commit suicide."

"The search for domination [...] is the fundamental basis for all human behavior, but this motivation remains completely unconscious."

Director's Comments

"I wanted to see if we could bring to the screen a deductive-type scientific discourse (like the kind we see in detective novels) and a work of fiction, mixing the two types of narrative together, the scientific and the fictional, to see if this mixture would create an interesting dramatic world."

"I found it intriguing, dramatically speaking, to interrupt the story and reproduce pieces of the narrative all of a sudden from another viewpoint. That's what got me excited: the idea of taking a second look from a different perspective at events which were first presented uncritically. I wanted to know if that would work on the dramatic level."

Cinématographe: "Did the characters in the film surprise you?"

Resnais: "Yes. For instance, we didn't expect Nelly Borgeaud (Arlette) to make all that commotion. We were rather astonished! We didn't expect things to end the way they did. We really thought that Jean and Janine were going to get back together. When Jean Gruault gave me the script with Jean Le Gall's speech, I was surprised. Even he didn't know what was going to happen the night before" (Decaux et al., p. 20).

Cinématographe: "What does the first shot represent?"

Resnais: "Originally it was a pendant from Hong Kong! A heart with a battery in it, to wear with a t-shirt. When it is turned on, it beats and blinks on and off. I had it at home and just brought it to the studio with me one day. There's nothing scientific about it at all" (p. 21)!

M. Chapsal: "Why do you insert black and white excerpts of old films into *My American Uncle*?"

Resnais: "It is generally recognized that we are influenced by the people we meet, by what we read, and by all the works of art we see in the course of our life. Why not by films? Just consider the emotional reaction of the public when a famous actor dies. At the same time I wanted to pay homage to great actors like Danielle Darrieux, Jean Gabin, and Jean Marais" (p. 18).

Excerpts for Discussion

Excerpt 1 (2'05-4'00): The beginning of the film (plastic heart, images of natural and cultural environments, beginning of the biographies).

Excerpt 2 (21'10-21'40): Jean and Arlette on the island; film excerpt with Danielle Darrieux.

Excerpt 3 (31'10-32'35): Janine furious with the director (film excerpt with Jean Marais); Janine meets Jean (excerpt with Jean Marais and Danielle Darrieux).

Excerpt 4 (59'35-1h02'00): Arlette tries sentimental blackmail to get her husband back.

Excerpt 5 (1h07'10-7'55): Jean's behavior on the island when he sees Janine; the laboratory rat.

Excerpt 6 (1h09'20-10'30): Jean with a rat's head; flight behavior by the three main characters.

Excerpt 7 (1h20'30-25'00): Janine learns that Jean's wife is not ill; laboratory rats; social constraints and inhibition.

Excerpt 8 (1h39'30-41'35): René is offered a new job; his reaction.

Excerpt 9 (1h53'20-54'55): Janine finds Jean at the wild boar hunt; Janine's behavior faced with Jean's attitude.

Excerpt 10 (1h58'10-59'15): Denouement: tracking shot in a slum neighborhood of New York City.

Quotations for Comment

René (whose stomach hurts): "It's nothing…it's just nerves. It's this guy, Veestrate. I've got to put up with him all day long. I feel like I'm on trial."

Thérèse: "That won't last forever."

René: "That's just it… They have to make a decision."

Thérèse: "Who do you mean, 'they'?"

René: "Oh, not Monsieur Louis or Monsieur Paul! It's the main office in Paris… People I've never seen…"

* * *

René: "Good grief, you remind me of my father! Every time we mentioned changing our farming methods or going to work in town, he brought up his American uncle…"

Thérèse: "… who ended up a beggar in Chicago!"

René: "That's what my father always said, but nothing proves he was right!"

* * *

Arlette: "Well… I wanted to ask you to let Jean come home to me and the children. Not forever, just for a few months."

Janine: "I'm afraid I don't understand."

Arlette: "You will understand. But first promise you won't say anything about this to Jean. It has to stay between us. I am sick too, much sicker than Jean… I've just been told. I have no hope. Mademoiselle… I'm going to die."

* * *

Janine: "…a chain of around forty food stores […] which would sell pre-packaged gourmet meals from the kitchens of the greatest chefs."

René: "I don't see how that concerns me."

Zambeaux: "We are going to need competent people to direct these stores."

René: "What would that involve?"

Janine: "Quality control, advising customers…helping them to compose a menu and choose the right wine…tasting the food…"

René (offended, ironical): "Do you furnish the apron and the chef's cap? My God…"

* * *

Janine: "No, no, I had to talk to you! We can't live with this lie the rest of our lives. It's just too stupid!"

Jean: "Listen to me! I think I know why you are here. When I told Arlette that I had seen you, she told me everything…confessed everything. I was terribly moved. You were marvelous, and I want to apologize for what she did… But Arlette was marvelous too…having the courage to tell such an enormous lie. How she must have suffered! At first I threw a tantrum. I didn't sleep all night. Then, in the morning, I understood… I'm sure that it was for the best. Arlette and I wept together…"

(Beside herself with indignation, Janine slaps Jean, who grabs her wrists; they struggle.)

Questions/Topics for Reflection

1. The relationship at the beginning of the film between the shots of rocks, bushes, seaweed, etc. and the shots of the little spoon, an inkbottle, a pair of scissors, a bicycle part, etc.
2. The social origins and ambitions of the three main characters (Jean, Janine, and René).
3. The role of the favorite movie stars of the main characters in this film.
4. Professor Laborit distinguishes between several basic patterns of human behavior. Examples of flight, fight, and inhibition behaviors in this film.
5. Arlette's recovery of her husband, who has been living with Janine. What instinct comes into play here, according to Laborit's theories?
6. The difference between the behavior of a rat in a cage subjected to an anguishing situation and a man in society. How does the situation of René, threatened by the rivalry with Veestrate, illustrate this difference? The (psychosomatic) consequences for René.

7. Laborit claims that aggressiveness is always a response to the inhibition or the impossibility of action, and that when it cannot be directed towards others, it can always be directed towards oneself. The best illustration of this thesis in the film.

8. The meaning of the title of the film, "*My American Uncle.*"

9. The three main characters: which one is the strongest? the weakest? Explain your opinion.

10. Do you find this film optimistic or pessimistic? Justify your opinion.

CRITICAL DOSSIER

Henri Laborit — René and Janine

In *My American Uncle* my ideas are not there to explain the behavior of the characters. They don't apply to them directly but serve to decode them.

We notice, for example, that if the character played by Depardieu does not succeed professionally, it is because his lack of education limits his imagination, his understanding of abstract ideas, his ability to process information and formulate new ideas. Consequently he is going to become inhibited, fall ill, and be driven to suicide.

On the other hand, Janine, the woman, is less "neurotic." Why? Because she is capable of fleeing [...]. She gets away, leaves her family, then her lover, changes milieus, and creates a new career for herself in the fashion world. She is perhaps the only one who is going to surmount her problems and succeed in inventing a new life for herself (Resnais, *Mon oncle d'Amérique*. pp. 25-26).

Jean-Pierre Oudart — René, Jean, Arlette

And then there is the world of the film, its space and time and characters which bring with them something other than their individual destinies. In moving from the country to the city, from a family business to a capitalistic enterprise, René Ragueneau represents a whole rural population which is constantly emigrating, a whole set of habits, beliefs, and prejudices that the film jostles, shatters, and, especially, distributes in a wide range of situations. As a result we are not confronted with a social type, a situation determined by class, nor even a privilege or a memory; it is a more subtle fabric. René isn't the same, for example, when he speaks to the young man that he is hiring or to his bosses. He hasn't achieved enough distance from his social origins, from his childhood, to be identified with his function. He is either too friendly to his inferiors or too submissive to his superiors, and at the same time he is angry with himself for it. He would like to rebel [...].

Jean Le Gall, this provincial journalist, arrivist, and failed writer who ends up in politics, does not assume his farcical position between Janine and his wife. He does not assume his membership in a social class, his fate, his professional situation [...]. He wanders about in a mobile milieu, a miniscule island which, with time, has expanded into a desert which is divided between this modern, chic actress whom he would like to love and his wife [...]. Arlette Le Gall is the character who knows the best what she wants and how to get it. Jean is lost in the vagaries of time, between the island of his childhood, of his grandfather, and these deserted spaces, this apartment and this villa where it is difficult to imagine any family living. And this ferociously faithful criminal wife is always there; she won't budge ("*Mon oncle d'Amérique*," pp. 49-50).

Marcel Oms — Jean's Island

In a certain way all of them have deep down the nostalgia of a child's world which fed their dreams and which is symbolized by the title of the film. The "American Uncle" is this mythical character who never comes, who is perhaps no longer alive and who, in any case, belongs to the world of fairy tales or legendary treasure islands. He has an initiatory function and isn't to be taken either word for word or literally.

Such is the function of Jean's island in the film. It is present virtually from the very first scenes, before returning as a leitmotif referring first to a group of happy memories, then to the broken promise of a solitary and hidden love, and finally to rupture and disillusionment. Beyond the island the last act of the film plays out until this final shot of a wall in New York, in a dilapidated decor, devastated and desolate, deserted, as empty as the hope of the return of the American Uncle [...].

Jean's island, which was where he was born, is a metaphor for earthly paradise and for the lost paradise whose memory changes as the demands, necessities, accommodations, and renunciations of the adult world transform our consciousness (*Alain Resnais*, pp. 140-142).

Jacques Chevallier — The Film Excerpts

The presence in the film of the images of Gabin, Danielle Darrieux, or Jean Marais is not just a matter of a film buff having fun; these are not simply quotations. We are dealing here — it should be self-evident — with "models," with anchoring points for the imagination of the characters within the socio-cultural realm of the imagination — the most powerful of all, the one imposed by cinema. However, they are specifically French models stuffed with connotations, tied to myths and to an ideology [...]. These are not precise reference points, but they are extremely strong ones. More subtly, the Gabin-Darrieux-Marais excerpts also refer to a certain type of French cinema to which Resnais's film is paying homage in its own way. If we ignore the set of images which surrounds them, we discover people brought together in perfectly conventional situations, repertory situations, obeying, for example, the codes of melodrama, indeed, of vaudeville [...]. To all appearances Resnais was inspired by popular cinema. He was trying to borrow the situations of this type of cinema, its dramatic resources and — let's not forget it, because it is extremely important — its comic resources (Chevallier et al., Panel discussion on "*Mon oncle d'Amérique*," p. 60).

Daniel Sauvaget — Behavioral Stereotypes

The meaning of the film may be found in what Resnais himself says about behavioral models and the codification of reactions, attitudes, and even the staging that individuals do of themselves. Here is a cinema which does the *staging* of the staging we do of ourselves. Laborit too gives a certain image of himself, and in this respect he functions like an actor in a story. The interest of the excerpts from old French films inserted into the film is also at this level; that is, they function as humorous commentaries and highlight behavioral stereotypes. While it is true that cinema constantly furnishes behavioral stereotypes, its raw material is behavioral stereotypes in life, and these stereotypes underlie both cinema and life. That is the essential of the dramatic mechanisms employed by Resnais (Chevallier et al., Panel discussion on "*Mon oncle d'Amérique*," p. 62).

Jacques Zimmer — The Last Shot of the Film

In my opinion the last shot closes the door completely. The solution that Laborit proposes is "Know thyself." The last image of the film shows us the wall of a building on which a magnificent landscape has been painted. As we approach it, the camera makes it increasingly indecipherable. The last close-up focuses on a few bricks. We thought we had understood the global structure; as we approach we realize that when we are at the heart of the matter, we still haven't understood anything. For me *My American Uncle* is a film filled with despair (Chevallier et al., Panel discussion on "*Mon oncle d'Amérique*," p. 62).

ALAIN RESNAIS'S FILMOGRAPHY
(FEATURE FILMS)

1959	*Hiroshima mon amour*
1961	*Last Year at Marienbad*
	(L'Année dernière à Marienbad)
1963	*Muriel, or the Time of Return*
	(Muriel, ou le temps d'un retour)
1966	*The War is Over (La Guerre est finie)*
1968-69	*Je t'aime, je t'aime*
1973-74	*Stavisky*
1976	*Providence*
1980	*My American Uncle (Mon oncle d'Amérique)*
1983	*Life is a Bed of Roses (La Vie est un roman)*
1984	*Love Unto Death (L'Amour à mort)*
1986	*Mélo*
1989	*I Want To Go Home*
1993	*Smoking No Smoking*
1997	*Same Old Song (On connaît la chanson)*
2003	*Not on the Mouth (Pas sur la bouche)*

WORKS CONSULTED

Benayoun, Robert. Conversation with Alain Resnais on *Mon oncle d'Amérique* in *Alain Resnais. Arpenteur de l'imaginaire: de Hiroshima à Mélo*. Paris: Stock, 1980.

.........."Le retour au pays natal. Sur *Mon oncle d'Amérique* d'Alain Resnais." *Positif,* 231 (June 1980): 33-40.

Chapsal, Madeleine. "Entretien avec Alain Resnais" in Gruault, *Mon oncle d'Amérique* (screenplay), pp. 7-19.

.........."Entretien avec Henri Laborit" in Gruault, *Mon oncle d'Amérique* (screenplay), pp. 21-32.

Chevallier, Jacques, and Olivier Gillisen, Robert Grelier, Jacqueline Lajeunesse, Marcel Martin, Philippe Pilard, Daniel Sauvaget, Jacques Zimmer. Panel discussion on "*Mon oncle d'Amérique.*" *La Revue du cinéma*, 352 (July-Aug. 1980): 57-62.

Decaux, Emmanuel, and Jean-Claude Bonnet, Bruno Villien. "Entretien avec Alain Resnais." *Cinématographe* 58 (June 1980): 15-22.

Gruault, Jean. *Mon oncle d'Amérique* (screenplay). Paris: Albatros, 1980.

Martin, Marcel. "*Mon oncle d'Amérique.*" *La Revue du cinéma*, 351 (June 1980): 23-24.

Oms, Marcel. *Alain Resnais*. Paris: Rivages, 1988.

Oudart, Jean-Pierre. "*Mon oncle d'Amérique.*" *Cahiers du cinéma*, 314 (July-Aug. 1980): 48-51.

Resnais, Alain. *Mon oncle d'Amérique* (screenplay). *L'Avant-Scène Cinéma* 263 (March 1981): 1-72.

Agnès Varda

Vagabond
Sans toit ni loi

(1985)

Agnès Varda, *Vagabond*: Mona, the vagabond (Sandrine Bonnaire) on the move. © Ciné-Tamaris

Director .... Agnès Varda
Screenplay and dialogues.. Agnès Varda
Assistant Directors .... Jacques Royer, Jacques Deschamps
Director of Photography ....Patrick Blossier
Music...Joanna Bruzdowicz
Film Editors .... Agnès Varda, Patricia Mazuy
Sound ....Jean-Paul Mugel
Art Directors.. Jean Bauer, Anne Violet
Script Girl (Continuity) ....Chantal Desanges
Producer .... Ciné-Tamaris, Films A2
Length .... 1 h 45

Cast

Sandrine Bonnaire (*Mona Bergeron, the vagabond*), Macha Méril (*Madame Landier, the plane tree specialist*), Stéphane Freiss (*Jean-Pierre, the agricultural engineer*), Yolande Moreau (*Yolande, Aunt Lydie's maid*), Patrick Lepczynski (*David, the "Wandering Jew"*), Yahiaoui Assouna (*Assoun, the vineyard worker*), Joël Fosse (*Paulo, Yolande's boyfriend*), Marthe Jarnias (*Aunt Lydie*), Laurence Cortadellas (*Eliane*).

STORY

One winter morning in the south of France a farm worker discovers a young women's filthy body in a ditch. She has apparently frozen to death during the preceding night. In voice-over a woman narrator who is most likely the filmmaker explains to us that the body, which no one has come to claim, was buried in a pauper's grave. She is interested in this young woman, whose name is Mona Bergeron, and is trying to learn as much as she can about her by talking to the people she met during the last weeks of her life, which she had spent roaming around the Nîmes region. The film consists largely of these peoples' memories of Mona, which are often presented as flashbacks. Their testimony —in front of the camera or filmed without their knowledge — is interspersed with the young woman's wanderings.

At the beginning of the film Mona walks out of the sea naked. Two suspicious characters on a motorcycle watch her from afar while she gets dressed, but they eventually leave. They will be the first two witnesses, followed by a truck driver who gave Mona a ride (but made her get out when she became obnoxious) and a worker who discovered her sleeping in an old shack that they were destroying. Mona knocks on the door of a house to ask for water, then at another door to ask for some matches. She smokes non-stop. The daughter of the family in the first house is envious of the vagabond and would like to be "free" like her. Mona is awakened the next morning by a gravedigger; she had put up her tent in a cemetery. Having only stale bread to eat, she accepts a sandwich in a café, then sets off down the road again. She hides when a police car passes. She finds work in a garage, where she washes cars, and then puts up her tent behind the service station and just lazes away the rest of the day. The owner speaks to us about her, saying that he didn't trust her (but we see him coming out of her tent pulling his pants up early in the morning…).

Facing the camera, Yolande the maid gives her testimony. She noticed the young woman in the castle where her uncle worked as a caretaker, asleep in the embrace of a young man. She envies them and would like to have the same kind of romantic relationship with her boy friend Paulo, who clearly has no feelings for her. Mona enjoys an idyllic existence at the castle with another vagabond, David, who refers to himself as "The Wandering Jew." They spend each day smoking marijuana, drinking wine, and making love. The idyll comes to an end abruptly when Paulo and his friends come to burglarize the castle one night and beat David up in the process. David offers his testimony on Mona, expressing his disappointment at her hurried departure when the burglars arrived.

Mona continues her wandering, then finds refuge with some aging hippies turned shepherds (a former philosophy student and his partner) who agree to take her in. However, finding it hard to tolerate her laziness and slovenliness, they soon force her to leave. She steals a few goat cheeses from the shepherds and sells them to a prostitute working the highway.

The film is dominated for a long while by the testimony of Madame Landier, a university professor specializing in the diseases of plane trees, who picks up Mona as she hitchhikes. Before we see the episode as a flashback, she relates the incident over the telephone to a friend, expressing astonishment at how bad the young woman smelled. She feeds Mona, explains her work to her, and lets her sleep in her car overnight. The next day she takes her to a place where she is studying some diseased trees and introduces her to a co-worker named Jean-Pierre, an agricultural engineer. We then see Jean-Pierre with his wife Eliane, who has set her sights on the apartment of her husband's great aunt Lydie. Eliane could not care less about the young vagrant her husband describes to her.

We catch up with Mona in a Red Cross trailer where she is giving blood before hitting the road again. She finds a job loading crates onto a truck. Jean-Pierre arrives at Mme Landier's home, just in time to save her from electrocution. Mme Landier is worried about Mona, who disappeared into the woods when she let her out of her car. Indeed, in the following episode Mona, who was camping out in the woods, is raped by a man who has stalked her.

In the following episode Mona is taken in by Assoun, a Tunisian vineyard worker whose lodgings and work she shares until the other workers, Moroccans, return and refuse to let her stay with them. Yolande picks her up next and puts her in a bedroom in Jean-Pierre's old aunt's apartment, where she is employed as a maid. Mona strikes up a friendly relationship with the old woman and gives her alcohol; the two of them get drunk together and break into uncontrollable laughter. Yolande returns and ejects Mona from the apartment (giving her some money) but is then kicked out herself at the insistence of Eliane. The police suspect her boyfriend Paulo of participating in a burglary of the castle where her uncle is caretaker.

We next find Mona with a group of dropouts, young drug addicts who have become derelicts. They spend their days at the train station and their nights squatting in an abandoned building. We receive the testimony of Jean-Pierre, who is horrified when he sees the young woman in an awful state as he is accompanying Yolande to her train. David "The Wandering Jew" arrives at the building where the group is squatting and gets into a fight with another vagrant over some money. They manage to set the building on fire, forcing Mona to leave. One of the dropouts speaks about Mona as he faces the camera. He is sorry about her departure: he would have liked to become her pimp.

Mona is now outdoors in the freezing weather. She tries to sleep in a large radish greenhouse with a plastic top, but she is too cold. The next day she is attacked and smeared with wine dregs by merrymakers celebrating a wine festival in a village where she had gone in search of bread. Terrified, she takes refuge in a telephone booth, then runs away. We see her finally in the middle of a vineyard covered with a filthy blanket, dragging her feet in boots which are falling apart at the seams. She walks across the vineyard towards the camera, stumbles, and falls forward into a ditch. She tries to get up but falls on her back and lies still. Fade to black.

CRITICAL RECEPTION

Ginette Delmas's opinion is typical of the enthusiastic critical reception accorded *Vagabond*: "Admirable film, faultless [...], the finest French film we've seen in years" (p. 39). For Alain Bergala it was "without a doubt one of the best films made by Varda, and in [his] opinion the best" (p. 6). This reaction was echoed by Claudine Delvaux, who declared that the film was "like the second wind not only of Agnès Varda's cinema but of French cinema, period. Absolutely new in its conception and the force which emanates from it, *Vagabond* is like the culmination of a complete body of works" (p. 33). "Lucid, powerful film" according to one critic, "moving film" or "great, beautiful film" according to others — the critical community was generally in agreement with Claude-Marie Trémois of the magazine *Télérama*, for whom "*Vagabond* is a masterpiece which richly deserved its Golden Lion at the last Venice Film Festival" (Dec. 4, 1985). The critics were not mistaken, and the prize received in Venice in September 1985 was only the beginning. Varda's film ran off with the International Critics Prize 1985, the Georges Méliès Prize 1985, the Prize of the International Catholic Cinema Organization 1985, the Prize for the Best Foreign Film 1986 in Los Angeles, the Prize for the Best Film and the Best Director at the Brussels Film Festival 1986, and the Prize for the Best Film at the International Film Festival of Durban (South Africa) 1987. For her acting in *Vagabond* (in which she "reached sublime heights," according to one critic), Sandrine Bonnaire was awarded the Cesar for the Best Actress at the Cannes Film Festival in 1985.

The opinion of the critics was vindicated by the public reception of the film. As Varda would later say, the film found a "vast and vibrant" public, abroad as well as in France, including the French provinces: "The film went everywhere, including out into the rural areas, where it was projected by the devoted film buffs of Ardèche-Images in a bus transformed into a forty-seat cinema. They did one showing in each town. (They managed to show the film to thirty thousand spectators in that region)" (*Varda par Agnès*, p. 181). Although this wasn't the first Varda film to win prizes (see below), *Vagabond*, as she foresaw, was after thirty years of filmmaking "the first of my films to enjoy a huge success in commercial terms" (Roumette, p. 35).

BEFORE *VAGABOND*

After studying art history, Varda became passionately interested in photography. Through photography she entered the entertainment world, having become the official photographer for Jean Vilar's Théâtre National Populaire at the Avignon Festival and at the Palais de Chaillot in Paris. When she decided to make her first film, *La Pointe Courte* (1954), Varda knew absolutely nothing about cinema. By her own admission she had seen only half a dozen movies in her whole life. She began her apprenticeship in the seventh art by talking with Alain Resnais, who would edit her film. *La Pointe Courte*, a small Mediterranean fishing village near Sète, is a mixture of documentary and fiction films. It is the story of a fictional couple combined with the story of the real struggle of a village whose economic survival was being threatened by large industry. This film was a harbinger of the nature of Varda's work in the cinema. She became just as interested in the documentary as in fictional stories, and she never hesitates to interweave the two genres in her films. As she said of herself, "I am drawn just as strongly to documentaries as to fiction films, and I like to mix the techniques and styles. I enjoy mixing all that together" ("Agnès Varda," *Séquences*, p. 35).

Varda's beginnings were promising: *La Pointe Courte* won the Grand Prize of the Avant-Garde Film in Paris in 1955 and, the same year, the Golden Age Prize in Brussels. Retrospectively, in the light of the first feature films of the young cineastes of the New Wave — Truffaut, Godard, Chabrol, and Resnais, among others — Varda would come to be perceived as one of the forerunners of that current or, as some liked to say, as the "grandmother of the New Wave." Before completely abandoning her career as a photographer in 1960, Varda made three short documentaries. These included two commissioned films, *O saisons, ô châteaux* (1957), on the Loire Valley castles, and *On the Coast* (*Du côté de la côte*, 1958), about the tourists of the French Riviera. The third was *L'Opéra-mouffe* (1958), in which we see, through the eyes of a pregnant woman, the people who frequent the open air market on the rue Mouffetard in Paris. Although Varda was no longer a professional photographer, she would never abandon photography completely. Her films, which are always striking by their formal beauty, often include photos and static images of all kinds which enrich their thematic register. *Salut les Cubains*, on Castro's Cuba (see below), is composed entirely of a montage of 1,500 photographs.

During the following twenty-five years, before making *Vagabond*, Varda directed seven feature films, including four fiction films: *Cléo de 5 à 7* (1961), *Happiness* (*Le Bonheur*, 1964), *Les Créatures* (1965), and *One Sings, the Other Doesn't* (*L'une chante, l'autre pas*, 1976). Her second feature film, *Cléo from 5 to 7*, identifies her clearly with the New Wave — at least its politicized, literary, and esthetically oriented branch known as the "Left Bank" group, which also included Alain Resnais and Chris Marker. In this film Varda shot in real time (from five o'clock to six-thirty) a critical moment in the life of a little Parisian pop singer who awaits anxiously the results of tests which will determine if she has cancer or not. The film was selected for both the Cannes and Venice Film Festivals in 1962 before receiving the Méliès Prize the same year. *Happiness* is a reflection on the nature of happiness, as well as on the right to happiness through love outside of conventional morality. A "scandalous" film, *Happiness* nonetheless won the Louis Delluc Prize in 1965 and the Golden Bear at the Berlin Film Festival the same year. The following film, *The Creatures*, which establishes a parallel between the life of a couple and the genesis of a novel, was characterized as a "cold and cerebral work" (Ford, 114). It was generally panned by both the critics and the public, despite its selection for the Venice Film Festival in 1966. *One Sings, the Other Doesn't*, which is devoted to questions concerning the right of women to decide to have children or not (contraception and abortion), relates the personal battle of two young women. It is clearly meant to be a homage to the feminist movement in France, which Varda supported unreservedly. Her film won the Grand Prize at the Taormina Film Festival in Italy in 1977.

In 1969 in Los Angeles Varda shot *Lions Love and Lies*, which is half documentary and half fiction. It depicts the hippie scene of avant-garde Hollywood actors, woven into the presidential campaign and the assassination of Robert Kennedy. In this period Varda devoted herself principally to documentaries, making a long series of short subjects, some of which were tied to leftwing politics, such as *Salut les Cubains* (1963) and *Black Panthers* (1968). The best known and some of the longest of these films include *Daguerréotypes* (1974-75), a documentary on the inhabitants of the rue

Daguerre in Paris, the street where Varda lives, and *Walls Walls* (*Murs murs*, 1980), a reflection on the people of Los Angeles based on mural paintings. *Documenteur* (1980-81), a mid-length film, is the portrait of a young woman and her son who live in exile in Los Angeles. The film is also about the woman's relations with other people and with the city itself, focusing on its poorest residents — the beggars, the abandoned, and the drunks. In 1982 Varda won a Cesar at Cannes for *Ulysse*, a short subject which explores an image from the past, a posed photograph she had taken nearly thirty years before in which we see a naked man standing on a pebble-covered beach and looking at the sea, a naked child sitting on the beach, and a dead goat.

ORIGIN

"The first emotion which paved the way for the film was my distress at the idea of people who freeze to death: vagrants in fields, beggars in the streets, and old women abandoned in unheated rooms" (*Varda par Agnès*, p. 40). However, Varda added, "You have to be close to the world of the dropouts, at least for a while, to dare to speak of them as if you knew them" (p. 168). Accordingly, Varda spent several weeks traveling around the Nîmes region meeting people, especially street people that she found in shelters and in train stations at night. She visited a Red Cross truck and gave some blood next to an "unemployed homeless man (a former drifter)" who told her stories about his life. She met "a certain shepherd with a beret, a wife, a child, goats and various cheeses" (p. 166). One day she picked up a hitchhiker, a girl who was traveling alone, a "wanderer" with an enormous backpack: "That had an even bigger impact on me than the young men. Well, my film is no more complicated than that: a girl alone on the road, alone in the woods, alone at night, outside. I really saw one who was camping near a cemetery, in the middle of winter. I put that in the film" (in Carbonnier and Revault d'Allonnes, p. 2).

When she returned to Paris at the end of November, she refused to write a screenplay, claiming, "The writing process paralyzes the imagination and is a useless expenditure of energy" (p. 2). She only agreed to submit to the eventual financial backers a two-page synopsis which described the general subject: "A girl who has rebelled against society walks alone along the road until she freezes to death." It is only afterwards that Varda came up with the idea of placing Mona's death at the beginning of the film. We would come to know the girl retrospectively, through the testimony of the people who met her. Varda rejected however the idea of a police investigation; the police aren't interested in this nameless drifter. "As for me, Varda the author, *I'm* interested in her" (p. 2). It is therefore the filmmaker who conducts the investigation by creating all sorts of people and studying what she calls "the Mona effect" on each of them.

Vagabond is thus deeply anchored in reality — with one exception. The story of Jean-Pierre, Mme Verdier's assistant, who lusts after his old aunt's apartment, is inspired by one of the characters of *Le Planétarium*, a novel by Nathalie Sarraute (1959). Varda, who was a great admirer of Sarraute, dedicated the film to her.

THE ACTORS AND THE SHOOTING

Varda had seen the remarkable acting of Sandrine Bonnaire when the actress was only fifteen years old, in Maurice Pialat's shocking film *To Our Loves* (*A nos amours*), which received the Cesar at Cannes for the Best Film in 1984. When Varda spoke to her about the role of Mona, Bonnaire accepted immediately. "What interested me," she explained, "was to play someone totally different from me. Varda told me that she wanted someone unpleasant, and I liked that idea, the idea of casting off an image, of playing a completely different role" (in Bergala and le Roux, p. 9). Varda had gotten some ideas and information from a young female drifter she had picked up on the road (Setina, an Algerian) and whom she had lodged in her home for a time. She left Bonnaire alone with this drifter in the woods for two days, "with some raw potatoes and a few matches in Setina's backpack" (*Varda par Agnès*, p. 168), so that the actress could "learn a few things from her," observe her attitude and demeanor.

Varda hired other professional actors for the roles which involved real acting: Macha Méril notably to play the role of the "college prof," the specialist in diseased plane trees, Stéphane Freiss to play her assistant Jean-Pierre, the agricultural engineer, and Yolande Moreau, a Belgian actress for the role of the maid Yolande. The rest of the cast, with very few exceptions, was composed of amateurs recruited locally in the Nîmes region, on location. These included the old aunt Lydie, the garage owner, Assoun the Tunisian (who plays himself), as well as the philosopher shepherd and his family, among others. Varda likes to film "real people," for both their authenticity and their frequently picturesque side. However, in *Vagabond* she required them to learn written dialogue, to rehearse their roles like the others actors, and to tolerate multiple takes now and then (Arbaudie, p. 18). Since she often had to deal with other non-professionals as well, she was confronted with some very unusual problems, as in the case of the shooting of the end of the episode of Mona's stay with Assoun. The Moroccans were genuinely hostile not only to the presence of "Mona," but to the presence of Varda's crew as well! Getting them to play their roles was a real challenge.

The film took two months to shoot, from March 8 to May 6, 1985, in the most makeshift conditions. The whole crew was lodged in a hostel lent by the city of Nîmes. They ate their breakfast together in the kitchen. A week before the shooting began Varda finally wrote the screenplay for her film, whose working title was *To Be Grasped* (*A saisir*): "I launched into the writing of a twenty-page framework broken up into sequences. The dialogue was just sketched out; I would complete it as the shooting progressed" (in Carbonnier and Revault d'Allonnes, p. 3). Indeed, every morning around five o'clock, before she got out of bed, Varda wrote the dialogues for the day. She would then photocopy them for the actors — unless she wrote them just before the takes. Bonnaire recalls, "I would wait in the car while she wrote the dialogues on the hood. Then we would shoot" (Bergala and le Roux, p. 9). Bonnaire emphasized nonetheless the rigor of Varda, who would not allow anyone to change a word: "Although Varda wrote the dialogue at the last minute, she insisted that it be scrupulously respected" (Dazat, p. 14). To help the young actress assimilate her character better, and for the sake of realism, she even had her wear Setina's old clothes during the filming (p. 14).

Because she was an independent producer, Varda enjoyed a large measure of freedom in her making of the film. This also permitted her to take some risks and to benefit from the unexpected. "The shooting was decided day by day," Bergala remarked, "and sometimes depended upon pure chance and upon whom they happened onto that day […]. This didn't prevent Agnès Varda from choosing the framing of the shots and determining the various camera movements with her usual meticulousness" ("La Repousse," p. 6). No less meticulous in her directing of the actors, Varda provided extremely precise instructions regarding the smallest details, the slightest movements of the characters — at the risk, she admitted, of appearing to be a fusspot.

After several months of editing and the presentation of the film at the Venice Festival, followed by two previews on November 25 in Paris and on December 2 in Nîmes, *Vagabond* opened to the public on December 4, 1985.

STRUCTURE AND STYLE

but we don't know what moves her at the end

Varda called *Vagabond* "the most rigorous and structured" film of her career (Roumette, p. 35). Often compared to *Citizen Kane* (1940), Varda's film begins by the death of the main character, whose life is then reconstructed by the testimony of people who had known her. However, while there is an "investigation" in both films, there is no journalist asking questions in *Vagabond*; it is Varda the filmmaker who leads the investigation. Also unlike Orson Welles's film, the series of flashbacks in Varda's film is based on testimony from people who have known the heroine only very briefly, or who simply crossed her path once. Owing to the juxtaposition of the various testimonies bearing on the behavior and character of Mona, commentators have often spoken of the "puzzle-like construction" of the film. However, the portrait we receive of Mona remains fragmentary. In truth, Varda wanted to create a "puzzle," and she intended for "one or two pieces" to be missing. Like the puzzle, her investigation will therefore remain incomplete.

The flashbacks in Varda's film are presented as "interludes" which interrupt the main thread of the narrative, that is, Mona's wandering. Her apparently aimless roving is documented by a dozen long tracking shots, each lasting about one minute, which accompany the heroine as she moves from place to place. Varda baptized these scenes the "traveling shots of the Grand Series." Varda conceives of this whole group of shots as a single tracking shot regularly interrupted by the testimonies, which often become flashbacks: "The whole film is a long traveling shot. We cut it up into pieces, separate the pieces, and place the 'adventures' between them" (in Dazat and Horvilleur, p. 19). In an attempt to render the continuity of the tracking shots more tangible, Varda often brings them to a halt on some object which we see again at the beginning of the next tracking shot of the "Grand Series." Sometimes it is a piece of farm equipment, other times a pile of tires, a section of wall, or simply a color (*Varda par Agnès*, p. 174).

The continuity between the traveling shots (which isn't necessarily perceived by the spectator) is reinforced by the original music written for these shots. This music not only compensates for Mona's silence but also "paraphrases her ever increasing solitude" (p. 209). Moreover, the orientation of these long tracking shots takes on a metaphorical value for Varda, who points out that all of the traveling shots of the "Grand Series" accompany the girl as she walks from right to left across the screen, "against the current" of society: "In our culture we read from left to right and any movement from right to left is a little strained and constraining" (p. 209).

As regards style Varda is particularly concerned with the esthetic quality of the shots, whose composition and lighting are meticulously prepared by her director of photography Patrick Blossier. She pays close attention to the lighting, which varies subtly according to the time of day or the environment in which the action is taking place. As Varda says, "Through his lighting Blossier was able either to reproduce natural daylight or evoke a certain sadness in poor peoples' homes, or still yet create in wealthy homes an even and regular light filled with depth and details, like at the old woman's apartment" (in Dazat and Horvilleur, p. 21). As for the style of the takes, Varda alternates a very mobile camera (to narrate Mona's "adventures") with static shots during the various testimonies. Despite the fact that Varda wrote every bit of the dialogue in these "interviews" — and despite the multiple takes — the utilization of real people looking directly into the camera gives a documentary flavor to her film. This characteristic is central to Varda's basic ambition as a filmmaker referred to above: "to make fiction films which have a documentary texture."

THEMES

Agnès Varda has a taste for plays on words. She calls *Vagabond* a "fait d'hiver" (a "fact of winter"), alluding to the death of the heroine during the winter. At the same time, "fait d'hiver" is homophonous with "fait divers," which is a French term meaning a newspaper article about a "trivial" event — such as Mona's death. Similarly, the French title of the film *Sans toit ni loi* ("Homeless and lawless"), which describes the case of Mona, is a pun on the expression "sans foi ni loi" ("faithless and lawless"), which refers to a person who has neither religion nor morality, which is no less the case of Mona. In any case, the film's French title reflects the fundamental antinomy of the vagabond's existence: the lack of a home — shelter, material comfort, and the company of others — is the ransom of the liberty which the wanderer enjoys. "Mona," the first name of the heroine, also seems to be a play on words suggesting both "nomad" and "monad," the latter word coming from the Greek *monos* or "alone" (Revault D'Allonnes, p. 5). Varda maintains that she simply chose a popular name, Monique, with its nickname Mona — while admitting that subconscious factors can play a role in choices of this kind.

Even the working title of the film contains a pun, since *A saisir* recalls the title of Varda's preceding film (*7P., cuis., s. de b… A saisir*), which is in the style of a classified ad for a rental unit (7 rooms, kitchen, bathroom…A bargain). However, the title also alludes to the character of the heroine of *Vagabond*, who is "*insaisissable*," that is, extremely elusive, impossible to understand. "*Insaisissable*" is the word which is repeated the most frequently by the film's commentators — along with "opaque," "unfathomable," and "impenetrable" — in speaking of the heroine. She is elusive, according to Bérubé, "because no one among those who knew her was able to understand her or stop her from wandering" (p. 56). "Opaque from the beginning to the end," says Prédal, who cites as proof the twelve long travel sequences (the Grand Series) "in which the camera tracks parallel to the girl as she walks. Whether she is happy or sad, rebellious or resigned, she can be accompanied but never really met in the true sense of the term" (p. 25).

It is only towards the end of the film, in the scene at the train station in which the camera tracks forward to a tight close shot of Mona as she awakens on a bench, that the camera really begins to "grasp" (or "seize") her. At the end of Mona's vagabondage, when she is lying on her back in the ditch where she has fallen, we see her in a static close shot angled sharply downward, which recalls the shot at the beginning in which the policemen photographed Mona's corpse. The film has come full circle. Since the young woman is no longer moving, she can finally be "grasped" — but only from the outside. As Varda remarks, at the end of the film "the mystery of Mona is still unresolved."

In all truth Varda doesn't even attempt to analyze Mona. She is no more interested in the psychology of her heroine than in the moral questions posed by her lifestyle. She scarcely bothers to suggest why she is a dropout; she just depicts her as she is. One could go so far as to say that Varda is less interested in Mona herself than in the reaction she provokes in others, what the filmmaker calls "the Mona effect": "As the author I invented an enigmatic Mona who doesn't answer my questions [...]. We do not really know why she is roving or what led her to do so. It is the fact of her passing through that is interesting. I would go even further: it is the effect of her passing through on all of us that interests me. Therefore, the subject is not so much the depiction of Mona herself as the depiction of the Mona effect" ("Agnès Varda," p. 35).

The brief contact with the girl who helps Mona pump some water, for example, provokes in the girl a realization that she yearns for liberty in her own life. Likewise, Yolande the maid becomes aware of the lack of love in her relationship with her boyfriend when she sees Mona and David sleeping in each others' arms at the castle — even though her reaction is based on a false, overly romantic impression of the couple's relations. The most profound effect, however, is certainly that exercised by Mona on the university professor Mme Landier, whose bourgeois lifestyle makes her feel guilty when confronted with the drifter's destitution. This effect is represented metaphorically by the electrical shock that she receives in her bathroom and which nearly electrocutes her. As Varda explained, "I needed for Mme Landier to have a little shock to help her let go and weep a little, to express her guilty conscience" (in Dazat and Horvilleur, p. 22).

Vagabond is a film which makes no concessions to the spectator; it is devoid of "romanticism." The ideal of liberty, the great attraction of wandering, is contradicted metaphorically by the lock and chain which David, Mona's momentary boyfriend, wears around his neck. Mona's so-called "liberty" is in fact severely circumscribed by material constraints (hunger, cold, solitude) and dangers (the police, theft, rape) of all kinds which turn her life into a constant struggle for survival. It is a struggle which she is condemned to lose, and Dazat speaks aptly of "a film on physical deterioration" (p. 11). The theme of deterioration is expressed both physically by Mona's growing filthiness, which produces nauseating odors, and metaphorically by the progressive delapidation of her boots and the loss of her personal belongings (tent, coat, sleeping bag) near the end.

Although for Mona the alternative to her vagabond's life is an unbearable confinement (represented by the goat attached to the tree and tormented by the dog in the wine grower' yard), the heroine's roving is no less a steady march towards the ultimate physical degeneration, that is, toward death. Death is one of the principal themes of the film. The opening shots, in which we discover Mona's corpse, establish immediately the "fate" of the young woman, just as the murder committed by François seals his fate at the beginning of the Marcel Carné film *Daybreak* (1939). However, unlike Carné's film, the flashbacks do not provide psychological explanations. They serve only to chronicle the last weeks of Mona's vagabondage, seen from the outside. Her route is strewn with "mortuary signs" (Picant, p. 146), beginning with the cemetery where she puts up her tent one evening. Other signs of death are the state of her boots (as noted above), the words of the philosopher shepherd (who points out to Mona that all of his former roving friends are dead), and the deadly disease which has infected the plane trees. As Mona herself says to the man who has hired her to load crates, "*I don't give a damn about your plane trees, but if they die, at least they'll remind you of me.*"

At first glance Mona seems to embody the world of the dropouts. However, we soon come to realize that she is even alienated from the typical dropouts (Toubiana, p. 11), such as the philosopher shepherd who is living his dream of returning to the land and complains that Mona has no desire to do anything: "*She isn't a dropout; she's just out.*" We may consider nonetheless that Mona represents the extreme limit of the dropout micro-culture. She embodies the absolutely incomprehensible, indeed repugnant side of this social phenomenon for those — including "productive" dropouts like the shepherd— who are attached to the traditional social values of industriousness, integrity, family, and cleanliness. Varda emphasizes in fact Mona's filth, knowing full well that this is what will especially disgust "respectable" people: "If we are sympathetic toward poverty," she observes, "we are much less tolerant of filth" (in Arbaudie, p. 18). She wants her heroine to be as antipathetic as possible. This is accomplished admirably by Sandrine Bonnaire, who makes no effort to be pleasant to others, even to those who help her. In this manner, while Varda introduces the spectator to the life of vagabonds, she also tests our capacity to accept the existence among us of people whom we not only do not understand, but whom we may find repulsive — as Jean-Pierre the agriculture engineer is repulsed by Mona at the train station. In short, Varda puts our humane instincts severely to the test. In a film which, according to Varda, has no intention of moralizing, the cineaste nevertheless gives us an important lesson: "Even antipathetic," she states, "Mona has the right to exist" (in Picant, p. 148).

*I wish to thank Agnès Varda for meticulously reading this introduction to her film and for providing valuable details and rectifications. The filmmaker reminds us of the appearance of a French DVD of *Vagabond* (December 2003) which contains a "bonus" entirely devoted to the "traveling shots of the Grand Series" and to the music composed for the film by Joanna Bruzdowicz. Other bonuses provide keys which are intended to facilitate the understanding of the particular film language (the "cinécriture") which Varda utilizes in the film.

STUDY GUIDE

Director's Comments

"What motivates me are the strong emotions which begin the process, and then using these emotions to make a movie. But my real passion is the writing, or rather the "film-writing" (*la cinécriture*). How am I going to express my emotions in a film, touch people, create a show which will be appropriate for millions of people and not just two or three? [...] I am an author; that's the only kind of films I make. I mean by that that I write the screenplays and I direct them" ("Agnès Varda," *Séquences*, p. 36).

"One day I pick up a brunette, very young, with an enormous backpack. She stinks something awful. After an hour of silence she finally speaks to me. Then I look for a restaurant. Two of them turn us away after one look at her. We find a pretty modest one which lets us in. We chat, and I'm thrilled by her. She is very attractive and has sensitive eyes. Alone, dirty, and rebellious. Hostile in any case. We leave. It is very cold, and I'm deeply troubled at the idea that she is going to sleep outside. I take her to several hostels, but they turn her away. There is no room, at least for a girl. In the car, having gotten over her nauseating odor, I listen to her talk about herself. Her name is Setina, and she comes from the Kabyle region in the Algerian mountains. She's cut her ties with her past. She explains why but talks mostly about her daily existence, breaking into laughter from time to time. When she needs money (she can get along on 500 francs a month, for bread, canned beans, potatoes, and cigarettes), she accepts small jobs like picking strawberries, gathering grapes, weeding greenhouses, or cleaning yards. What is important is not to stay on these jobs very long, not to settle down anywhere. I give her a few addresses, places she can stay if she is in need, a little money, and I let her off where she asks, at the entrance to a forest that she is familiar with. It's still light outside. Bye! Goodby!" (Varda, *Varda par Agnès*, p. 167).

"I want the spectator to react to this girl who is a vagabond, a drifter, and who is dirty. Dirtiness is a subject which fascinates me, because we live in a pasteurized, aseptic world where deodorant reigns. You know, people realize that they have to reach out to others, but there are always conditions. They are happy to try to help people who are out of work, provided that those people want to work. If a guy is unemployed and lazy, that's unacceptable. They are glad to do something for the poor, but they have to be clean. A poor person who smells bad is going to be rejected. Holes in his clothes, unkempt, that's okay, since he's poor. But he must keep his dignity. Well, Mona keeps her dignity, but she is dirty and could care less" (Jean Roy, p. 19).

"Mona is beautiful because she is not a victim. Beautiful because she is proud. She does not say thank you. She is proud like the nomads of the Sahara and the gypsies; she has the noble bearing of the nomads. Mona the nomad. And she isn't very pleasant. She makes love with anyone, but without love. Sandrine didn't want Mona to have sexual relations with anyone, but I wanted her to sleep with another drifter, in the castle, and with other men, and that's what's suggested in the film. Because she simply isn't Joan of Arc. Drifters have a sexual life too, even it it's on and off. Very happy to be playing a role in which she could show her talent rather than her buttocks, Sandrine wanted to eliminate any form of sexuality from her role. But I convinced her that Mona wasn't a saint. Mona sleeps with guys but doesn't give a damn about them" (in Carbonnier and Revault d'Allonnes, p. 3).

"People who rove are neither camping nor sightseeing. They are poorly equipped: they don't have walking shoes, and they carry a kitchen knife rather than a Swiss knife. They live surrounded by nature but don't pay any attention to it. You never hear them talking about beautiful landscapes or sunsets. Moreover, most of them are detached from reality and are bored. I almost said that they are inside boredom and feel fine that way. Sandrine was introduced to this state of mind in two days of half-conversations and half-silence. In addition to surviving, drifting is doing nearly nothing and learning to live like that" (Varda, *Varda par Agnès*, p. 168).

"*Vagabond* is a work of fiction, a wickedly realistic fiction in which I used real people in a simulated documentary style. Mona is a character who is magnificently understood and played by Sandrine Bonnaire, but she is "documented" by people that I had met by chance, picked up on the highway and taken back home (particularly a girl that we had met when we had nearly begun shooting).

Mona, who eventually freezes to death, is described by those who have seen her or met her as she passed by. This fictional character becomes real because she is described by 'real people': a shepherd, a garage owner, a road worker, a mason, a farmer, a Tunisian laborer. They didn't make up their comments themselves, since I wrote their testimony, but I only wrote it after having imagined that I was going to do a documentary on them. I tried to imagine what they themselves would think or say, their way of speaking, their body language, their manner of being [...].

In *Vagabond* they "acted like actors," but as if it were a documentary. I am always using a mixture of methods. I think that *Vagabond* is a success. I say that immodestly, because after thirty years of cinema, it's the film in which my ambition to make fictional films with a documentary texture is best fulfilled. I could say the same thing about my goal of "cinema-writing" ("*cinécriture*"), that is, the desire to make shots structured in space, without psychology (the tracking shots during Mona's walking scenes, for example), one of the very subjects of my film" ("Agnès Varda" in Devarrieux and De Navacelle, pp. 48-49).

Excerpts for Discussion

Excerpt 1 (2'10-5'05): The first sequence of the film: the discovery of Mona's corpse, the police "investigation", the narrator's voice-over; Mona comes out of the sea.

Excerpt 2 (6'00-7'45): The truck driver picks up Mona; he makes her get out, recounts the episode to his friend.

Excerpt 3 (14'15-14'50): "Traveling of the Grand Series" accompanying Mona's walking (just before the sequence with the garage owner): framing of the tractor; Mona's arrival revealed by the tracking shot; the police car goes by (Mona hides); Mona catches up to and moves beyond the tracking shot, which stops on the sign for the service station.

Excerpt 4 (14'50-18'05): The garage owner sequence (first testimony, flashback: second testimony).

Excerpt 5 (37'50-41'25): Mona with the shepherds; she moves into the trailer; Mona kicked out.

Excerpt 6 (59'40-1h00'50): The "electrocution" of Mme Landier.

Excerpt 7 (1h02'20-03'20): The rape of Mona.

Excerpt 8 (1h40'00-43'25): The wine festival episode (the Clowns and the Whites), last "Traveling of the Grand Series," the end.

Quotations for Comment

Voice-over (Varda):

"No one claimed the body: it went from the ditch to the potter's field. This corpse which had resulted from a natural death left no trace. I wondered who among those who knew her when she was little still thought about her. But the people she had met recently remembered her. These witnesses helped me to tell about the last weeks of her last winter. She had made a strong impression on them. They spoke of her unaware that she was dead. I didn't think that it was useful to tell them that, nor that her name was Mona Bergeron. Personally, I know little about her, but it seems to me that she came from the sea."

* * *

The Girl at the water pump: "I would prefer to leave. That girl who asked for water is free. She goes wherever she wants."

Her Mother: "Maybe she doesn't get three meals a day, served by her mother."

The Girl: "Sometimes it would be better not to eat. I'd like to be free … I'd like to be free."

* * *

The Garage Owner: "These drifters are all the same: flirts, lazy good-for-nothings. [*We next see him crawling out of Mona's tent early in the morning, pulling up his pants.*] She had the gall to complain about my dirty hands. No, that's not what she said. She told me, 'You have a dirty mind.' She's got some nerve!"

* * *

Yolande: "Paulo, why aren't you nice to me? […] I know a couple of lovers who do everything together: eat, smoke, sleep, listen to music."

* * *

The Shepherd: "Maybe you're freer than I am. Good for you. I chose a middle ground between solitude and liberty."

Mona: "People hassled me for a long time. Not anymore."

The Shepherd: "You've chosen absolute liberty, but you also have absolute solitude. There comes a time when if you go on like that, I think you destroy yourself. You head for destruction. If you want to live, you stop. Anyway, all of my friends who kept on drifting are dead…or they've become wrecks — alcoholics, drug addicts — because the loneliness got to them."

* * *

The Shepherd (to Mona in the trailer): "Come on! Come on out of there so we can talk about this."

Mona: "What's the matter? What do you want?"

The Shepherd: "You're the one who doesn't want anything. We give you a piece of land, you do nothing with it. You've got nothing in your head."

Mona: "Why? I've got to have something in my head? I have to be a shepherd like you? Yours isn't the only way to drop out."

The Shepherd: "You're not a dropout, you're just *out*. You don't exist."

[...]

Mona: "Look, I hated being a secretary. I left all the little office bosses, so I'm not going to put up with one out here in the country."

The Shepherd: "I think you've read too many dime novels. You're dreaming."

＊ ＊ ＊

The Old Woman (to her husband): "She's strong willed. She knows what she wants. If I had sent you packing when I was her age, I would be better off. Because when you're married to the wrong person, it's for life... I liked that hippie."

＊ ＊ ＊

Mme Landier: "You studied English?"

Mona: "Yeh...all through high school."

Mme Landier: "Did you graduate from high school?"

Mona: "Yeh, I have a secretary's diploma."

[...]

Mme Landier: "So why did you leave everything?"

Mona: "Traveling and drinking champagne is better."

＊ ＊ ＊

Eliane: "When I think that your aunt has a seven-room apartment for herself alone! It's not fair! [...]"

Jean-Pierre: "Well, Aunt Lydie won't live forever!"

Eliane: "Yes, but we're wasting our best years just because we don't have enough money — or room."

Jean-Pierre: "Listen, quit complaining, OK? If you had seen this drifter...She doesn't have anything. Nothing at all, no shelter, no money, let me tell you..."

Eliane: "Spare me your crap about that filthy girl who took you and your Landier in, that prof who's always getting worked up about something. Quit wasting your sympathy on a run-away. She's probably a fugitive, or a mental patient, or a drug addict..."

＊ ＊ ＊

Mme Landier (to Jean-Pierre): "I almost died...electrocuted. I almost died. It's true what they say. I saw my life flash before my eyes...a bunch of images. It seemed so long [...]. How strange. That girl I picked up, I saw her several times, like a reproach. [*Flashback: Mme Landier lets Mona out of her car at the entrance to a forest and gives her some food and money. Return to the present.*] We can't just leave her like that. The woods are too dangerous. Jean-Pierre, you have to help me. Go look for her. I'll show you the place in the woods on the map [...]. I'm very worried about her, so alone. I should have done something. I don't even know her name."

* * *

The Shepherd: "She passed through like a gust of wind. No plans, no goals…no desires, she didn't want anything. We tried to suggest things to her … she wasn't interested in anything, anything at all. She's not roving, she's just wrong. She's useless, and by proving that she's useless, she's showing that the system she's rejecting is right about her. She's wrong, she's not a real rover."

* * *

Jean-Pierre (on the telephone): "I'm at the train station, and she's here. Boy, if you could only see her. She's horrible, a complete ruin. It makes me sick to see her [...]. Of course you can understand her state. Sometimes I feel so down and out myself. But to fall that low [...]. When I met her before, she asked me, 'Are you afraid of me?' Yes, I'm afraid of her. She frightens me because she disgusts me."

Questions/Topics for Reflection

1. The first sequence of the film (the discovery of the body, the police "investigation," the voice-over narration, Mona and the sea). Its thematic importance for the film in general.
2. Mona's lifestyle. How does she survive? The importance of the time of year at which the film's action takes place.
3. Mona's character, her behavior towards others (for instance: the truck driver at the beginning, the young man who buys her a sandwich in the café).
4. The role of the "witnesses" in this film; the manner in which they are filmed; the mixture of fiction and documentary film.
5. The "Mona effect" on the witnesses; for example, the girl at the pump, the garage owner, the shepherd, the old woman, Mme Landier, Eliane and Jean-Pierre, the dropout who wanted to be Mona's pimp.
6. The conflict between Mona and the philosopher-shepherd and its relationship with the question of "dropping out."
7. Mme Landier's character. Why is she interested in Mona? Connection between Mona and the plane trees. The role of Mme Landier's "electrocution."
8. After Mona's arrangement with Assoun, her expulsion by the group of immigrant workers (their hostility).
9. The thematic interest of the relationship between Mona and Aunt Lydie.
10. The meaning of the village festival episode in which Mona is smeared with wine dregs.
11. Mona's evolution, beginning with her dip in the sea at the beginning of the film. The signs of this evolution.
12. The connection between the "traveling shots of the Grand Series" and the episodes of Mona's life (the structure of the film).

CRITICAL DOSSIER

Alain Bergala — Mona's Otherness

What is the real subject of this film? It's not exactly Mona's character, or the film would be completely different and would tell us about Mona, would succeed in framing her and in accompanying her, in short, in understanding and loving her. The true subject of the film is the relationship between the filmmaker and her character. This relationship is based on a fundamental ambivalence: Agnès Varda is attracted to the character of Mona precisely because she rejects her desire to understand and like her. This is of course Mona's most pronounced character trait: her absolute refusal to accede to other people's expectations of her whenever that goes beyond her own needs or her own desires [...]. This stubborn refusal to respond to other people's expectations or to be considerate of them (including Varda who is filming her) creates a radical otherness for Mona's character. This otherness extends not only to the petty bourgeois people she meets along the way, but also to those who belong to the same general social category as she — David, Assoun, or the dropouts at the train station. She will remain to the end "the other," even in relation to the other "others," whether it be a wandering Jew or a Moroccan, since that is the essence of her character. Varda is thus struggling with this dilemma: how to film a character who repulses her as much as she attracts her, who threatens her as much as she fascinates here ("La Repousse," p. 5).

Serge Toubiana — "An Impregnable Being"

It is impossible to get anything out of Mona, to know anything about the feelings of this girl who is drifting, who is on the periphery of the other dropouts, this girl who goes beyond the limits. The film bumps up against her; there is a sort of hiatus between Varda's cinema and the cold, indomitable character who refuses to play anyone's game. When Mona meets the character played by Macha Méril, who is devoted to saving plane trees, she stays cloistered in the car, indifferent to the world. It is this stubborn refusal by Mona to play the game that makes this film so moving. As the film develops, Mona sinks deeper and deeper into her intractability vis-à-vis the world, just as the filmmaker's silence becomes progressively heavier and more anguishing as her inability to explain her character, to reduce her to human proportions, sinks in.

Mona's story would only be worth a few lines in the local paper. What is moving is the tenacity with which Varda draws the material for a story from an impossible subject and character [...]. To learn about Mona, Varda brings before the camera to testify several characters who have met her by chance during her travels or who have spent a little time with her along the way. They have the right to speak, but their words are empty: the documentary is pure illusion. Mona is an impregnable being who cannot be apprehended by language. It is because of her manner of eluding comprehension that Mona is so moving, like an autistic child, both cut off from the world and yet existing in the universe [...] ("L'Ombre d'un doute," pp. 11-12).

Raymond Lefèvre — "Common Voyeurism"

A film of gazes, *Vagabond* is a brilliant variation on the theme of common voyeurism. Mona's wandering takes on a different tone depending on whether she meets indifference, greed, kindness, envy, aggressiveness, violence, or cowardice;

that is, the whole spectrum of emotions which are attached to the gazes which she meets and which serve to mark her way. This includes a few high points like the extraordinary drunkenness and the wild laughter of an elderly woman momentarily liberated from her gloomy dependent existence. The testimonies are stages in the course of which Mona asserts her personal identity through her successive refusals. In a kind of rehabilitation of original insolence, Agnès Varda has created a character who has deliberately rejected the elementary taboos of early upbringing. She would choke on the words "thank you" and feels no need to wash, even if she stinks to high heavens. She doesn't want to be taken care of, rebuffs any orders, and brooks no advice. Refusing shelter to live without laws, Mona breaks off any tie which puts a limit on her independence. Even the long tracking shots which accompany her in her random roving and which stop dead on a farming implement or on a tree stump have no purchase on this equally moving and disconcerting character, magnificently portrayed in the young Sandrine Bonnaire's performance.

Such a stylistic emphasis excludes any moral judgment. Agnès Varda neither accuses nor excuses. Her character's vagabondage is not a form of fleeing; it is simply the expression of an extreme liberty which leads to an absolute solitude which we are not expected to pity, even if Mona furtively wipes away a few tears ("*Sans toit ni loi*," p. 26).

Fabrice Revault d'Allonnes — "First Name Mona"

Alone and needing no one, Mona is first and foremost a *monad*. Although nomadism is a community phenomenon, she passes alone through the sedentary "community." That is Varda's goal in making Mona move about and what makes her, as Varda says, a rebel [...]. Everything considered, Mona represents *absolute liberty*. Being a nomadic monad in a saturated and conformist world; being a wolf in a sheep's world: if that implies the risk of being a social "subhuman" being (including the risk of famine), it means by the same token acquiring the "divine" power — because it is super-human — of dissociating oneself from others, of not living like them [...]. It represents our phantasm, our common image of liberty. And what strange force is necessary to claim this liberty, from our standpoint of shackled social animals. The price you have to pay to have even *her* liberty — this price, we know, is solitude...until death ("Prénom: Mona...," p. 5).

Jérôme Picant — The Rape of Mona

Mona's character eludes fiction itself; she is a character off whom all events, even those which are *a priori* "dramatic," seem to slide without leaving a trace. The episode of the rape of Mona in the woods after her meeting with Mme Landier is a perfect illustration. The sequence is shot by a camera which never stops moving: it frames the man who is stalking her, then Mona, before moving away during the attack itself. The filmmaker doesn't use any near shots or close-ups which would increase the emotional charge of the sequence. The only element of tension is the music, which increases until it fills the theater. This episode, of which Mme Landier had had a premonition, will never be mentioned again. Dire events slide off of Mona, and so it seems normal that they slide off the witnesses also. With the exception of Mme Landier when she is faced with death, no one is conscious of the extreme distress of the young woman. Mona's character is not intended of course to attract sympathy. Her episode with David demonstrates her profound self-centeredness and her indifference to what happens to other people. Refusing to submit to fictional conventions, Agnès Varda makes no attempt to make her heroine likeable. Mona is certainly rejected, but she rejects everyone else too ("Sans toit ni loi ou La boucle imparfaite," p. 147).

Bernard Bastide — From Aphrodite to Dionysius

This time once again, like *Cléo from 5 to 7* twenty-five years earlier, *Vagabond* is a journey — in this case a movement from the sea to the land, from cleanliness to putrescence, accompanied by gradual degradation. Mona's life, like that of any human being, is a (slow) process of auto-destruction.

"*Since the beginning of the project I had this picture in my mind: Mona, with no family, coming out of the sea,*" Varda remarks. Like Aphrodite (Venus) who was born from the waves and foam near Cythera, Mona was born from the water: clean, not yet sullied by the gaze or contact of others. This first shot in which she appears is in fact a double birth: her arrival in the world and her appearance on the screen seem to be superimposed, erasing from the outset any allusion to Mona's social or cultural past. She exists, period. In what follows Agnès Varda steadfastly maintains her viewpoint: just show what happens without explaining, and above all without judging. With a mixture of attraction and repulsion rendered palpable in the lateral tracking shots which accompany Mona without approaching her, the filmmaker simply provides a set of situations, a range of meetings in which, like in *Cléo*, Eros and Thanatos are constantly intertwined.

Mona's sexual relationships are numerous (the garage owner, the squatter), but they are devoid of love, performed mechanically like a tribute which she must pay in exchange for her freedom. As for Thanatos, it is present at many levels, death appearing symbolically [...].

We find the symbolic register in the cemetery — the one where Mona camps out, the one behind the prostitute working the highway — and in Rita Mitsuko's song which speaks of "the cancer which killed you," the same cancer which, called colored chancre, is poisoning the sap of the plane trees [...].

But the theme of death in *Vagabond* refers especially to Mona the solitary nomad, and it is inscribed in the film from the prologue when her dead body is discovered. Mona is presented in several phases, with an entomologist's meticulousness, and is represented not only visually and auditorily, but, we might say, on the tactile and olfactory planes as well. The cold which numbs Mona, the bread which is too hard to eat, and the water frozen into ice all belong to this register. The progress of death is likewise intimately related to the individuals who meet the drifter, activating or noting this process of deterioration. There is first of all the rapist, a kind of satyr, in both the mythological and realistic senses, whom she meets in the woods. Then there are those, from Mme Landier to the philosopher shepherd, who give testimony about her filthiness, her stench, and her vomiting (see the scene at the train station). Finally there is this ultimate sullying, the one which Mona has to endure at the Fête des Paillasses, which we would like to discuss further.

Inherited from the Dionyses, classical festivals in honor of Dionysos (Bacchus), this kind of carnival takes place every Ash Wednesday at Cournonterral, a little village in the Hérault department. The participants, nearly all of them natives, split into two clans: *les Paillasses* (Clowns) and the *Blancs* (Whites). The first group of people chases the second in order to smear them, by any means possible, with wine dregs. Agnès Varda discovered this festival during her initial scouting for the film. It is rather troubling to see how the filmmaker's taste for mythology was combined with this still lively tradition, how the documentary was channeled into the narrow framework of a fictional work. If we look more closely, we can see that the Paillasse scene, actually a film within the film, possesses a two-fold logic, one dramatic, the other symbolic. At the level of the scenario, it is because of the village festival that Mona can find no food, that she loses her blanket and dies from both hunger and the cold. The symbolic interpretation turns out to be particularly instructive. Indeed, coming on the heels of other incidents of soiling, the wine dregs are the preeminently "excrementous part of wine." Thus Mona, like all the victims of the festival, moves toward *"that part of the self that we normally suppress or reject or refuse. Our excrementous side. Our death side. Our side already putrid or destined to putrify"* (Charles Camberoque and Yves Rouquette, *Les Paillasses* [Paris: Verdier, 1985], p. 8). When Mona escapes from the festival, she is already dead. Dead socially because she is excluded from a ritual whose rules are unfamiliar to her. Dead physically because her body smeared with wine dregs has already begun to resemble a corpse in a state of putrefaction. Her fall into the ditch — an image which contrasts sharply with her rising out of the waves at the beginning — is the logical conclusion of this long process of deterioration ("Mythes cachés, mythes dévoilés dans l'oeuvre d'Agnès Varda," pp. 78-80).

Jérôme Picant — The Image and Its Commentators

The puzzle-like construction of this film, noted by Agnès Varda, emphasizes the fundamental role which falls to the image in her work: even unfinished and unfinishable the puzzle is an image [...].

The image's power of representation and not of explanation — which supposes an active role on the part of all the commentators of the image, both in the film (the witnesses) and outside of the film (the spectators) — appears to be the keystone of this film. Numerous episodes of Mona's life are connected to photos whose representational function alone is clear: Mona's body photographed by the gendarmes offers no explanation of her life or her death. Later in the film, filmed from the back and from above, Mona sits and looks at a series of seven postcards: the photo of a girl, a photo of an antique mask (which she picks up), a wooded landscape, a painting by Van Gogh, and a series of landscapes. Apparently devoid of any personal character, these photos furnish no information on Mona's itinerary or her past. During her short stay in Aunt Lydie's apartment, Mona leafs through the old lady's photo album, but the contents only become meaningful when Aunt Lydie explains who each character is. It is thus the commentary that gives meaning to the images. The film's organization is a good illustration of this idea: the testimonies intervene as commentaries on the images which compose the sequences of the narrative. These testimonies have no documentary value. They are just part of the fictional construct, and their sense may be absolutely contradictory to what the image reveals. Two episodes are particularly illustrative of this. During the writing of the report on Mona's death, the gendarmes conclude that it was a "natural death given the position of the body," which is contradicted by the relaxed position of the body (the arm lifted up), hardly commensurate with the normal image of a person who has frozen to death. During the episode at the garage, the owner slanders Mona's behavior when interviewed but neglects to mention that he had slept with her to recover, so to speak, the money he had paid her for her work.

[…] The spectator is thus caught in a game of *mise en abyme* : he is expected to comment both the images of the episodes of Mona's life and the images of the testimonies ("Sans toit ni loi ou La boucle imparfaite," pp. 152-154).

AGNÈS VARDA'S FILMOGRAPHY
(FEATURE FILMS)

1954	*La Pointe Courte*
1961	*Cléo de 5 à 7*
1964	*Happiness (Le Bonheur)*
1965	*Les Créatures*
1969	*Lions Love and Lies* (in English)
1974	*75 Daguerréotypes* (documentary)
1976	*One Sings, the Other Doesn't (L'une chante, l'autre pas)*
1980	*Walls Walls (Murs murs,* documentary)
1985	*Vagabond (Sans toit ni loi)*
1986-87	*Jane B. par Agnès V.*
1987	*Kung-Fu Master*
1990	*Jacquot de Nantes, L'Univers de Jacques Demy* (documentary)
1995	*One Hundred and One Nights (Les Cent et une nuits)*
2000	*The Gleaners and I* (*Les Glaneurs et la Glaneuse,* documentary)

WORKS CONSULTED

"Agnès Varda" (interview), *Séquences* 126 (Oct. 1986): 33-37

Arbaudie, Marie-Claude. "Faits d'hiver.", *Le Film français* 2064 (Nov. 22, 1985): 18.

Audé, Françoise. "*Sans toit ni loi.* La Zone." *Positif* 299 (Jan. 1985): 64-65.

Bastide, Bernard. "Agnès Varda photographe ou L'apprentissage du regard." *Etudes cinématographiques* 179-186. Paris: Minard, 1991 (pp. 5-11).

………."Mythes cachés, mythes dévoilés dans l'oeuvre d'Agnès Varda." *Etudes cinématographiques* 179-186. Paris: Minard, 1991 (pp. 71-83).

Bergala, Alain. "La Repousse." *Cahiers du cinéma* 378 (Dec. 1985): 4-8.

Bergala, Alain, and Hervé le Roux. "Au risque du tournage." *Cahiers du cinéma* 378 (Dec. 1985): 9-10.

Bérubé, Robert-Claude. "*Sans toit ni loi.*" *Séquences* 123 (Jan. 1986): 55-57.

Billard, Ginette. "Venise : La Sélection française." *Le Film français* 2051 (Aug. 23, 1985): 3-4.

Bonnaire, Sandrine. "Au risque du tournage." *Cahiers du cinéma* 378 (Dec. 1985): 9-10.

Carbonnier, Alain. "*Sans toit ni loi.*" *Cinéma 85* 322 (Dec. 4, 1985): 5.

Carbonnier, Alain, and Fabrice Revault d'Allonnes. "Mona, nomade" (interview). *Cinéma 85* 322 (Dec. 4, 1985): 2-3, 11.

Dazat, Olivier. "Marche funèbre." *Cinématographe* 114 (Dec. 1985): 11.

.........."Jouer à la belle étoile" (conversation with Sandrine Bonnaire). *Cinématographe* 114 (Dec. 1985): 13-15.

Dazat, Olivier, and Gilles Horvilleur. "Agnès Varda de 5 à 7." *Cinématographe* 114 (Dec. 1985): 18-22.

Delmas, Ginette. "*Sans toit ni loi.*" *Jeune Cinéma* 171 (Dec.-Jan. 1985-86): 38-39.

Delvaux, Claudine. "Varda, *Sans toit ni loi*… Nouvelles Vagues." *Revue belge du cinéma* 20 (Summer 1987): 32-34.

Devarrieux, Claire, and Marie-Christine De Navacelle. *Cinéma du réel.* Paris: Editions Autrement, 1988 (chapter written by Varda, pp. 46-52).

D'Yvoire, Christophe. "A saisir." *Première* 100 (July 1985): 50.

Fieschi, Jean-André, and Claude Ollier. "La grâce laïque." *Cahiers du cinéma* 165 (April 1965): 42-50.

Ford, Charles. *Femmes cinéastes.* Paris: Denoël/Gonthier, 1972 (esp. pp. 110-116).

Flitterman-Lewis, Sandy. "*Sans toit ni loi* : le 'portrait impossible' de la féminité." *Cinémaction* 67 (March 1993): 171-176 (excerpted from her book *To Desire Differently. Feminism and the French Cinema* [New York: Columbia UP, 1996]).

Lefèvre, Raymond. "*Sans toit ni loi.*" *La Revue du cinéma* 411 (Dec. 1985): 25-26.

Picant, Jérôme. "Sans toit ni loi ou La boucle imparfaite." *Etudes cinématographiques* 179-186. Paris: Minard, 1991 (pp. 141-154).

Prédal, René. "Agnès Varda. Une oeuvre en marge du cinéma français." *Etudes cinématographiques* 179-186. Paris: Minard, 1991 (pp. 13-33).

Revault d'Allonnes, Fabrice. "Prénom : Mona…" *Cinéma 85* 322 (Dec. 4, 1985): 5.

Roud, Richard. "The Left Bank." *Sight and Sound* 32.1 (Winter 1962-63): 24-27.

Roumette, Sylvain. "Portrait d'Agnès Varda (1986)." *Revue belge du cinéma* 20 (Summer 1987): 35.

Roy, Jean. "La Routarde qui monte au nez." *L'Humanité* 12842 (Dec. 4, 1985): 19.

Smith, Alison. *Agnès Varda.* Manchester : Manchester UP, 1998.

Toubiana, Serge. "L'Ombre d'un doute." *Cahiers du cinéma* 376 (Oct. 1985): 8-17 (esp. pp. 10-12).

Varda, Agnès. *Sans toit ni loi* (screenplay). *L'Avant-Scène Cinéma* 526 (2003).

.........*Varda par Agnès.* Paris: Cahiers du cinéma, 1994.

.........Un jour sous le ciel." *Cahiers du cinéma* 378 (Dec. 1985): 11-15.

Historical Context of the Films

1928 Buñuel and Dalí, *An Andalusian Dog.*

1929 U.S. stock market crash and economic crisis in Europe.

1933 Adolf Hitler elected Chancellor of Germany; the Nazi Party in power.

1933 Jean Vigo, *Zero For Conduct.*

1936 Civil War in Spain; General Franco in power.

1936 Jean Renoir, *A Day in the Country* (edited and first shown in 1946).

1936-37 The Popular Front (left-wing government) in power in France.

1937 Jean Renoir, *Grand Illusion.*

1939 (Sept. 1) Nazi Germany invades Poland; France declares war on Germany. The "Phoney War" (the French troops wait behind the Maginot Line).

1939 Jean Renoir, *The Rules of the Game.*

1939 Marcel Carné, *Daybreak.*

1940-44 France occupied by the Nazis.

1941 (Dec. 7) The Japanese attack Pearl Harbor; the U.S. enters the war.

1944 (June 6) D-Day; the Allies land in Normandy and in Provence.

1945 (May 8) Germany surrenders.

1945 Marcel Carné, *Children of Paradise.*

1945 (August 6) Atom bomb dropped on Hiroshima; Japan surrenders.

1946 Beginning of the French 4th Republic.

1946 Jean Cocteau, *Beauty and the Beast.*

1946-54 French Indochinese War.

1948 The Marshall Plan adopted.

1950-53 Korean War.

1951 Beginning of the European Common Market.	*1951* René Clément, *Forbidden Games.*
	1953 Jacques Tati, *Mr. Hulot's Holiday.*
1954 Indochina wins independence.	
1956-62 Algerian War.	*1956* Robet Bresson, *A Man Escaped.*
1958 General De Gaulle President of the Republic; beginning of the 5th Republic.	*1959* François Truffaut, *The 400 Blows.*
	1959 Alain Resnais, *Hiroshima mon amour.*
	1960 Jean-Luc Godard, *Breathless.*
1962 Algeria wins independence.	*1962* François Truffaut, *Jules et Jim.*
1964-72 U.S. War in Vietnam.	
1968 "The Events of May" (student and worker revolt in France).	
1969 De Gaulle resigns; Georges Pompidou President of the Republic	*1969* Eric Rohmer, *My Night at Maud's.*
1973 Yom Kippur War (Israel and the neighboring Arab countries).	
1974 Death of Pompidou; Valéry Giscard d'Estaign President of the Republic.	
	1980 Alain Resnais, *My American Uncle.*
1981 François Mitterrand President of the Republic.	
	1985 Agnès Varda, *Vagabond.*

To Broaden Your Knowledge of French Cinema

(films not mentioned in the preceding chapters)

1931 Alexandre Korda, *Marius*

1932 Marc Allégret, *Fanny*

1933 Jean Benoît-Lévy, *Nursery School* (*La Maternelle*)

1934 Marcel Pagnol, *Angèle*

1935 Julien Duvivier, *Escape from Yesterday* (*La Bandéra*)
      Jacques Feyder, *Carnival in Flanders* (*La Kermesse héroïque*),
         Pension Mimosas

1936 Julien Duvivier, *They Were Five* (*La Belle Equipe*)
      Sacha Guitry, *The Story of a Cheat* (*Le Roman d'un tricheur*)
      Marcel Pagnol, *César*

1937 Julien Duvivier, *Pépé le Moko*
      Jean Grémillon, *Lover-Boy* (*Gueule d'amour*)

1938 Marcel Pagnol, *The Baker's Wife* (*La Femme du boulanger*)

1940 Marcel Pagnol, *The Welldigger's Daughter* (*La Fille du puisatier*)

1941 Jean Grémillon, *Tugboats* (*Remorques*)

1942 Henri-Georges Clouzot, *The Raven* (*Le Corbeau*)

1943 Jacques Becker, *It Happened at the Inn* (*Goupi-Mains-Rouges*)
      Jean Grémillon, *Summer Light* (*Lumière d'été*)

1944 Jean Grémillon, *The Sky Is Yours* (*Le Ciel est à vous*)

1945 Jean Dréville, *The Nightingale Cage* (*La Cage aux rossignols*)

1946 Jean Delannoy, *La Symphonie pastorale*
      Juien Duvivier, *Panique*

1947 Claude Autant-Lara, *Devil in the Flesh* (*Le Diable au corps*)
      Henri-Georges Clouzot, *Quai des Orfèvres*
      Georges Rouquier, *Farrebique*

1948 André Zwobada, *Noces de sable* (Maroc)

1949 Yves Allégret, *Such a Pretty Little Beach* (*Une si jolie petite plage*)
      Jean-Pierre Melville, *The Silence of the Sea* (*Le Silence de la mer*)

1950 Max Ophuls, *La Ronde*

1951 Jacques Pottier, *Dear Caroline* (*Caroline chérie*)

1952 Jacques Becker, *Golden Marie* (*Casque d'or*)
André Cayatte, *We are All Assassins* (*Nous sommes tous des assassins*)
Christian–Jacque, *Fanfan-la-Tulipe*
Max Ophuls, *House of Pleasure* (*Le Plaisir*)

1953 Henri-Georges Clouzot, *Wages of Fear* (*Le Salaire de la peur*)

1954 Jacques Becker, *Grisbi* (*Touchez pas au grisbi*)
Sacha Guitry, *Royal Affairs in Versailles* (*Si Versailles m'était conté*)

1955 Alexandre Astruc, *Les Mauvaises Rencontres*
Henri-Georges Clouzot, *Les Diaboliques*
Jean-Pierre Melville, *Bob the Gambler* (*Bob le flambeur*)
Max Ophuls, *Lola Montès*

1956 Claude Autant-Lara, *Four Full Bags* (*La Traversée de Paris*)
Roger Vadim, *And God Created Woman* (*Et Dieu créa la femme*)

1957 Louis Malle, *Elevator to the Gallows* (*L'Ascenseur pour l'échafaud*)

1958 Claude Chabrol, *Bitter Reunion* (*Le Beau Serge*)
Louis Malle, *The Lovers* (*Les Amants*)

1959 Marcel Camus, *Orfeu negro*
Georges Franju, *The Keepers* (*La Tête contre les murs*)
Jean Rouch, *I, a Black Man* (*Moi, un Noir*)
Roger Vadim, *Dangerous Liaisons 1960* (*Les Liaisons dangereuses 1960*)
Henri Verneuil, *The Cow and I* (*La Vache et le prisonnier*)

1960 Jacques Becker, *The Night Watch* (*Le Trou*)
Costa Gavras, *Z*
Louis Malle, *Zazie dans le métro*

1961 Jacques Demy, *Lola*
Jacques Rivette, *Paris Belongs To Us* (*Paris nous appartient*)

1962 Serge Bourguignon, *Sunday and Cybele* (*Les Dimanches de Ville-d'Avray*)
Robert Enrico, *The Beautiful Life* (*La Belle Vie*)
Chris Marker, *The Pretty May* (*Le Joli Mai*)
Yves Robert, *War of the Buttons* (*La Guerre des boutons*)

1963 Phillipe de Broca, *That Man from Rio* (*L'Homme de Rio*)
Louis Malle, *The Fire Within* (*Le Feu follet*)
Jacques Rozier, *Adieu Philippine*

1964 Alain Cavalier, *L'Insoumis*
Jacques Demy, *The Umbrellas of Cherbourg* (*Les Parapluies de Cherbourg*)

1965 René Allio, *La Vieille Dame indigne*
Phillipe de Broca, *Chinese Adventures in China*
    (*Les Tribulations d'un Chinois en Chine*)
Luis Buñuel, *Diary of a Chambermaid*
    (*Le Journal d'une femme de chambre*)
Gérard Oury, *The Sucker* (*Le Corniaud*)
Pierre Schoendoerffer, *La 317e Section*

1966 Claude Lelouch, *A Man and a Woman* (*Un homme et une femme*)
Jean-Pierre Melville, *The Second Breath* (*Le Deuxieme Souffle*)
Gérard Oury, *Don't Look Now We're Being Shot At* (*La Grande Vadrouille*)

1967 Claude Berri, *Two of Us* (*Le Vieil Homme et l'enfant*)
Luis Buñuel, *Belle de jour*
Jean-Pierre Melville, *Le Samouraï*
Edouard Molinaro, *Oscar*

1968 Jacques Rivette, *The Nun* (Suzanne *Simonin, la Religieuse de Diderot*)

1969 René Allio, *Pierre et Paul*
Jean-Pierre Melville, *The Shadow Army* (*L'Armée des ombres*)
Marcel Olphus, *The Sorrow and the Pity* (*Le Chagrin et la pitié*)
Maurice Pialat, *Naked Childhood* (*L'Enfance nue*)
Claude Sautet, *The Things of Life* (*Les Choses de la vie*)
Henri Verneuil, *Le Clan des Siciliens*

1970 Marcel Camus, *The Wall of the Atlantic* (*Le Mur de l'Atlantique*)
Jean Girault, *Le Gendarme en balade*

1971 Louis Malle, *Le Souffle au coeur*

1972 Luis Buñuel, *The Discreet Charm of the Bourgeoisie*
(*Le Charme discret de la bourgeoisie*)
Claude Sautet, *César et Rosalie*

1973 René Allio, *Hard Day for the Queen* (*Rude Journée pour la reine*)
Yves Boisset, *R.A.S.*
Jean Eustache, *The Mama and the Whore* (*La Maman et la putain*)
Gérard Oury, *Les Aventures de Rabbi Jacob*
Bertrand Tavernier, *The Clockmaker of Saint-Paul*
(*L'Horloger de Saint-Paul*)

1974 Chantal Akerman, *I, You, He, She* (*Je, Tu, Il, Elle*)
Bertrand Blier, *Going Places* (*Les Valseuses*)
Yves Boisset, *Dupont Lajoie*
Louis Malle, *Lacombe Lucien*
Claude Pinoteau, *The Slap* (*La Gifle*)
Jacques Rivette, *Céline and Julie Go Boating*
(*Céline et Julie vont en bateau*)
Claude Sautet, *Vincent, François, Paul and the Others*
(*Vincent, François, Paul… et les autres*)

1975 Chantal Akerman, *Jeanne Dielman, 23 Quai du Commerce,*
1080 Bruxelles
Marguerite Duras, *India Song*
Bertrand Tavernier, *The Judge and the Assassin* (*Le Juge et l'assassin*)
André Téchiné, *Memories of France* (*Souvenirs d'en France*)

1976 Robert Enrico, *The Old Gun* (*Le Vieux Fusil*)
Joseph Losey, *Mr. Klein* (*Monsieur Klein*)
Bertrand Tavernier, *Let Joy Reign Supreme* (*Que la fête commence*)

1977 Diane Kurys, *Diabolo menthe*

1978 Bertrand Blier, *Get Out Your Handkerchiefs* (*Préparez vos mouchoirs*)
Claude Chabrol, *Violette Nozière*
Edouard Molinaro, *La Cage aux folles*

1979 Bertrand Blier, *Cold Cuts* (*Buffet froid*)
Christian de Chalonge, *L'Argent des autres* (*Other People's Money,* my trans.)
Maurice Pialat, *Passe ton bac d'abord* (*Finish High School First,* my trans.)

1980 Maurice Pialat, *Loulou*
Claude Pinoteau, *La Boum* (*The Party,* my trans.)
Claude Zidi, *L'Inspecteur la bavure* (*Inspector Screw-up,* my trans.)

1981 Jean-Jacques Beinex, *Diva*
Alain Corneau, *Choice of Arms* (*Le Choix des armes*)
Bertrand Tavernier, *Clean Slate* (*Coup de torchon*)
Daniel Vigne, *The Return of Martin Guerre* (*Le Retour de Martin Guerre*)

1982 Claude Miller, *Under Suspicion* (*Garde à vue*)
Jean-Marie Poiret, *Le Père Noël est une ordure* (*Santa Claus is a Louse,* my trans.)
Ettore Scola, *La Nuit de Varennes* (*The Night of Varennes,* my trans.)
Andrzej Wajda, *Danton*

1983 Jean-Jacques Beinex, *The Moon in the Gutter* (*La Lune dans le caniveau*)
Claude Berri, *Tchao Pantin!*
Diane Kurys, *Entre nous* (*Coup de foudre*)
Maurice Pialat, *To Our Loves* (*A nos amours*)
Francis Veber, *Les Compères* (*The Buddies,* my trans.)

1984 Luc Besson, *Subway*
Michel Deville, *Peril* (*Péril en la demeure*)
Bertrand Tavernier, *A Sunday in the Country* (*Un dimanche à la campagne*)

1985 Coline Serreau, *Three Men and a Cradle* (*Trois hommes et un couffin*)
Claude Zidi, *My New Partner* (*Les Ripoux*)

1986 Jean-Jacques Annaud, *The Name of the Rose* (*Le nom de la rose*)
Jean-Jacques Beinex, *Betty Blue* (*37,2° le matin*)
Claude Berri, *Jean de Florette, Manon of the Spring* (*Manon des Sources*)
Bertrand Tavernier, *'Round Midnight* (*Autour de minuit*)

1987 Alain Cavalier, *Thérèse*
Louis Malle, *Goodby Children* (*Au revoir les enfants*)
Maurice Pialat, *Under the Sun of Satan* (*Sous le soleil de Satan*)

1988 Jean-Jacques Annaud, *The Bear* (*L'Ours*)
Luc Besson, *The Big Blue* (*Le Grand Bleu*)
Claire Denis, *Chocolat*
Jean-Loup Hubert, *The Grand Highway* (*Le Grand Chemin*)

Patrice Leconte, *Monsieur Hire*
Claude Miller, *The Little Thief* (*La Petite Voleuse*)
Bruno Nuytten, *Camille Claudel*

1989 Bertrand Blier, *Too Beautiful For You* (*Trop belle pour toi*)
Louis Malle, *May Fools* (*Milou en mai*)
Bertrand Tavernier, *Life and Nothing But* (*La Vie et rien d'autre*)

1990 Claude Berri, *Uranus*
Luc Besson, *La Femme Nikita*
Jacques Doillon, *The Little Criminal* (*Le Petit Criminel*)
Jean-Paul Rappeneau, *Cyrano de Bergerac*
Brigitte Rouan, *Overseas* (*Outremer*)

1991 Alain Corneau, *All the Mornings of the World* (*Tous les matins du monde*)
Jean-Pierre Jeunet, *Delicatessen*

1992 Jean-Jacques Annaud, *The Lover* (*L'Amant*)
Cyril Collard, *Savage Nights* (*Les Nuits fauves*)
Claude Miller, *L'Accompagnatrice*
Claude Sautet, *A Heart in Winter* (*Un coeur en hiver*)
Régis Wargnier, *Indochine*

1993 Claude Berri, *Germinal*
Krzysztof Kieslowski, *Trois Couleurs: Bleu*
Jean-Marie Poiré, *Les Visiteurs*
André Téchiné, *My Favorite Season* (*Ma saison préférée*)

1994 Patrice Chéreau, *Queen Margot* (*La Reine Margot*)
Jean-Pierre Jeunet et Marc Caro, *The City of Lost Children*
    (*La Cité des enfants perdus*)
Krzysztof Kieslowski, *Trois Couleurs: Blanc*, *Trois Couleurs: Rouge*
Hervé Palud, *An Indian in the City* (*Un Indien dans la ville*)

1995 Josiane Balasko, *French Twist* (*Gazon maudit*)
Karim Dridri, *Bye-Bye*
Mathieu Kassovitz, *Hate* (*La Haine*)
Jean-Paul Rappeneau, *The Horseman on the Roof* (*Le Hussard sur le toit*)
Claude Sautet, *Nelly et Monsieur Arnaud*
André Téchiné, *Wild Reeds* (*Les Roseaux sauvages*)

1996 Jacques Audiard, *A Self-Made Hero* (*Un héros très discret*)
Patrice Leconte, *Ridicule*

1997 Claire Denis, *Nénette et Boni*
Benoît Jacquot, *Seventh Heaven* (*Le Septième Ciel*)
Bertrand Tavernier, *Capitaine Conan*

1998 Patrice Chéreau, *Those Who Love Me Can Take the Train*
    (*Ceux qui m'aiment prendront le train*)
Benoît Jacquot, *The School of Flesh* (*L'Ecole de la chair*)
Francis Veber, *The Dinner Game* (*Le dîner de cons*)
Eric Zonca, *The Dreamlife of Angels* (*La Vie rêvée des anges*)

1999 Patrice Leconte, *The Girl on the Bridge* (*La Fille sur le pont*)
      Régis Wargnier, *East-West* (*Est-Ouest*)

2000 Patrice Leconte, *The Widow of Saint-Pierre* (*La Veuve de Saint-Pierre*)
      Pitof (Jean-Christophe Comar), *Vidocq*
      Francis Veber, *The Closet* (*Le Placard*)

2001 Agnès Jaoui, *The Taste of Others* (*Le Goût des autres*)
      Jean-Pierre Jeunet, *Amélie* (*Le Fabuleux Destin d'Amélie Poulain*)

Sources for Research on French Films

Electronic Data Bases

Academic Search Elite

Art Abstracts (before 1984, Art Index)

Arts and Humanities Citation Index (since 1980)

Expanded Academic ASAP (Infotrac)

FIAF International Filmarchive Database (on CD-ROM and on line)

JSTOR (some journals on line, with entire articles available)

Lexis Nexis (includes articles in French)

MLA Bibliography

Project Muse (some journals on line, entire articles available)

Some Current Websites (for quick information)

The Internet Movie Database: http://www.us.imdb.com (a large variety of information on films from all countries).

Bibliothèque du Film (BIFI): http://www.bifi.fr (bibliographical information; in French).

Cinefil: http://www.cinefil.com (recent films especially; in French).

Monsieur Cinéma: http://www.mcinema.com (recent films, video clips; in French).

Forum des Images: http://www.forumdesimages.net (very summary information; in French).

*There are websites devoted to virtually all of the major French filmmakers, with a wealth of information.

Bibliographies, Encyclopedias, Dictionaries, etc.

Alternative Press Index (entries by categories: "Film and Literature," "Film and Politics," "Filmmakers," etc.; the "Film Reviews" are located at the end).

L'Avant-Scène Cinéma (usually presents one major film per issue, with an introduction, the screenplay, and a selection of review articles; in French).

Bibliographie des Französischen Literaturwissenschaft (founded by Otto Klapp, 1956– to the present, 1 vol. per year ; books published on French cinema followed by entries by director; articles in French, English, and German).

Dictionnaire du cinéma. Passek, Jean-Loup, ed. New updated edition. Paris: Larousse-Bordas, 1998 (summary biographies: directors, actors, technicians, etc.; winners of the most important prizes, by year; in French).

Dictionnaire mondial des films. Rapp, Bernard, and Jean-Claude Lamy, eds. Paris: Larousse, 2000 (in French).

L'Encyclopédie du cinéma. Boussinot, Roger, ed. Paris: Bordas, 1980 (in French).

Film Literature Index (entries by subject, since 1973).

Film Review Index (vol. 1 1882-1949, vol. 2 1950-1985; entries by film and by chronological order; only Anglophone sources).

Film Study: An Analytical Bibliography. 4 vols. Manchel, Frank, ed. Rotherford, N.J.: Fairleigh Dickinson UP, 1990 (entries by historical period and by country).

Pallister, Janis L. *French-Speaking Women Film Directors: A Guide*. Madison, N.J.: Fairleigh Dickinson UP.

International Directory of Films and Filmmakers. 4 vols. Pendergast, Tom, and Sara Pendergast, eds. ("Films", "Directors", "Actors and Actresses", "Writers and Production Artists"; for the volume "Films": entries by film, with credits and relevant books and articles — very rich bibliographical source).

International Index to Film Periodicals

MLA Bibliography

New York Times Film Reviews (film reviews published since 1913)

New York Times Index (see "Motion Pictures": articles published in the *New York Times* on all aspects of cinema).

Oxford Guide to Film Studies (historical and theoretical survey of world cinema: critical approaches, genres, movements, national cinemas, directors, etc.).

Reader's Guide to Periodical Literature (see "Motion Pictures," "Motion Picture Reviews," etc.: entries by director, by film, by genre, by country, etc.).

Variety International Film Guide, 1990-1996 ; former title was *International Film Guide*, 1964-1989 (one volume per year: entries by country, with an introduction for each country, statistics on film production and number of spectators).

World Encyclopedia of Film. Smith, John, and Tim Cawkwell, eds. New York: Galahad Books, 1974 (very brief biographical entries).

Index

Key

BB *Beauty and the Beast*
BR *Breathless*
CP *Children of Paradise*
DB *Daybreak*
DC *A Day in the Country*
FG *Forbidden Games*
FHB *The 400 Blows*
GI *Grand Illusion*
HC1 History of Cinema I
HC2 History of Cinema 2
HMA *Hiroshima mon amour*

JJ *Jules et FGm*
MAU *My American Uncle*
ME *A Man Escaped*
MHH *Mr. Hulot's Holiday*
MNM *My Night at Maud's*
NW The New Wave
PR Poetic Realism
RF "Reading" a Film
RG *The Rules of the Game*
VB *Vagabond*
ZC *Zero For Conduct*

History, Theory, Criticism

Autant-Lara, Claude CP 143 **NW** 229
Astruc, Alexandre **RF** 23 BB 163 ME 211 **NW** 230
Barthes, Roland **RF** 27
Bazin, André **RF** 19, 22, 27 DC 57, 60, 68 GI 82, 83, 84, 89 RG 100, 104, 107, 108, 114 DB 124, 126, 127, 128,129, 133, 134, 135 BB 163 MHH 191, 194, 195, 196, 201, 202 ME 208, 215 FHB 236, 237, 239 MNM 313
Becker, Jacques **PR** 37 **NW** 229
Bresson, Robert **NW** 230
Buñuel, Luis **HC2** 11-16
Carné, Marcel **HC2** 16 **RF** 22, 28 **PR** 37-38 ZC 46 **NW** 229
Chabrol, Claude **NW** 229, 230, 231
Chaplin, Charles **HC1** 5, 6 **HC2** 7 **RF** 28
Christian-Jaque **NW** 229
Clément, René **NW** 229
Clair, René **HC2** 9-11 **RF** 23 **PR** 37 **NW** 229
Clouzot, Henri-Georges **NW** 229
Cocteau, Jean **PR** 38 **NW** 229, 230
Dalí, Salvador **HC2** 11-16
DeMille, Cecil B. **HC2** 7
Delannoy, Jean **PR** 38 **NW** 229
Demy, Jacques **RF** 38 **NW** 229, 231
Doniol-Valcroze, Jacques **NW** 229
Delluc, Louis **HC2** 9

Dovzhenko, Aleksandr **HC2** 7
Dulac, Germaine **HC2** 9 **ME** 217
Duvivier, Julien **PR** 37
Eastman, George **HC1** 1, 6
Edison, Thomas **HC1** 1-2
Eisenstein, Sergei **HC2** 7 **RF** 25, 26, 27-28 ZC 42 HMA 255
Epstein, Jean **HC2** 9
Feuillade, Louis **HC1** 5
Feyder, Jacques **HC2** 8, 9 **PR** 37
Flaherty, Robert **HC2** 7
Ford, John **HC2** 7 **NW** 230
Franju, Georges **NW** 229
Freud, Sigmund **HC2** 11, 14-15 **DB** 135 **BB** 167-168, 175 **FHB** 241
Gance, Abel **HC1** 6 **HC2** 8-9 **RF** 23 **NW** 229, 230, 231
Gaumont Léon **HC1** 5
Giroud, Françoise **NW** 229
Godard, Jean-Luc **RF** 26, 32, 40 **NW** 229-230
Grémillon, Jean **HC2** 9 **PR** 37 **NW** 229
Guitry, Sacha **PR** 37 **NW** 229
Griffith, D.W. **HC1** 4, 6 **HC2** 7,8 **RF** 25
Hawkes, Howard **NW** 230
Hitchcock, ARFred **RF** 22 **NW** 230
Hoerner **HC1** 1
Ince, Thomas **HC1** 4, 6
Kast, Pierre **NW** 229
Keaton, Buster **HC2** 7

Koulechov, Lev **HC2** 7 **RF** 25
L'Herbier, Marcel **HC2** 9
Lang, Fritz **HC2** 7
Langdon, Harry **HC2** 7
Legrand, Michel **NW** 231
Linder, Max **HC1** 5
Lloyd. Harold **HC2** 7
Lubitsch, Ernst **HC2** 8
Lumière, Auguste **HC1** 2
Lumière, Louis **HC1** 2-3
Malle, Louis **NW** 230, 231
Marey, Etienne-Jules **HC1** 1,2
Marker, Chris **NW** 229
Martin, Marcel **RF** 19-20, 22, 23, 24, 27, 28
Méliès, Georges **HC1** 3-4, 5
Metz, Christian **RF** 20, 21
Murnau, F.W. **HC2** 7,8
Muybridge, Eadweard **HC1** 1
Ophuls, Max **NW** 229, 230
Pagnol, Marcel **PR** 37 **NW** 229
Pathé, Charles **HC1** 5,6
Plateau, JosCPh **HC1** 1
Prévert, Jacques **PR** 37-38
Pudovkin, Vsevolod **HC2** 7
Ray, Nicholas **NW** 230
Renoir, Jean **HC2** 9, 16 **RF** 21-24, 28-31, 35 **PR** 37 **NW** 229-230 **FHB** 237, 241
Resnais, Alain **RF** 22, 28 **NW** 229-230
Reynaud, Emile **HC1** 2
Rivette, Jacques **NW** 229
Rohmer, Eric **NW** 229
Rossellini, Roberto **NW** 230
Sennett Mack **HC1** 4, 6
Sjöstrom, Viktor **HC2** 8
Truffaut, François **RF** 23, 28, 35 **NW** 229, 231
Stroheim, Erich von **HC2** 8
Vadim, Roger **NW** 231
Varda, Agnès **NW** 229, 230
Vertov, Dziga **HC2** 7
Vigo, Jean **HC2** 15, 16 **RF** 23, 28 **PR** 37
Visconti, Luchino **NW** 230
Welles, Orson **RF** 27 **NW** 230
Wiene, Robert **HC2** 7

Directors and Technicians

Agostini, Philippe **DB** 121 **CP** 139
Alekan, Henri **BB** 161, 165, 169
Almendros, Nestor **MNM** 309, 313

Aubert, Pierre **MHH** 189
Aurenche, Jean **FG** 177, 181
Auric, Georges **BB** 161, 165, 169
Bachelet, Jean **RG** 97
Barsacq, Léon **CP** 139, 140, 145
Bassiak, Cyrus **JJ** 289, 293, 313
Baudrot, Sylvette **HMA** 253
Bauer, Jean **VB** 353
Beauregard, Georges de **BR** 271
Becker, Jacques **DC** 55 **GI** 75, 81 **CP** 143
Bérard, Christian **BB** 161, 165, 169, 170
Bertrand, Paul **FG** 177
Bertrand, Pierre-André **ME** 205, 217
Bilinsky, Boris **DB** 121
Blossier, Patrick **VB** 353, 361
Bocquet **ZC** 39
Bost, Pierre **FG** 177, 181
Bouché, Claudine **JJ** 289
Boyer, François **FG** 177, 180
Braunberger, Pierre **DC** 55, 58, 62
Bresson, Robert **CP** 143 **BB** 164 **ME** 205-227 **FHB** 237 **BR** 279 **JJ** 300
Bretagne, JosCPh de **GI** 75 **DC** 55 **RG** 97
Briaucourt, Roger **MHH** 189
Brun, Philippe **MAU** 333
Bruzdowicz, Joanna **VB** 353, 363
Burel, Léonce-Henry **ME** 205
Calvet, P. **HMA** 253
Capel, Fred **JJ** 289
Carné, Marcel **DB** 121-137 **CP** 139-160 **BR** 276, 277 **VB** 362
Carrère, Jacques **BB** 161 **MHH** 189
Cartier-Bresson, Henri **DC** 55 **RG** 97, 103
Chabrol, Claude **NW** 229, 230, 231 **FHB** 237 **BR** 271 **MNM** 312 **VB** 357
Chanel, Coco **RG** 97
Charbonnier, Pierre **ME** 205, 210
Clément, Claude **FG** 177
Clément, Jean-Paul **ME** 205
Clément, René **BB** 163, 167, 172 **CP** 145 **FG** 179-189 **MHH** 194, 204
Cocteau, Jean **CP** 143 **BB** 161-176 **FG** 180 **ME** 209 **BR** 277, 285 **HMA** 256 **MAU** 339 **FHB** 230, 235, 237
Colpi, Henri **HMA** 253, 266, 267
Constantin, Jean, **FHB** 233, 239
Cosson, Roger **MHH** 189
Costa, Lucile **BB** 161
Cottrell, Pierre **MNM** 309
Courant, Curt **DB** 121

Coutard, Raoul *BR* 271, 273, 274, 279 *JJ* 289, 294, 304

De Broca, Philippe *FHB* 233

Decae, Henri *FHB* 233

Decae, Jacqueline *FHB* 233

Decrais, René *GI* 75

Decugis, Cécile *BR* 271 *MNM* 309

Delerue, Georges *HMA* 253 *JJ* 289, 294

Desanges, Chantal *VB* 353

Deschamps, Jacques *VB* 353

Desormières, Roger *RG* 97

Devigny, André *ME* 205, 210, 212, 213, 214

Dorfmann, Robert *FG* 177

Dubouillon, Annie *ME* 205

Duras, Marguerite *HMA* 253, 255-256, 259

Dussart, Philippe *MAU* 333

Duyre, Roger *FG* 177

Dzierlatka, Arié *MAU* 333

Esaka *HMA* 253

Escoffier, Marcel *BB* 161

Evein, Bernard *FHB* 233

Faye, Suzanne *BR* 271

Freire, Dido *RG* 97

Fusco, Giovanni *HMA* 253, 257, 258 267

Gabutti, Raymond *CP* 139

Giroud, Françoise (GourdFG) *GI* 75, 80

Godard, Jean-Luc *ZC* 42 *RG* 116 *FHB* 237 *BR* 271-286 *HMA* 255 *MNM* 312, 313, *VB* 357

Goldblatt, Charles *ZC* 39

Grassi, Jacques *MHH* 189

Gruault, Jean *JJ* 289, 292 *MAU* 333, 337, 342, 343, 345

Gys, Robert *DC* 55

Houllé-Renoir, Marguerite *DC* 55 58 *GI* 75 *RG* 97

Hubert, Roger *CP* 139

Ibéria, Claude *BB* 161

Ito *HMA* 253

Jaubert, Maurice *ZC* 39, 44, 46, 47, 51, 52 *DB* 121, 128, 136

Juillard, Robert *FG* 177, 179

Jurgenson, Albert *MAU* 333

Kaufman, Boris *ZC* 39, 43

Koch, Carl *GI* 75, 80

Kosma, Joseph *DC* 55, 58, 61-62, 67 *GI* 75 *CP* 139, 140, 145, 152

Laborit, Henri *MAU* 333-351

Lagrange, Jacques *MHH* 189

Lamy, Raymond *ME* 205

Le Henaff, René *DB* 121

Lebreton, Jacques *BB* 161 *FG* 177

Léon, Jean *MAU* 333

Leterrier, Catherine *MAU* 333

Lourié, Eugène *GI* 75, 81 *RG* 97

Machetti, Jean-Claude *FHB* 233

Machuel, Emmanuel *MNM* 309

Malle, Louis *ME* 205

Malraux, Florence *MAU* 333

Marquet, Henri *MHH* 189

Matras, Christian *GI* 75

Maumont, Jacques *BR* 271 *MNM* 309

Mayo, Antoine *CP* 139 *HMA* 253

Mazuy, Patricia *VB* 353

Mercanton, Jacques *MHH* 189

Melville, Jean-Pierre *BB* 174

Méresse, Raymond *BB* 161

Michel-Ange *MHH* 189

Michio, Takahashi *HMA* 253, 256

Miyakuni *HMA* 253

Mouqué, Georges *CP* 139

Mousselle, Jean *MHH* 189

Moussy, Marcel *FHB* 233, 238, 245-246

Mozart, Amadeus *RG* 113 *ME* 205, 216, 222, 223 *BR* 277, 279, 283, 286 *MNM* 309

Mugel, Jean-Paul *VB* 353

Orain, Fred *MHH* 189

Paulvé, André *BB* 161 *CP* 139, 140, 144, 146

Petitjean, Armand *DB* 121

Pinkévitch, Albert *GI* 75

Petri *HMA* 253

Prévert, Jacques *DC* 58 *GI* 79 *DB* 121, 125, 126, 127, 129, 133, 134 *CP* 139-160

Rabier, Jean *FHB* 233

Rachline, Nicole *MNM* 309

Raichi, Henri *ME* 205

Renault, R. *HMA* 253

Renoir, Claude *DC* 55, 67, 70 *GI* 75, 80, 86

Renoir, Jean *ZC* 44, 46 *DC* 55-73 *GI* 75-95 *RG* 97-119 *DB* 123, 124 *CP* 143 *BB* 165 *MHH* 194 *ME* 212 *FHB* 235, 237, 241 *JJ* 291 *BR* 282

Resnais, Alain *ZC* 44 *HMA* 253-270 *JJ* 294 *MNM* 313 *MAU* 333-351 *VB* 356, 357

Rohmer, Eric *ME* 208, 214, 217 *FHB* 237 *MNM* 309-332

Rollmer, Frank *GI* 75

Romans, Alain **MHH** 189
Royer, Jacques **VB** 353
Royné **ZC** 39
Ruh, Jean-Pierre **MNM** 309 **MAU** 333
Rust, Henry **CP** 139
Saint-Saëns, Camille de **RG** 99, 106
Saulnier, Jacques **MAU** 333
Schiffman, Suzanne **JJ** 289
Schmitt, Henri **MHH** 189
Schroeder, Barbet **MNM** 309
Sébillotte, Hélène **MAU** 333
Solal, Martial **BR** 271, 276
Spaak, Charles **GI** 75, 78, 79, 80, 85
Tati, Jacques **MHH** 189-204
Teisseire, Robert **CP** 139
Thiriet, Maurice **CP** 139, 140, 145
Trauner, Alexandre **DB** 121, 125, 127, 129
    CP 139, 140, 144, 145, 152
Truffaut, François **ZC** 42 **GI** 81 **FHB** 233-
    252 **BR** 271, 274, 277, 278, 279 **JJ**
    289-307 **MNM** 312, 313 **VB** 357
Varda, Agnès **VB** 353-374
Vérité, Yvette **FG** 177
Vierny, Sacha **HMA** 253, 257 **MAU** 333
Vigo, Jean **ZC** 39-54 **GI** 80 **FHB** 241, 243
    HMA 255
Violet, Anne **VB** 353
Viot, Jacques **DB** 121, 125, 129
Visconti, Luchino **DC** 55
Witta, Jeanne **DB** 121
Yamamoto **HMA** 253
Yepes, Narciso **FG** 177, 183
Yoyotte, Marie-Josèphe **FHB** 233
Zwobada, André **RG** 97

Actors and Actresses

Adlin, Georges **MHH** 190
Amédée **FG** 178
André, Marcel **BB** 162
Arditi, Pierre **MAU** 334
Arletty **DB** 122, 124, 125 **CP** 140, 145,
    147, 153
Assouna, Yahiaoui **VB** 354
Auclair, Michel **BB** 162, 165, 170
Auffray, Patrick **FHB** 234
Badie, Laurence **FG** 178 **MAU** 334
Balducci, Richard **BR** 272
Barbaud, Pierre **HMA** 254
Barrault, Jean-Louis **CP** 140, 144, 150, 153,
    MNM 315

Barrault, Marie-Christine **MNM** 310, 315
Batcheff, Pierre **HC2** 12
Bassiak, Cyrus **JJ** 289, 293, 297
Bataille, Sylvia **DC** 56, 57, 58, 61, 63, 67,
    68
Baumer, Jacques **DB** 122
Bedarieux, Gérard de **ZC** 40
Beerblock, Maurice **ME** 206, 210
Belmondo, Jean-Paul **DB** 125 **BR** 272, 273,
    274, 276, 281, 282, 284
Berry, Jules **DB** 122, 125, 126, 127, 129,
    133, 135 **BR** 274
Berry, Mady **DB** 122
Blanchar **ZC** 40, 44
Blier, Bernard **DB** 122
Bonnaire, Sandrine **VB** 354, 356, 359, 363,
    365, 370
Borgeaud, Nelly **MAU** 334, 345
Boulanger, Daniel **BR** 272
Boverio, Auguste **CP** 140
Brasseur, Pierre **CP** 140, 145, 153, 159
Brialy, Jean-Claude **FHB** 234
Brunius, Jacques B. **DC** 56, 58 **DB** 125,
    128
Camax, Valentine **MHH** 190
Carette, Julien **GI** 76, 79, 80, 89, 91, 97
    RG 98, 114
Carl, Raymond **MHH** 190
Casarès, Maria **CP** 140, 145 **ME** 212
Cortadellas, Laurence **VB** 354
Courtal, Suzanne **FG** 178
Dalio, Marcel **GI** 76, 79, 80, 81, 92 **RG** 98,
    102, 114, 116
Darnoux, Georges **DC** 56, 58
Darrieu, Gérard **MAU** 334
Dassas, Stella **HMA** 254
Dasté, Jean **ZC** 40, 44 **GI** 76, 80 **MAU** 334
David, Liliane **BR** 272
Day, Josette **BB** 162, 165
Debray, Eddy **RG** 98
Decomble, Guy **FHB** 234
Decroux, Etienne **CP** 140
Delhumeau, Jean-Paul **ME** 206
Demange, Paul **CP** 140
Delphin **ZC** 40
Depardieu, Gérard **MAU** 334, 338, 348
Diener, Jean **CP** 140
Doude, Van **BR** 272
Douking, Georges **DB** 122
Dubois, André **MHH** 190
Dubois, Marie **JJ** 289, 293 **MAU** 334

Dubost, Paulette *RG* 98, 102
Duverger, Albert *HC2* 13
Emile, Mme *ZC* 40, 44
Ertaud, Jacques *ME* 206
Fabian, Françoise *MNM* 310, 315
Fabre, Michel *BR* 272
Flament, Georges *FHB* 234, 241
Florencie, Louis *CP* 140
Fontan, Gabrielle *DC* 56, 57 *DB* 122
Fosse, Joël *VB* 354
Fossey, Brigitte *FG* 178, 181
Francoeur, Richard *RG* 98
Frankeur, Paul *CP* 140
Frégis, Lucien *MHH* 190
Freiss, Stéphane *VB* 354, 359
Fresnay, Pierre *GI* 76, 79,8 80, 86, 89, 91
Fresson, Bernard *HMA* 254
Gabin, Jean *GI* 76, 78, 79, 80, 81, 86, 89,
    92 *DB* 122, 123, 125, 126, 127, 129,
    130, 133, 134, 135, 136, *CP* 152 *FG*
    196 *BR* 278, 281 *MAU* 334, 339, 341,
    341, 345, 349
Gabriello, André *DC* 56, 57
Garcia, Nicole *MAU* 334, 338
Gérard, Claire *RG* 98
Gérard, Marguerite *MHH* 190
Germon, Nane *BB* 162
Godard, Jean-Luc *BR* 272
Golstein, Coco *ZC* 40
Grégor, Nora *RG* 98, 102
Hanin, Roger *BR* 272
Haudepin, Sabine *JJ* 289
Heil, Carl *GI* 76
Herrand, Marcel *CP* 140, 145, 153
Houllé-Renoir, Marguerite *DC* 56, 58
Hubert, Lucien *FG* 178
Huet, Henri-Jacques *BR* 272
Itkine, Sylvain *GI* 76
Jarnias, Marthe *VB* 354
Kanayan, Richard *FHB* 234, 248
Laborit, Henri *MAU* 334-351
Lacourt, René *MHH* 190
Larive, Léon *ZC* 40 *RG* 98
Laudenbach, Philippe *MAU* 334
Laurent, Jacqueline *DB* 122, 125
Le Flon, Robert *ZC* 40
Léaud, Jean-Pierre *FHB* 234, 235, 238,
    239, 240, 241, 248
LeClainche, Charles *ME* 206
Lefèbvre, Louis *ZC* 40
Léger, Père Guy *MNM* 310

Lepczynski, Patrick *VB* 354
Leterrier, François *ME* 206, 210, 211, 214
Loris, Fabien *CP* 140
Magnier, Pierre *RG* 98
Mansard, Claude *FHB* 234 *BR* 272
Manson, Héléna *MAU* 334
Marais, Jean *BB* 162, 164, 165, 166, 170,
    171 *FG* 180 *MAU* 334, 339, 341, 345,
    349
Marco, Raoul *BB* 162
Mareuil, Simone *HC2* 12
Marin, Jacques *FG* 178
Marken, Jane *DC* 56, 57 *CP* 140
Maurier, Claire *FHB* 234, 239
Mayen, Anne *RG* 98
Melville, Jean-Pierre *BR* 272, 277
Méril, Macha *VB* 354, 359, 369
Mérovée, P. *FG* 178
Modot, Gaston *GI* 76, 80 *RG* 98 *CP* 140
Monod, Roland *ME* 206, 210, 211, 212
Montero, Germaine *DC* 62
Moreau, Jeanne *FHB* 234 *JJ* 289, 293
Moreau, Yolande *VB* 348, 353
Nay, Pierre *RG* 98
Okada, Eiji *HMA* 254, 256
Parély, Mila *RG* 98, 102 *BB* 162, 165, 166
Parlo, Dita *GI* 76, 80, 92
Pascaud, Mr *MHH* 190
Pascaud, Nathalie *MHH* 190, 193
Pérès, Marcel *CP* 140
Perronne, Denise *FG* 178
Peters (la petite) *GI* 76
Pierre, Roger *MAU* 334, 338, 343
Poujouly, Georges *FG* 178, 181
Pruchon, Gilbert *ZC* 40
Rémy, Albert *FHB* 234, 239
Renoir, Alain *DC* 56, 58
Renoir, Jean *DC* 56, 58 *RG* 98, 102
Renoir, Pierre *CP* 140, 145, 146
Repp, Pierre *FHB* 234
Rignault, Alexandre *MAU* 334
Rispal, Jacques *MAU* 334
Rognoni *CP* 140
Riva, Emmanuelle *HMA* 254, 256, 263,
    264, 265
Rolla, Michèle *MHH* 190
Saintève, Louis *FG* 178
Salou, Louis *CP* 140, 145, 153
Seberg, Jean *BR* 272, 274, 276, 282, 284
Serre, Henri *JJ* 289, 293, 298
Silver, Véronique *MAU* 334

Stroheim, Eric von **GI** 76, 80, 86, 89, 91, 92
Subor, Michel **JJ** 289, 293
Talazac, Odette **RG** 98
Tati, Jacques **MHH** 189-204
Temps, Paul **DC** 56, 58
Toutain, Roland **RG** 98
Tréherne, Roger **ME** 206
Trintignant, Jean-Louis **MNM** 310, 314, 315, 321

Urbino, Vanna **JJ** 289
Vacchia, Gaston **MAU** 334
Vialle, Max **MAU** 334
Virlogeux, Henri **FHB** 234
Vitez, Antoine **MNM** 310, 315
Wasley, André **FG** 178
Werner, Oskar **JJ** 289, 293, 298, 303

Credits

Illustrations

Museum of Modern Art Film Stills Archive: pp. xvii, 3.
Les Grands Films Classiques F-Paris: p. 12.
Les Grands Films Classiques F-Paris and Janus Films NY: p. 97.
Gaumont: pp. 39, 205.
Films du jeudi: p. 55.
Studio Canal Image: p. 73, 177.
Collection André Heinrich: pp. 121, 139.
Société Nouvelle de Cinématographie: p. 161.
Les Films de Mon Oncle: p. 189
MK2: pp. 233, 333.
Argos Films: p. 253.
Raymond Cauchetier-Paris: Cover photo, pp. 271, 289.
Les Films du Losange: p. 309.
Ciné-Tamaris: p. 353.

Article and Book Excerpts

Arts, p. 226
L'Avant-Scène Cinéma: pp. 48, 64-65, 87-88, 111-112, 131-132, 154-156, 159, 172-173, 183-184, 220-221, 260, 261-262, 280-281, 298-300, 323-325, 338-339, 346-347, 348. 365-368.
Cahiers du Cinéma: pp. 108-110, 114-115, 133-136, 187, 197-200, 245-246, 263-264, 278-279, 282, 303-304, 322-323, 329, 348-349, 364, 368-369.
Cinématographe: p. 345.
Editions Albatros: p. 224-225, 345.
Editions de l'Archipel: pp. 129-130, 152-153.
Editions Armand Colin: p. 268.
Editions Autrement: p. 365.
Editions du Cerf: pp. 201-202, 222-223, 223-224.
Editions Flammarion: pp. 85-86, 108-110, 157.
Editions Hatier: pp. 69-70.
Editions Henri Veyrier: p. 157.
Editions de l'Herne: p. 322.
Editions Ivréa: pp. 68, 89-91.
Editions J.-C. Lattès: p. 116.
Editions Jean-Pierre Delarge: p. 158.
Editions Kimé: p. 328-329.

Editions Méridiens-Klincksieck: pp. 70-71.

Editions Pierre Belfond: pp. 110-111.

Editions Pierre Lherminier: pp. 49-50, 52-53, 247-248, 327-328.

Editions Pierre Waleffe: p. 134.

Editions Minard: pp. 326, 327, 371-372.

Editions Nathan: pp. 70, 93, 246-247, 264-265, 284-285, 300, 301-303, 304.

Editions Ramsay: pp. 157-158, 200.

Editions Rivages: pp. 282-283, 327, 349.

Editions du Rocher: pp. 170-171.

Editions Seghers: pp. 113-114, 115, 129, 174, 185-86, 267-268.

Editions du Seuil: pp. 51-52.

Editions Temps Libres (Cinéma): pp. 201, 222, 260-261, 281-282, 301, 322-323, 364, 370.

Editions Universitaires: p. 224.

Etudes: p. 223.

Film Criticism: pp. 249-250.

Guislain, Pierre: pp. 115-116.

Hammond, Robert: pp. 171-172.

Le Monde: p. 279.

Literature/Film Quarterly: p. 175.

Positif: pp. 47, 109, 133, 281.

Premier Plan: pp. 49, 50-51, 53, 84-85, 91-92, 168-169, 264-265, 266-267.

Revue belge du cinéma: pp. 283-284.

La Revue du cinéma: pp. 67, 68, 116-117, 185, 186-187, 200-201, 263, 349-350, 369-370.

Roy, Jean: p. 364.

Script: pp. 304-305.

Séquences: p. 363-364.

Télé-Ciné: pp. 249, 303.